Gerhard Richter   Painting After All

Gerhard Richter Painting After All

Sheena Wagstaff
Benjamin H. D. Buchloh

With essays by
Briony Fer / Hal Foster /
Peter Geimer / Brinda Kumar /
André Rottmann

THE
MET

The Metropolitan Museum of Art, New York
Distributed by Yale University Press, New Haven and London

Contents

Director's Foreword

Over the past six decades, Gerhard Richter has developed an astonishingly diverse practice that underscores a resolute commitment to painting. *Gerhard Richter: Painting After All* highlights the artist's long engagement with postwar avant-garde art movements, especially his investigation into the formal and conceptual possibilities of painting through both abstract and representational means. Conceived in close collaboration with the artist, the selection of more than one hundred works featured in the exhibition and this accompanying book—ranging from early photo paintings to portraits to later large-scale abstract series—presents an incisive overview of Richter's career from the early 1960s to the present. The result is a vivid demonstration of the artist's reckoning with history and memory in both collective and personal terms.

Gerhard Richter: Painting After All brings together many iconic paintings but also features lesser-known works such as a series of monoprints from 1957 titled *Elbe*. Key works will be exhibited for the first time in the United States, from the early paintings *Group of People* (1965), *Alps* (1968), and *Townscape Paris* (1968) to the important later series *Cage* (2006) and *Birkenau* (2014), which engage with painterly abstraction from markedly different perspectives. In addition, the architectonic *House of Cards (5 Panes)* (2020)—a new glass work being debuted in the exhibition—will be especially resonant within gallery spaces designed by Marcel Breuer.

As the concluding exhibition at The Met Breuer, *Gerhard Richter: Painting After All* will be the culmination of a boundary-pushing program that has considered the practices of modern and contemporary artists from across the globe, often within the context of the deep histories of art at The Met. This exhibition was sensitively and intelligently curated by Sheena Wagstaff, Leonard A. Lauder Chairman of the Department of Modern and Contemporary Art at The Met, and Benjamin H. D. Buchloh, Andrew W. Mellon Professor of Modern Art in the Department of History of Art and Architecture at Harvard University, with Brinda Kumar, Assistant Curator of Modern and Contemporary Art at The Met. This catalogue includes important essays by the curators as well as those by Briony Fer, Hal Foster, Peter Geimer, and André Rottmann that each extend the curatorial insights proposed by the exhibition.

We are delighted that the Museum of Contemporary Art, Los Angeles, has partnered with The Met on this exhibition. Following its presentation in New York, *Gerhard Richter: Painting After All* will travel to Los Angeles, where it will be the first monographic museum exhibition of the artist in that city.

In closing, we are grateful to Gerhard Richter and his studio and archive for their support of this project, as well as to the many individuals and institutions who have lent Richter works from their collections. We also deeply appreciate the generosity of donors, especially Barrie A. and Deedee Wigmore, who made the exhibition possible, as well as Morgan Stanley for its lead corporate sponsorship. Major support was provided by David S. Winter and members of the Modern and Contemporary Art Visiting Committee, including Jane C. Carroll, Renée E. Belfer, Victoria Newhouse, Denise Saul, Malcolm H. Wiener, Bettina Bryant, Michael Ringier, Linda M. Lindenbaum, and Linda Macklowe. We are also grateful to Angela A. Chao and Jim Breyer, the Horace W. Goldsmith Foundation, Kenneth and Rosalind Landis, and Stuart and Gina Peterson for their important additional funding. We extend our thanks to Christie's for its support of the exhibition's opening, related programs, and catalogue. We also recognize the important contributions of the Mary C. and James W. Fosburgh Publications Fund to this beautiful book, and Joan and Donald J. Gordon for their commitment to the education programming at The Met Breuer. Final thanks are due to the countless staff members at The Met whose tireless work continues to support the excellence of our modern and contemporary programming.

Max Hollein
Director
The Metropolitan Museum of Art

Acknowledgments

Devoted to the work of one of the greatest and most prolific artists of our time, this exhibition and publication are the result of years of careful and considered planning and have entailed the collaboration of numerous individuals and institutions across Europe and America. Our sincere gratitude is thus commensurate with the magnitude of the project.

For making this exhibition possible, we thank the Barrie A. and Deedee Wigmore Foundation for its exemplary generosity, and Morgan Stanley for its corporate sponsorship. Major support was provided by David S. Winter, along with Jane C. Carroll, Renée E. Belfer, Victoria Newhouse, Denise Saul, Malcolm H. Wiener, Bettina Bryant, Michael Ringier, Linda M. Lindenbaum, and Linda Macklowe of the Modern and Contemporary Art Visiting Committee. For the additional funding provided to the exhibition, we are grateful to Angela A. Chao and Jim Breyer, the Horace W. Goldsmith Foundation, Kenneth and Rosalind Landis, and Stuart and Gina Peterson. We also extend our gratitude to the Mary C. and James W. Fosburgh Publications Fund and Christie's for their commitments to this catalogue. For their generous support of the exhibition's related education programs, we thank Christie's and Joan and Donald J. Gordon.

Working in close collaboration with Gerhard Richter himself to develop this oeuvre-spanning exhibition and book has been a rare experience and great pleasure. Our foremost thanks and profound respect are thus due to the artist for his generosity and for his interest in and intense engagement with the project. Our many visits to his studio in Cologne were always lively, convivial, and stimulating, and allowed for deeper insights into his practice that helped us more keenly identify the possibilities and priorities for this exhibition. We are also grateful for the abiding support of Sabine Moritz, the artist's wife, during the course of this project's development.

Over the years, members of the artist's studio, especially Konstanze Ell and Juliane Au, have been exceptionally helpful in fielding numerous organizational and logistical requests. This show would not have been possible without their supreme efficiency, and we truly appreciate their assistance along the way. Also essential was Benjamin Farr's engineering guidance for Richter's glass works, two of which are making their first public appearances in this exhibition.

We wish to extend particular thanks to Dietmar Elger, head of the Gerhard Richter Archiv, with whom we have worked fruitfully in preparation for this exhibition. We have been fortunate to draw on the expertise that Dr. Elger has garnered from his long-standing stewardship of the artist's archives and his deep knowledge of Richter's works; both the exhibition and the publication have benefited from his involvement.

Scholarship on Richter's work is enriched by fresh perspectives on his practice. We are delighted to include new essays by our esteemed coauthors Briony Fer, Hal Foster, Peter Geimer, and André Rottmann, whose insightful contributions distinguish this volume.

Gerhard Richter: Painting After All is the first major U.S. exhibition focused on the artist in nearly two decades. The exhibition's success relies on the generosity of many private individuals and the collegiality of institutional partners across two continents. We have been heartened by the interest that collectors and curators alike have taken in our project and their willingness to entrust us temporarily with precious works by Richter from their collections. The names of these lenders may be found on page 12 of this publication, and we sincerely thank them and those who wish to remain anonymous for their loans. In addition, we would like to especially acknowledge the assistance of Corinna Thierolf (Bayerische Staatsgemäldesammlungen, Munich); Judith Irrgang (Museum Frieder Burda, Baden-Baden); Nimfa Bisbe ("la Caixa" Foundation, Barcelona); Anne Pontegnie (Cranford Collection, London); Hendrik Driessen, Martijn van Nieuwenhuyzen, and Maria Schnyder (De Pont Museum, Tilburg, The Netherlands); Laura Satersmoen (Fisher Art Foundation, San Francisco); Anita Froehlich (Froehlich Collection, Stuttgart); Andreas Stolzenburg and Brigitte Kölle (Hamburger Kunsthalle); Anton and Annick Herbert (Herbert

Foundation, Ghent); Randall Suffolk and Amy Simon (High Museum of Art, Atlanta); Hans-Jürgen Schwalm and Kerstin Weber (Kunsthalle Recklinghausen); Martina Lehmannová (Lidice Memorial, Czech Republic); Heike Munder and Nadia Schneider Willen (Migros Museum für Gegenwartskunst, Zurich); Stephan Diederich (Museum Ludwig, Cologne); Susanne Pfeffer and Mario Kramer (Museum MMK für Moderne Kunst, Frankfurt); Glenn Lowry and Ann Temkin (Museum of Modern Art, New York); Sylvia Weber (Würth Collection, Germany); Kaywin Feldman (National Gallery of Art, Washington, D.C.); Neal Benezra and Gary Garrels (San Francisco Museum of Modern Art); Eva Müller-Remmert (Ströher Collection, Bochum); and Maria Balshaw and Frances Morris (Tate). We also appreciate the time and behind-the-scenes efforts of countless collection managers, registrars, and art handlers, whose work is crucial to such loan exhibitions.

At The Met, we are fortunate to rely on the outstanding support of a number of colleagues across the museum in the realization of such exhibitions. This volume was expertly produced by our colleagues in The Met's Publications and Editorial Department, managed by Mark Polizzotti, Gwen Roginsky, Michael Sittenfeld, and Peter Antony. Elisa Urbanelli carefully and sensitively edited the texts, while our bibliographer Kate Norment judiciously verified all notes and references. This elegant volume was thoughtfully designed by Daphne Geismar and, at The Met, steered by the production skill of Paul Booth. Josephine Rodriguez-Massop was instrumental in securing images and permissions. We also wish to recognize Jennifer Bantz's editorial assistance for the exhibition.

Special thanks are owed to Daniel H. Weiss, President and CEO, and Max Hollein, Director, for their steadfast support of not only this show but also the pioneering program of exhibitions at The Met Breuer over the last four years, of which this will be the culminating presentation. The Met's Exhibition's Office played a key role in this project, and we duly acknowledge the immense work of Quincy Houghton, Katy Uravitch, Martha Deese, and Marci King. In the Counsel's Office, we appreciate Sharon H. Cott, Amy Desmond Lamberti, and Nicole Sussmane for their aid in exhibition-related documentation. In the Department of Modern and Contemporary Art, we are grateful to Pari Stave, Rebecca R. Kusovitsky, Elizabeth Doorly, Padget Sutherland, and Kolleen Ku for their assistance through the many administrative and planning stages of this project.

The vibrancy of Richter's art is best understood firsthand, when its complexity and range of media can be effectively experienced. In this endeavor we have relied on the expertise and invaluable guidance of our deeply knowledgeable and meticulous conservators, in particular Isabelle Duvernois, Nora Kennedy, The Met's Sherman Fairchild Conservator in Charge of Photograph Conservation, Rachel Mustalish, Shawn Digney-Peer, and Kendra Roth. In The Met's Design Department, Patrick Herron and Anna Rieger created a thoughtful and sophisticated design for the exhibition and graphics. The exhibition was made accessible to a wide audience through educational, digital, audio, and Live Arts programs. Many colleagues have developed these initiatives, including Frederick P. and Sandra P. Rose Chairman of Education Sandra Jackson-Dumont, Ann Meisinger, Limor Tomer, Rebecca McGinnis, Kate Farrell, William Fenstermaker, Bryan Martin, Melissa Bell, Nilam Agrawal, and Paul Caro. Brian Healy and Mahin Kooros in Merchandising devised creative retail accompaniments to the exhibition, while Kenneth Weine, Ann M. Bailis, Alexandra Kozlakowski, and Micol Spinazzi in External Relations have enthusiastically and astutely promoted the project to the public. We also extend our thanks to our team at The Met Breuer, including Allison Barone, Patrick Paine, Robin Madray, and Seth Goodwin. We are also grateful to Taylor Miller and Deborah Gul Haffner in Buildings and Construction for their advice. Finally, our acknowledgements are due to those in the Development Department who, together with Max Hollein, helped to secure the necessary funds for the exhibition, publication, and opening events: Clyde B. Jones III, Jason Herrick, John L. Wielk, Jennifer Brown, and Elizabeth Burke.

Ambitious exhibitions such as this rely on a number of individuals outside the museum as well. We would like to recognize Marian Goodman, who has been a dedicated supporter of Richter's work for many decades; Philipp Kaiser and Katharine Arnold, who have facilitated certain loans; and Cheyenne Westphal and her colleagues, who assisted with our application for United States Government Federal Indemnity. We are also grateful to Wojciech Płosa and Szymon Kowalski of the Auschwitz-Birkenau State Museum for their guidance on images sourced from their archives.

Finally, we wish to acknowledge Klaus Biesenbach, the Maurice Marciano Director of the Museum of Contemporary Art, Los Angeles, and his colleagues—Jill Davis, Bennett Simpson, Rebecca Lowery, Meridith Gray, and Patrick Weber—who have ensured that *Gerhard Richter: Painting After All* is presented to great effect in Los Angeles. We are delighted that through this collaboration audiences on both the east and west coasts of the United States will thus have the opportunity to experience in person Richter's innovative and challenging work. As this exhibition comes up to date with Richter's artistic practice, it is also very timely. At a moment when younger generations of artists find it increasingly imperative to deal with the current disjuncture between the political and personal, there is a renewed momentum to consider how identity and memory can be refracted within the materiality of painting. Richter's practice, so relevant to both the long history of art and the current role art can play in society, make this exhibition's presentation at both the encyclopedic Metropolitan Museum of Art and the Museum of Contemporary Art especially pertinent.

Sheena Wagstaff
Leonard A. Lauder Chairman, Modern and Contemporary Art
The Metropolitan Museum of Art

Benjamin H. D. Buchloh
Andrew W. Mellon Professor of Modern Art
Harvard University

Brinda Kumar
Assistant Curator, Modern and Contemporary Art
The Metropolitan Museum of Art

Lenders to the Exhibition

ARTIST ROOMS: Tate and National Galleries of Scotland

Stefan Asbrand-Eickhoff, Hessen

Bayerische Staatsgemäldesammlungen, Pinakothek der Moderne, Munich

Museum Frieder Burda, Baden-Baden

"la Caixa" Collection of Contemporary Art

Cranford Collection, London

De Pont Museum, Tilburg, The Netherlands

Friedrich Christian Flick Collection

Froehlich Collection, Stuttgart

Lyn and Jerry Grinstein

Anne Simone Kleinman and Thomas Wong

Hamburger Kunsthalle

Herbert Foundation, Ghent

Samuel and Ronnie Heyman, Palm Beach, Florida

High Museum of Art, Atlanta

Kunsthalle Recklinghausen

The Robert Lehrman Revocable Trust, Courtesy of Aimee and Robert Lehrman

Lidice Memorial, Czech Republic

Ruth McLoughlin, Monaco

Migros Museum für Gegenwartskunst, Zurich

MKM Museum Küppersmühle für Moderne Kunst, Duisburg / Germany, Ströher Collection

Museum Ludwig, Cologne

Museum MMK für Moderne Kunst, Frankfurt

The Museum of Modern Art, New York

National Gallery of Art, Washington, D.C.

Gerhard Richter Archiv, Staatliche Kunstsammlungen Dresden

San Francisco Museum of Modern Art, The Doris and Donald Fisher Collection

James and Dana Tananbaum

Tate

Würth Collection, Germany

and multiple private collections

Contributors

Benjamin H. D. Buchloh
Andrew W. Mellon Professor of Modern Art, Harvard University, Cambridge, Massachusetts

Briony Fer
Professor of the History of Art, University College, London

Hal Foster
Townsend Martin, Class of 1917, Professor of Art and Archaeology, Princeton University, Princeton, New Jersey

Peter Geimer
Professor of Art History, Freie Universität Berlin

Brinda Kumar
Assistant Curator, Modern and Contemporary Art, The Metropolitan Museum of Art, New York

André Rottmann
Research Fellow and Lecturer, Department of Art History, Freie Universität Berlin

Sheena Wagstaff
Leonard A. Lauder Chairman, Modern and Contemporary Art, The Metropolitan Museum of Art, New York

Sheena Wagstaff

Introduction: The Excavation of Memory

This book, and the exhibition it accompanies, arose from a conversation with Benjamin Buchloh about how to articulate the complexity of Gerhard Richter's art and, in so doing, how to encapsulate his remarkable six-decade career. We settled on a core focus that would actively demonstrate both the artist's highly inventive investigation into the very nature of painting and his quest to test the medium's ability—through dual modes of representation and abstraction—to address the history and memory of the image over time. One way to introduce these intertwined themes is by exploring a small selection of paintings that span his career: *Table* (1962), deemed formally by the artist to be his first "mature" painting; *September* (2005), a diffident yet paradoxically assured response to the destruction of the twin towers of the World Trade Center on September 11, 2001; and the *Birkenau* paintings (2014), which attempt to reckon with Holocaust imagery and its inconceivable historical implications. All of these paintings are notable for originating in photographs, though they engage with their sources in tellingly different ways, and as a group they speak to the conceptual and philosophical significance of the image in Richter's oeuvre.

This pictorial sensibility finds its origins in *Table* (p. 104), in which image re-creation and painterly abstraction, often regarded as two distinct aspects of Richter's practice, demonstratively coalesce. Expounding on how he came to embrace the role of the photograph in his approach to picture making, Richter once commented: "I was able to see [the photograph] differently, as a picture... without all those conventional criteria which I formerly attached to art. There was no style, no composition, no judgment. It liberated me from personal experience. There was nothing but a pure picture."[1] *Table* is a watershed painting for Richter. Based on a photograph from the design magazine *Domus* of a modern white table, the image is of the most prosaic of objects. "I wanted to make a new start after my work in East Germany.... I wanted to draw a line... and so set *Table* at the top of my worklist."[2]

Richter's painting began with a rendering of a table in the center of the canvas; when the surface had dried, he wiped a solvent-soaked cloth rapidly in spiral motions over the image, dissolving and partially obliterating it, leaving aggressive, gestural swirls of pigment as evidence of his performative act of erasure, or unmaking (fig. 1). By depicting the actual defacement or even eradication of the image, through what Tom McCarthy describes as "a sense of some kinetic violence" that lies in the act of making the work, the radical transfiguration of photograph to painting is an emphatic demonstration of coming to terms with this perceived binary.[3] *Table* anticipates the way in which Richter introduces a form of distortion or destruction into the creative process of his subsequent practice. Through these means, he confronts us with painting's quintessential nature by invoking the illusion of realism along with its simultaneous deterioration. The same dialectic between presence and absence enacted in formal terms by obliterating the photographic traces of a table is embodied metaphorically within the fragmented image of the object itself, one whose quotidian function spans the arc of human existence over millennia. *Table* thus carries the aura of memory into our present.

More than forty years after the gestural deletion of the image in *Table*, a similar process takes on a direct allegorical significance in the painting *September* (p. 185), a small, photo-based work that attests to Richter's considered approach to a deeply emotive topic. In co-opting one of the most ubiquitous media images from the early years of our century—capturing the precise moment of explosive impact caused by the hijacked plane hitting the second of the twin towers—he takes the reproduction of a photograph to a different register (fig. 2). His painterly iteration of the cataclysm, witnessed in real time by people in New York and by millions worldwide on television, and documented extensively in other media, reads at first as abstract, and yet the ghostly image, seared into our collective memory, is instantly recognizable.

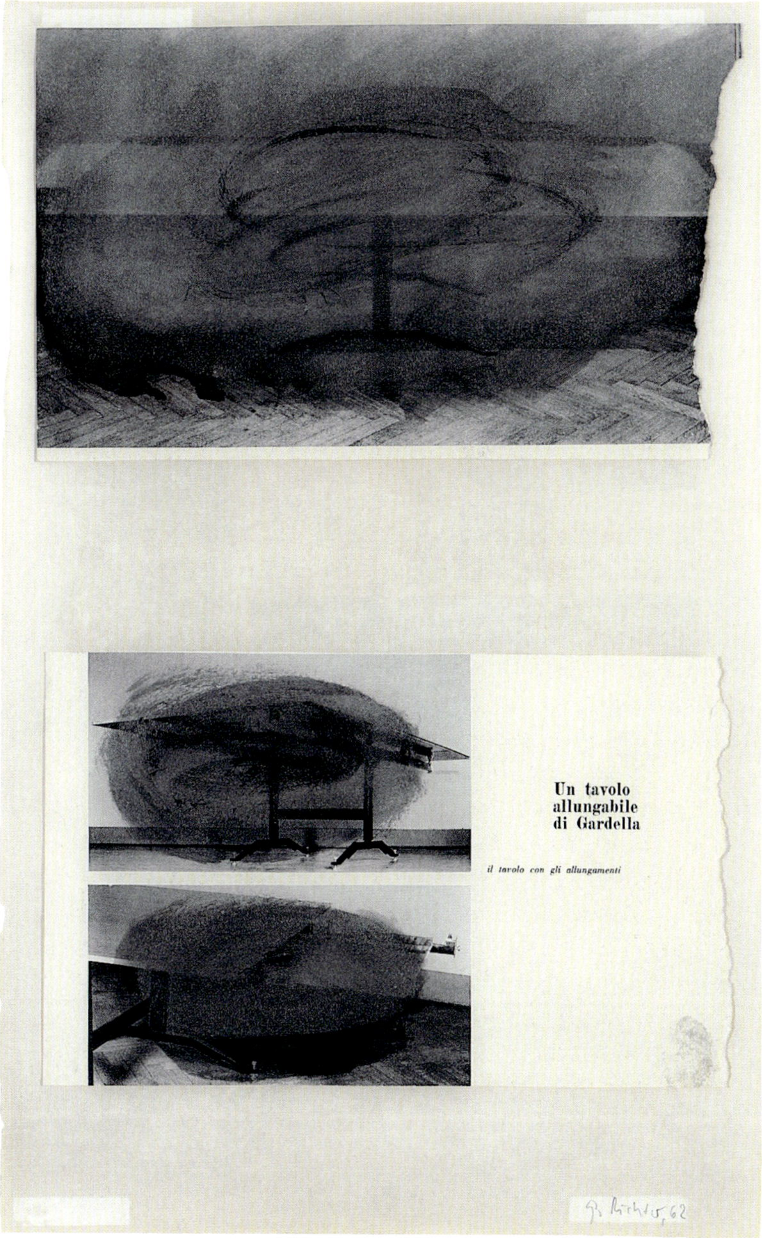

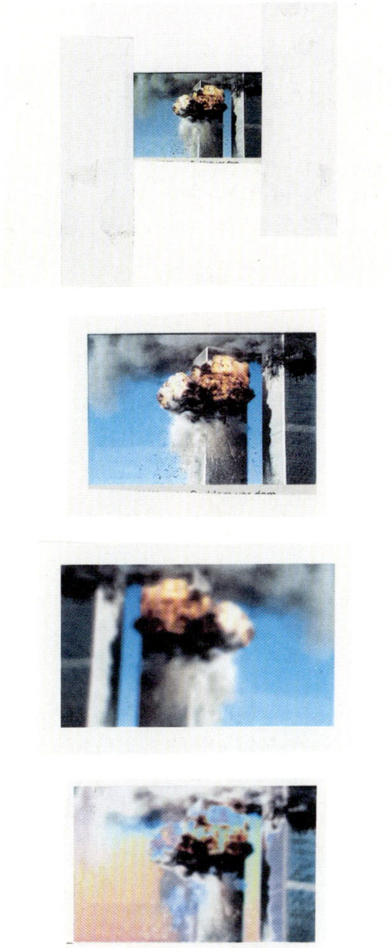

FIG 1
Gerhard Richter, maquette for *Table*, 1959. Magazine clippings on paper, 18 ⅞ × 11 ⅞ in. (48 × 30 cm). Private collection, Frankfurt

FIG 2
Gerhard Richter, *Atlas* sheet 744, "Stripes, WTC" (detail), 2006. 22 ⅛ × 28 ¾ in. (56.2 × 73 cm)

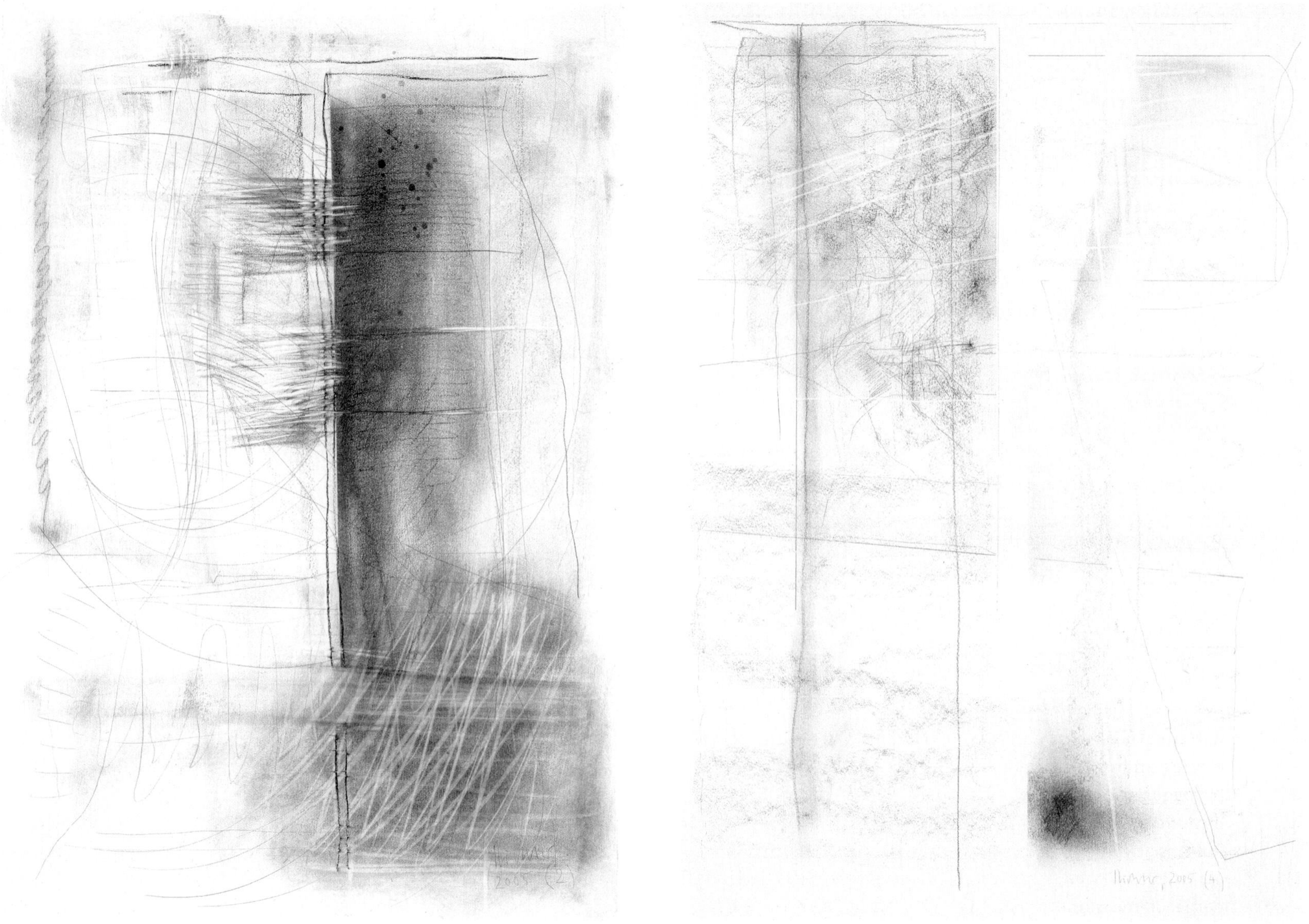

FIG 3
Gerhard Richter, *Drawing II* and *Drawing IV*, 2005. Graphite on paper, each 59 ½ × 40 ⅛ in. (151 × 102 cm). Drawings CR 05/2 and CR 05/4

On the day after the 9/11 terrorist attacks, the *New York Times* reported that we had "witnessed the inexpressible, the incomprehensible, the unthinkable."[4] A range of artistic responses have subsequently attempted to understand and give meaning to a seismic event that felt inconceivable. There was a particular need for literary interpretations to address the trauma of this visual spectacle, about which Don DeLillo wrote, "There is no logic in apocalypse.... There is something empty in the sky. The writer tries to give memory, tenderness and meaning to all that howling space."[5] Novels by DeLillo, Jonathan Safran Foer, Claire Messud, Jay McInerney, and others, which began to appear in 2005 (the same year Richter painted *September*), are notable because their attempts to express the inexpressible all focus on narratives of how New Yorkers dealt with the catastrophe. While their explorations of the human condition were designed to counter or mitigate the spectacle of 9/11, their failure to engage with its larger philosophical implications caused a fierce debate about the difficulty of writing fictional accounts of real, though "unimaginable," events, and whether the "realism" of fiction was capable of dealing effectively with crisis or trauma in the twenty-first century.

The notion that the visual medium of painting could intelligently and sensitively reckon with such a phenomenal visual spectacle in more meaningful terms than the written word has been regarded with skepticism. Yet, as the academic literature on the topic acknowledges, studies of trauma "elaborate on the paradoxical juxtaposition of a strong demand for representation and the simultaneous impossibility to represent."[6] Richter tackles this paradox directly.

At the time he painted *September*, four years after 9/11, Richter was among only a handful of visual artists to venture into the realm of rendering the traumatic collective event. He was acutely aware of the challenge of depicting such a disaster from a neutral standpoint, given that the image's reception as a document of trauma is inevitably entwined with its colossal affective power. The danger was that by reiterating an image turned cliché he might also trigger a tremor of voyeuristic sensationalism. Having worked up many preliminary studies, four drawings (fig. 3), and other paintings, Richter acknowledged his sensitivity to this dilemma in his comment to Hans Ulrich Obrist: "Probably September 11 bothered me more than I expected."[7] As with *Table*, the genesis of the final painting emerged from the destruction of the image. He commented that, in comparison to older works, it was "more spontaneous, more abrasive, less aesthetic, somewhat painful. The little picture of the two towers was very colorful to start with, with the garish explosion beneath the wonderful blue sky and the flying rubble. That couldn't work; only when I destroyed it, so to speak, scratched it off, was it fit to be seen.... On the one hand, it's a perfectly harmless picture, small, and not at all sensational. On the other, it has such a spectacular title."[8]

FIG 4
Detail of *September* (2005; see p. 185)

The image of the towers came into existence through a labored process of applying layers of paint that were then successively scraped, overlaid, rubbed, and so on, until the picture came to hover between representation and abstraction. The artist's broad, sweeping strokes of thick pigment back and forth across the surface of the canvas resulted in the tactile, palpable, final layer of the painting (fig. 4). Through gestures that simultaneously erase and complete the image, the painting attempts a pictorial equilibrium, holding in tension both the formal polarities of abstraction and representation and the oppositional forces of destruction and reconstruction. Indeed, to paraphrase Buchloh, it is "an allegorical reiteration"—one might say reconstruction—"of a destruction already fully accomplished by history."[9]

September is a palimpsest epitomized by clear evidence of its facture. Richter mediates his qualms about giving in to the spectacular nature of the subject by distancing the image through an act of excavation, preventing its facile consumption. In the end, he hopes that this work, as well as other emotionally weighted works, exists only as "a painting... but not a spectacle and not an illustration."[10] It speaks precisely to the complex synthesis of history, memory, subject, and space that lies at the heart of Richter's artistic practice, which reaches its apotheosis in the *Birkenau* paintings.

In the early postwar period, Richter was one of the few visual artists who approached the imagery of the Holocaust. W. G. Sebald, Richter's peer and one of Germany's most respected authors, described those years as a time when "there was a tacit agreement, equally binding on everyone, that the true state of material and moral ruin in which the country found itself was not to be described. The darkest aspects of the final act of destruction, as experienced by the great majority of the German population, remained under a kind of taboo like a shameful family secret, a secret that perhaps could not even be privately acknowledged."[11] Cultural figures like Richter who ventured into this territory were aware of "the extremely precarious position of those [artists] in a society that was morally almost entirely discredited."[12]

In 1964, not long after he made *Table*, Richter attempted to articulate why he began a group of so-called photo paintings based on images selected from newspaper articles and family photo albums that depicted perpetrators, sympathizers, or victims of the Nazi regime: "What fascinates me is the alogical, unreal, atemporal, meaningless occurring of an occurrence which is simultaneously so logical, so real, so temporal and so human, and for that reason so compelling. And I would like to represent it in such a way that this clash is maintained."[13] Three years earlier, Richter had seen one of four extant photographs taken in early 1945 by a prisoner at Auschwitz-Birkenau, a copy of which he included in his *Atlas* (see fig. 15). And nearly fifty years later, in 2008, he encountered a photograph from the same series again in a newspaper review of Georges Didi-Huberman's book *Images in Spite of All* and framed it on the wall of his studio (fig. 5).[14] As he told Nicholas Serota, "You see a concentration camp yard, with people walking around in it quite calmly, moving corpses.... There's an appalling contrast between the contents and the look of the picture."[15] Perhaps Richter's technique of making paintings as palimpsests, refined in *September* through his reconciliation with the documentary imagery of 9/11, enabled his eventual reckoning with these enormously powerful photographs attesting to the inhumanity of mankind. As he recalls, "When I bought the book, I saw that there were four photographs. I decided to paint them after all, despite my doubt that it could be possible to create 'pictures' through painting. In autumn 2014 I began to transfer these four pictures to canvas but soon realized that it did not work. So I scratched the paint away and painted anew until I had the four abstract works. It is not unusual for me to start with something representational and end up with something abstract."[16]

The *Birkenau* paintings (pp. 225–28) embody a narrative process that began with the projection of photographs onto four primed canvases. Richter then rendered each image in graphite directly on the surface (fig. 6). Successive layers of paint—a pink-beige color, followed by red, then green, and finally black—became disfigured through repeated rupturing, gouging, and incising, wet into wet, to create an undulating, pitted surface that partially exposes the dark strata of its history of creation (see fig. 20). The fragmented topographical sediments are not only analogous to the experience of prolonged suffering without losing consciousness—both physically and philosophically—but also suggestive of the precarious nature of memory, here in its descent into the archives of Germany's past.

Whereas *September* retains the specter of its source, the *Birkenau* paintings bear no such visual cues. With no visible trace left of their photographic origins, they deny any voyeuristic gratification. Richter purposefully titled them to denote the pictures' subject and to affect and "influence our way of seeing or hearing" through the historical resonance of the concentration camp's name.[17] As a result, the abstract paintings are perceived as being inextricably associated with their title.

Richter's artistic practice has long been deeply concerned with questions of representation while reflecting on the problematics of Germany's history, arriving at a treatment that involves the active construction of a new way of regarding the past. It resuscitates and transcends the traditional genre of history painting, proposing "memory painting" as a vehicle for memorialization. As such, the *Birkenau* paintings speak to a silent history of post-Holocaust Germany, in which "imagistic representation[s] of a reality... reflect the fragile, transitory nature of the depicted subject, the risk that it may pass into oblivion."[18]

Like the work of his literary counterpart Sebald, Richter's paintings can be seen as projects of rescue in response to a collective memory crisis. Theodor Adorno (avidly read by both

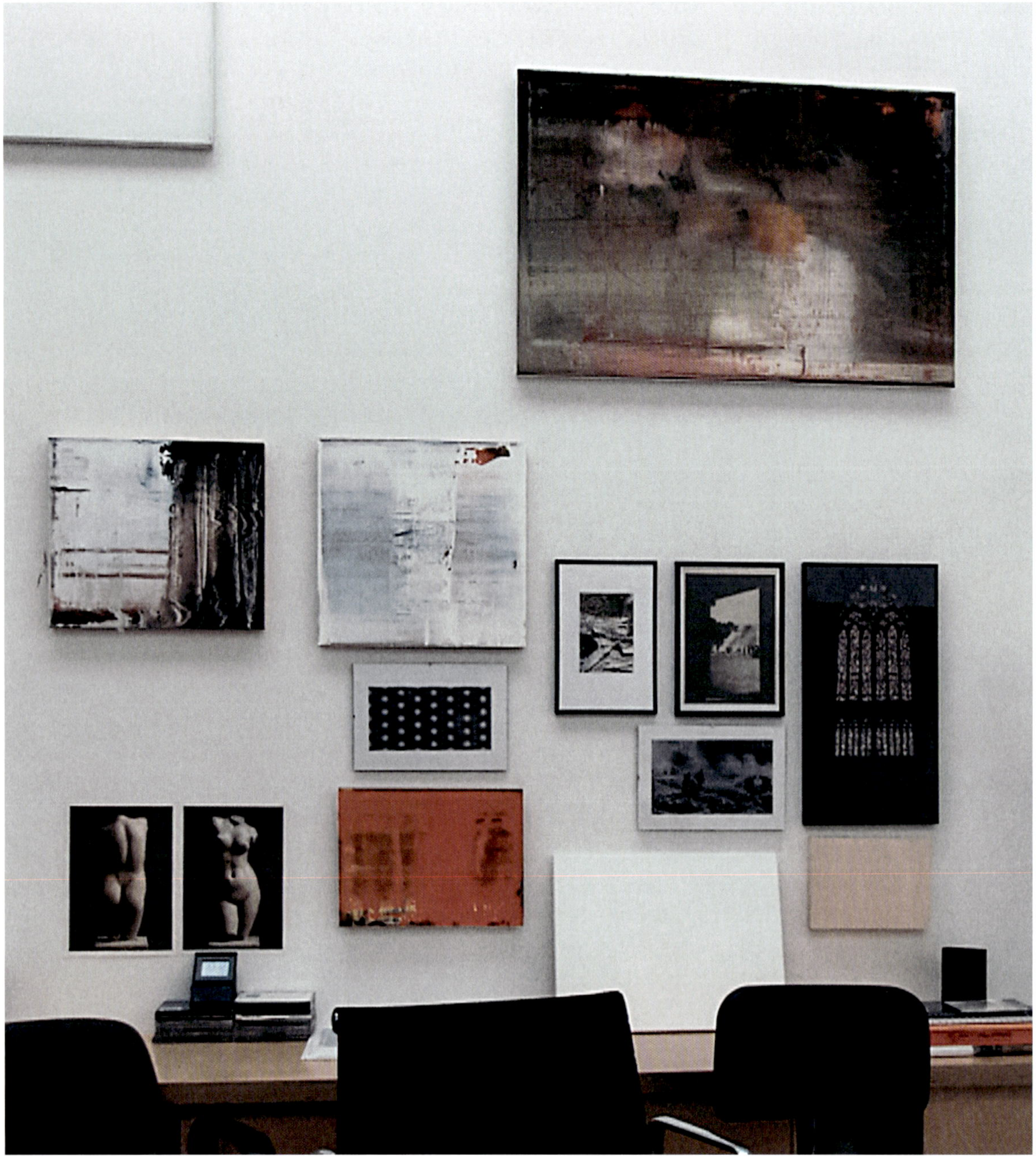

FIG 5
Framed Birkenau photograph among other images on the wall of Richter's studio, 2009. Film still (detail) from Corinna Belz, *Gerhard Richter Painting* (2012)

Sebald and Richter) once suggested that when the living disappear into death, as was the case in the photograph of unidentified bodies strewn across the ground at Birkenau, memory for each individual in that morass is their only means of rescue: "Our memory is the only help that is left to them. They pass away into it, and if every deceased person is like someone who was murdered by the living, so he is also like someone whose life they must save, without knowing whether the effort will succeed."[19] As allegorical reflections on memory, the *Birkenau* paintings embed the reality of the Holocaust within their palimpsests, which become abstract statements connecting past to present—statements of continuity through both form and title.

Ultimately, the artist's project is analogous to visually replicating the slippage of memory and the attendant disappearance of the image: "Richter's gaze at history is... not fixed merely on the historical event, but in equal measure on the *conditions of the possibility of memory* in the arena of art."[20] The *Birkenau* paintings thus challenge our collective memory and invite reflective commemoration; they are not so much a means to understand the Holocaust as a way perhaps to make us realize that there is no possibility of understanding the Holocaust. Richter's new type of history-painting-as-memory-project arises from his belief that he is "still very sure that painting is one of the most basic human capacities... that make sense, that stay with us, as something human."[21] It is painting, after all, that endures.

Gerhard Richter is regarded as one of the most serious painters of our time, whose sensitive intelligence and artistry have reckoned with the gravest questions of history and the ability of painting to communicate a retrieval of collective memory. His entire artistic project over six decades has reinvigorated and expanded the conventional genres of painting. It has also restored confidence in the importance of forms of abstraction. At a time when the power of the image is central to a resurgence in both figurative and abstract painting, Richter's reconciliation of both approaches to picture making is evident throughout his oeuvre. Asked what he regards as the purpose of art, Richter answered: "For surviving this world.... [Art] has the measure of all the unfathomable, senseless things, the incessant ruthlessness of our world. And art shows us how to see things that are constructive and good, and to be an active part of that."[22]

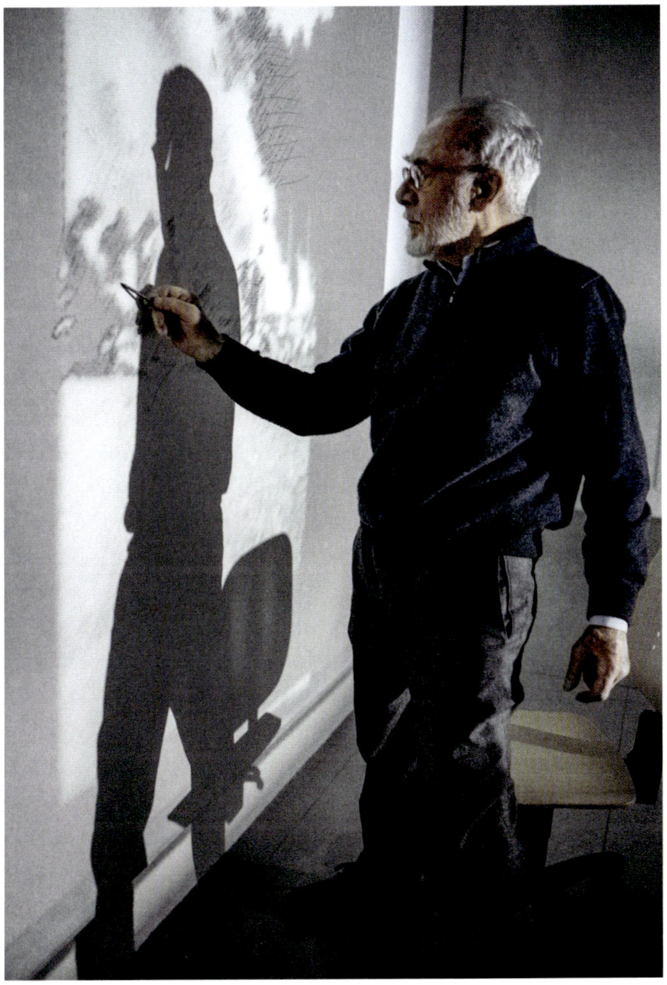

FIG 6
Richter working on the initial stage of *Birkenau*, February 1, 2014. Photograph by Joe Hage

Benjamin H. D. Buchloh

Documents of Culture, Documents of Barbarism: Richter's *Birkenau* Paintings

Among the many discontinuities and epistemic ruptures in Gerhard Richter's life and oeuvre, several deeply connected strands run across a trajectory of six decades, from 1957 to 2017. One is Richter's repeated return to the question of whether any artist, and more improbably any German painter, could possibly construct a credible mnemonic representation of the destruction of European Jews under the rule of German Nazi Fascism. Despite this ongoing preoccupation in his work, his statements on the topic are often opaque. For example, when queried on several occasions about his awareness of artists Lea and Hans Grundig,[1] who were prominent faculty members at the Academy of Fine Arts in Dresden, where Richter had studied—and who were among the first German artists in the immediate post–World War II period to have engaged in representing the concentration-camp system and the Holocaust—Richter either claimed to have been hardly aware of their activities or dismissed them as irrelevant to his artistic formation. Thus, we must assume that the artist, at that stage of his development, simply doubted the Grundigs' artistic competence, or that he was indifferent to the testimonies of witnesses and victims of Nazi Fascism, or that his indifference suggested a fundamental skepticism about the qualifications of painting—as opposed to poetic, philosophical, or photographic means—for the mnemonic representation of the Shoah (to use the Hebrew term for the Holocaust).

Yet already in 1957, having just graduated from the Dresden Academy as a Socialist Realist mural painter, Richter made a series of twelve drawings to illustrate *The Diary of Anne Frank* (figs. 7–9).[2] Regardless of the drawings' almost painfully naive Picassoesque features, their subsequent withdrawal from exposure and documentation seems to attest to the young artist's growing insight that a highly stylized, benevolent homage to one of the most prominent Jewish victims among six million was no less problematic than the cruelly realistic depiction of the anonymous victims of industrialized mass murder in Lea Grundig's drawings and print portfolios (fig. 10).[3]

Shortly after his flight from State Socialism in 1961 and his arrival in West Germany, Richter returned to the challenges of whether and how his paintings could confront the historical legacies of German Fascism and the Holocaust. One of his earliest works, painted in 1962, was a pathetic attempt at a portrait of "der Hitler" (as Theodor Adorno had called him in a famous 1959 lecture); the canvas, which he soon erased, became the verso of *Deer* (see fig. 64). Two other paintings with explicit Holocaust imagery were displayed in his first group exhibition in the West, which opened on May 13, 1963, in an empty butcher shop in Düsseldorf's Kaiserstrasse.[4] One, titled *Erschießung* (*Execution*) (fig. 11), juxtaposed a painted photographic image documenting a Fascist execution of political prisoners with a serialized image of an eerily smiling starlet, inverted to form a Warholian frieze below the hanging corpses. The other (fig. 12) combined the enigmatic letters *Tagebu* (undoubtedly a fragment of the German title of the *Tagebuch* [Diary] *der Anne Frank*) with a large-scale, crudely painted depiction of a headless photographic pinup. Soon after the exhibition, the artist destroyed both paintings.

Adorno's above-mentioned 1959 lecture, called "The Meaning of Working through the Past," was soon recognized as one of the most important of his early philosophical reflections on the conditions of collective disavowal and the concomitant destruction of historical and mnemonic abilities in postwar West Germany. Surprisingly to some, Adorno had referred to the German cult of Anne Frank's diary (which had even been adapted to a stage production) precisely as a paradoxical psychosocial symptom of that disavowal, in which the erosion of authentic compassion, resulting in the inability to actually mourn and remember the victims, had become painfully evident:

I was told the story of a woman who, upset after seeing a dramatization of The Diary of Anne Frank*, said: "Yes, but* that *girl at least should have been allowed to live." To be sure, even that was good as a first step toward understanding. But the individual case, which should stand, and raise awareness about, the terrifying totality, by*

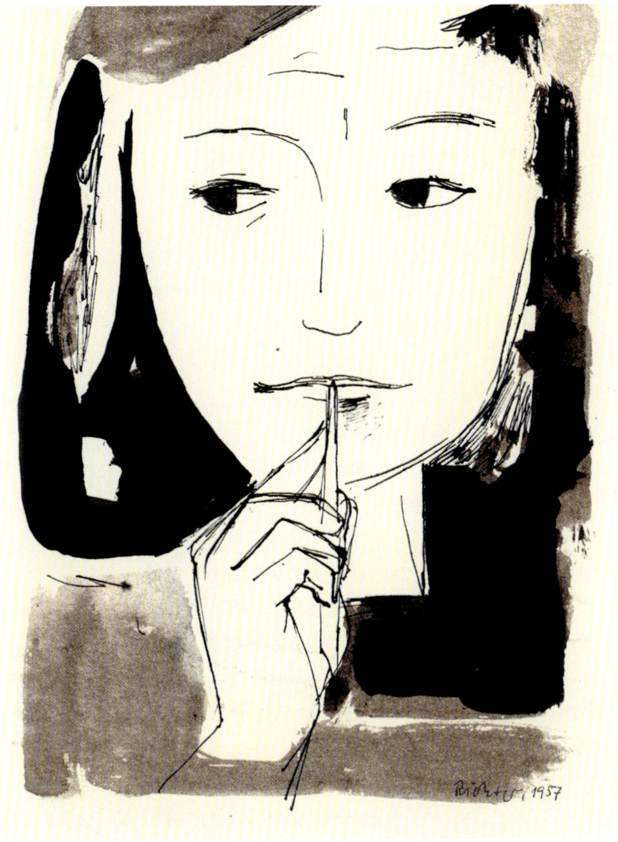

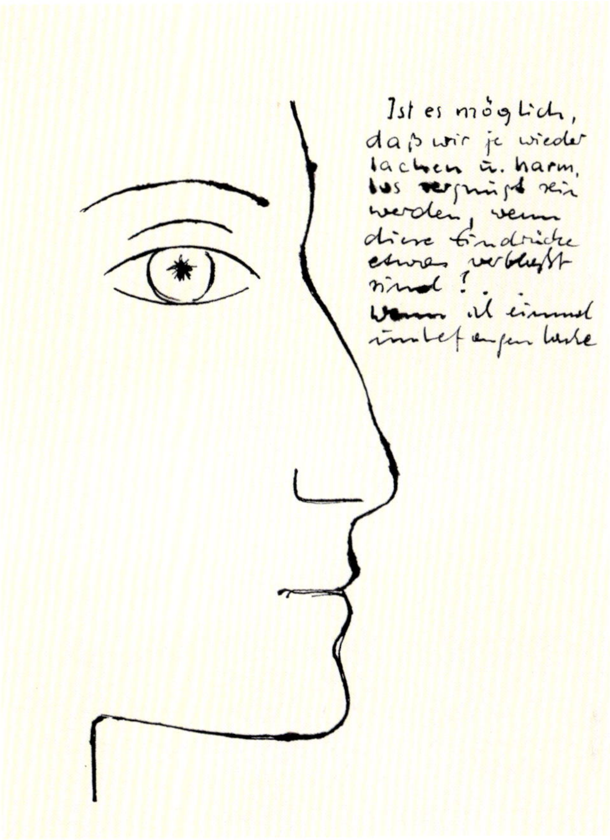

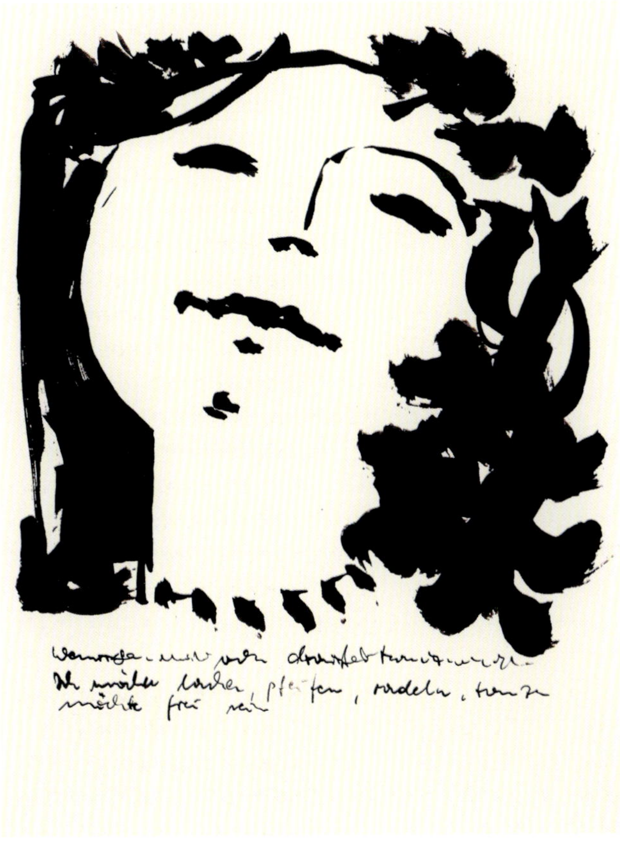

FIGS 7–9
Gerhard Richter, illustrations for *The Diary of Anne Frank*, ca. 1957. Ink on paper, each 11 ⅝ × 8 ¼ in. (29.6 × 21 cm). Gerhard Richter Archive, Dresden (inv. 497/13, 500/13, 501/13)

its very individuation became an alibi for the totality the woman forgot. The perplexing thing about such observations remains that even on their account one cannot advise against production of the Anne Frank play and the like, because their effect nonetheless feeds into the potential for improvement, however repugnant they also are and however much they seem to be a profanation of the dignity of the dead.[5]

Richter read this published lecture only many years later, and since then Adorno's writings have increasingly informed his thinking, all the way up to his recently renewed reflections regarding the viability of his *Birkenau* paintings (2014), which are discussed at length below.[6] But the artist's seemingly disrespectful, diffident fragmentation of *Tagebuch* in the title of his 1962 painting might well have signaled his own awareness of and increasing discomfort (precisely along the lines of Adorno's criticism) with the emerging state-sponsored memory culture. Officially titled *Vergangenheitsbewältigung*, this "mastering of the past" had shifted from the mute repression of the initial postwar years into mandated forms of ritualistic remembrance. After Richter's arrival in West Germany, it became obvious that he was facing not only the ethical challenge to rupture the mechanisms of this enforced memory culture but also the aesthetic challenge to define his speaking position as an artist emerging from that history and attempting to construct means and modes of representation.

Like his fellow citizens in the West, Richter could neither claim a place of ethical transcendence and historical exemption due to his age nor identify himself as a subject removed from responsibility and collective guilt (a role that the Communist East's mythical history of collective anti-Fascism had falsely posited for its citizens). It is highly unlikely that Richter would have read Hannah Arendt's then-recently published series of essays in the *New Yorker*, reporting from the 1961 trial of Nazi war criminal Adolf Eichmann in Jerusalem, yet her diagnosis of postwar German mentalities (including yet another comment on the German cult of Anne Frank) corresponded to Richter's, as it articulated the Germans' increasingly manifest conflicts in the processes of subject and cultural identity formation.

It is quite gratifying to feel guilty if you haven't done anything wrong: how noble! Whereas it is rather hard and certainly depressing to admit guilt and to repent. The youth of Germany is surrounded, on all sides and in all walks of life, by men in positions of authority and in public office who are very guilty indeed but who feel *nothing of the sort. The normal reaction to this state of affairs should be indignation, but indignation would be quite risky—not a danger to life and limb but definitely a handicap in a career. Those young German men and women who every once in a while—on the occasion of all the* Diary of Anne Frank *hubbub and of the Eichmann trial—treat us to hysterical outbreaks of guilt feelings are not staggering under the burden of the past, their fathers' guilt; rather, they are trying to escape from the pressure of very present and actual problems into a cheap sentimentality.*[7]

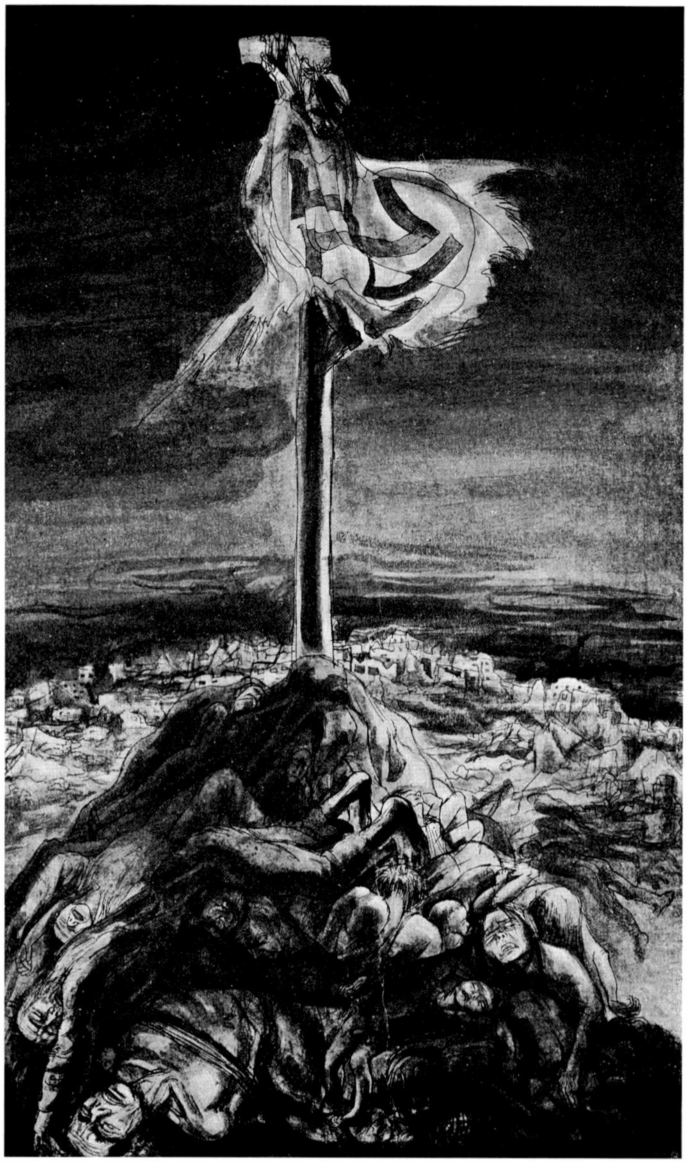

FIG 10
Lea Grundig (German, 1906–1977), *Eternal Shame*, folio 17 from the artist's lithographic portfolio *In the Valley of Slaughter*, published in Tel Aviv, 1944

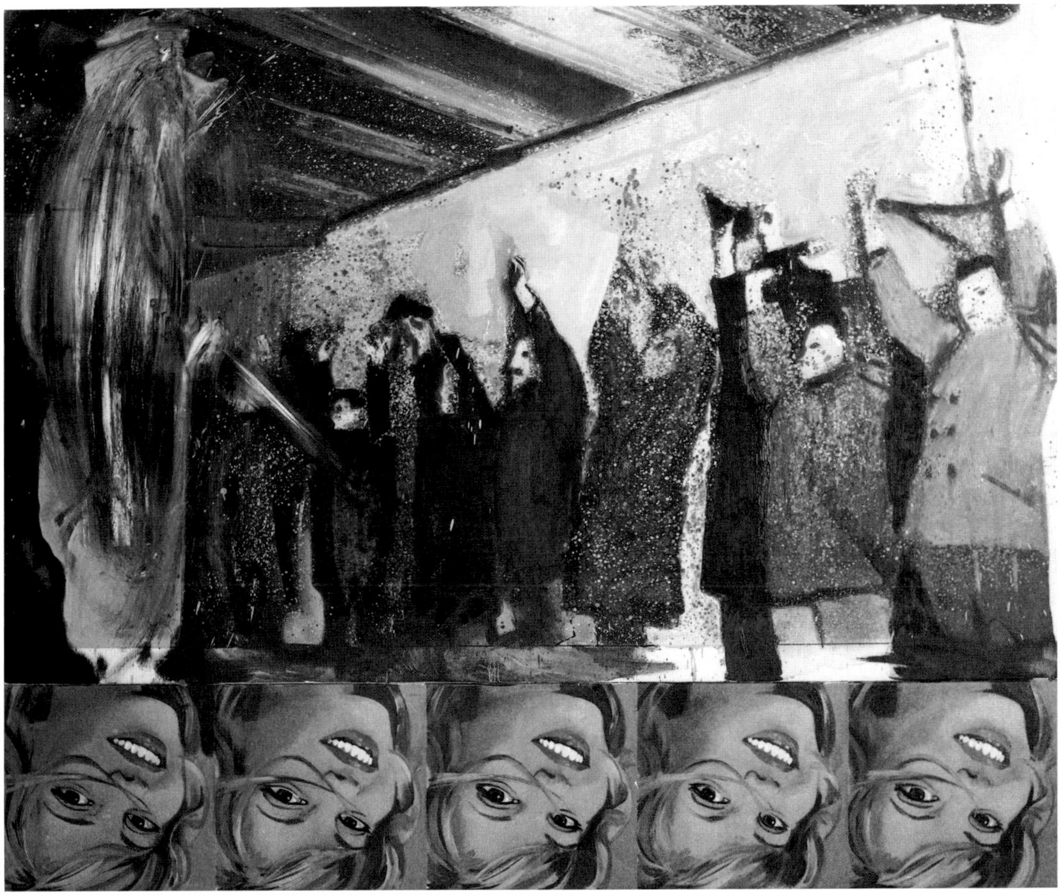

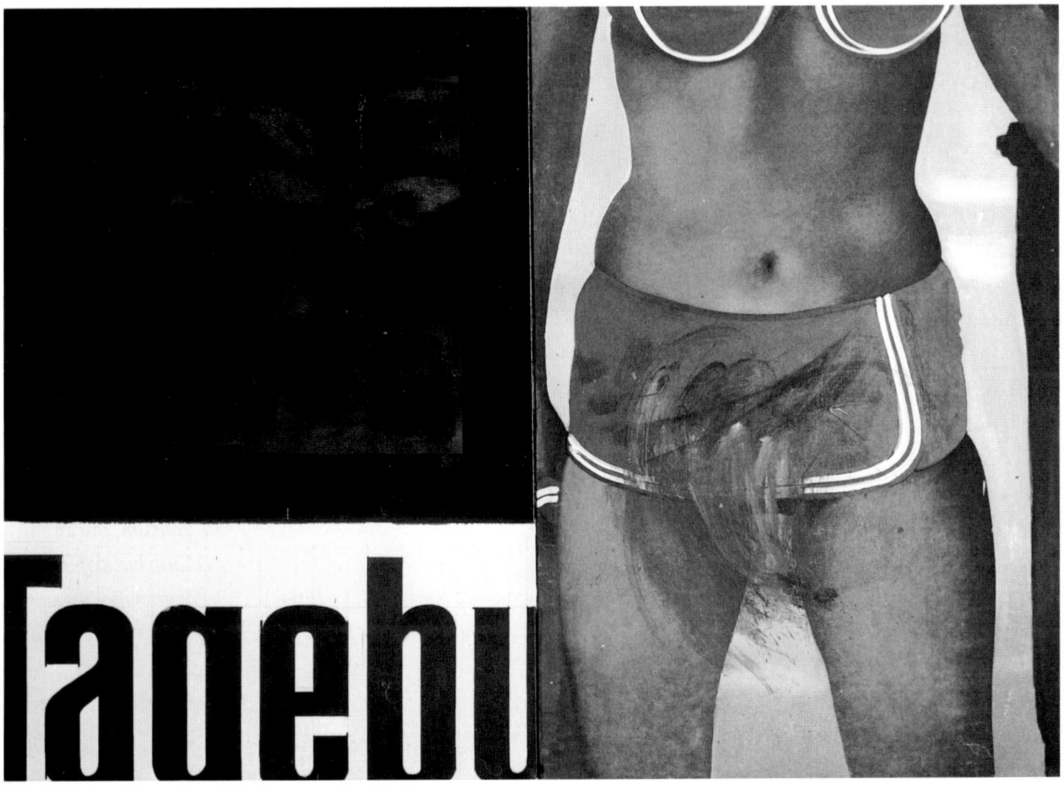

FIG 11
Gerhard Richter, *Erschießung* (*Execution*), 1962. Mixed media on canvas, 66 ⅞ × 78 ¾ in. (170 × 200 cm). Destroyed

FIG 12
Gerhard Richter, *Tagebu(ch)* (*Diary*), 1962. Mixed media on canvas, dimensions unknown. Destroyed

As a new West German citizen and as an artist, Richter was defined within these extremely contradictory parameters of ethical and aesthetic demands. The ethics mandated, more urgently than in the East, that he be politically conscious in order to counteract both the collective condition of disavowed guilt and the repression of Fascist history. And the aesthetics demanded that the geopolitically repositioned artist represent what had been previously utterly unthinkable and was now rightfully considered—and might well prove to remain—utterly impossible to represent. One would only have to think of some of Richter's prominent contemporaries in Europe such as Yves Klein or Piero Manzoni (or, even less comparable, an American like Jasper Johns) to recognize the fundamentally different spectrum of historical, political, and social challenges that Richter actually chose to confront.

Although this spectrum of critical reflection was atypical for most visual artists of Richter's generation, it had already been explored by a number of philosophers, poets, and writers in the immediate aftermath of the war. The resulting theoretical analyses were formulated not only by Arendt and Adorno, German Jewish philosophers writing from the perspective of exile,[8] but equally by writers such as Georges Bataille and Jean-Paul Sartre, coming out of the French Resistance. Therefore, Richter's growing consciousness of the Holocaust was not motivated merely by aesthetic questions concerning the possibilities, or rather, the impossibilities of representation. To an equal if not greater measure, it was defined precisely by those ethical questions that the philosophers posed. The first question concerned the indisputable condition of collective German guilt, which Karl Jaspers had already addressed in 1946:

Metaphysical guilt: There exists a solidarity among men as human beings that makes each co-responsible for every wrong and every injustice in the world, especially for crimes committed in his presence or with his knowledge. If I fail to do whatever I can to prevent them, I too am guilty. If I was present at the murder of others without risking my life to prevent it, I feel guilty in a way not adequately conceivable either legally, politically or morally. That I live after such a thing has happened, weighs upon me as indelible guilt.[9]

The second question asked not only how a post-bourgeois and post-national subjectivity could be credibly constituted after Auschwitz, but also whether any artistic or cultural identity could be reconceived that would not recognize the genocide of the Jewish population of Europe as one of its foundational historical paradigms. Bataille posed this very question in response to Sartre's notorious essay "Anti-Semite and Jew":

In being a man, there is generally an oppressive, sickly element that must be overcome. But this weight and this repugnance were never as heavy as they have become since Auschwitz. Like you and me, those responsible for Auschwitz had nostrils, a mouth, a voice, human reason, they could unite, could have children. Like the Pyramids or the Acropolis, Auschwitz is the fact, the sign of man. The image of man is inseparable, henceforth, from a gas chamber.[10]

The Italian social historian Enzo Traverso has argued that if neither philosophy—in Traverso's argument, primarily Marxist philosophy—nor anthropology has proven capable of understanding and adequately addressing the legacies of Auschwitz, then these disciplines themselves have to be rethought accordingly. That this argument applied equally to the epistemology of aesthetic representation and cultural production in the immediate postwar period, if not the following decades, seems to be a compelling proposition, even though the artistic and art-historical evidence of that period contradicts it, with very few exceptions.[11]

The first and most frequently quoted of Adorno's critical reflections on the possibilities of cultural production after Auschwitz had been formulated shortly after the philosopher's return to Europe from the United States in 1949.[12] While it stated absolutely that "the production of lyrical poetry after Auschwitz was barbaric," the sentence remained relatively vague in determining the criteria of this qualification. Did a poet's mere claim to have survived with a voice intact qualify as barbaric, or did the verdict of barbarism apply generally to poetry's traditional promises to enunciate privileged forms of experience, ranging from the sacred to the spiritual, or from the ravishing to the ravaged recordings of the unconscious, as in recent Surrealist automatism? Or did Adorno's prohibition of poetry situate itself in the lineage of the most advanced epistemology of poetic practices, beginning with Stéphane Mallarmé and reaching a first climax in Dada during World War I? This lineage had defined twentieth-century poetry as a negation of all traditional lexical, phonetic, and grammatical principles, and it had refused the conventions of poetic substitution and condensation precisely in order to foreground those collective forms of linguistic articulation and self-representation that the bourgeois hierarchy of literary genres had perpetually prevented. Not surprisingly, Samuel Beckett, the writer who had fused a narrative of the somatic annihilation of historical experience with the phonetic anti-aesthetics of the Dada avant-garde, emerged as both Adorno's and Richter's favorite post–World War II author.

It has gone previously unnoticed that Adorno's verdict might well have been inspired by Walter Benjamin's seventh thesis from his "Theses on the Philosophy of History," which had—now famously—stated:

There has never been a document of culture that is not simultaneously one of barbarism. And just as it is itself not free from barbarism, neither is it free from the process of transmission, in which it falls from one set of hands into another. The historical materialist thus moves as far away from this as measurably possible. He regards it as his task to brush history against the grain.[13]

It is also little known that Adorno subsequently revised his initial position on poetry on several occasions. His second major statement concerning the conditions of postwar cultural production no longer voiced a prohibition, but rather a fulminating, if not outright nihilistic, critique of culture that resuscitated the most radical anti-aesthetic positions of the first decades of the twentieth century, from Marcel Duchamp's urinal to the writings of Bertolt Brecht. These had already insisted that all artistic propositions should simultaneously enunciate their proper negation, visibly signal the inevitable failures of their utopian promises, and underline the dialectics of culture and barbarism as being inextricably innate to their practices. Thus, Adorno stated in 1965:

Culture intensifies and perpetuates the stench, since it is stench itself, since its palaces are built from dog turds—as Bertolt Brecht once stated in a wonderful passage. A few years after these lines were written, Auschwitz gave us the incontrovertible evidence that all culture had failed. . . . Thus all culture after Auschwitz, including its own urgently necessary critiques, ends up as mere garbage.[14]

We should not forget that modernism's first truly nihilistic epistemology—the post–World War I anti-aesthetic—had defined itself simultaneously within a dialectic of previously unimaginable forms of collective and subjective self-determination while it registered the impact of equally unimaginable catastrophe, annihilation, and trauma. Adorno's surprising citation of Brecht (whose work he generally disparaged) draws on the tropes of scatological debasement to discredit any aspirations for one's privileged elevation in the acts of cultural production and consumption. Yet, while this dialectic of the documents of culture and barbarism might have prevailed during the first three decades of the twentieth century, inevitably, authentic culture after World War II would have to take barbarism as its primary, if not singular, point of departure, bereft of any utopian or redeeming powers that culture might have previously promised. Adorno's philosophical trajectory was modified a third time, in 1965:

I once said that after Auschwitz one could no longer write poetry, and that gave rise to a discussion I did not anticipate. . . . Just as I said that after Auschwitz one could not *write poems—by which I meant to point to the hollowness of the resurrected culture of that time—it could equally well be said, on the other hand, that one* must *write poems, in keeping with Hegel's statement in his* Aesthetics *that as long as there is an awareness of suffering among human beings there must also be art as an objective form of that awareness.*[15]

The author's spectrum of theoretical aesthetic demands, beginning with a fundamental prohibition of poetic language (and, by implication, all forms of cultural depiction and narration), passing through an annihilating anti-aesthetic, and culminating in the declaration of artistic production as an act of mourning and solidarity in human suffering, could well be cited as a model for Richter's own shifting and increasingly differentiated positions. Following the Anne Frank drawings of 1957 and the now-destroyed paintings of 1962, his third attempt to address these ever more urgent and complex questions was a group of particularly important paintings completed in 1964–65 that differed dramatically from his earlier efforts to engage explicitly with German political history; among them are *Family at the Seaside* (p. 106), *Uncle Rudi* (p. 109), *Aunt Marianne* (p. 108), and *Mr. Heyde* (p. 113). In them, he avoided the fallacies of a transcendental position of exemption; they are neither falsely affirmative and treacherously sentimental, like the Anne Frank drawings, nor deceptively self-righteous, like the disturbing juxtaposition of Holocaust references with pinup imagery. In contrast, Richter's photo paintings of 1964–65 almost ostentatiously implicate their author and his family within the very triangulation of actual complicity, guilt, and disavowal. Consider, for example, the portrait of his uncle Rudi, a German Wehrmacht soldier in uniform, who had died in the first six months of the war. The painting was destined to be a gift to the Czech town of Lidice on the occasion of a commemorative exhibition, organized by the Berlin dealer René Block. This exhibition aimed to remind Germans of the massacre of the town's population and the destruction of its buildings that German soldiers had performed in retribution for the 1942 execution of Reinhard Heydrich, the Nazi commander in the so-called Protectorate of Bohemia and Moravia (the part of Czechia occupied by the Germans), by Czech and Slovak resistance fighters. In his apparently affirmative identification with the perpetrator in his own family and with the photographic memories of the family album, the artist explicitly opposed the false sentimentality of commemorative postures promoted by the emerging official memory culture. Even more provocative was Richter's decision to paint Werner Heyde, a protagonist of the Nazi euthanasia program, thus inverting the traditional function of the portrait genre, which was to portray admired agents of history or beloved subjects. The erosion of this convention through the depiction of a high-ranking (yet now seemingly anonymous) Nazi criminal was both a public incrimination of the German people at large—for crimes committed during the freely elected and voluntarily sustained Fascist regime—and an indictment of the scandalous protection former Nazis had received during the period of reconstruction under the government of Konrad Adenauer.[16]

Thus, Richter's portraits of 1964–65 achieve a dual resolution of the conflicts he had faced during his first years in the West by abolishing the false distancing position of both affirmative sentimentality and pseudo-critique. Furthermore, by conflating photographs of Heyde and other perpetrators with the hallowed genre of the portrait, Richter collapsed the difference between the documents of culture and the documents of barbarism, in fact, positing the latter as the primary reference

FIGS 13, 14
Gerhard Richter, *Atlas* sheets 16 and 18, "Photographs from Books," 1967. Each 26 ¼ × 20 ⅜ in. (66.7 × 51.7 cm)

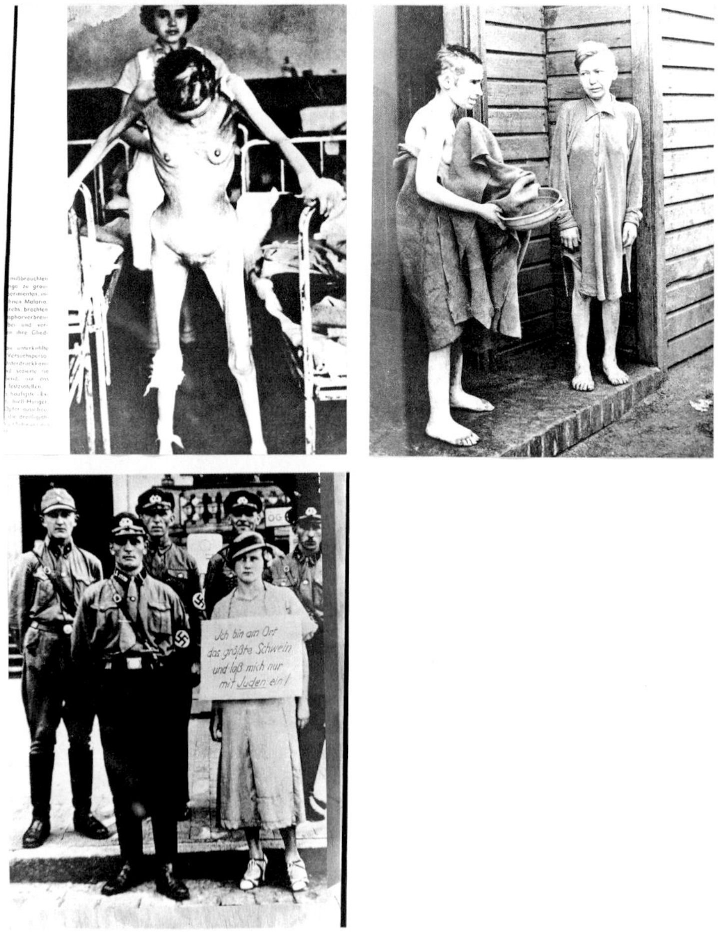

13

and point of departure for any critical reflection.[17] And finally, even on a purely epistemological level, the artist's mapping of the two types of documents generated a fundamental transformation of the ready-made aesthetic itself, whose substitution by the rule of the photographic image had permeated painterly production since Robert Rauschenberg and had culminated with Andy Warhol (both of whom had left an immensely important imprint on Richter's formative years in the West). Richter's iconographic choices finally uncovered and incorporated the photograph's actual historical and political abysmal depths to include the images of trauma and devastation, originating from their ultimate reference to the instantiation of extreme political barbarism, as both Bataille and Adorno had diagnosed.

It might not be accidental at all that these paintings—constituting the first fully credible painterly project to address the history of German Fascism and its consequences for the formation of a new post-Fascist and post-national subjectivity—would emerge as if in tandem with the famous Auschwitz trials conducted in Frankfurt, under the leadership of General Attorney Fritz Bauer, between 1963 and 1965. After all, as is now generally understood, the initiation of these trials not only began a serious process of collective reflection and recognition but also prompted critical interventions by the emerging generation of students and intellectuals who finally dared to confront the silence of the generation of the Fascist fathers.[18]

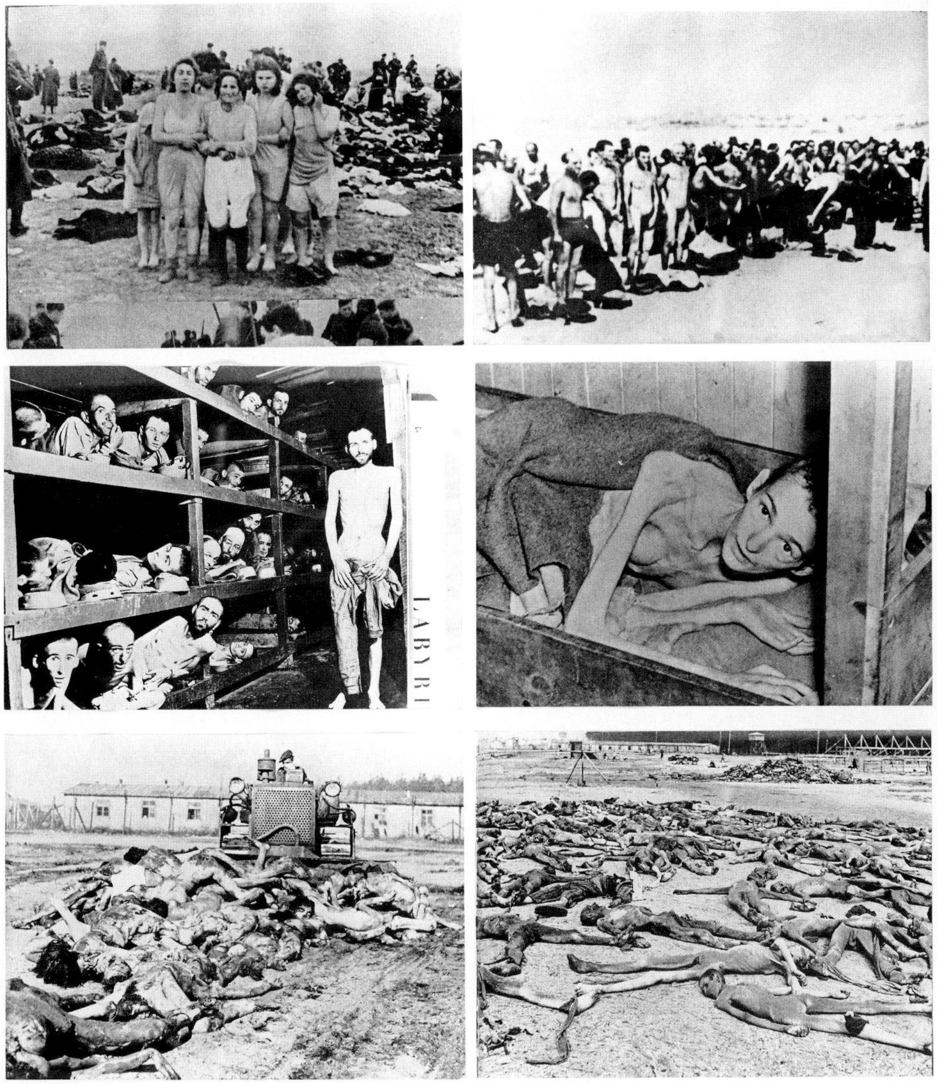

14

Two years after making the photographic paintings, the artist again forced these questions about the representation of the Holocaust. This time, however, he reached for a threshold beyond which any further debates seemed decisively canceled. Deploying two equally offensive strategies, Richter appeared to suggest that, given the historical context, even the very desire for documentary imagery depicting that history would more likely originate from obscene and parasitical voyeuristic compulsion than from evolving forms of belated compassion. Enacted in Richter's *Atlas*, the first strategy juxtaposed photographs from the concentration camps with pornography, and the second one—being no less offensive—inflicted a layer of garish felt-tip marker colors on the former (figs. 13–17).[19] As is by now well known, the scandalous confrontation between traumatic images of bodily annihilation and images of extreme pornographic banality had already occurred in at least two instances, both certainly unknown to Richter in 1967. Five years earlier, Boris Lurie, a survivor of Buchenwald and a member of the NO!art group violently attacking Pop art in New York,[20] made photocollages in which he compiled similarly insufferable juxtapositions of imagery, asserting the paradox that the phenomena of the Holocaust were unspeakable and unthinkable, yet apparently not unviewable. And, as Georges Didi-Huberman has pointed out, Jean-Luc Godard in his film *Une femme mariée* (1964) had forged a constellation of pornographic sex scenes along with clips from Alain Resnais's *Night and Fog* (1956), a

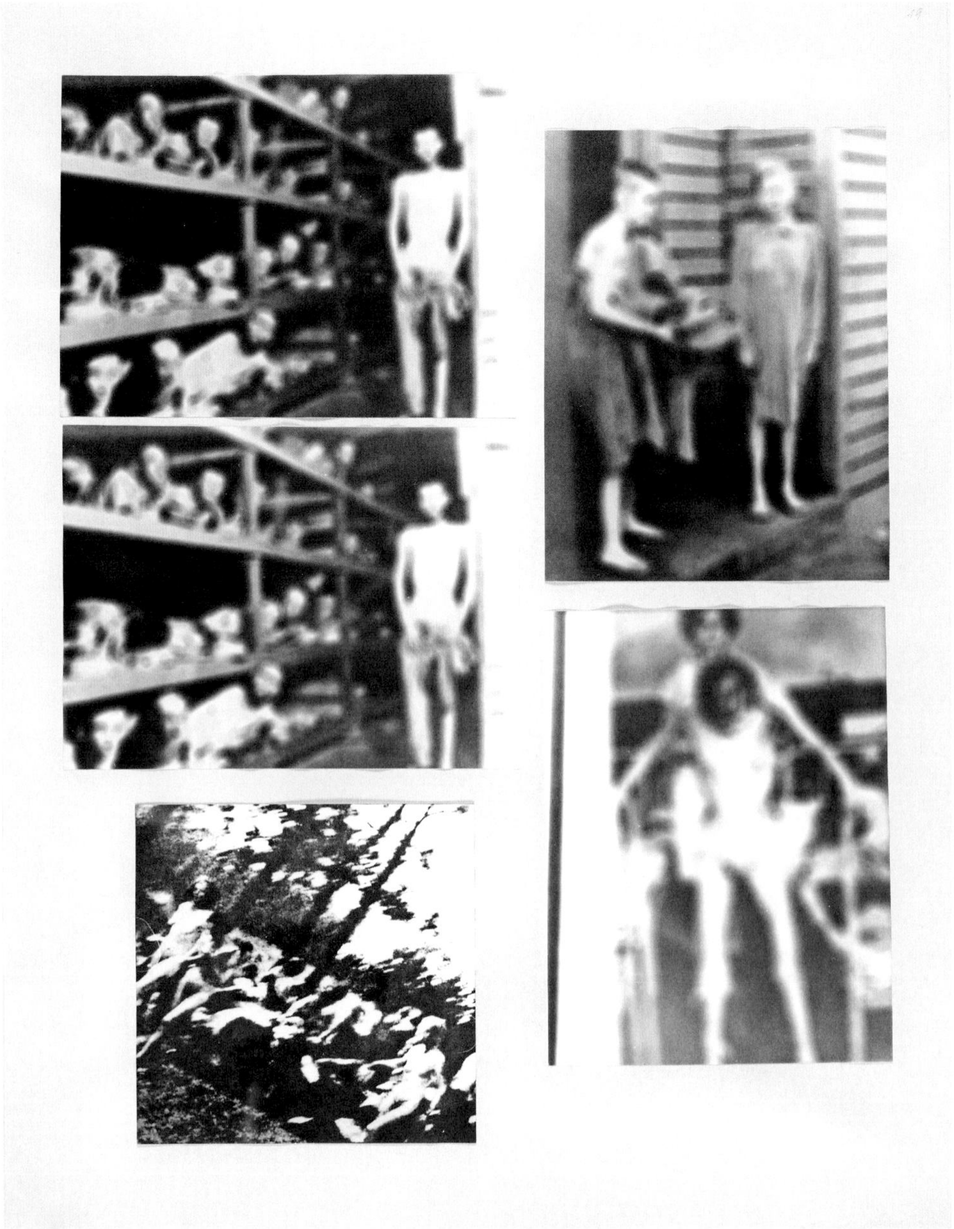

15

FIGS 15, 16
Gerhard Richter, *Atlas* sheets 19 and 20, "Photographs from Books," 1967. Each 26 ¼ × 20 ⅜ in. (66.7 × 51.7 cm)

concentration-camp documentary that had become the most important early documentary film for the broader dissemination of the history of the Holocaust and one of the first films to present the subject with actual photographic material taken at the camps immediately after their liberation.

One preliminary explanation of this startling tactic, practiced by three artists more or less simultaneously, recalls an observation by the German Jewish writer and literary historian Ruth Klüger, who stated, "There was something resembling the pleasure of pornography about the interest at the time in the Holocaust which had not yet been given that name."[21] A second explanation draws on Richter's frequent references to the fact that these photographs of the camps had haunted him since his days as a student in Dresden,[22] when he first encountered them in American and British publications, and that a final reckoning with them in a prospective exhibition and publication might have promised a cathartic relief from years of fixation.[23] And a third, more conclusive interpretation suggests that Richter recognized these images—the ultimate documents of barbarism of the twentieth century—as a paradigmatic dialectical negation of any possible, easily achievable painterly representation in the future. From the painter's perspective, therefore, the true scandal of these images is not just the voyeuristic compulsion that draws the viewer but the fundamental and irreparable schism of vision and desire that they have imposed, complemented by the degradation of painting,

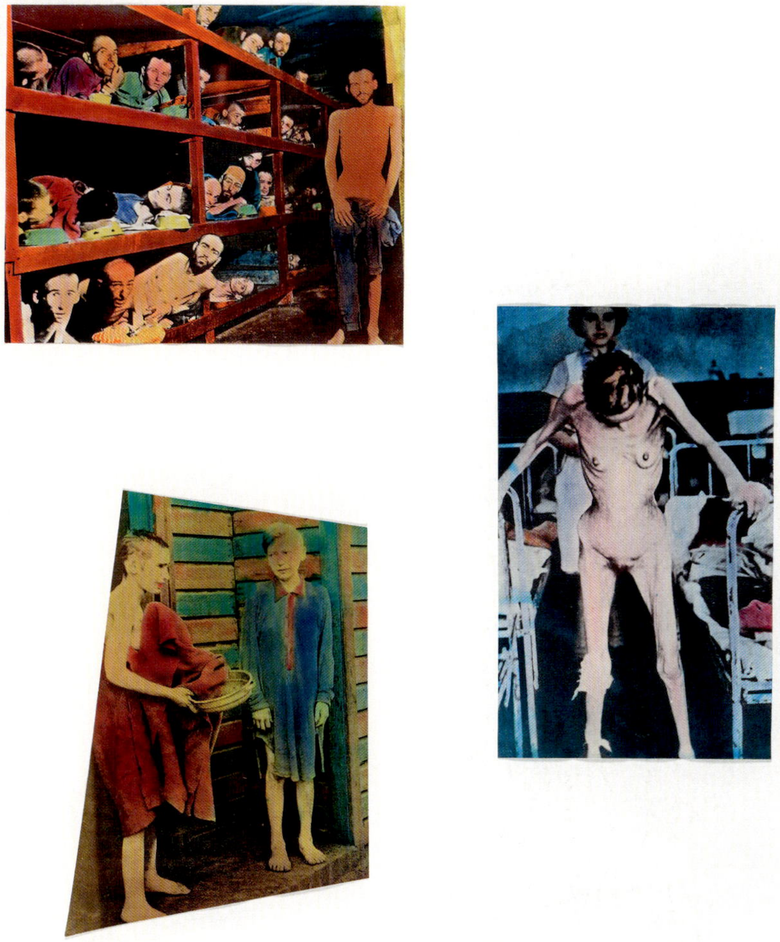

16

that is, even the mere act of coloring a surface. Thus, even the very matter of color—ultimately, the practice of painting itself—aspires to, or inevitably succumbs to, that status of allegorical annihilation.

The Banality of Color

It seems appropriate then to recognize that the garish Warholian application of paint on these photographs not only offends us visually but also devalues color itself as one of painting's traditional essences, corresponding to photography's erasure of painting. Richter's almost exclusive deployment of grisaille in the first five years of his practice had initiated this dual cancellation of painting's presumably essential foundations. Simulating the regime of the photograph, this monotonal scheme insisted that, *sub specie* of (recent) history, any conventional denotative use of color could only betray naïveté, banality, or conciliatory delusions.

Richter's iconic and chromatic *Atlas* images, in contrast, explicitly present themselves as actual documents of barbarism. As such, they exemplify a paradigm of absolute negativity that altered the epistemology of painterly practices in the second half of the twentieth century, similar to the impact of the initial paradigm formations in the 1910s that ranged from abstraction to the ready-made. Taking such imagery as their point of departure, Richter's *Birkenau* paintings (pp. 225–28),

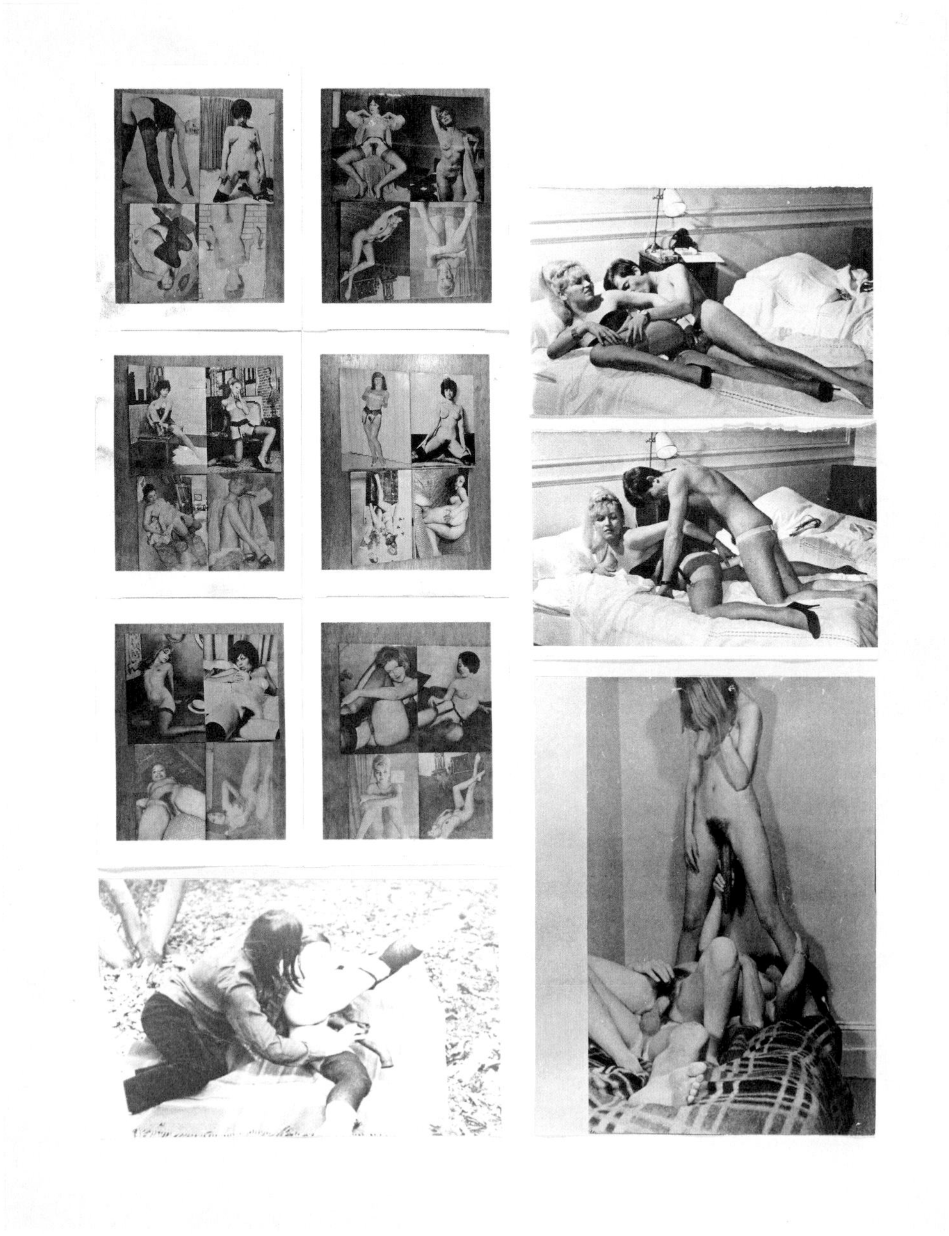

FIG 17
Gerhard Richter, *Atlas* sheet 22, "Photographs from Magazines," 1967. 26 ¼ × 20 ⅜ in. (66.7 × 51.7 cm)

his most recent major work, extend the artist's meditations on the Holocaust and its impact on culture, subjectivity, and nation-state identity into the present, expanding this opposition between photographic documents of barbarism and painterly documents of culture into an almost monumental form.[24]

This group of four paintings is complemented by four digitally produced copies (pp. 224, 229), each of which is divided into four quadrants. The paintings and the copies are to be installed on opposite walls, accompanied by reproductions of four photographs (pp. 230–31) that had been taken secretly in August 1944 by Alex, a Greek prisoner at Auschwitz and a member of the Sonderkommandos, who risked his life smuggling them to the Polish resistance in order to inform the world what was happening in the death camp. As early as 1967, Richter had inserted one of these photos into sheet 19 of his *Atlas* (fig. 15), indicating that he had been familiar with these images before rediscovering them in a review of Didi-Huberman's crucial study *Images in Spite of All*.[25]

Working from initial studies (figs. 18, 19), Richter attempted to transform these four photographs into paintings, at first projecting them and subsequently sketching them in graphite on four large, equally sized canvases, possibly planning to execute them in the manner of the dark grisaille paintings of his cycle *October 18th, 1977* (1987). His work on this project started and stalled over almost a year, a lengthy period of hesitation that ended only when the artist decided he could not achieve what he had first intended. He erased the figurative drawings by overpainting them, starting a slow and prolonged process of producing palimpsests of four large-scale, abstract paintings (fig. 20 illustrates the stages of execution for one of the group).

Once completed, these four paintings covered the drawings of the photographs with a netlike abstraction, an irregular grid structure consistent on all four surfaces, whose facture, rather than being gesturally expressive, appears hesitant, insecure, and confined. And chromatically, these canvases are limited—rather atypically among Richter's abstract works of the last twenty years—mostly to the interaction of the complementary colors of red and green and the noncolors of black and white. If one compares *Birkenau* to Richter's recent large-scale abstract paintings such as the Forest (2005; pp. 188–89) and Cage (2006; pp. 196–201) series, their intrinsic differences in color, texture, and facture become instantly evident. Such a comparison also forces us once again to confront the questions of whether and how painterly abstraction could actually represent a fundamentally unrepresentable historical subject. In the *Birkenau* paintings, where would one find the marks of distinction and the criteria of differentiation between the mnemonic and spectacular morphologies of Richter's abstraction? After all, in Richter's large-scale abstractions, the transubstantiation of visual structures and chromatic contrasts into registers of seemingly pure optical delectation often borders on the spectacular, a condition—as Guy Debord famously argued in 1967—that subordinates all other forms of communication and experience to specular exchange and gratification.[26] Could one discern the documents of culture and barbarism within the register of texture, facture, and gesture, or would one more likely discover their fundamental incompatibility and incomparability within the chromatic register? Or, if neither, what other specific criteria would the paintings offer to develop a credible differentiation?

Structure and facture in the *Birkenau* paintings manifestly suspend, if not terminate, the principles that had previously ruled Richter's abstractions. They exchange the grand gesture, even if it had been semi-mechanically produced with a squeegee, for a painterly procedure that appears almost as a stultified stutter. And the paintings' chromatic differentiations correspond to this facture with a closed circularity, given that the spectral flows and glissandos of Richter's previous abstractions have been reduced to the arrested bipolarities of green and red, black and white. If they indeed convey a sense of recalcitrance against the chromatic opulence and seductive plenitude of Richter's earlier abstract paintings, they demarcate a decisive difference from the spectacular in painting itself, a difference that at times might not have been all that clearly defined. All hopes that color might be redeemed seem finally vanquished; a perfidious green, for example, reminds us that this hue can never be extracted from its attachment to the referents of nature. And the complementary red—strangely never condemned by the great avatars of abstraction,[27] even though its referential bonds with nature (ranging from roses to blood) are just as fixed—appears here as an equally impertinent hue, suggesting that red and green serve as the two foundational colors of a cruel cycle of growth and destruction, of remembering and forgetting, as if their complementarity could naturalize the eradication and resuscitation of life. In their juxtaposition with red and green, the small units of black and white, remnants from Richter's melancholic grisaille paintings, are equally fragmented and particularized. Thus, the hesitant morphologies and confined chromatic constellations seem to trace the contradictions operative within the mnemonic process itself, as both an inevitable necessity and an inevitable failure, echoing Beckett's famous statement: "I can't go on, I must go on."

Given that no traces of the photographs or the drawings of them remain visible in the paintings, the only connection to the images published in Didi-Huberman's study is the eventual choice of the title, *Birkenau.* Prior to their first presentation, at the Dresden Albertinum in 2015, Richter had simply identified the works as *Four Abstract Paintings.* Only after a period of additional reflection did the artist reluctantly decide to refer to these works as the *Birkenau* paintings, thus making explicit their origins and historical references.

The Duplicate

One of the stranger features in Richter's conception and execution of *Birkenau* was his decision to subject these paintings immediately after completion to a process of digital duplication. On the occasion of the Dresden exhibition, the artist decided to install the two groups—the four original paintings and the four reproductions—on opposite walls. The digital duplications are differentiated from the paintings by the partitioning of each into equally sized quadrants, the demarcation of which inserts a negative white space into the previously unified and unique painterly body. Viewers might associate this partition with a cruciform grid (like a window frame), the crosshairs of a weapon's scope, or the religious emblem of a cross. Given that Richter had previously duplicated some of his paintings photographically (at first in 1972, after the sale of his *48 Portraits*) and more recently had reproduced key paintings (including *Ema [Nude on a Staircase]*, *Uncle Rudi*, and *Mr. Heyde*) in photographic editions without partitioning the prints, we must assume that the spatial and perceptual division of the *Birkenau* reproductions was motivated by more complex demands.[28]

The first reason might have been to sustain the dialectical opposition between singularity and multiplicity, which has served as a formal and conceptual strategy in many of Richter's crucial works and has permeated his thinking since the mid-1960s. Painting's innate claims to be unique and singular were always challenged by the potential for proliferation and

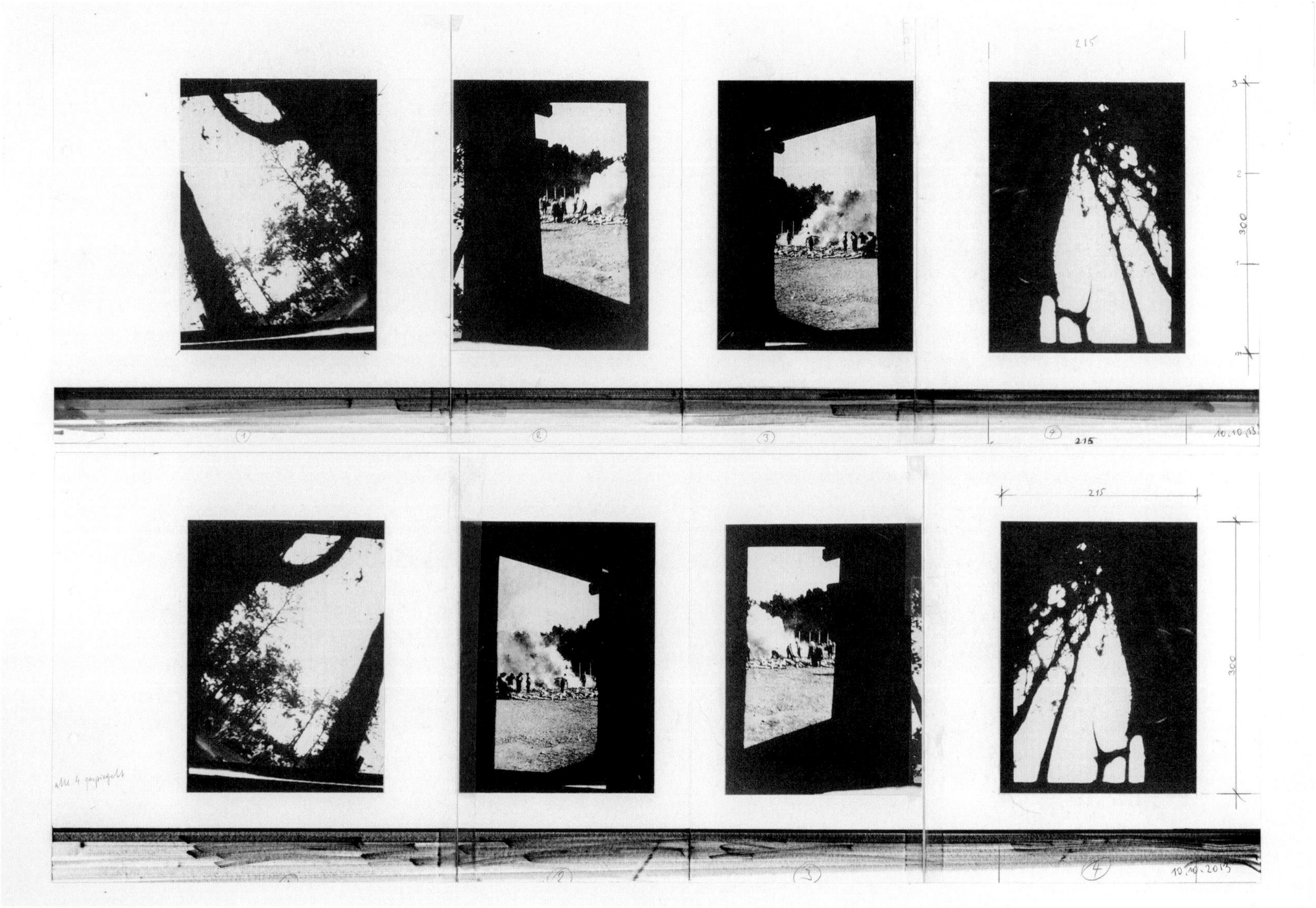

FIGS 18, 19
Gerhard Richter, *Atlas* sheets 807 and 808, "Studies for Birkenau," 2013. Each 19 ¾ × 27 ½ in. (50 × 70 cm)

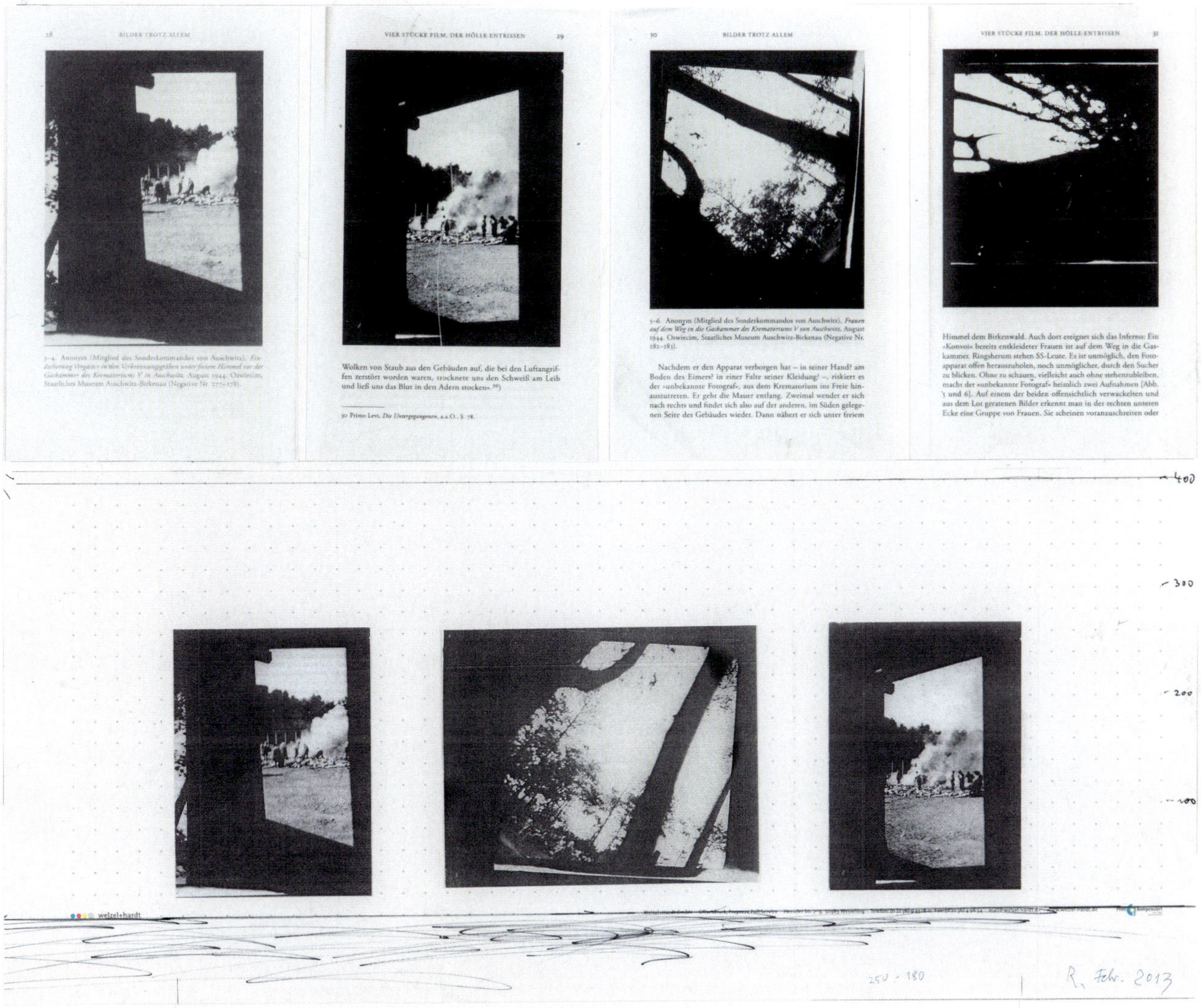
28 BILDER TROTZ ALLEM
3–4. Anonym (Mitglied des Sonderkommandos von Auschwitz), *Einäscherung Vergaster in den Verbrennungsgräben unter freiem Himmel vor der Gaskammer des Krematoriums V in Auschwitz.* August 1944. Oświecim, Staatliches Museum Auschwitz-Birkenau (Negative Nr. 277–278).
VIER STÜCKE FILM, DER HÖLLE ENTRISSEN 29
Wolken von Staub aus den Gebäuden auf, die bei den Luftangriffen zerstört worden waren, trocknete uns den Schweiß am Leib und ließ uns das Blut in den Adern stocken«.[30])
30 Primo Levi, *Die Untergegangenen*, a.a.O., S. 78.
30 BILDER TROTZ ALLEM
5–6. Anonym (Mitglied des Sonderkommandos von Auschwitz), *Frauen auf dem Weg in die Gaskammer des Krematoriums V von Auschwitz.* August 1944. Oswiecim, Staatliches Museum Auschwitz-Birkenau (Negative Nr. 282–283).
Nachdem er den Apparat verborgen hat – in seiner Hand? am Boden des Eimers? in einer Falte seiner Kleidung? –, riskiert es der »unbekannte Fotograf«, aus dem Krematorium ins Freie hinauszutreten. Er geht die Mauer entlang. Zweimal wendet er sich nach rechts und findet sich also auf der anderen, im Süden gelegenen Seite des Gebäudes wieder. Dann nähert er sich unter freiem
VIER STÜCKE FILM, DER HÖLLE ENTRISSEN 31
Himmel dem Birkenwald. Auch dort ereignet sich das Inferno: Ein »Konvoi« bereits entkleideter Frauen ist auf dem Weg in die Gaskammer. Ringsherum stehen SS-Leute. Es ist unmöglich, den Fotoapparat offen herauszuholen, noch unmöglicher, durch den Sucher zu blicken. Ohne zu schauen, vielleicht auch ohne stehenzubleiben, macht der »unbekannte Fotograf« heimlich zwei Aufnahmen [Abb. 5 und 6]. Auf einem der beiden offensichtlich verwackelten und aus dem Lot geratenen Bilder erkennt man in der rechten unteren Ecke eine Gruppe von Frauen. Sie scheinen voranzuschreiten oder
400
300
200
100
welzel+hardt
250 · 180
R., Febr. 2013

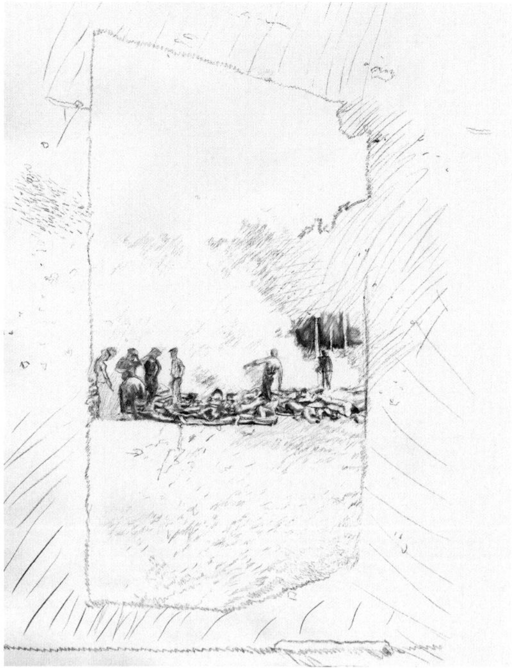

July 15

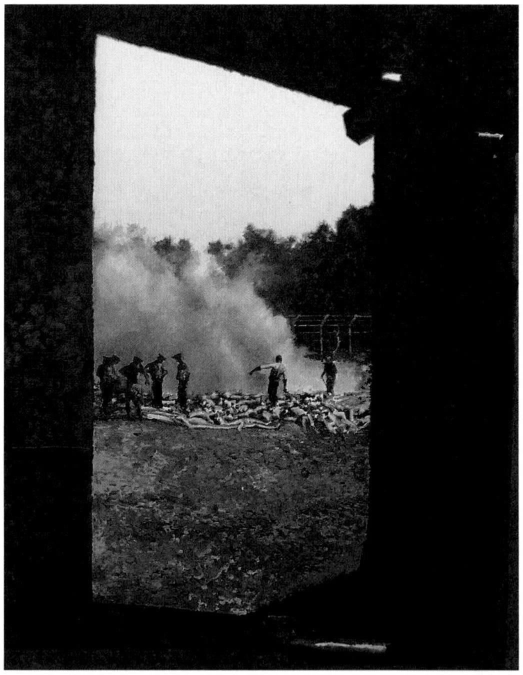

July 29

FIG 20
Eight states of *Birkenau* (CR 937-2), 2014. Each 102 ⅜ × 78 ¾ in. (260 × 200 cm)

August 3

August 3

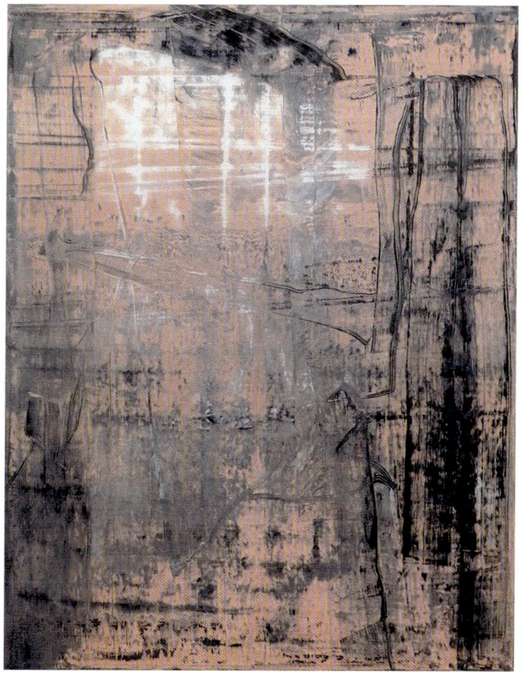
August 4

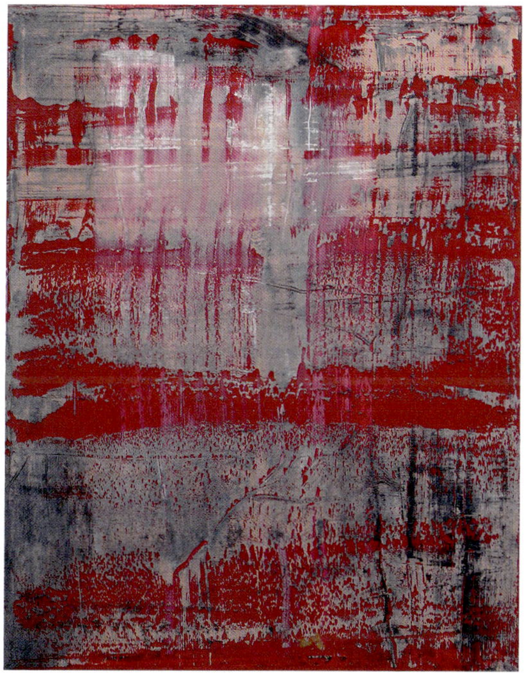
August 13

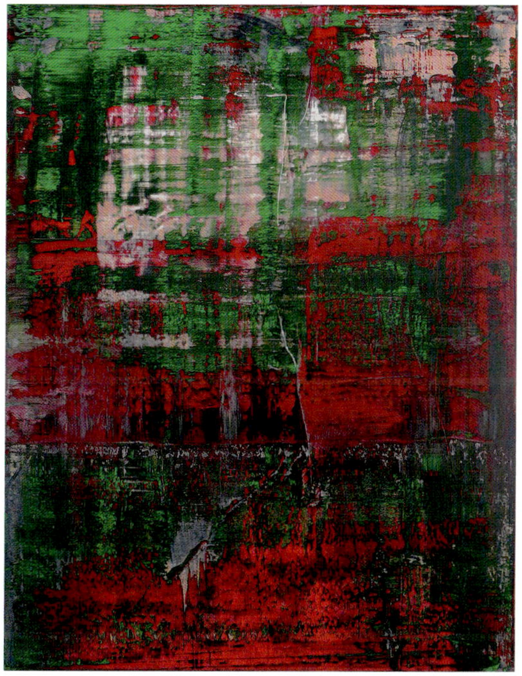
August 14

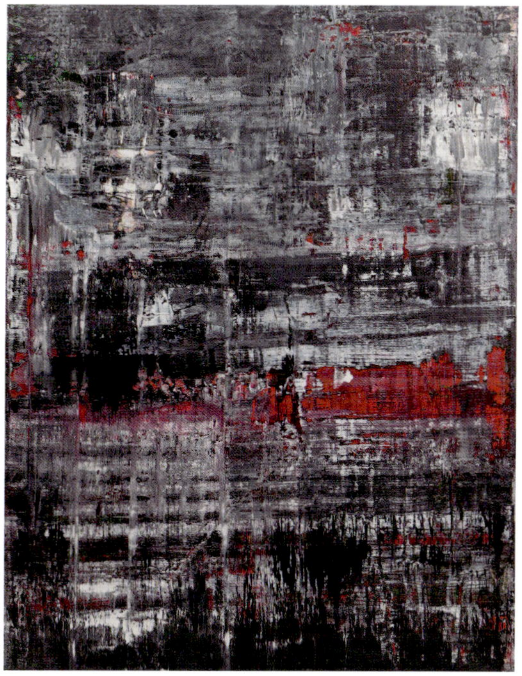
August 25

confronted with the inevitable multiplicity of reproduction. A second motivation for the digital duplication of the *Birkenau* group could have been the desire to simultaneously resist both the work's incumbent monumentality and its equally inevitable fetishization as spectacularized painting, the principal modes of reception with which contemporary culture obstructs any intrinsically mnemonic project. And even a third reason, an economic calculation, might have motivated the digital reproductions. Unlike the paintings, which Richter has identified explicitly as originals that cannot be sold, the two sets of reproductions, each comprising sixteen digital prints, can paradoxically realize their immense potential in the art market.[29]

Thus, one may wonder whether the paintings' duplication should be read primarily as an allegorical devaluation of their singularity, or whether this technological permutation augments their importance, as if functioning almost like a proliferating parthenogenesis of mnemonic images. One may also consider whether this extension from unique painting to digital copy transforms a memory image that meditates on the past—and represents the singular history of the Shoah—into an operative document that confronts the present and future, recognizing an apparently iterative cyclical structure of violence and barbarism within the current political sphere. Thus, the relationship between the original *Birkenau* paintings and their reproductions appears to actually dehistoricize the legacy of the death camps and to redirect the emphasis toward conditions of extreme political violence today.

If read in this manner, Richter's diptych (composed of the two groups) probes further philosophical questions that relate to the theorization, historicization, and representation of the Holocaust. The first one queries to what degree any attempt to construct a mnemonic representation of historical trauma in the present is itself inevitably and involuntarily implicated in the very process of spectacularization, a social tendency whose primary motivation aims precisely at the elimination of mnemonic and historical thinking. Whether any painting, particularly Richter's large abstractions, can resist its immediate subjection to spectacle culture is a challenge that his work has faced for several decades, one that the artist had to confront all the more in the *Birkenau* series. That Holocaust memory can and will all too easily be transformed into a product of the culture industry was lamented by the Hungarian writer and Holocaust survivor Imre Kertész:

> *Many more are those who steal the Holocaust from its guardians only to make cheap junk of it. . . . A Holocaust conformism was formed, as well as a sentimentalism, a Holocaust canon, a system of taboos and its ritual language, Holocaust products for the consumption of the Holocaust.*[30]

The second theoretical question Richter's *Birkenau* addresses is the seemingly unresolvable conflict among historical, ethical, and aesthetic demands. If some historians contend that all images of the Holocaust should be publicized, others insist that only abstraction—as an ethical and aesthetic prohibition—can abolish the repression of history and induce mnemonic representations without (re-)activating the viewer's sadistic desires for spectacle that victimize the victims once again. Richter's *Birkenau* precisely stages this dialectical tension between the photographic document of trauma and the mnemonic, if not redemptive, painterly sublimation.

The most incisive distrust of photographic documents as authentic traces that promise to bring the viewer closer to the unimaginable but, in fact, veil it or parasitically share its scopic violence was voiced by Adorno. In his 1962 text "Commitment," one of the first philosophical critiques of the representation of trauma in Holocaust imagery, the philosopher warned against the tendency among politically committed artists to aestheticize suffering.[31] Even the most faithful image of suffering positions viewers at a safe, almost pornographic remove from the event, allowing them to feel in control of the depicted scene. Though he was not specifically differentiating between painting and photography, Adorno's critique of the iconic mimesis of suffering is decisive:

> *The so-called artistic representation of the sheer physical pain of people beaten to the ground by rifle-butts contains, however remotely, the power to elicit enjoyment out of it. The moral of this art, not to forget for a single instant, slithers into the abyss of its opposite.*[32]

In the mid-1980s, Adorno's prohibition of representation was voiced even more forcefully by Claude Lanzmann, ironically a close ally and friend of Sartre, who had been at the center of Adorno's critique in "Commitment." Eleven years in the making, Lanzmann's *Shoah* (1974–85), a documentary film of almost ten hours, consists solely of present-day footage of Holocaust survivors and members of the resistance, as well as, on occasion, interview attempts with some of the Nazi perpetrators. In certain ways, Lanzmann opposed and inverted the principles of Resnais's *Night and Fog* by programmatically rejecting the use of archival footage and documentary photographs. Coining the phrase "obscenity of understanding," he insisted that the iconic and mimetic representation of the victims, no matter how pedagogical the shock might be, amounted to an obscene act—one that would essentially comfort viewers by placing them in the mastering position of the perpetrators. Taking a position similar to Adorno's, he negated the assumption that a historical trauma of the magnitude of the Shoah could ever be visually grasped and understood.

And the third question—possibly the most difficult—posed by Richter's *Birkenau* is whether the Shoah should, and can, be historicized at all, as authors like Enzo Traverso have extensively argued. Or whether the Shoah, following Elie Wiesel's theological demand, should be considered a unique and singular catastrophe that solely concerns the Jewish people, a catastrophe that cannot be theorized outside the history of European anti-Semitism and should not be compared with other genocides in different historical and political contexts, let alone with any present situation. Richter's strategy of subverting the unique sanctity of the *Birkenau* paintings by replicating them with their digital mirror, and thereby increasing their circulation, suggests that he shares the former position, implicitly stating that the violence of Nazi Fascism, while the most horrendous of the crimes against humanity in the twentieth century, should not be isolated and singularized. Rather, the multiplication of the works could suggest that any commemorative approach to understanding the Shoah inevitably has to expand the scope of its critical reflection to include the catastrophes of the present and the imminent future.

Naming Abstraction

In his groundbreaking study *Abstraction and the Holocaust,* Mark Godfrey traces both the history of post-World War II American modernist abstraction and the various efforts—successes and failures—of artists, historians, and critics in that period to either utterly ignore the intersection of Holocaust history and the culture of abstract painting or to confront it in a variety of complicated maneuvers.[33] The first of the few possible challenges to his important thesis, as much as to our own interpretation of Richter's *Birkenau* paintings, derives from the insight that actually only a very small number of works could be explicitly positioned within the historical trajectory that took the caesura of the Holocaust as its point of departure. Thus, a first question emerges concerning the formal and morphological status of these abstract paintings: having been produced by these postwar artists before, during, and after their temporary engagement with that history, would they now not have to appear totally indifferent to, if not outright defiant of, any such contextualization? Among the few figures for whom this engagement was momentous or foundational (i.e., Barnett Newman, Morris Louis, and Frank Stella), only Stella, in his early Black Paintings,[34] allows for a productive comparison with Richter; both belong to the same generation (they were born in 1936 and 1932, respectively), and both respond to the powerful legacy of American Abstract Expressionism. Taking Godfrey's extensive discussion of Stella into account,[35] our brief comparison will allow us also to pose a second question: Can the mere act of establishing a reference by naming a nonrepresentational painting, such as Stella's *Arbeit Macht Frei* (fig. 21), in 1958, or Richter's *Birkenau*, in 2014, possibly justify the work as a credible, critical, or mnemonic attempt at painterly representation after the Holocaust?

If our first question acknowledges that post-World War II artistic cultures could not possibly have fulfilled the aesthetic mandate that all artistic practices after Auschwitz (and historical trauma) would have to depart from documents of barbarism, it also entails another acknowledgment, namely, that all common cultural production since then has inevitably acquired the condition of compensatory, if not fraudulent, consolation. Similarly, if our second question acknowledges that the ethical

FIG 21
Frank Stella (American, born 1936). *Arbeit Macht Frei*, 1958. Enamel on canvas, 85 × 121 ½ in. (215.9 × 308.6 cm). Private collection

aspiration for cultural practices is to initiate processes of forming truly post-national identities, then we would have to admit in analogue that the actual features of national identities provided by cultural production inevitably always reveal the fraudulence of all identitarian claims.

Stella's nominalist incursion in 1958—what we could call an act of deictic voluntarism—reminded the emerging American art world (at the time about to be newly renovated with a post-Duchampian aesthetic) of the actual historical and sociopolitical conditions of experience that determined the conception of painting after the Holocaust. His diffident gesture was as powerful as a provocation as it was temporary in its effects on the new concepts driving cultural production. Richter's naming of his work in 2014, almost fifty years later, performs a similarly provocative, if not more profound, staging of the near-impossible aspirations to induce and sustain a mnemonic, critical, and political practice, given the universal rule of spectacle and exchange value in the art world. The mere act of naming by both painters seems to acknowledge, after all, that abstraction will inevitably have to fail in the face of its immense task to represent the unrepresentable with painterly means. And only the chasm between the act of naming and the gesture of a nameless and comparatively meaningless painting can confront viewers with the actual demands to be literally faced.

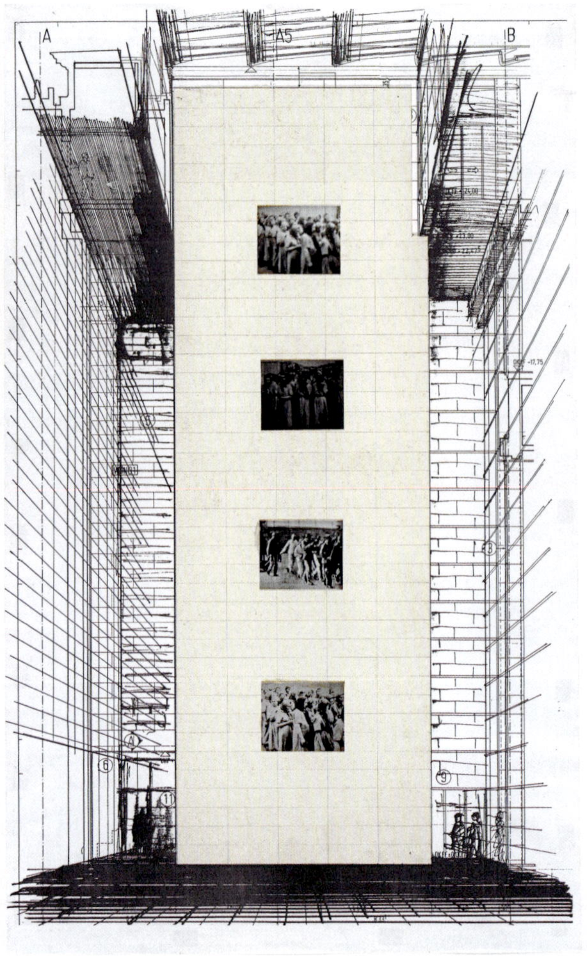

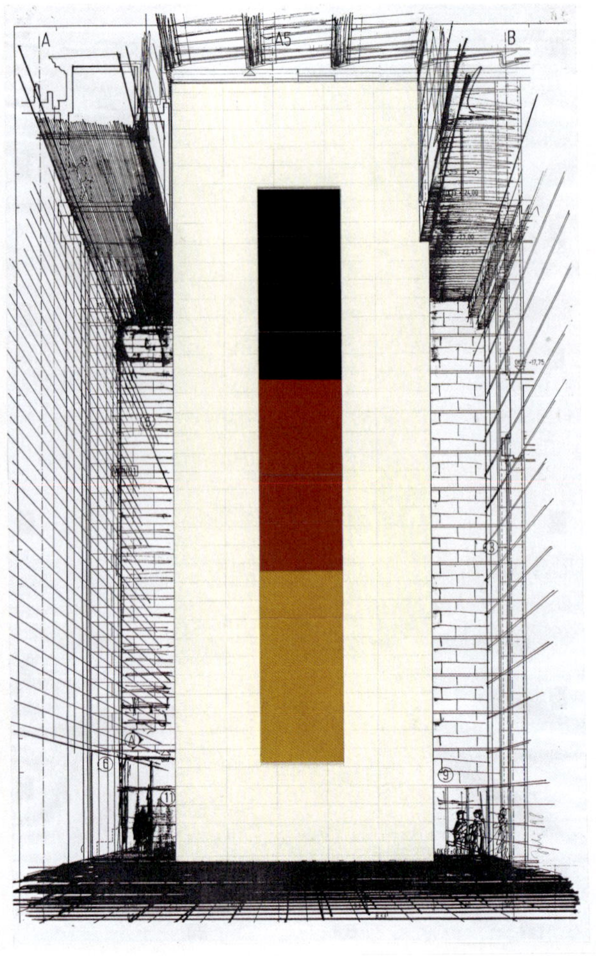

FIGS 22, 23
Gerhard Richter, *Atlas* sheets 648 and 655, "Reichstag," 1997.
Each 28 × 20 ⅜ in. (71 × 51.7 cm)

Nation-State Culture after Auschwitz

In 1997, almost ten years before the *Birkenau* project, Richter had returned once more to the photographs of the concentration camps in his *Atlas*. The occasion was a commission from the German government to contribute a site-specific work to the restored Reichstag in Berlin, which had become the seat of parliament in the recently reunified Germany. And again, Richter's initial conception to take the documents of barbarism as his point of departure—this time, by installing the photographs as mural-size billboards in the building's entrance hall (fig. 22)—was eventually rejected by the artist. Clearly, we must assume that he recognized once more that the photographic depiction of the victims would only amount to renewed spectatorial scopic abuse. More importantly, the artist figured that the monumental and ostentatious display of these presumably mnemonic devices could only legitimize a reconstituted, self-righteous nation-state ideology. Thus, in a perplexing reversal, Richter submitted a comparatively bland final project that merely decorates the wall space assigned to him with a monumental construction of six large, enameled-glass panels in the three colors of the German flag (fig. 23). Anticipating the fate of his work, like all cultural production, to be subjected to a "process of transmission, in which it falls from one set of hands into another," as Walter Benjamin stated, Richter knew that, at this moment in history, memory itself would be recruited to the ceremonious celebration of a newly found nation-state pride.

Yet, Richter's resuscitation of the memory of Auschwitz in the *Birkenau* paintings might not have been motivated only by his desire to contest these conditions of assimilation to nation-state culture, or by his almost compulsively cyclical return to the question of how his painting could serve as a mnemonic project reflecting the possibilities of cultural production by a German artist after the Holocaust. It might have been actualized by the recognition of an evolving insight that artistic practices under present political circumstances increasingly face the near-universal renewal of proto-Fascist nationalist ideologies that urgently warrant a manifest cultural and political opposition. Consider the following random sampling of recent symptoms from the actual sociopolitical climate in which Richter created *Birkenau*, drawn from a broad spectrum of current German class society and its semblance of universal economic might.[36] We can start the ladder with the proto-Fascist Berlin Islamic *lumpenproletarian* rappers Farid Bang and Kollegah, who mock the bodies of Auschwitz victims in their "songs" and announce a "future Holocaust"—only to receive the highest official annual award of the German music industry, appropriately named the Echo. Or we can step up the social ladder to hear a German corporate superpower broker, the CEO of Volkswagen, entertaining his stockholders at a conference with the slogan "Ebit Macht Frei," a pun on the notorious inscription "Arbeit Macht Frei" (work sets you free) on the gates at Auschwitz and other concentration camps.[37] Or we can quote a petty bourgeois middle-class politician, reminted as the reactionary leader of a new right-wing populist party, stating in 2019: "Hitler and the Nazis are only a bit of bird shit on over a thousand years of successful German history."[38] Or we can read seemingly liberal art historians, devoted to triumphantly restoring an innately patriarchal discourse of mastery and national identity, asserting: "Germany is now recognized worldwide for its exemplary responsibility in engaging with history. . . . All four artists (Baselitz, Kiefer, Polke, Richter) represent what one could call an *Ur-deutsche phenomenon* evident in their works embedded in German history since the early 1960s."[39] All of these statements claim a new nationalist legitimacy and strike identitarian poses that emulate the legacy of Auschwitz within a new cocoon of national pride and a decisive repression of historical memory.

The most sinister of these maneuvers in the cultural register is perhaps to be found in a seemingly elegant passage by the art historian Götz Adriani, suggesting that now even the poet Paul Celan's famous phrase "Death is a master from Germany" can be convincingly dismissed and traded for a reference to Richter and others as the new "Masters from Germany":

> *How could art now take the place of death that had been implored by Celan as the Master from Germany? This interest in a quality brand "Made in Germany," paired with a seemingly irreducible market demand, was not a foregone conclusion, since German art in the course of its history for the most part had lived in the shadow of Dutch, Italian, French and American models. . . . In the course of its 500-year history only Albrecht Dürer, Hans Holbein the Younger, and Adam Elsheimer achieved international recognition beyond Germany during their lifetime.*[40]

And once the master discourse of this patriarchal Mercedes mentality is spun into action and out of control, we learn that those four male masters are the sole and the first German artists to ever have achieved international recognition (as though Käthe Kollwitz, John Heartfield, Kurt Schwitters, Hannah Höch, Eva Hesse, Hanne Darboven, and Isa Genzken had never existed and had not been known in the world). It is precisely this recruitment of painting, and of cultural practices in general, for the purpose of sustaining the nationalist and masculinist discourses of the so-called imagined communities that Richter's *Birkenau* opposes. The work undermines those discourses with the weak and pervasive negativity of allegorical abstraction, a visual language that had to define itself historically in the dialectical negation of its utopian origins and aspirations, without, however, yielding even the slightest impulse of its critical opposition to ideological deployment. After all, Adorno's insight that the "unspeakable dimensions of utopian thought are only to be represented in absolute negativity"[41] determines Richter's oeuvre to this very moment.

Peter Geimer

Seeing One Medium through Another: Richter's Photo Paintings of the 1960s

Gerhard Richter's *Dead* (fig. 24), one of the artist's earliest paintings based on a photograph, takes its motif from an article in the West German illustrated magazine *Quick* about the mysterious sinking of a steamship off the coast of Long Island, New York. Of the article's illustrations, Richter selected the photo showing one of the three corpses that had washed ashore, half hidden beneath a huge block of ice (fig. 25). Richter first exhibited the painting in May 1963, in an empty Düsseldorf storefront at Kaiserstrasse 31A that he and his friends Manfred Kuttner, Konrad Lueg, and Sigmar Polke had rented for a joint exhibition. As the four artists wrote in a letter to the city officials, "The exhibition does not have a commercial purpose, but seeks to inform about a new figurative direction in art and to exhibit for the first time a group of young Düsseldorf artists."[1] Coined Capitalist Realism, this "new figurative direction" was both a play on Soviet Socialist Realism and a response to the ascendancy of Pop art in the West. Richter had left Dresden, in East Germany, two years before and enrolled at Düsseldorf's Art Academy. As a refugee he received a state stipend, but his financial situation was still precarious, and in order to support himself he sold pigments at the academy, helped out at artist parties, and, with Kuttner and Lueg, designed parade floats for the Rhineland's Carnival.

All this occurred more than half a century ago, and today it is by no means easy to understand the political and cultural climate of 1963, let alone Richter's thinking about art in only his second year residing in the Federal Republic of Germany. Nevertheless, it is necessary to discard the notion that in the year it was painted *Dead* was an "early work" of Richter's, for everything that could have rendered it one lay in the future and was accordingly incalculable: the Townscapes and Abstract Paintings, the color panels and Strips, the gray mirrored surfaces, the overpainted photographs, and the later paintings based on photos, from the *48 Portraits* and the cycle *October 18, 1977* to *September* and, finally, to the four abstract canvases titled *Birkenau*. Art historians tend to think that an artist's entire production can be traced back to hidden, inner linkages, latent sources, and foreshadowing of later works. It is from these factors that the "strange unit designated by the term, work"[2] arises, and in this line of thinking one of the most dubious, though persistent, notions is that of the "early work." An "early work" is identified as such only later, forming the basis of a teleology that sees an artist's development through time as being driven by an inner, predetermined logic. This essay attempts to avoid this teleological constraint and to look at Richter's early paintings not from the vantage point of a clearly contoured oeuvre but within the contingency of his beginnings, not so much as his "early work" but as examples of contemporary picture making in the 1960s. Needless to say, when considering Richter's photo paintings in their historical context, one cannot fully ignore what we know of all that followed. Yet, it makes a difference whether one takes the later work as the basis for an interpretation of the earlier pieces or opts to avoid such a teleological short circuit.

The painting *Coffin Bearers* (p. 105) is also based on a tabloid photograph—in this case, one taken from an article in the February 1963 issue of *Neue Illustrierte* about a serial killer who ultimately poisoned his wife in her sleep. The image captures the moment when funeral home employees were removing the victim's coffin from her house (fig. 26; see also fig. 36). In his painted version, Richter largely suppressed any indication of the setting, shifting the event into an abstract picture space. A gray veil obscures portions of the picture. Above the coffin rises a vortex of black pigment in clearly visible brushstrokes, beneath which drips of paint have trickled down into the light rectangle of the coffin. In the painting, the man standing on the far left in the photograph has become like a stele figure, isolated from what is taking place, and a speech bubble containing a series of arbitrary numbers issues from his mouth. *Coffin Bearers* captivates with its direct juxtaposition of two different modes of representation: on the one hand, nonobjective, gestural forms in blurred or dripping paint, and on the other,

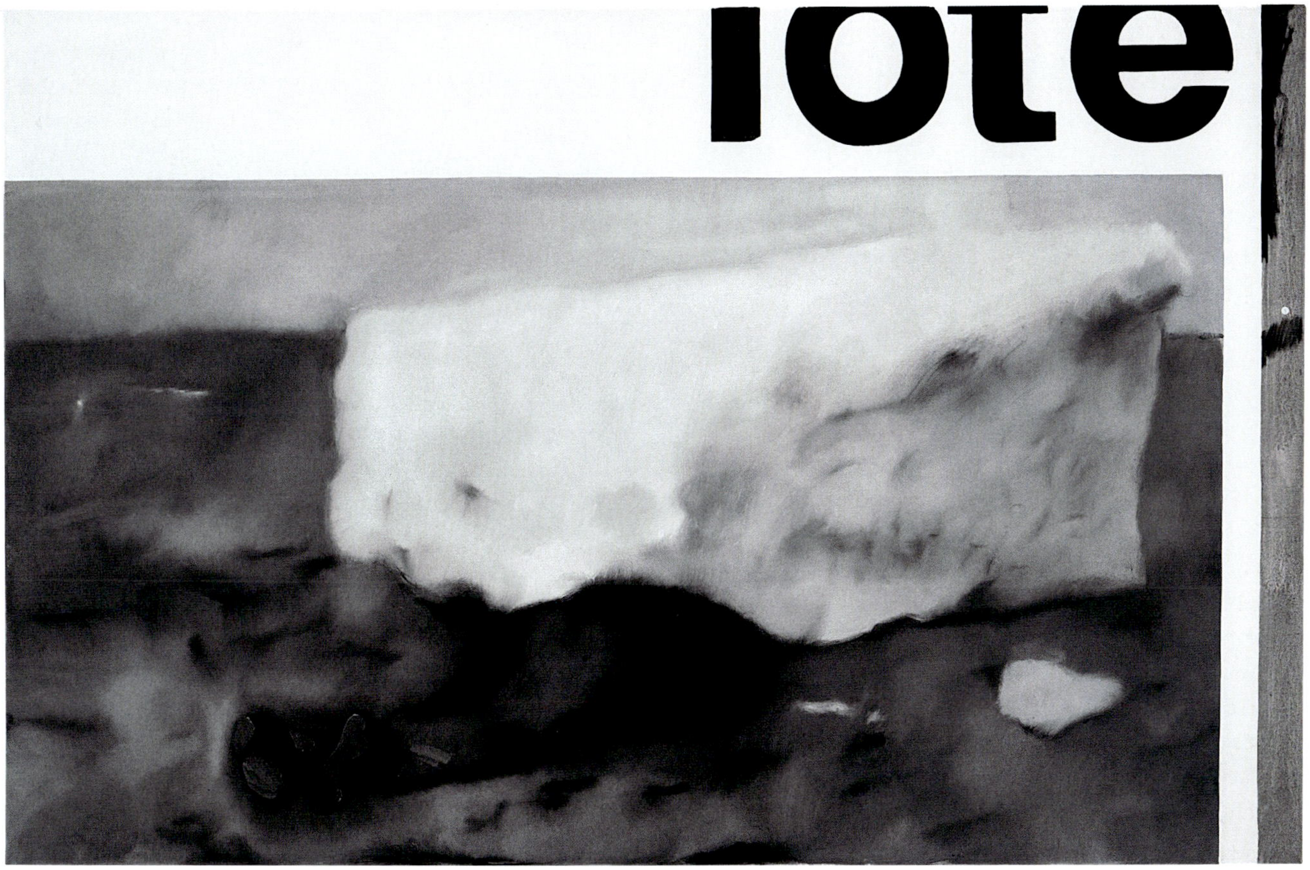

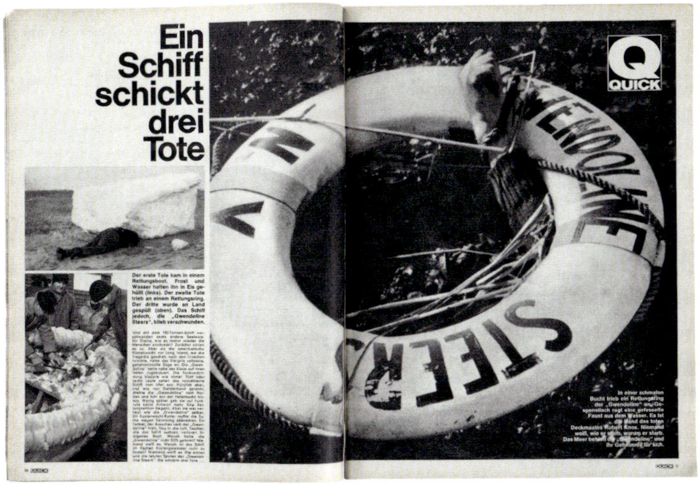

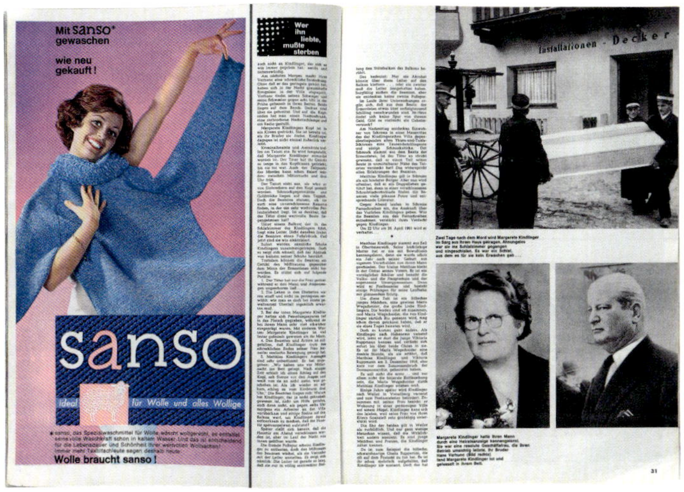

FIG 24
Gerhard Richter, *Dead* (*Tote*), 1963. Oil on canvas, 39 ¾ × 59 ½ in. (101 × 151.1 cm). CR 9. The Museum of Modern Art, New York, The Sidney and Harriet Janis Collection, by exchange (741.2013)

FIG 25
"A Ship Gives Up Three Dead," *Quick*, March 3, 1963

FIG 26
"Anyone Who Loved Him Had to Die," *Neue Illustrierte*, February 3, 1963

clearly delineated figural forms whose outlined elements loom out from the fog of color like islands of objective realism. The outline of the center figure seen from the back becomes less distinct toward the picture's bottom edge, while his white hatband stands out sharply, as in a photograph. Similarly, Richter repeats the crisply outlined rectangle of the coffin with an amorphous, unidentifiable field of blurred pigment immediately below it. Significantly, these zones of "free" painting do not suggest the virtuoso expressionism we know from action painting or Art Informel. Instead, they seem like quotes of such expressiveness, as if, for purposes of demonstration, different samples from the available scale of abstract painting have been combined into one tableau.

At the same time, the original's photographic quality is still clearly recognizable in the painting, and not only owing to the objective sharpness of certain details and the picture's black-and-white palette. The loose arrangement of the four figures also suggests the randomness of a snapshot, even if one has no knowledge of the original photograph. The photographic element appears only indirectly, as adapted in genuinely painterly ways, and this juxtaposition of the two modes dominates the picture. Such simulation of painting-as-photograph already characterized *Table* (p. 104) from the year before, a painting that Richter based on a photograph from the Italian design journal *Domus*. To quote Benjamin Buchloh, *Table* places the "epistemological conflicts between painting and photography once again almost literally on the table/tableau as the surfaces of their most cogent display."[3] Before I come back to these "conflicts" below, it would be useful to briefly review the long history of the reciprocal influences of painting and photography and of the latter's special status—during a time when it was still far from being officially recognized as an independent art.[4]

Painting and Photography: The History of a Relationship

As is well known, photography was not accorded the status of an independent art from the beginning; it first had to become established and institutionally recognized. It was generally defined by way of comparison with other pictorial arts, especially drawing and painting. According to Roland Barthes, "Photography has been, and is still, tormented by the ghost of Painting . . . ; it has made Painting, through its copies and contestations, into the absolute, paternal Reference."[5] This comparative approach automatically imposed itself in the first decade of the new medium, in the 1840s. With the introduction of the mechanically produced and photochemically fixed image, a new iconography appeared, one that needed to be placed in the context of the established arts. Thus, William Henry Fox Talbot identified his first photographic experiments as "photogenic drawings" and called the new technique the "pencil of nature." Although Talbot used these terms to make distinctions between photography and drawing—the mechanical, automatic process of the former, as distinguished from the manual execution of the latter—drawing remained the standard, the model against which he sought to define his new medium.[6] As Walter Benjamin rightly noted, a similar comparative approach characterizes later theoretical definitions of photography. The first theorists "sought nothing beyond acquiring credentials for the photographer from the judgment-seat which he had already overturned."[7] Especially writers who conceived of the photographic image as a photochemical trace, imprint, or—in the tradition of Charles Sanders Peirce's theory of semiotics—index tended to point to painting in order to demonstrate *ex negativo* the wholly different way photography functioned.[8] André Bazin, for example, remarked: "Clearly the fascinating objectivity of Chardin is in no sense that of the photographer."[9] Bazin was referring to Jean-Baptiste-Siméon Chardin, an eighteenth-century painter whose realism is frequently described as a precursor to that of photography. Bazin qualifies the seeming similarity between painting and photography, evident in their iconography, in order to highlight the far greater differences in the processes of their production. As for the representatives of the index or imprint theory—from Siegfried Kracauer and Rudolf Arnheim to Susan Sontag, Rosalind Krauss, and Roland Barthes—and for Bazin as well, the basis for comparison between painting and photography "is not to be found in the result achieved but in the way of achieving it."[10] And to these writers, the distinct differences in production predominate: iconographic similarities between photographic and painted images cannot obscure the fact that the processes and techniques of the two mediums are very different.

In his *Theory of Film* (1960), Kracauer likewise derives his determination of the position of photography from a reciprocal elucidation of the mediums. He writes, "The achievements within a particular medium are all the more satisfying aesthetically if they build from the specific properties of that medium."[11] In this play of differences, photography and painting occupy contrary positions. Along a continuum of mediums, he insists photography "has its legitimate place at the pole opposite that of painting." Instead of helping to express "human intentions," like a painter, the photographer needs to take into account the "camera's recording function." The photographer comes closest to that recognition when he abstains as much as possible from styling, composing, and technical manipulation, and instead admits randomness and the unexpected into his pictures. Accordingly, Kracauer emphasizes photography's "tendency toward the unorganized and diffuse," its "concern with unstaged reality."[12] Painting appears as the extreme opposite to this "realistic tendency." In sum, to be true to its special aesthetic role, a photograph needs to be as unpainterly as possible. Kracauer's deliberations on the specifics of the medium thus touch on the fundamental question of photography's artistic nature as well. He distinguishes its "form-giving tendency," whose proponents rely on composition, staging, and artistic expression, from its "realistic tendency." In his view, those who focus on the former produce little more than hybrid forms of pictures that do justice to neither the fundamental aesthetic principle of photography nor the creative potential of the fine arts. "It is as if the use of photography for strictly artistic purposes led into a sort of no man's land somewhere between reproduction and expression."[13]

Kracauer's "fundamental aesthetic principle" clearly accommodates opposing ideals, for the same holds true in the reverse direction; when photography's value as art is determined through an emphasis on its structuring potential, there is little interest in defining its recording function. For example, toward the end of the nineteenth century, the Pictorialists wished to secure photography's status as art by largely underplaying its mechanical, registering qualities. The role of the photographer was shifted completely away from snapping a picture with his camera to his subsequent treatment of it, which involved manually developing the negative, creating elaborate, elegant prints, and reducing the sharpness of detail through artificial blurring (fig. 27). That paradoxical attempt to establish a genuine aesthetics of photography by forcing it to imitate another art was short-lived. Later generations of photographers—such as the proponents of the New Vision movement in the 1920s and 1930s—no longer tried to show the medium's uniqueness by displaying its ability to mimic painting; rather, they identified its uniquely photographic qualities.

Yet, there were very different ideas about whether photography should achieve singular status as an art form or as an independent image-making technique whose relationship with art was virtually neutral. These competing positions characterized photographic debate well into the twentieth century and were still at odds in the 1960s. Consider, for example, the conflicting theories of the postwar German photographers Otto Steinert and Albert Renger-Patzsch. In 1948, Steinert introduced the first course in photography at Saarbrücken's Staatliche Schule für Kunst und Handwerk, and a year later, together with five other photographers, founded the artists' group Fotoform.[14] Like Kracauer a few years later, Steinert was interested in defining what was specific to photography, but he placed it at the opposite end of the scale—emphasizing not the camera's recording function but rather "*absolute photographic figuration,* in its freest form." Such figuration had to relinquish "any kind of objective description" and abstract the object to the point "that it becomes only a formal element, a compositional building block."[15] Steinert sought to defend this aesthetic against the "collective preconceived notion" that photography mainly registers actual events and is manifested in the "amateur souvenir photo" or the "vast production of utilitarian photos and millions of meaningless snapshots."[16] As he wrote, "This pervasive recording stands in absolute contrast to the essential idea behind all artistic endeavor, namely abstraction, the ability to

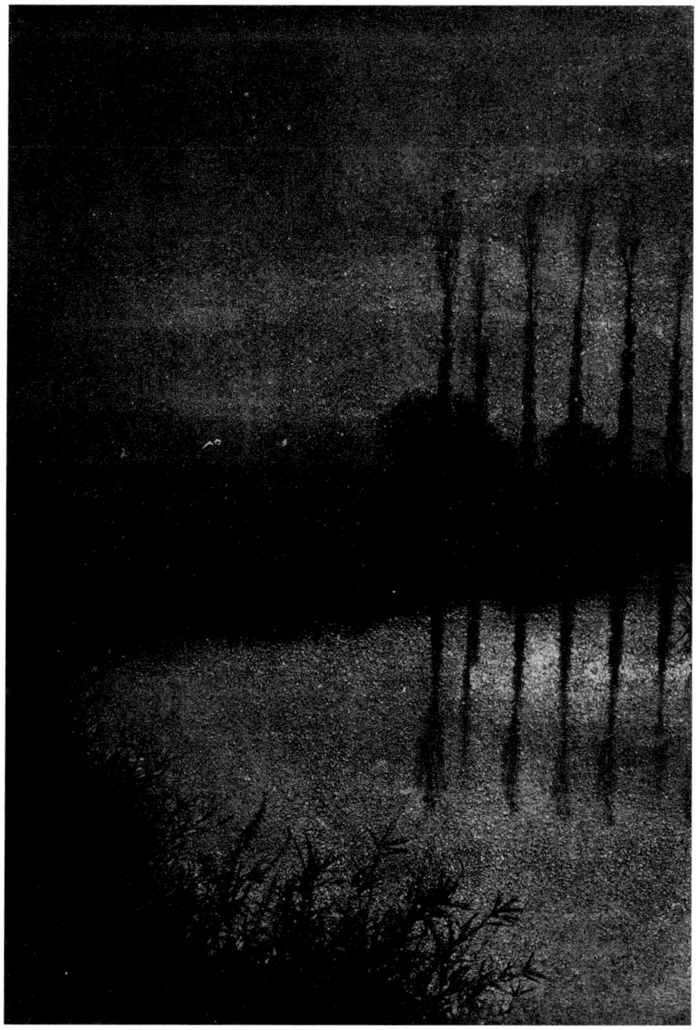

FIG 27
Robert Demachy (French, 1859–1936), *Twilight near Croissy*, 1879/1914, printed 1975. Collotype, 8 ⅝ × 5 ¾ in. (22 × 14.7 cm). Art Institute of Chicago, Kathleen W. Harvey Memorial Fund (1976.207f)

separate the essential from the incidental."[17] In 1951, at the Kunsthochschule Saarbrücken, Steinert organized *Subjective Photography*, an international exhibition that was presented again two years later at the George Eastman House in Rochester, New York. By displaying photographs by László Moholy-Nagy, Man Ray, and Herbert Bayer alongside works of the Fotoform group, he aimed to create ties to the avant-garde movements of the 1920s and thereby provide a prehistory for his own efforts to achieve "absolute photographic figuration." Accordingly, the aesthetic program of so-called subjective photography included the renewed use of techniques such as the photogram, the negative print, solarization, and time exposure. An example is a *Luminogramme* from 1952 that Steinert made at night in Paris's place de la Concorde (fig. 28). By moving his camera in a circle with the shutter open, he turned the glowing streetlights into abstract lines of movement with no visible connection to the surrounding cityscape. Any objective reference was further removed by his subsequent reversal of the image's tonal values. Even in this photograph what Kracauer emphasized as the "camera's recording function"—or its "pervasive description," as Steinert put it—could not be fully eliminated; however, it was reduced and placed wholly in the service of photographic design. The seemingly expressive image is not a record of something in the world but rather of the photographer's movement. Similarities have been rightly observed between the *Luminogramme* and gestural, Art Informel painting, especially works by Hans Hartung.[18] Beginning in the late 1940s the Cologne photographer Chargesheimer (Karl-Heinz Hargesheimer) also aimed for a connection with abstract painting with his "gelatin paintings" (fig. 29). In them, he completely eliminated mechanical and optical elements of photography and manipulated photo chemicals like a painter's pigments. A photo like Steinert's *Points and Lines* (fig. 30) exhibits no such expressive desire. But even in that work—whose title is an obvious allusion to Vasily Kandinsky's *Point and Line to Plane*—the motif is stripped of any topographical or functional coordinates and is simply a two-dimensional geometric pattern.[19]

To be sure, the trend toward abstraction in photography was neither predominant around 1960, nor were its aesthetic premises unchallenged. For example, in 1955 Albert Renger-Patzsch, who continued to produce his works in the New Objectivity style, like those from the prewar years, noted: "The direction photography has taken in recent years doesn't much please me." Photography "has once again attached itself to the coattails of art, only now it is abstract art."[20] In "Versuch einer Einordnung der Fotografie" (1956), translated as "An Essay toward the Classification of Photography," Renger-Patzsch roundly criticized the fact that photography had become "dependent on art." The turn away from the medium's mechanical nature produced nothing more than "a species that is neither art nor photography." Like Steinert, Renger-Patzsch saw photography as "a graphic process sui generis," but one that was "neither art nor craft." Photography's value "is determined partly through aesthetic, partly through technical judgments; and on the basis of its mechanical structure, it seems to me to be better suited for doing justice to an object than for expressing an artistic individuality."[21] In contrast to Steinert, who isolated his motifs photographically, Renger-Patzsch generally included elements

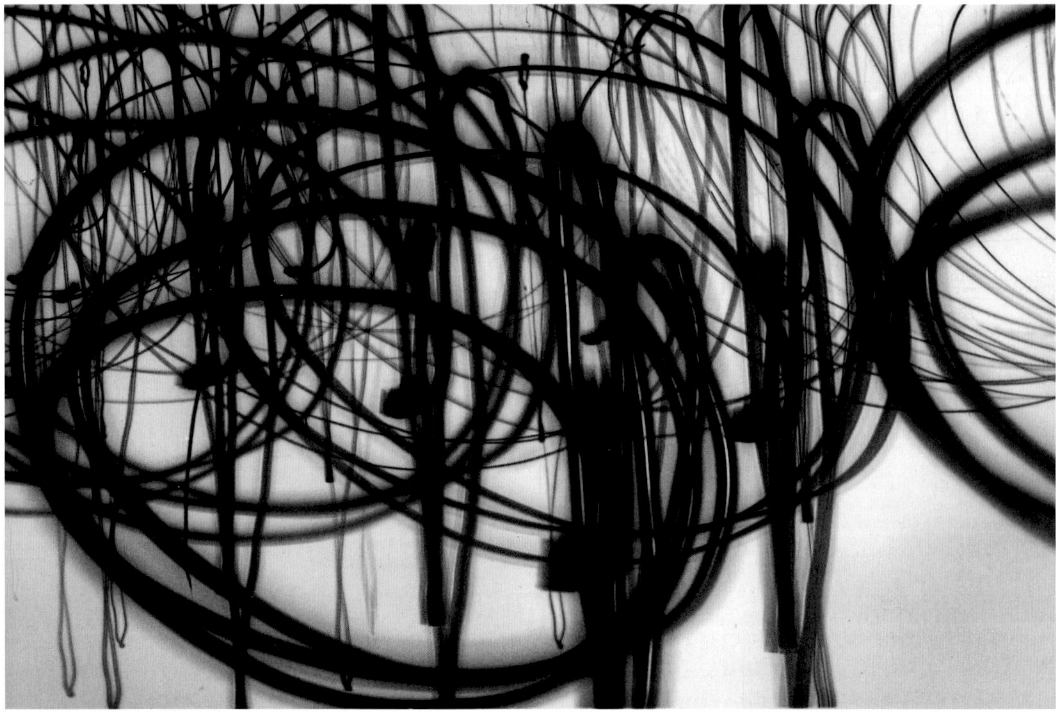

FIG 28
Otto Steinert (German, 1915–1978), *Streetlights on the place de la Concorde III*, 1952. Gelatin silver print, 16 ⅜ × 23 ⅝ in. (41.5 × 60 cm). Museum Folkwang, Essen

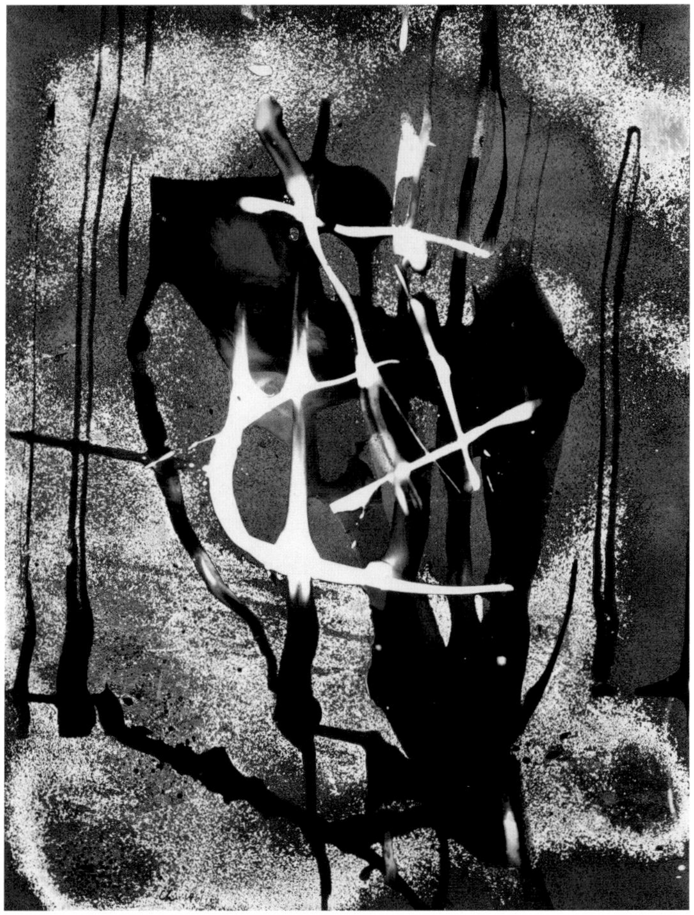

29

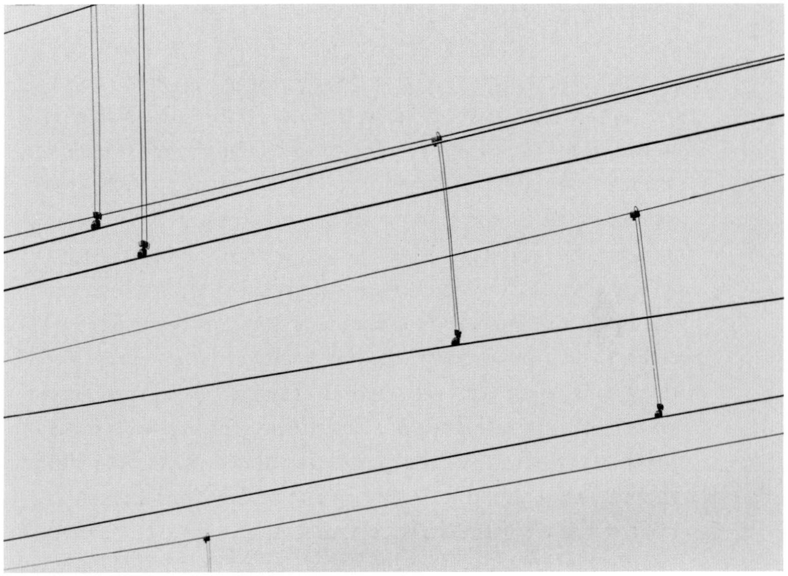

30

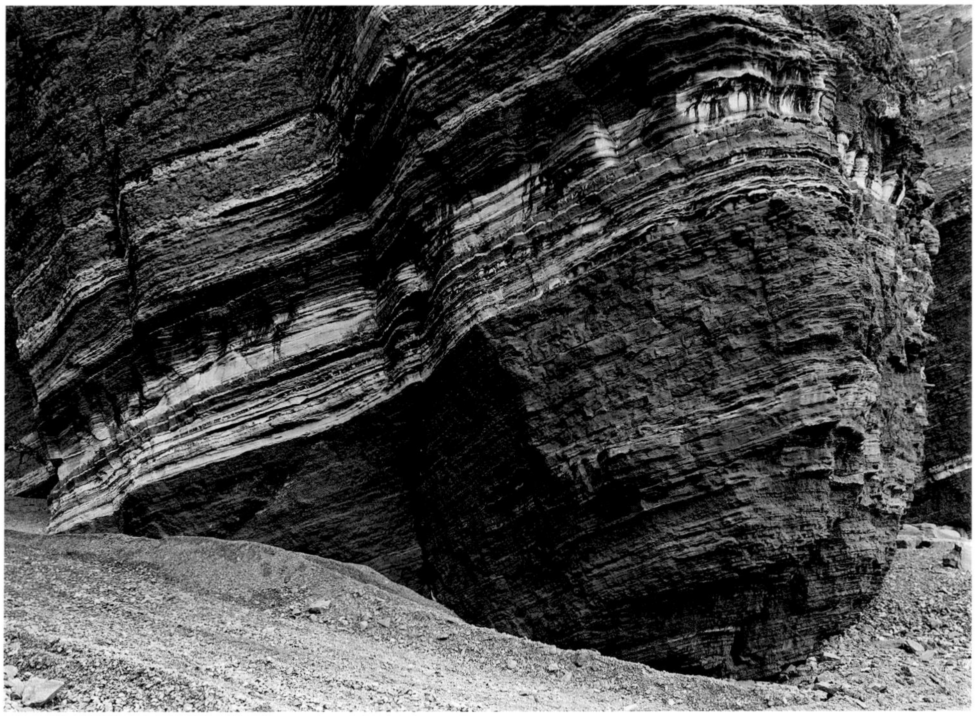

31

FIG 29
Chargesheimer (Karl-Heinz Hargesheimer) (German, 1924–1971), *Skriptur*, from the book *Lightgraphics, Monoscriptures*, 1961. Gelatin silver print, 15 × 11 1/16 in. (38.1 × 28.1 cm). Harvard Art Museums/Busch-Reisinger Museum, Gift of The Cultural Council in the Federation of German Industry (1991.16.1)

FIG 30
Otto Steinert (German, 1915–1978), *Points and Lines*, 1952. Gelatin silver print, 11 ½ × 15 ¾ in. (29.3 × 39.9 cm). Museum Folkwang, Essen

FIG 31
Albert Renger-Patzsch (German, 1897–1966), *Buntsandstein from Helgoland, North Sea, Sedimentite*, 1961. Gelatin silver print, 11 ⅜ × 15 ⅛ in. (28.8 × 38.3 cm)

of their physical surroundings (fig. 31). A stone appears as an object in a specific setting, and the resulting geological pattern is presented as an inherent formal characteristic, not as evidence of the photographer's sense of design.

In the early 1960s, criticism of attempts to make photography conform to the demands of art also came from a very different camp, namely the proponents of *Life* magazine's photographic style. In 1960, the Austrian photographer Karl Pawek wrote that photographic abstraction produced little more than "wallpaper patterns." Pawek's criticism was rooted in a passionate devotion to the medium's immediacy and authenticity: "Photography is the world itself, photography is reality itself, photography is what is taking place in this reality, what happens there, what bleeds, lives, suffers, develops there."[22] In 1964, in response to Edward Steichen's exhibition *Family of Man* (1955), Pawek put together the *World Photography Exhibition*, a collection of more than five hundred photographs meant to answer the question, "What is man?" Pawek's egalitarian show was met with reservations similar to those Roland Barthes expressed in his critique of *Family of Man*.[23] Barthes described that exhibition as an attempt to tame history and replace social and political differences with the ahistorical "myth" of the human condition.[24]

This sketch of postwar German photography cannot convey a complete picture, of course, but it does identify some of the main trends in and uses of photography at the time when Richter arrived on the scene with his photo paintings. From Richter's remarks about photography from that time it is impossible to associate him with any of the positions described—certainly not with the attempt to ennoble photography as art by aligning it with abstract painting.[25] Given that he had only recently disclaimed his earlier experiments with Art Informel and Tachisme, even physically destroying some of the paintings, and had declared the painting *Table* to be the first work in his catalogue raisonné, it would have been illogical for him to take delight in abstraction in, of all places, the medium of photography. The degree to which Richter consciously registered the trends described is difficult to reconstruct. In any case, his surviving works themselves are more informative than his often contradictory statements.

Whereas art photography attempted to achieve the qualities of painting, Richter turned the equation around; as a painter, he imitated the look of photography. He was not the first to do so. In the history of painting's changing relationship with photography, there are obvious precursors: Eugène Delacroix and Gustave Courbet both used photographs as models for paintings; Edgar Degas imitated the arbitrary features of the camera shot, such as cropping, in his compositions; and Ernest Meissonier made ample use of Eadweard Muybridge's movement studies. But unlike these painters, Richter flaunted his use of photographs by painting in black and white and reproducing the blur that is typical of the medium. It is a mistake to think of Richter's photo paintings in terms of a hierarchy among mediums, the lingering claims that one is superior to another. It has been said that in Richter's photo paintings "it becomes perfectly clear that for him, painting, having become obsolete, needed to avail itself of the truthful, compelling nature of the photograph."[26] But this is unconvincing. It perpetuates the idea described above, namely that a faltering medium might find support from the example of a more secure one—only this time the direction is reversed; it is no longer that painting affords a certain artistic legitimacy to photography, but conversely, that photography has rescued painting. Also, the description of this process as a "transfer of the principle of mimicry from nature into art" sees Richter's recourse to photography as a "rescue," one that was able to "provide a new authority to painting, for decades repeatedly declared to be dead."[27] The biological metaphor suggests that in his painting Richter hoped "to appropriate the qualities of the rival medium," as if painting and photography were natural antagonists locked in a struggle for greater artistic legitimacy. To my mind, Richter's recourse to photography seems more a reflection on one medium (photography) in terms of another (painting), not an appropriation for the sake of survival. His photo paintings of the 1960s represent a new synthesis, in which the two mediums are evolving no longer in competition but rather in response to each other. Accordingly, Richter's paintings after photographs are not imitation or mimicry, intended to deceive the viewer. Their large format (one unavailable for the presentation of photography in the 1960s) and their clearly visible brushstrokes preclude their being mistaken for photographs.[28] They are painterly adaptations of photography and are meant to be seen as such.

Richter's recourse to photography is even more apparent in paintings such as *Pedestrians* (1963), *Mrs. Marlow* (1964), and *Secretary* (1963) (figs. 32–34) than in *Coffin Bearers* and *Table*. These works quote characteristic features of photography in the medium of painting. In *Pedestrians* and *Mrs. Marlow* it is the frozen movement typical of photographs, the way the camera extracts a static image from a sequence of movements in time, and in doing so frequently fails to obey the rules of "good" composition, instead fixing what is only incidental and fragmentary. It has been said that the snapshot "refers to the fluency of time without conveying it," that it "stole a life it could not return."[29] Walter Benjamin famously described this alienating effect in his *Short History of Photography* as photography's "optical unconscious" and referred to the "other nature" that the camera, as opposed to the eye, captures. "It is possible, for example, however roughly, to describe the way somebody walks, but it is impossible to say anything about that fraction of a second when a person *starts to walk*."[30] Richter's *Pedestrians* depicts just such a pose, in that split second when its subjects start to walk—to some extent the very opposite of what in the history of painting has been traditionally referred to as the "fruitful moment."[31] It is a painted snapshot whose elements fail to fuse

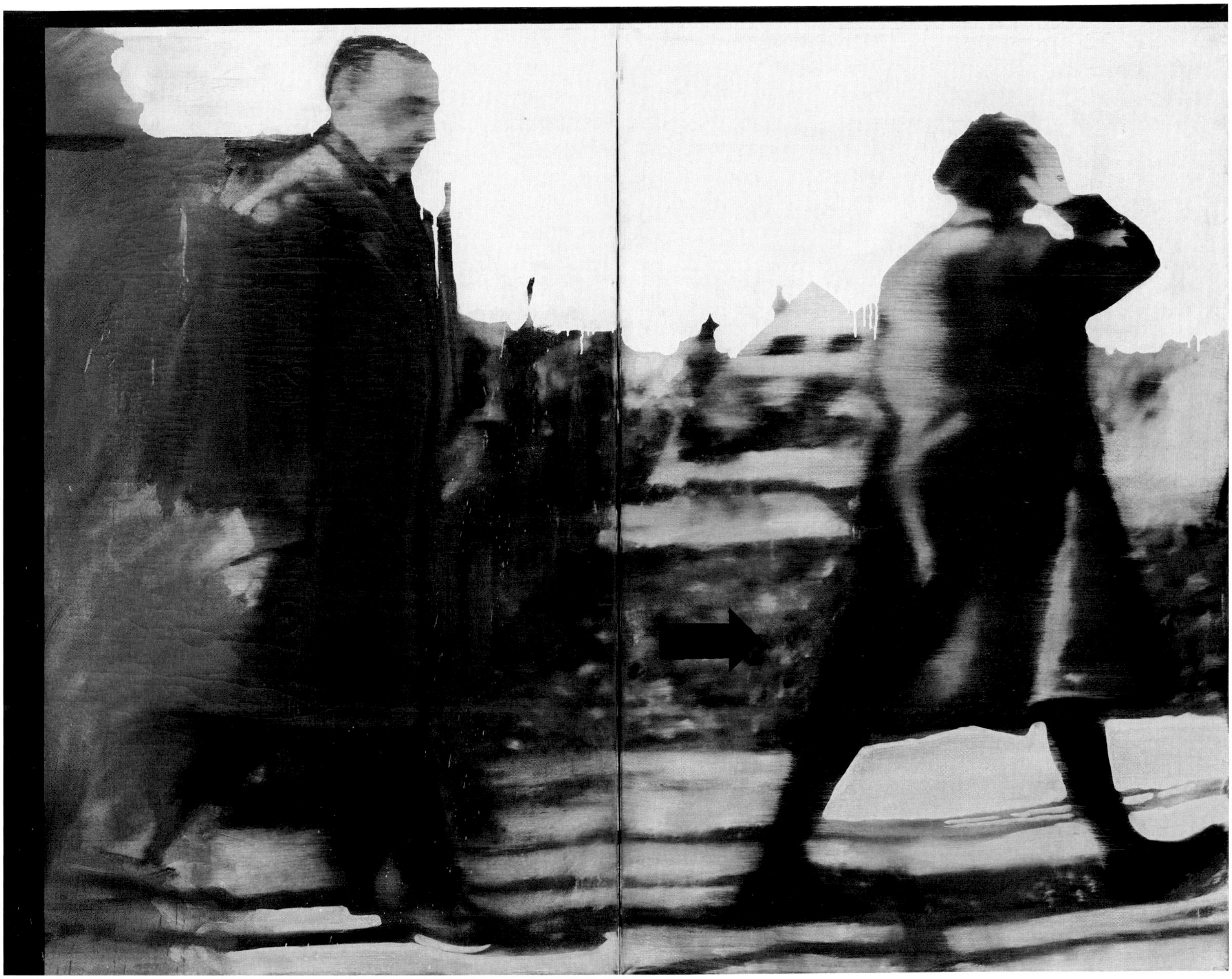

FIG 32
Gerhard Richter, *Pedestrians* (*Fußgänger*), 1963. Oil on canvas, 2 parts, in total, 55 ⅛ × 69 5/16 in. (140 × 176 cm). CR 6. Museum MMK für Moderne Kunst, Frankfurt

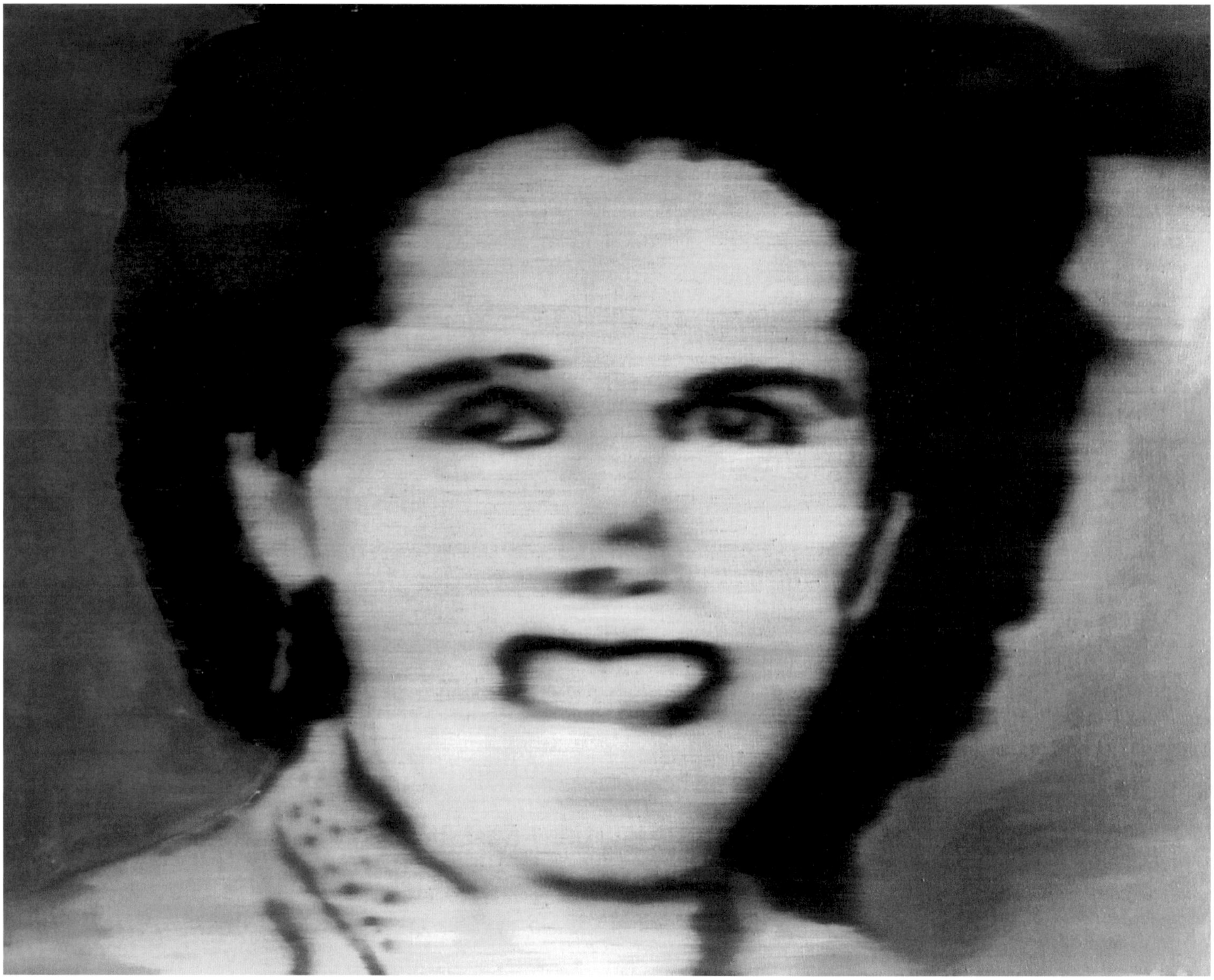

FIG 33
Gerhard Richter, *Mrs. Marlow* (*Frau Marlow*), 1964. Oil on canvas, 30 ⅜ × 37 ¾ in. (77 × 96 cm). CR 28. Private collection, Switzerland

into a single impression. In *Mrs. Marlow* the effect is seen in the subject's artificially frozen smile, a momentary expression the camera happened to capture and that Richter reproduced on his canvas. *Secretary*, moreover, renders a typical photographic defect: the figure's double shadow is a common feature of unprofessional photos taken with a flash. Finally, there is the frequently mentioned blurring in the pictures, an optical artifact unknown in painting that is a clearly recognizable characteristic of photography. Both the blurring and the shadow produced by a flash are listed as technical flaws in the photo manuals of the time, mistakes to be avoided. If one subscribes to the theory that a technique or a medium is more clearly manifested in its accidents and defects—its disruptive features—than in the normally smooth course of its use, one could say that in his adoption of precisely these elements Richter captured in painting one essential quality of photography.[32] They set his works apart from those of the Photorealists, which tend to retain the sharp focus, clarity, and transparency of the photographic original.

While death or murder play a role in some of Richter's photo paintings of the 1960s, as a group they are by no means confined to an iconography of mayhem. Taken from illustrated magazines and reproduced without the accompanying text, the images no longer carry an aura of the spectacular; only his titles (*Dead*, *Coffin Bearers*) retain an echo of the sensational. He also based paintings on advertisements for consumer goods, as in *Two Fiats* (1964) and *Folding Dryer* (1962), and on photographs of banal, utilitarian objects, as in *Toilet Paper* (1965) and *Kitchen Chair* (1965; p. 112). His time-consuming process of selecting the source images, enlarging them with an opaque projector, and patiently tracing their contours necessarily brought an element of concentration and focus to the paintings, regardless of their iconography. "It was not the sheer abundance of images that occupied Gerhard Richter—as it did Robert Rauschenberg or Wolf Vostell" (and here one might add their serial repetition, as practiced by Andy Warhol) "but the single, striking picture, the significant photograph in its actuality and with its potential for further development as a painting."[33] This observation by Uwe Schneede is supported by the few comments Richter made, more than four decades later, about the selection of his motifs; in the case of *Secretary*, for example, he emphasized particular details in a manner reminiscent of Roland Barthes's theory of the *punctum*: "the odd way she looks to the side, her conspicuous hands, the little jacket."[34]

Schneede suggests that what Richter refers to in his works is the photographic image's "semblance of reality," and to my thinking that explains his interest in photography better than the assumption that it was motivated by a fundamental skepticism or a desire to unmask the apparent referentiality of an image. The blurring in Richter's photo paintings has been interpreted as a commentary on the photograph's "claim to authenticity" and an expression of "fundamental perceptual

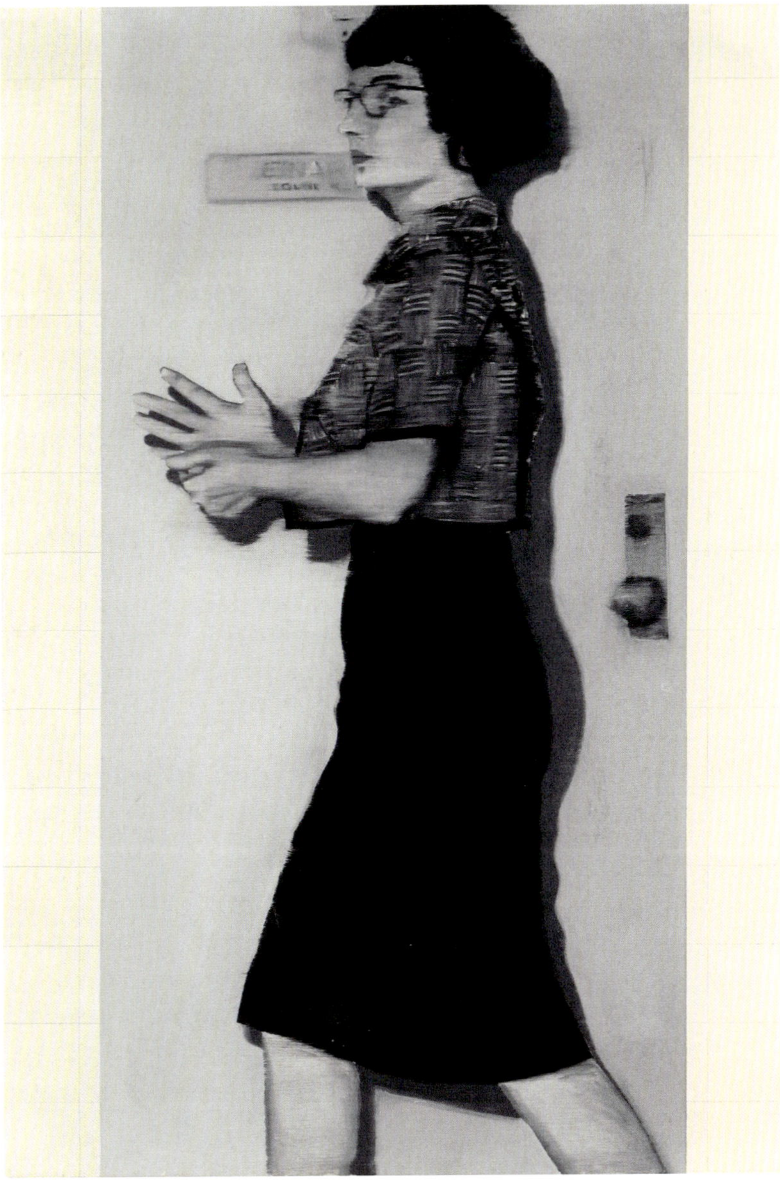

FIG 34
Gerhard Richter, *Secretary* (*Sekretärin*), 1963. Oil on canvas, 59 × 39 ⅜ in. (150 × 100 cm). CR 14. Galerie Neue Meister, Albertinum, Staatliche Kunstsammlungen, Dresden

doubt."[35] Accordingly, painting, now self-confident, could claim authority and primacy. But all the same, whether one conceives of the photo painting as the "salvation" of painting through photography or, conversely, as painterly criticism of the photograph's promise of authenticity, one ultimately remains entangled in the traditional antagonism between two mediums whose relationship is always considered hierarchical.

The Unpainted Pictures

Above all, this reading places Richter closer to a fundamental criticism of photography as elsewhere expressed in the 1960s. As early as 1956, Günther Anders criticized photography as a technical surrogate for direct experience in his essay "Ikonomanie": "Anyone who has had an opportunity to observe tourists, namely people from highly industrialized countries, on the move in Rome or Florence will have noted how greatly it confuses them to encounter *singularities*; those imposing historical relics standing about as unique specimens in the serial world."[36] He argues that such people compensate for their insecurity in dealing with uniqueness through excessive use of their cameras: "Since they no longer know any existence except one among effigies—the serially produced wares of their world, between, with, and from which they live—reproductions, copies from patterns, replicas are simply their reality."[37] Similarly, on a trip to Greece in the spring of 1962, Martin Heidegger interpreted his fellow travelers' feverish picture taking in the ruins at Delphi as a symptom of their ontological innocence: "everywhere people taking pictures. They throw their memories in the technically produced picture. They abandon without clue the feast of thinking that they ignore."[38]

A few years later, in 1965, Pierre Bourdieu criticized photography for very different reasons in an essay titled "Un art moyen: Essai sur les usages sociaux de la photographie" (translated as "The Social Definition of Photography"). In addition to interpreting empirical data on class-specific attitudes toward photography, he included some fundamental thoughts on the medium's function and expressed skepticism of its supposed realism. Unlike Kracauer, Bourdieu felt that there were no qualities unique to photography. Instead, what can be said of it follows from its social uses. For that reason, Bourdieu does not ask what photography's characteristics are, what it can do, or what it is, but rather what qualities modern society ascribes to it. Its realism thus proves to be a mere convention: "It is commonly agreed that photography can be seen as a model of veracity and objectivity." Using his terminology, it is up to the sociologist to expose this convention as a "social representation" and point out the "false evidence" on which it is based.[39]

To my thinking, Richter's work can hardly be understood against the background of such a skeptical view of photography. This is certainly true of a series of pictures Richter added to his *Atlas* in 1967, which Buchloh characterized as "rupturing the entire field."[40] These were photographs of the Holocaust, some of them taken immediately after the liberation of the concentration camps by members of the Allied forces. Their appearance in the *Atlas* recalls Buchloh's observation that "there is still one link that binds an image to its referent within the apparently empty barrage of photographic imagery and the universal production of sign exchange-value: the trauma from which the compulsion to repress had originated."[41] To understand how these pictures were seen in the 1960s, it is necessary to review their history in postwar Germany.

The Allies began publishing photographs from the liberated camps in late April 1945. Pictures from Buchenwald, Bergen-Belsen, Dachau, and Falkenau appeared in newspaper articles and on handbills; they were distributed as postcards, posters, and brochures; and they were viewed in shopwindow displays and on newsreels. As Habbo Knoch observes, the circulation of these disturbing pictures was meant to "unleash a cathartic shock, with which the 're-education' of an entire populace was to begin." However, instead of leading to enlightenment and reflection, "the visual enormity of the piles of corpses initially drew attention away from the regime's everyday techniques."[42] We now recognize that the pictorial reports of the time were incomplete and undifferentiated: there was no distinction between the different kinds of camps or between different groups of prisoners and the reasons for their incarceration and killing. The systematic nature of the Nazis' crimes disappeared behind the pictures' shocking presentation of atrocities and their overwhelming emotional effect instead of bringing the Germans to think about their own potential guilt and responsibility. As Cornelia Brink has written: "It is not the fact represented by the photographs that is rejected [by the German population]—the power of their authenticity has hardly ever been challenged—but their projective tendency, the moral appeal connected to them."[43] The failed attempt at collective reeducation was followed by a "visual amnesia,"[44] in which a great number of Germans, faced with a war-centered memory culture, simply began to see themselves as victims as well. When Hannah Arendt visited Germany in 1950, she witnessed "a deep-rooted, stubborn, and at times vicious refusal to face and come to terms with what really happened."[45]

But in the mid-1950s, the pictures reappeared. Despite widespread resistance, Alain Resnais's *Night and Fog* (1956), a documentary film about the Nazi concentration camps mainly consisting of historical footage and photographs, was screened before varied audiences in numerous German cinemas. Many of its viewers had been born in the 1930s and 1940s. As Richter later recalled, he first saw photographs from the camps when a fellow student at Dresden's Academy of Fine Arts circulated a publication about the film during a break.[46] Then, in 1960, Gerhard Schoenberner published *The Yellow Star*, the first picture book devoted exclusively to documenting of the annihilation of Europe's Jews. Finally, in 1963, the Frankfurt Auschwitz trials began, followed by the public with tremendous interest.

The fate of the photographs from the camps can be clearly traced using the example of one that Richter included in his *Atlas*. Showing prisoners inside a barracks (see fig. 14), it was taken by a member of the United States Army in April 1945 after the liberation of the Buchenwald camp and appeared only a few weeks later in the brochure *KZ: An Illustrated Report from Five Concentration Camps*, published by the Allies as part of their intended reeducation campaign. After the subsequent phase of collective amnesia, this picture, like many others, went into circulation again in the 1960s. We now find it difficult to imagine what it meant as testimony in that era and to understand its historical uniqueness, given that since then the picture has been reproduced thousands of times in the most varied contexts. This in no way detracts from the photograph's documentary value. However, it is important to recognize that it only gradually attained such iconic status. In 1967, when Richter included the image in his *Atlas*—at that time an unpublished, personal sourcebook—pictures from the concentration camps were by no means so overexploited.

The same photograph appears in the *Atlas* three more times. It occurs twice on the next page in an extremely blurred copy (see fig. 15), followed by a reproduction to which Richter applied color (see fig. 16), as he had already done to two pictures, one of two female inmates in prison clothing and the other of Margit Schwartz, thirty-one years old, taken in the infirmary of the Bergen-Belsen camp in May 1945.[47] Needless to say, Richter's addition of color had nothing in common with the widespread practice, begun in the nineteenth century, of tinting "unfinished" black-and-white photographs to make them appear more realistic. His strong, glowing colors are more reminiscent of garish makeup and are entirely unsuited to the photographic subject; they lead a grotesque life of their own as a second, artificial layer. Richter apparently used colored felt-tip pens, which, according to Buchloh, were "at that moment one of the most innovative bureaucratic marking devices (comparable in many ways to the initially shocking deployment of ballpoint pens in drawings by Andy Warhol or Sigmar Polke thereafter)."[48] To my thinking, his use of such dubious implements was a kind of commentary on art's possibilities and the limits of its competence. His inclusion in the *Atlas* of the Buchenwald photograph in three different forms—as an unaltered reproduction shown with other photos of the camp, then doubled and blurred, and finally colored—suggests that he was approaching it almost hesitantly, stalking it. Another experiment follows on the next pages of the *Atlas*: not another reproduction, but rather an abrupt contrast—a series of pornographic images. At that time, Richter was planning, with Konrad Lueg, to exhibit such a juxtaposition of pornography and concentration-camp photos at Düsseldorf's Galerie Niepel; the gesture would have placed the photos in the framework of an art institution.[49] They abandoned their plan, as Richter later remarked, out of "fear that it went too far."[50]

So pictures from the camps continued to be only latent possibilities, potential sources in the reservoir of the *Atlas*, never the subjects of independent works. The same is true of countless other pictures in the *Atlas*, but without question, the camp photos have a significantly different importance. According to Antoine de Baecque, who reproduced a series of photos from the liberation of the camps at the beginning of his book on the history of film, these shots function as a "traumatic emblem": the prisoner's gazes are effective as a "generic form."[51] De Baecque here describes the fact that the prisoners' gazes had been burned into the collective memory and continued to haunt the screen even when entirely different gazes were seen. The photos were operative even without being actually reproduced. Similarly, these pictures were not simply absent from Richter's artistic production of the 1960s; they also doubtless played a role—not directly visible, but at work in the background.

Should we then consider the photographs in the *Atlas* part of Richter's oeuvre? A comment by Georges Didi-Huberman about the use of found pictures in the work of the experimental documentary filmmaker Harun Farocki might well answer this question. Farocki, Didi-Huberman writes, did not stamp his own mark on historical photographs or motion pictures; instead, he emancipated them and gave them back to the public, to whom they properly belong.

> *It is neither the question of the commodity nor that of art as such that determines his decision to* take, *here or there, the images that interest him. What he leans toward is, rather, the disappearance of* copyright *in the field of visual archives of history. He takes only to learn, never to impose his maker's mark: thus, the woman of the* Auschwitz Album, *in* Images of the World and the Inscription of War, *will never become a stylistic indicator for Farocki's art.*[52]

Something similar might be said with regard to Richter, bearing in mind all the differences between the two artists. Richter did not transform the photos of Buchenwald into stylistic indicators for his art. In that he dealt with them only hesitantly, virtually circling around them, yet ultimately leaving them in the reservoir of the *Atlas*, he preserved their status as historical evidence. Even so, these pictures are not simply absent from Richter's work from the 1960s. Their presence in the *Atlas* attests that Richter ultimately chose *not* to use them as photographic patterns for paintings of his own but rather to preserve them as photographs. Art historians generally deal with what has actually taken place, what has been realized by an artist and is manifested in his or her work. But, occasionally, what only hovers in a latent state is also worthy of attention—an unpainted picture, an unrealized exhibition. In considering Richter's photo paintings of the 1960s, one also needs to consider what was *left out*.

Briony Fer

Chrono-Technics: Richter's Family Pictures

What would it be to see Richter's family pictures—including the paintings of his aunt, his uncle, his father-in-law, his wives, his children, and so on—as part of the artist's lifelong speculation on painting rather than the product of his own biographical narrative? I'm suggesting that we need to set up some degree of friction between a "family picture"—which signals a type of picture—and a "family portrait," indicating a stronger tie to its sitters. My aim is not necessarily to refute the powerful interpretations grounded in the artist's own family history but to argue that the family picture also offered Richter a number of pictorial possibilities beyond the more immediate demands on a portrait to represent its subjects. I shall suggest instead that the family motif, understood as a unit of composition, serves as a temporal device within a body of work that first and foremost is concerned with the relation between painting and time. That such a temporal device can never be "pure," but is also mediated and even compromised by personal and historical experience, I take as a given.[1] Art history has been adept at describing spatial techniques and yet the temporal *as* technique has barely a vocabulary to help us. In part, therefore, my aim is simply to try to find a form of description for the family pictures that allows us to think what it might mean for a picture-type to recur so often and in so many different versions of itself.

Richter's preoccupation with families, both his own and other people's, both known and not known to him, was unusual from the outset and as anomalous for an artist of his generation as his ongoing commitment to painting.[2] Yet, the sheer number and array of his protagonists puts the category of family in jeopardy, not least suggesting a fundamental lack of clarity as to where one family ends and another begins. In the first and perhaps most concentrated episode in which he produced his family pictures, between 1964 and 1966, the likenesses between the various groups that he chose to depict come to override the differences. A generic cast of characters creates a strong sense of collective anonymity. Figures generally take on the informal poses and grisaille textures more typical of a mass image culture than of the formal traditions of portraiture. There is always a constant copresence of the look of the photograph (the slight blur) with the fact of the painting (the strokes of paint).

It is hard to overestimate the disruption wrought on this supposedly affectless ground by the moment of recognition of Richter's family ties to his uncle Rudi (p. 109), a soldier in the Wehrmacht, or his SS doctor father-in-law (p. 106). I do not intend to suggest that we should or even could "unsee" what we see, knowing what we do of their subjects. Nor can we forget, once we know, that *Aunt Marianne* is a painting of Richter's schizophrenic aunt, who was killed in 1945 under the Nazi euthanasia program (a digital print of the work appears on p. 108). But I am also interested in the relation of typology to temporality—and how this picture, which Richter originally called *Mother and Child*, can be seen as receptive to time rather than idealized as "timeless" or "universal." When it was first exhibited, at the Galleria Tartaruga in Rome in 1966, *Aunt Marianne* was merely one of twenty paintings shown, at least a dozen of which were based on either photographs from Richter's family album or generic family pictures drawn from newspapers and magazines. Among them are *The Schmidt Family*, *Woman with Child (Beach)*, *Infant on a Table*, *Three Siblings*, and four individual paintings of the Baker family. In this extended group—or family—of pictures, personal and pictorial genealogies play off one another. Different generations and moments in time are brought together only to make their temporal distance from one another and from us more difficult to gauge.

Another painting shown in Rome was *Family after Old Master* (fig. 35), painted after a newspaper photograph of the American artist John Singleton Copley's 1776 portrait of his family. A page from Richter's *Atlas* (fig. 36), his repository of photographic material, shows a medley of different sources, including the grainy news clipping of Copley's picture. As a historical group portrait, the Copley is unusual in the *Atlas*, placed alongside mainly amateur or else documentary photographs recording moments of birth, marriage, and death—as if a life cycle is also a life cycle of pictures. Richter may not have known that Copley painted the portrait while exiled in London, unable to return home because of the American Revolutionary War.[3] But even if the subject matter coincidentally resonates with Richter's personal history, the artist having left his family behind when he emigrated from East Germany to the West in 1960, the juxtaposition of this painting with the other images has something absurd about it—as if an "American Old Master" were in itself a slightly kitsch proposition from a European point of view at the time; you can almost hear the sound of clashing of new and old worlds. The typological consistencies, that is, the fact that the paintings conform to certain conventions that attach to the family group, set in train any number of temporal and genealogical confusions. For example, we are invited to ask, in what possible way could an Old Master relate to the self-portrait-of-the-artist-as-an-infant that is Richter lying on a table or sitting on Aunt Marianne's lap? Well, in none that is easy to pin down, except insofar as both are part of a group of paintings in which such fortuitous connections might—by chance—coalesce for a moment. Needless to say, other groupings would make different conjunctions.

The tension between naming and not naming his subjects is not confined to the paintings of the artist's close family. Especially early on, Richter was keen that his work not be read simply as biographical or personal. Rather, it was important to him to leave the viewer guessing and with a sense of uncertainty.[4] The conceptual wedge between pictures and persons is driven home all the more dramatically in the family pictures precisely because they refuse deeply culturally ingrained assumptions about portraits—not least the idea that we are required to empathize with their subjects. Instead Richter makes sure that the most supposedly personal and the most impersonal representational traits are virtually impossible to tell apart. It is likely that the Copley painting appealed to him not because of its identification with exile but because it was so generic and anonymous and faintly ludicrous. Still, *Family after Old Master* seems something of a one-off, a kind of kitschy ancestor-picture that has to be seen in a group for its comic timing to be felt. Tradition, if we could even call it that, is worn lightly, creating a deflationary effect consonant with a radical avant-garde gesture that goes back to Marcel Duchamp's *L.H.O.O.Q.* (1919), his moustachioed Mona Lisa, or Francis Picabia's ink-splat *La Sainte Vierge* (1920), rather than to, for example, Picasso's monumental *Mother and Child* paintings of the early 1920s (fig. 37), which bear the heavy weight of history associated with the period's classicizing return to order.

What *Family after Old Master* shows us, as atypical as it is, is how a traditional compositional structure such as the family motif can act as a measure of temporal distance through which painting can telescopically contract time and so make it both palpable and strange.[5] Richter continued to use pictorial tradition in this way, working with motifs that have almost the status of the cliché, such as the stereotypical image of the mother and child. The conventions of compositional structure embedded within the history of Western painting are devices that are just as powerful as the iconographic subjects that they traditionally served. Portrait photographs and even snapshots conform to the same paradigm of representation. Yet their protocols are also remarkably elastic and staged in the family pictures as a prolific series of choreographed movements veering between formality and informality.

There were plenty of paintings of children in the 1966 show: the Baker boy and girl, the three siblings, and Aunt Marianne, of course, who at fourteen held the baby Gerhard, a few months old at the time, in the source photograph taken in the early 1930s. Their formats consistently mine the formal trope of the child looking out and toward a future. The very act of painting after portrait photographs of this type produces a ricochet effect of looking back over a life in order to look forward to a life as yet unlived, which, in Marianne's case, was brutally cut short. Rather than unbroken, this version of genealogy is perversely

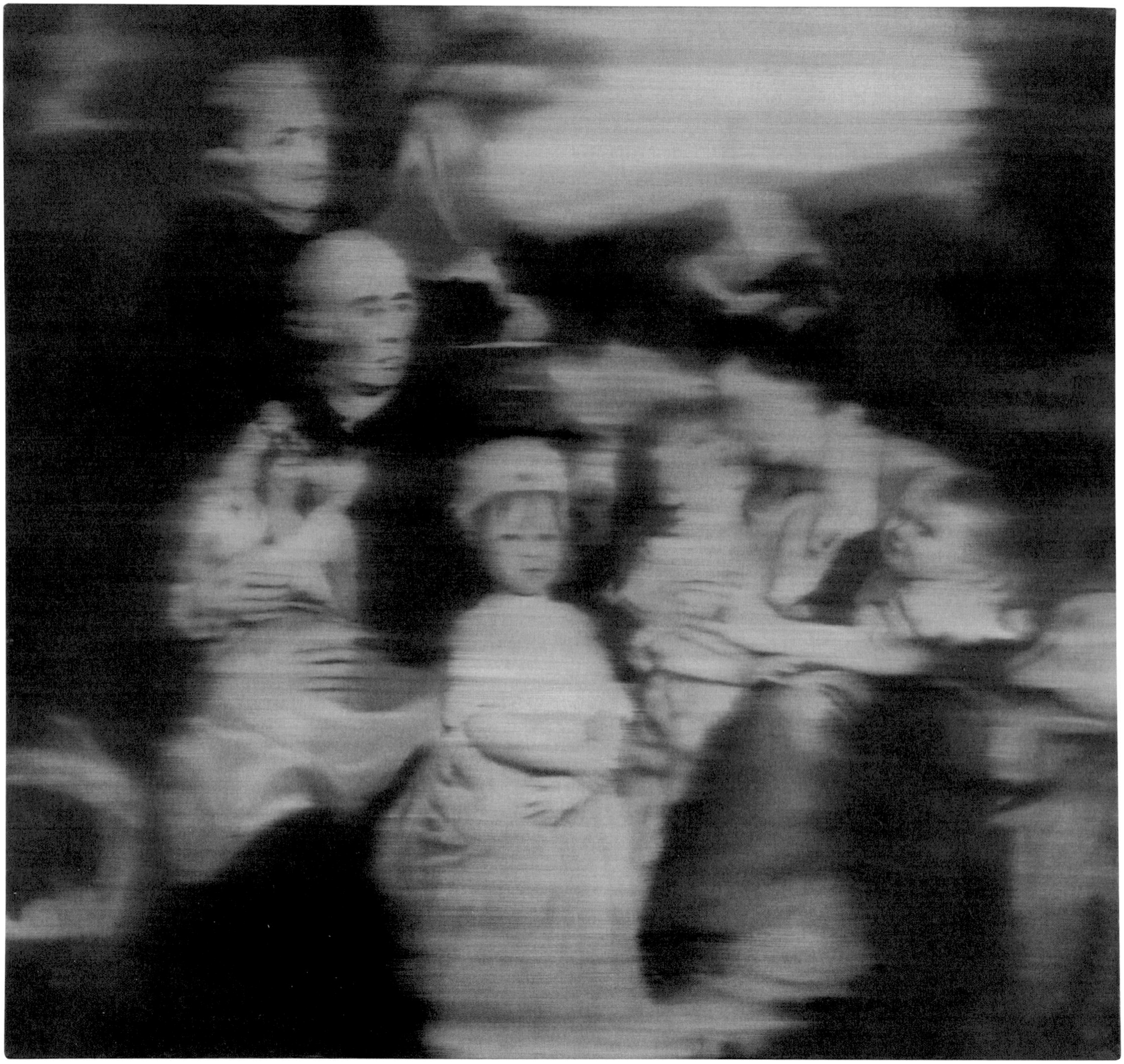

FIG 35
Gerhard Richter, *Family after Old Master* (*Familie nach Altem Meister*), 1965. Oil on canvas, 57 ⅞ × 61 in. (147 × 155 cm). CR 26. Museum Brandhorst, Munich

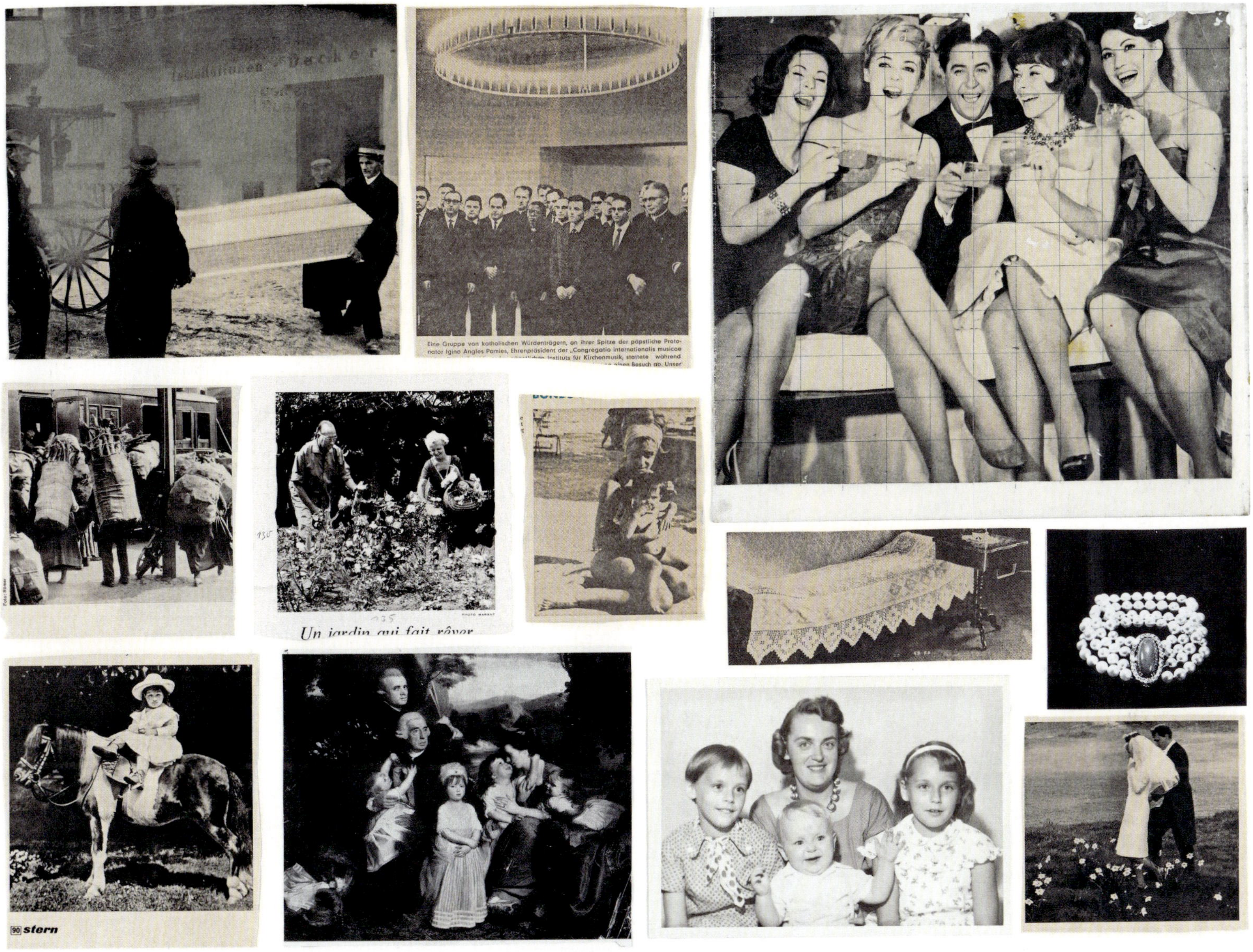

FIG 36
Gerhard Richter, *Atlas* sheet 9,
"Newspaper and Album Photos,"
1962–68. 20 ⅜ × 26 ¼ in. (51.7 × 66.7 cm)

truncated by the cruel severance of her death. Marianne, half-hidden behind the infant Richter's head, is happy and smiling, both startlingly vivid and a ghost of herself. Yet the arrangement of the family group suggests an even stronger connection to the painting *Three Siblings* (fig. 38), a painting based on a newspaper photograph that Richter found out much later depicted the Danish royal princesses.[6] These lateral, metonymic connections between pictures are in this context as important as the recognition of the paintings' ostensible subjects.

Richter has spoken about the way in some instances he discovered the identities of a group of figures only after the fact or recognized a relation of one painting to another only many years later.[7] That is to say, there are a host of chance connections or even coincidences that attach to a painting once it has been made—and to which the work is necessarily open. The newspaper sources may have provided him with a trigger for a painting, then, but do not provide its explanatory key. Often, much earlier pictorial traditions are also in play, and although more hidden, equally insistent. The reaching back through time becomes a habit for Richter, but just as the paintings don't simply mean what the photographs they are based on mean, so they don't necessarily replicate the authority of past tradition either. Rather, I think we could more fruitfully compare Richter's method to Marcel Proust's—bearing in mind what Walter Benjamin referred to as Proust's exploration of "convoluted time, not boundless time."[8] The famous idea of involuntary memory, where the taste of a madeleine suddenly triggers the past to erupt into the present, is only one aspect of Proust's literary method, where his obsession with time is constantly being filtered through reference to the "convolutions" of a history of painting. Arguably, Proust, at least in the first few volumes of *In Search of Lost Time*, offers a kind of pictorial atlas to rival Richter's own. Proust's character Swann has a mania for seeing everything and everyone through painting—a mania for seeing likenesses, as he put it,[9] to paintings by Giotto, Chardin, Vermeer, and literally hundreds of other artists—including his own fictional painter, Elstir—conjured up in the novel at a level of frequency only found otherwise in works of art history. There is a persistent sense of paintings being haunted by one another, as well as by the act of painting itself.

The sudden proliferation of people that enters Richter's paintings in 1964, from the single figure to couples to family groups to crowds, creates a social panorama. There are young and old, public and private, rich and poor; there are scenes of birth and death. These kinds of groupings contrast in obvious ways with Warhol's screenprinted portraits of the famous but also cut against the grain of a more general prohibition on figure painting among the neo-avant-gardes of the early sixties. Paradoxically, perhaps, Richter's family pictures would veer in another direction, making time and the temporal the main business of his painting. When developing his photo paintings, he was categorical: "A portrait must not express anything of

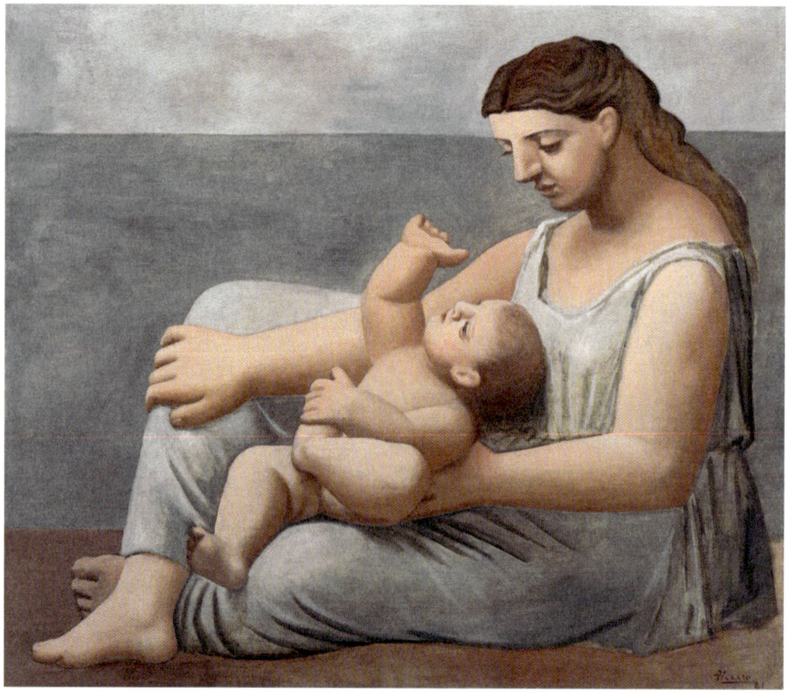

FIG 37
Pablo Picasso (Spanish, 1881–1973), *Mother and Child*, 1921. Oil on canvas, 56 ¼ × 68 in. (142.9 × 172.7 cm). The Art Institute of Chicago, Restricted gift of Maymar Corporation, Mrs. Maurice L. Rothschild, and Mr. and Mrs. Chauncey McCormick; Mary and Leigh Block Fund; Ada Turnbull Hertle Endowment; through prior gift of Mr. and Mrs. Edwin E. Hokin (1954.270)

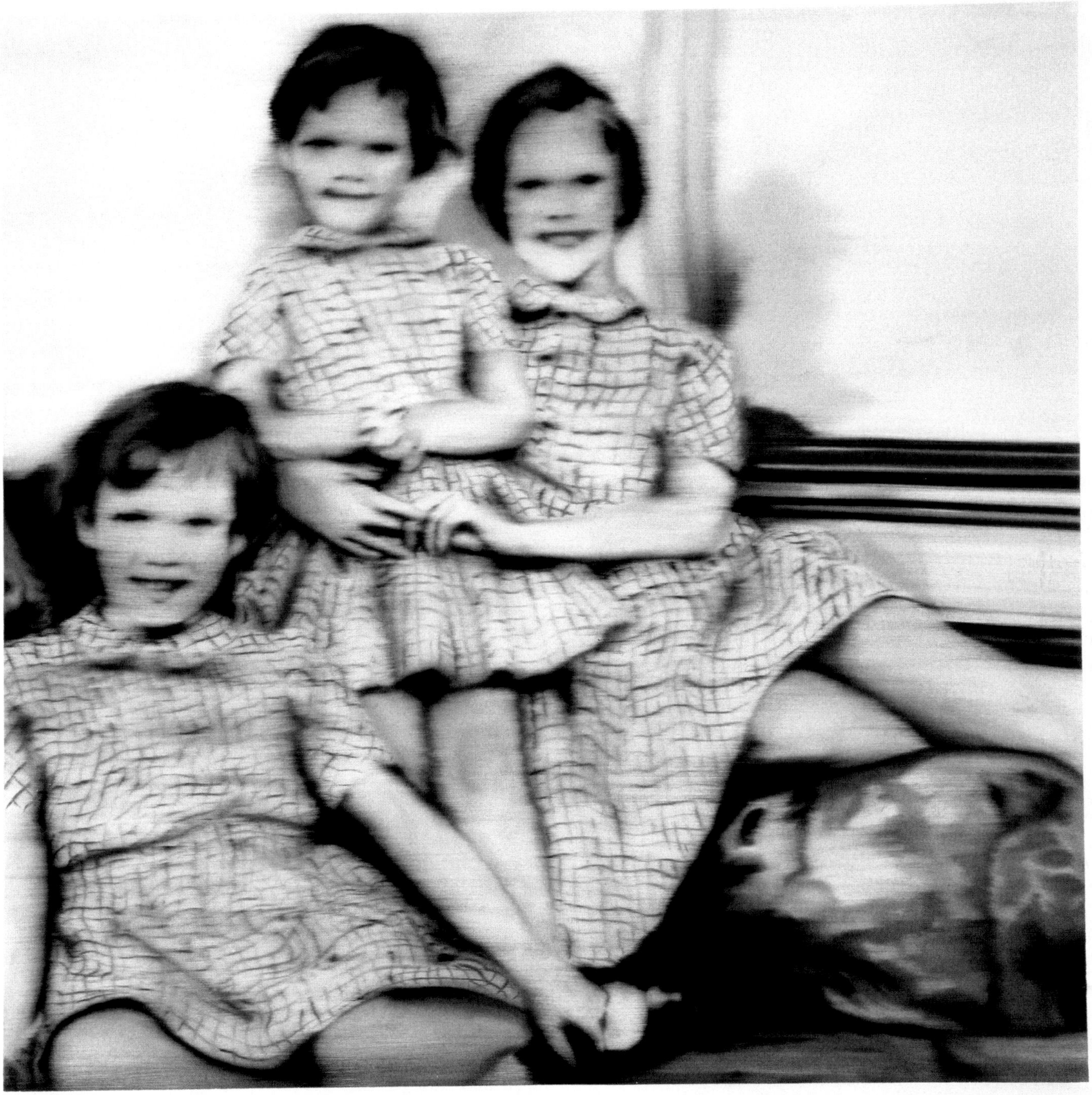

FIG 38
Gerhard Richter, *Three Siblings* (*Drei Geschwister*), 1965. Oil on canvas, 53 ⅛ × 51 ⅛ in. (135 × 130 cm). CR 82. Private collection, Chicago

the sitter's 'soul,' essence or character."[10] Many statements of this type pepper the notes he was writing at the time. Of course, Richter is by no means the only artist to use the photograph as a tool to create psychological distance. Think, for instance, of his contemporary Vija Celmins, who based her small, mute, grisaille—and always unpeopled—paintings on found photographs of German warplanes. Or think of Ed Ruscha, who, especially with hindsight, can be seen to have developed an interest in the processes of degradation enacted by time quite as intense as Richter's, albeit in a comic rather than a tragic mode. For example, *Babycakes with Weights* (fig. 39) was one of only a few books Ruscha made to commission, yet on one level it was his most personal, in the sense that it took the form of a chronicle of the growth of his baby son. The photo of infant Eddie at the front of the book, with the caption "15 lb. 8 oz.," is entirely out of place in the context of Ruscha's work, which is otherwise almost entirely devoid of human subjects, and so brings with it the full force of a comedic "baby picture." The subsequent pages of the book are devoted to photographs of numerous celebratory cakes given with their weights, in random order—cakes that gradually break down into abject mess. The earliest months of life are weighed in metrics and in cake-time. Of course, in tone and content Ruscha's *Babycakes* could not be more different from Richter's versions of what Freud refers to as the "king baby"[11]—in many cases, himself—that seem to degrade and decompose through the strangely tactile apparitions of his paintings.

Despite the pictorial ironies that Richter was exploring at the time, there was nothing ironic in the statement he made in his notes: "I use photography to make a painting, just as

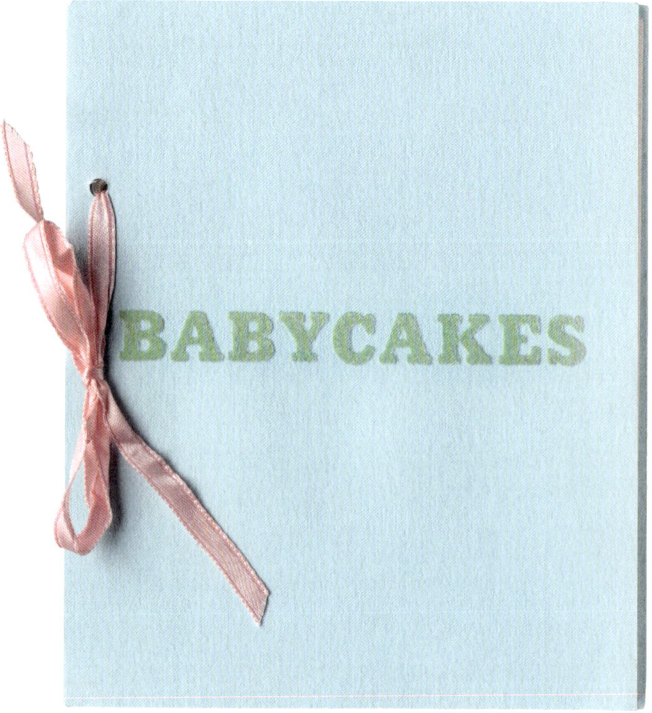

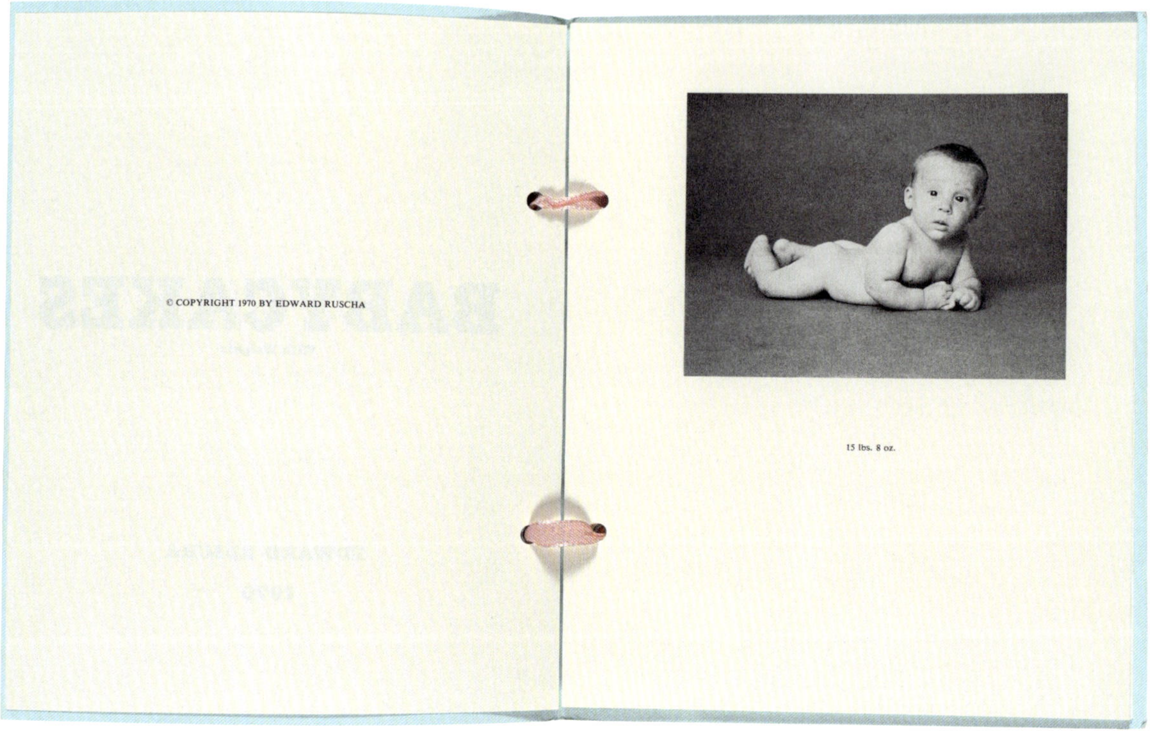

FIG 39
Ed Ruscha (American, born 1937), *Babycakes with Weights*, 1970. Black-and-white offset printing, 7 ½ × 6 × ⅛ in. (19.1 × 15.2 × .3 cm). The Metropolitan Museum of Art, New York, Purchase, Joyce F. Menschel Photography Library Fund, 2016 (2016.78.16)

Rembrandt uses drawing or Vermeer the *camera obscura*."[12] Yet, it has been harder to think critically about Richter's deeply serious engagement with artistic tradition than about his relationship to photography, perhaps because tradition has historically been so tied to notions of retrogression within avant-garde discourse.[13] Arguably, "tradition" operated for Richter as both good and bad object from the outset—though it is also true that his underlying concern with Vermeer, especially, has been entirely consistent. And increasingly, over the decades, Richter's engagement with Vermeer and pictorial tradition has come to involve much more than the camera obscura as a prototypical modern camera. Nowhere is this investment in traditional schema clearer than in the second sustained set of family pictures that Richter painted roughly thirty years after the first: those of his third wife, Sabine, and the series titled S. with Child from 1995 (pp. 170–73, figs. 40, 41). These later works seem to restore tradition rather than break it down, as if marking a reparative phase, in contrast to his photo paintings of the 1960s with their traumatic memory traces. The urge to equate these pictures of his wife and baby son, Moritz, with the artist's personal life may be strong, but in the face of an encounter with them, these works are as unyielding and inaccessible at the level of their subject as any other.

When they were first exhibited, at the newly opened Carré d'Art in Nîmes in 1996, the eight S. with Child paintings seemed to disrupt the narrative of Richter's work to date; I admit to being both puzzled and intrigued by them.[14] They were small, intimate, and introverted in a way that his previous work had not been. On the one hand, they seemed to echo the most extreme formulation of an established pictorial schema, the Madonna and Child, an association exacerbated by the title. On the other, they were decidedly not a closed group but belonged to an extended family of paintings of the same kind and size that behaved very differently. They have the look of snapshots, for sure: the casual composition, the slight indistinctness, the blur at the edges of the contours. But they are not simply replications of the *Atlas* photographs (figs. 42, 43). Compared to its source, the image in the paintings on pages 170 and 172 top (CR 827-1 and CR 827-3) has been cropped, making it tighter and bringing us closer, and Richter's characteristic use of the squeegee has totally transformed it. The action of taking off layers of still-damp paint in emphatic horizontal movements *undoes* the image, in the process distressing the surface that we see, allowing slivers of light to break through (or so it appears).

Richter himself had noted much earlier, "Everyone has produced his own 'devotional pictures'; they are the likenesses of the family."[15] As a compositional type, a "mother and child" is the most hieratic of pictures and the most deeply embedded within a Western Christian tradition, so ubiquitous and internalized that it is reproduced in family snapshots. But even within the most conventional pictorial traditions one finds incredible inventiveness and malleability that belie the ready cliché. Certainly, if one compares a roomful of Bellini pictures—and only a modern viewer would—one sees the formal schema or prototype constantly adapting, setting in train multiple possible versions of itself, including the switch from portrait to landscape format, and presenting a textbook case of repetition maximizing difference. Older understandings of time as

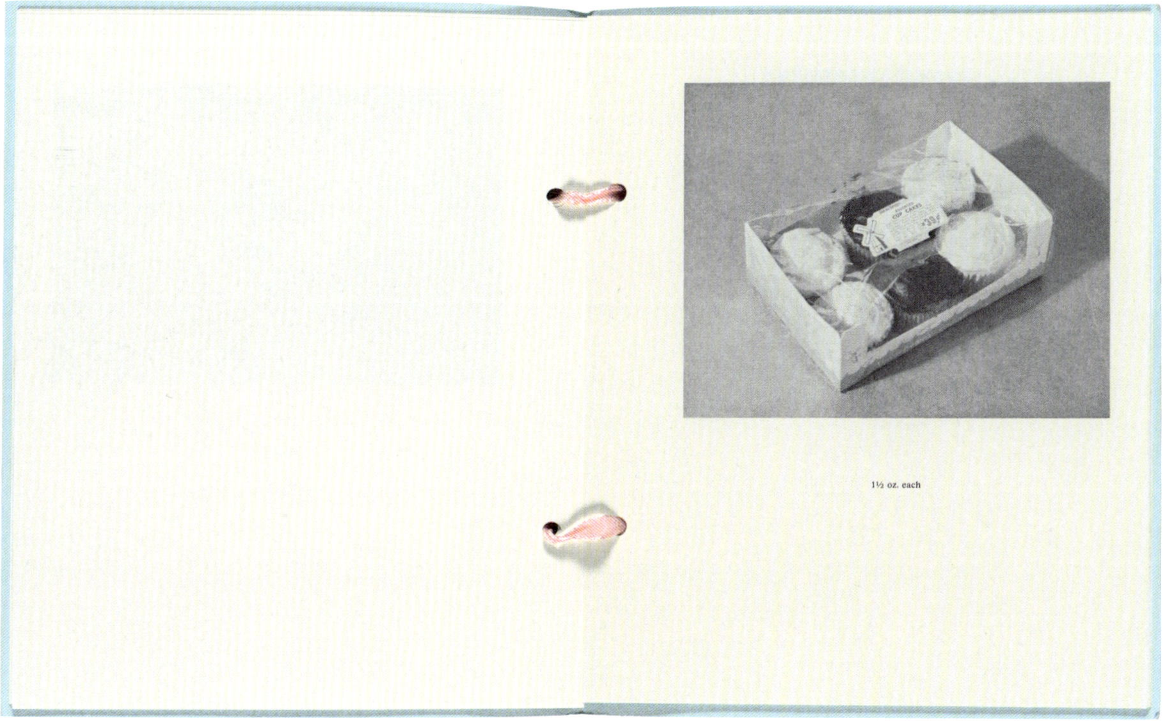

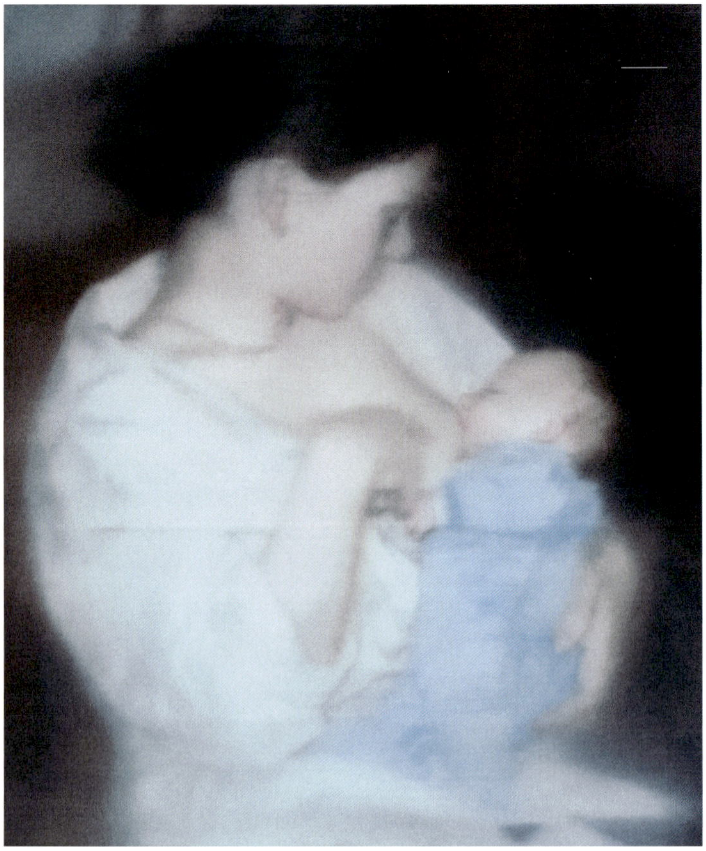

40

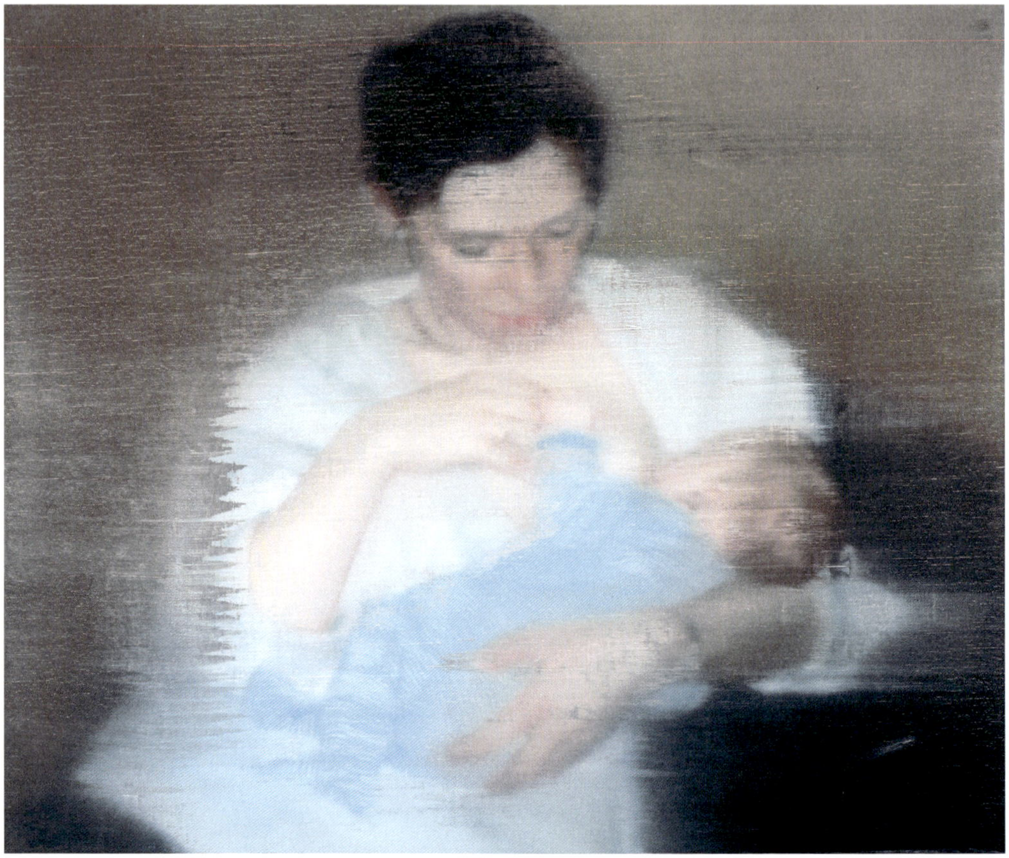

41

FIG 40
Gerhard Richter, *S. with Child* (*S. mit Kind*), 1995. Oil on canvas, 24 × 20 ⅛ in. (61 × 51 cm). CR 827-5. Hamburger Kunsthalle, Hamburg

FIG 41
Gerhard Richter, *S. with Child* (*S. mit Kind*), 1995. Oil on canvas, 24 ⅜ × 28 ⅜ in. (62 × 72 cm). CR 827-6. Hamburger Kunsthalle, Hamburg

FIG 42
Gerhard Richter, *Atlas* sheet 614, "S. with Child," n.d. 20 ⅜ × 26 ¼ in. (51.7 × 66.7 cm)

FIG 43
Gerhard Richter, *Atlas* sheet 615, "S. with Child," n.d. 20 ⅜ × 26 ¼ in. (51.7 × 66.7 cm)

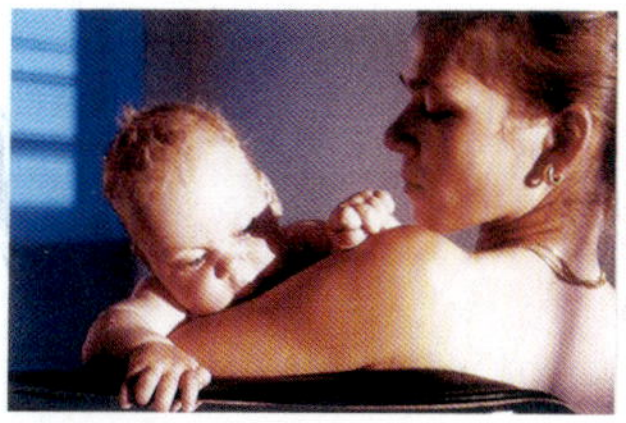

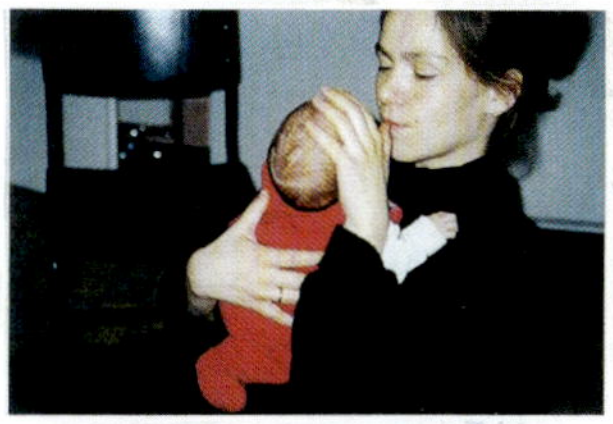

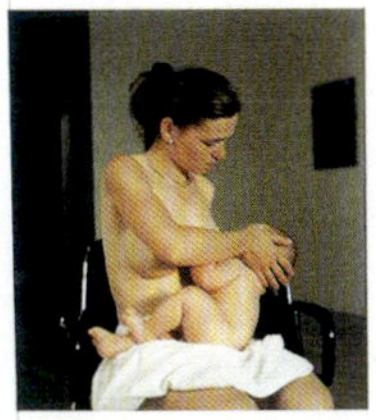

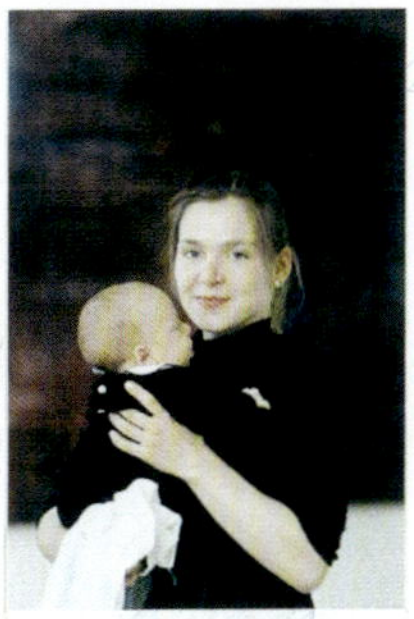

42

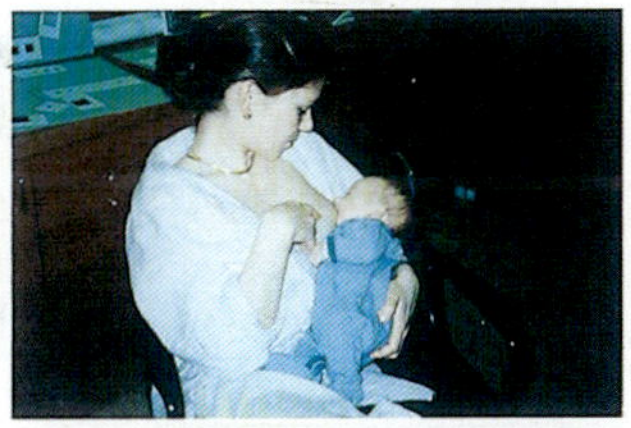

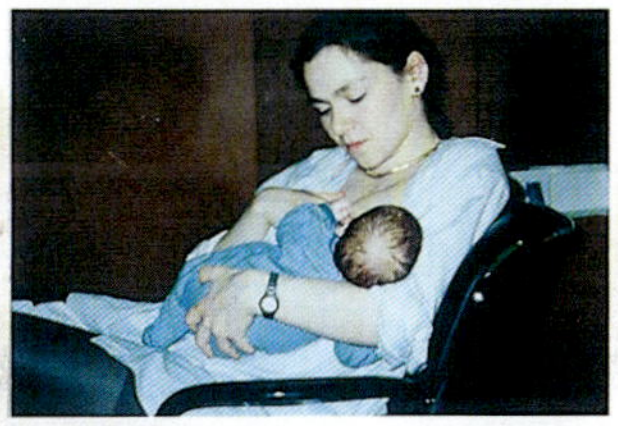

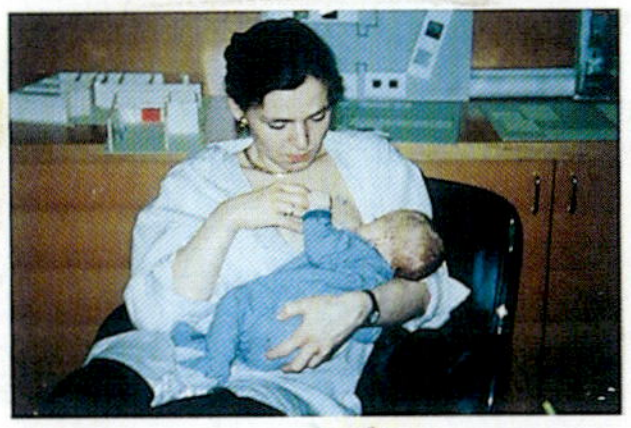

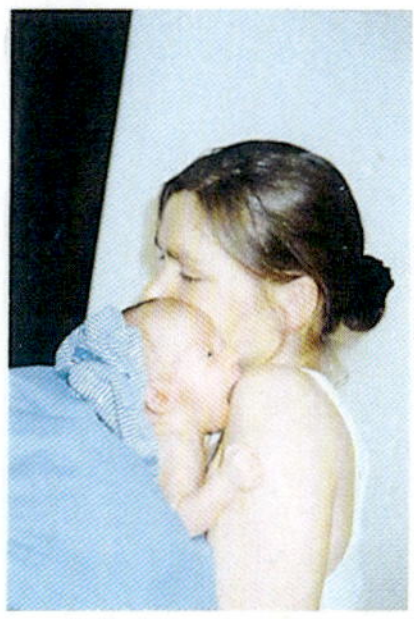

43

prophetic, as so often conveyed in the Madonna and Child image, translate for a modern viewer into something both more secular and speculative. In Bellini's *Madonna of the Meadow* (fig. 44), for instance, with her eyes half closed, the Virgin looks to be in a suspended, dreamlike state, as if she were herself experiencing the very apparition that she appears in.

Richter is highly attuned to such strictures and possibilities of pictorial convention, not with respect to the authority of tradition, but rather, as Theodor Adorno wrote of Marcel Proust, because pictures "are part of the life of the person who observes them."[16] Adorno was contrasting Proust's sense of the afterlife of the work of art with Paul Valéry's sense of the historically preserved but lifeless object to which the observer no longer has any possibility of a vital relationship. Rather than retrogressive, then, let's imagine Richter's visual atlas as more attuned to Proust's than to Valéry's museumlike (in the German *museal*) stasis. At a certain point in *In Search of Lost Time*, Swann, who is in the process of writing an essay on Vermeer over the whole course of the novel, begins to formulate an idea about the way art opens onto and allows one to imagine not just one but multiple worlds: "worlds which, centuries after the extinction of the fire from which their light first emanated, whether it is called Rembrandt or Vermeer, send us still each one its special radiance."[17] Past art refuses to stay in the past, just as the present refuses to stay present, frequently losing itself and lapsing into another time and constantly scrambling the measure of temporal distance. How long ago "then" was is continually moving and spreading out. Richter's family pictures, which supposedly capture a moment in a life, in fact unravel in time, always already the subject of retrospection. The just-born human—the original origin myth—comes into being in a painting only to begin to vanish and fade into the striations across its surface.

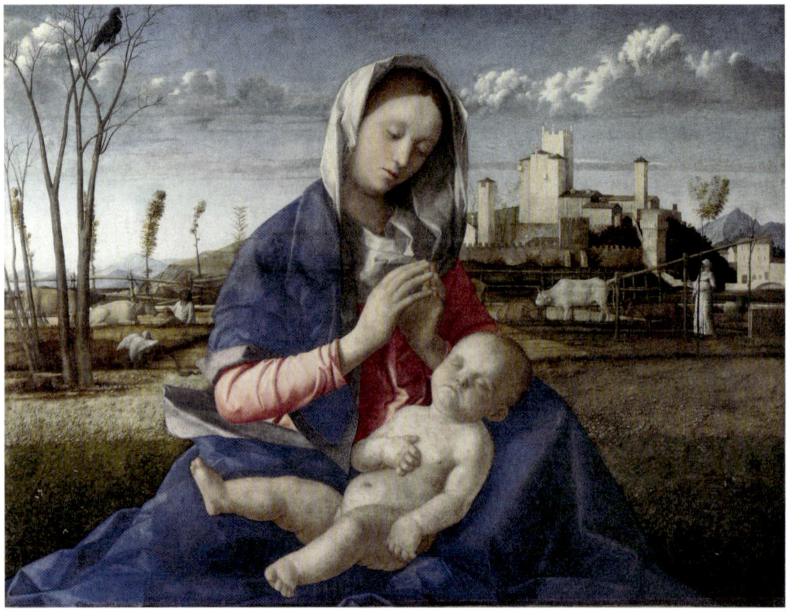

44

Unsurprisingly, Richter's interests in Vermeer have changed—though even at the outset, he was never *only* interested in the camera obscura as a technical apparatus that the Dutch artist famously used to make his paintings.[18] Later on, there are moments when he seems instead completely in thrall to Vermeer's emanating light, such as in the 1994 paintings of Sabine that vividly recall a picture like *Woman Reading a Letter* (fig. 45). But more compelling still is the way Vermeer was somehow able to create a complex and enigmatic sense of time in painting.[19] Surely, that was why Proust was so drawn to him in the first place. The most articulate, as well as mysterious, demonstration of this is Vermeer's allegorical work *The Art of Painting* (fig. 46), in which we see the artist from the back, at work at his easel, painting the very work that we are witnessing before us. That is to say, we are watching the painter painting the very scene we are looking at. Proust would do something similar for modern literature, basing his novel on the conceit that—as we gradually discover—the narrator is in the process of writing the same novel that we are in the

FIG 44
Giovanni Bellini (Italian, ca. 1435–1516), *Madonna of the Meadow*, ca. 1500–1505. Oil on panel, 26 ⅛ × 33 ½ in. (66.5 × 85.1 cm). National Gallery, London (NG599)

FIG 45
Johannes Vermeer (Dutch, 1623–1675), *Woman Reading a Letter*, ca. 1663. Oil on canvas, 18 ¼ × 15 ⅜ in. (46.5 × 39 cm). Rijksmuseum, Amsterdam (SK-C-251)

FIG 46
Johannes Vermeer (Dutch, 1623–1675), *The Art of Painting*, 1666–67. Oil on canvas, 47 ¼ × 39 ⅜ in. (120 × 100 cm). Kunsthistorisches Museum, Vienna (GG 9128)

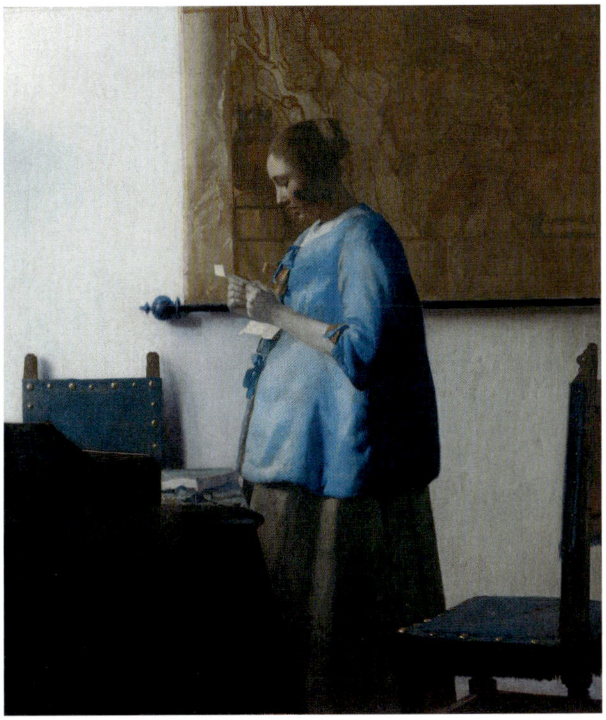

45

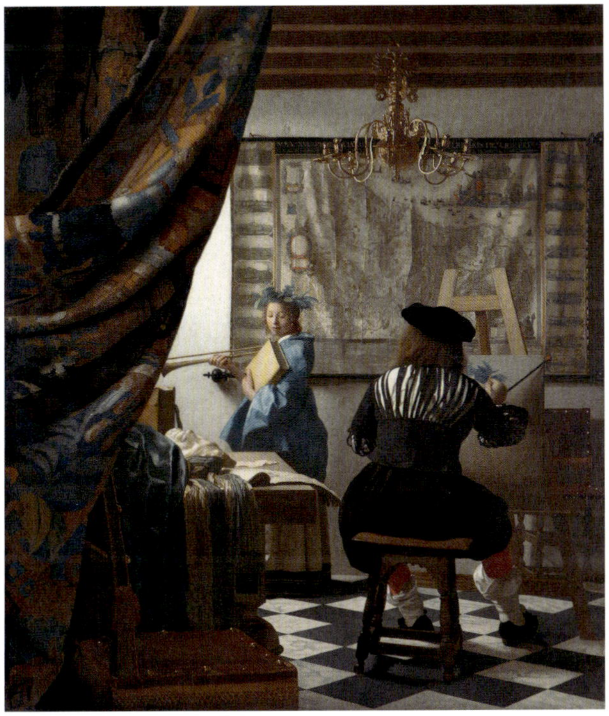

46

process of reading. In this double movement, different temporalities overlay and reverse one another simultaneously.

Richter does not need to paint himself into a painting in order to reveal its temporal aspects. Or, I should say, he's not concerned with revealing hidden allegorical meanings or parallel narratives as such. Rather, his method generally involves, or at least is intensified by, working laterally across several pictures, creating small groups of two or three related works, as in the 1995 series S. with Child. These are paintings that show us the process that made them, but they also seem to act out painting's evanescence. The image is both present and in danger of absenting itself entirely. The pair of paintings mentioned above (pp. 170, 172 top) seem to move in and out of vision. The first painting is thinned out of so much of its substance that it appears like a ghost. The second, by contrast, seems to have accrued so much viscosity that the paint threatens to drown the image, leaving only fragments to be glimpsed—a larger hand here, a part of a tiny arm there. The mottled shower of black paint that rains down over the surface, marking the drift of the squeegee as it was pulled over the canvas, links the work to the series of abstract paintings of the same size made at the same period. Although it is one of the eight S. with Child paintings, its subject is barely visible. It is surely as much an abstract painting as it is a family picture, as if it lies at some outer edge of this group and might morph into a completely abstract one. The series moves toward a degradation of the image as a legible subject. In the process, the painting itself becomes somehow a much more material entity, whereas it almost seems as if the materiality of the image has migrated elsewhere.

Richter repeats this movement again and again, not only in the S. with Child series but also notably in the many still lifes he worked on during the same period, especially the flower paintings. Perhaps the word *cycle* better describes these small clusters of works, although, strictly speaking, a cycle generally consists of more than a pair of paintings. Antinarrative and abbreviated, they are extreme contractions of Richter's larger cycles of abstract paintings. Some mimic a *vanitas* still life with a wilting flower. Others *act out*, like the small cycle of three paintings of a vase of tulips on Richter's desk (figs. 47–49), which we see metamorphosing from figuration to abstraction. The aftereffect of the flash of light in the Polaroid on which the painting was based becomes a diffuse, inchoate, and strangely luminous surface. The image ends up as precarious and transient as a flower in bloom. And while it would be wrong—and far too melodramatic in this context—to say that painting itself is subject to its own symbolic death, there is, especially in these small works, an implied sense that painting is always necessarily a matter of mortality, whether we like it or not.

It is often surprising how much of the materiality of painting seems to have been lifted from these small figurative works, making them somehow lighter, more like a visionary apparition

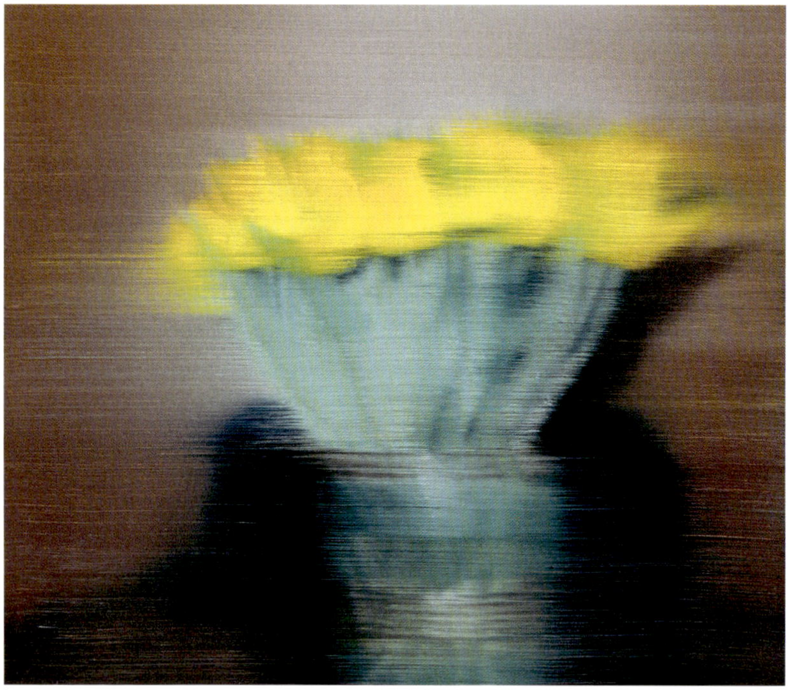

47

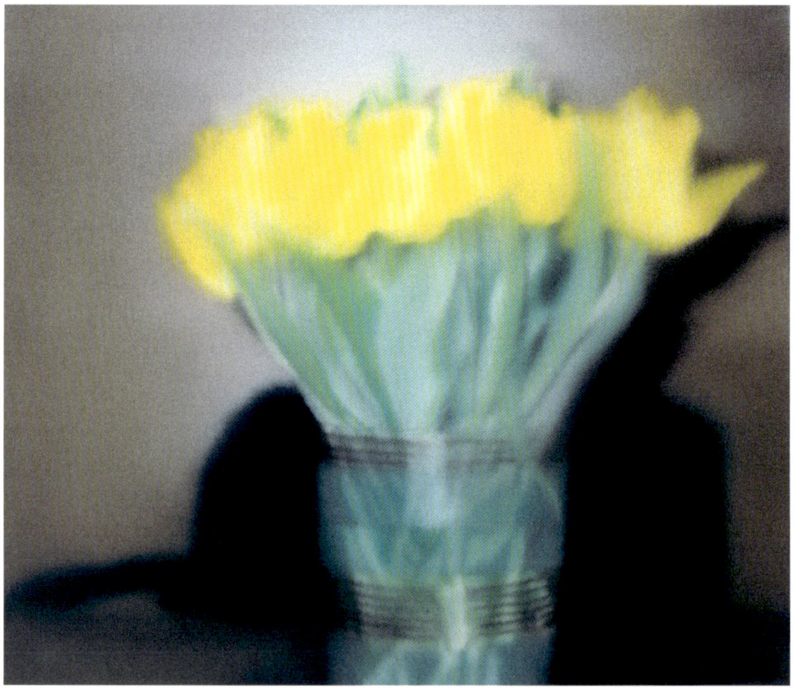

48

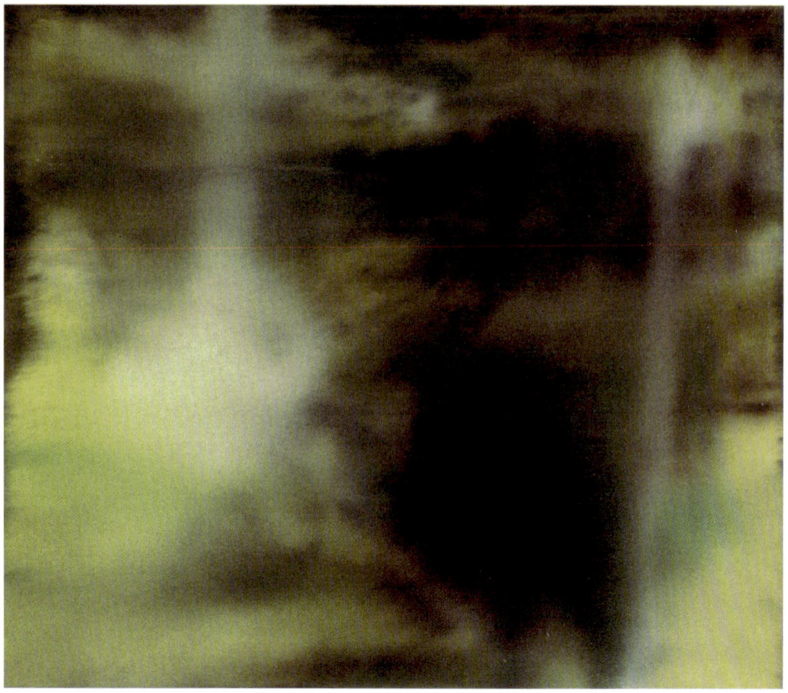

49

FIG 47
Gerhard Richter, *Tulips* (*Tulpen*), 1995. Oil on canvas, 14 ⅛ × 16 ⅛ in. (36 × 41 cm). CR 825-1. Österreichische Galerie Belvedere, Lower Belvedere, Vienna

FIG 48
Gerhard Richter, *Tulips* (*Tulpen*), 1995. Oil on canvas, 14 ⅛ × 16 ⅛ in. (36 × 41 cm). CR 825-2. Private collection, Cologne

FIG 49
Gerhard Richter, *Abstract Painting* (*Abstraktes Bild*), 1995. Oil on canvas, 14 ⅛ × 16 ⅛ in. (36 × 41 cm). CR 825-3. Collection Vanmoerkerke, Belgium

in a state of suspension. The surface layer can be thinly painted and feel insubstantial. It is as if the concreteness of the world—evocative at times of the material thickness of a Courbet landscape (fig. 50)—does not belong to the painted human figure anymore but adheres more convincingly to the ground of abstraction. It turns out that families of pictures are just as unstable as any other kind of family. Different possible groupings continually emerge, which, far from maintaining the typological categories of picture that had initially seemed so generative, now positively encourage us to think of painting types themselves as remarkably porous. With hindsight, *Aunt Marianne* asks us to imagine a more spacious sense of how a painting might hold multiple temporalities, in this case, as a time of childhood, not only evocative of the infant Richter as a subject, but also reminiscent of the archaic compositional protocols of a Bellini painting. However obscurely felt, that nuance—that sudden throwback to the tradition of an old prophetic motif—only highlights the poignancy of loss in the subject's actual fate. Such contingencies are as unpredictable as they are inevitable. This might be the case in any artist's work, but Richter positively courts them through his process.

If pictures become part of the life of the person who observes them, as Adorno succinctly summed up Proust's distinctively modern way of thinking, then it is not always easy to live with a "mania for likenesses" that seems, in due course, to turn everyone into a picture. The family group is one way to organize people within a social panorama, and, as we have seen in Richter's hands, it is a constantly mutating cast of characters who are always viewed in the perspective of time, making them hard to place. The increasing interest that Richter has shown in older pictorial traditions, especially in the pictures from the 1990s, would at first glance seem to mark a rather more conservative relation to tradition than he had previously demonstrated. However, paintings have the capacity to do something rather different from what we might have expected of them. The unstable quality of the family pictures and the effect of fleeting evanescence that flickers across them simply make us aware of time as a sliding scale, upon which we have only a precarious hold. The ricochet effect of looking back and looking forward—an effect that can feel like either a sudden bounce or a gradual turning around different viewpoints—is not confined to Richter's pictures of his family. But the family as a trope offers him several possible ways of imagining how a friction between personal and pictorial genealogies might be generative. The look on the slightly smudged face of his own infantile self inside the picture of Aunt Marianne—the look that turns outward toward us—becomes a token of a fluid and mobile and ultimately temporal point of view.

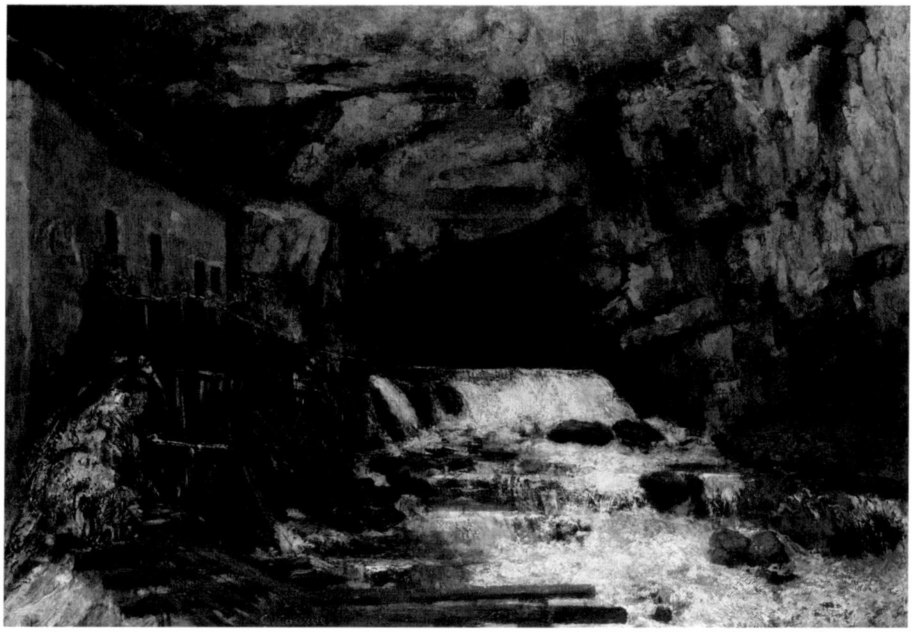

FIG 50
Gustave Courbet (French, 1819–1877), *The Source of the Loue*, 1864. Oil on canvas, 39 ¼ × 56 in. (99.7 × 142.2 cm). The Metropolitan Museum of Art, New York, H. O. Havemeyer Collection, Bequest of Mrs. H. O. Havemeyer, 1929 (29.100.122)

Brinda Kumar

Terrains of Paint: Richter's Landscapes

For the cover of the catalogue of his first large-scale retrospective, in 1986,[1] Gerhard Richter chose a photograph of the interior of his Cologne studio (fig. 51). In the background, two large abstract paintings lean against a wall. The mid-ground features an H-frame easel on which rests a landscape that will become *Venice (Island)* (1985). In front of it is a chair, on which is a small handheld mirror used by the artist to verify the compositional logic of his paintings.[2] In a related photograph found inside the catalogue, Richter is doing just that,[3] but the cover image leaves us to contemplate the setting in his absence. The mirror faces outward, perhaps as an invitation to the viewer to take a closer look—to shift his or her perspective. At first glance, the composition typifies the manner in which Richter has straddled the positions of seeming polarity—photographic realism and abstraction—that have characterized many accounts of his work. Yet Richter himself often disavowed the distance between abstract and photo-based paintings, and so the staging can also be read as an artistic conceit designed to exaggerate those oppositional terms of his practice. In a subsequent series of closely related works also titled *Venice* (fig. 52), the artist scumbled and scratched the surfaces of the landscapes, thwarting the very dichotomy he had highlighted so prominently on the cover of his catalogue. Therefore, Richter's placement of the photographic landscape at the heart of the studio scene allows one to consider that the form occupies a liminal space in his oeuvre and is thus germane to understanding it in terms of contrasts and continuities. At this mid-career reckoning, this introductory image represents Richter's acute awareness of his simultaneous commitment to and ambivalence toward painting, as both a historical and personal medium. The setting also creates the opportunity to consider Richter's relationship to nature and the landscape form as broadly generative and as an important passage into realizing his artistic concerns.

By now, it is a truism that the transformation of the photographic image has been foundational for Richter's practice, starting with his breakthrough work in the early 1960s of blurred photo paintings that draw upon found images and family pictures. His arrival at landscapes, however, was much more oblique and occurred in two precursory periods. Landscapelike scenes appeared intermittently beginning in the mid-1960s, but the presence of nature in his paintings precedes even those works that could classify as landscapes—for example, *Deer* (see fig. 64). In Richter's own account, he identified a series of landscapes from 1964–69 that were "anonymous, brochure-like, not individually experienced; Sphinx, pyramids, etc."[4] A discrete series, these works are in keeping with the photo paintings he was making in the 1960s (fig. 53). Through their obvious man-made markers (sphinx, pyramid), they identify a distant elsewhere, producing a sense of double displacement that is underscored by the fact that the paintings reproduce images taken from various print sources.[5] Traces of the foundness of the landscapes, such as the original explanatory text and captions, further connect them to the contemporaneous photo paintings.

The other precedents for Richter's investigation of naturalistic landscapes are his Townscapes and closely related paintings of mountains from 1968 (pp. 118, 119, 120–23). Mark Godfrey has persuasively argued for the reading of these works as the artist's means to "think through problems about history without ever making conventional history paintings and instead making landscapes."[6] For example, Godfrey identifies in Richter's approach to his alpine compositions a refusal "to see the mountain as a 'majestic force' and to associate it with nationalist strength. . . . Rather than allowing his viewer to feel a sense of empowerment with a prospect seen from the peak of a mountain, Richter conjures a sense of impenetrability and disorientation."[7] This is amplified by the stark gestures and thick impasto used to create these images, which are more or less in focus depending on one's position in relation to the painting. Tellingly, Richter decided to include the Townscapes and his alpine works in his installation at the German pavilion at the Venice Biennale in 1972. At the time, he slyly noted that

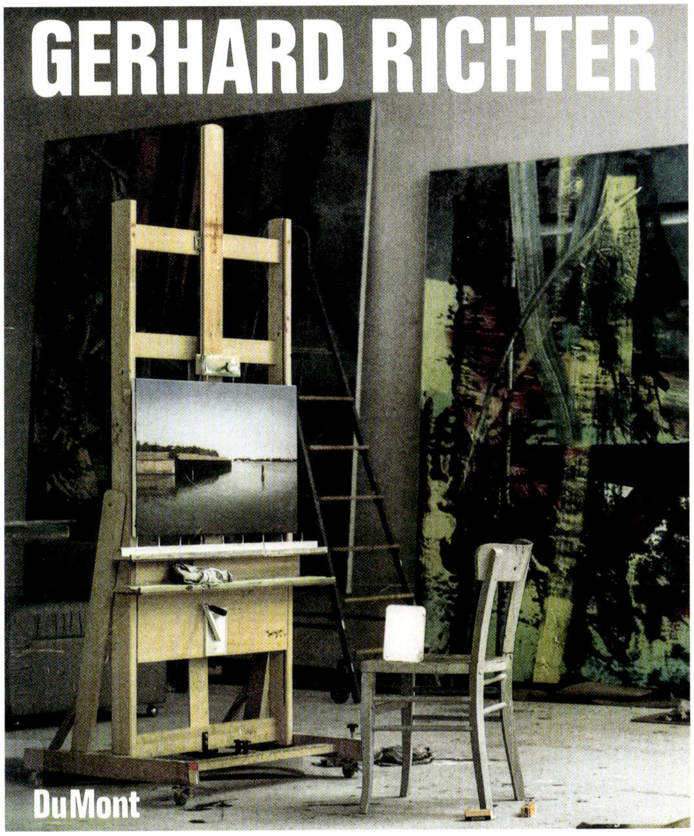

51

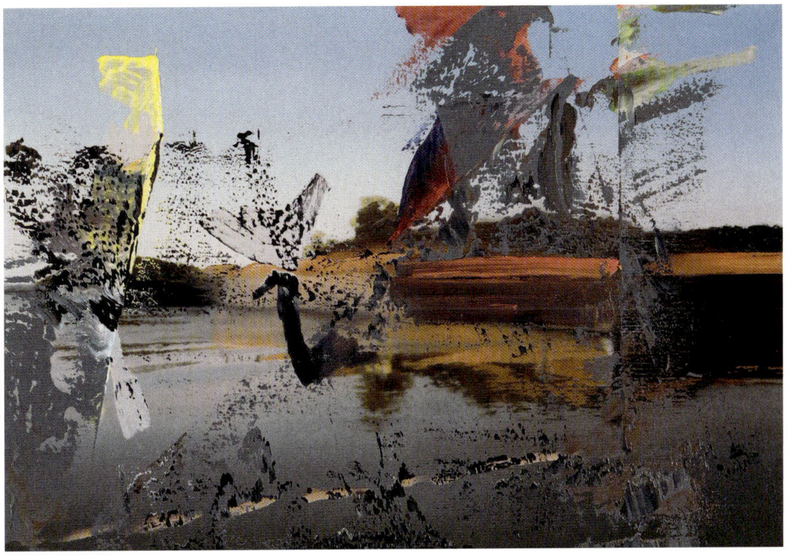

52

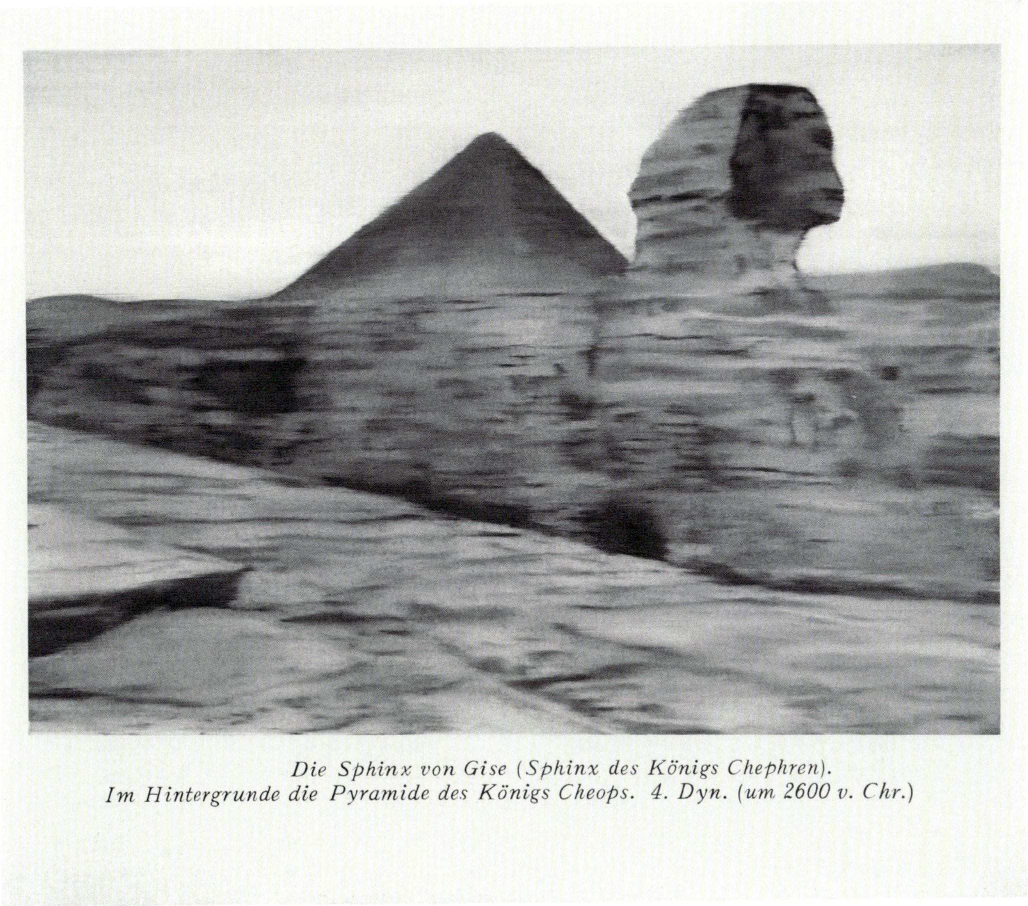

53

FIG 51
Cover of *Gerhard Richter: Bilder; 1962–1985*. Cologne: DuMont, 1986.

FIG 52
Gerhard Richter, *Venice* (*Venedig*), 1986. Oil on canvas, 33 ⅞ × 47 ⅝ in. (86 × 121 cm). CR 606-3. Museum Frieder Burda, Baden-Baden

FIG 53
Gerhard Richter, *Great Sphinx of Gizeh* (*Große Sphinx von Gise*), 1964. Oil on canvas, 57 ½ × 65 ½ in. (146.1 × 166.4 cm). CR 46. Glenstone Foundation, Potomac, Maryland

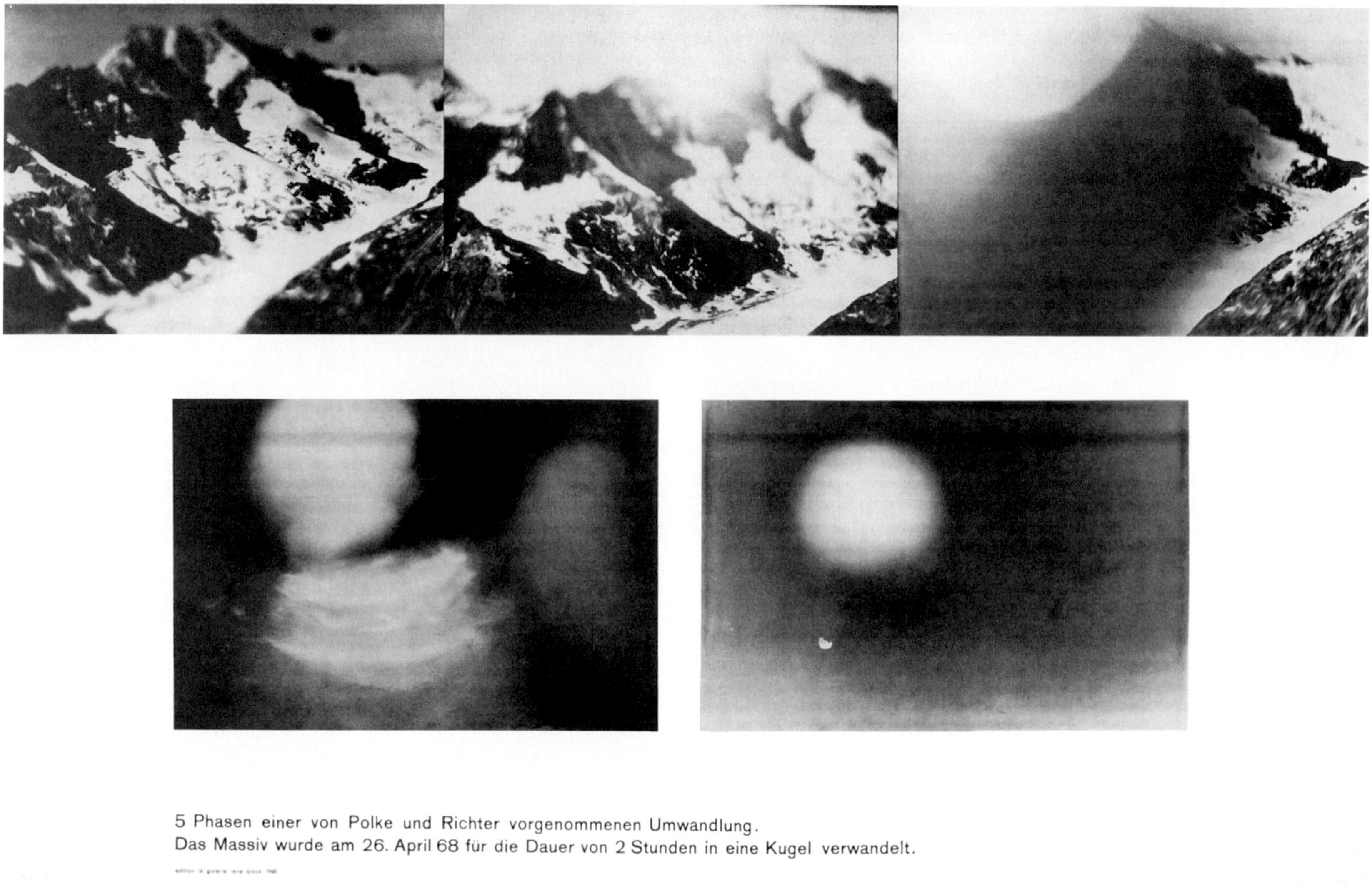

FIG 54
Gerhard Richter and Sigmar Polke (German, 1941–2010), *Transformation* (*Umwandlung*), 1968. Offset print on lightweight card, 18 ⅜ × 26 ½ in. (46.6 × 67.2 cm). Editions CR 14

he "fancied the idea that [he] alone could represent Germany."[8] The center of the Venice project was undoubtedly Richter's *48 Portraits*, a series featuring white European and American men, all prominent in the late nineteenth and early twentieth centuries in the fields of literature, science, philosophy, and music. The portraits, rendered in a uniform black-and-white encyclopedic format, have been interpreted by some as paternal progenitors—a particularly fraught subject in the context of postwar Germany. By hanging them in the central room of the pavilion, which was built by the National Socialists in the 1930s, Richter—who had arrived in West Germany just ten years prior—deliberately inserted this complex and disquieting series into a narrative that necessitated navigating German national identity.[9] Significantly, however, also arranged in the adjacent rooms were the Townscapes, the Alps and other mountain paintings, a trio of Cloud paintings, and a number of brushy green canvases, including *Park Piece*, *Jungle Picture* (fig. 63), and the related *Untitled (Green)*. This arrangement in the installation further implies a reading of these Ur-landscapes as history paintings against the grain. It also suggests an early recognition of how Richter's paintings of nature are key to understanding the subtly subversive politics of his work.[10]

This conjunctive positioning is instructive in considering Richter's approach to the landscape form, and especially the mountain motif, at a slightly earlier moment. In 1968, amid the charged climate of radical leftist politics—toward which Richter, having come from East Germany, was unsurprisingly ambivalent—Richter and Sigmar Polke, his friend and occasional collaborator, produced an offset lithograph titled *Transformation* (fig. 54). Created at about the same time as the Alps group, the print humorously suggests the synchronous omnipotence and impotence of the artist.[11] The caption matter-of-factly notes, "5 stages of a transformation undertaken by Polke and Richter. On April 26, 1968, the mountain was transformed into a sphere for a duration of two hours." Formally, the work harks back to Richter's earlier preoccupation with found images accompanied by captions and explanatory notes, but here he instead produced his own simulated photographs and pseudo-descriptive text. In the political context of the day, the transformation can be seen as an absurdist and ironic interpretation of the hubris and futility of human intervention in cosmic matters.[12] Many years later, in 1992, Richter would return to the climactic sphere, producing steel orbs engraved with the name of their "source" peaks in the Swiss Engadin: Piz Fedoz, Piz Lagrev, etc. (fig. 55).[13]

Richter's works that are most closely associated with landscape painting, not least because of their visual affinity to the art-historical traditions of the genre, first appear in 1968. They are a series of paintings based on the artist's own photographs from a trip to Corsica, the first vacation he was able to take with his family since moving to the West (fig. 56). The landscapes in this series are characterized by low horizons, deep distances across the sea, silhouetted mountains, and hovering clouds through which burst shafts of light. The misty vistas produce a natural blurring that dovetails with Richter's recurring use of this effect, while all the constitutive elements—sea, mountains, and clouds—would become focused subjects of inquiry in his subsequent practice. Thus, the Corsica series marks the beginning of a fitful engagement with the genre, one that began quite personally, but through which Richter would find new possibilities for thinking of painting historically and conceptually.

At about this time, Richter found sympathy with Gilbert & George, two artists who likewise were consciously stepping outside the mainstream by returning to antiquated forms. Richter has often acknowledged that they were the first to appreciate his landscapes.[14] The affinity between the artists is unsurprising; in 1971–72 Gilbert & George were interested in conceptual photo and video works that addressed the English countryside,[15] in a manner that paralleled Richter's own arboreal fascinations, which engaged with the larger national

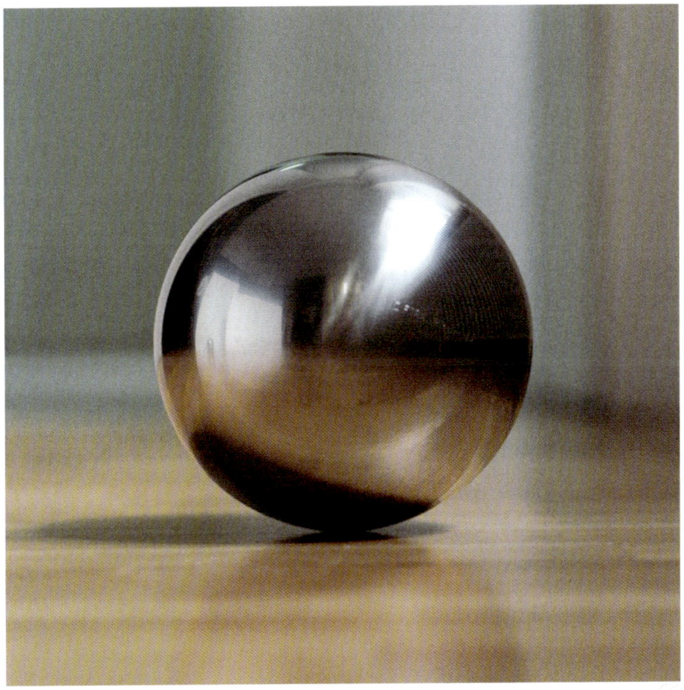

FIG 55
Gerhard Richter, *Sphere III* (*Kugel III*), 1992. Stainless steel, diam. 6 ¼ in. (16 cm). Editions CR 77

and cultural resonances of the forest. A plan was formed for Richter to create portraits of the duo from preparatory photographs taken in the Alps or in a garden setting, but that project was never realized.[16] Instead, in 1975 Richter painted a series of portraits of the two men employing doubled or overlaid photographs, occasionally with landscapes in the background. In spite of this association with his fellow artists, not to mention the conceptual implications of his work, contemporary critics identified Richter's early landscapes as sentimental, conservative, and self-indulgent, and perhaps because of this reaction, Richter was even more determined to amplify their effect: "It was a kind of act of defiance on my part."[17]

Paintings of nature appear occasionally in Richter's output, punctuating his much larger and astonishingly diverse corpus of abstract works. Although landscapes dominate the folios of the *Atlas*, few ended up the focus of paintings. As Richter explained: "It is... untrue that I have nothing specific in mind. As with my landscapes: I see countless landscapes, photograph barely 1 in 100,000, and paint barely 1 in 100 of those that I photograph. I am therefore seeking something quite specific; from this I conclude that I know what I want."[18] The folios of the *Atlas* nevertheless reveal that, for a brief period in the early 1970s, landscapes unlocked certain conceptual possibilities for the artist, especially in his "Rooms" pages. These include sketches of architectural interiors, ranging from Rococo spaces to modernist white cubes, in which Richter placed cloudscapes and landscapes on the walls, floor, and ceiling—usually photographs that he took himself and that sometimes correlate to actual paintings. Some of these plans for the display of works represent actual or realistic gallery interiors, while others depict more obviously imaginary spaces. These latter drawings are sometimes read as utopian, but in Richter's own telling, they are in fact decidedly different and much more complicated.[19] The scale and details of certain drawings suggest a radical revisiting of the idea of making murals, as he had done for political ends in the GDR, although here the imagery is stripped of figurative and narrative context. Instead, the putatively Romantic assumptions of landscape are deliberately tuned to an extreme pitch through a range of strategies, including the scenes' usurpation of all the room's surfaces (fig. 57) and the monumentalizing of the imagery to an estranging degree (fig. 58), so much so that these "total pictures" could be visually all-consuming, or, in Richter's words, "so overwhelming in effect that they could have been used to torture or kill."[20]

Underlying this approach is an ambivalence toward nature and especially toward the tradition of Romantic landscapes. In their disorienting presentation, the spaces Richter proposes in these "Rooms" offer a place of suspended perception that resists the Romantic. This resistance allows Richter to contend with the enduring tendency toward Romanticism and to see its darker sides. As he told Irmeline Lebeer, "I simply think that we have not yet got over the Romantic epoch. The pictures of that period still constitute a part of our sensibility... if not, we would no longer look at them. Romanticism is far from dead. Exactly like fascism."[21] That is not to say that Richter elided the distance between his era and that of Caspar David Friedrich. Rather, as Godfrey points out, "we could argue that Richter wanted to invoke Friedrich precisely to make visible the caesura separating his age from Friedrich's."[22] In other words, Richter is acutely aware that the events of the midcentury had irrevocably rendered the historical German landscape a place of no return, while also recognizing the inevitable need to grapple with it as a cultural touchstone.

Even though his approach to landscape was always more complex than and fundamentally different from sentimental nostalgia for Romantic traditions, Richter found it difficult to shake the association with conservativism. Much of this is attributable to the fact that his landscapes have been interpreted in terms of Friedrich's art-historical legacy ever since

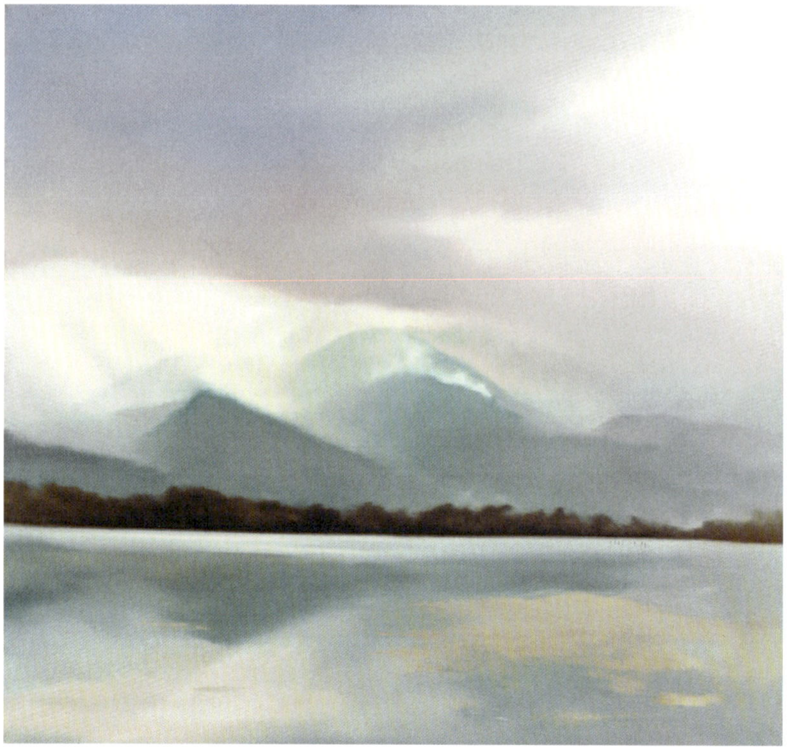

FIG 56
Gerhard Richter, *Corsica (Korsika)*, 1968. Oil on canvas, 33 ⅞ × 35 ⅞ in. (86 × 91 cm). CR 199. Private collection, Switzerland

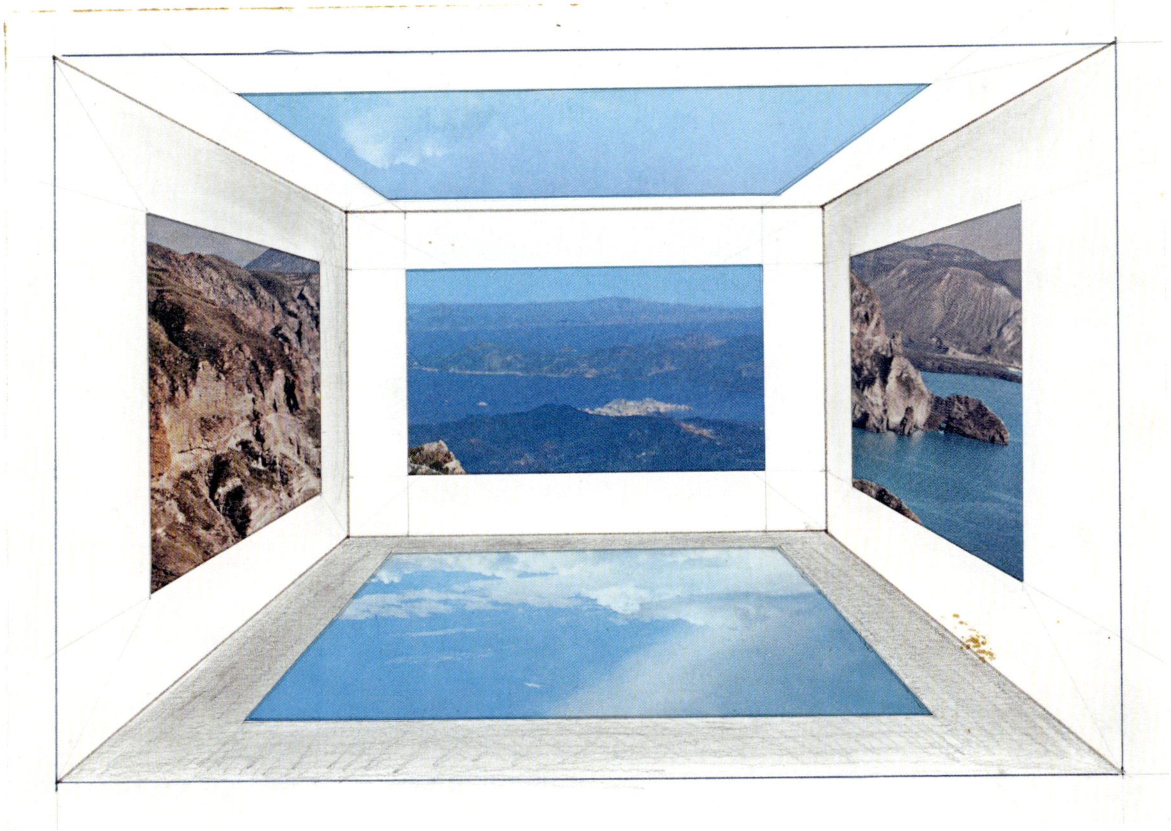

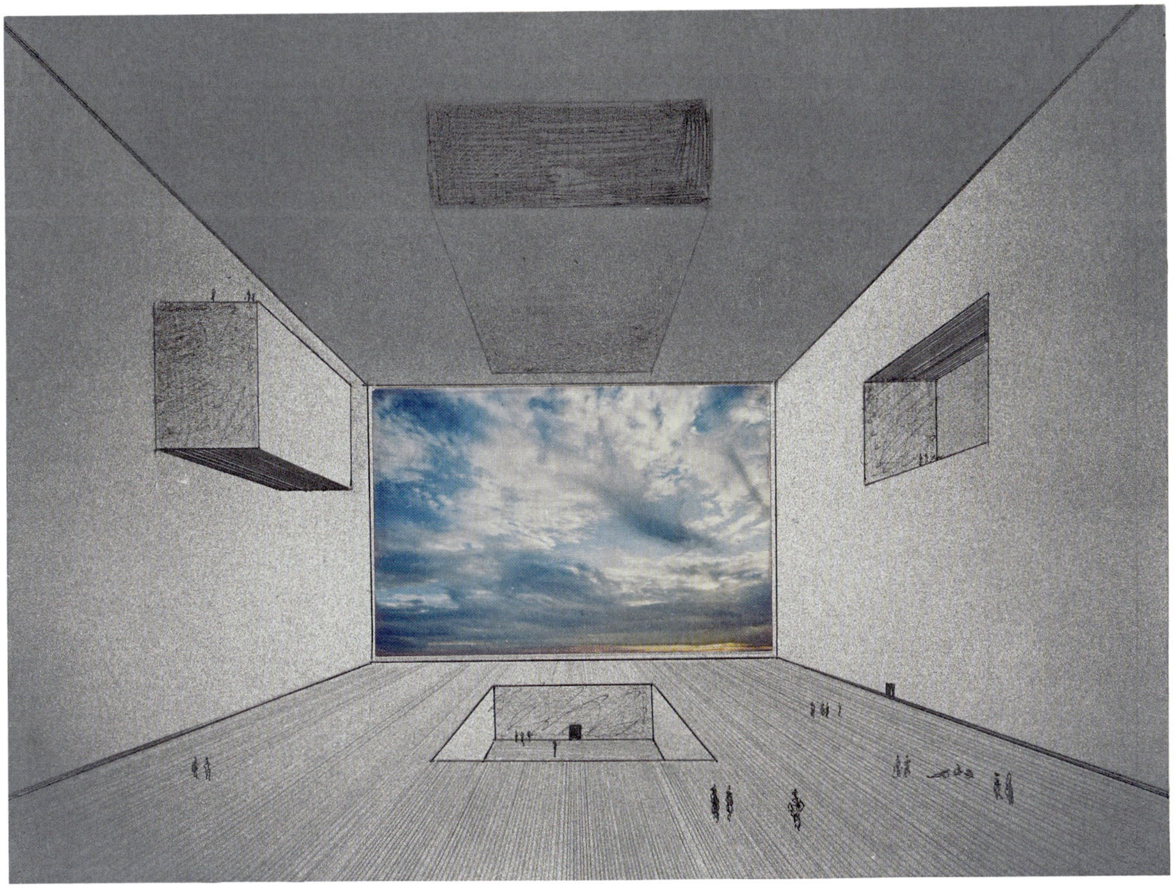

FIG 57
Gerhard Richter, *Atlas* sheet 222, "Rooms" (detail), 1970. 20 ⅜ × 14 ½ in. (51.7 × 36.7 cm)

FIG 58
Gerhard Richter, *Atlas* sheet 249, "Rooms" (detail), 1971. 26 ¼ × 20 ⅜ in. (66.7 × 51.7 cm)

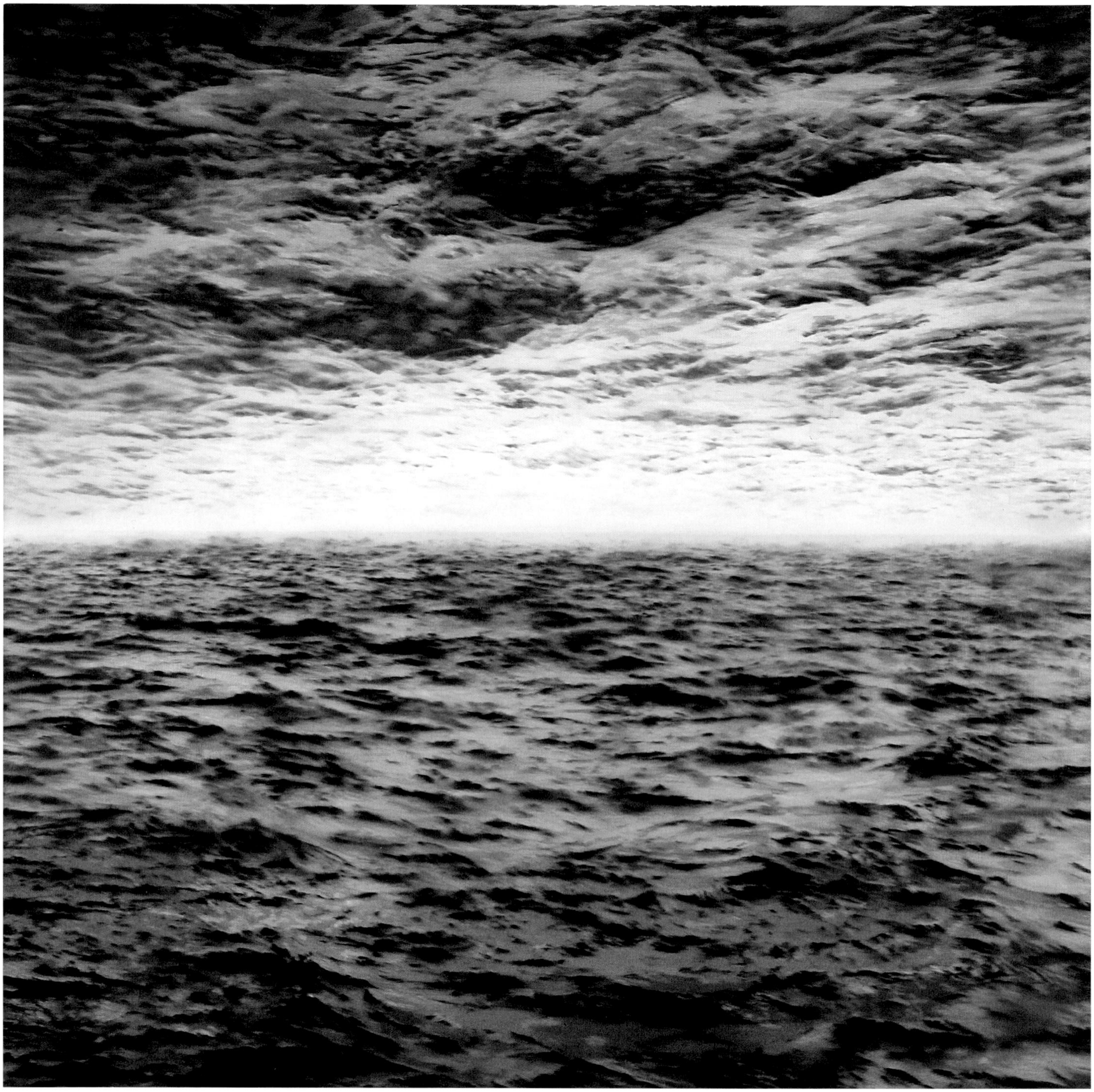

FIG 59
Gerhard Richter, *Seascape (Sea-Sea)* (*Seestück [See-See]*), 1970. Oil on canvas, 78 ¾ × 78 ¾ in. (200 × 200 cm). CR 244. Nationalgalerie, Staatliche Museen zu Berlin

FIG 60
Gerhard Richter, *Eis* (*Ice*). Cologne: Walther König, 2011

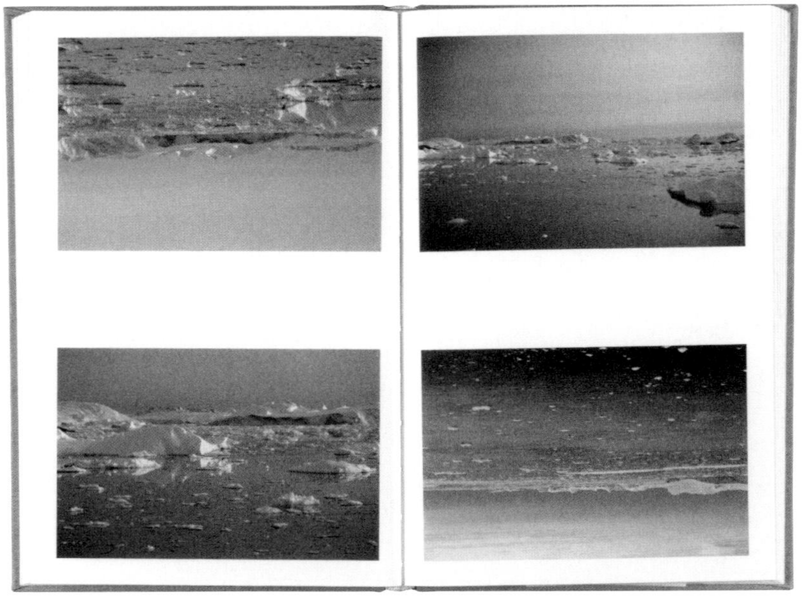

they were first seen in public in the early 1970s, not least because of Richter's admitted affinities for his predecessor. At the time, Richter's explanations of his interest in landscape had been seemingly twee,[23] leading contemporary critics to accuse the works of being "too beautiful, too romantic, too shallow."[24] But perhaps this perspective failed to consider that Richter's determined, though not exclusive, commitment to painting had always been slightly anachronistic with regard to prevailing attitudes toward the medium. By the late 1960s, an acute desire to break away from his familiar, well-known works led him to a fertile period of experimentation, out of which emerged many of the approaches that would preoccupy him for much of the 1970s: the Details, the Color Charts, the Inpaintings, the Gray Paintings, the later Abstract Paintings, and some landscapes. While these categories of work seem discrete and stylistically divergent, there is discernible connective tissue between them—something that Richter has always conceded. In this context, his conscious return to the archaism of the landscape genre can be seen as a further way to radically subvert expectations by looking simultaneously backward and forward at painting from what Robert Storr has described as a "Janus-like position."[25] Thus, Richter's approach to landscape is a knowing and deliberate embrace of a recognizably traditional and loaded genre that has allowed him to self-consciously probe the material, historical, and conceptual conditions of painting.

This is most evident in his paintings of the sea, both the early square paintings of 1969–70 and the later horizontal Seascapes of 1975. When the former were first displayed, in 1971 in Düsseldorf, they were deliberately shown in a row, and their cumulative presentation created an interplay between repetition and difference that anticipated some of the display strategies of the "Rooms" in the *Atlas*. There are aspects of the paintings that also thwart a Romantic reading, such as a horizon line articulated by the splicing of two source photographs, typically in a sea-and-sky combination but also in a sea-and-sea formation, as indicated in the title of two works (for example, fig. 59). Godfrey has interpreted this incongruence allegorically as "a situation facing painting and German culture in general: no matter the desire for continuity with the past, one is left with a consciousness of a break that makes cohesion impossible."[26] The horizon line in these paintings functions as an imperfect mirror that seemingly (but not fully) conceives a whole that is profoundly denatured. Its evident artificiality defies an easy lapse into a simpler apprehension of its beauty. Richter has deliberately noted this disjunction:

Of course, my landscapes are not only beautiful or nostalgic, with a Romantic or classical suggestion of lost Paradises, but above all "untruthful" (even if I did not always find a way of showing it); and by "untruthful" I mean the glorifying way we look at nature—nature, which in all its forms is always against us because it knows no meaning, no pity, no sympathy, because it knows nothing and is absolutely mindless: the total antithesis of ourselves, absolutely inhuman.[27]

The pitiless nature to which Richter alludes finds a more personal expression in photographs he took on a solitary retreat to Greenland in 1972, during a period of private tumult.[28] Benjamin Buchloh recognizes them as referring less to the actual landscape than to Richter-the-tourist-photographer's experience associated with it.[29] Occupying several folios of the *Atlas*, the Greenland photographs are a direct response to Friedrich's painting *The Wreck of Hope/Sea of Ice* (1823–24) and became the basis for four large Seascapes from 1975 (pp. 136, 137) and a series of three paintings from the early 1980s, including *Ice* (p. 147) and *Iceberg in Mist* (p. 149). Adrift like the occasional floes seen in some compositions, the paintings at first glance seem sublime and mesmeric, but they consciously preclude possibilities for symbolic interpretation, as haze blurs the horizon, and sea and sky become barely distinguishable.[30] The source photographs from this same trip are further subjected to the estranging effects of mirroring in the composition of Richter's artist's book *Eis* (*Ice*) (fig. 60). Indeed, mirroring had preoccupied Richter for a long time—from photographic double exposures, to his *Sea-Sea* paintings, to the portraits of Gilbert & George (pp. 134, 135) that anticipate the visual effects of the mirrored glass pieces he would make in the 1980s.

Richter's doubling down on painting in the early 1970s also reveals a fascination with the physical properties of oil paint that goes beyond the ocular production of the blur and is distinct from the surface effects of gestural abstraction. About the same time that Richter painted his early landscapes based on personal holiday photos, he also created a series that explored

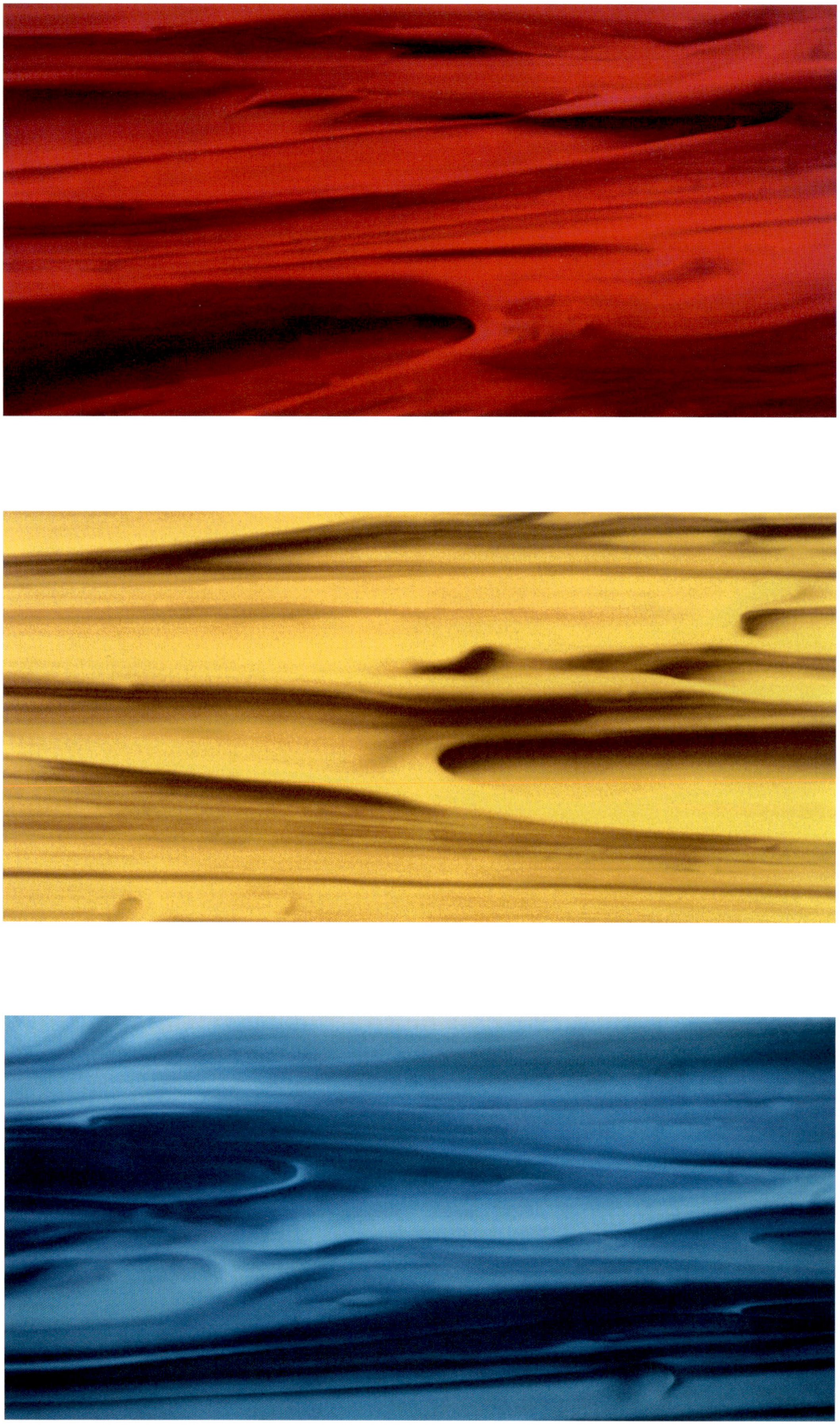

FIG 61
Gerhard Richter, BMW Paintings: *Red, Yellow, Blue* (*Rot, Gelb, Blau*), 1973. Oil on canvas, each 118 ⅛ × 236 ¼ in. (300 × 600 cm). CR 345-1–3. BMW Headquarters, BMW Group, Munich

the visual texture of the medium. To make his Details (1970–71), he used a knife to smear a palette with viscous oil paint, photographed it, enlarged the image, and painted close-up details of the melding pigments. Jürgen Harten sees in the Details a similarity to congealing lava and connects them to Richter's paintings of Vesuvius (p. 139).[31] However, they are visually more analogous to "terrains" of paint, especially when scaled to the extent of the BMW Paintings (fig. 61), which portray monochromatic slathers of primary colors. This kinship between the Details and his landscapes is further discernible through their similar presentation in the *Atlas* (fig. 62). It is also worth considering these blown-up microcosms of oil paint as a sort of material DNA that connects the brushy Townscapes and alpine paintings to the Inpaintings and later Abstracts—from the works that began as photographs of details of abstract paintings to the later squeegee paintings. Moreover, focused compositions of details would recur in Richter's work, from the Halifax series to artist's books such as *Obrist* (featuring a tactile cover) to *War Cut* and *Birkenau*, which zoom in on cropped topographies of the painted surface. These iterative and duplicative moves in Richter's oeuvre—across mediums, formats, and genres—are predicated on a "tenuous relationship to realism," what Richter once described as "a healthy distance from painting."[32]

Counterintuitively, the archaism of landscape painting allowed Richter a way to create this necessary distance. He was keenly aware that it is impossible to return to the historical Romanticism of the landscape form but also understood that working *through* that form might yield possibilities for painting and for contending with history. Circumventing the binds of realism gave him a means to explore the genre, but never indulgently—his landscapes evince a commitment to approaching nature in unstable, relational terms. He is drawn to shimmering light, the serial presence of trees and mountains, and the constant flux of clouds and seas rather than to the portrayal of places that propose a sense of the transcendence of time. Viewing Richter's relatively few landscapes among the large number of abstract paintings he made from the 1970s onward, one can recognize his contention that there was no difference to him between his abstractions and his photo painting.[33] Time and again, he produced landscapes in series of closely related compositions—variations on a theme—that afforded both painterly exploration and the opportunity for cumulative display. The paintings in the Venice series, for example, are landscapes on the verge of abstraction that demonstrate the successive erosion of form over several canvases through either a gradual blur or overtly strident brushstrokes that interrupt the harmony of the surface.[34] Richter's acute understanding of the creative potential unlocked at the intersection of nature and chromatic material is evident in a letter from 1973 to the Swiss art historian and curator Jean-Christophe Ammann:

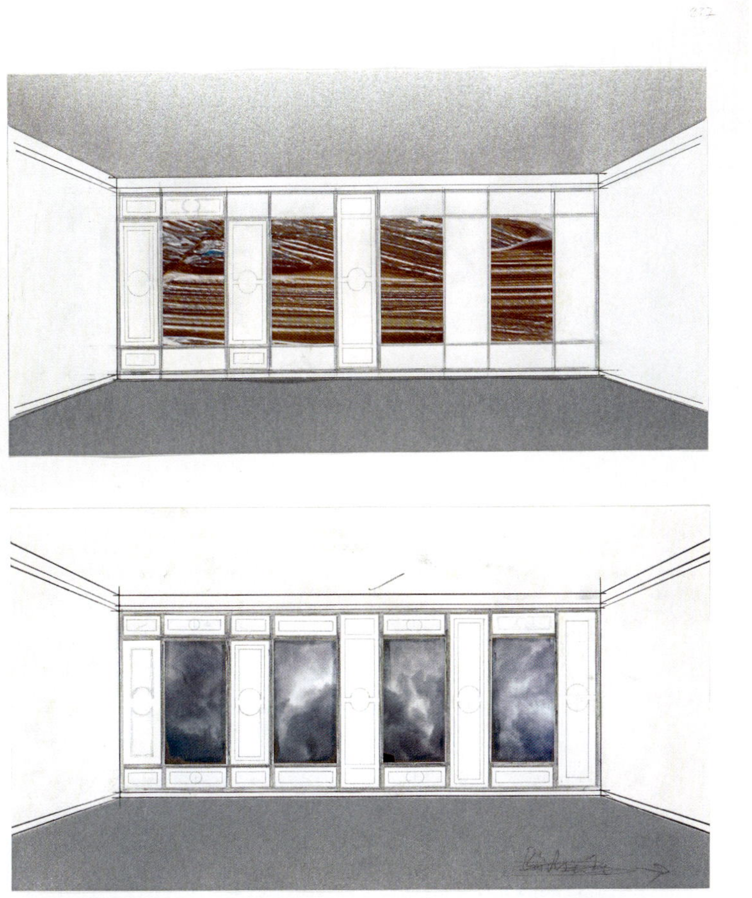

FIG 62
Gerhard Richter, *Atlas* sheet 252, "Rooms," 1971. 26 ¼ × 20 ⅜ in. (66.7 × 51.7 cm)

FIG 63
Gerhard Richter, *Jungle Picture* (*Dschungelbild*), 1971. Oil on canvas, 78 ¾ × 78 ¾ in. (200 × 200 cm). CR 312. Private collection

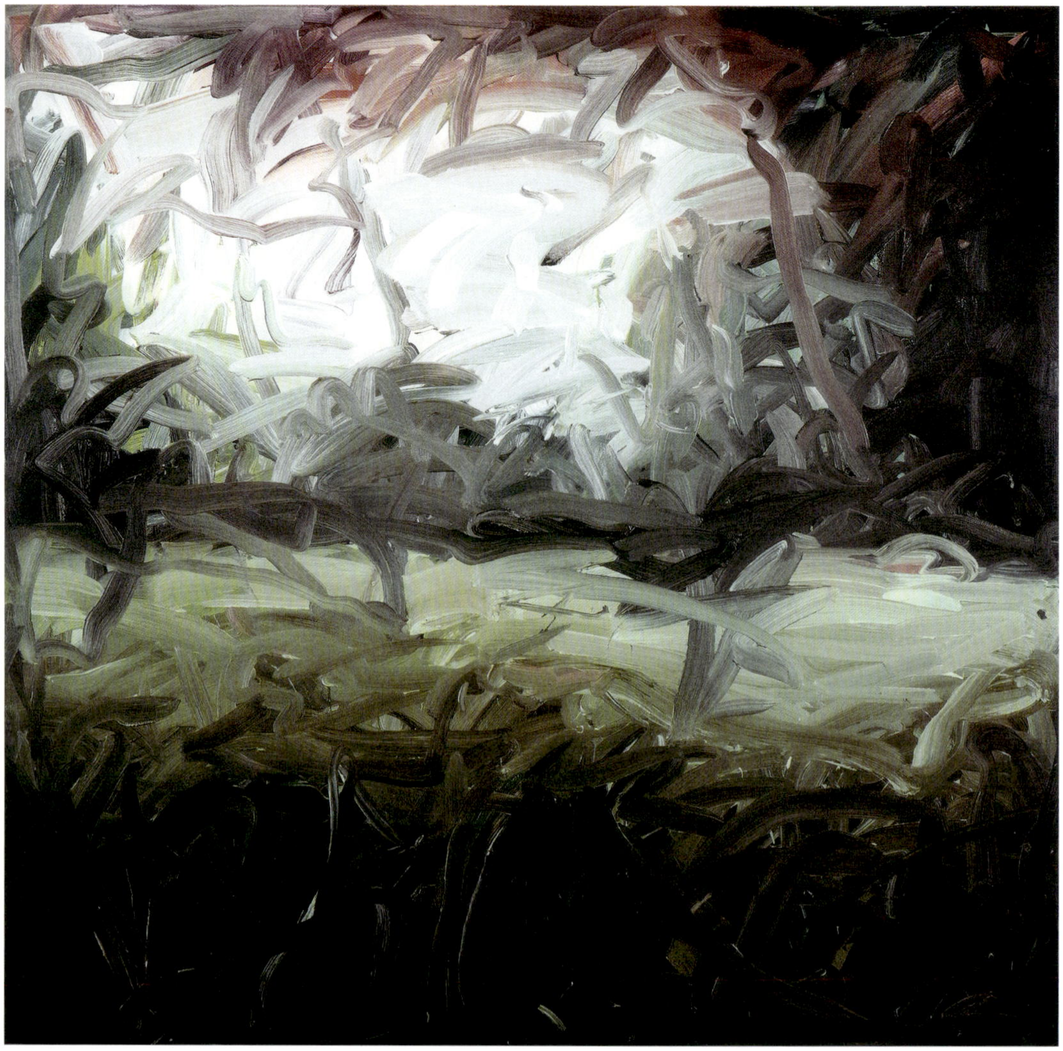

The Jungle Pictures [fig. 63] at the Biennale take their colours from nature; it took me a little time to remember that I have tools with which I can make anything: Red-Blue-Yellow (and light = white). Pictures as the result of process. Three primary colours, as the source of endless sequences of tones: either tone by tone, systematically multiplied and accurately presented (colour charts) or this artificial jungle. The shades and forms emerge through the constant blending of brushstrokes; they create an illusionistic space, without any need for me to invent forms or signs. The brush goes on its allotted way, from patch to patch of paint, first mediating and then to a greater or lesser degree destroying, mixing, until there is no place left intact. It is almost a soup, a non-hierarchical interweaving of form with space and colour. Pictures which emerge, which result from the making. Not creations; definitely not creative, in the sense of that mendacious work (I mention this, because I so loathe the word) but creaturely. To illustrate the fascination of these jungle-like, interlacing forms hold for me: as a child I traced with my finger, on my own empty, slightly greasy supper plate, bows and curves that constantly intersected to produce fantastic spatial structures that changed with the light and could be altered unendingly. I find this more interesting than fixed form, the posited sign.[35]

Richter's assertion of nature as a nonhierarchical interweaving of form afforded a conceptual freedom for landscapes to approach abstractions and vice versa. The artist is ever conscious of how his canvases are exercises that revel in the lusciousness of oil paint, which he daubs, feathers, and blends or stretches, rolls, drags, and scrapes in additive and subtractive processes that create irresolute surfaces. He has spoken of how, especially when he is working with a squeegee, his canvases become "veiled,"[36] a term he used to describe the surface of a series of paintings titled Forest (pp. 188–89). The description calls to mind one of his earliest paintings, *Deer* (fig. 64), in which the blurry, dimensionally rendered titular beast is par-

FIG 64
Gerhard Richter, *Deer* (*Hirsch*), 1963.
Oil on canvas, 59 × 78 ¾ in.
(150 cm × 200 cm). CR 7. Fondation
Louis Vuitton, Paris

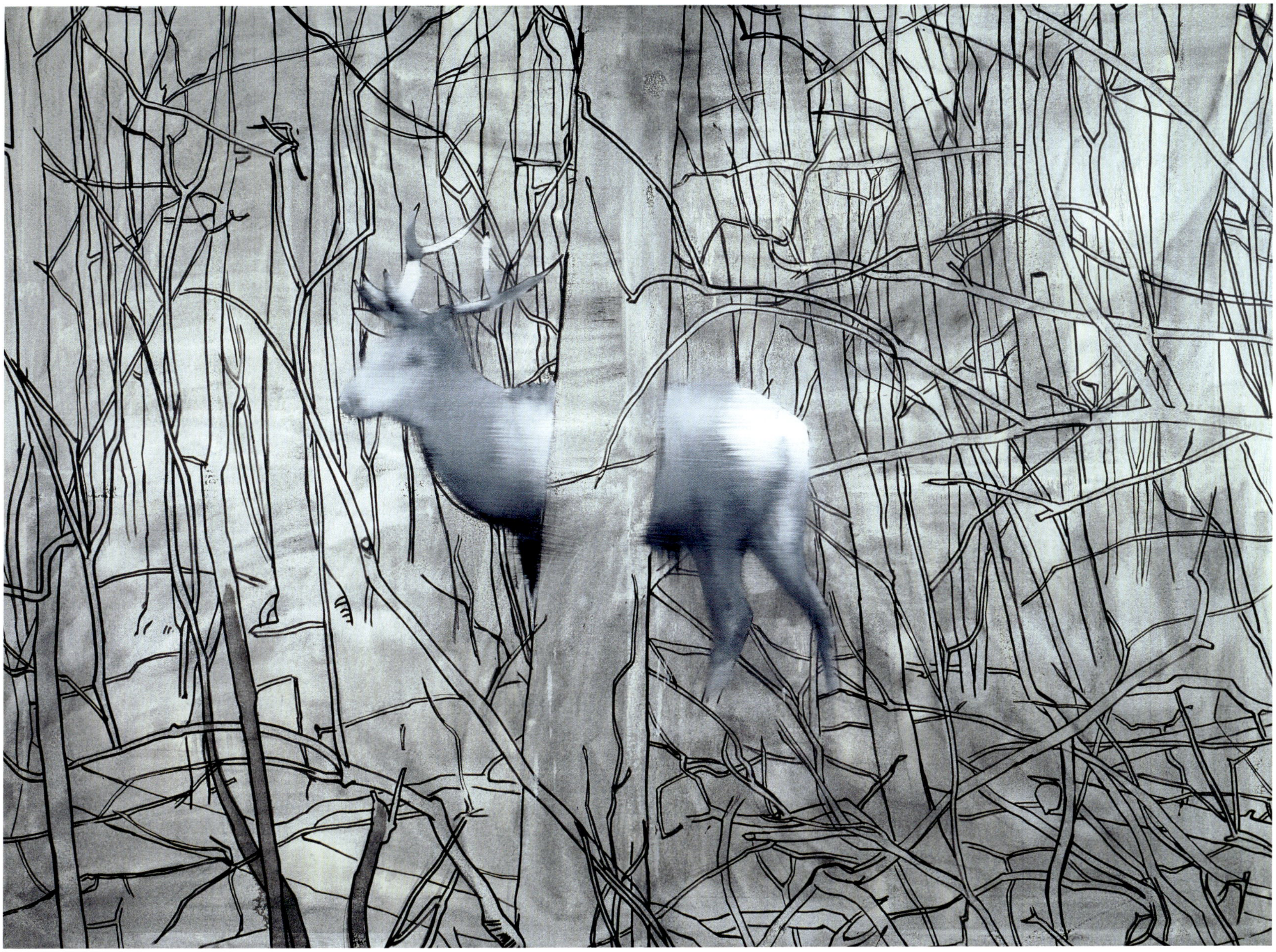

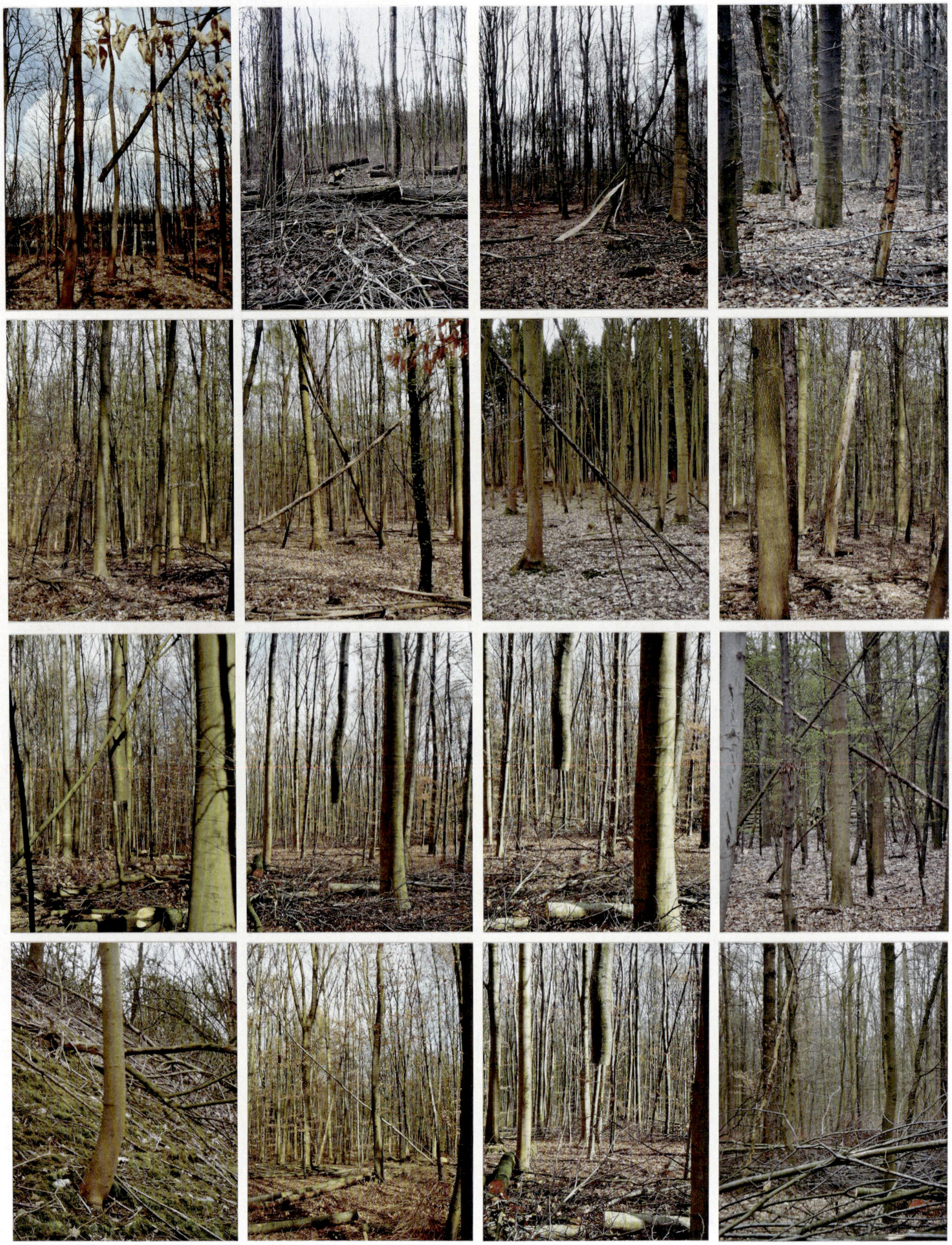

FIG 65
Gerhard Richter, *Atlas* sheet 758, "Hahnwald," 2006. 28 ¾ × 22 ⅛ in. (73 × 56.2 cm)

tially hidden by a tangle of simply outlined trees. Based on a photograph taken by Richter, the painting evokes a seeming unfinishedness that disallows an otherwise conventional composition to lapse into kitsch. About the subject, he told Sabine Schütz:

For us Germans, in particular, relating to forests as strongly as we do, the stag does of course have a symbolic quality. I wanted to be a forester when I was young, and I was really excited when I found a real stag in the forest and took a photograph. Later I painted him, and the painting was a bit less romantic than my youthful photograph.[37]

This acknowledgment of the romance of the forest recurs in his writings and interviews, and while sometimes he leans in to this characterization, he remains wary of the darker seductions and mysteries of the woods.[38]

These simultaneous gestures of recognition and resistance run through the trees and forests of Richter's canvases, both the landscapes and the abstracts. Although the latter's associations with the arboreal may seem impressionistic, they are nevertheless keenly understood and articulated.[39] Richter originally titled the works in the Forest series *Abstract Paintings* in 2005 but rechristened them the following year at the time of the exhibition *From Caspar David Friedrich to Gerhard Richter* at the J. Paul Getty Museum in Los Angeles. While the connection to Friedrich is one explanation for the change, it is worth noting that during this same period Richter took a number of photographs of Hahnwald, a forested suburb near Cologne where the artist lives and works, and included them in the *Atlas* (fig. 65).[40] Although there is no direct correspondence between the *Atlas* images and the paintings, the similarities between them are unmistakable; compare, for example, the suspended felled branches and the abruptly halted vertical strokes, or the murky depths of the woods and the richly painted blacks. These shared forms are evocative of both the personal experience of a particular place and a collective signification of the forest. Yet Richter recognizes that the disaggregation inherent in this latter sense is deeply unmooring. About the cycle, he told Hans Ulrich Obrist:

Helplessness is the great theme in painting, or rather the strongest motivation for and during painting. And the forest in general has special significance, perhaps more so in Germany than anywhere else. You can lose your way in forests, feel deserted, but also secure, held fast in the bosom of the undergrowth. A fine romantic subject.[41]

Interestingly, Richter invokes a sense of disappointed hope that spurs a mode of striving in his work in order to conjure the forest as a place of ambiguity or suspension that resists the Romantic, even as he insists on its persistence. These contradictions not only characterize Richter's writings but also underscore an enduring ambivalence toward Romanticism and history that finds an abiding expression in his landscapes and his approach to nature more generally.

Richter evokes forests one final time in the series initially called *Abstract Paintings* and later titled *Birkenau* (pp. 225–28). As Buchloh notes, "Only after a period of additional reflection did Richter decide to refer to these paintings explicitly as the Birkenau paintings, thus making their origins and their historical references explicit even though no visual traces of the photographs remained."[42] The birch trees that gave the forests around the Nazi concentration camp at Auschwitz-Birkenau their name feature in the four photographs by Sonderkommandos on which the artist originally based the paintings (pp. 230–31).[43] In two photographs, the trees appear in the far distance and form a horizon before which the atrocities were being committed; in the other two, the black silhouettes of trunks and branches appear aslant, a testament to the necessarily covert circumstances under which the images were recorded. Indeed, in one of these two photographs, the camera was inadvertently focused on the trees alone. It is worth noting that a detail from one of the photographs was added to Richter's *Atlas* as early as 1967, along with other images of prisoners in camps, under the heading "Photographs from Books" (see fig. 15). For decades, Richter struggled with a satisfactory way to address the photographs of the camps, and Godfrey has argued that his approach to nature is bound up with them: "The trees around Birkenau . . . haunt the forests in his works."[44]

Richter's interest in painting landscapes based on photographs of nature has waned in recent years, and he has chosen instead to focus largely on abstraction. Nevertheless, to view his landscapes in contrast to either his photo paintings or his abstract works, or simply as a bridge between them, is insufficient. By tracing the material and conceptual relationships between his various approaches, one becomes aware that working through the representation of nature as he did allowed Richter to ground a practice that seriously considers the cultural and personal entanglements of history and of painting, across the divides of genre and style.

André Rottmann

Randomizing Painting: Notes on Richter's Abstractions

In hindsight, the work of Gerhard Richter seems to bifurcate in 1966, five years after he defected from the German Democratic Republic and moved to Düsseldorf. The artist's practice until that year had been exclusively grounded in transferring allegedly meaningless black-and-white photographs—found in newspapers or family albums, or, increasingly after 1965, taken by Richter himself—into manifestations of an ostentatiously indifferent kind of painterly figuration. In these early works, the provocative banality of the object (be it a piece of furniture, a view of contemporary architecture, a natural vista, or a portrait) is complemented, even amplified, by the artist's distinctive method of using a broad brush to cautiously blur contours soon after applying the paint. Destined to submerge representation into diffuse gradations of gray, this peculiar process makes "everything equally important and equally unimportant," as Richter stated in one of his typically laconic notes from that period. And despite the labor invested in this form of mimesis, which involves projecting the photographic motif onto the canvas and tracing its contours, this technique—and thus the artist—supposedly makes the painting "technological, smooth and perfect."[1]

Richter's famous blur indeed approximates surfaces and screens—or, more precisely, painterly mediation and photographic mediatization. At the same time, as British philosopher Peter Osborne has argued, the effect not only engages in a critical epistemology of visual representation in the age of technological reproducibility but also serves to draw attention to the sheer presence of paint, creating "complex dialectics of transparency and opacity, proximity and distance, forgetting, remembering, and expecting."[2] In this configuration of contradictions, Richter both debased and defended painting through the concurrent introduction of the mechanical. While this phase of his career roughly paralleled the emergence of Pop art in the United States and the United Kingdom, unlike contemporaneous works by Andy Warhol, Richard Hamilton, and Ed Ruscha, Richter's paintings, while partaking in the deconstruction of the medium, refrained from purging it of its logic and legacy entirely. In the words of Hal Foster, "the debasement of pictorial content on the one hand, the preservation of pictorial form on the other... renders his painting intensely ambiguous, skeptical of its traditional authority yet committed to this tradition nonetheless."[3]

Time and again, Richter's oeuvre over the past six decades has engaged the contradictions of painting's continuation in the aftermath of modernism and, perhaps even more importantly, amid an exponentially intensifying technological situation in which, according to the clairvoyant account of Friedrich A. Kittler, the "general digitalization of information" eventually would erase "the difference between individual media."[4] As the German media theorist further explicates:

> *Sound and image, voice and text have become mere effects on the surface, or, to put it better, the interface for the consumer. Sense and the senses become mere glitter.... In computers everything becomes number: imageless, soundless, and wordless quantity. And if the optical fiber network reduces all formerly separate data flows to one standardized digital series of numbers, any medium can be translated into another. With numbers nothing is impossible.*[5]

Against the backdrop of this *Gestell*, the "enframing," or framework—which, as defined by philosopher Martin Heidegger, is the entirety and essence of modern technology as a way of both revealing and shaping the appearance of phenomena otherwise inaccessible to human perception[6]—this essay demonstrates how the practices and matrices of abstraction within, but also beyond, the confines of aesthetic concerns assume particular relevance in Richter's body of work.

Apart from the 1957 monotypes titled *Elbe* (pp. 210–11), which merely display the traces of a roller used to spread black paint, and notwithstanding the gestural marks in *Table* from 1962 (p. 104), the artist's first official painting, which effectively encroach on and erase the subject, Richter's nascent dialectic of the rejection and retrieval of painterly traditions

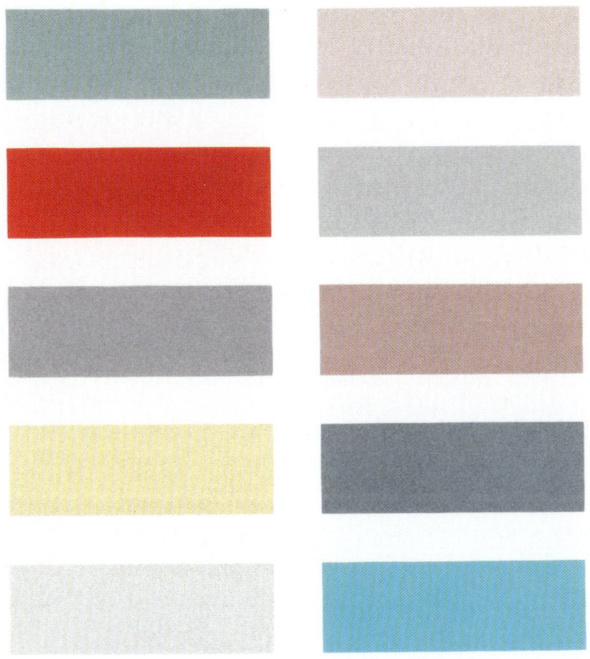

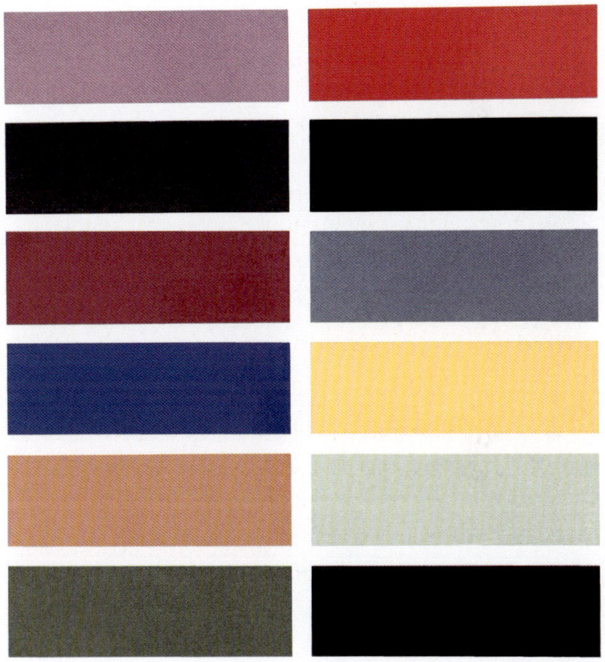

FIG 66
Gerhard Richter, *Ten Colors* (*Zehn Farben*), 1966. Enamel on canvas, 53 ⅛ × 47 ¼ in. (135 × 120 cm). CR 135-1. Collection of Julie and Edward Minskoff

FIG 67
Gerhard Richter, *Twelve Colors* (*Zwölf Farben*), 1966. Enamel on canvas, 27 ½ × 25 ⅝ in. (70 × 65 cm). CR 137. Private collection

FIG 68
Marcel Duchamp (American, born France, 1887–1968), *Tu m'*, 1918. Oil on canvas, with bottlebrush, safety pins, and bolt, $27\frac{1}{2} \times 119\frac{5}{16}$ in. (69.8 × 303 cm). Yale University Art Gallery, New Haven, Connecticut, Gift of the Estate of Katherine S. Dreier (1953.6.4)

and techniques at first was solely committed to the vestiges of realism under the impact of the photographic image. It is only with *Ten Colors* from 1966 (fig. 66) that the self-reflexivity of abstraction, as well as references to the history of nonobjective art, enter into Richter's aesthetic fabric and critical outlook. Since then, his work has evolved in recursions, notoriously encompassing an entire panoply of painterly idioms, procedures, styles, and genres. From this so-called Color Chart onward, abstraction and figuration—to the bewilderment of many viewers and critics—have existed in Richter's practice simultaneously rather than successively.

At first, it must seem puzzling, even incomprehensible, that Richter's approach to abstraction over time hardly became uniform or predictable. With the Gray series (1968), panels of nonexpressive paint enter Richter's repertoire. In 1976, the geometrically ordered Color Charts and the mournful monochromes that capture the "degree zero" of painting begin to take turns with nonobjective, yet seemingly gestural, brightly colored (non)compositions, incipiently derived from photographic blowups of details found in previous paintings, now rendered miragelike and out of focus.[7] Oscillating strokes and surfaces, for which the work *Gray Streaks* (1968) served as a prelude, disintegrate into chromatic ciphers of painting's entanglement with imaging (and other) technologies. Under the aegis of such media, abstraction, far from being synonymous with a modernist tabula rasa of representation, appears in works like *Abstract Painting* from 1978 (pp. 144–45) as parasitical, in the sense (provided by French philosopher Michel Serres) as both reliant on (or feeding off) other media, in a way that renders visible this very process of mediatization: fuzziness, for instance, reads as noise, static, or interference.[8] It is as if, in these works, abstraction—for the longest time conceptualized as painting relying only on its own means—is reformatted and filtered through the optics and protocols of contemporary systems and apparatuses of transmission. And, finally, since the mid-1980s Richter in his so-called Large Abstracts has developed a process of execution based on the successive application and removal of coats of paint, primarily with the help of a squeegee, resulting in palimpsest-like iridescent layers, fractured polychromatic screens punctuated by scratches and spatters, and uneven sedimentations of differentiated hues and textures. In these painting series, abstraction suddenly seems antithetical, almost as an antidote to the rules of repetition and replication governing Richter's overall oeuvre.

This contradictory, at times paradoxical, configuration of painterly facets and factors makes Richter's work truly post-conceptual and consequently contemporary.[9] Devoted to an analysis of his multifarious modes of abstraction from the mid-1960s until today, the present study seeks to advance and substantiate two interrelated propositions. Tracing the development of the artist's Color Charts, the first proposition argues that Richter defines abstraction as an effect of and correlation to modernity rather than an avenue to transcend it; concomitantly, he renders the grid, the quintessential template of modernist self-reflexivity, tangible as a "cultural technique," to use German media scholar Bernhard Siegert's term, of exercising power through discipline and control. The second attempts to demonstrate that within Richter's abstract projects—whether geometric or gestural—he introduces chance as a means to suspend the medium of painting in a dialectical tension between increasingly technologically induced formats of control and aesthetic forms of dissent or even resistance.

The Matrix of Color

Richter's *Ten Colors*, a midsize painting in panel format, presents ten rectangular swatches of colors ranging from light gray and dusky pink to subdued yellow and dull auburn to radiant red and bright teal, arranged in two columns on a white background. Even on prolonged inspection, the distribution of chromatic values within this rigid noncompositional order does not register as following a predetermined system. Quite to the

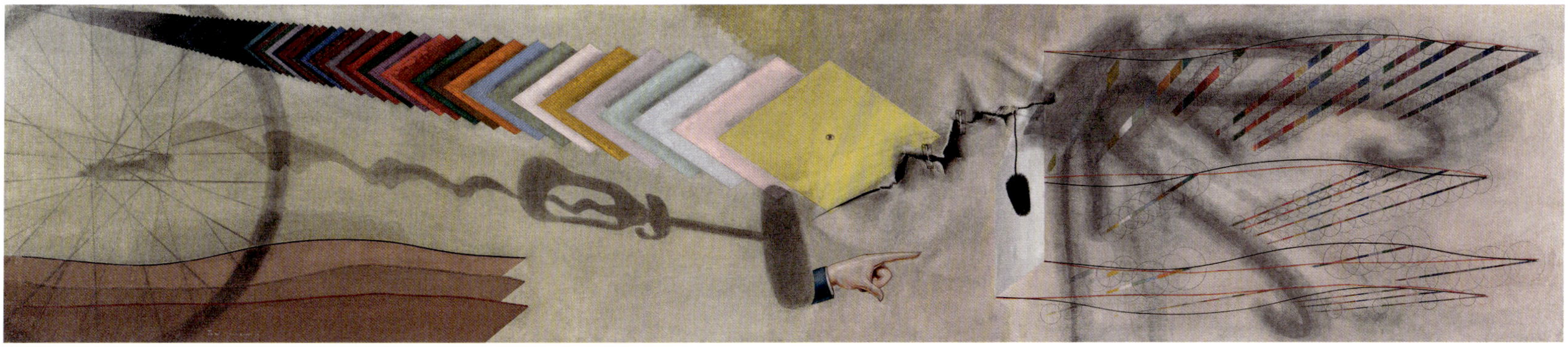

contrary, it appears absolutely random. Irrespective of the strict template structuring it, *Ten Colors* remains grounded in the manual skills of traditional painting, revealed by visible brush marks. As in the blurred photo paintings, mediation did not strive to negate the impressions of materiality. In fact, *Ten Colors* was an abstraction in disguise. Just as Richter had copied black-and-white photographs, he now produced an enlarged replica of commercial color samples of the type found at hardware stores. Soon after, the artist repeated the process with the complementary work *Twelve Colors* (fig. 67), foreshadowing the seriality of his Color Charts to come. Repudiating Neo-Constructivist aspirations to restitute the lost supposed primacy and politics of the prewar monochrome—while also engaging with the work of his friend and colleague Blinky Palermo, Pop, and (slightly later) Minimalism[10]—Richter provocatively defined color as a readily available, prefabricated commodity rather than an original substance or ingenious sign.

Made the same year as Richter's overtly Duchampian rendition of his wife, *Ema (Nude on a Staircase)*, his (pseudo)abstract paintings of 1966 declare color to be nothing other than a readymade. In *Tu m'* (fig. 68), a painting that combines silhouettes of famous ready-mades with a stretched sequence of industrially produced color samples, Marcel Duchamp had dismantled the pretensions of "pure" abstraction (found, for instance, in the works and writings of his contemporaries Vasily Kandinsky, František Kupka, Robert Delaunay, and Paul Klee), which sought to induce experiences of spiritual, sensual, or somatic plenitude. More than four decades later, on the occasion of the "Art and Assemblage" symposium at the Museum of Modern Art in New York in 1961, Duchamp even went so far as to claim that precisely because tubes of paint are mass-manufactured, modern painting at large belonged to the industrial culture of the ready-made.[11] By 1966, Richter evidently shared Duchamp's skepticism regarding color's supposedly intrinsic aesthetic value, and with *Ten Colors* he directly confronted its commercial exploitation. However, whereas Duchamp had taken the devaluing of color as reason enough to abandon painting altogether, in favor of a generic conception of art based on the ready-made principle, Richter, in contrast, concluded that the commodification of color still had to be explored within (rather than beyond) the specific, however precarious, boundaries of the medium. In doing so, the artist did not address color as an isolated phenomenon but rather aligned its standardization to models and methods of application, distribution, and composition. Richter's practice in this respect stands in a lineage of a kind of painting that ever since Georges Seurat's pointillist dots—which severed referential and spatial ties between mark and matter—had explicitly linked the support of the picture plane with what art historian Carol Armstrong has called a "matrix of materialities": an ensemble comprising interrelated media, practices, and techniques, such as (in the case of Seurat) halftone reproduction, the autochrome plate, and the industrial Jacquard loom.[12]

Richter's art since 1966 can be understood as igniting a reflection on the sociopolitical correlates and changed currency of abstraction as a pictorial episteme. If nonobjective painting once claimed to radically transcend the conditions of modern society, or if it depicted modern society's rationale in negative terms by its refusal of traditional representation, then for a variety of reasons this discursive scaffolding, as Dutch art historian and critic Sven Lütticken has argued, became untenable in the second half of the twentieth century. Movements such as the Bauhaus had already designed products whose ornamental surfaces were clearly indebted to industrial technologies and mechanical apparatuses that prefigure today's digital programs.[13] Under the conditions of ever-tightening concatenations between modern rationality and aesthetic ambition in the postwar period, abstraction finally amounted to the Pyrrhic victory of the avant-garde's utopian thought: "Abstract art," Lütticken writes, "was based on the supposition that abstracting from visible appearances enabled one to reach a higher truth, but now abstraction penetrates society to the core."[14]

Epistemologies of the Grid

It seems pertinent to explore the ways in which Richter's painterly reproduction of a color chart evokes the grid—that is, the geometric, flattened, regular, and almost compulsively repeated structure of lateral coordinates that purports to avoid any relation to the real in order to secure the alleged autonomy of abstraction. The mimicry of a color sample performed by *Ten Colors* already belied this quintessential "modernist myth," later famously debunked by art historian Rosalind Krauss.[15] In other words, Richter had departed from the recognition that abstraction cannot help but communicate with what Heidegger has called the "standing-reserve" of the modern world, i.e., the reality (or truth, even) of a technological world that ultimately cannot but inform abstraction's appearance and procedures, despite its aspiration to be an end in itself. Nonetheless, the 1966 work goes beyond parody or pastiche. Paradoxically, his putatively ironic citation of a color chart inhabiting the grid is a means to gauge, not deny, the grid's validity and potential for painting in the aftermath of the medium's concomitant claims for self-referentiality and self-sufficiency. Assuming such an epistemological function, *Ten Colors* initiated intermittent deployments of this device in the artist's oeuvre. Richter's confrontation with the dominant structure (or *dispositif*) of organizing surface and composing color in avant-garde and postwar abstraction—practiced by artists from Piet Mondrian and Josef Albers to Ad Reinhardt and Frank Stella to Agnes Martin and Sol LeWitt—intensified over time with works such as *192 Colors* (1966), *180 Colors* (1971), and *1,024 Colors* (1973 and 1974), culminating in *4,900 Colors with 196 Single Pictures* (2007; see fig. 72), presenting a virtually inexhaustible array of algorithmically allocated color chips.

In her essay from the late 1970s (which does not address Richter's work), Krauss distinguishes between the centrifugal dimension of the grid, operating "from the work of art outward, compelling our acknowledgement of a world beyond the frame," and the centripetal one that casts "an introjection of the boundaries of the world into the interior of the work."[16] Created over the course of more than four decades and taking on varied forms and formats, Richter's grids, however, not only present "the given work of art... as a mere fragment, a tiny piece arbitrarily cropped from an infinitely larger fabric,"[17] but also invariably attest to the habitually disavowed exterior orientation of the grid. His Color Charts steer painterly abstraction toward preexisting procedures and protocols of representation and governance, of deixis and administration based on the entanglement of power, knowledge, and technology in modernity.[18] In this way, his work radicalizes the centrifugality, which, according to Krauss, is immanent to the modernist paradigm of the grid. In Richter's later serialized grids of randomly distributed colors, especially, abstraction increasingly registers as not only positing "the theoretical continuity of the work of art with the world."[19] Rather, in the artist's probing dialectic of the medium of painting, it appears as almost nothing more than an effect—however enthralling, even exhilarating—of the *Gestell* or framework undergirding the real.

In a slightly later text—in which she connects the axiom of repetition inherent to the grid to the repressed role played by the copy in modern art—Krauss argues that the grid, in fact, is not "an indisputable zero-ground beyond which there is no further model, or referent, or text."[20] Countering the notion of the grid's supposed opacity and originality, she observes, it "*follows* the canvas surface, doubles it. It is a representation of the surface, mapped, it is true, onto the same surface it represents, but even so, the grid remains a figure, picturing various aspects of the 'originary' object."[21] The grid's pretension of nonreferentiality, in other words, serves to cover over its actual pretexts. Repetition does not escape representation, but enacts it; in this sense, Krauss redefines the modernist grid in terms of a summation rather than negation of those ground planes used to measure, construct, and constrain space, whether in abstract painting, printing technologies, perspectival construction, or architectural renderings.[22]

Directing attention away from the realm of art, Bernhard Siegert, in turn, analyzes the grid as one of the preeminent "cultural techniques" in the Western Hemisphere from the sixteenth to the twentieth century, insofar as it instigated the modern understanding of occupied and empty place.[23] In his definition, cultural techniques are "operative chains that precede the media concepts they generate" while always presupposing a "historically given micronetwork of technologies and techniques."[24] Transforming preexisting relationships among devices, actions, discourses, and subjects, cultural techniques form assemblages of processes and practices "involved in operationalizing distinctions in the real."[25] Accordingly, the grid in Siegert's assessment constitutes "an imaging technology that by means of a given algorithm enables us to project a three-dimensional world onto a two-dimensional plane" and hence "is a general diagrammatic procedure that uses specific addresses to store data that can be implemented in the real as well as in the symbolic."[26] Put differently, the grid encompasses a notion of order that, on the one hand, allows for surveying and administering space based on the distinction between data and addresses, and, on the other hand, makes it possible to either identify a location or register any absence therein. "The grid," Siegert concludes, "is a medium that operationalizes deixis. It allows us to link deictic procedures with chains of symbolic operations that have effects in the real."[27] Rather than representing a system devoid of reference, the grid refers to a system of representation "turning humans into retrievable objects" and establishing "the universal practice that constitutes the basis of modern disciplinary societies."[28]

Chance and Control

Richter's Color Charts—especially the various series produced since the early 1970s—are indeed instances of "diagrammatic abstraction," which, according to Benjamin Buchloh, can be defined as "*one* variety of abstraction that explicitly recognizes *externally* pre-existing systems of spatial temporal quantification, or schemata of statistical data collection as the necessary and primary matrices determining a pictorial/compositional order."[29] Here Buchloh identifies and theorizes a heretofore unacknowledged, even repudiated, variety within the historical gamut of abstract painting that arguably only Richter has fully addressed and brought to the fore. Eschewing the traditional exposure of gesture, facture, or ductus (i.e., the mode of applying paint), diagrammatic abstraction—this long-overlooked paradigm—according to Buchloh, counters the claims made by biomorphic and automatist works because it "would neither register cosmic nor somatic plenitude; nor would it record spiritual correspondences. It would neither promise acts of psychic liberation, nor would it trace desire."[30] Less obvious, but more importantly, diagrammatic abstraction also did not subscribe to the idea—guiding, for instance, Mondrian's Checkerboard paintings (fig. 69), to which Richter's charts have been compared many times—that the abolition of hierarchies in pictorial representation (i.e., the introduction of formal equivalences through the organization of the compositional field by way of identical rectangular units, each containing a monochrome surface) would grant self-reflexive painting the status of a premonition of an egalitarian social order.[31] So while Mondrian's utopian modernism filled the grid with constellations of colors suggesting—within the rational confinement of a (centripetal) lattice—harmony, equilibrium, and systematism (which, in political terms, might signify communication, equality, and accountability), purely "diagrammatic abstraction records the forms of the disenchantment of the world, the subject's submission to legal and administrative control."[32] In other words, the modern(ist) diagram renders the grid tangible not only in "its structure as myth"[33] but also as a cultural technique of power putting "persons or things in their place, to objectify and subjugate them."[34]

In 1966, Richter's work took the first steps toward diagrammatic abstraction. No longer mimetically based on a preexisting source, the commercial color chart, *192 Colors* was executed in oil paint instead of enamel, further amplifying the aspect of anonymity. The artist opted for a chance-based approach to disseminating chips of color on the surface of the canvas by

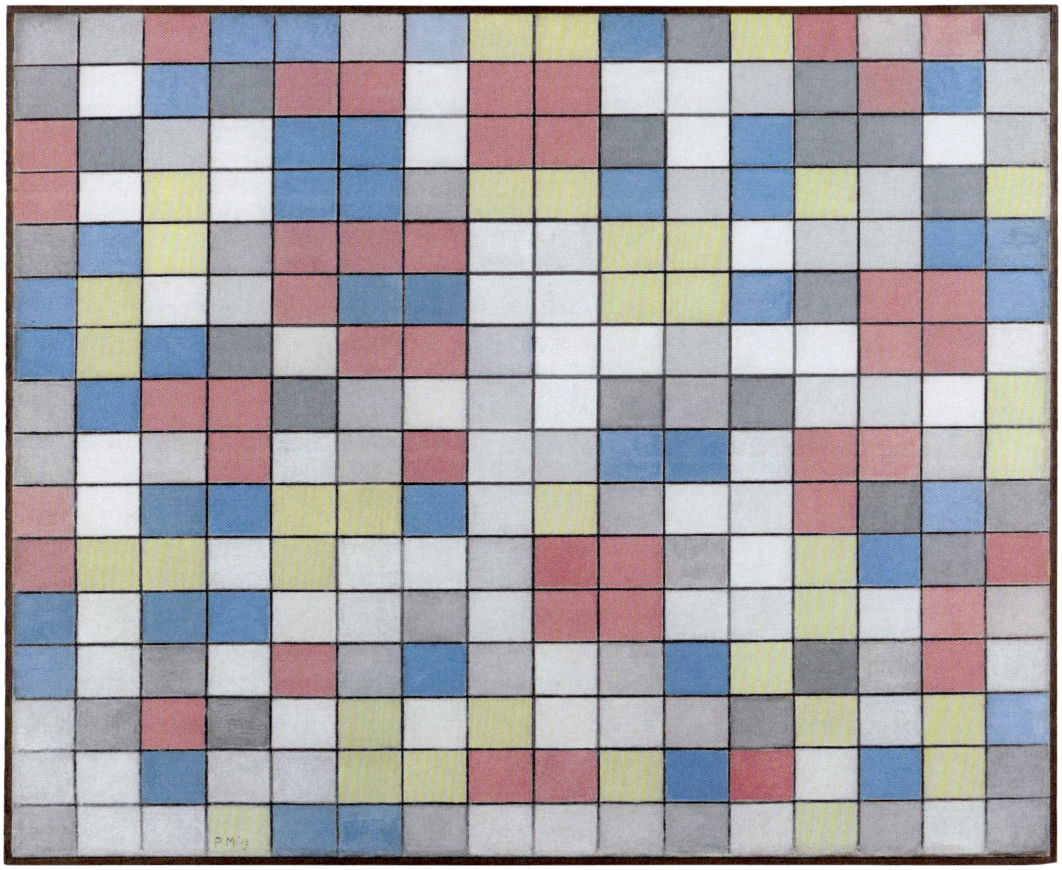

FIG 69
Piet Mondrian (Dutch, 1872–1944), *Composition with Grid 9: Checkerboard Composition with Bright Colors*, 1919. Oil on canvas, 33 ⅞ × 41 ¾ in. (86 × 106 cm). Gemeentemuseum Den Haag, The Hague (0334325)

randomly picking a sample, or, as sometimes reported, by following the instruction given by someone else—Palermo, for instance—who called out the names of colors without any intentional preference. In a manner comparable to earlier works such as Ellsworth Kelly's *Colors for a Large Wall* (fig. 70) and François Morellet's *Random Distribution of 40,000 Squares Using the Odd and Even Numbers of a Telephone Directory, 50% Blue, 50% Red* (1960), *192 Colors* combines the inhabitation of a template with a principle of indeterminacy, and the austere and confining order of the chart with the playful, yet limited, process instigated to distribute tones randomly and without repetition. However, it is only from 1971 onward that the artist's grids are governed by a truly diagrammatic conflation of a systematic chromatic categorization and equally stringent methods of making the placement of the colors register as coincidental. The Color Charts made in that year, most prominently *180 Colors* (fig. 71), in the words of curator Robert Storr, were based on Richter's decision to abandon "the sampler as a pretext, along with the improvised changes he had rung on that formal given." Instead, he devised "a mathematical system for mixing the three primary colors in graduated amounts so as to dramatically expand the number of combinations and refine the distinctions among them."[35]

Following this development, more precisely after 1973, Richter not only eliminated the grid's frame or armature from his charts, so that drawn and allotted colors abutted one another and covered the entire visual field without boundaries, but also multiplied the components exponentially. As a result of adding two shades of gray and later a green to his arsenal of colors, which had been previously restricted, as in avant-garde models, to the primaries red, yellow, and blue (and their respective gradations), by 1974 Richter had produced a series of twenty-six canvases that progress algorithmically. The works range from having 4 or 16 colors to 64, 256, 1,024, and finally 4,096 colors, all applied with lacquer. "The aim," according to Belgian critic Birgit Pelzer, "was to obtain a neutral chromatic scale by starting with multiplication of the number 4."[36] In the largest and final panel, repetition enters the random logic of Richter's Color Charts (1,024 chips were painted twice, with the help of assistants), although it is almost impossible to discern the duplications amid the sheer abundance of chromatic permutations dispersed among the sequences of interconnected grids.[37] The chance-driven, increasing proliferation of possible combinations in this body of work not only dynamized geometric abstraction but also transposed it onto a visual field at once meaningless and seemingly inexhaustible. In one of his rare reflections on contemporary art, media theorist Friedrich Kittler speculated in a 1996 interview about the continuing relevance of Richter's work:

Looking at it from the angle of information technology and computer science, the last possibility to still talk, for instance, about beauty

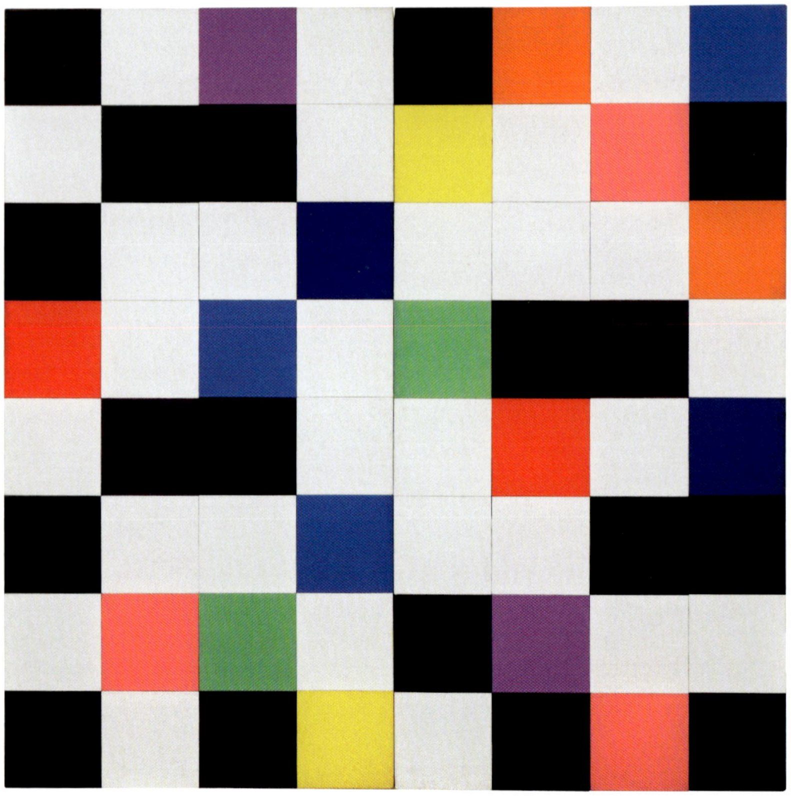

FIG 70
Ellsworth Kelly (American, 1923–2015), *Colors for a Large Wall*, 1951. Oil on canvas, sixty-four panels, overall 94 ½ × 94 ½ in. (240 × 240 cm). The Museum of Modern Art, New York, Gift of the artist (1067.1969.a-b)

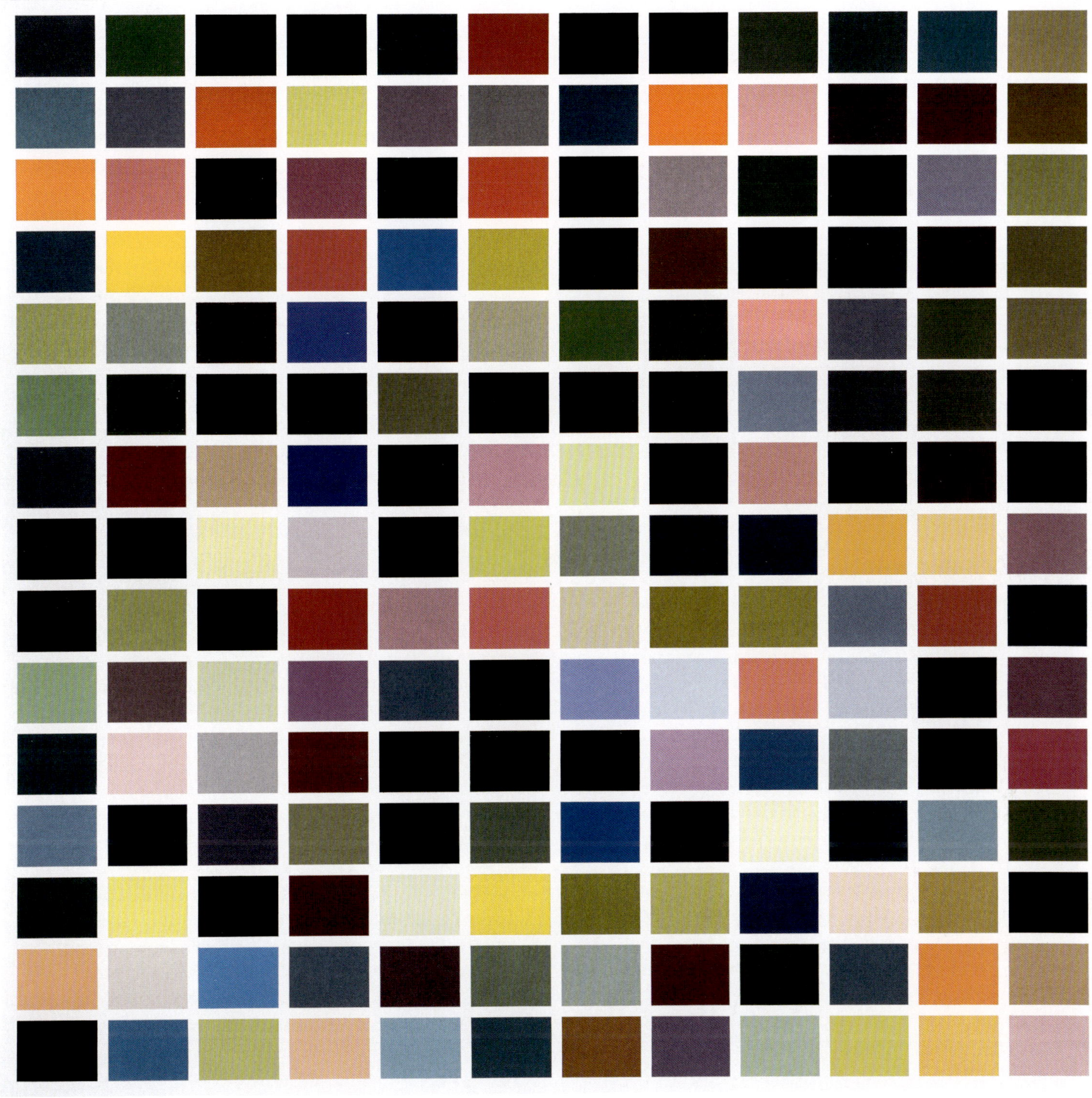

FIG 71
Gerhard Richter, *180 Colors* (*180 Farben*), 1971. Enamel on canvas, 78 ¾ × 78 ¾ in. (200 × 200 cm). CR 300-1. Private collection, New York

lies in the challenge to inquire into the complexity and orderliness of aesthetics. The fact that certain developments in modernity to such a degree have reduced complexity and visualized themselves in such a reductive manner, necessarily provokes a cab driver to argue, I could have done that myself. . . . I do not have the impression in the case of Mondrian, for example, that the geometric figures really have been calculated in a complicated way, and that people like Richter or Ligetti sustained complexity under highly modern conditions of production and present people with a riddle.[38]

This assessment seems all the more apt for Richter's *4,900 Colors* (fig. 72, pp. 202–3), which exists in eleven versions and coincided with the commission to design a window in the Cologne Cathedral. After a hiatus of more than three decades, Richter returned to the complex trope of the color chart, using computer algorithms to create abstract paintings in a context where "writings and texts no longer exist in perceptible times and spaces, but rather in the transistor cells of computers."[39] No longer—proverbially or actually—rolling the dice or drawing a lot, Richter in this series ultimately shifted to employing a digital program responsible for the random selection and distribution of colors, which assistants sprayed onto the surface of individual lacquer squares that were then, according to the respective protocol, glued and taped onto an Alu Dibond support. Using this process of generating tonal permutations, Richter produced 196 unique panels, each composed of twenty-five color plates measuring 9.7 centimeters square. The artist chose the twenty-five colors in a scale, picking tones that would result in an even chromatic spectrum of gradation from light to dark. Every color was numbered and subsequently allocated to a place within the invariant grid by the automated numeric sequences of calculated chance, which, as in the case of *4,096 Colors* from 1974, allowed for the repetition of one or more elements.[40] When a second version of this immense painting was exhibited at the Serpentine Gallery in London in 2008, the 196 panels were combined in forty-nine blocks consisting of four panels (or one hundred chips) each, the exact arrangement of which was determined by a roll of the dice. Finally, the artist decided the sequence of the panels on the gallery walls.

Undoubtedly, *4,900 Colors* is the epitome of Richter's confrontation with diagrammatic abstraction. At the same time, all stages of the production and dissemination of the work, in all its versions, were permeated by instances of chance. As evinced by his 2006 series of six large, nondiagrammatic, abstract paintings titled after the composer John Cage (pp. 196–201), Richter had earlier been an astute, yet distant, observer of Fluxus activities, and certainly he was fully aware of the legacy of chance operations in the realm of music that had combined constriction and accident, confinement and randomness. Particularly in light of the explicitly technological dimension of Richter's latest Color Charts, Cage's concept of sound, itself precipitated by the capacity of magnetic tape to register the totality of tonal or acoustic possibilities, seems to resonate in the painter's practice. In his analysis of chance and indeterminacy in Cage's work of the early to mid-1950s, art historian Branden W. Joseph stresses that the mechanical apparatus's capabilities of not only "reproducing *any* sound but, through various means of manipulation, producing *every* possible sound" made sound "conceivable as a continuous expanse without gap, division, or lacuna."[41] In Kittlerian parlance, chance resides in the real, which is only revealed by technology.[42] According to Joseph, for Cage, disorder and chance become relative terms, with the latter's multiplicity holding the potential for actualizing virtualities from the unfathomable complex totality of the former.[43] Whereas unexpected, haphazard encounters could liberate the subject from the strictures of modern rationality and instrumental reason, as claimed earlier by the avant-garde (the Surrealists, most notably), media technology here is understood as the prerequisite for the mobilization of chance.

Buchloh has argued that Richter's protocols of abstraction do not confirm and consolidate "the administrative order and quantifying power of the diagram" but rather counter the disciplinary dimension of the grid through the introduction of chance. With "aleatory chromatic constellations" intervening into a predetermined, restricted pictorial order, he thus contends, "Richter grasps the inevitable aesthetic necessity of inserting a fundamental contradiction within the essentially positivist project of diagrammatic abstraction."[44] Precisely because only fractions and figments of the disorder of the real can be actualized through the randomized technological operations that bring these works into existence, Richter's most recent Color Charts display an almost abysmal and vertiginous sense of pulsation and boundlessness, which the artist achieved by putting painting in the thrall of relentlessly progressing systems of permutation and variation.[45] One might even go so far as to describe *4,900 Colors* as a matrical painting that manifests itself beyond the threshold of our senses. The very fact that this work articulates a passage from the modular order of closed entities that governed the artist's earlier aleatory works to a state of perpetual change and recombination—or modulation—does not necessarily exclude and expel the subject, as Pelzer has declared.[46] On the contrary, beholders of this numerically based, never finalized artwork are addressed as subjects of the very new regime of power that allows the work to come into being, and in which, according to Gilles Deleuze, individuals are "undulatory, in orbit, in a continuous network."[47] In other words, the viewing subject is not bypassed by the forces of constant transmutation at the basis of *4,900 Colors* but sutured into their logic all the more thoroughly, albeit at the cost of being decentered, destabilized, and disoriented. If Richter's project indeed undermines the grid's discipline by injecting chance, then these abstract assemblages do not counter control, let alone transgress its purchase and impact on the real. Even the rapport between disorder and chance becomes ambivalent in this

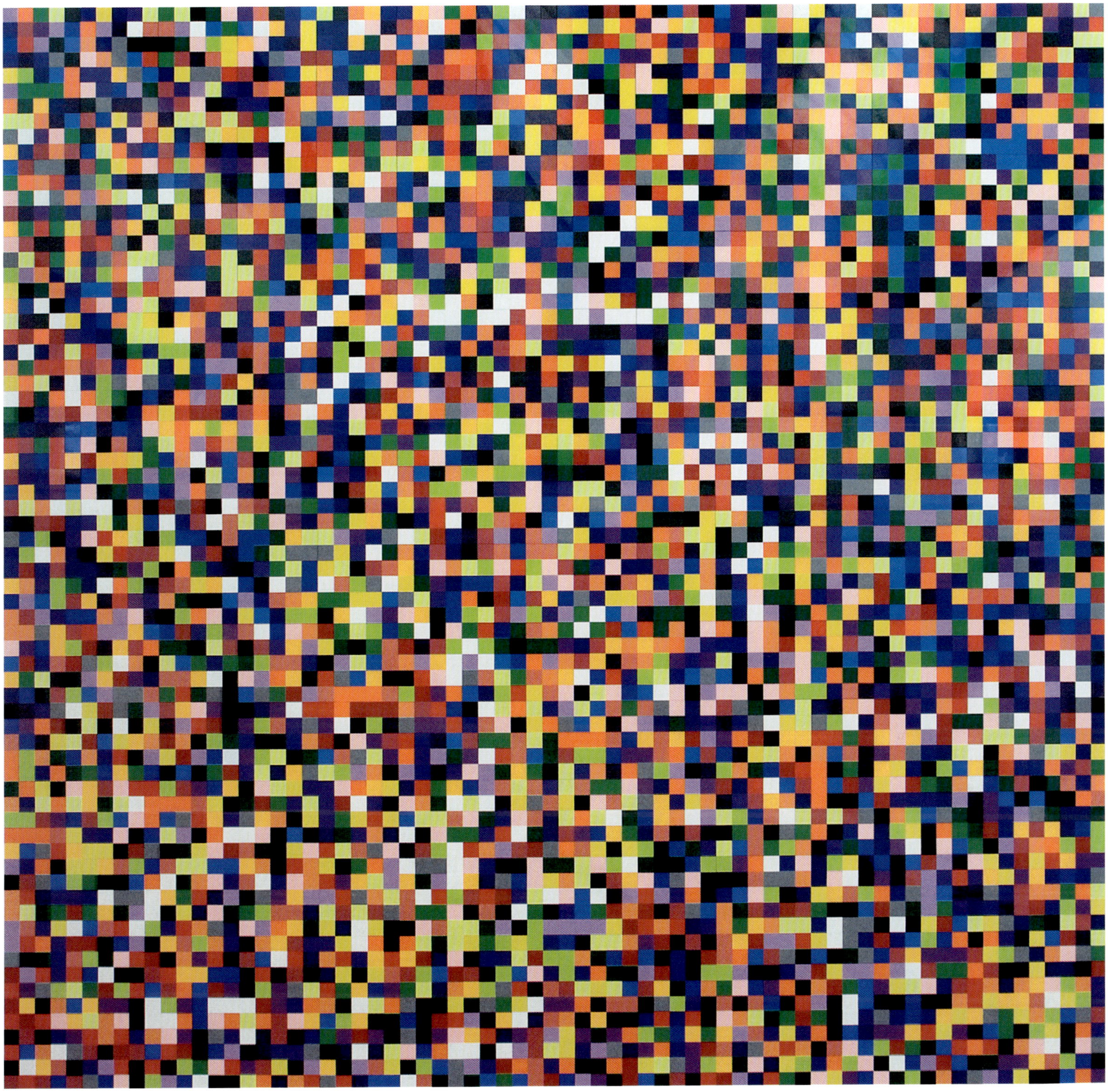

FIG 72
Gerhard Richter, *4,900 Colors* (*4,900 Farben*), 2007. Lacquer on Alu Dibond, 196 plates, 267 ¾ × 267 ¾ in. (680 × 680 cm). CR 901. Fondation Louis Vuitton, Paris

sustained painterly dialectic, as the artist's work seismically gauges and confronts control in the full meaning of contemporary sociotechnological mechanisms.

In his "Postscript on the Societies of Control," written in about 1990, Deleuze describes the passage from discipline to control—which, according to fellow philosopher Michel Foucault, was established and operated through sites of enclosure designed to exercise, as becomes evident by the deployment of the grid in Western modernity, surveillance and regimentation in order to distribute individuals in space—as a development in which machines tend to be eclipsed by computers, factories by corporations, salaries by bonuses, examinations by constant testing, signatures by codes, the gold standard by fluctuating currencies, energy by information, products by services, and distinct spaces by isomorphic networks. The analogical, in short, becomes numerical.[48] Overturning and liquefying stable forms and fixed entities or enclosures of all kinds, control brings into existence a sprawling spatial order in which sites and subjects find themselves in constant transition and inflection. In such a "universal system of deformation," individuals become *dividuals*, i.e., an internally split subjectivity no longer formed by pressure from the outside but intimately wired with exterior techniques and assemblages.[49]

"Enclosures," Deleuze has noted, "are *molds*, distinct castings, but controls are a *modulation*, like a self-deforming cast that will continuously change from one moment to the other, or like a sieve whose mesh will transmute from point to point."[50] With regard to artistic production from the early 1970s, Joseph, in a short commentary on Deleuze's concept and its relevance for art history, argues that the processes of dissolution and expansion brought about by the ascent of control directly concern the "autonomy and integrity of the modernist object," as "electronic imagery and information technology" transform medium specificity.[51] Richter's Color Charts, it would seem, not only share this recognition of a demise of medium specificity but have departed from it—and paradoxically use it to advance painting and its aesthetic experience in the present, against all odds.

Accident and Calculation

Given Richter's radical submission of the epistemes of abstraction to contemporary forces of technology and laws of control (a process that, as argued above, signals the mathematical randomization even of chance itself), it is hardly surprising that the artist produced a series dedicated to John Cage. Made between late October and early December 2006 (and first shown in the central pavilion at the 52nd Venice Biennale in 2007), Richter's six Cage Paintings confront viewers with a sequence of singular canvases, each entirely covered in multiple broken strata of paint. Through the contamination, scraping, or removal of material substance, Richter partially revealed layers, segments, and sections underneath the surface. The tonal values of these works range from black and dark green (predominant especially in the cycle's first painting) to light gray and brilliant white, interspersed with comparatively scarce remnants of pungent yellow, dark blue, and bright red. Yet these colorful pigments, for the most part concealed by leaden coats and fractured textures, do not serve to animate the surfaces. On the contrary, their hiddenness and latency only contribute to an overall sense of destitution, dereliction, and deterioration exuded by the ash gray, their ruinous textures dominating the overall impression of the ensemble.

In producing these subdued, even melancholic, works (reportedly while listening, at least intermittently, to Cage's music), the artist departed from creating formulaic abstract sketches with the help of long wood rulers (with the exception of *Cage (1)*, which is based on a previously existing image from the Silicate series of 2003). Richter then obliterated these non-objective figures by adding strokes and daubs, and, more decisively, by exerting the pressure of a squeegee, his hallmark tool. In this case, he equipped the squeegee with a transparent piece of acrylic that allowed him to observe the effects of his actions.[52] As in his 1972 series Inpaintings, Richter defines abstraction in these works as a mode of perpetual cancellation or even destruction of gestures, formerly understood as expressing one's active intentions and unconscious dispositions. Remotely reminiscent of the graphic method devised by nineteenth-century physiologist Étienne-Jules Marey to trace and analyze (human and animal) animation or locomotion, the squeegee's impressions on the surface register the artist's bodily movements, resulting in prominent vertical lines at the right side and other places across the pictorial field that indicate where he paused. At the same time, indices of equally repeated horizontal trajectories create a rhythm in the painting's texture, revealing a gridlike system of coordinates.[53]

Whereas Richter's Color Charts expose the grid as the epitome of modernity's administration of spaces and subjects, while also addressing, through the incorporation of chance protocols, its changed relevance under the sociotechnological conditions of control societies, the Cage Paintings simultaneously evoke the grid and submerge it in collisions of colors and textures. Hence, the very traces of Richter's paradoxical process of making and unmaking marks bring forth a kind of painting that signifies absolute singularity in terms of both execution and experience. None of these works could ever be repeated. Yet, they are the result of a semimechanized painterly procedure in which "tactile control and manual dexterity" are radically diminished and enunciation is accessible only through erasure.[54] Richter's technique concurrently anticipates and attempts to contain moments of chance. Accident and command coalesce. In the artist's tribute to Cage, chance is not technologically derived from the disorder of the real but instead becomes manifest in indeterminate incidents that punctuate the palimpsest-like screen of paint. In these works, Richter

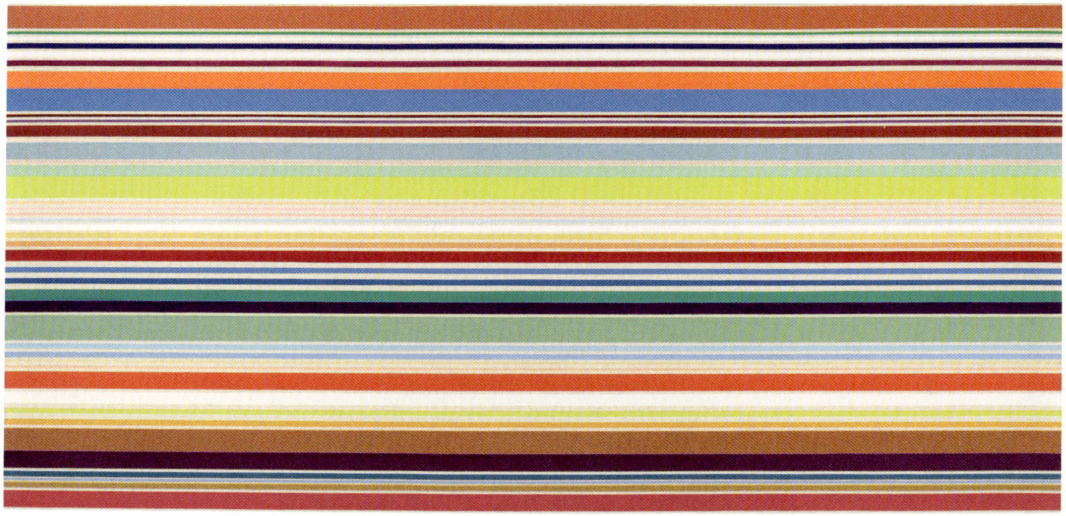

FIG 73
Kenneth Noland (American, 1924–2010), *New Day*, 1967. Acrylic on canvas, 89 ⅜ × 184 ¼ in. (227 × 468 cm). Whitney Museum of American Art, New York, Purchase, with funds from the Friends of the Whitney Museum of American Art (68.18)

programmatically stages an aporetic conception and practice of abstraction as the promise and potential of chance—once a viable, or so it seemed, means of systematically escaping from the constraints and constrictions of everyday mechanisms of control—which are both redeemed and (literally and figuratively) buried under innumerable layers of mostly gray matter. Thus, the paintings' reflection on the afterlife of chance directly confronts viewers with, to quote a related analysis by Buchloh, the "highly contradictory structures of Richter's abstraction... since the radical negation of rationalist instrumentality... perpetually operates in tandem with a mnemonic dimension of the failed historical trajectories of abstract painting."[55]

In Richter's complex practice, which arguably has advanced to define painting in the present, the dialectics of the medium's depletion and continuation necessarily cannot come to a halt. In 2011, Richter made his first Strip painting, based on his own *Abstract Painting* from 1990. The elongated panel, which would initiate an entire series produced until 2015 (pp. 220–21), is a digitally rendered abstraction composed of thin bands of color printed on paper and mounted on Alu Dibond behind Perspex. These bewildering striations are the products of a process in which the source chosen by the artist was first divided vertically into two parts and then each part was multiplied and mirrored. After this procedure was repeated twelve times, the plentiful painterly details increasingly collapsed into a radiant flickering of progressively thinner lines (at the end consisting of 8,190 elements, each measuring no more than .8 millimeters).[56] This process of division, reflection, and refinement could be continued virtually ad infinitum; however, its effects no longer would be discernible to the human eye. Once based in the sustained, self-reflexive pictorial order of bodily performance, Richter's abstraction, ruled by conditions of media technologies—which, according to Kittler, only "may yield historical traces of the unknown called the body"[57]—becomes nothing but an interface of a recursively advancing codification of all matter as mere data. Whereas Kenneth Noland, in works such as *New Day* (fig. 73), applied paint with rollers, sponges, and brushes to create the impression of continuous lines of color merging with the surface, Richter's algorithmic evacuations of facture and gesture deliberately subject the aesthetic medium to the leveling logic of technology. The Strip paintings, as Buchloh has concluded, make us recognize the proximity of "aleatory chromatic expansion to a technocratic and administrative quantification of the infinite."[58] In this respect, the artist's work appears to partake in the crucial insight that "it is not what humans do or want according to their interiorities which defines the scope for action of a given epoch; it is the exteriority of codes and signs, letters and numbers that allows, but also limits, what can be thought and achieved."[59] In Richter's abstract work, we are confronted, time and again, with "events that number among the arbitrariness of what can be written down and the stringency of calculation at the same time."[60] The artist's immense and eminent practice of (abstract) painting can be sustained and advanced only through his unrivaled attentiveness to the technological world and, concomitantly, his unsurpassed ingenuity, even audacity, to confront and explore it—without ever mistaking randomization for randomness.

Hal Foster

In a Glass, Darkly

Over the years, Gerhard Richter has held different views about his glass works. In a note from 1971, he writes, "Perhaps the Doors, Curtains, Surface Pictures, Panes of Glass, etc. are metaphors of despair, prompted by the dilemma that our sense of sight causes us to apprehend things, but at the same time restricts and partly precludes our apprehension of reality."[1] Richter refers here to *4 Panes of Glass* from 1967 (p. 117, fig. 74), his first piece in glass, which consists of the titular elements set vertically in iron frames and attached with iron rods from floor to ceiling in a way that (at least originally) allowed viewers to rotate them. The work appears very matter of fact; yet, as in related Minimalist objects such as *Untitled (Mirror Cubes)* (fig. 75) by Robert Morris, *4 Panes* sets up a double tension: the first between the sheer opticality of the panes and the obdurate physicality of the frames and rods, and the second between what we *know*—there are four large identical rectangles in front of us—and what we *perceive*—different framings, reflections, and refractions caught in the angled glass. Through this double tension Richter stages an almost Cartesian doubt about "our apprehension of reality."

A year later, in 1972, Richter returns to this glass piece: "Illusionism has never interested me, with the exception of the *Large Curtain* painting, the *5 Doors* and the *4 Panes of Glass*. Those rather structured paintings are out of the frame, and in fact I rather disappointed myself, because I don't really want to think structurally in this way. I prefer to go through destruction to construction."[2] This dense statement intimates a new caution about *4 Panes*—that it moved too quickly "out of the frame" of painting into the actual space of "structure"—which can be read, in turn, as an implicit critique of the Minimalist shift from painting to the "specific object" and the architecture around it, a shift associated, above all, with Donald Judd, Carl Andre, and Dan Flavin.[3] Richter is "disappointed" by this shift, or rather, he is disappointed that he followed it (etymologically, a "disappointment" is a "loss of position"): it led him to stray from his preferred path "through destruction to construction," that is, from the making of painting through its (difficult) undoing rather than its (simple) obviating, as is the case with Minimalist objects.

Several years on, in 1977, in an important letter to his close interlocutor Benjamin Buchloh, Richter again alters his view of the glass piece and its Minimalist associations: "In the Grey Pictures it's lack of differentiation, nothing, nil, the Beginning and the End; in the Panes of Glass it's the analogy with attitudes and possibilities; in the Color Charts it's chance, anything is correct, or rather Form is Nonsense; in the new Abstract Pictures it's arbitrariness, almost anything is possible."[4] In this litany of negatives, the relatively positive assessment of *4 Panes* stands out, obscure though it is. With his doubt about perception and his skepticism about structure now abated, Richter is intrigued by "the analogy with attitudes and possibilities" that *4 Panes* suggests, by which I take him to mean the way that the framings, reflections, and refractions of the glass permit an experience of actual and virtual positions of both panes and viewers in space. In short, he sees *4 Panes* as involved in the phenomenological dimension of Minimalism—with its special attention to the interrelationship among artwork, perception, and environment.

A few years later, in a telegraphic note of 1981, Richter focuses on yet another aspect of glass, its mirror effect, which he would soon explore directly in his work. "Picture in itself," Richter writes, "cropped effect, likeness to photograph, readymade character."[5] This is cryptic, but it does highlight both the automatic illusionism of mirrored glass and its everyday quality as furniture. Richter then adds an abrupt "polemic" about mirrored glass: "devaluing of all other pictures; provocation of the viewer, who sees himself instead of a picture."[6] On the one hand, a mirror is the very "picture in itself" because it shows whatever is placed before it, and, as Richter comments later, it is "the only picture that always looks different."[7] As such, it trumps and so "devalues" other kinds of representation. On the other hand, mirrored glass is "devalued" in turn because it

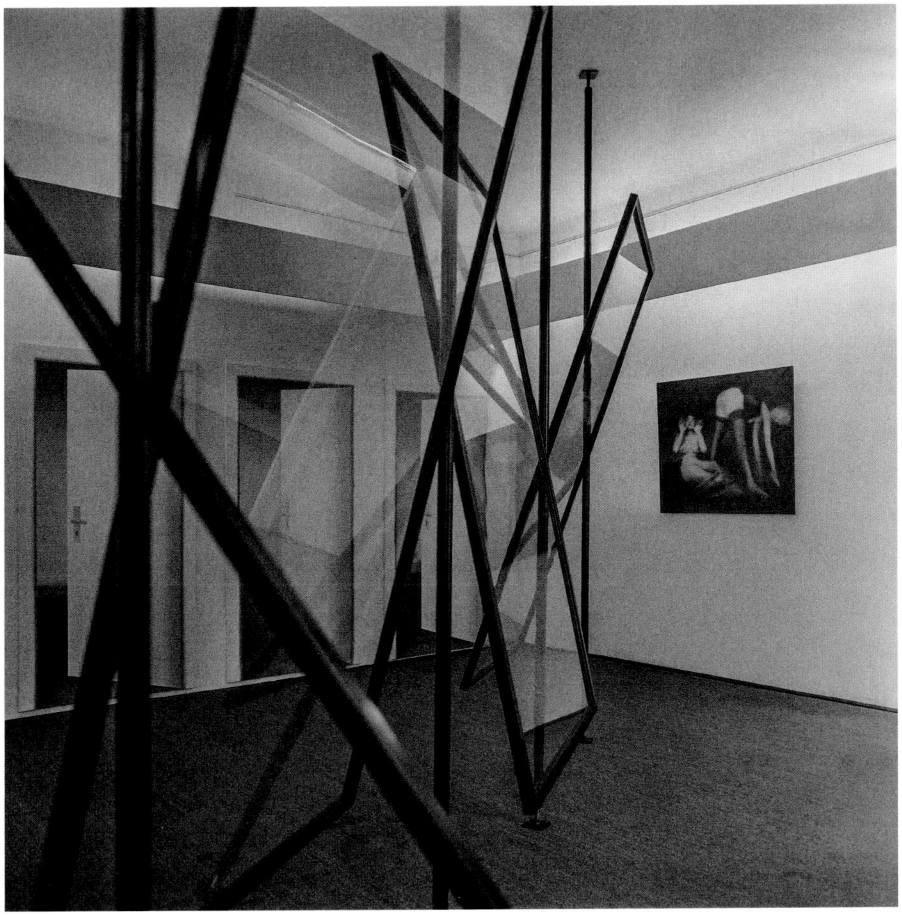

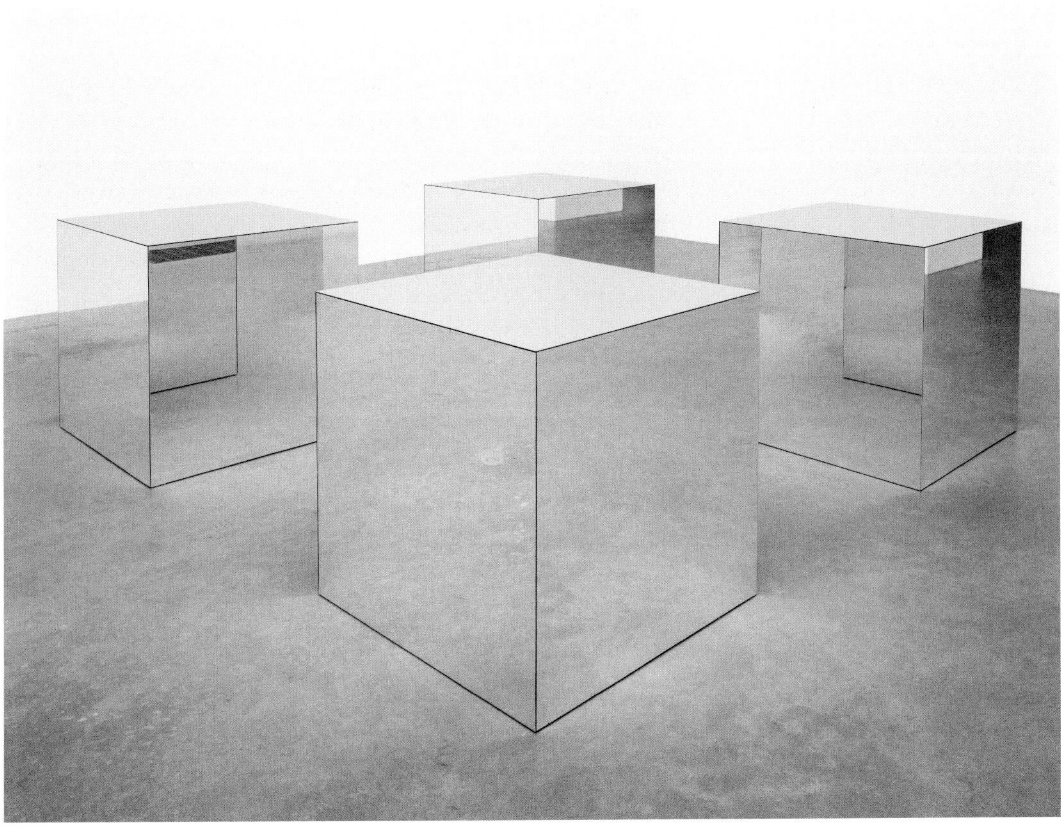

FIG 74
Gerhard Richter, *4 Panes of Glass*, installed at the Galerie Heiner Friedrich, Munich, 1967

FIG 75
Robert Morris (American, 1931–2018), *Untitled (Mirror Cubes)*, 1965, reconstructed 1971. Mirror glass and wood, each cube 36 × 36 × 36 in. (91.4 × 91.4 × 91.4 cm). Tate Modern, London

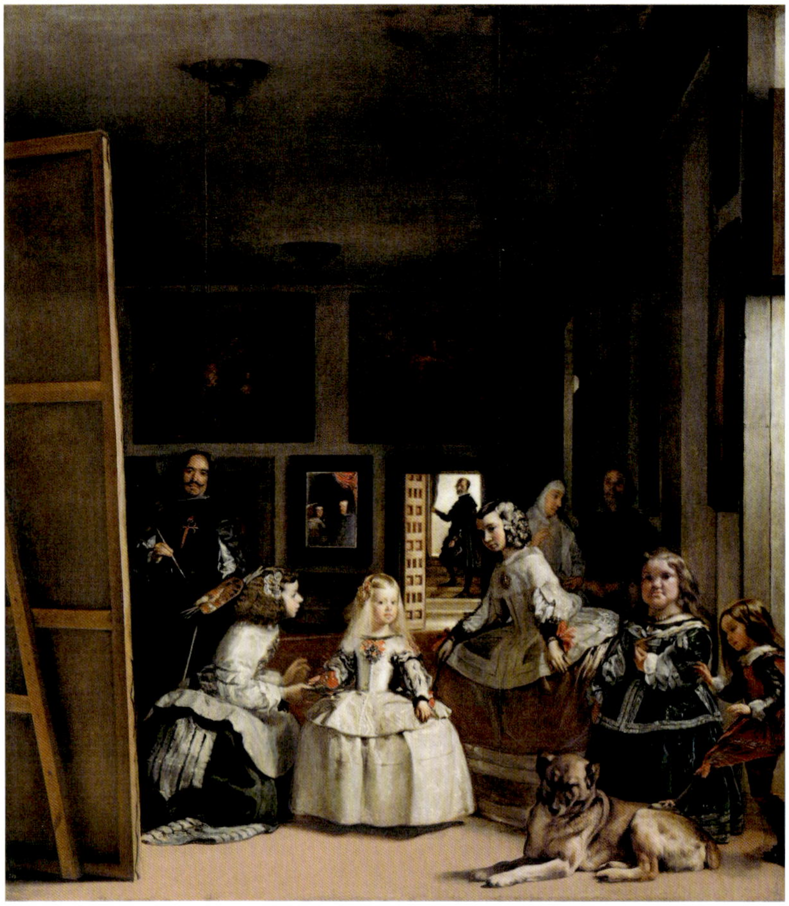

FIG 76
Diego Velázquez (Spanish, 1599–1660), *Las Meninas*, 1656. Oil on canvas, 126 ¼ × 110 ⅞ in. (320.5 × 281.5 cm). Museo del Prado, Madrid (P001174)

confounds the viewer, who cannot get around her own reflection to see the glass properly. Traditional paintings, especially in a vertical format, invite our bodily identification (the ego is first and foremost an image, Freud tells us, a basic point that Lacan underscores in his celebrated account of "the mirror stage" in our development). In fact, the felt analogy between a composed painting and a contemplative viewer is so fundamental that we are not aware of it until it is interfered with. And this is precisely what the glass pieces do: our reflection, in the sense of our mirrored image, disrupts our reflection, in the sense of our contemplation. "I see the mirror as a metaphor of your work as a whole," Hans Ulrich Obrist once commented to Richter. "The word 'reflect' has two planes of meaning, which bring the viewer into the picture, and thus the viewer is in two states at once."[8]

Finally, in 1991, at a time when Richter was at work on glass pieces coated with single colors, such as *Mirror, Blood Red* (p. 165), he has this to say: "In the case of the colored mirrors, the result was a kind of cross between a monochrome painting and a mirror, a 'Neither/Nor'—which is what I like about it."[9] This is another rich statement, one that Richter repeats, so it deserves special attention. If some of the glass pieces like *4 Panes* evoke windows, others like *Blood Red* double as mirrors, and both allude to the monochrome as well. The window and the mirror were the primary paradigms of Western painting from the Renaissance onward, often challenged but never overthrown, until the monochrome, a prized device of the twentieth-century avant-garde, canceled both.[10] Buchloh has situated the glass pieces brilliantly in this modernist context, so little more needs to be added on that score.[11] Still, the question remains: Why did Richter call up these old models of painting, not only after the postwar repetition of the monochrome by Robert Rauschenberg, Piero Manzoni, and others, but also during the Minimalist and Post-Minimalist move from painting into ambient space? According to Buchloh, Richter effectively voids the old paradigms of window and mirror, and "the monochrome seems to have become an affectless record of loss" as well, no longer "mystical in its purity or critical in its self-reflexivity," as it was for Kazimir Malevich and Aleksandr Rodchenko, respectively.[12] Moreover, the glass pieces attest to "the extreme negation of the very promises of an emancipatory potential of perceptual and social experience with which monochromy and transparency were initially endowed."[13] I mostly agree with this assessment, but it does not account fully for the ambiguity of the "neither/nor" quality that Richter also values in these works.

In his epochal treatise *De Pittura* (1435), the Italian polymath Leon Battista Alberti proposed the window as the paragon of painting. According to Svetlana Alpers in *The Art of Describing: Dutch Art in the Seventeenth Century* (1983), this southern model became so dominant in the Renaissance that it occluded a paradigm favored in the north, one based on the mirror. For Alpers the window positions the viewer as primary (I see the world arrayed before me), while the mirror puts the world first (it is reflected in the image as if my presence were not required). However, theorists such as Michel Foucault and Louis Marin ignored this north/south dichotomy, which runs deep in the discipline of art history, and argued that "classical representation" actually combines the models of window and mirror. For Foucault the masterpiece of such representation is *Las Meninas* (1656; fig. 76) by Velázquez, for Marin it is *Et in Arcadia Ego* (ca. 1638) by Poussin, and the essence of both paintings is a "reflecting transparence."[14] With great panache, Velázquez depicts not only a window and a mirror but also the back of the very canvas that he seems to work on, the subject of which is the king and the queen (who appear dimly in the distant mirror). Again, whereas Alpers sees *Las Meninas* only as an anomaly, one caught between northern and southern orientations, Foucault regards it as an epitome of classical representation.[15]

In his glass pieces, Richter literalizes the use of windows and mirrors and, in doing so, produces a very unclassical representation, one that we experience as neither "I see the world" nor "the world is seen." These works also defy the first purpose of traditional painting and photography, which is to fix an image, to still a figure.[16] ("The pleasant thing," Richter comments about glass, "is that it makes the pictorial space even more variable and more subject to chance than it is in photography."[17]) Often, even as the panes turn our bodily substance into virtual shadow, they also transform nonexistent light into actual illumination.[18] They thus destabilize not only the objects in front of them—again, no motif is arrested once and for all—but also the viewers, whose images are reflected and refracted in protean ways. This effect directly counters the fundamental goal of classical representation, for both paradigms of traditional painting, the window and the mirror, were dedicated to the mastery of the subject as well as the control of the object. In fact, Foucault claimed *Las Meninas* as an epitome of classical representation precisely because it locates the viewer in "the place of the king," which allows us to feel that we are sovereign over a world given to us to behold and to possess. "I see the world"—I summon it into appearance—is a clear expression of such imaginary power, but so too is "the world is seen." On the one hand, the fiction that the world simply appears before us undergirds the empiricist belief that we can know the world objectively and manipulate it instrumentally. On the other hand, the same fiction allows us to look on the world as though secretly, from a position that combines unobserved command with voyeuristic pleasure.

Richter collapses the models of the window and the mirror in his glass works. In the more transparent pieces we struggle to see or to be seen clearly at all; in the more reflective ones we cannot get out of our own way. Objects as well as subjects appear and disappear in a manner that cannot be predicted or controlled; they loom up and fade away; they look distorted, obscured, or otherwise lost in space. Jacques Lacan once argued that the primary function of traditional painting is not trompe l'oeil, to fool the eye, but *dompte-regard*, to tame the gaze.[19] Often the glass pieces do much the opposite: they render the gaze wild. Sometimes the effect approximates the schizophrenic sense of space once evoked by the Surrealist associate Roger Caillois. Caillois describes a subject who, possessed by space, becomes "similar, not similar to something, but just *similar*," susceptible to endless shape-shifting.[20]

Frequently in the glass pieces forms become formless, even anamorphic (an anamorphic image appears legible only from an oblique angle). The most celebrated instance of anamorphosis in Western art is *The Ambassadors* (1533; fig. 77) by Hans Holbein the Younger. Another fine example of classical representation, this painting presents two French diplomats at the English court surrounded by tokens of wealth, power, and knowledge, while an apparition rises up from the bottom of the picture as though out of a hallucinated grave, a nacreous

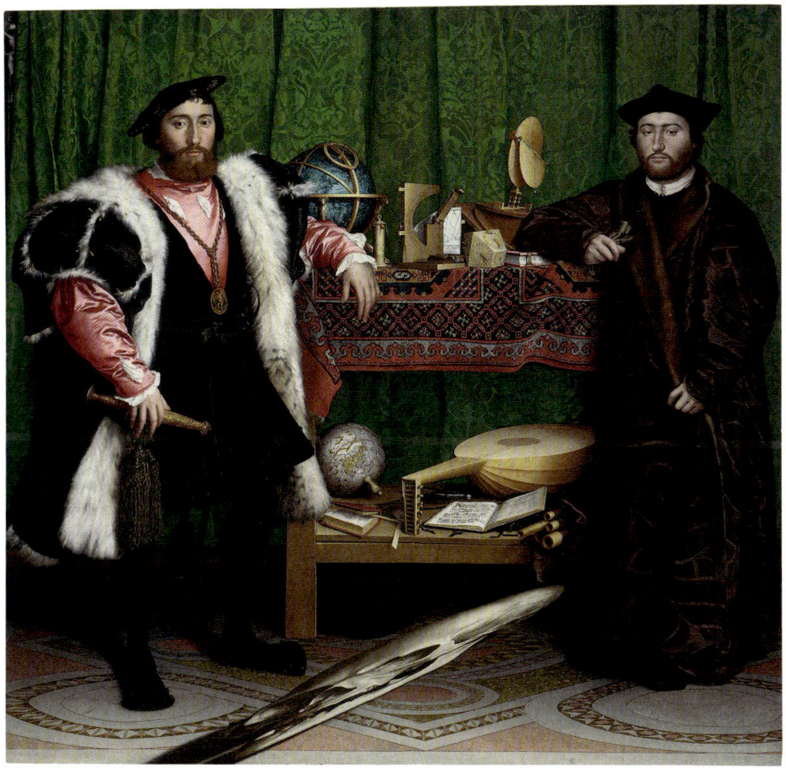

FIG 77
Hans Holbein the Younger (German, 1497/98–1543), *The Ambassadors*, 1533. Oil on wood, 81 ½ × 82 ½ in. (207 × 209.5 cm). National Gallery, London (NG1314)

thing that the aristocrats cannot detect. Viewed from the extreme left of the painting, however, the anamorphic object is revealed to us as a skull, which suddenly shifts *The Ambassadors* to the category of the *vanitas*: the memento mori of the death's-head is a reminder that none of us, no matter how rich, mighty, or cultured, can transcend our mortality. Whereas the message of *The Ambassadors* is "We too will die" (*Et in Arcadia Ego* delivers the same pronouncement), the implication of the glass pieces is that we never fully existed in the first place—or, as the Austrian satirist Karl Kraus would say, "You don't even live once." Often the viewer becomes her own spectral shadow, her own anamorphic skull.

How does this dark view of the glass work jibe with the positive comment about its "analogy with attitudes and possibilities"? In part, Richter seems to stage his ambivalence about Minimalism in these pieces; certainly, they register the changed valence of Minimalism over time.[21] Initially, according to Judd, the Minimalists turned to specific objects in order to defeat the illusionism of painting once and for all, a mission that Richter first supported (again, "illusionism has never interested me," he wrote in 1972). Yet, the reflective surfaces of many Judd boxes (fig. 78) and shelves (not to mention the diffusive glow of all Flavin lights) belie this Minimalist rhetoric, and illusionism became rampant in work by Robert Irwin, James Turrell, and others who followed the example of Judd and Flavin: with these artists, the pictorial is not negated by objecthood so much as atomized in space. Initially, too, the Minimalists underscored the spatial parameters of the artwork in order to guide the phenomenological experience of the viewer. Yet the elaboration of Minimalism since then—from Turrell to Olafur Eliasson and beyond—has had much the opposite effect: it confounds rather than articulates space and subject alike.[22] In short, Minimalist theory is largely contradicted by subsequent practice that purports to develop it, and the Richter glass pieces can be seen to have anticipated this problem then and to demonstrate it now.

Historically, interest in phenomenological experience has deepened at times of technological transformation; it is as though a focus on the body might offer some cover from the distractions of new media. It is no surprise, then, that Minimalism emerged alongside Pop. But phenomenology cannot save us from a world given over to the commodity-image, especially now in its digital form. As Dan Graham has suggested in works and writings alike, both the subjects and the spaces posited by Minimalism are never as pure as the phenomenological account of this art suggests; they are always already social and mediated (fig. 79). Seen from a contemporary perspective, Richter makes a similar point. In this way, his glass pieces are neither aligned with Minimalism nor opposed to it. Put positively, they allow for a kind of viewing that is

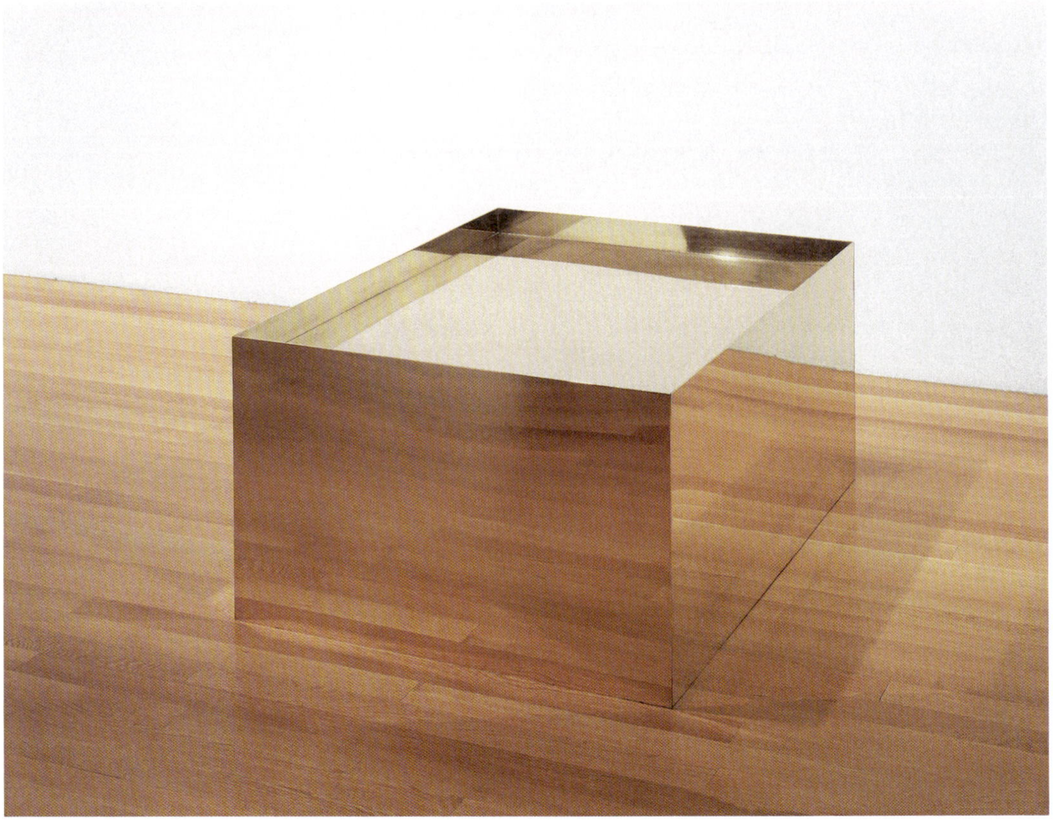

FIG 78
Donald Judd (American, 1928–1994), *Untitled*, 1968. Brass, 22 × 48 ¼ × 36 in. (55.9 × 122.6 × 91.4 cm). The Museum of Modern Art, New York, Gift of Philip Johnson (687.1980)

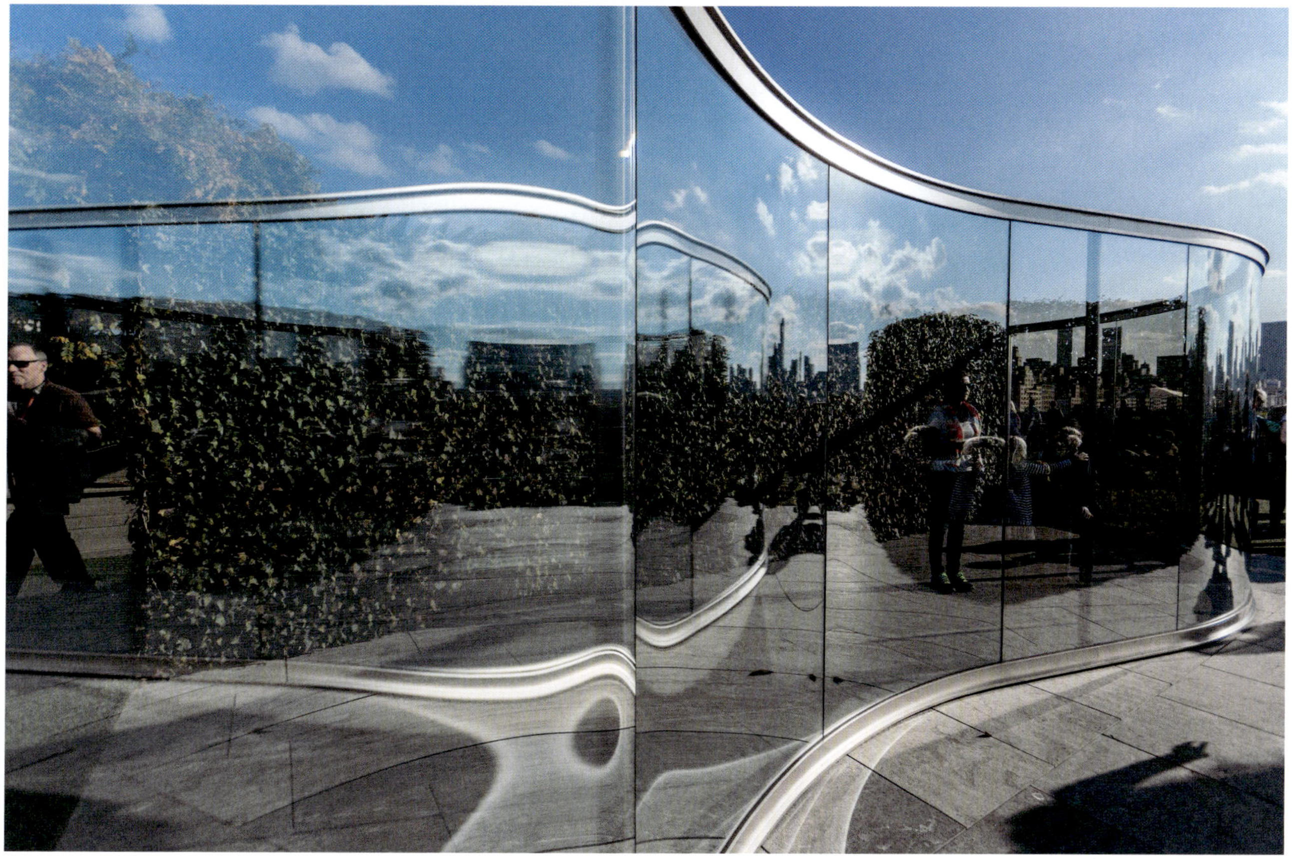

both durational, of the sort associated with Minimalism, and punctual, even transcendental, of the sort that Michael Fried, the great antagonist of Minimalism, associated with abstract painting.[23]

Here again Richter reveals his penchant for a "neither/nor" stance, which also speaks to his discomfort with ideological oppositions. This neutrality is the apparent aim of a good number of his key devices: the nonstyle of his snapshot paintings, the blandness of his encyclopedia portraits ("which neutralizes everything and all ideology"[24]), the evasive quality of his blurred images, the blasé indifference of his Gray Paintings, the arbitrary nature of his Color Charts, and so on. Distinct from negativity, this neutrality serves as a protection against ideological confinement, and it aligns Richter with Roland Barthes, for whom the neutral does not cancel meaning so much as "baffles" it. "I define the Neutral as that which outplays the paradigm," Barthes writes, with "paradigm" defined here linguistically as "the opposition of two virtual terms from which, in speaking, I actualize one to produce meaning." "Or rather," he continues, "I call Neutral everything that baffles the paradigm. . . . Whence the idea of a structural creation that would defeat, annul, or contradict the implacable binarism of the paradigm by means of a third term."[25] It is this third term, this elusive way through restrictive oppositions, that Richter seeks: "Something has to

FIG 79
Dan Graham (American, born 1942), with Günther Vogt (Swiss, born 1957), *Hedge Two-Way Mirror Walkabout*, 2014. Iris and Gerald B. Cantor Roof Garden, The Metropolitan Museum of Art, New York

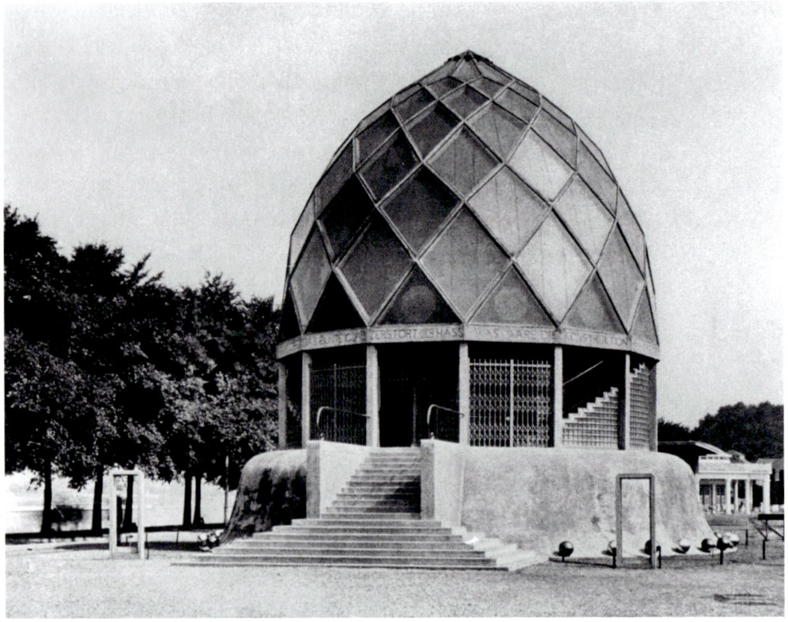

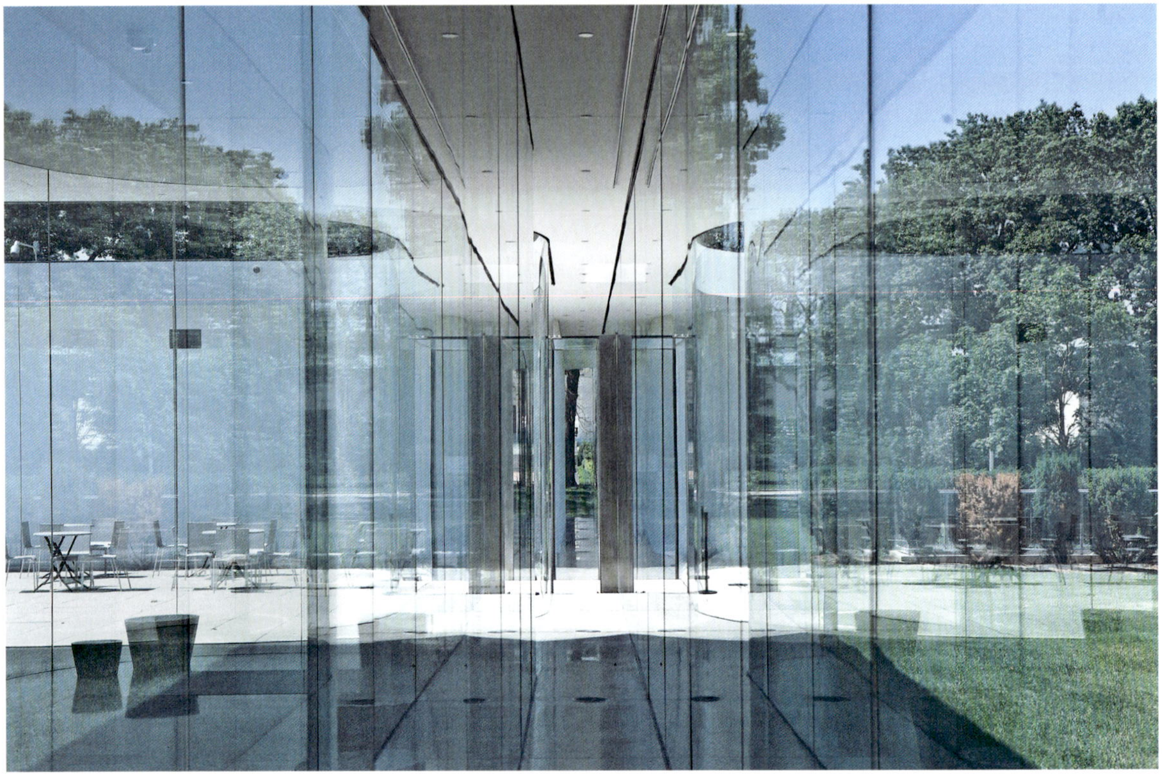

FIG 80
Bruno Taut (German, 1880–1938), Glass Pavilion for the Deutscher Werkbund Exhibition, Cologne, 1914

FIG 81
SANAA (Sejima and Nishizawa and Associates) (Japanese, founded 1995), Glass Pavilion at the Toledo Museum of Art, 2006

be shown and simultaneously not shown, in order perhaps to say something else again, a third thing."[26] That is precisely what the glass pieces attempt through an equal insistence not only on window and mirror but also on picture and object. In this same way they treat Minimalism as both "a new alphabet"[27] and a problematic phenomenology, and affect a viewer who feels both activated and "baffled."

Yet can an artist truly outplay a dominant regime of visuality? Might "the third thing" be an avoidance strategy of its own?[28] Such questions come into focus when we consider the glass pieces in relation to architecture, both modern and contemporary, especially with an eye to the vaunted transparency of its glass construction. Buchloh has shown how Richter counters the utopian hopes projected onto glass architecture in the 1910s by architects such as Bruno Taut (fig. 80), and how he also brackets the disenchanted values of New Objectivity associated with glass architecture in the 1920s and 1930s by critics such as Walter Benjamin. So, too, Richter invites us to look back on the co-option of architectural transparency when the International Style of Mies van der Rohe and others became the template for corporate buildings in the postwar period. In addition, the glass pieces allow us to think critically about more recent developments in design culture.

In 1963, not long before Richter first took up glass, the architectural historian Colin Rowe and the artist Robert Slutzky published an influential essay titled "Transparency: Literal and Phenomenal." Rowe and Slutzky demoted the "literal" (or actual) transparency of structure permitted by glass construction and advanced the "phenomenal" (or perceived) transparency of space, which they defined as a matter of Cubist surfaces that "interpenetrate without an optical destruction of each other."[29] In retrospect, this text anticipates the moment in architectural discourse more than a decade later when the articulation of surface became as important as that of space, and the understanding of skin as important as that of structure; that is, it anticipates the discursive advent of the postmodern emphasis on scenographic facades. Key here is that Rowe and Slutzky wrote positively of "the equivocal emotions" that a play between literal and phenomenal transparency can provoke. In our own time, many prominent architects—Rem Koolhaas, Jacques Herzog and Pierre de Meuron, Jean Nouvel, and SANAA (fig. 81) among them—have worked hard to produce such ambiguous effects by means of luminous skins and translucent envelopes. Yet often these devices only dazzle or confuse, and, as the architectural historian Anthony Vidler has remarked, the viewing subject is "suspended in a difficult moment between knowledge and blockage."[30] This "difficult moment" is structurally similar to fetishization; indeed, as with the commodity fetish according to Marx, we cannot readily understand how such buildings are produced, and, as with the sexual fetish according to Freud, they promise an emotional intensity at the possible cost of cognitive arrest ("the subject is suspended"). In other words, such architecture can be beautiful, but it can also be spectacular in the sense given the word by the Situationist Guy Debord—a fetish on a grand scale, the production of which, again, is mystified, and whose primary effect might well be mystification.[31] With glass pieces such as *House of Cards (5 Panes)* (p. 245) Richter helps us to question this architectural condition at a remove.

The window and the mirror are not only old paradigms of artistic representation or modern instruments of architectural transparency. They are also familiar devices of commercial display that support the narcissistic blandishments of consumer capitalism, not to mention common instruments of security and surveillance used to police both corporate and governmental spaces. "Seeing oneself and watching oneself seeing have become the almost exclusive modus of being in the world," Buchloh has commented, and this is even more the case with the dominance of social media today.[32] Today, too, the window and the mirror are largely reformatted, often quite literally, by the digital screen, which has become our primary model of visuality, one that has already transformed film and television beyond recognition. "Windows" was trademarked long ago, and what is the selfie universe of Facebook and Instagram but an endless hall of mirrors? Several of the glass pieces—perhaps the multilayered *11 Panes* (p. 183) above all—challenge our narcissistic drive for mirroring, as our images are both multiplied and dispersed by them. In fact, reflected darkly in this entire body of work is a whole history of uses and abuses of glass in the world around us.

Plates

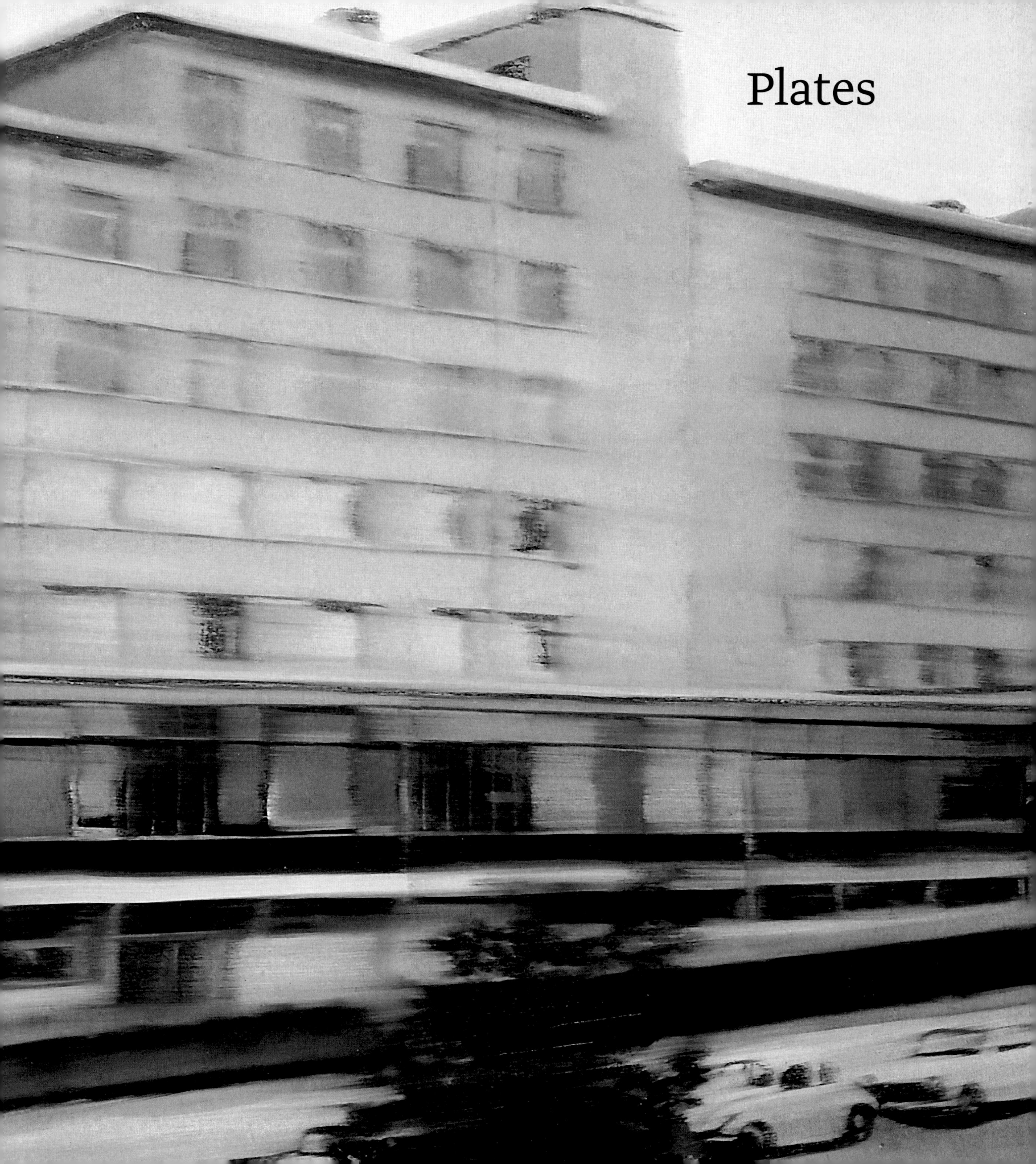

Table, 1962 35 7⁄16 × 44 ½ in. (90 × 113 cm)

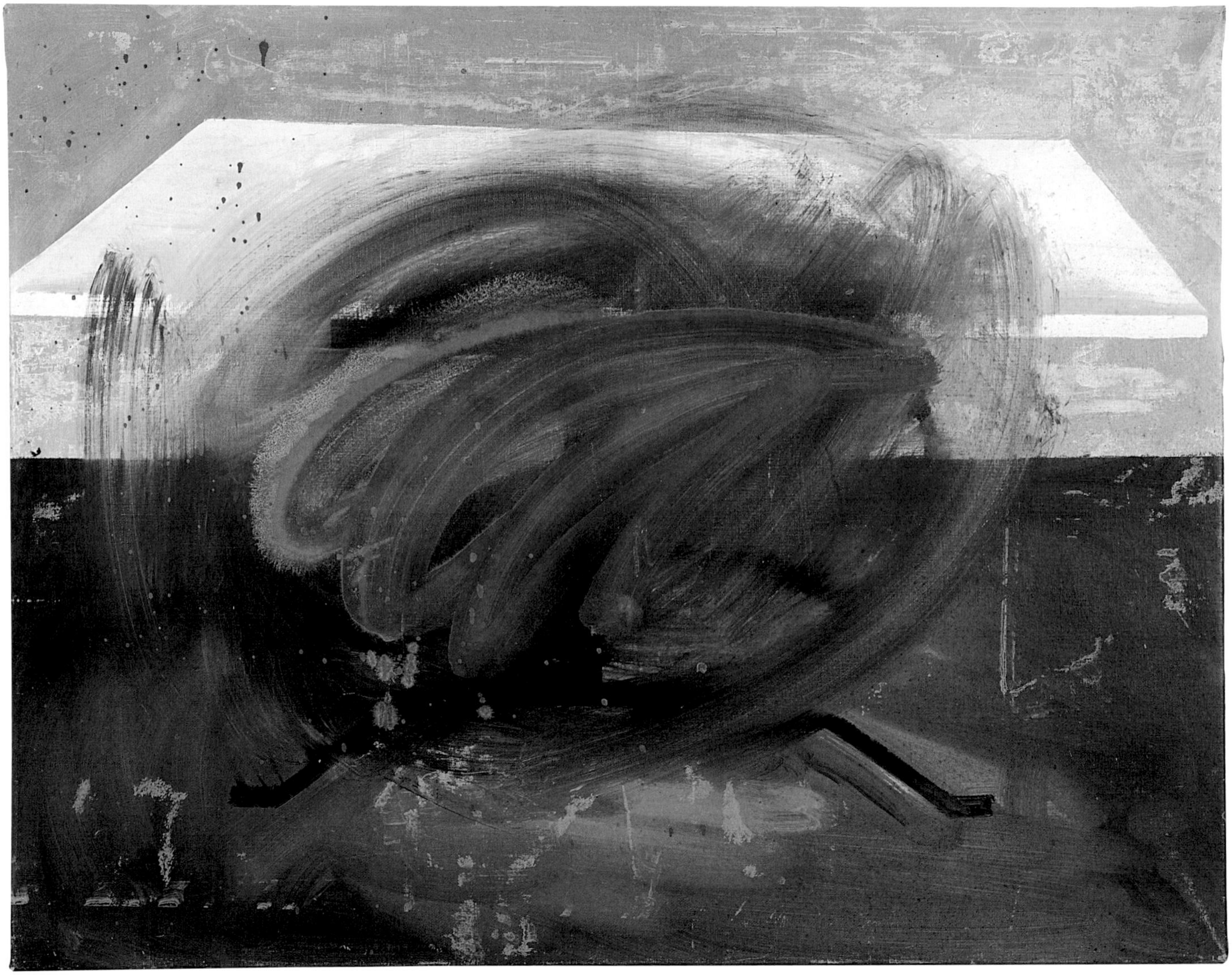

Coffin Bearers, 1963   53 ⅛ × 70 ⅞ in. (135 × 180 cm)

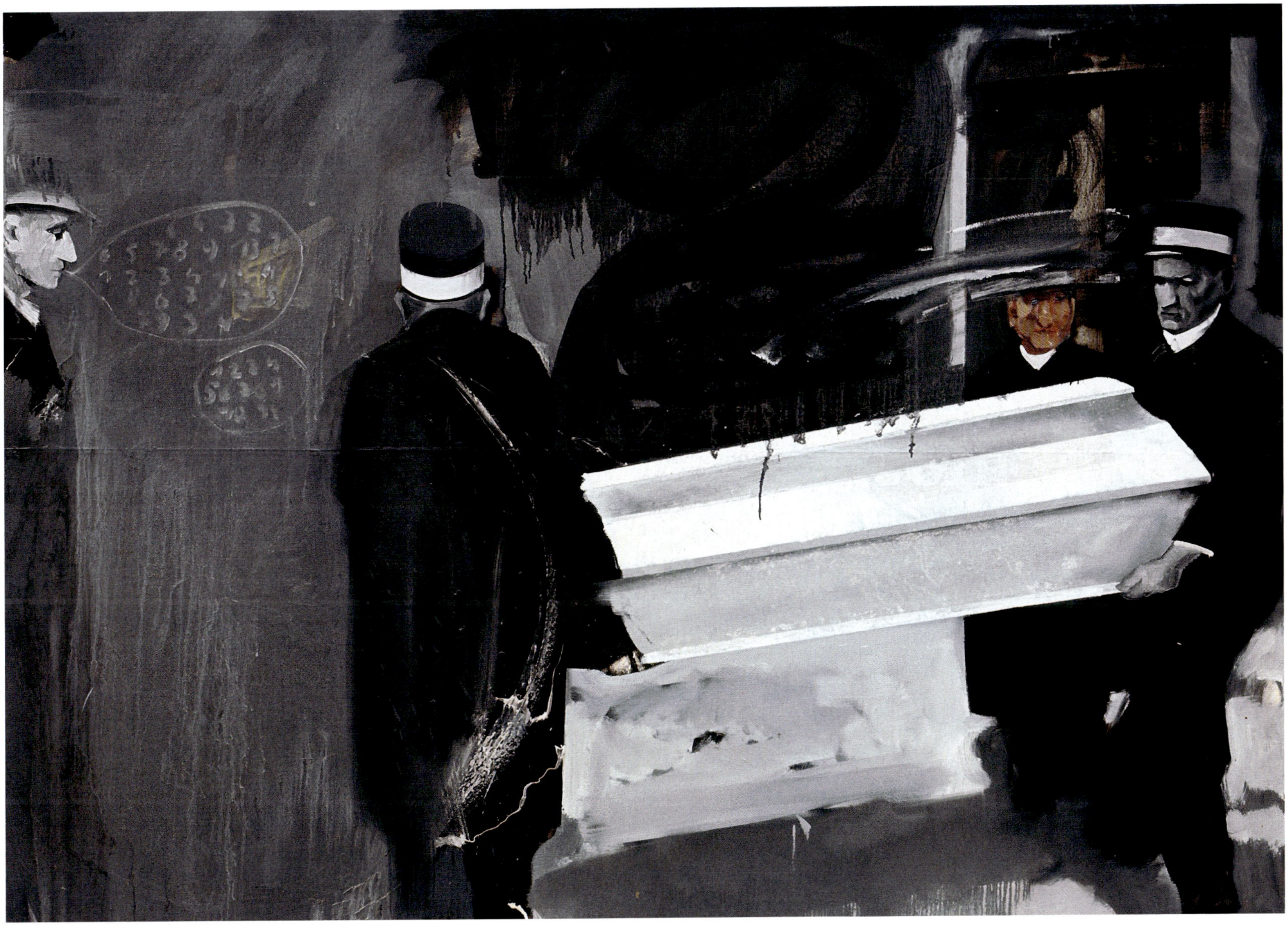

Family at the Seaside, 1964 59 1/16 × 78 3/4 in. (150 × 200 cm)

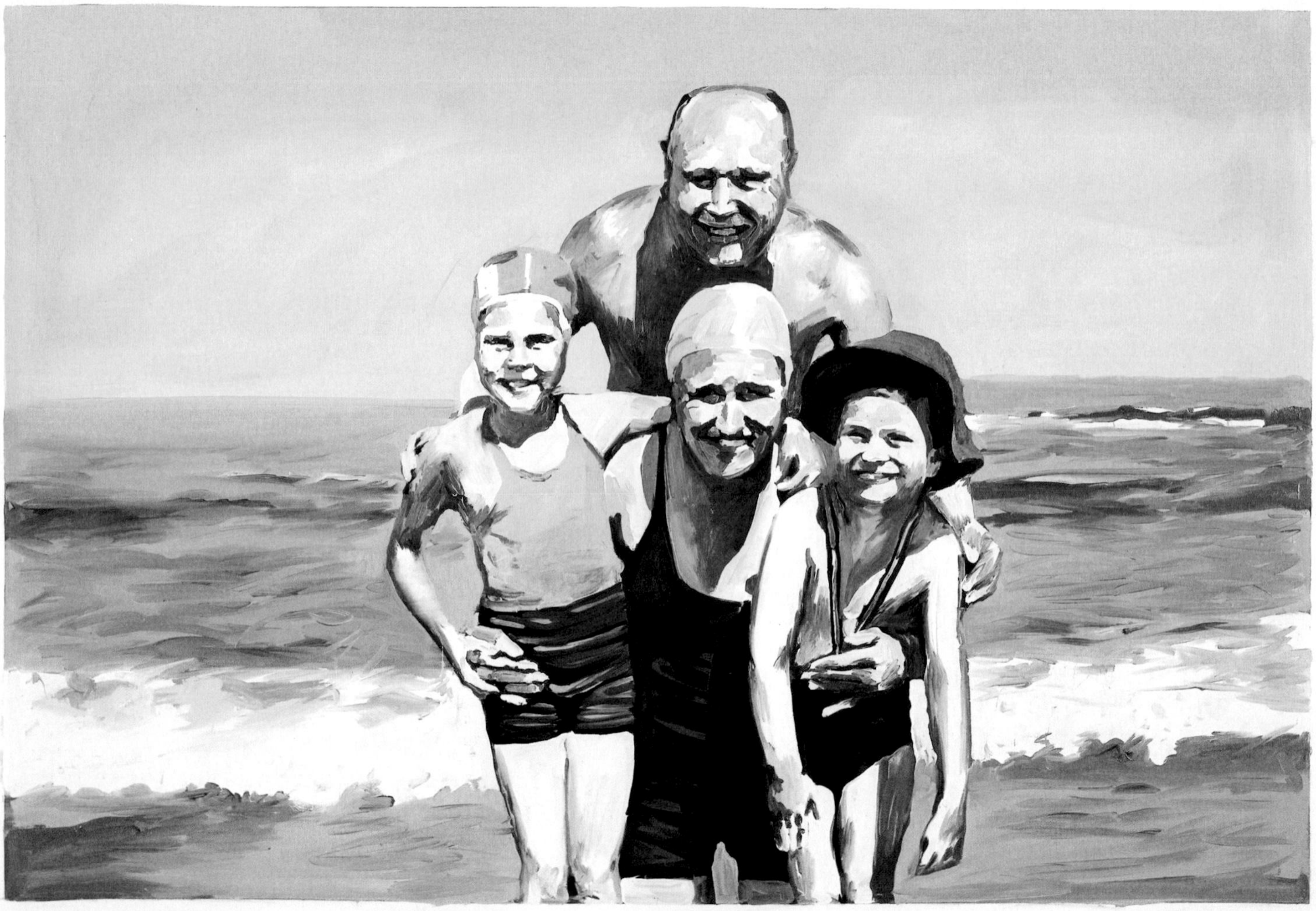

Administrative Building, 1964   38 9/16 × 59 1/16 in. (98 × 150 cm)

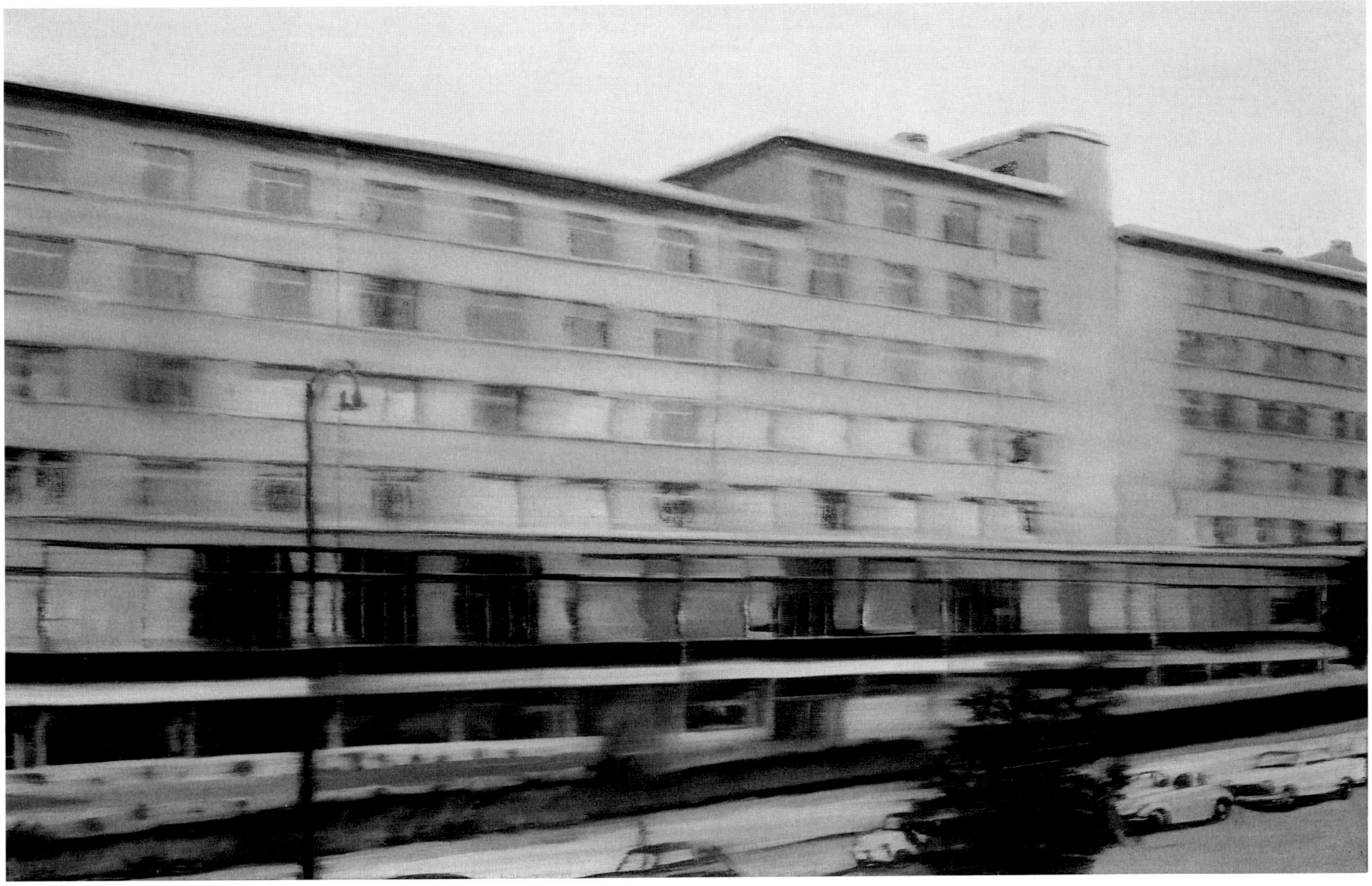

Aunt Marianne, 1965/2018 $39\,^3/_8 \times 45\,^1/_4$ in. (100 × 115 cm)

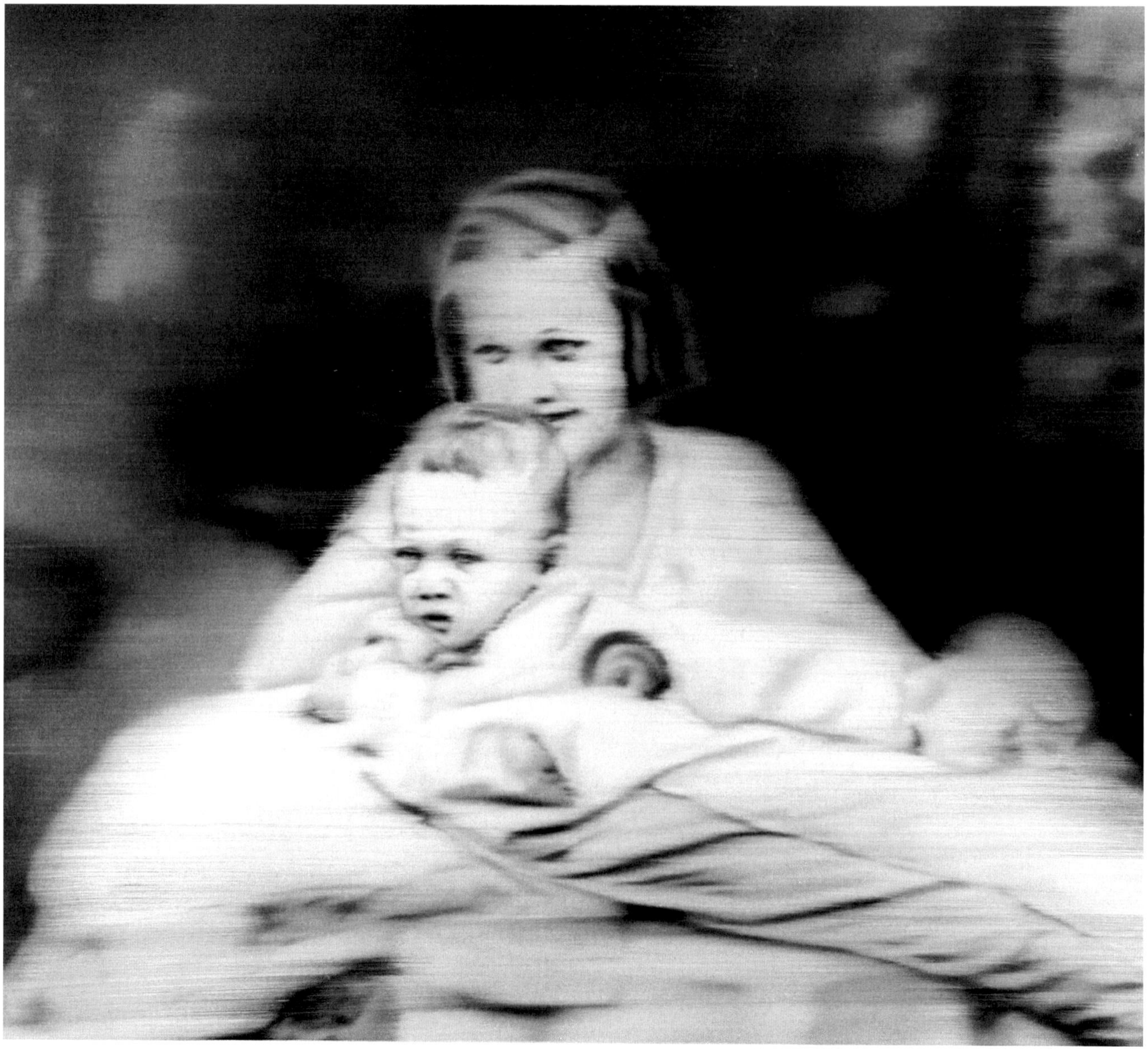

Uncle Rudi, 1965 34 ¼ × 19 ¼ in. (87 × 50 cm)

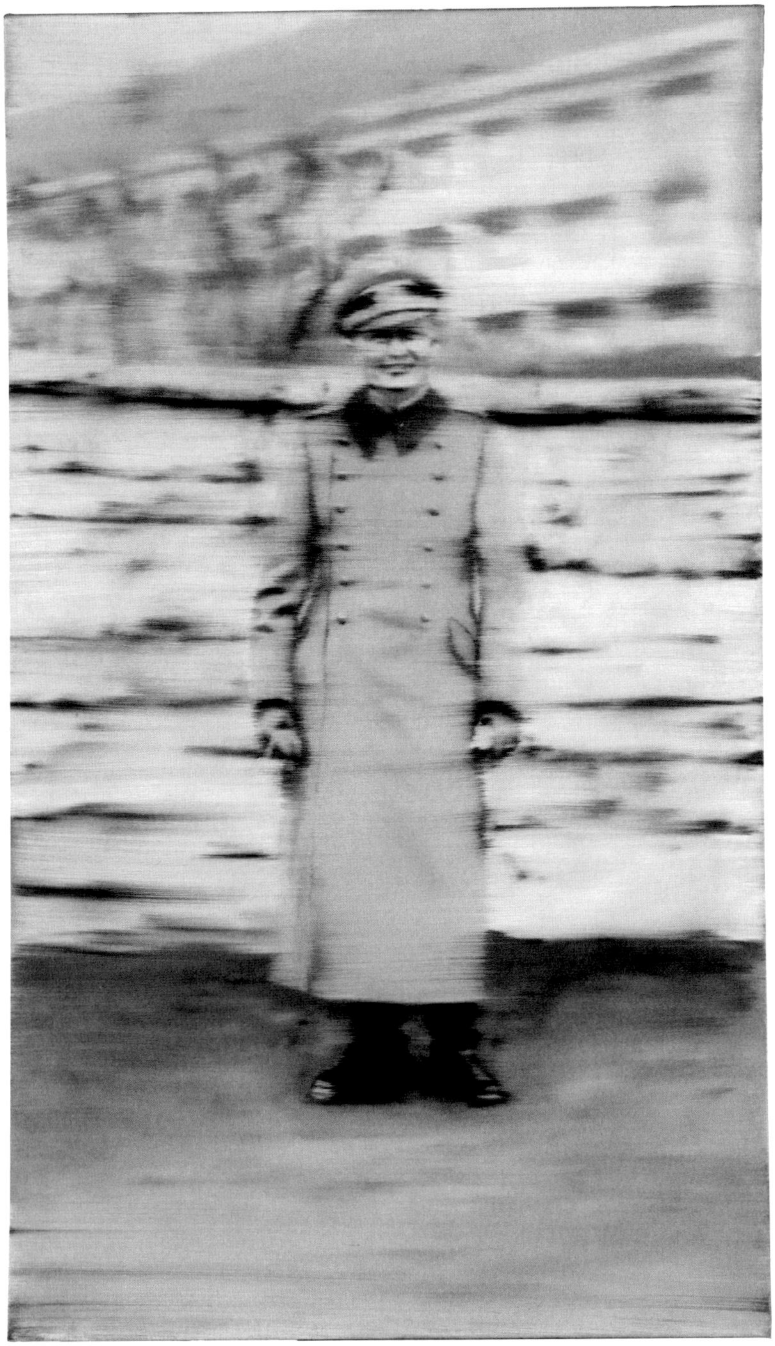

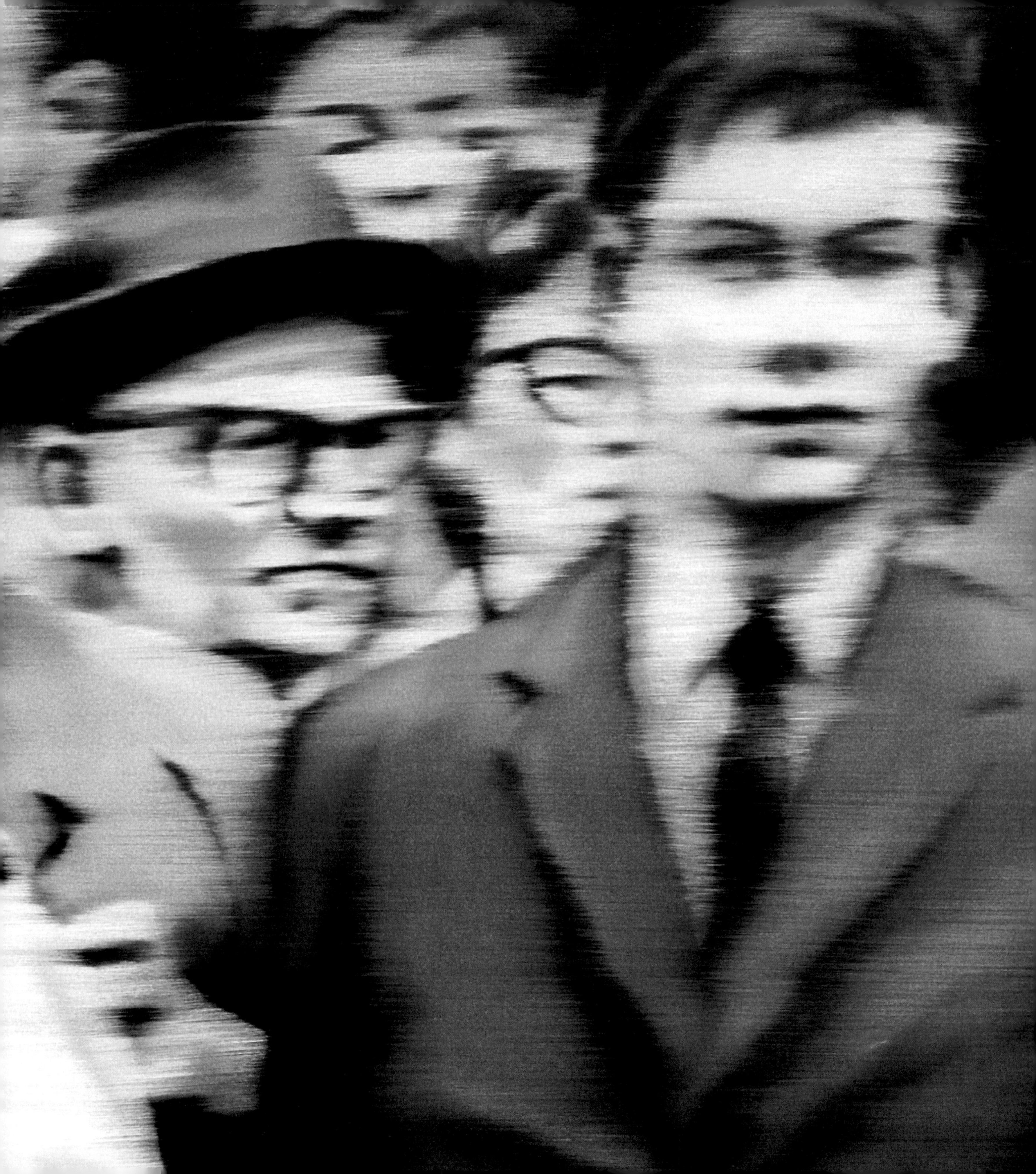

Group of People, 1965   66 15⁄16 × 78 ¾ in. (170 × 200 cm)

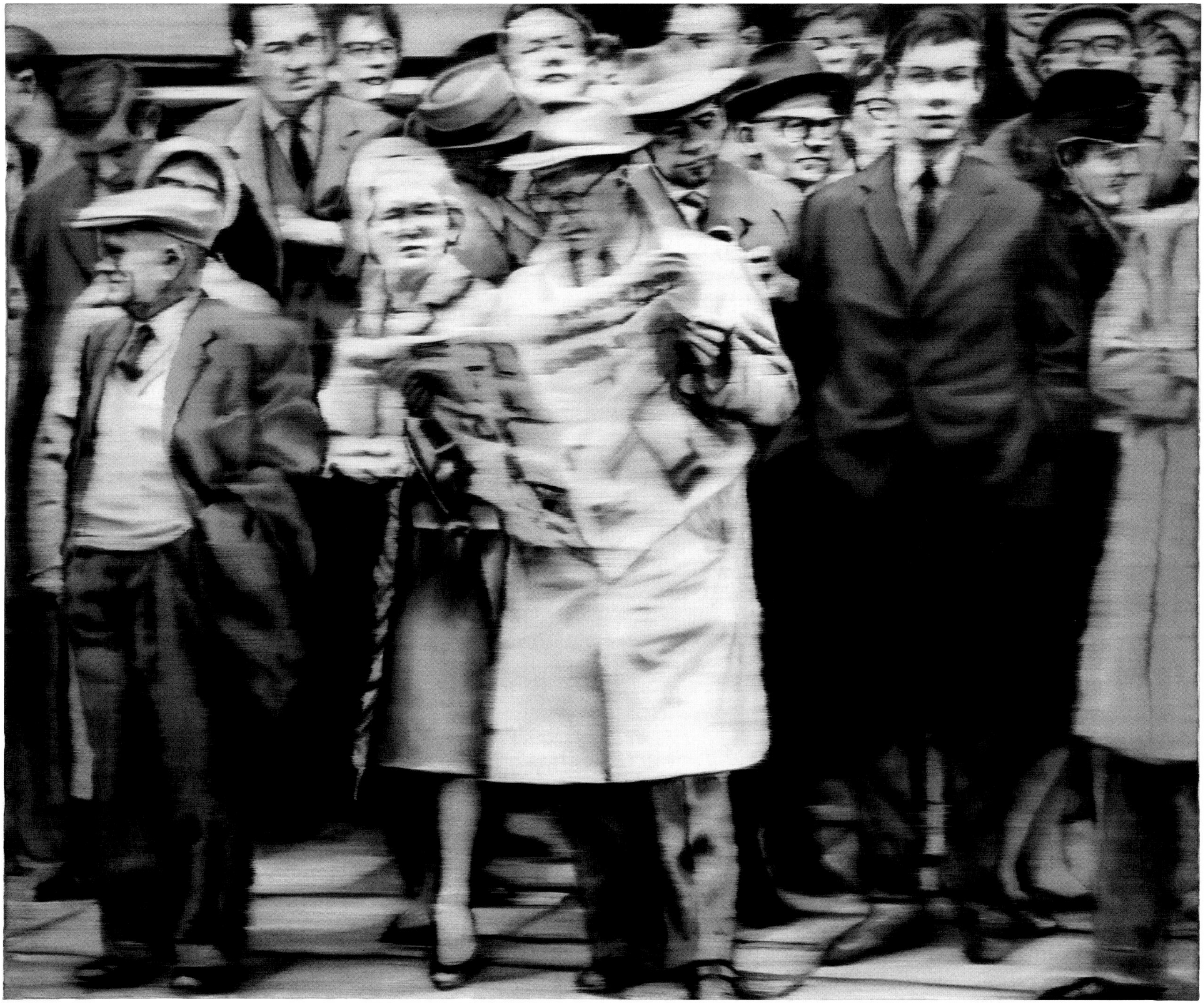

Kitchen Chair, 1965   39 3/8 × 31 1/2 in. (100 × 80 cm)

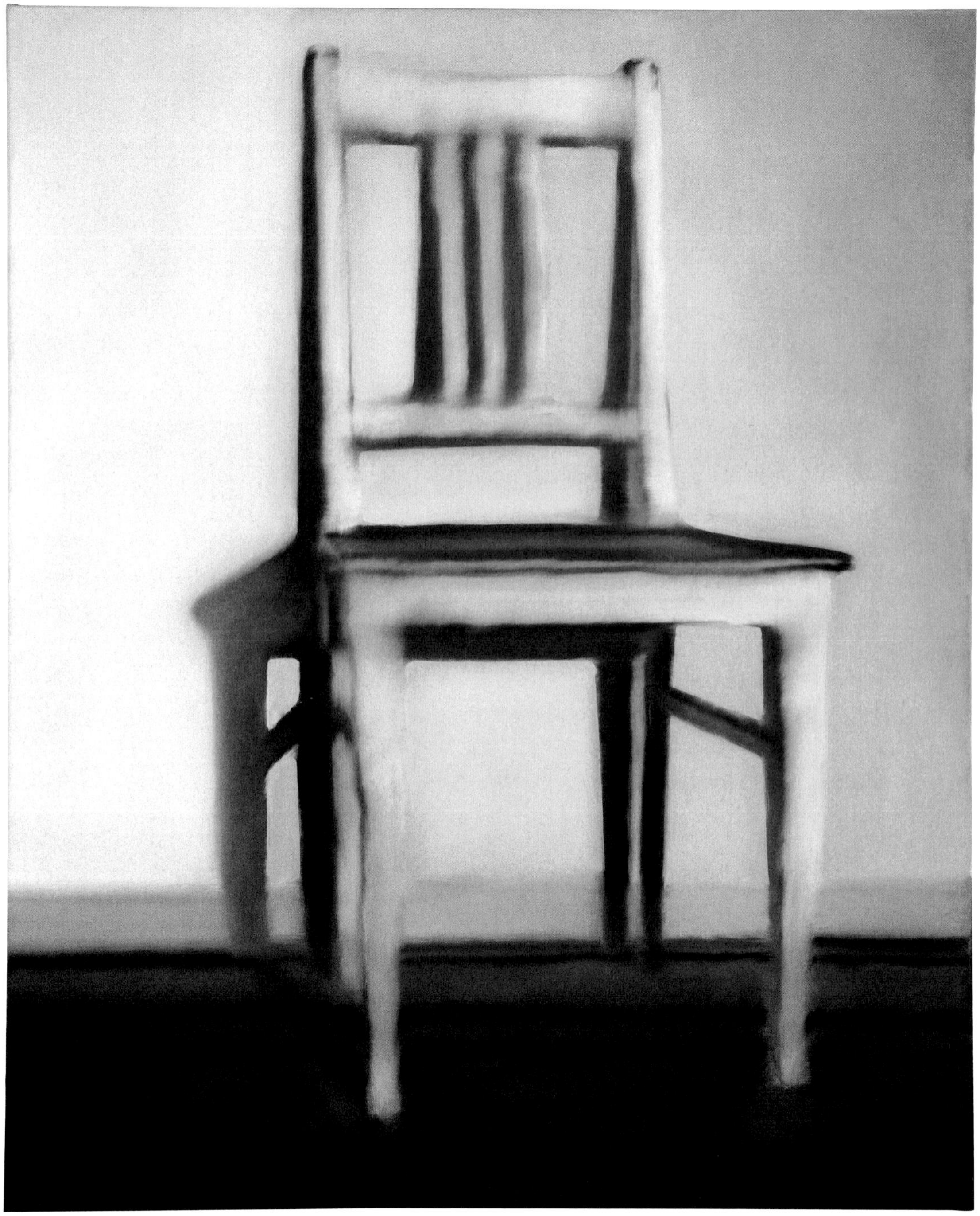

Mr. Heyde, 1965   21 ⅝ × 25 ⁹⁄₁₆ in. (55 × 65 cm)

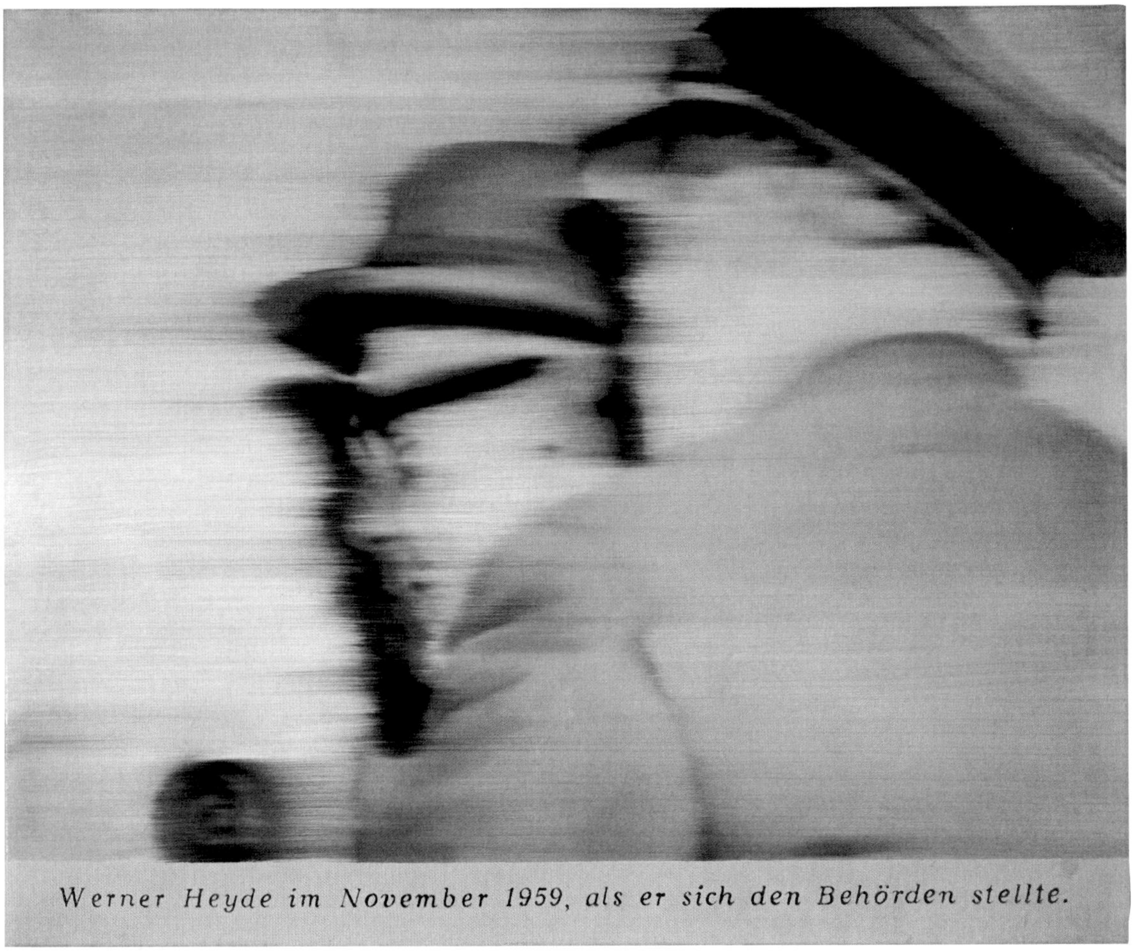

Eight Student Nurses, 1966   each panel 37 ⅜ × 27 ½ in. (95 × 70 cm)

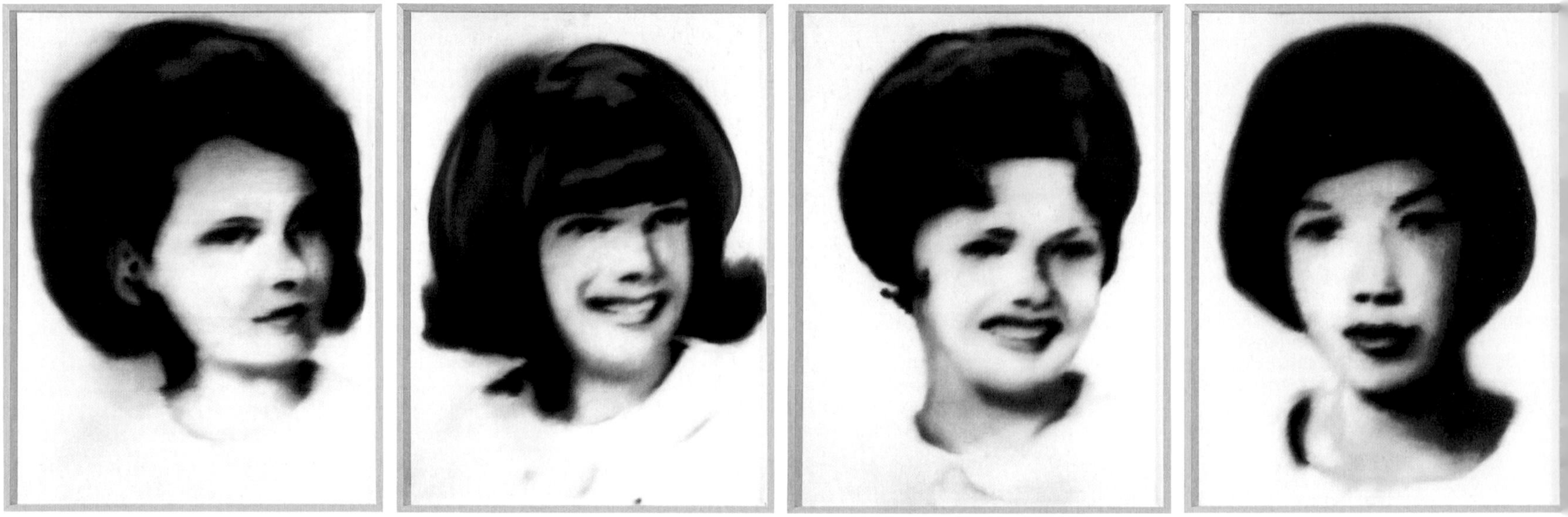

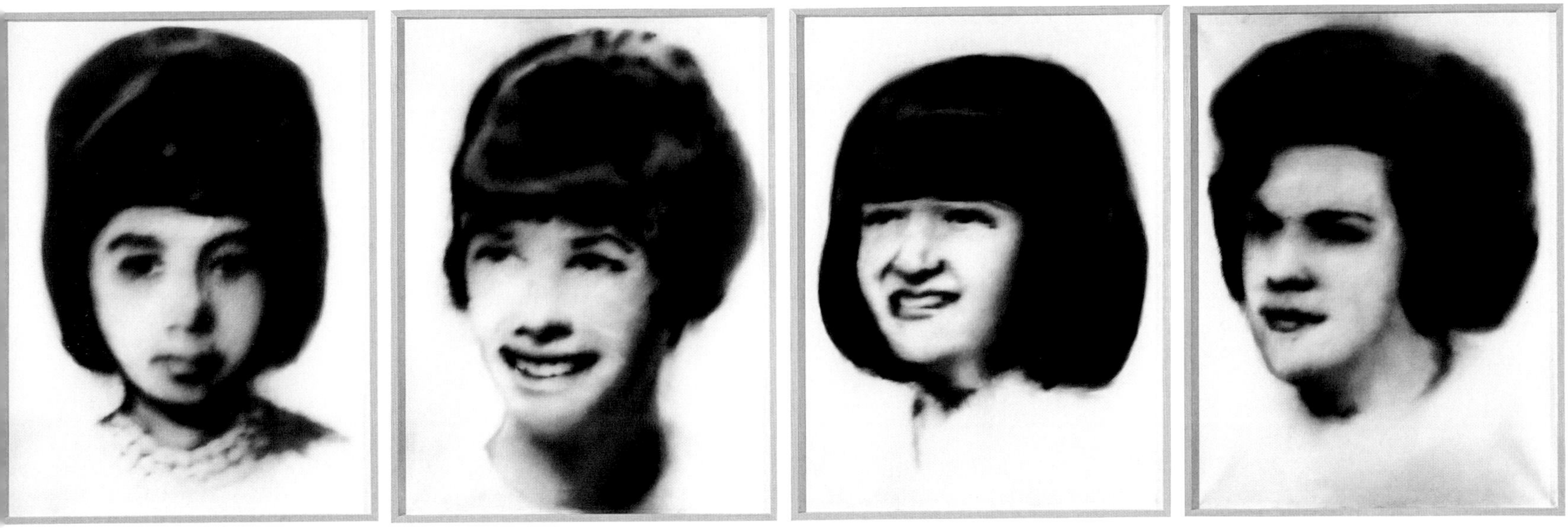

4 Panes of Glass, 1967 each framed pane 77 3/16 × 41 ¾ in. (196 × 106 cm)

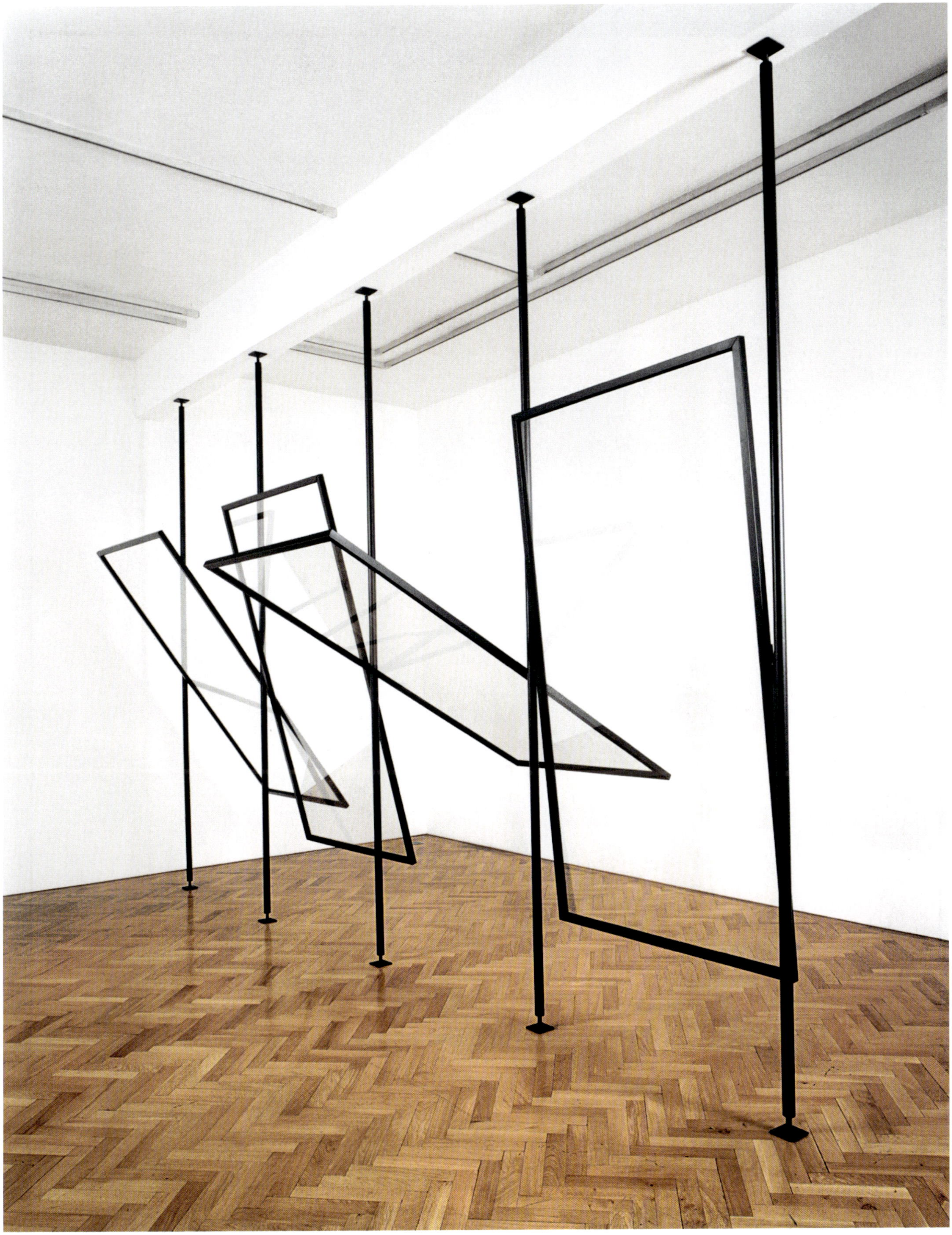

Townscape Paris, 1968 78 ¾ × 78 ¾ in. (200 × 200 cm)

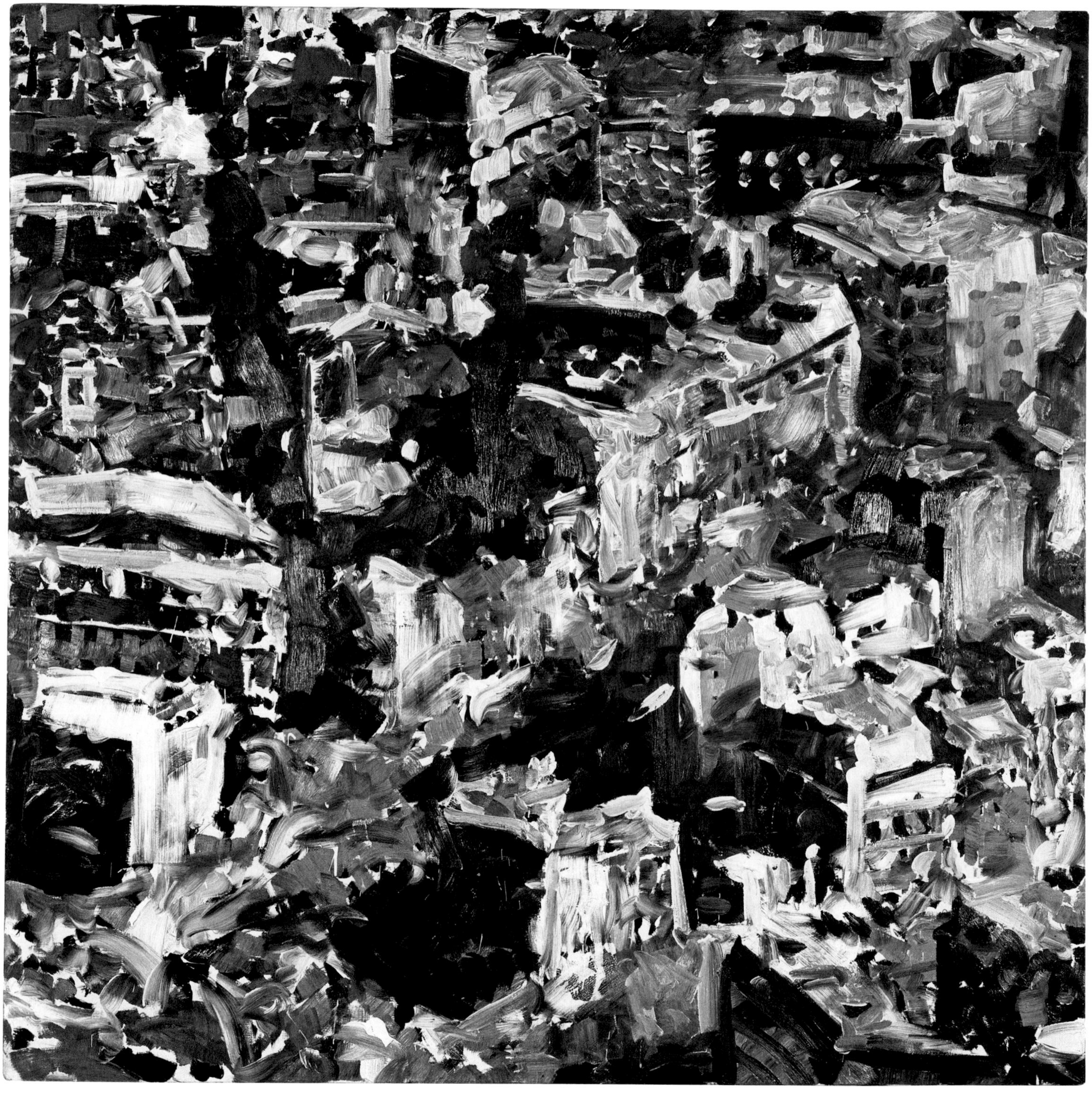

Townscape Madrid, 1968 9 ft. 1 1/16 in. × 9 ft. 6 15/16 in. (277 × 292 cm)

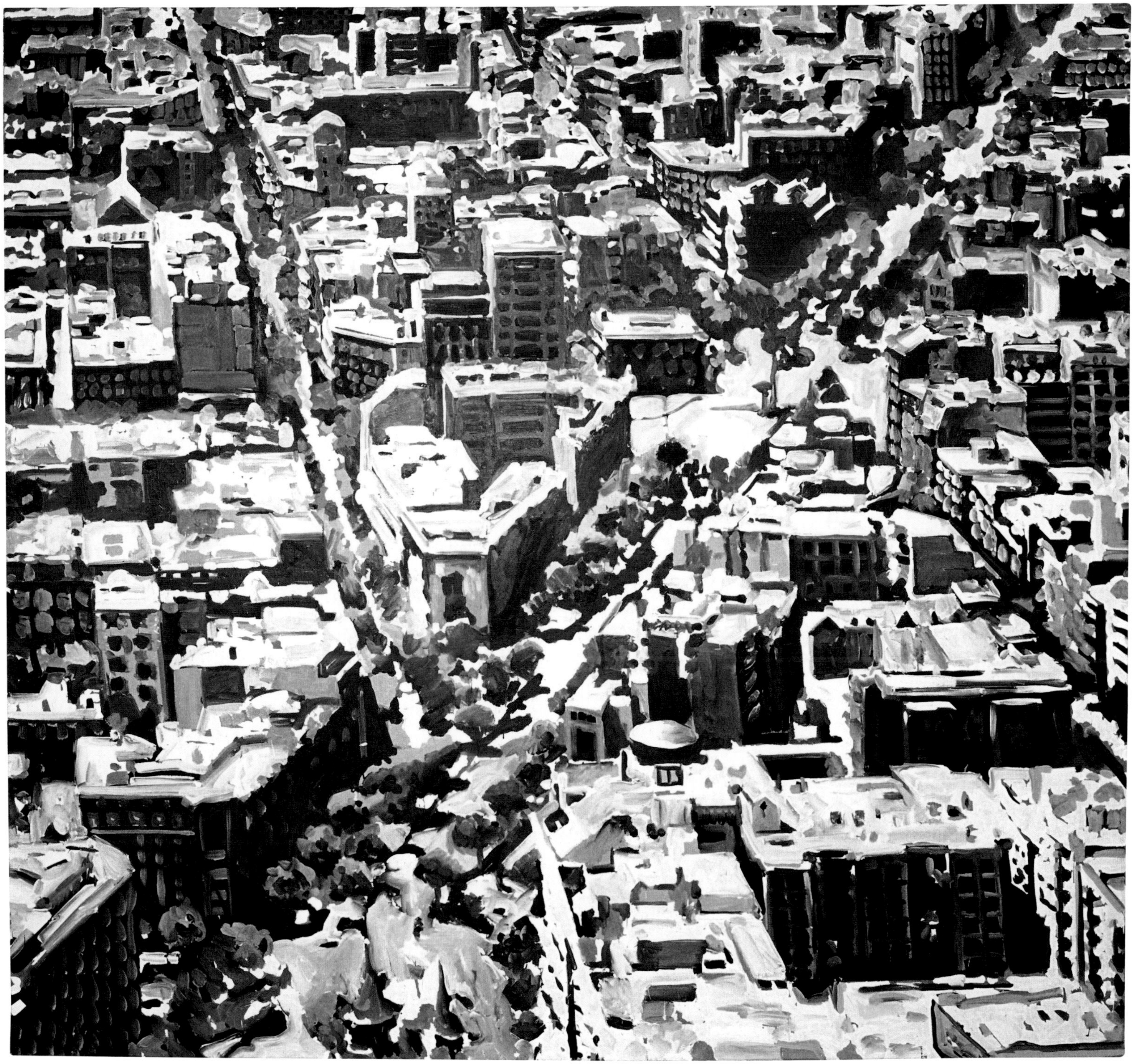

Alps, 1968   78 ¾ in. × 21 ft. 3 ⅞ in. (200 × 650 cm)

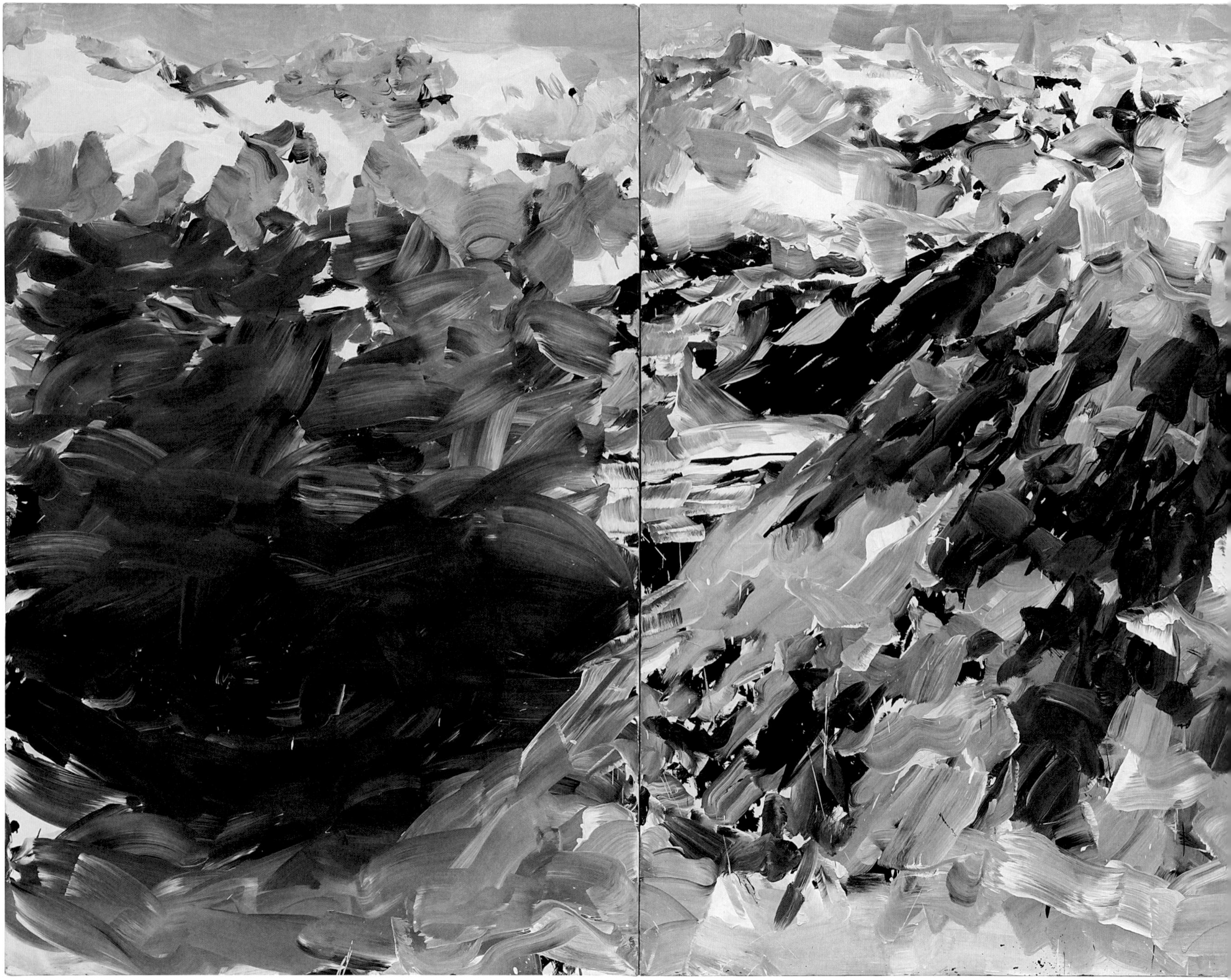

Untitled, 1968 31 ½ × 15 ¾ in. (80 × 40 cm)

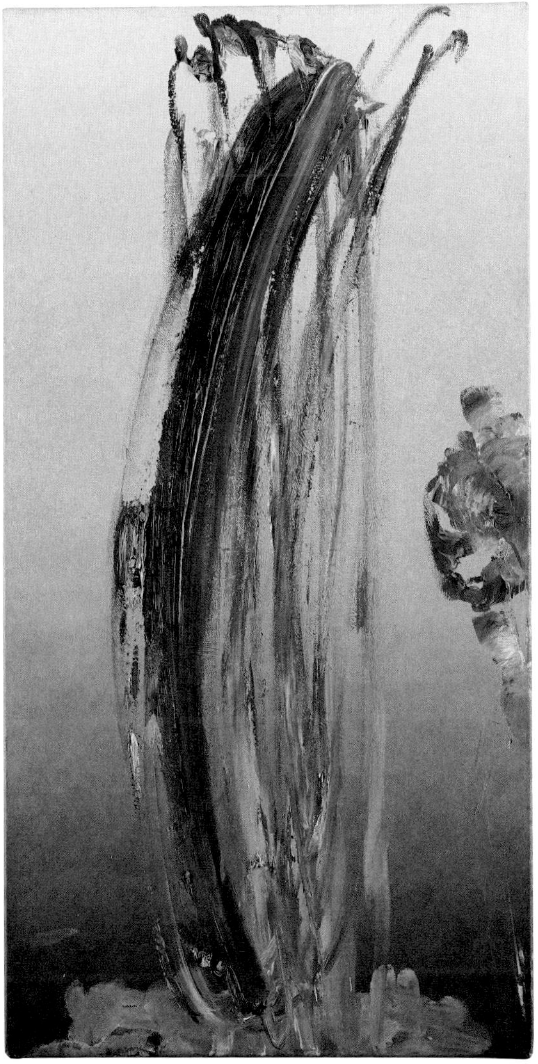

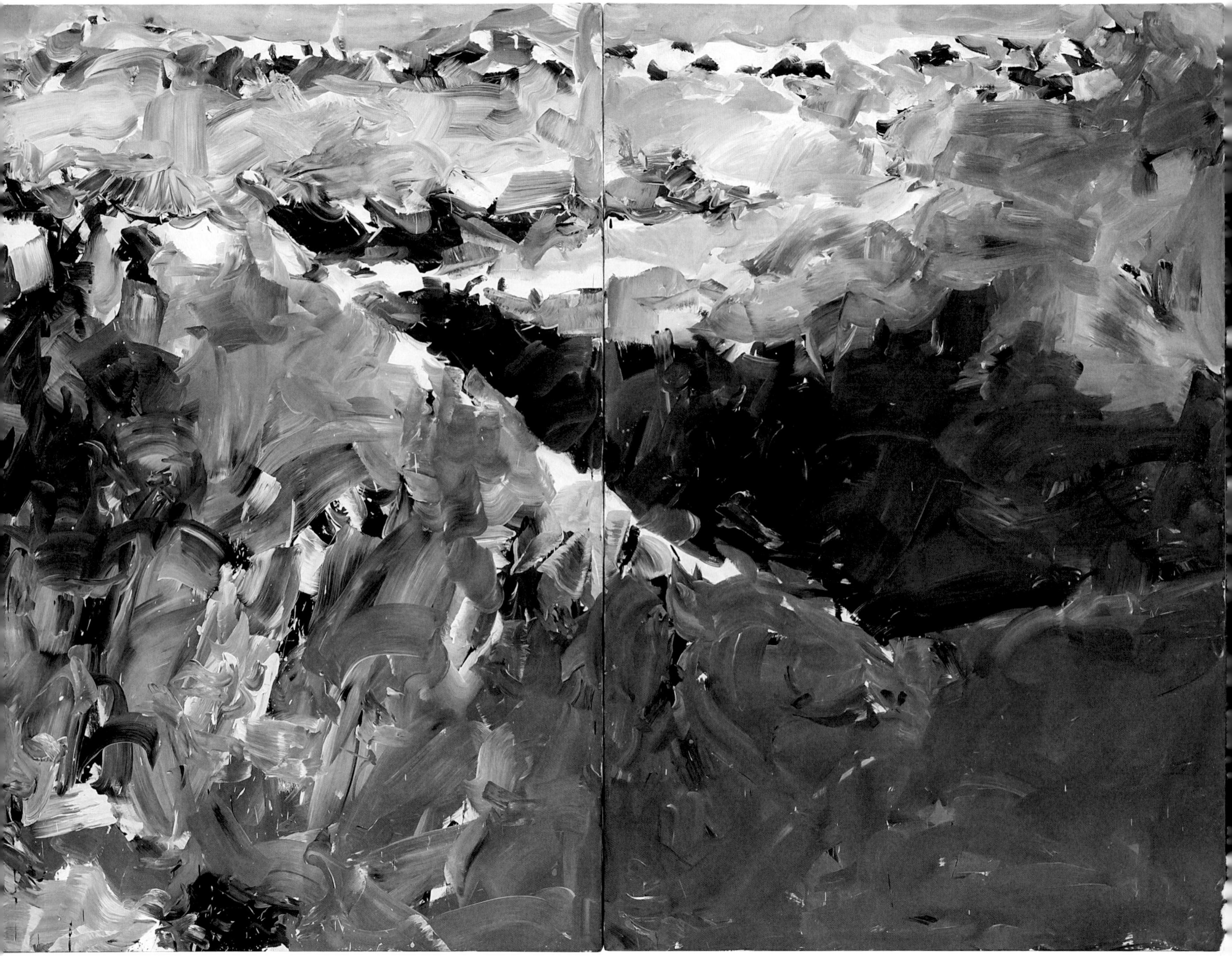

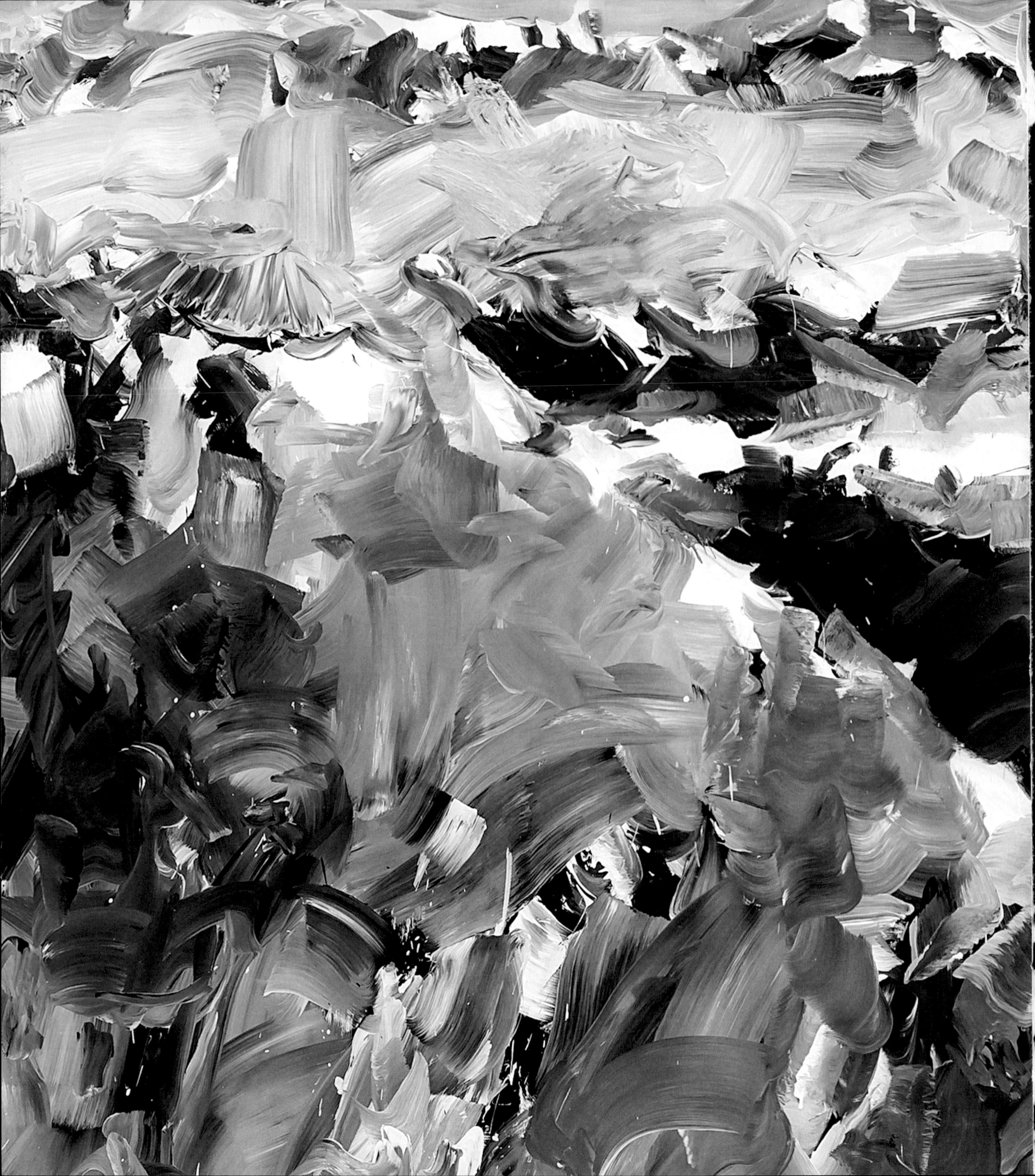

Vintage, 1968 $37\frac{3}{8} \times 45\frac{1}{4}$ in. (95×115 cm)

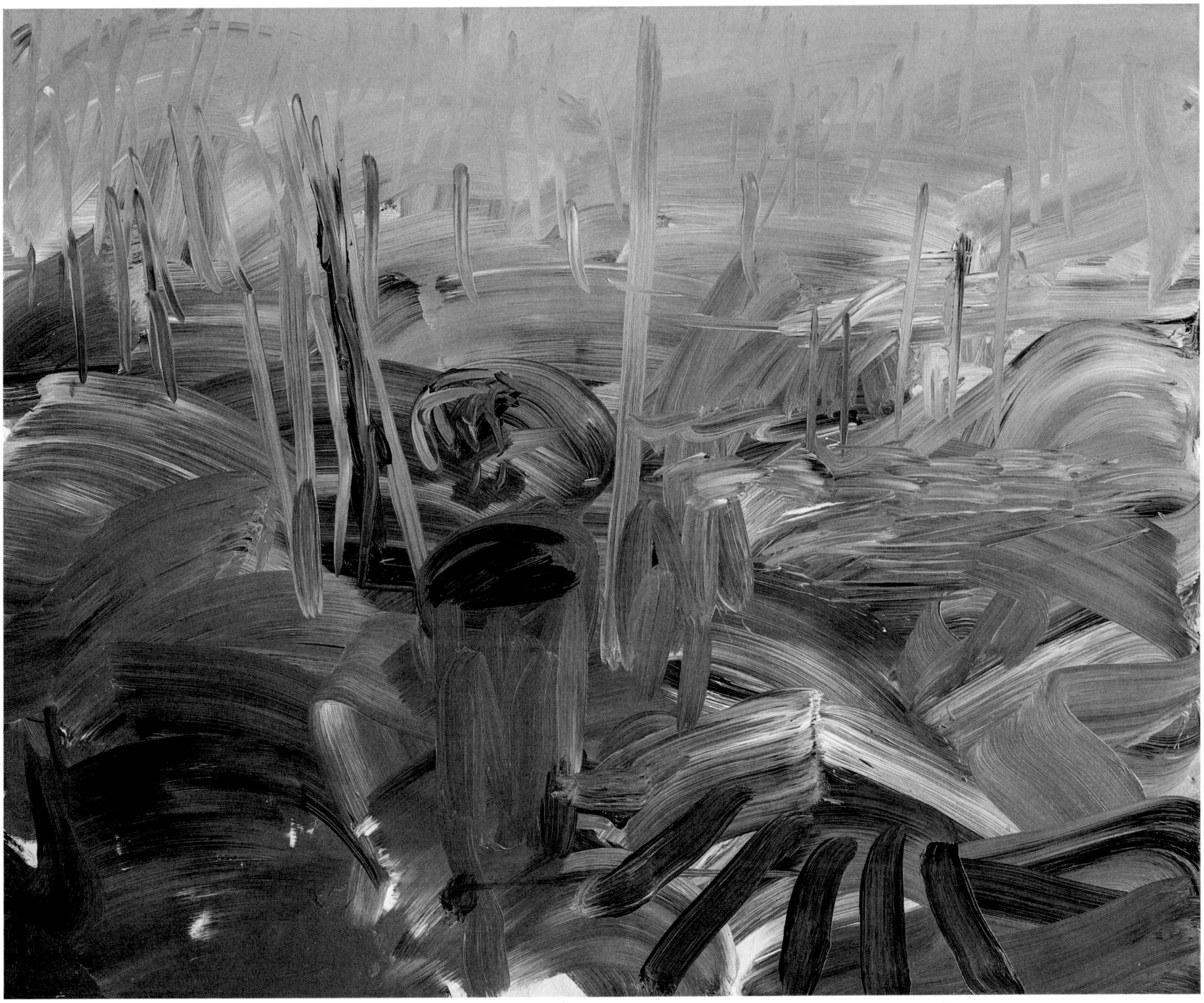

Star Picture, 1969 27 9/16 × 27 9/16 in. (70 × 70 cm)

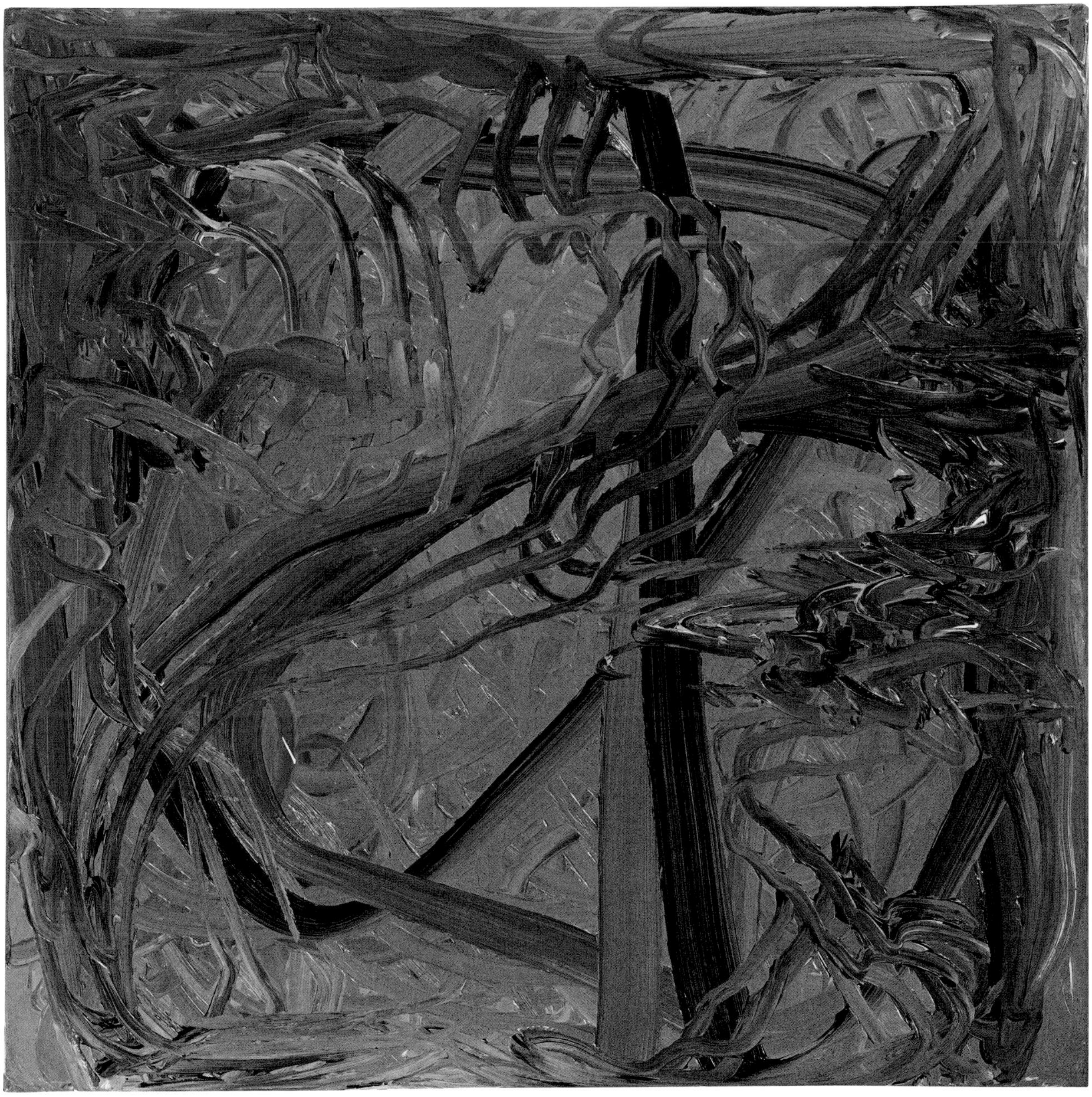

Star Picture, 1969 $27\frac{9}{16} \times 27\frac{9}{16}$ in. (70 × 70 cm)

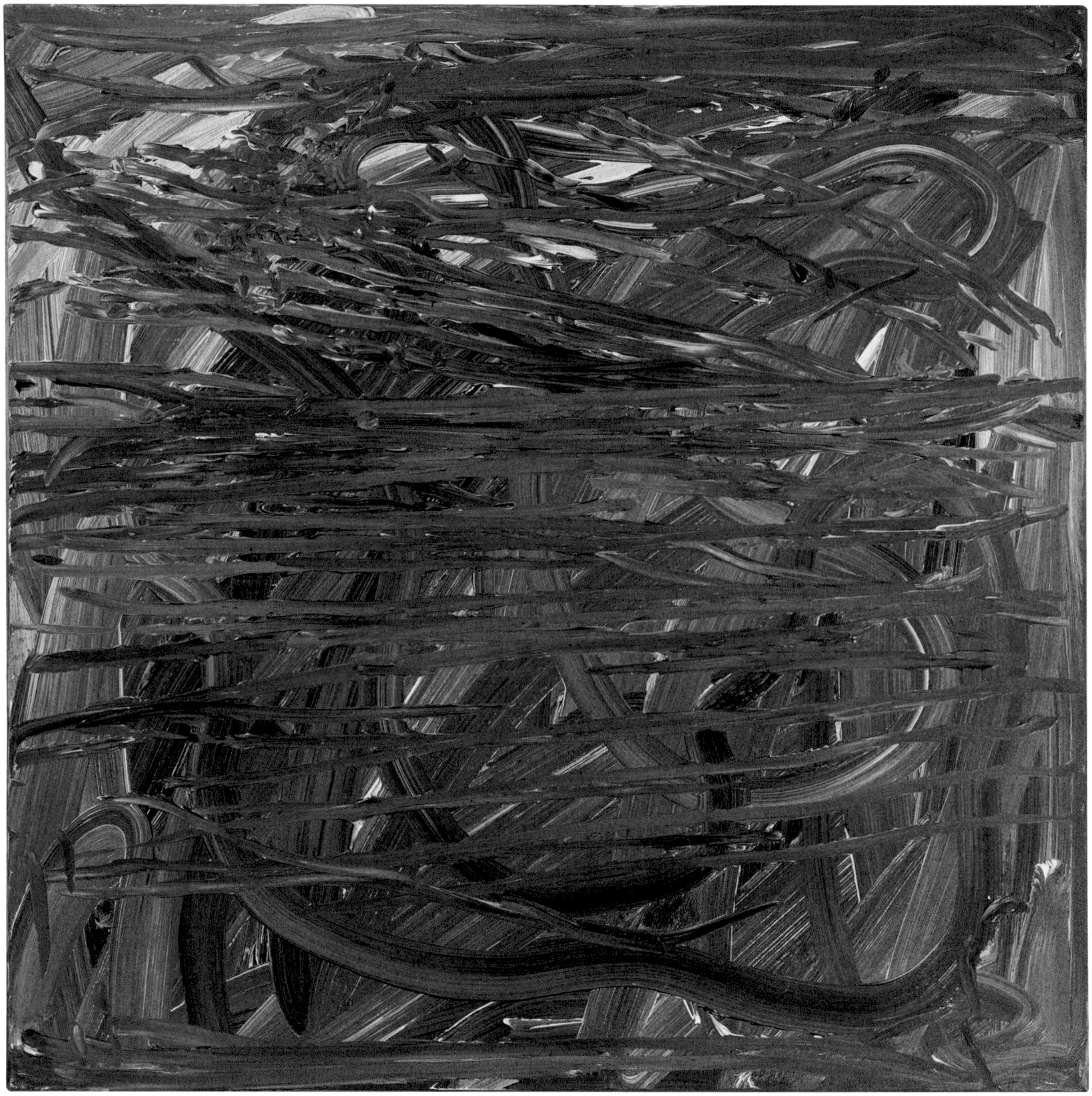

Star Picture, 1969 27 9/16 × 27 9/16 in. (70 × 70 cm)

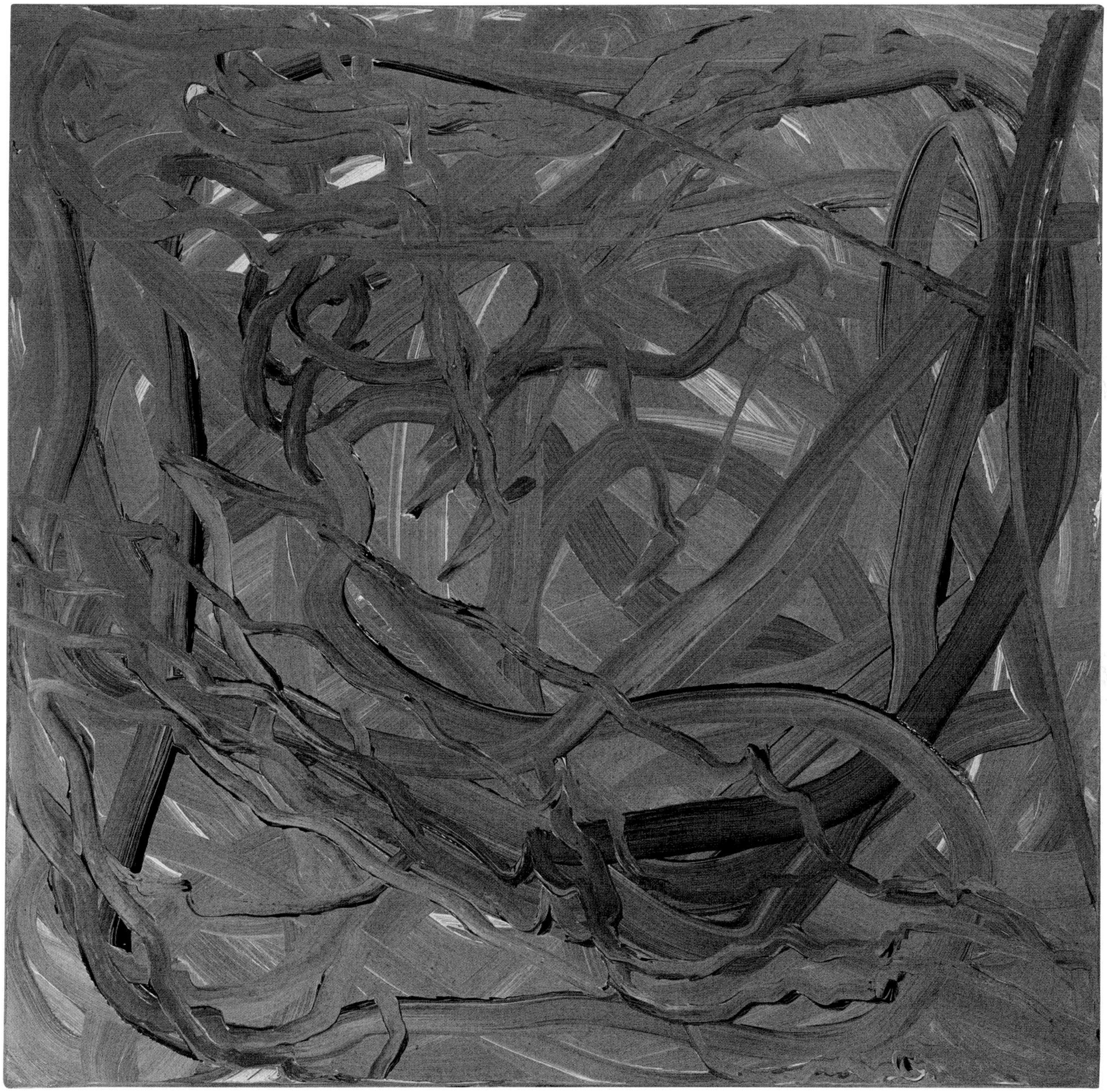

Study for Clouds (Contre-jour), 1970   31 ½ × 39 ⅜ in. (80 × 100 cm)

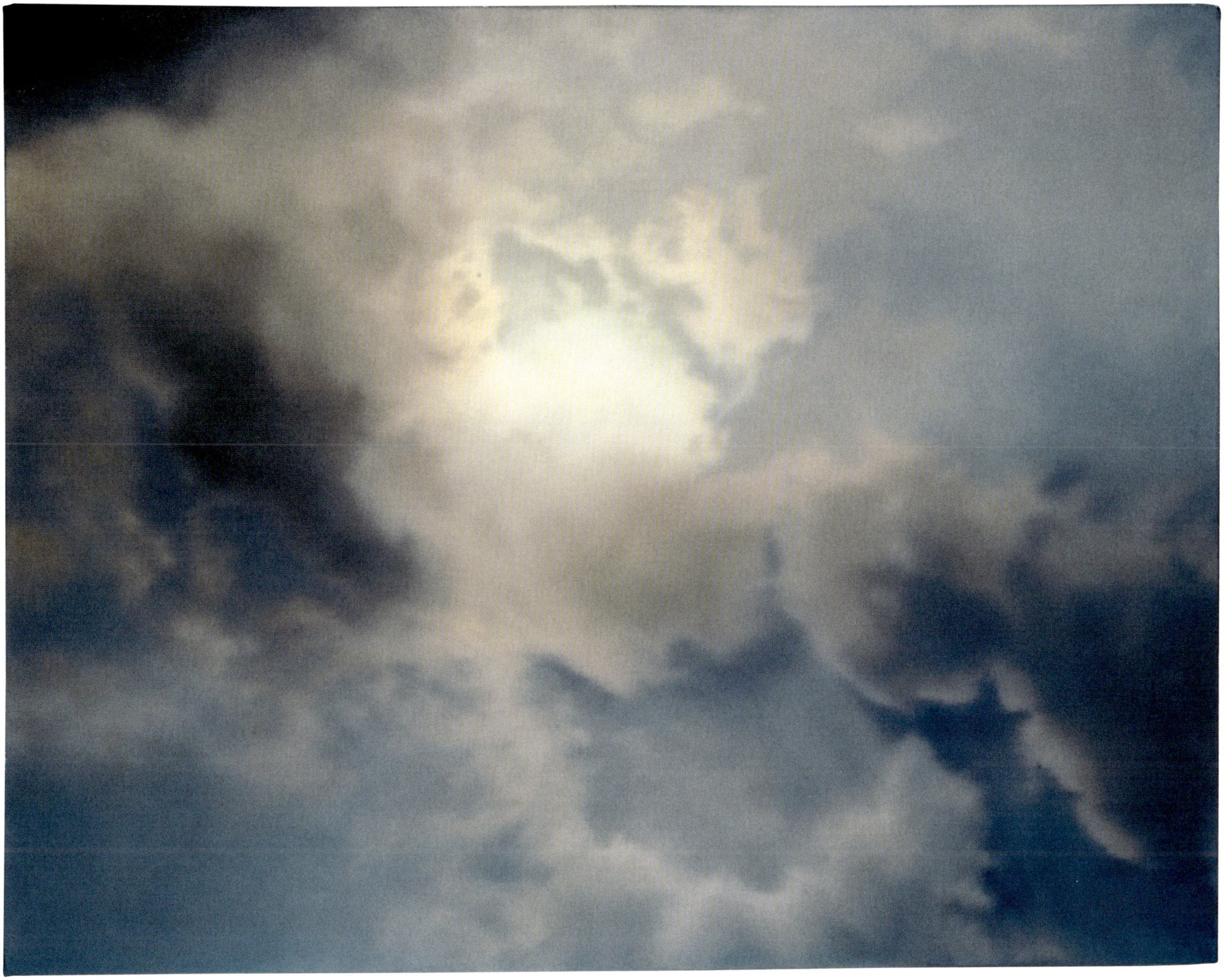

Brigid Polk, 1971   39 ⅜ × 49 3/16 in. (100 × 125 cm)

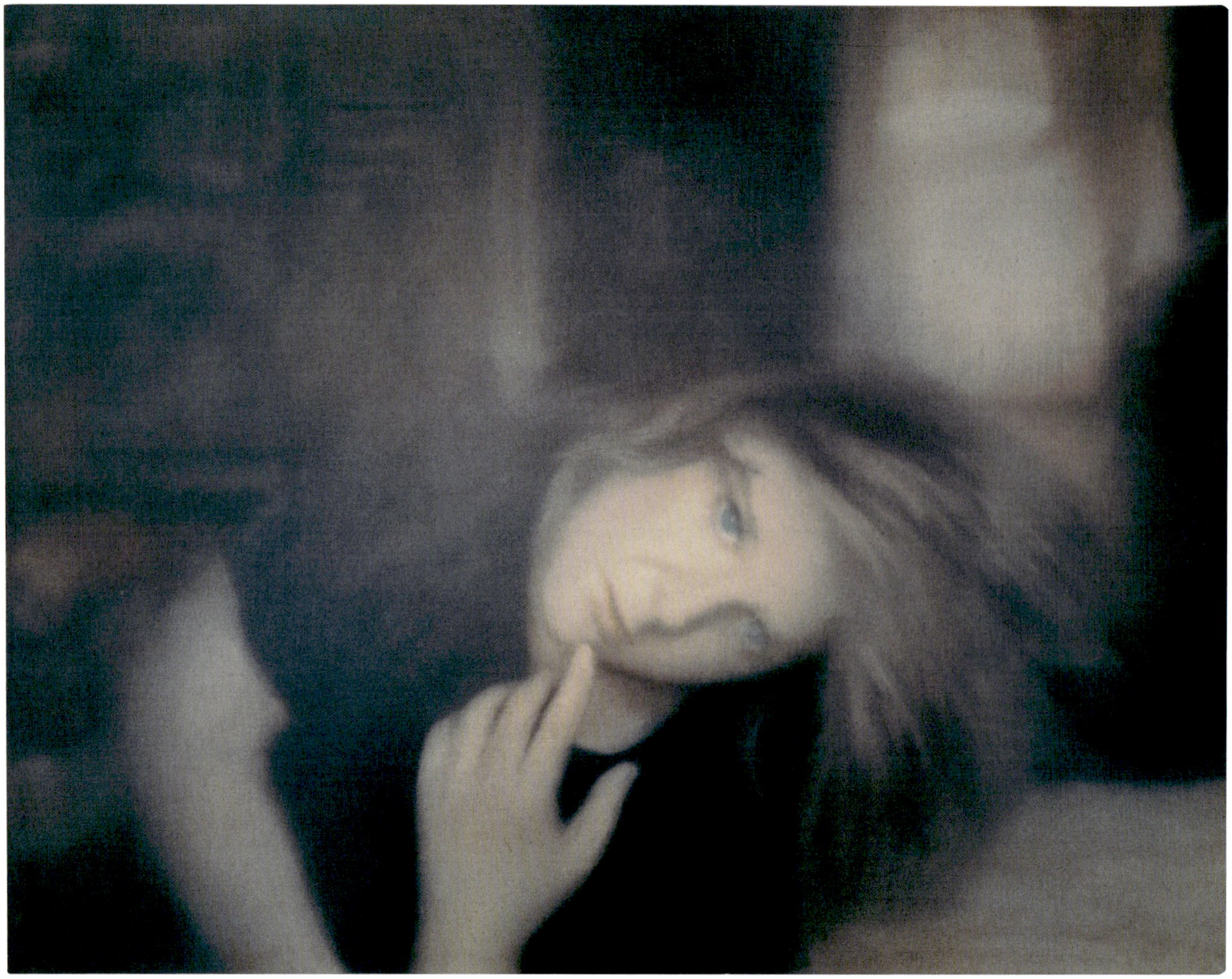

Gray (Bark), 1973   35 7/16 × 25 9/16 in. (90 × 65 cm)

Gilbert, 1975 25 9/16 × 23 5/8 in. (65 × 60 cm)

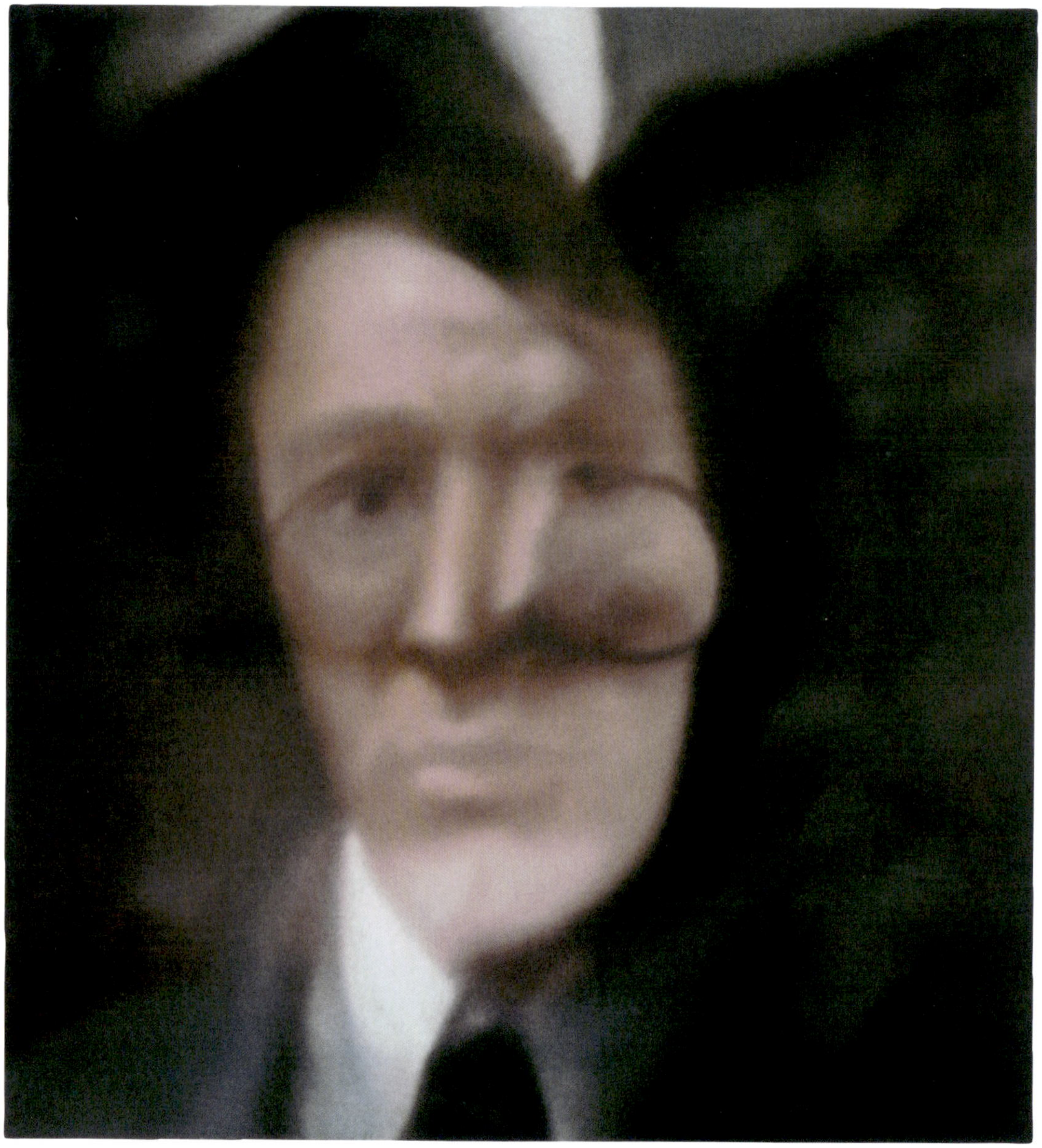

George, 1975 25 9/16 × 23 5/8 in. (65 × 60 cm)

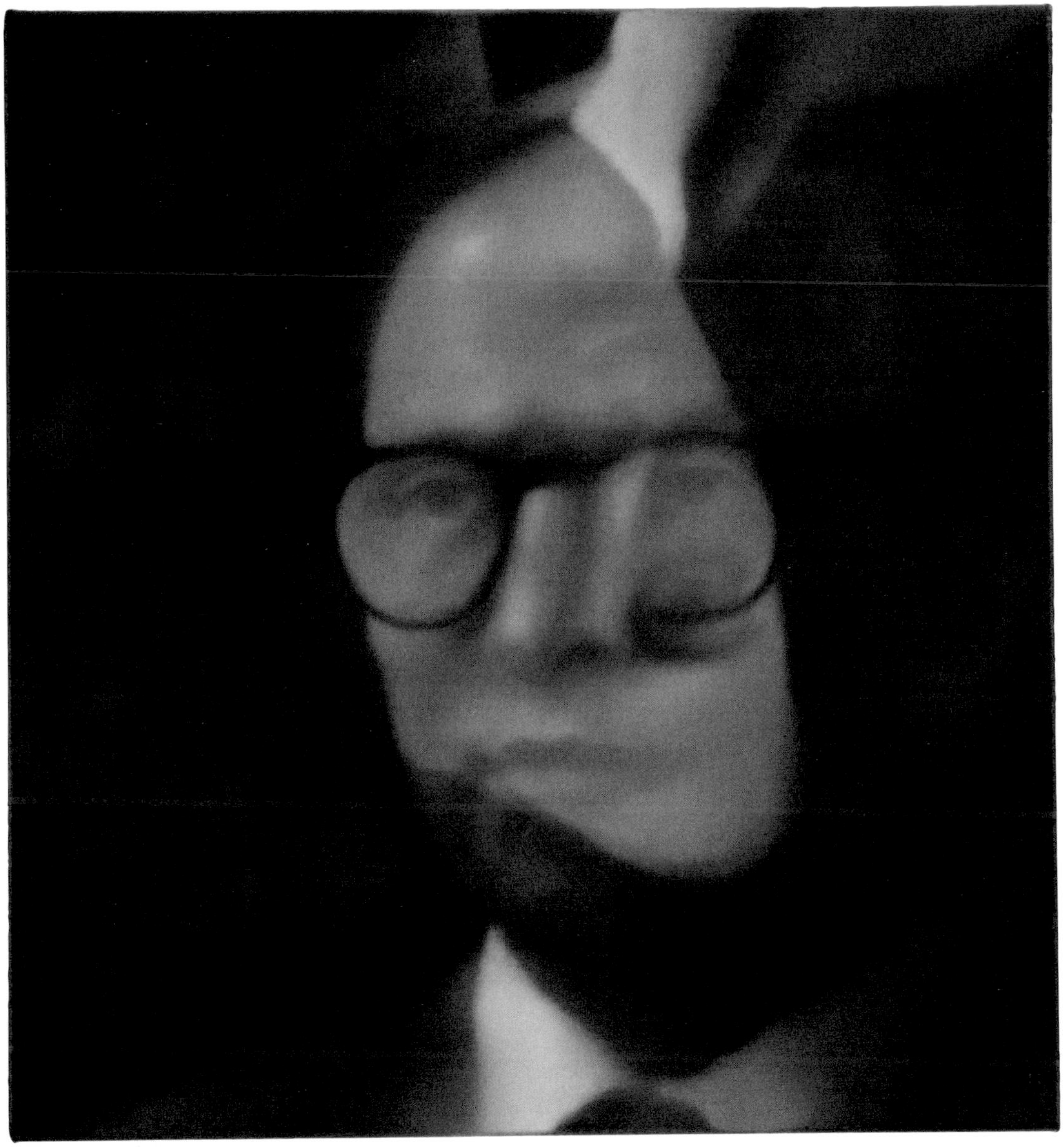

Seascape, 1975 78 ¾ in. × 9 ft. 10 ⅛ in. (200 × 300 cm)

Seascape, 1975   78 ¾ in. × 9 ft. 10 ⅛ in. (200 × 300 cm)

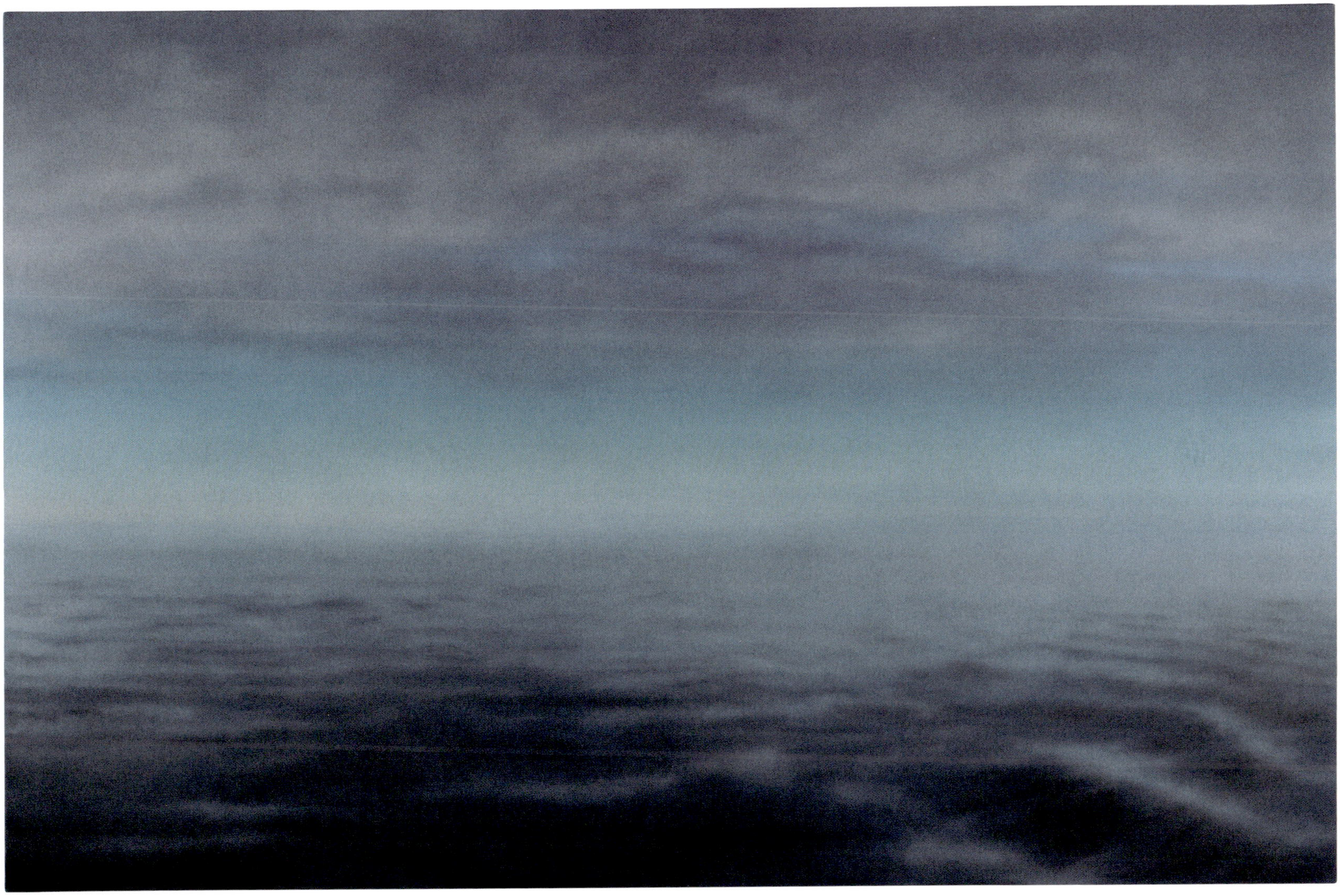

Vesuvius, 1976 28 ¾ × 41 5⁄16 in. (73 × 105 cm)

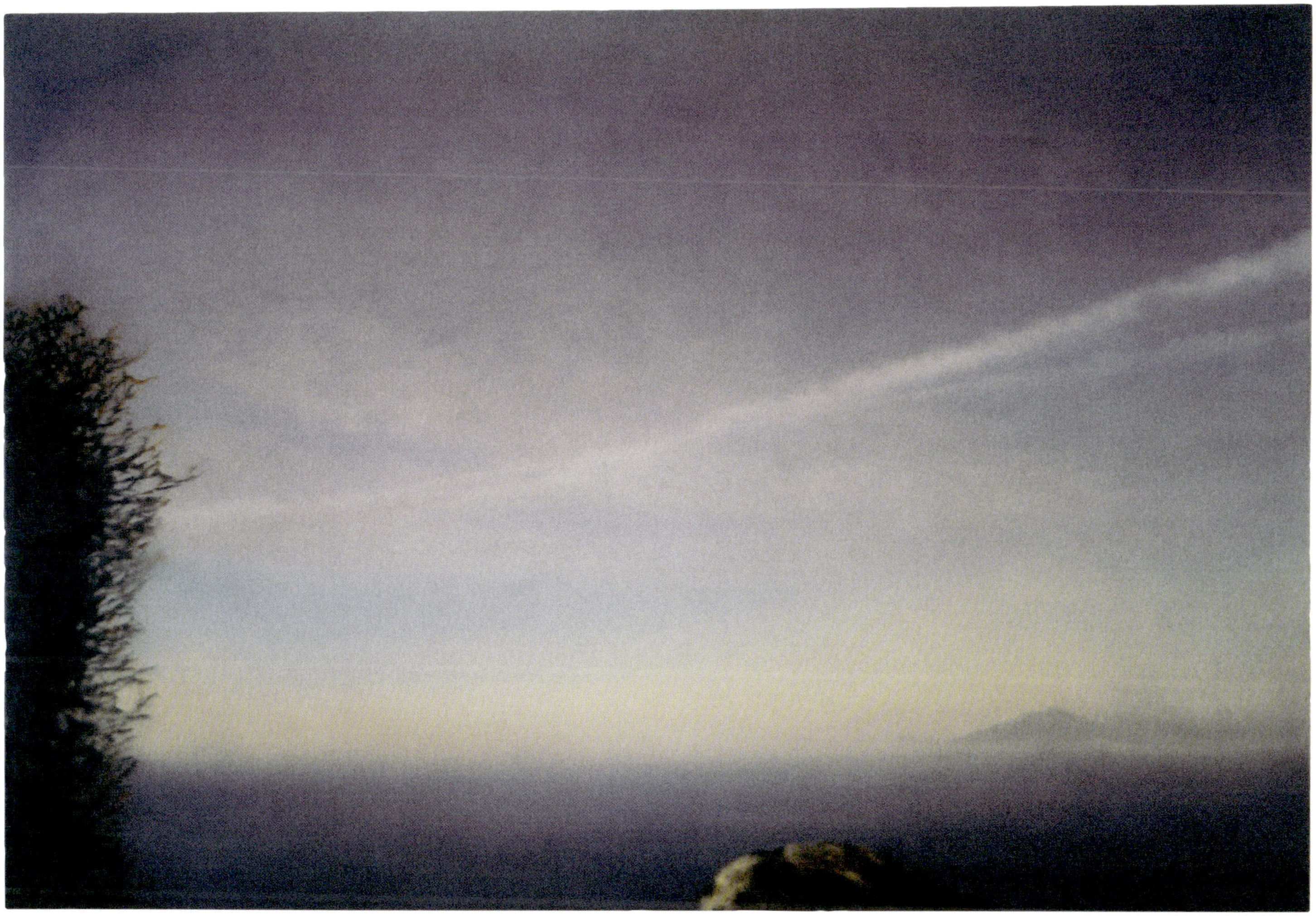

Betty, 1977   11 $^{13}/_{16}$ × 15 ¾ in. (30 × 40 cm)

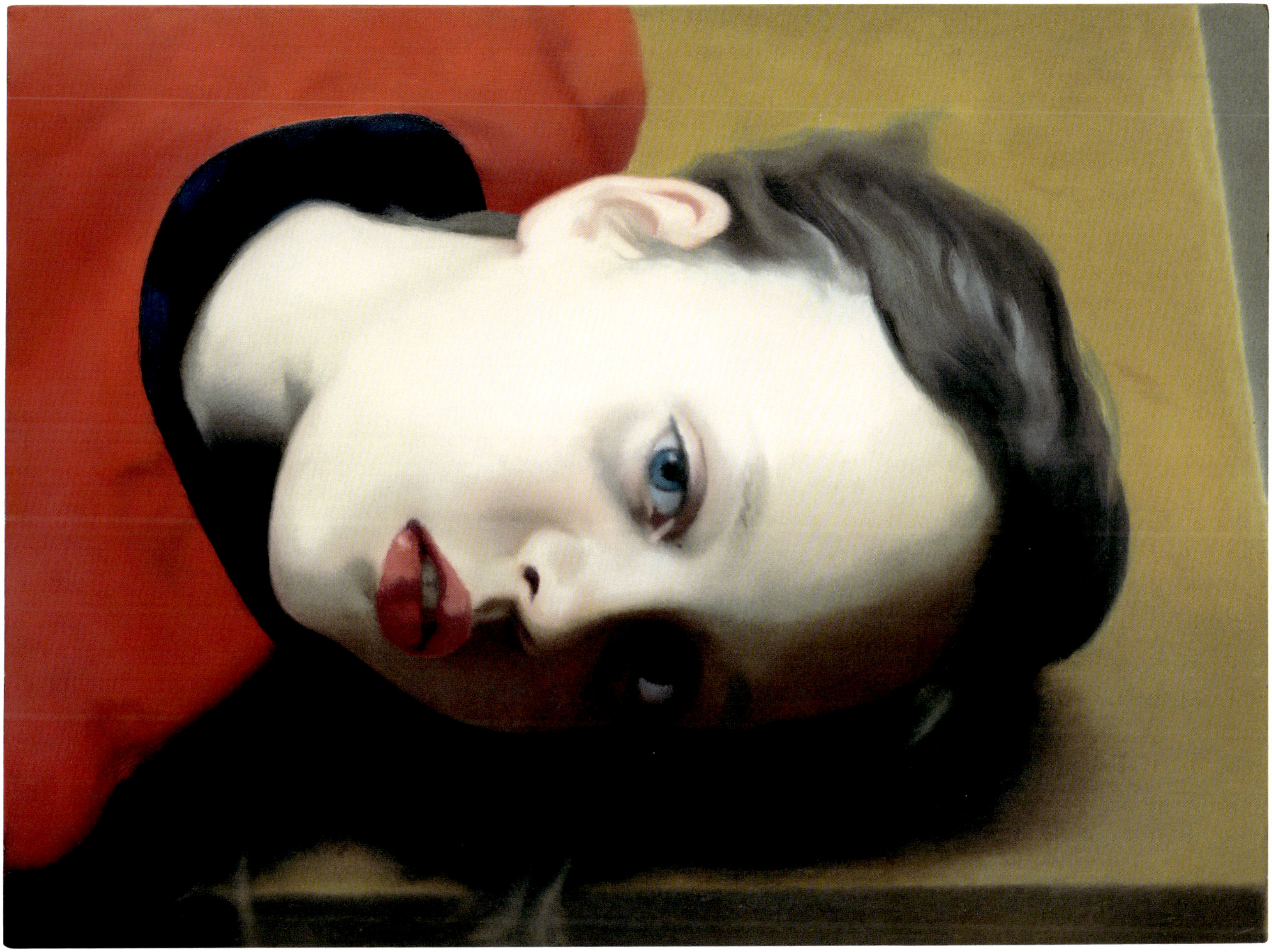

Betty, 1977 19 11/16 × 15 3/4 in. (50 × 40 cm)

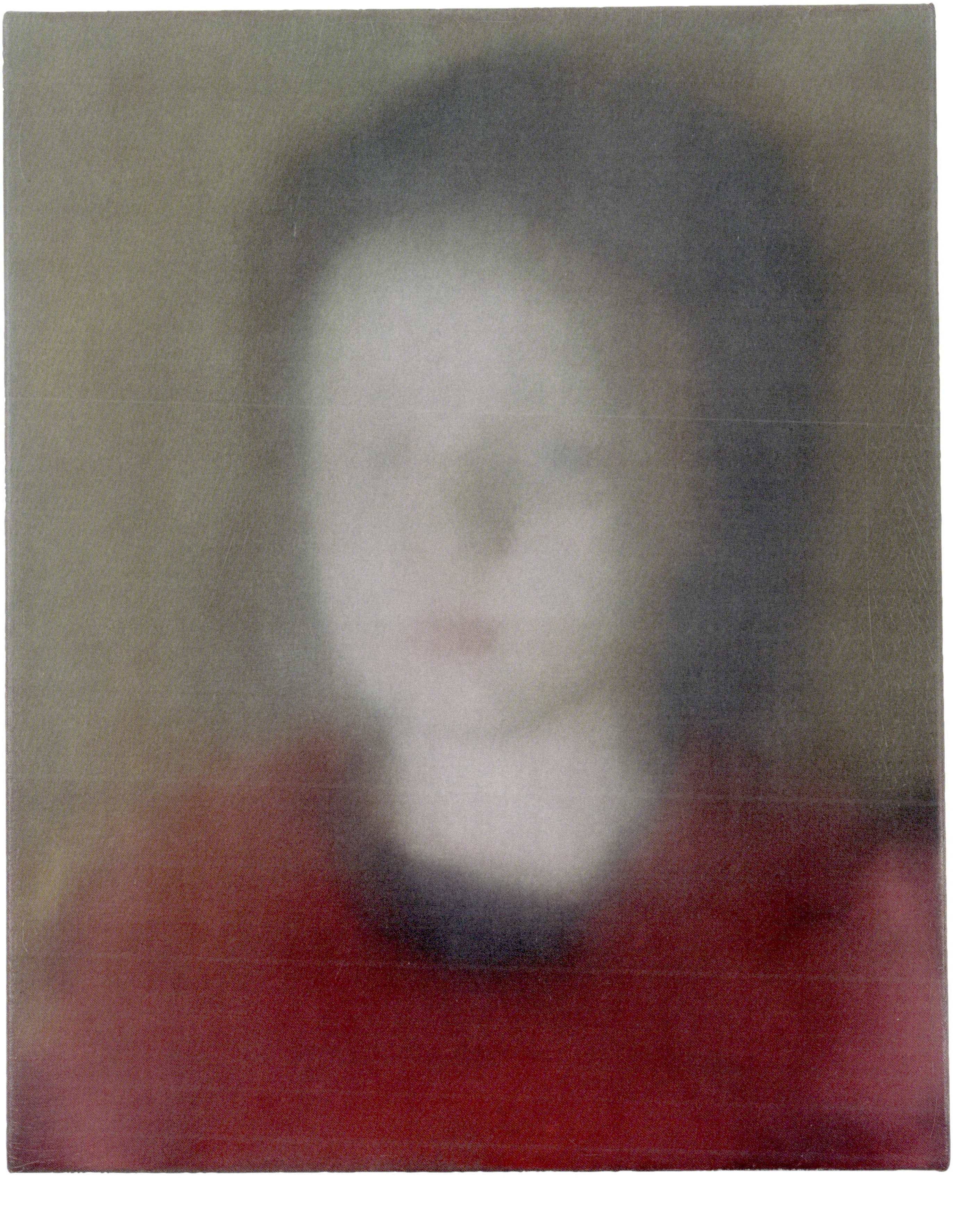

Abstract Painting, 1978   78 ¾ in. × 10 ft. 11 ⅞ in. (200 × 335 cm)

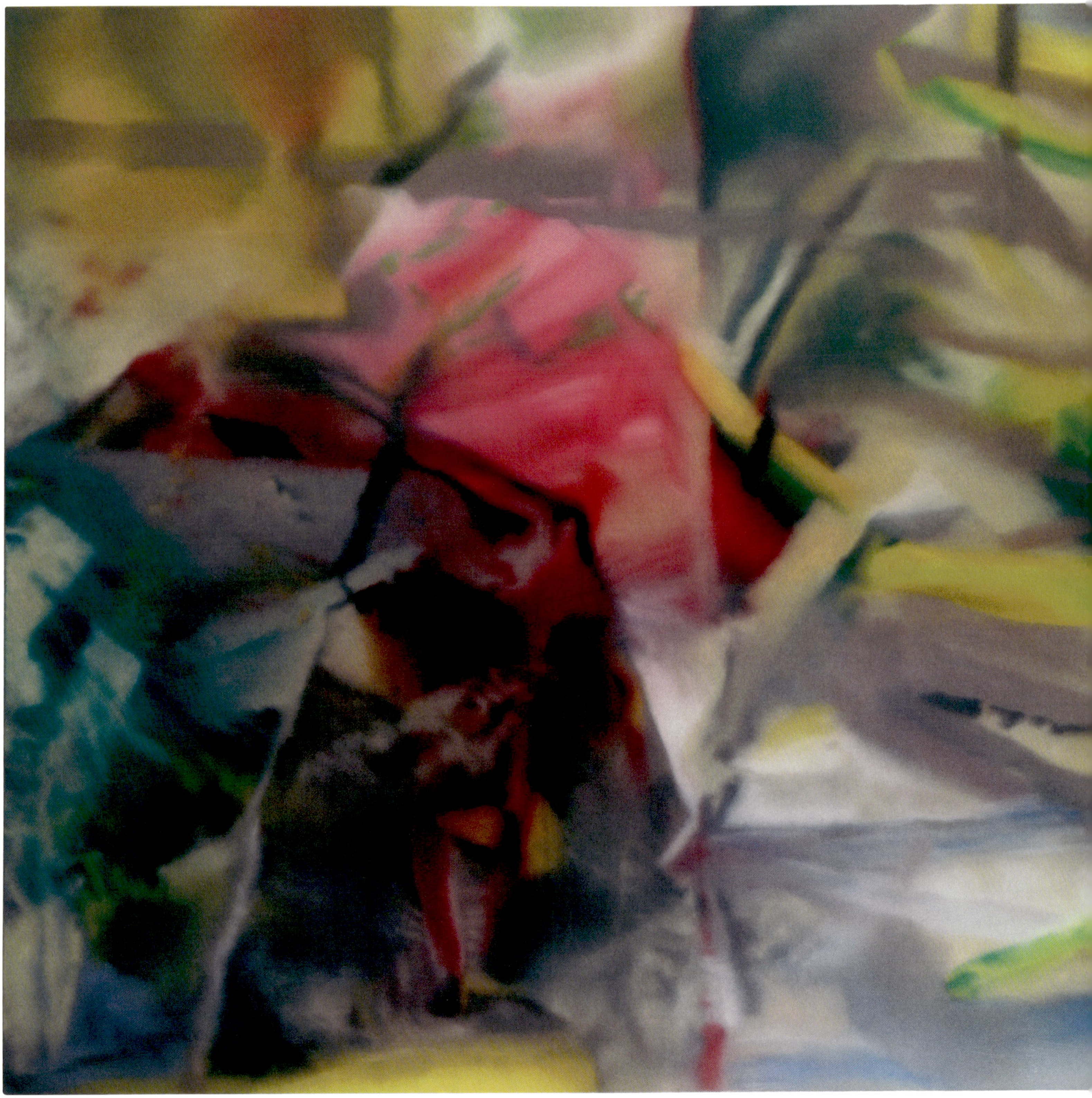

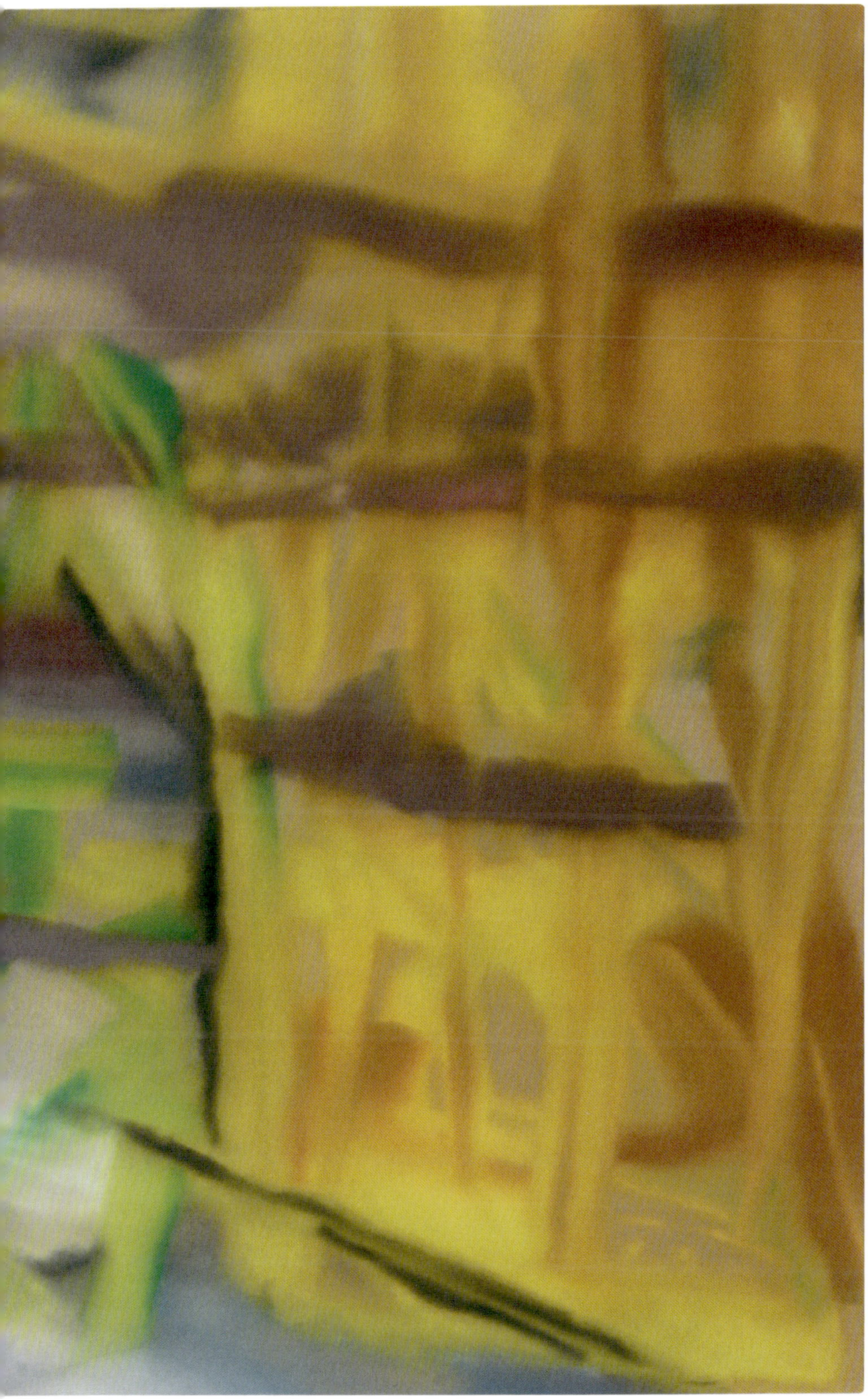

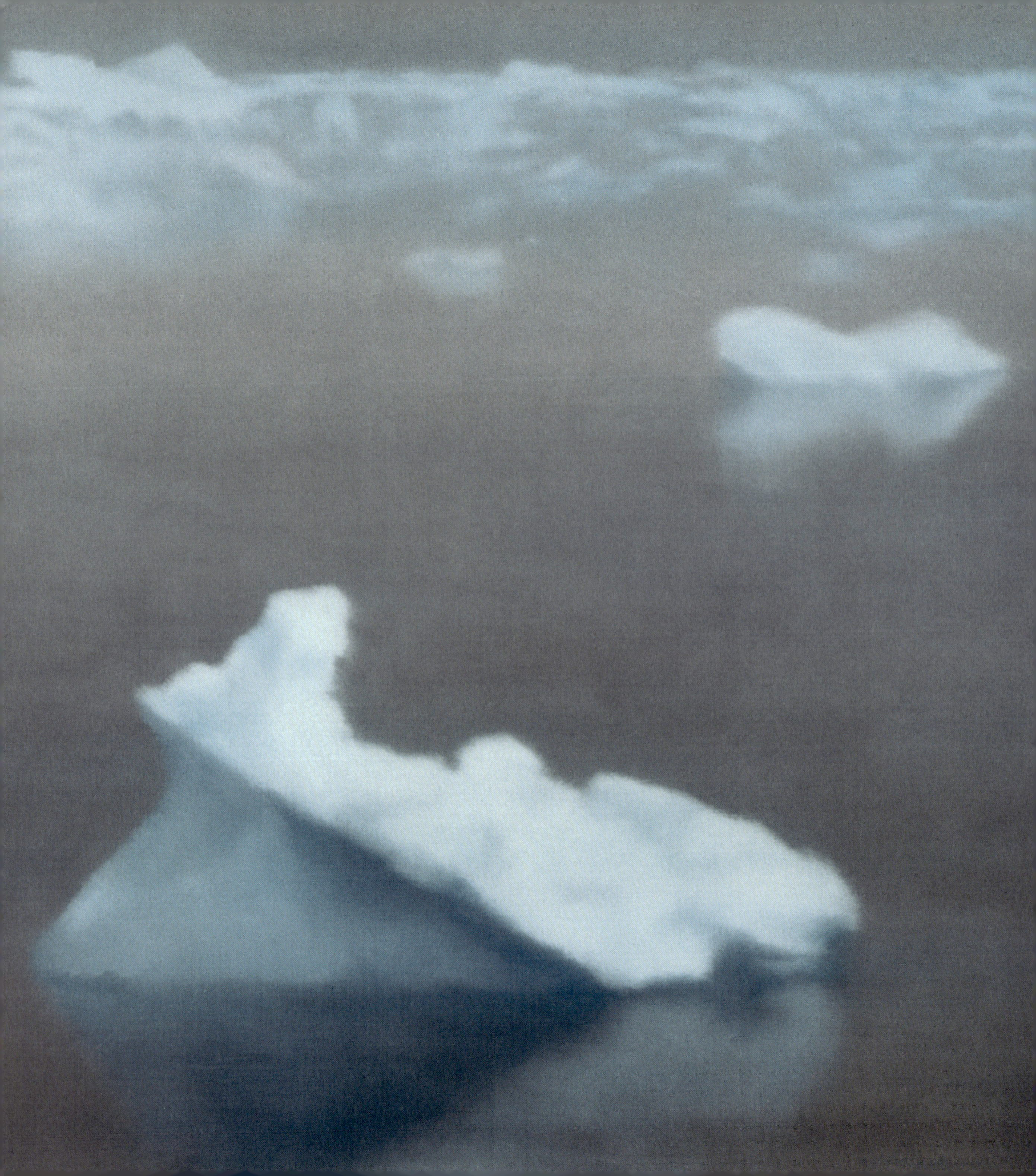

Ice, 1981   27 9/16 × 39 3/8 in. (70 × 100 cm)

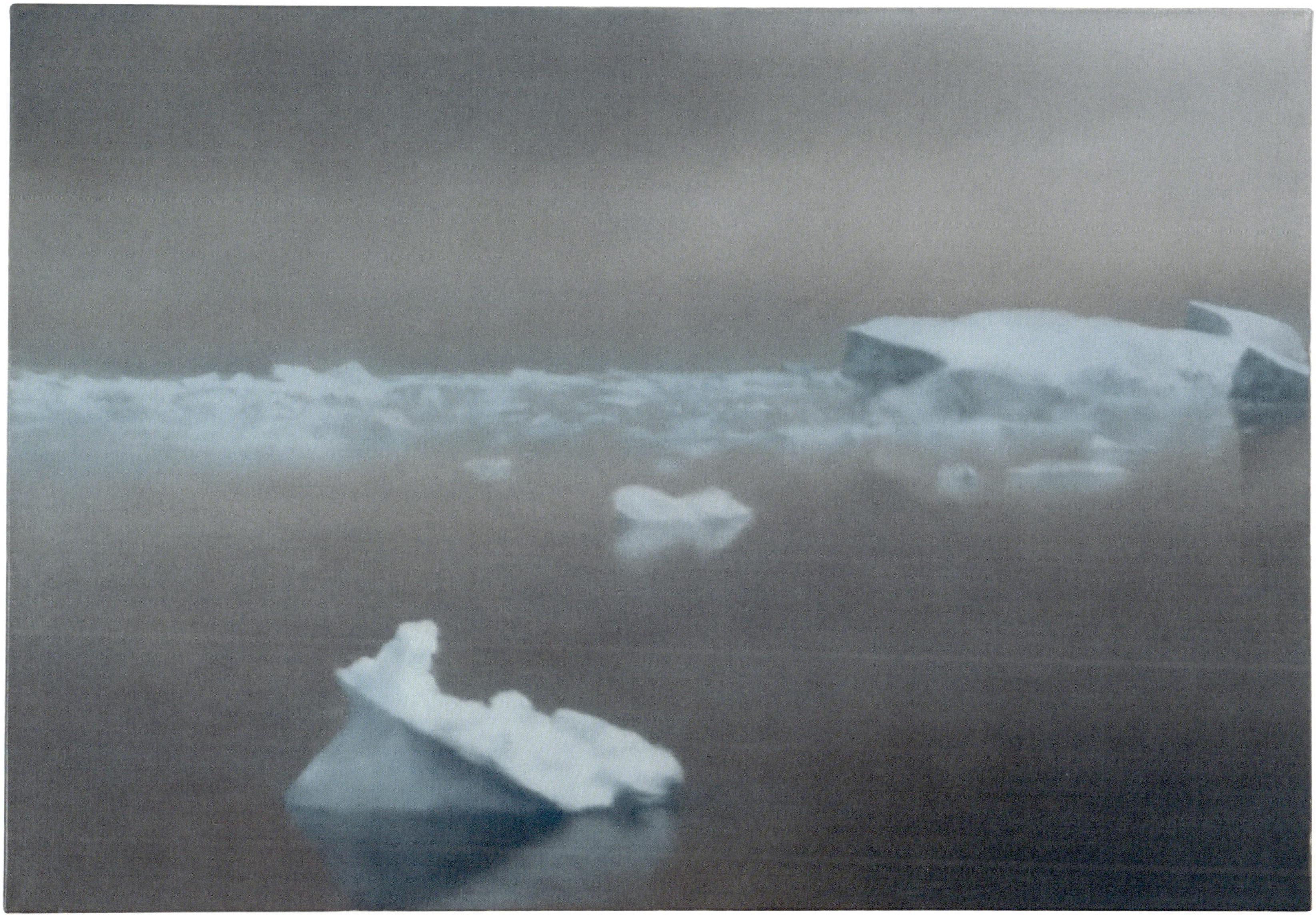

Iceberg in Mist, 1982   27 9/16 × 39 3/8 in. (70 × 100 cm)

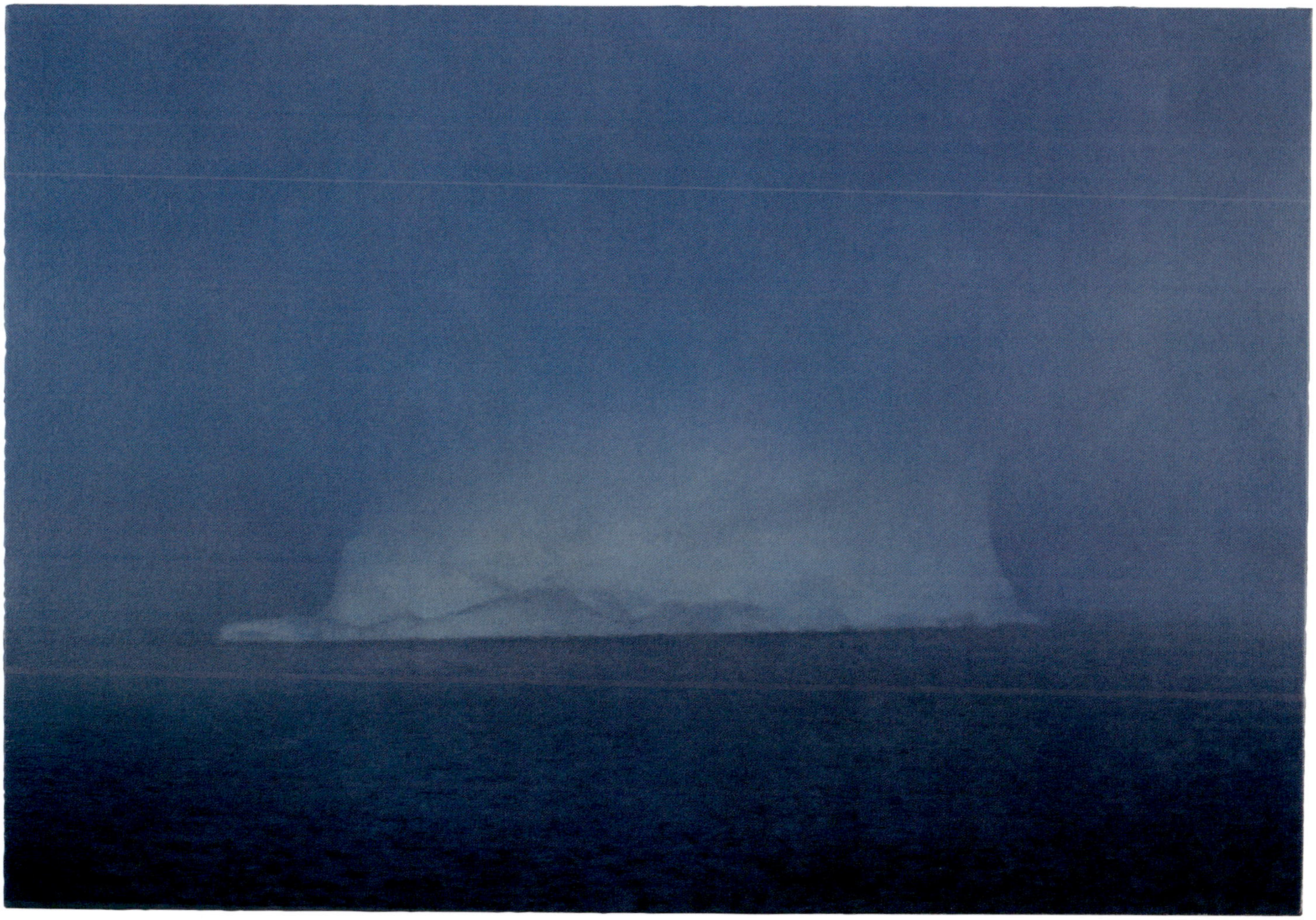

Skull, 1983 31 ½ × 25 9/16 in. (80 × 65 cm)

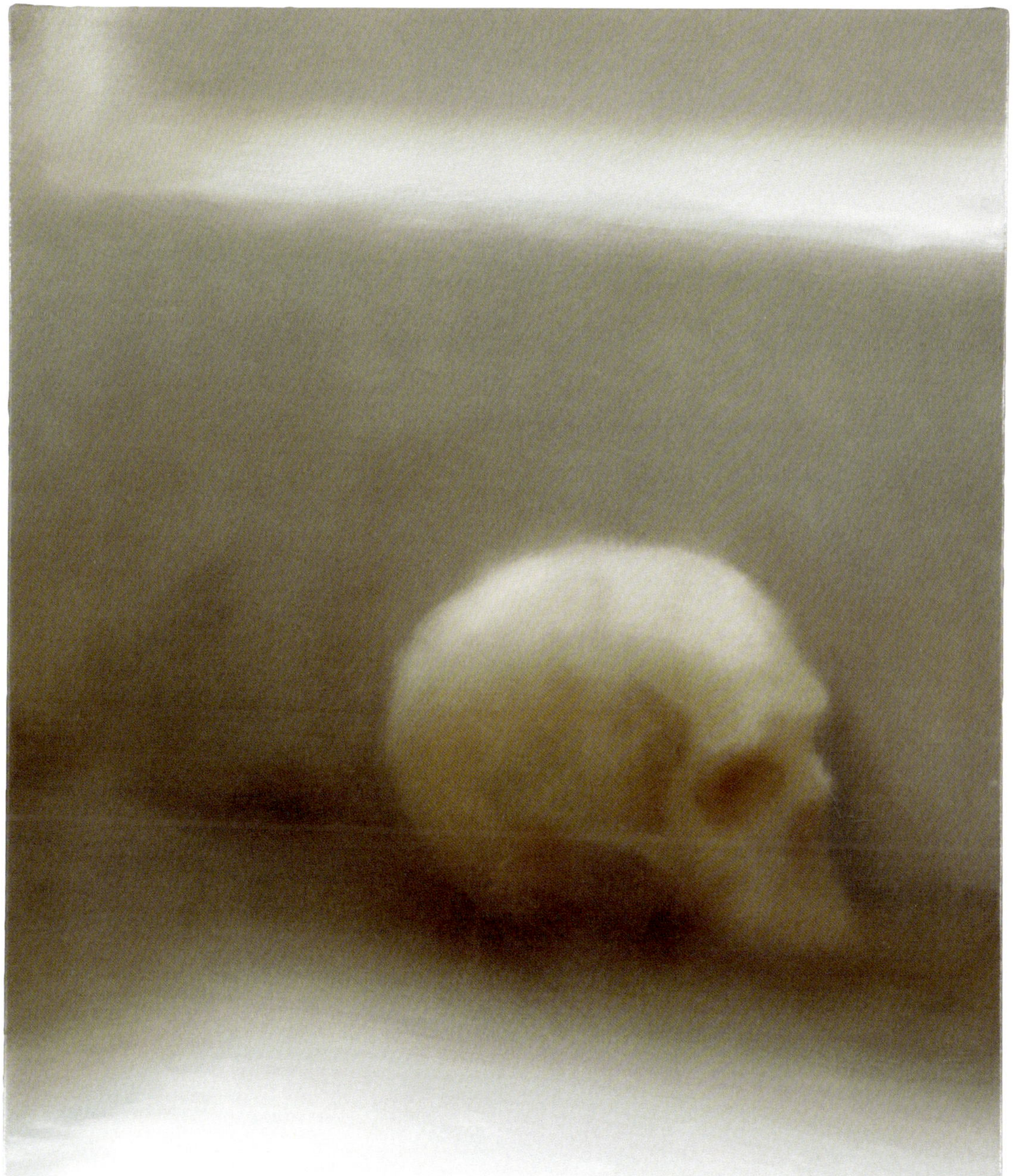

July, 1983 $98\frac{7}{16} \times 98\frac{7}{16}$ in. (250 × 250 cm)

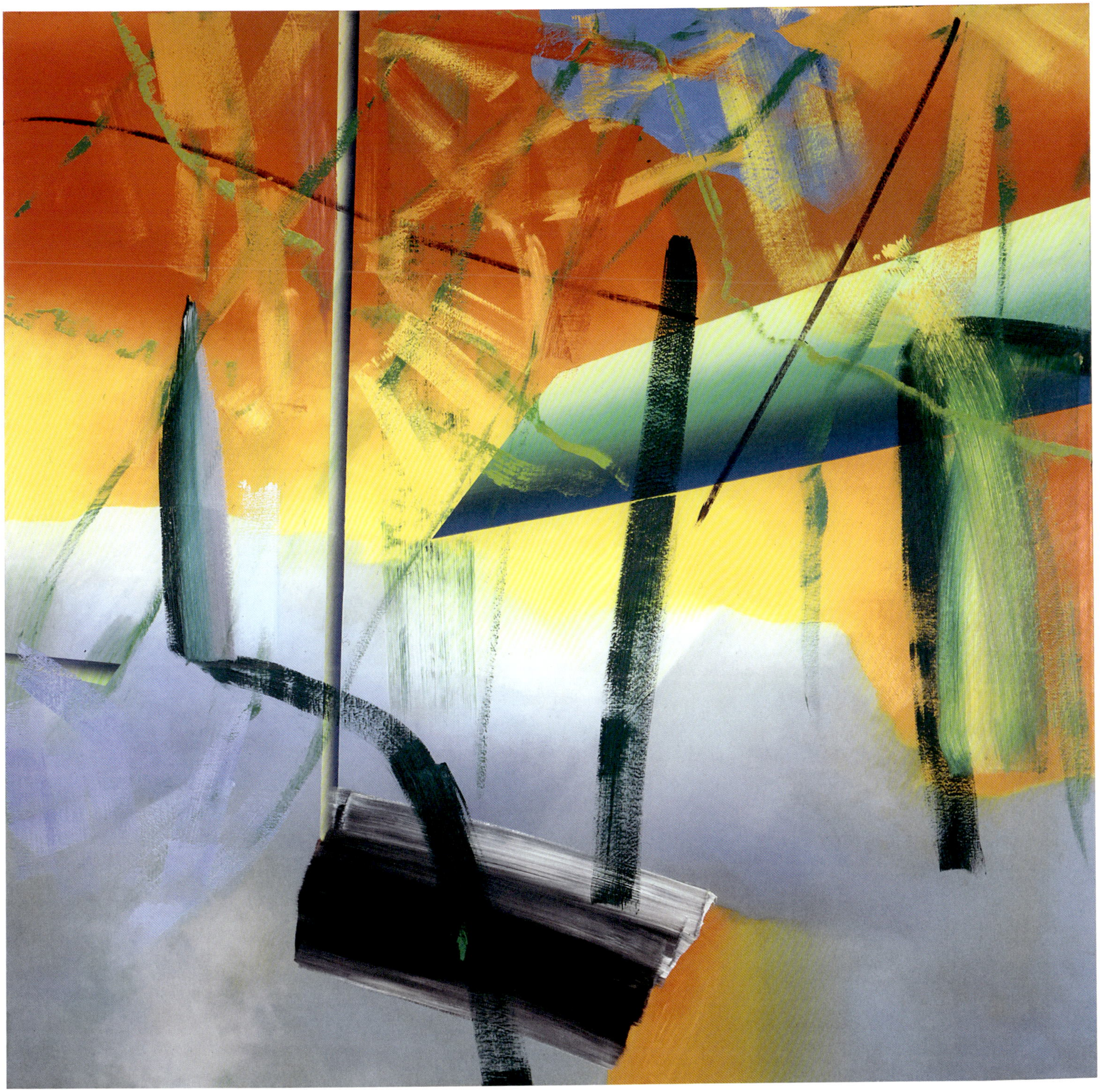

Mirror, 1986   78 ¾ × 70 ⅞ in. (200 × 180 cm)

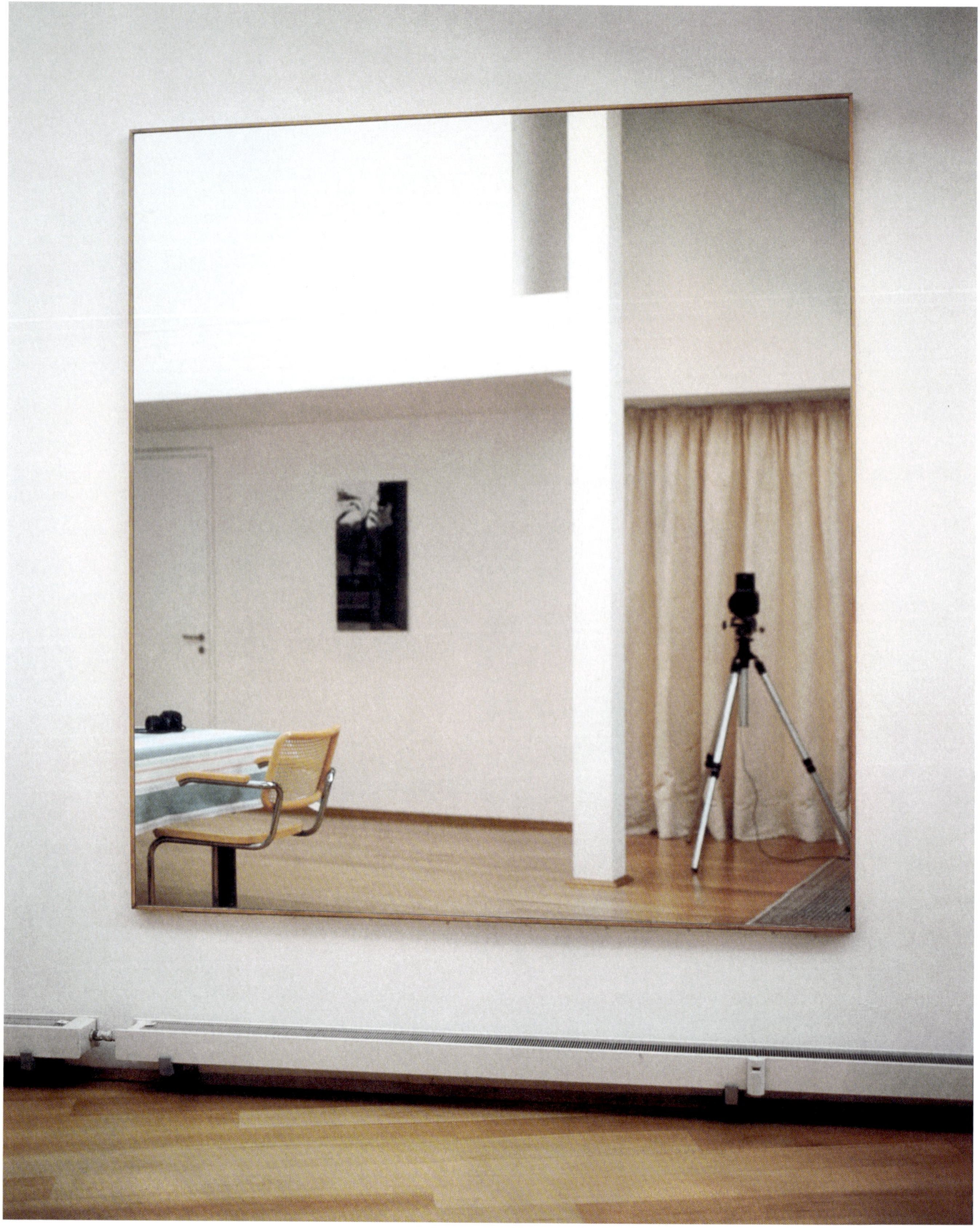

Cathedral Corner, 1987   48 × 34 ¼ in. (122 × 87 cm)

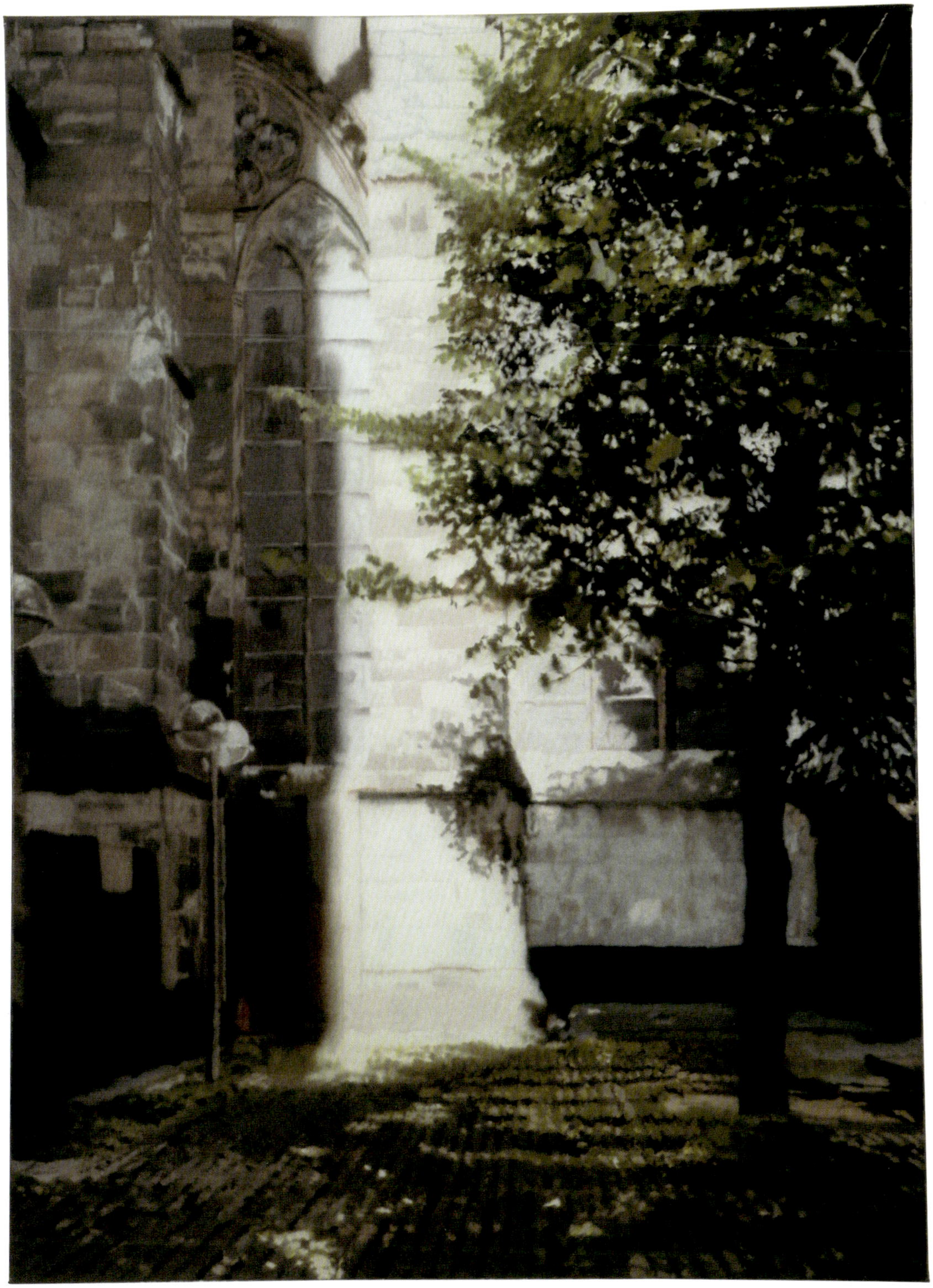

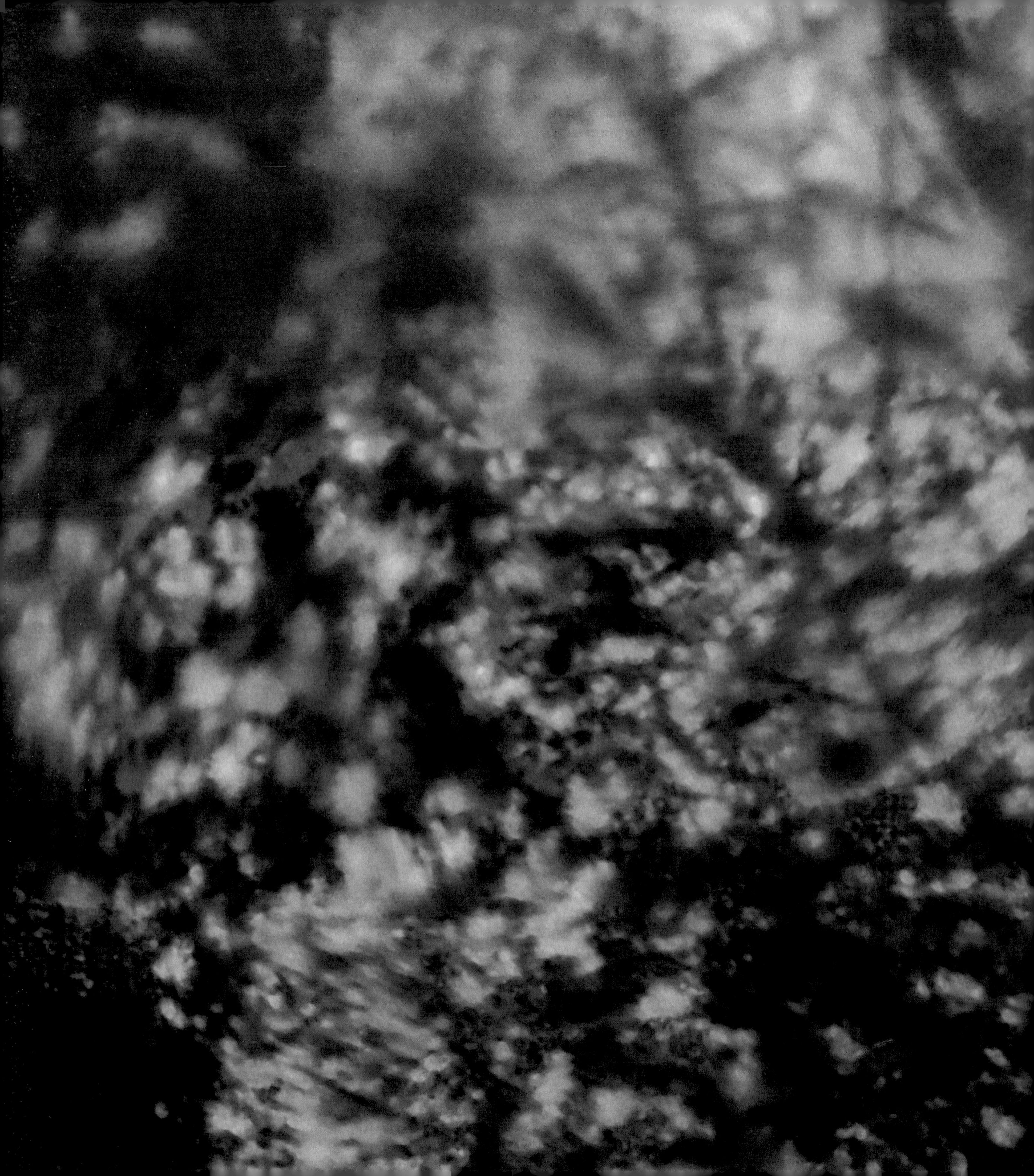

Squatters' House, 1989   32 5/16 × 44 1/8 in. (82 × 112 cm)

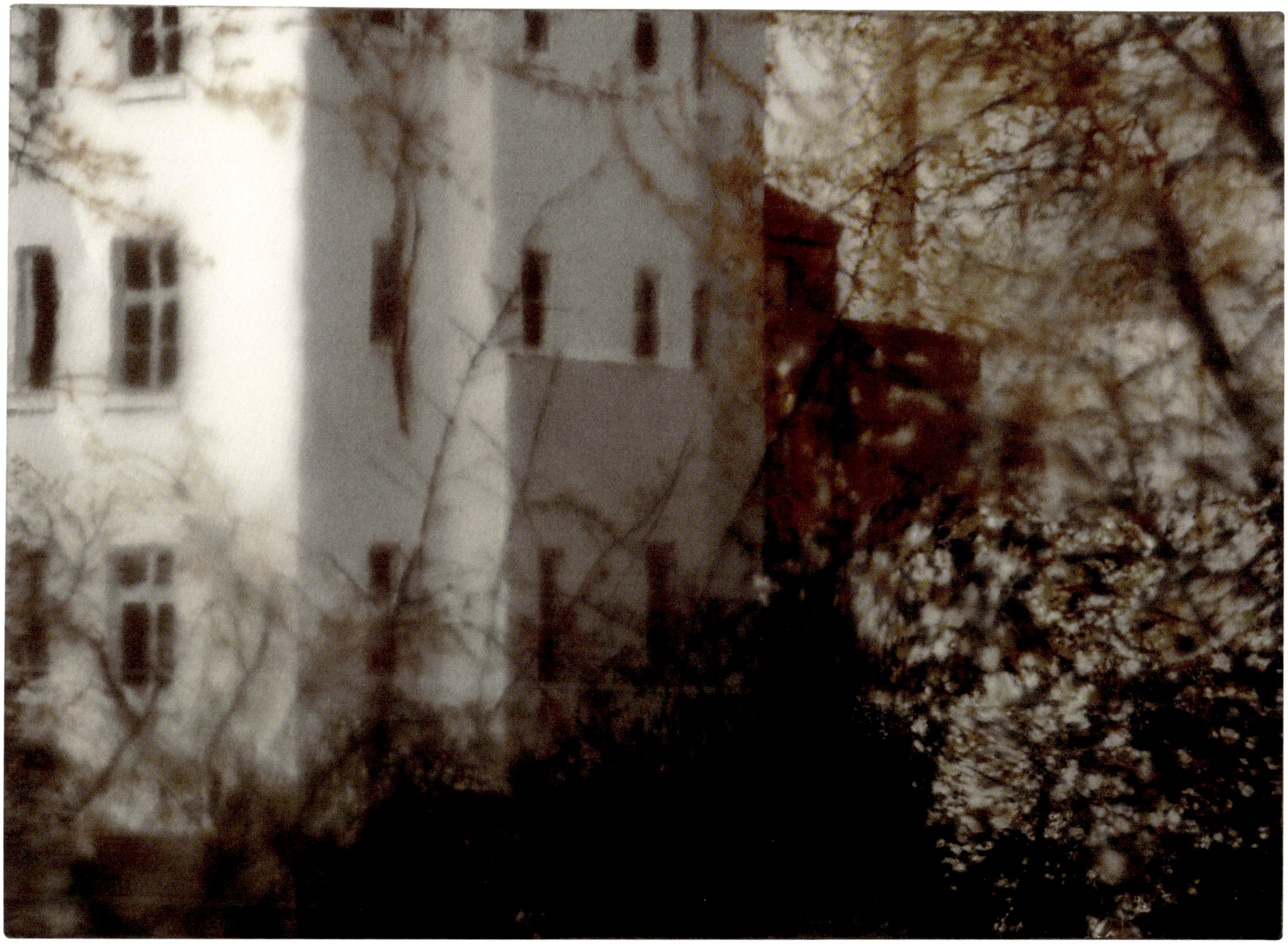

Passage (Leipzig), 1990 28 3/8 × 40 3/16 in. (72 × 102 cm)

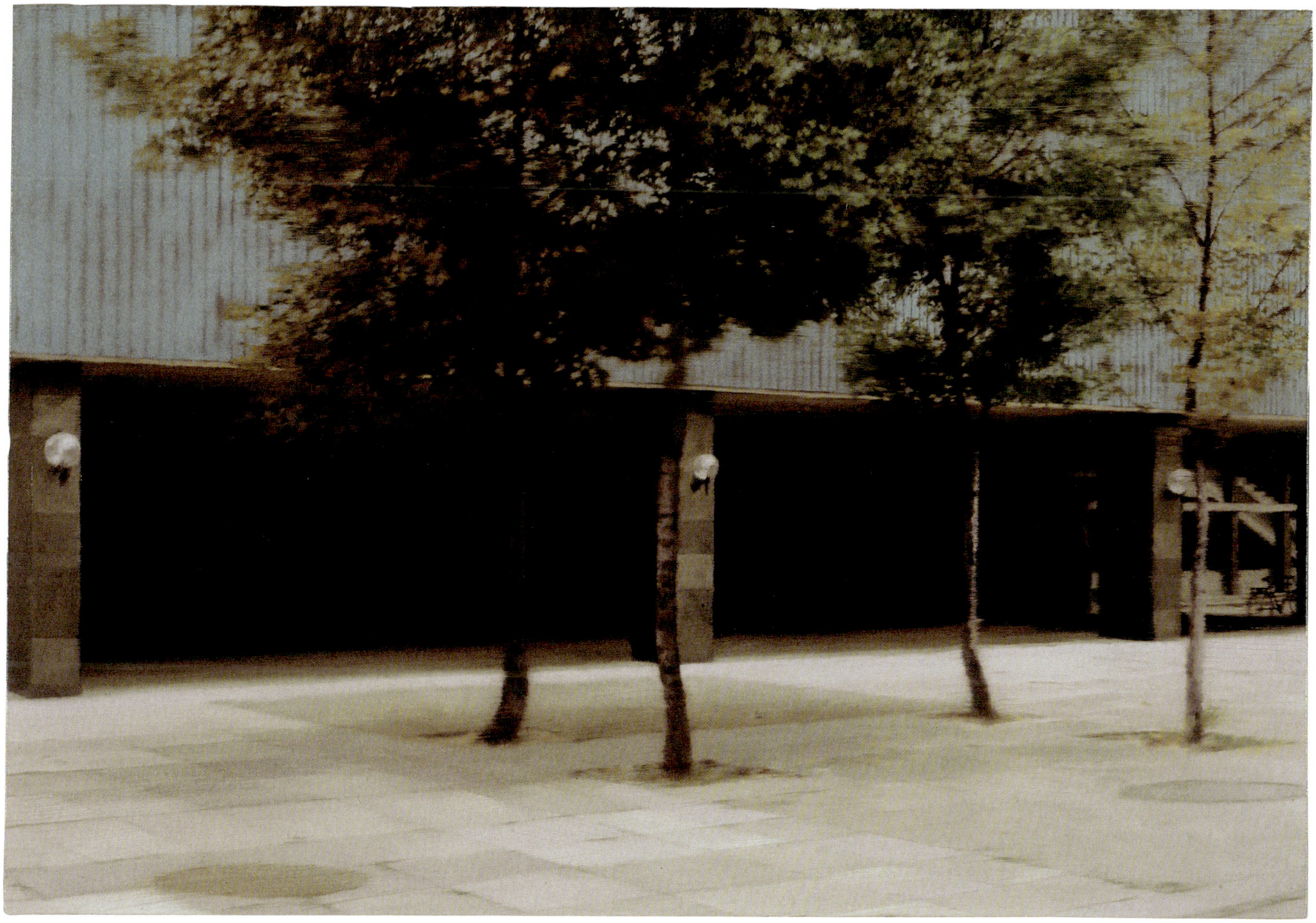

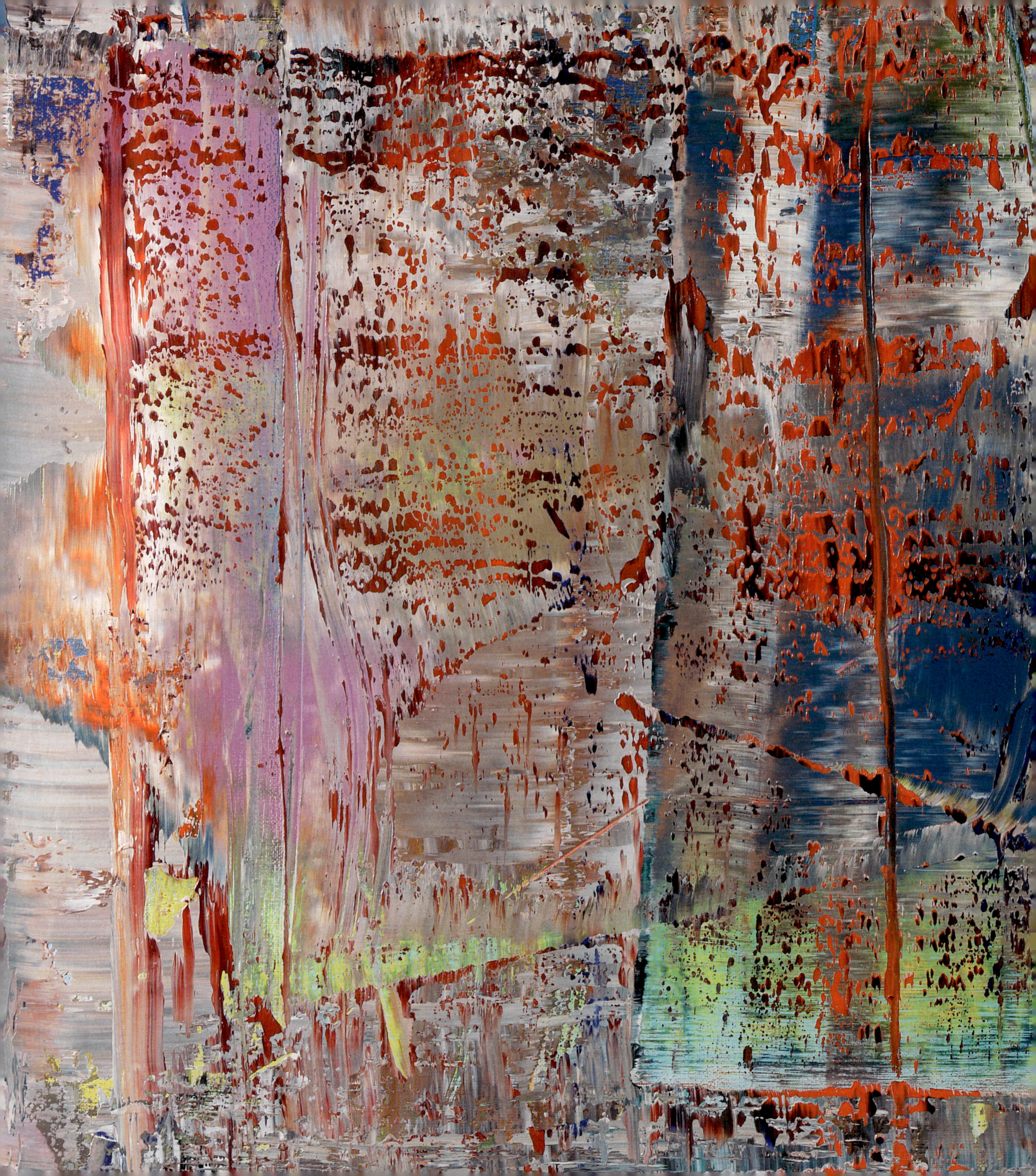

Abstract Painting, 1990 36 ¼ × 49 ⅝ in. (92 × 126 cm)

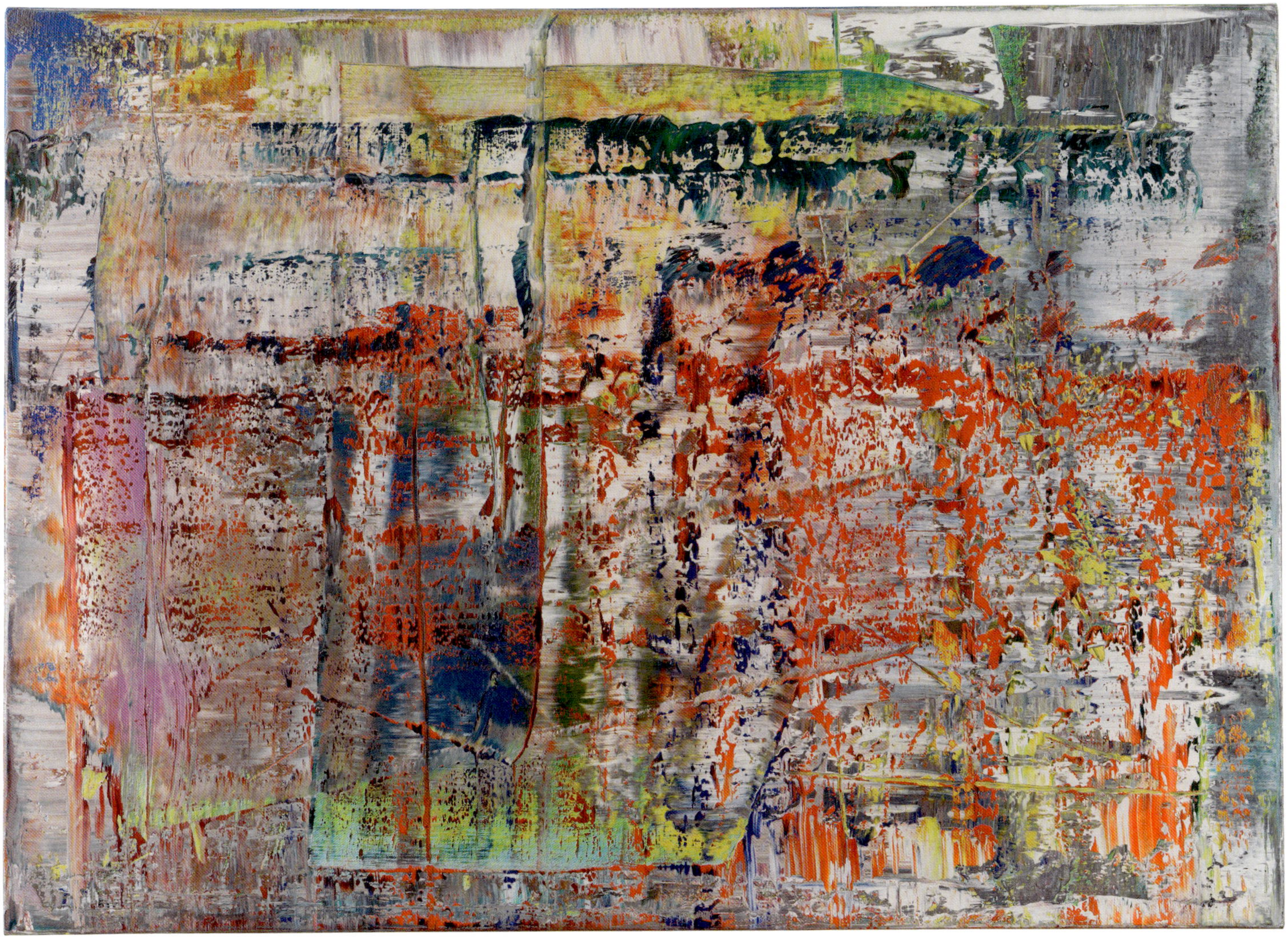

Six Photos, May 2–7, 1989, 1991 each 13 ¾ × 20 in. (35 × 50.8 cm)

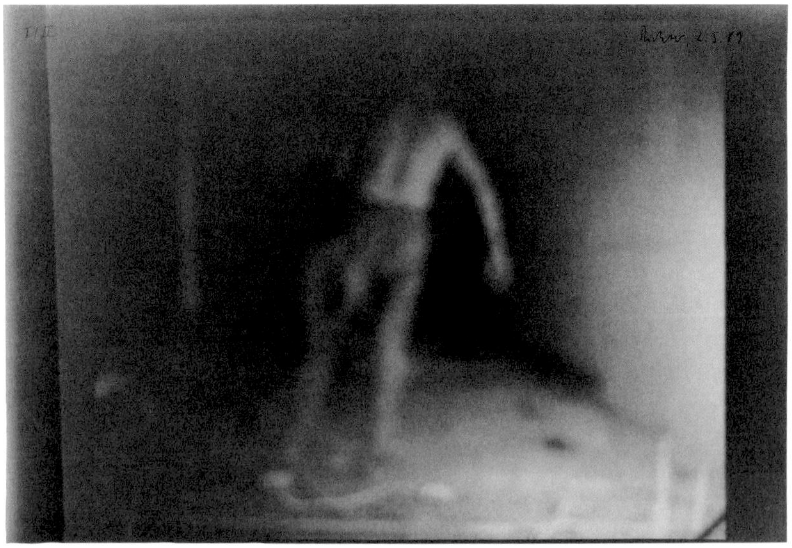

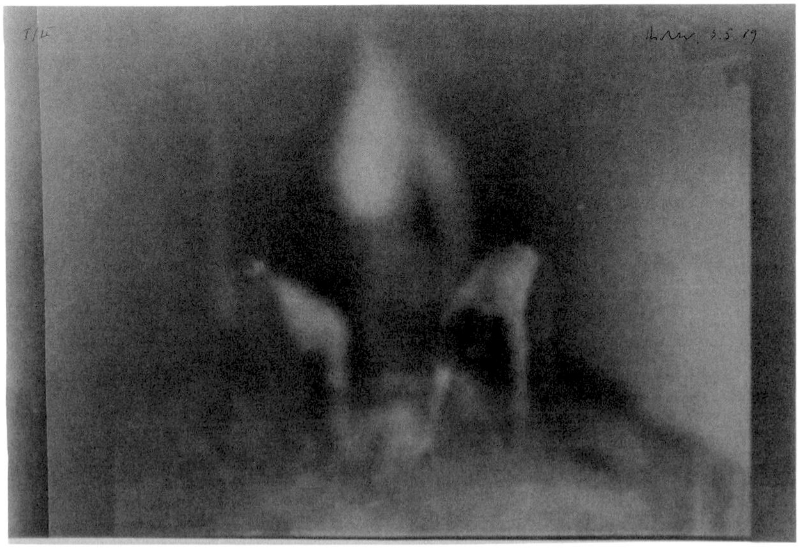

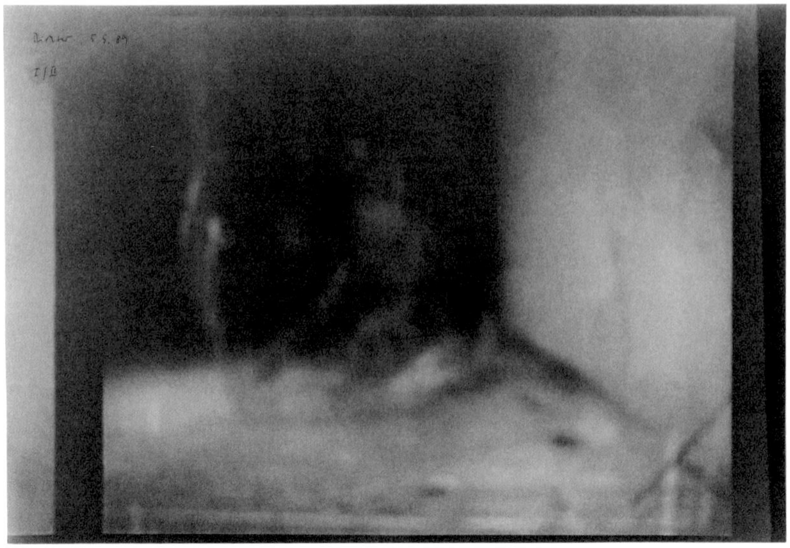

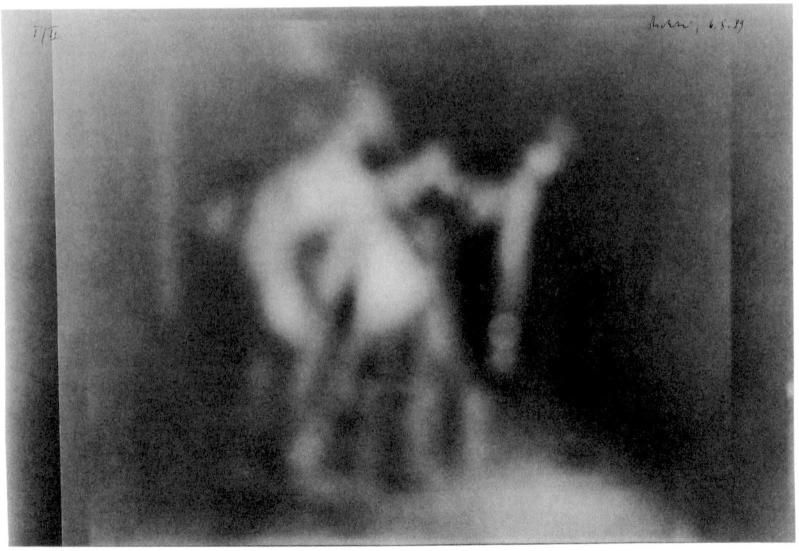

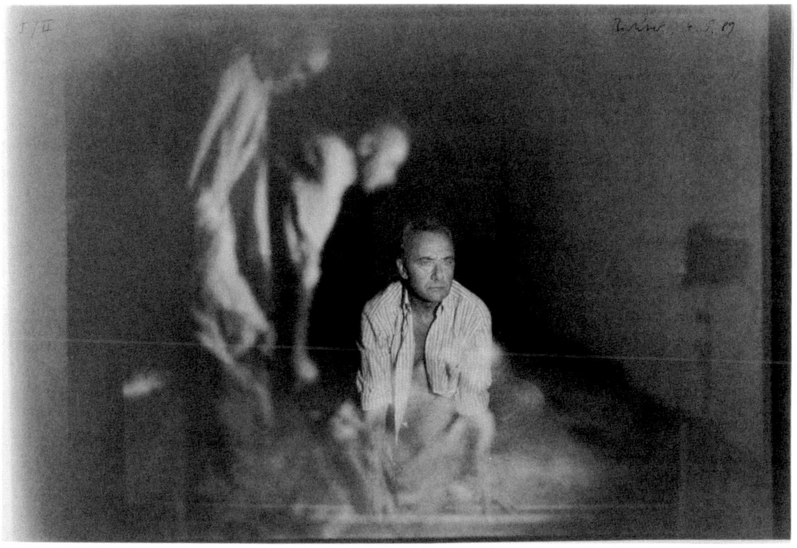

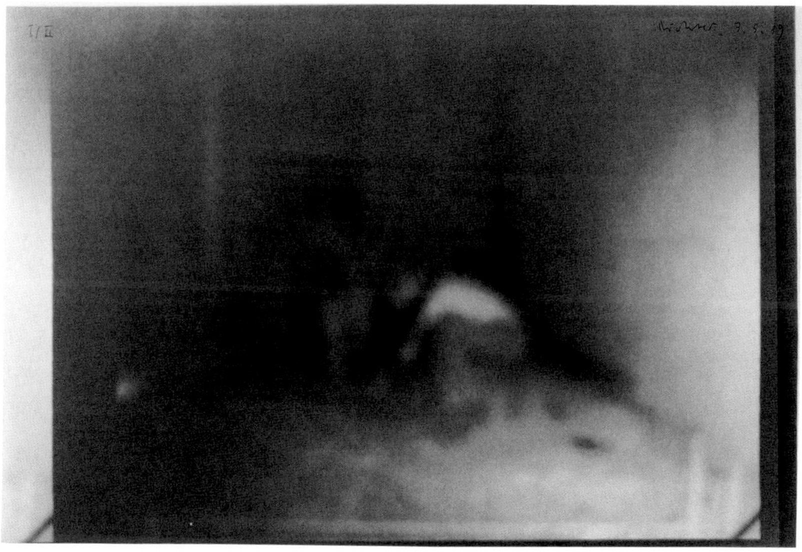

Mirror, Blood Red, 1991 35 1/16 × 36 1/4 in. (89 × 92 cm)

I.G., 1993 32 ¼ × 36 ¼ in. (82 × 92 cm)

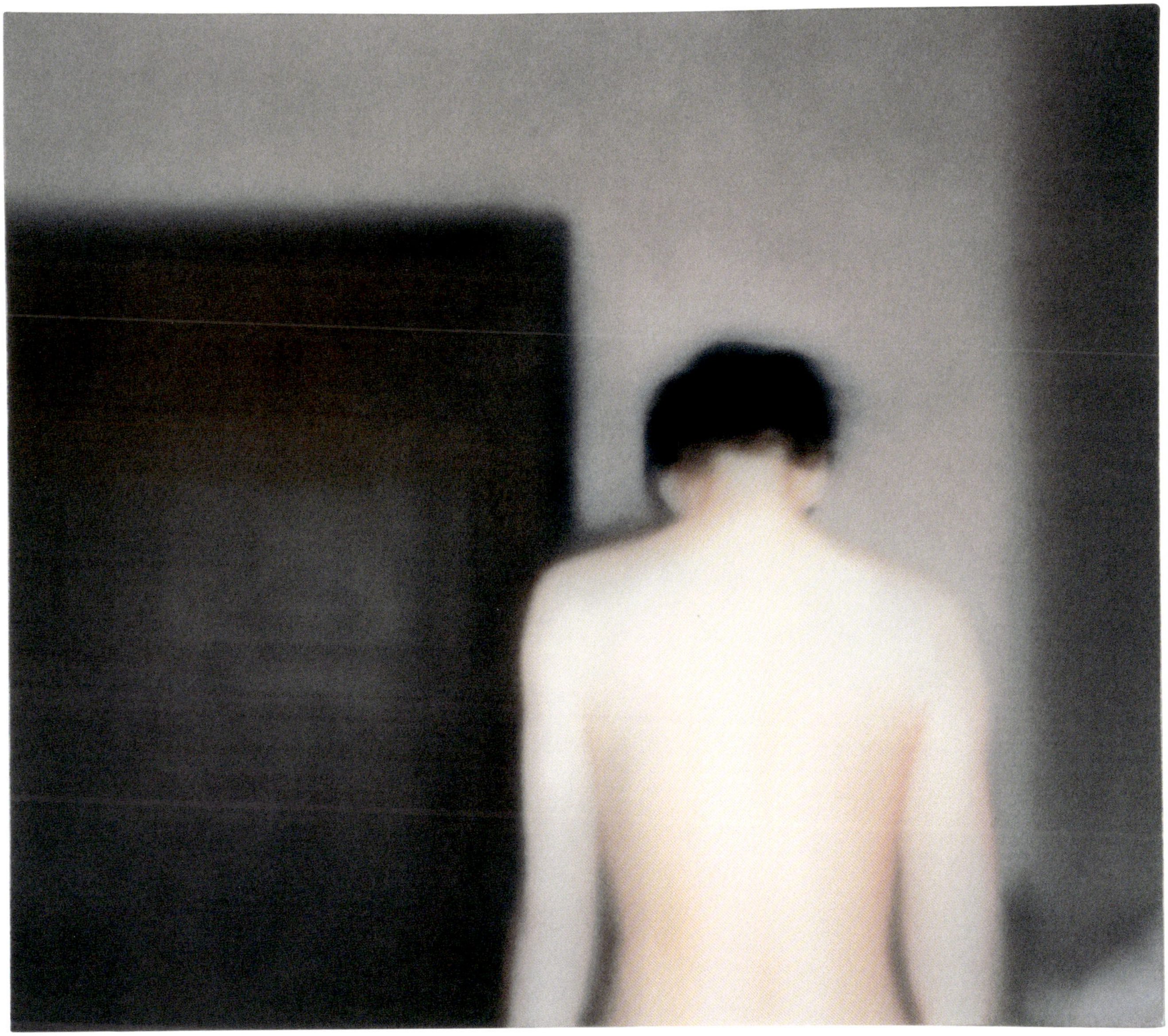

I.G., 1993 28 3/8 × 40 3/16 in. (72 × 102 cm)

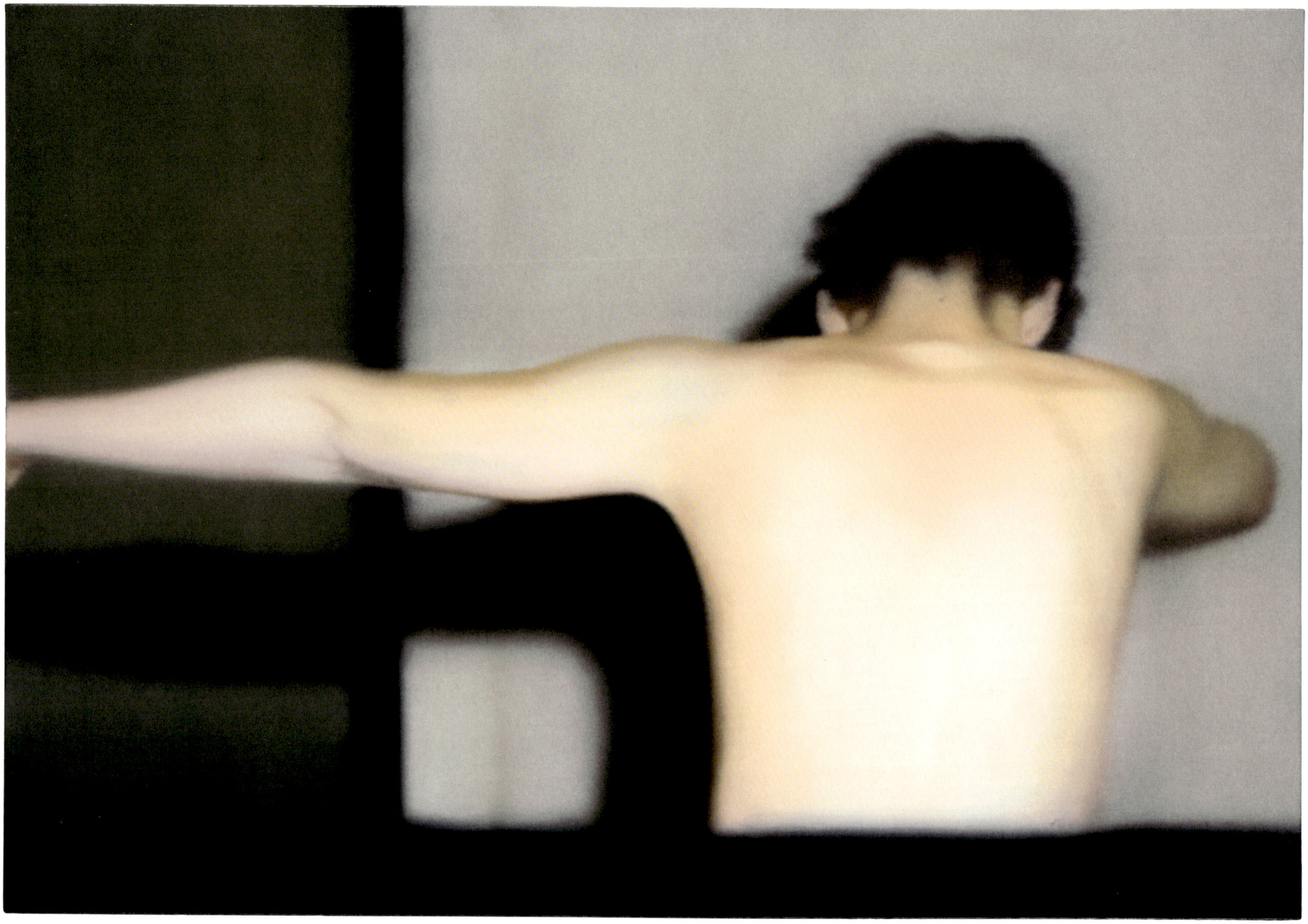

I.G., 1993 28 ⅜ × 32 5/16 in. (72 × 82 cm)

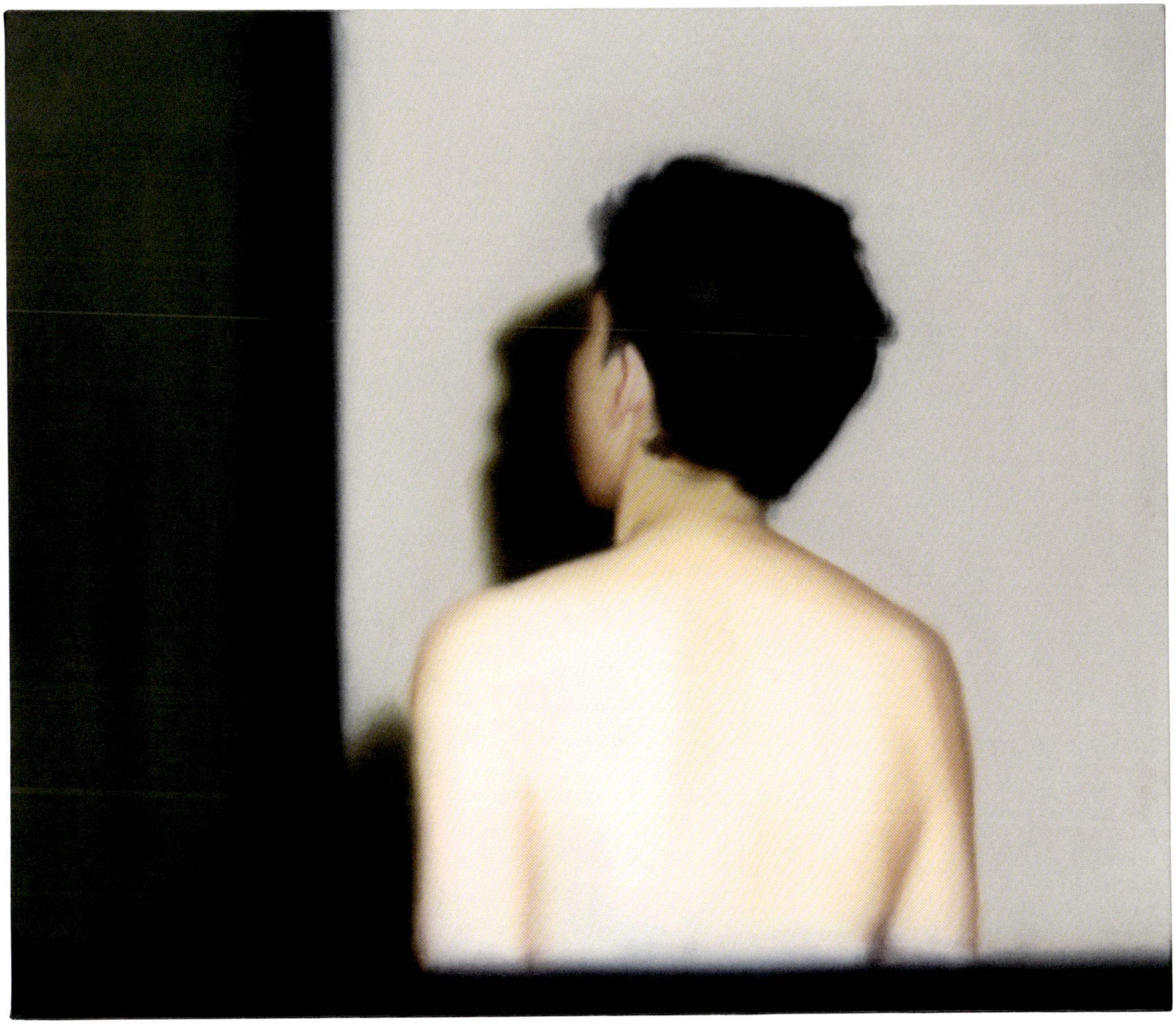

S. with Child, 1995 14 3/16 × 16 1/8 in. (36 × 41 cm)

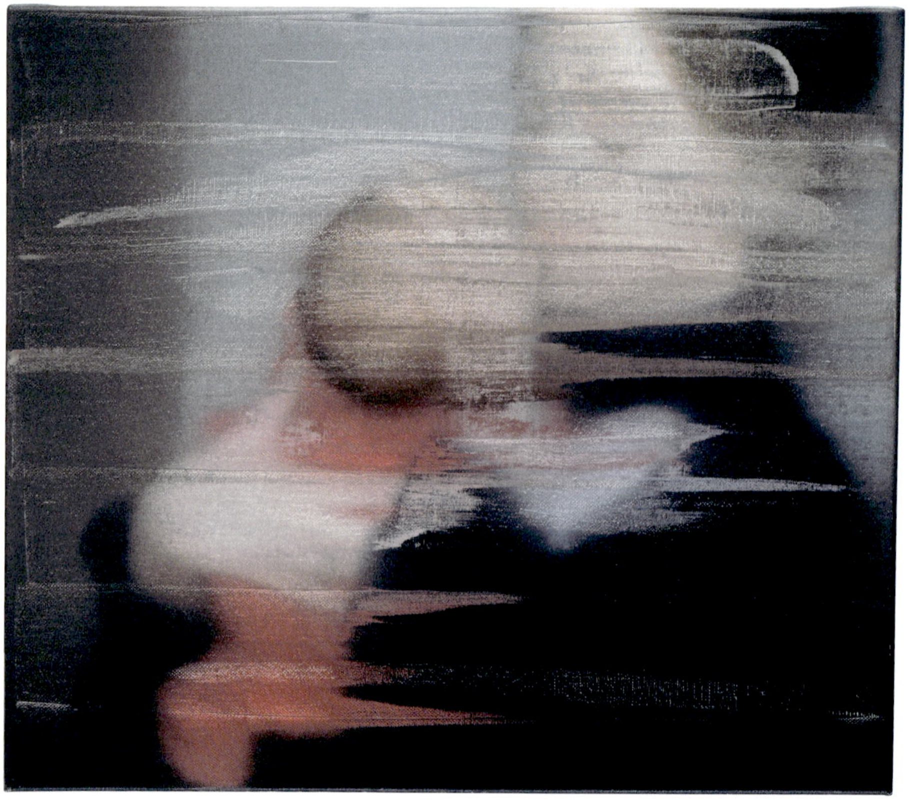

S. with Child, 1995 16 ⅛ × 14 3/16 in. (41 × 36 cm)

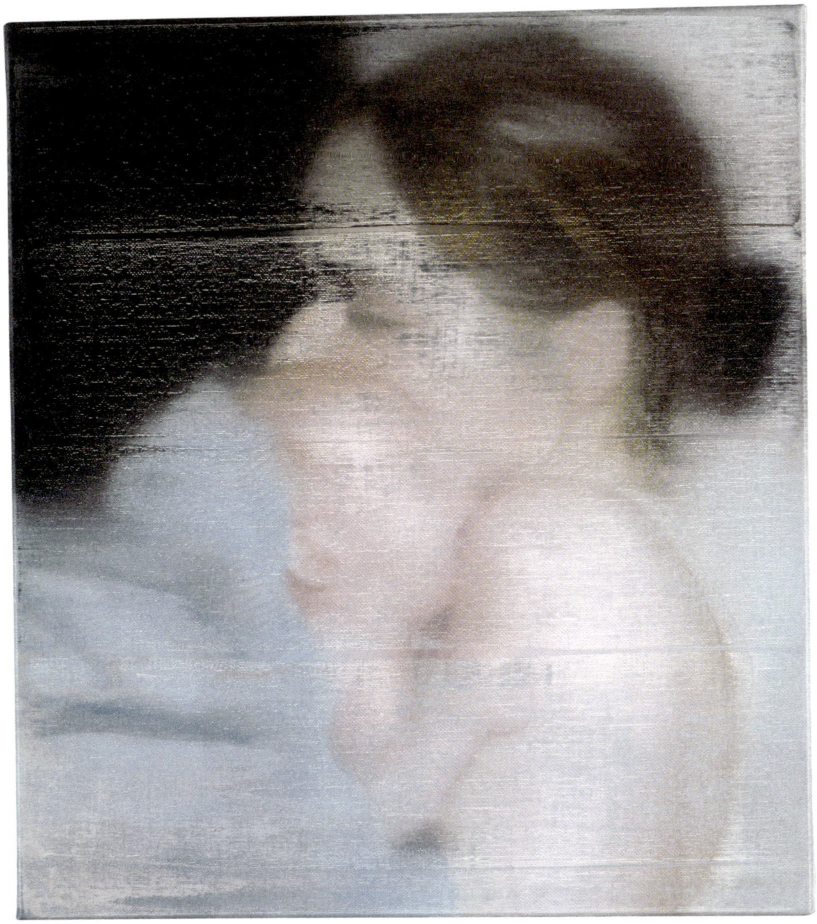

S. with Child, 1995 20 ½ × 24 7/16 in. (52 × 62 cm)
S. with Child, 1995 20 ½ × 22 1/16 in. (52 × 56 cm)

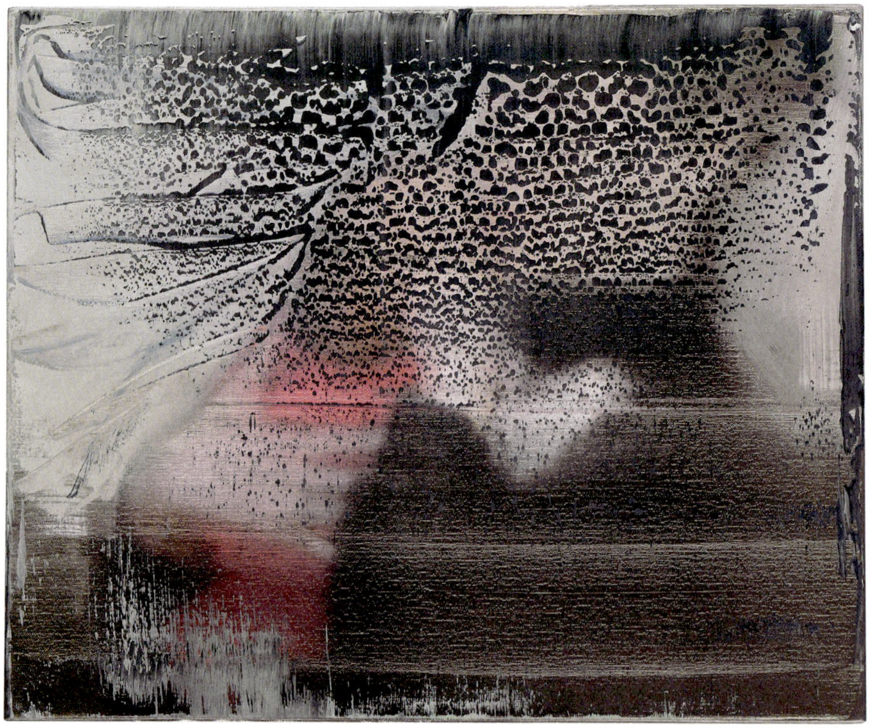

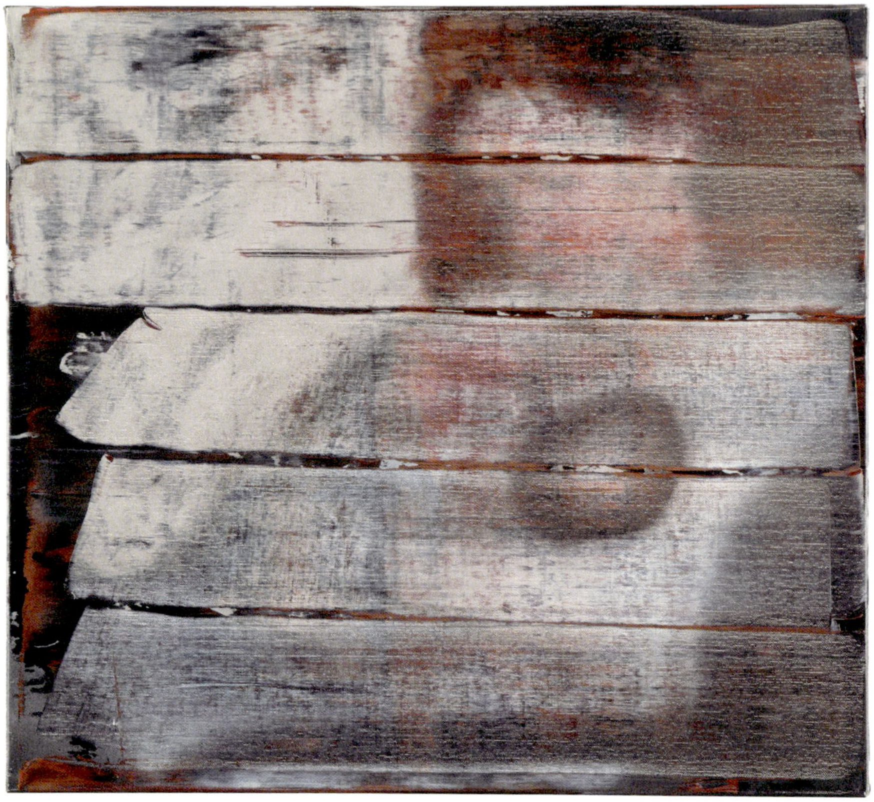

S. with Child, 1995 14 3/16 × 20 1/16 in. (36 × 51 cm)

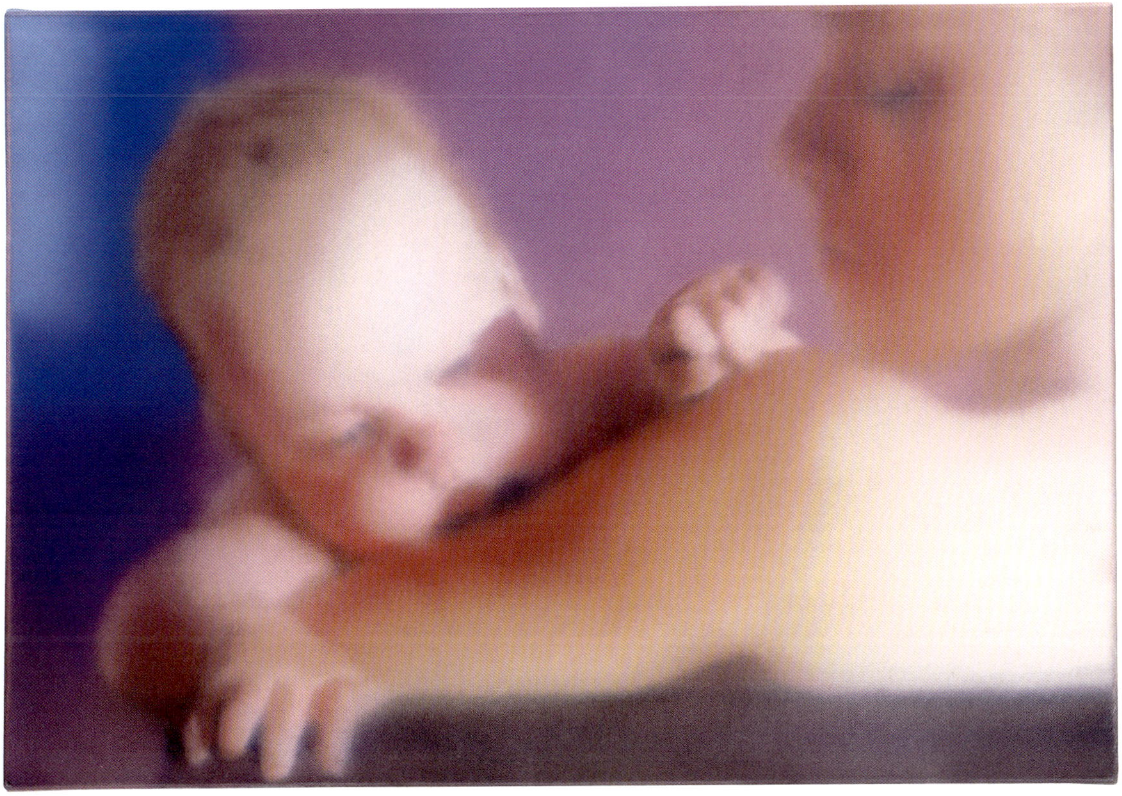

Self-Portrait, 1996 20 1/16 × 18 1/8 in. (51 × 46 cm)

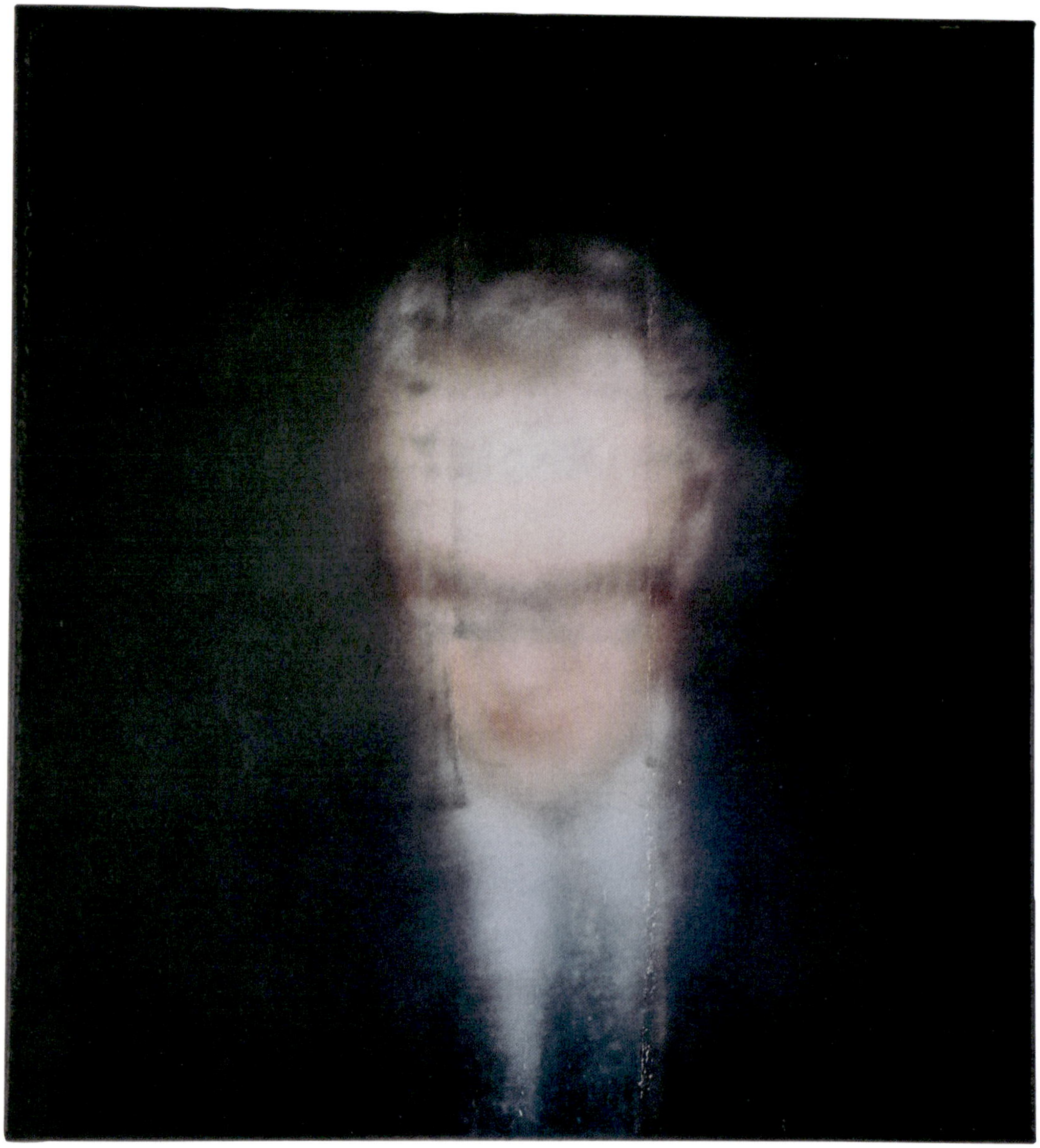

Self-Portrait, 1996 20 1/16 × 18 1/8 in. (51 × 46 cm)

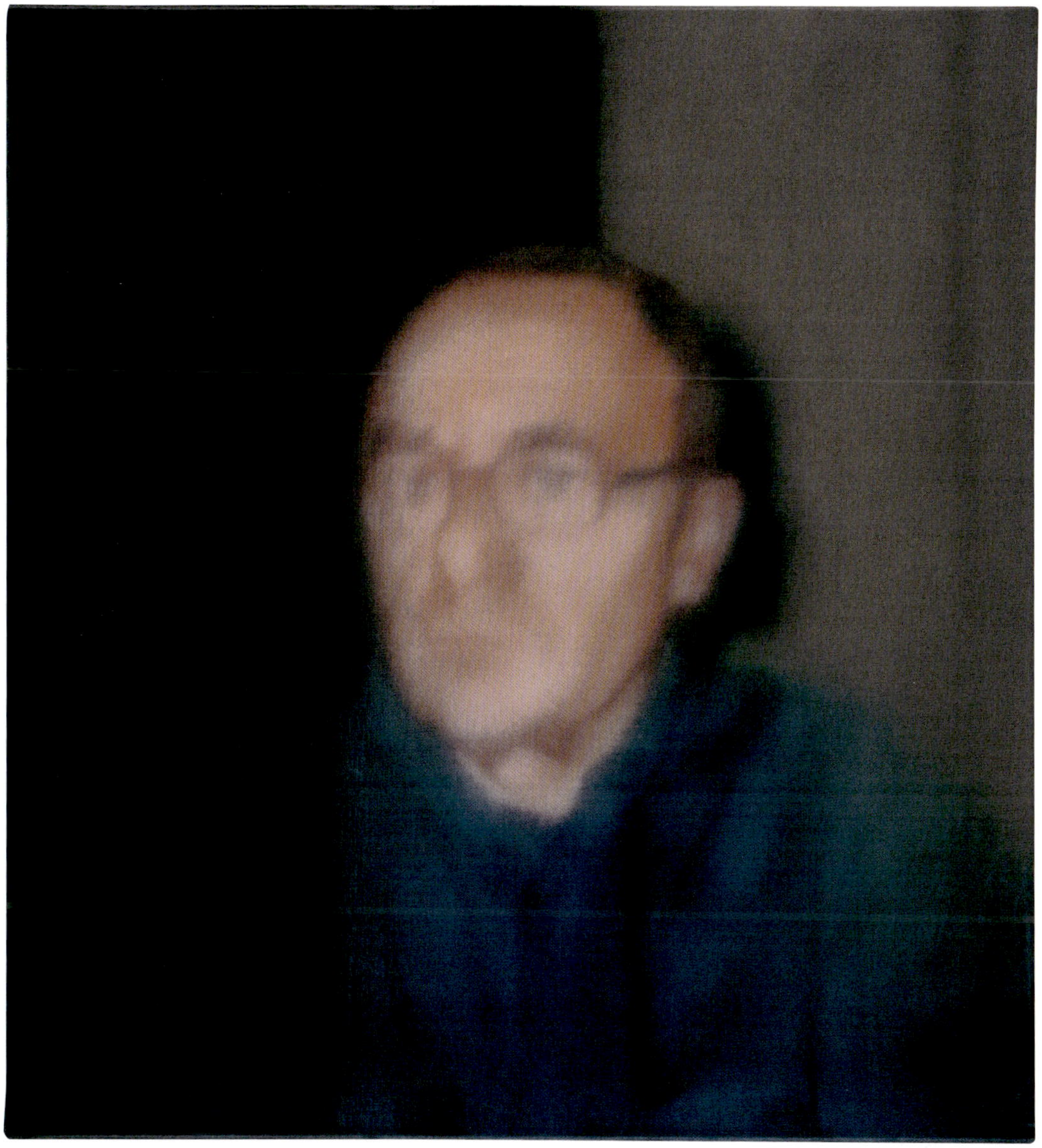

Snow, 1999 22 1/16 × 20 1/8 in. (56 × 51 cm)

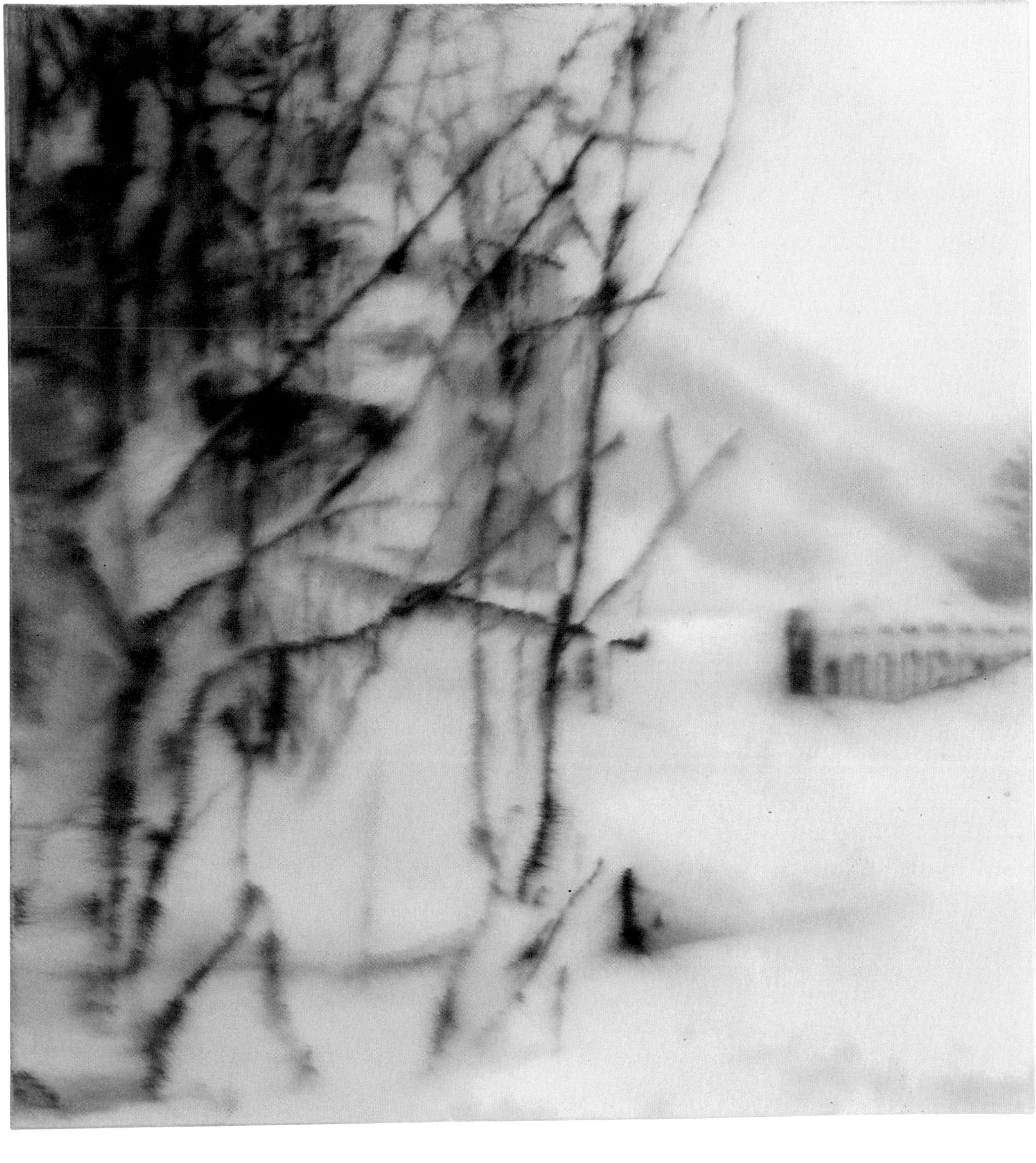

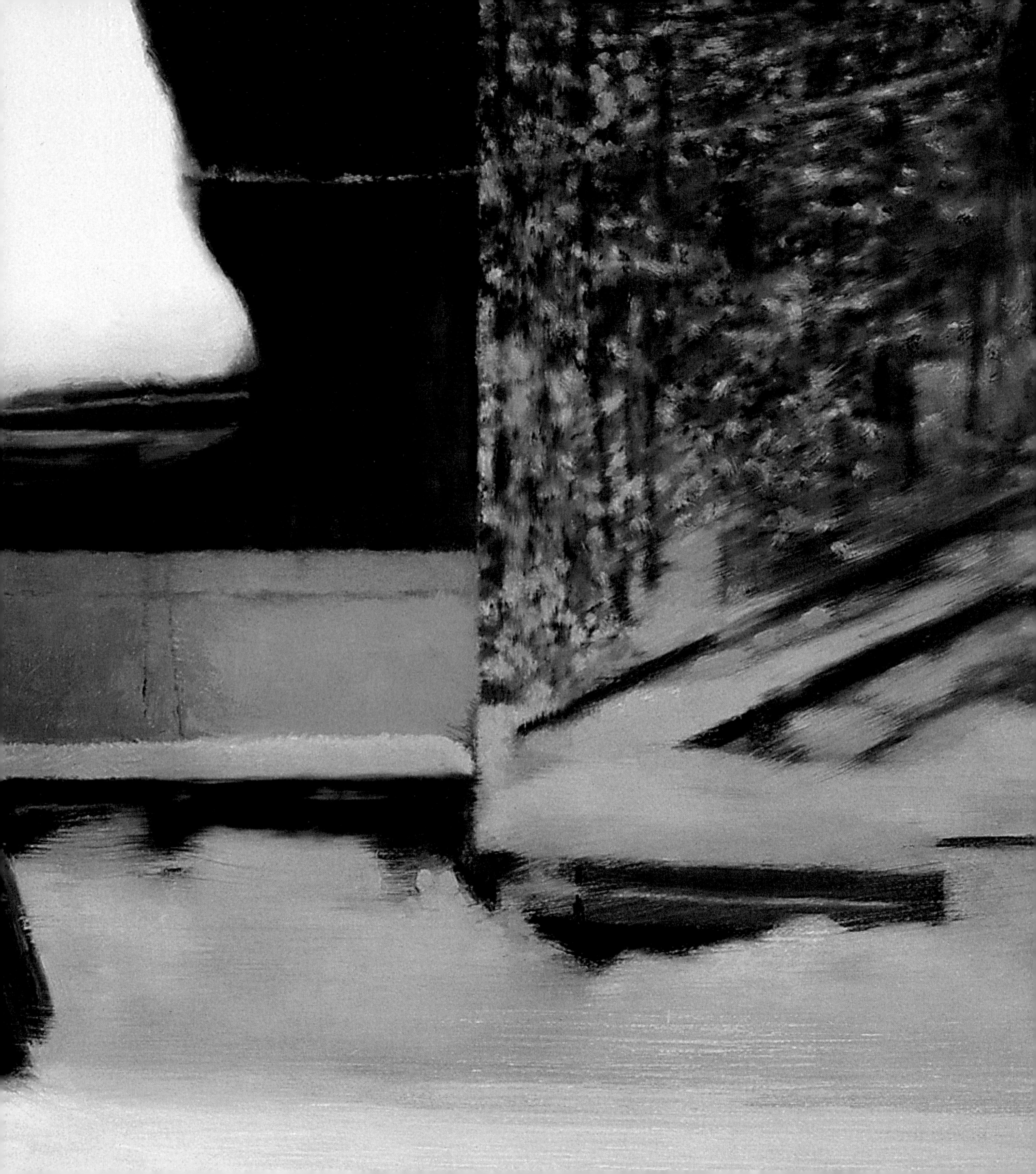

Farm, 1999 18 ⅛ × 20 1/16 in. (46 × 51 cm)

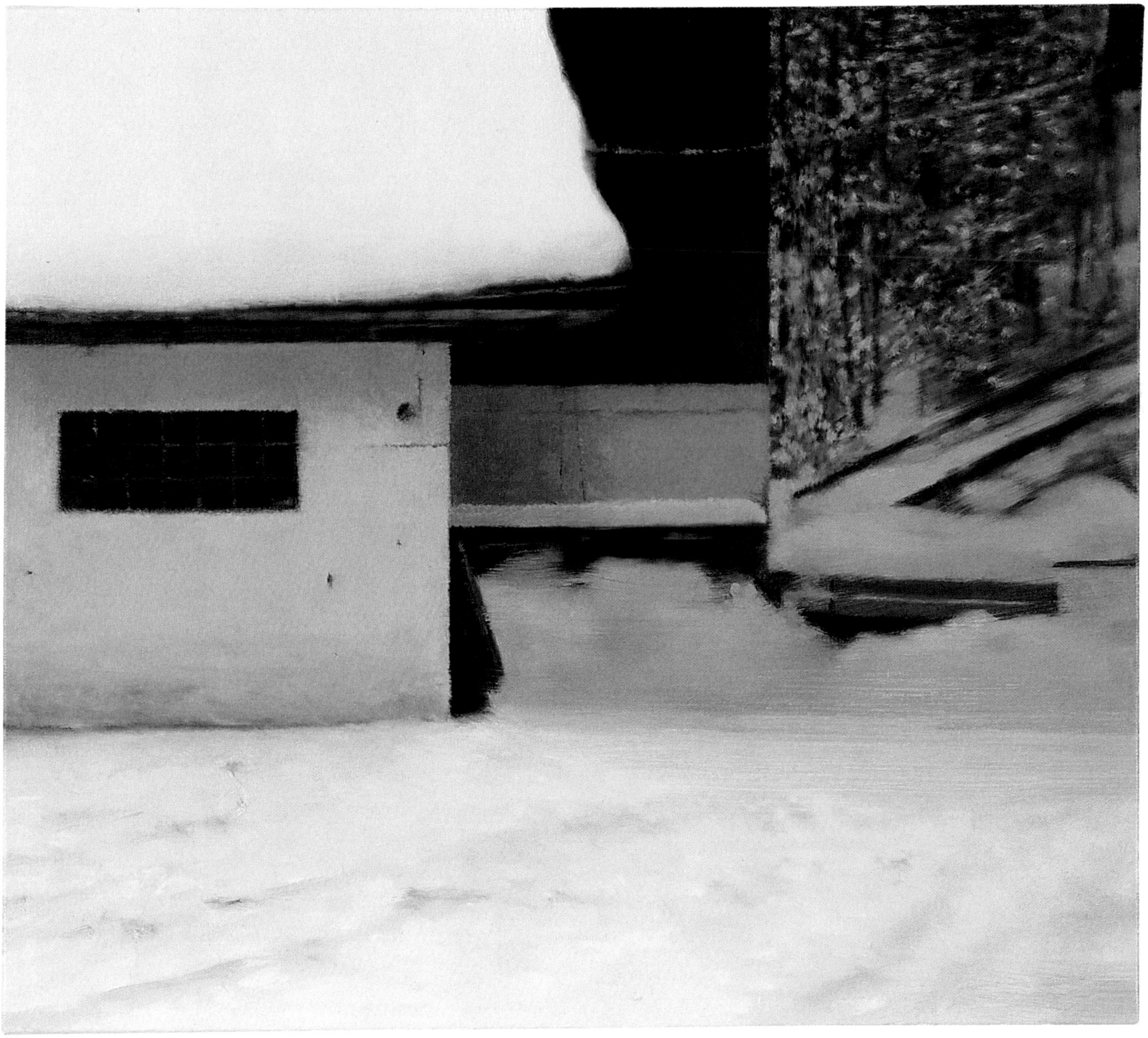

Moritz, 2000 20 $\frac{1}{16}$ × 18 $\frac{1}{8}$ in. (51 × 46 cm)

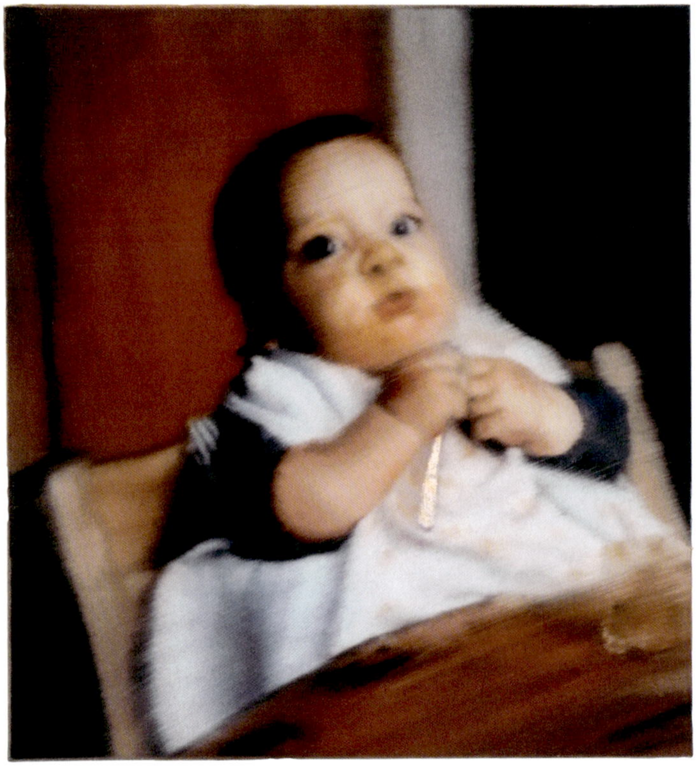

Moritz, 2000 $24\frac{7}{16} \times 20\frac{1}{2}$ in. (62×52 cm)

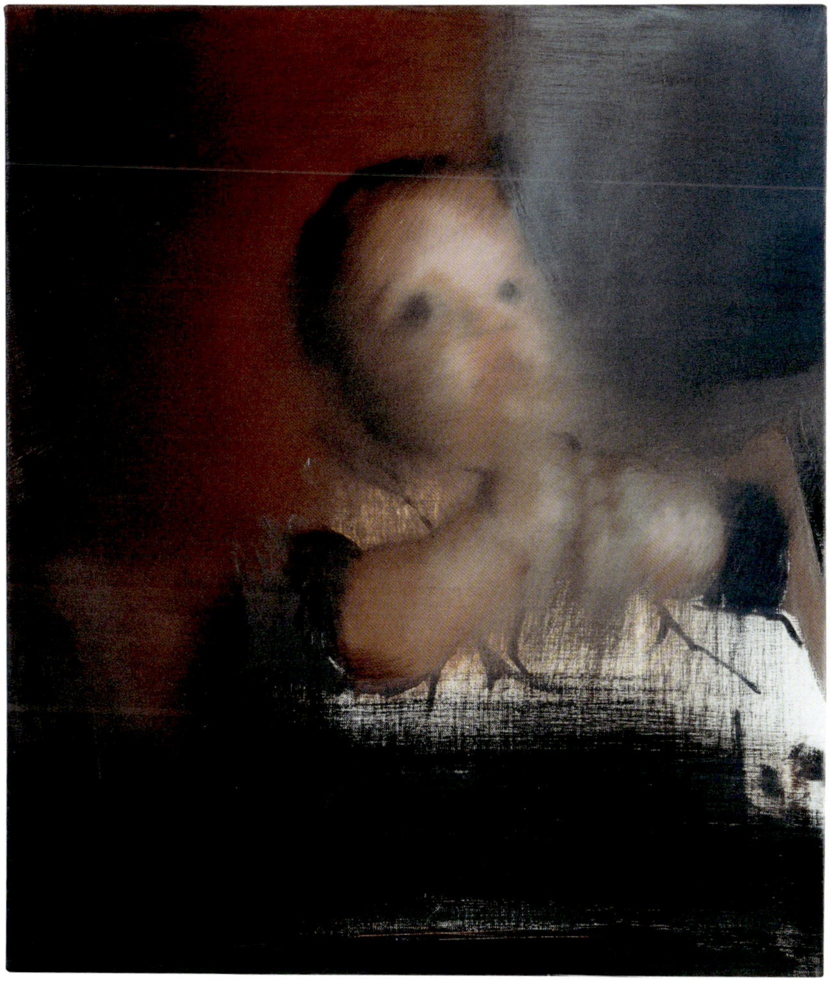

11 Panes, 2004   10 ft. 11 ⅞ in. × 82 $^{11}/_{16}$ in. × 22 $^{13}/_{16}$ in. (335 × 210 × 58 cm)

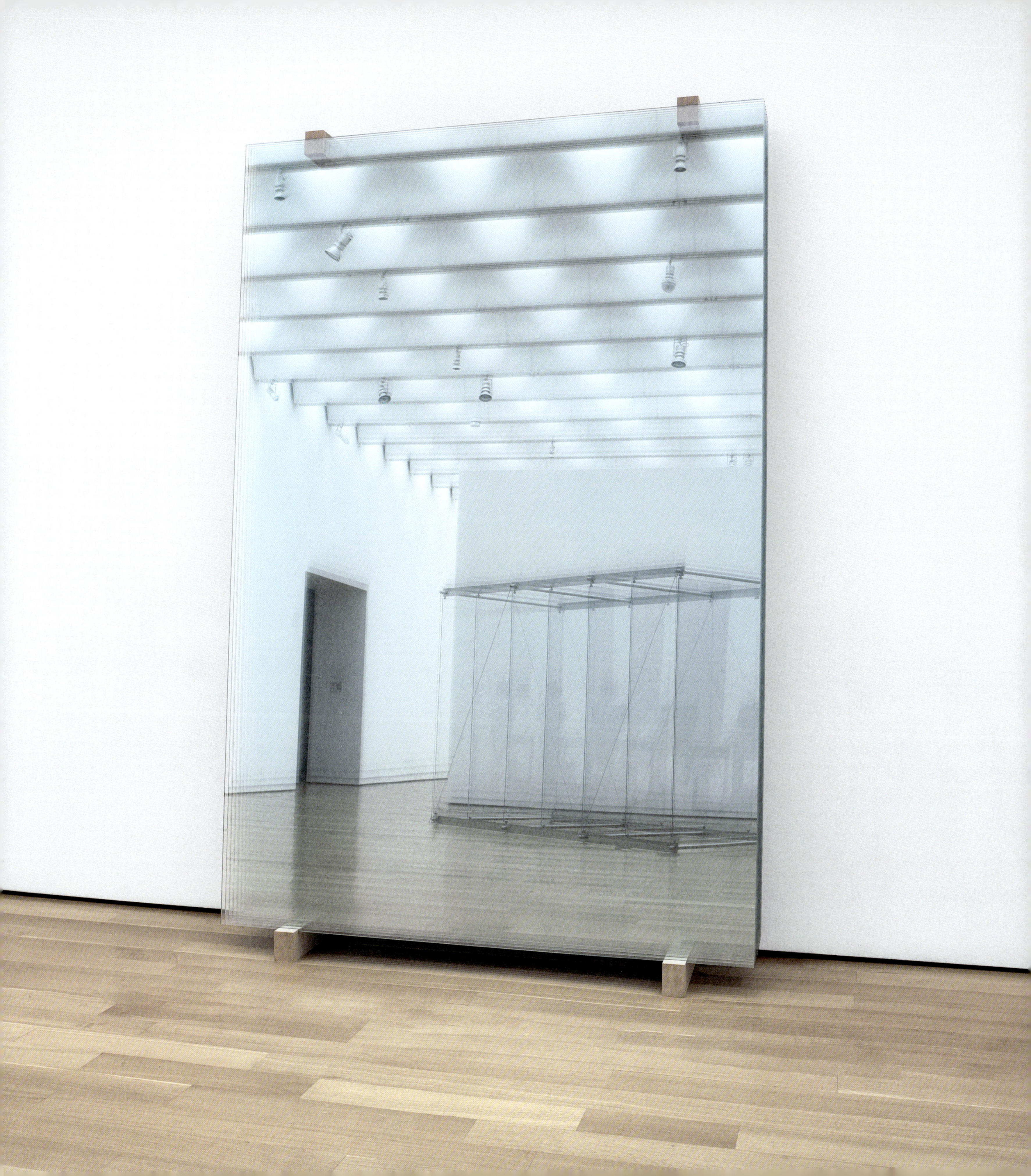

September, 2005 20 ½ × 28 ⅜ in. (52 × 72 cm)

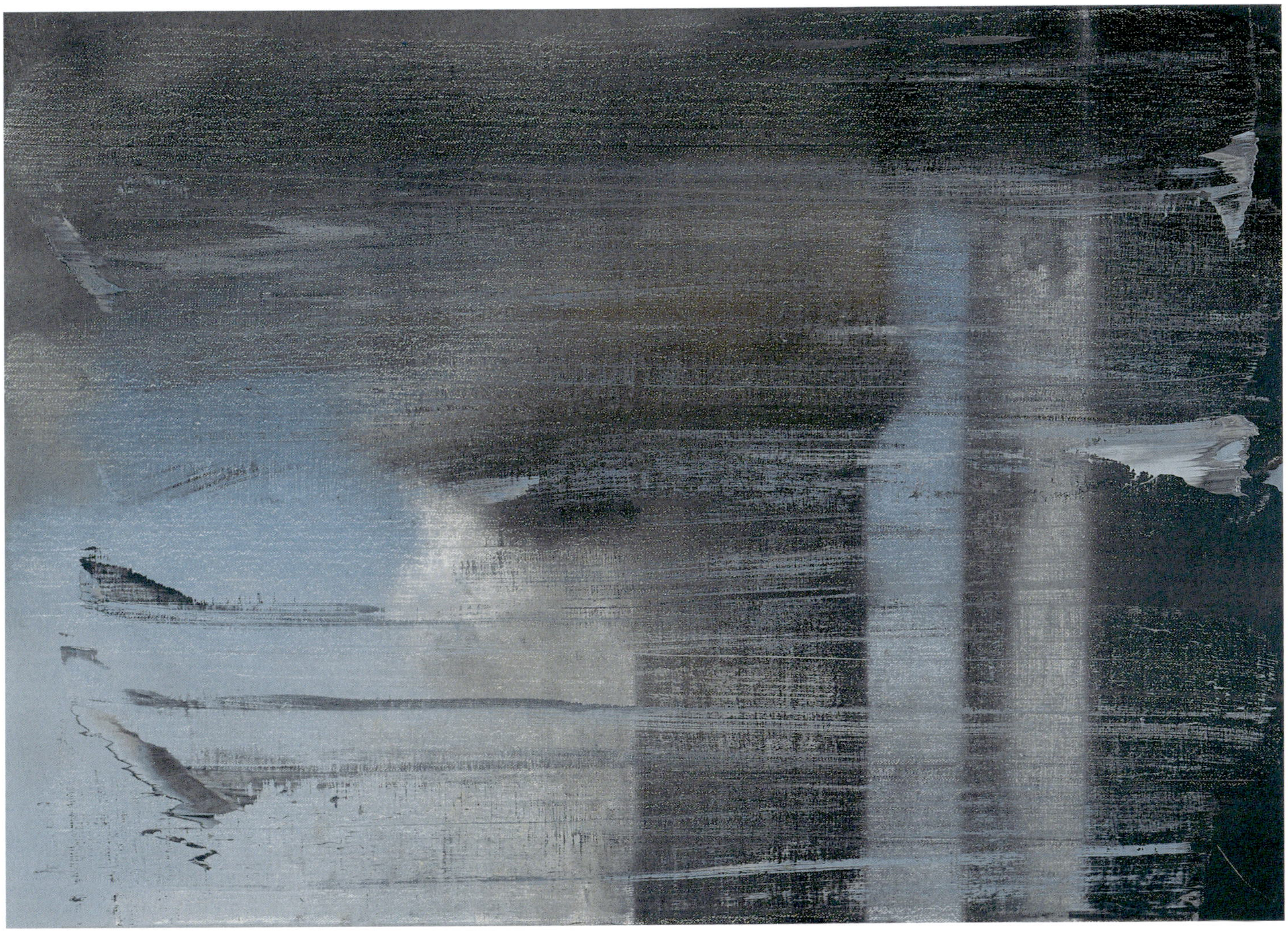

Juist, 2005 $24\,{}^{7}\!/_{16} \times 22\,{}^{7}\!/_{16}$ in. (62×57 cm)

Forest (1–12), 2005 each 77 9/16 × 51 15/16 in. (197 × 132 cm)

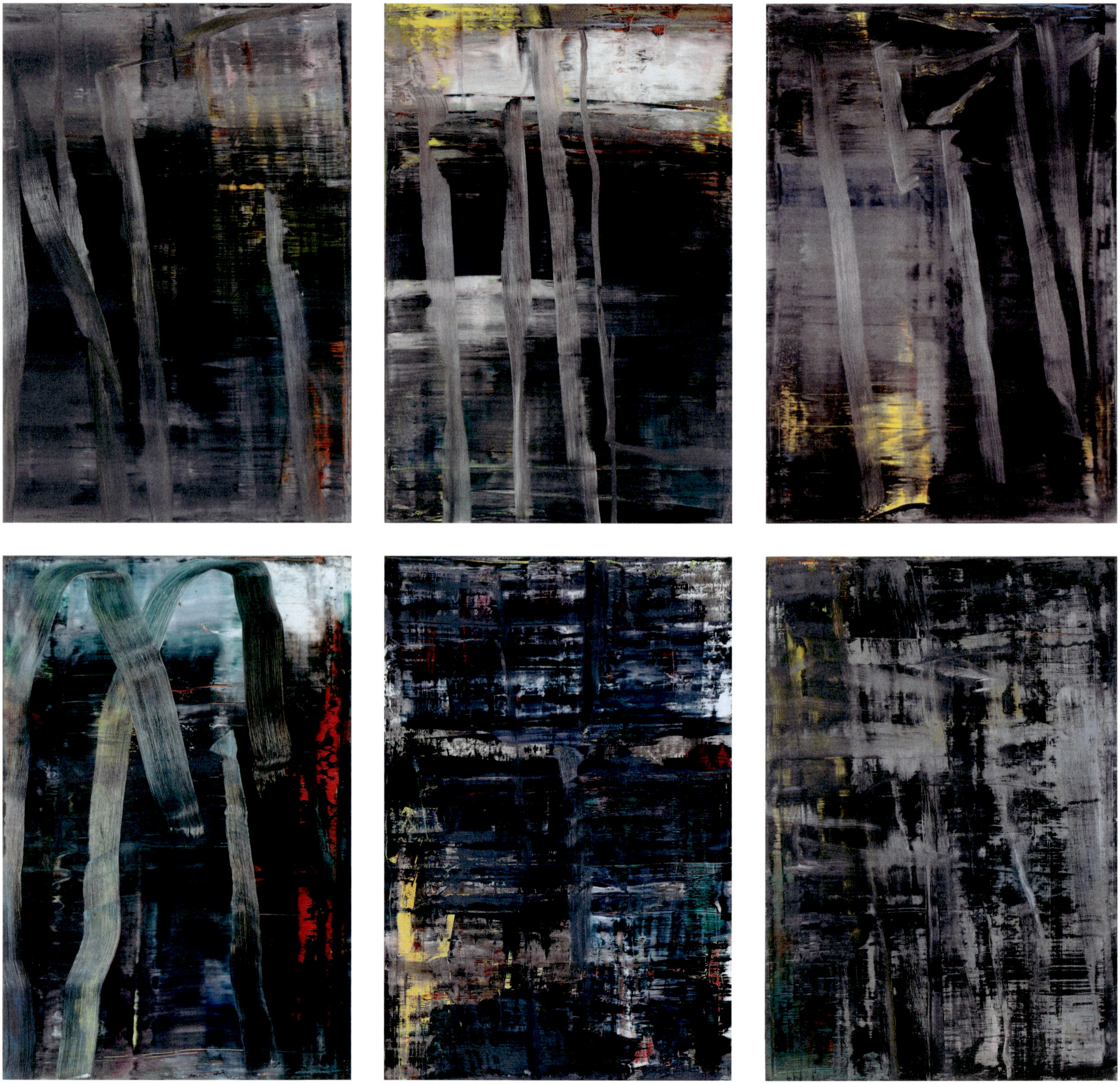

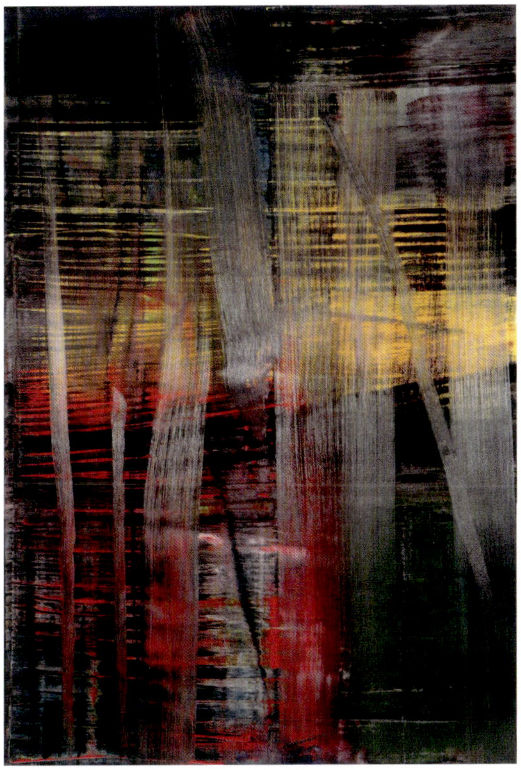
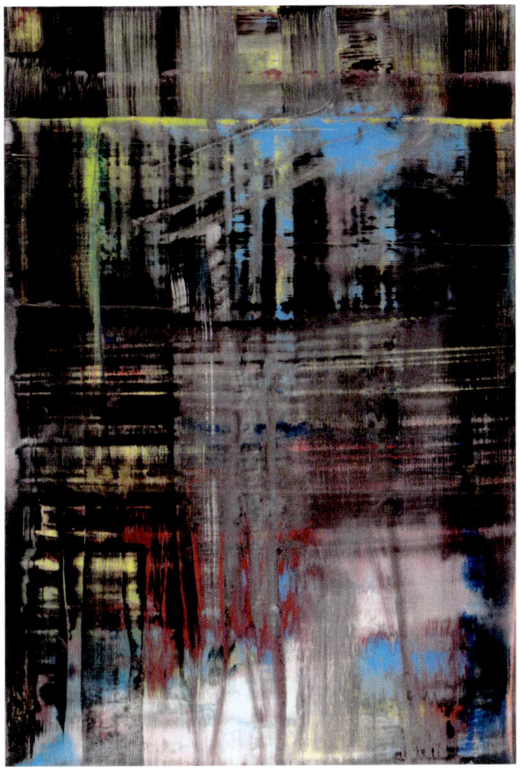
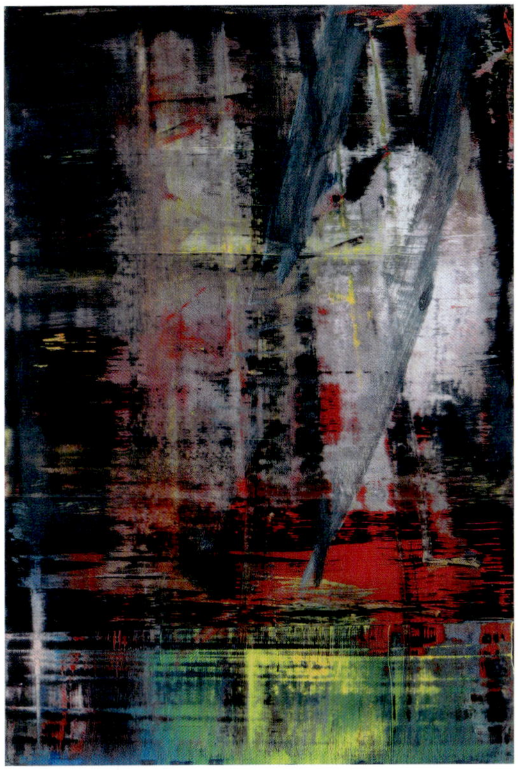
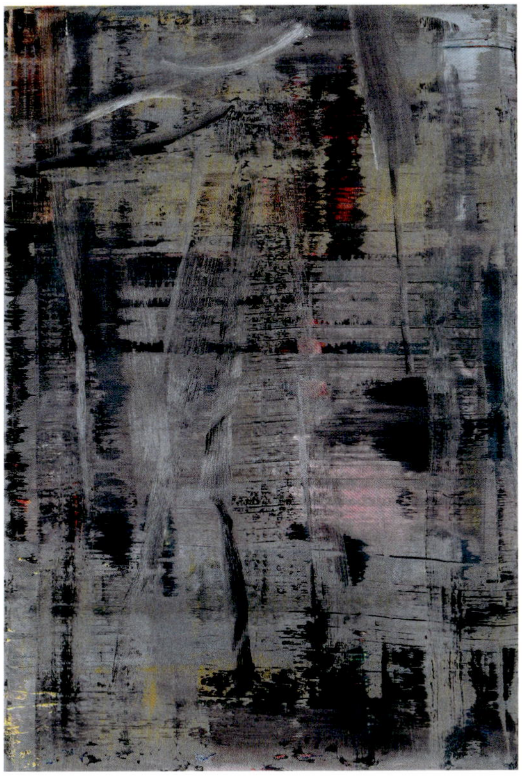
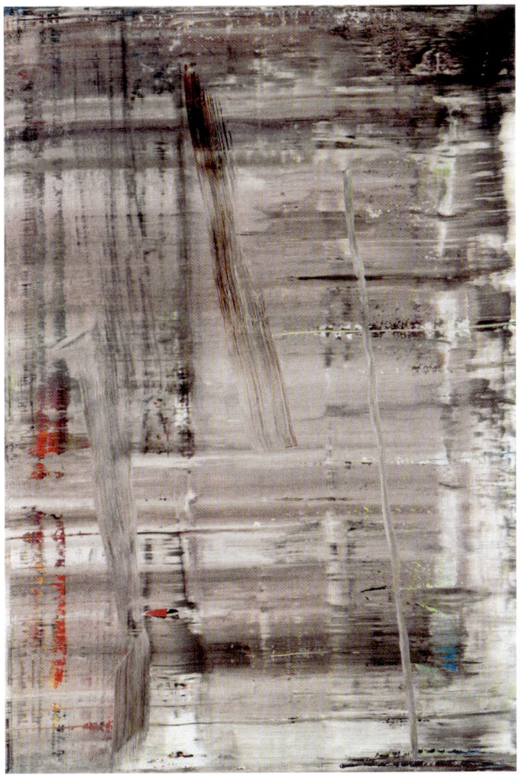
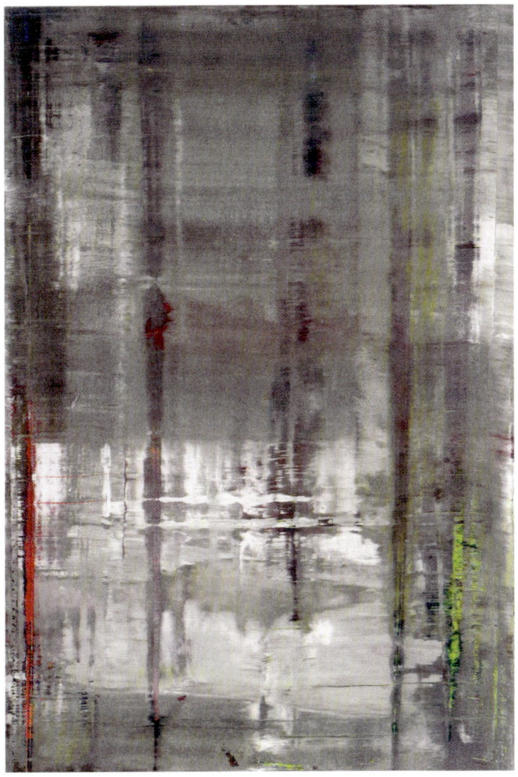

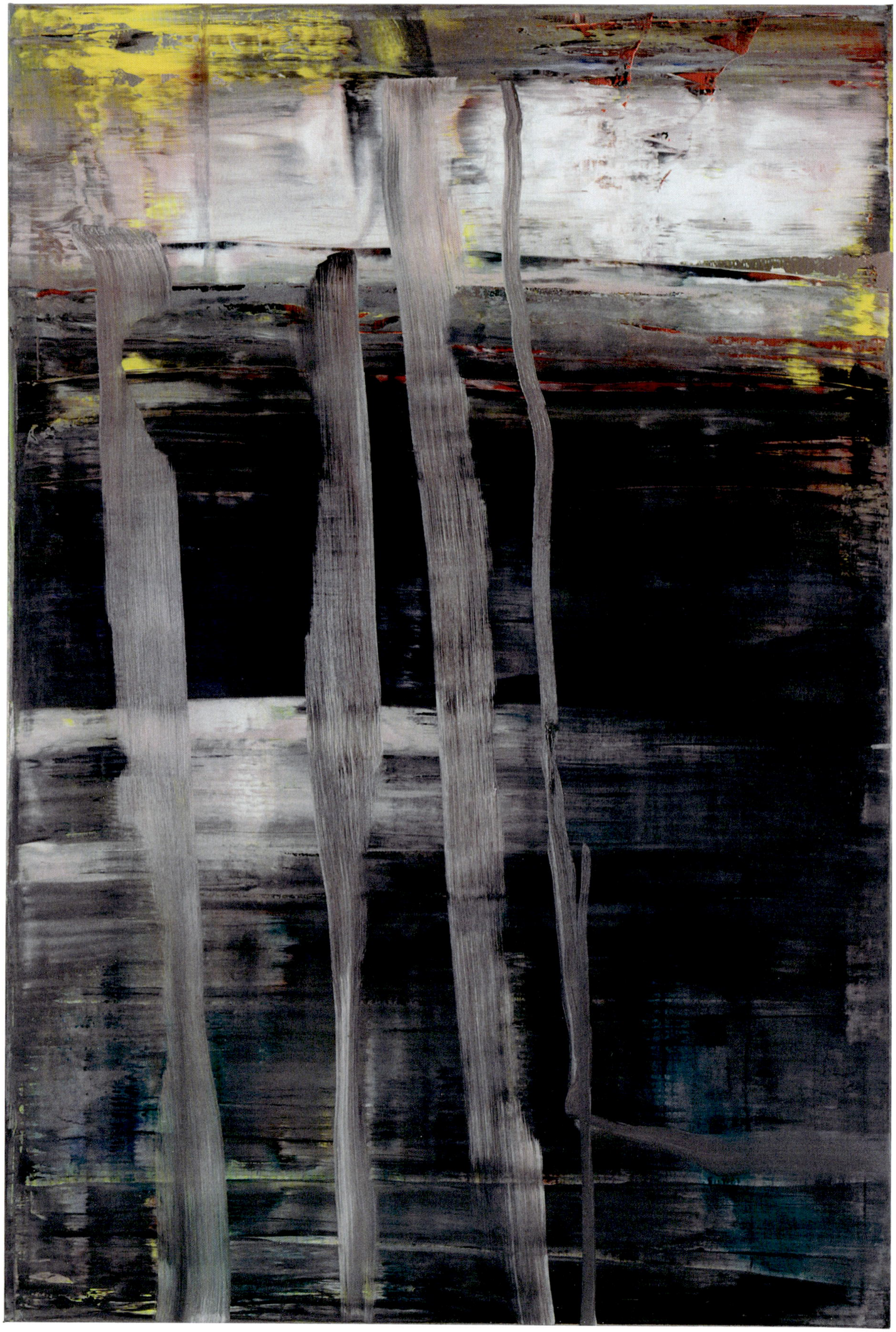

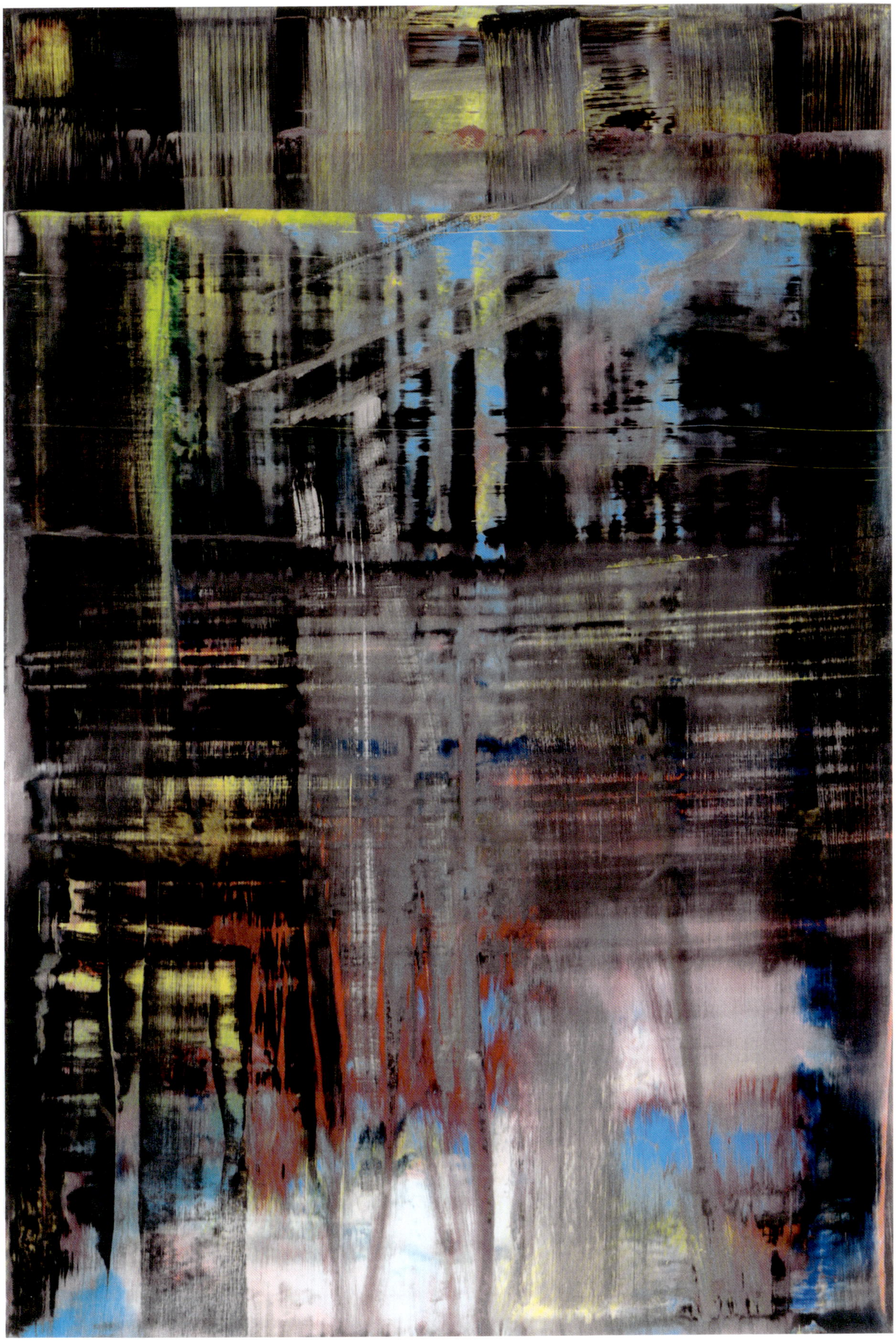

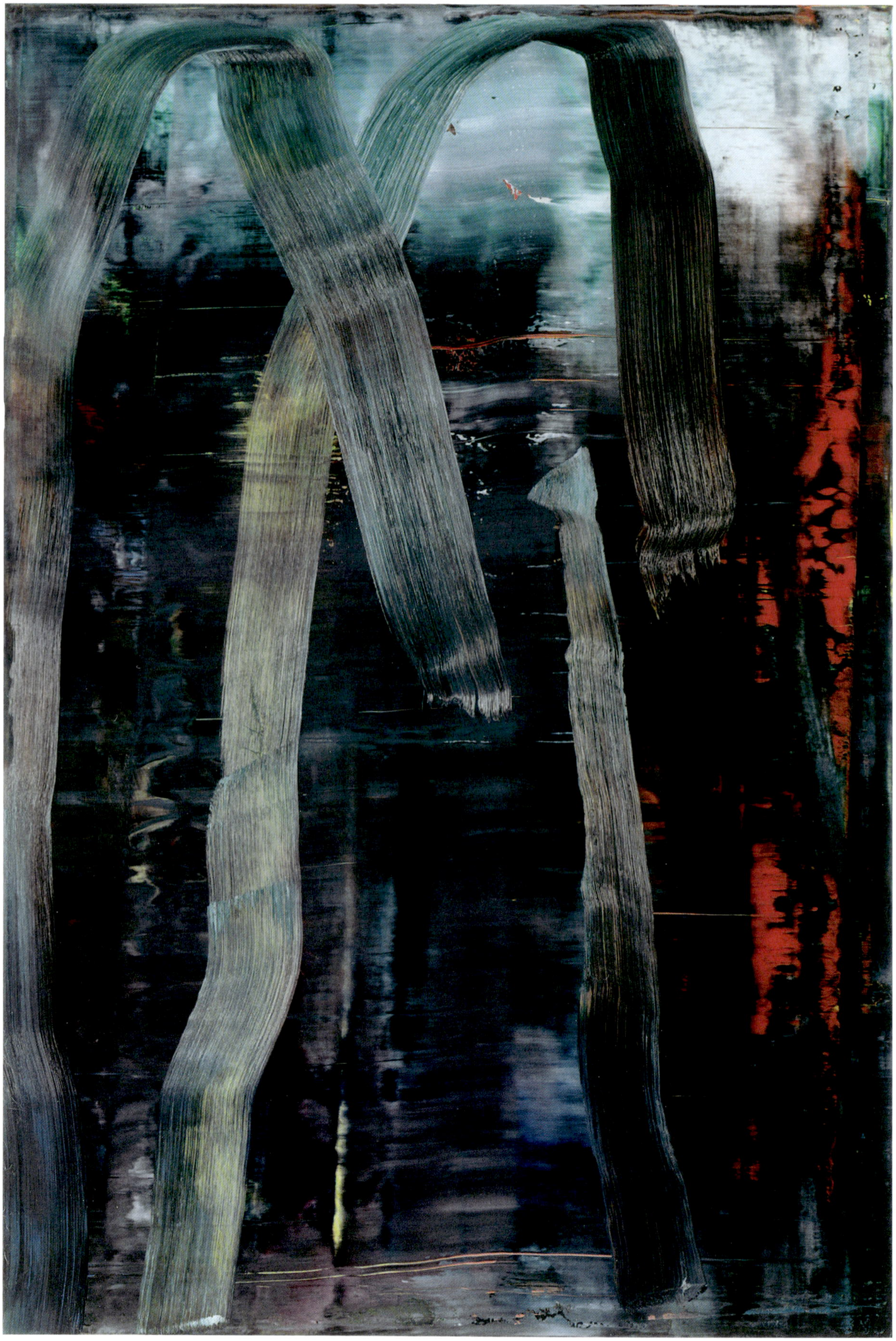

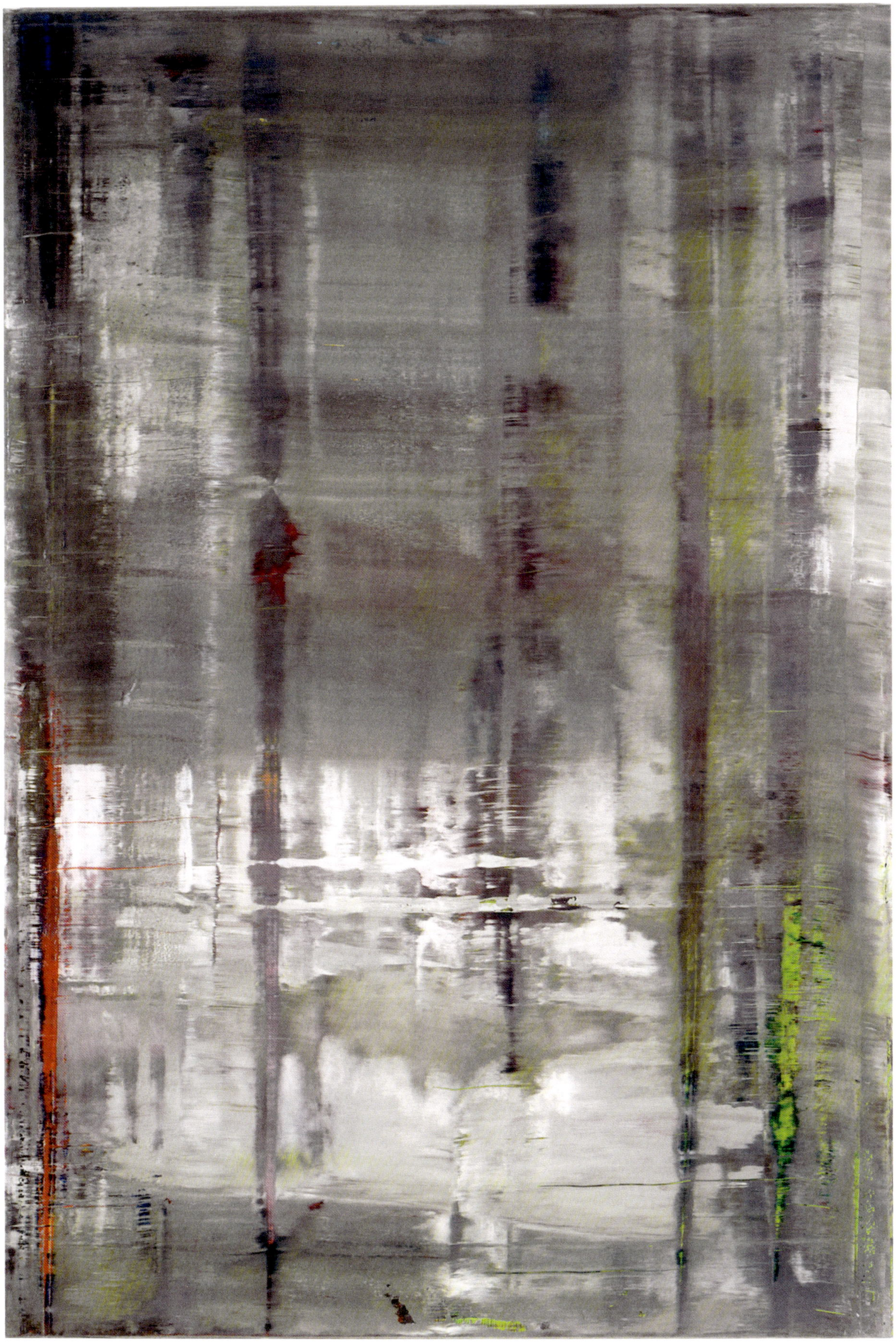

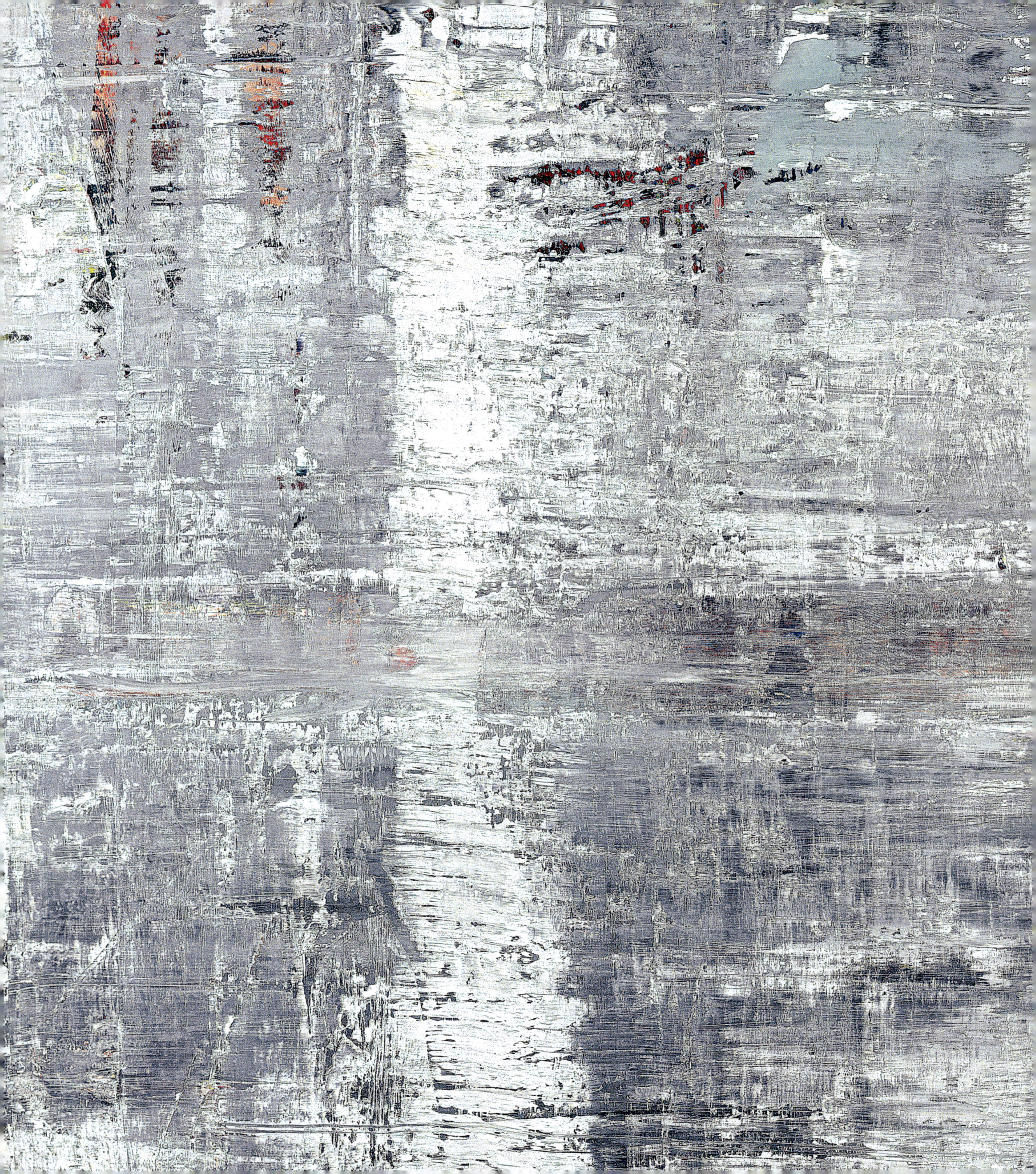

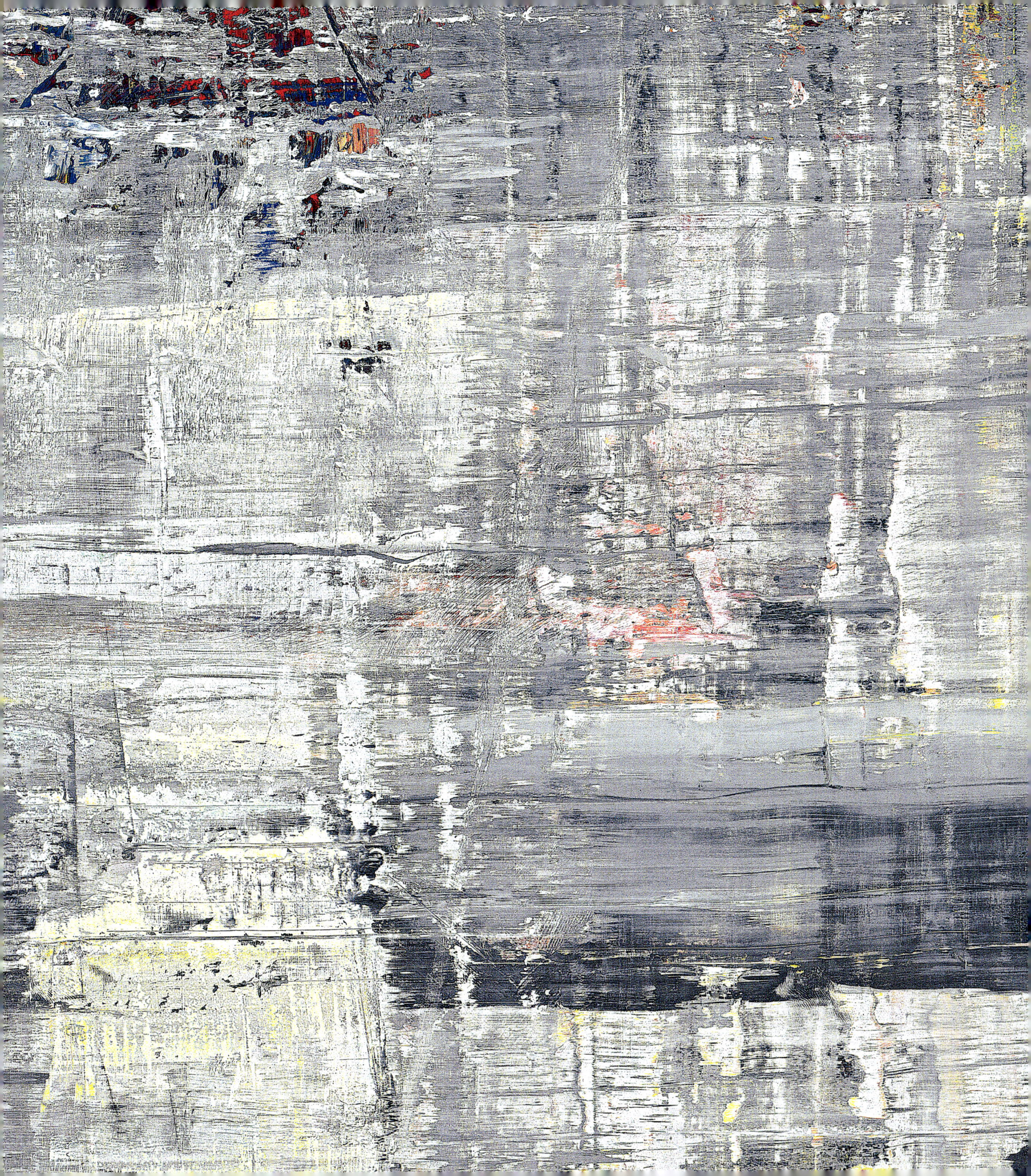

Cage (1), 2006 9 ft. 6 3/16 in. × 9 ft. 6 3/16 in. (290 × 290 cm)

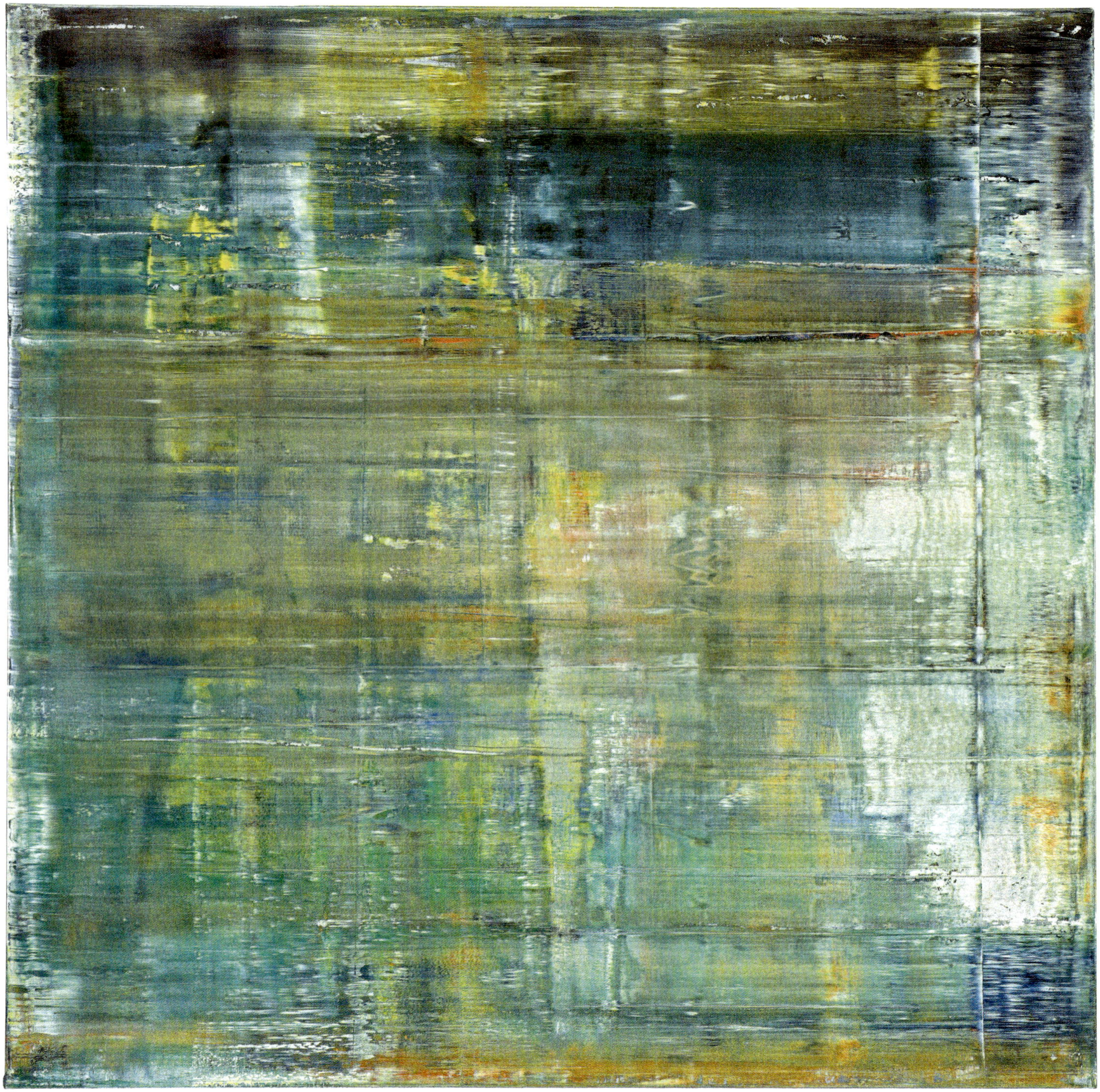

Cage (2), 2006 9 ft. 10 ⅛ in. × 9 ft. 10 ⅛ in. (300 × 300 cm)

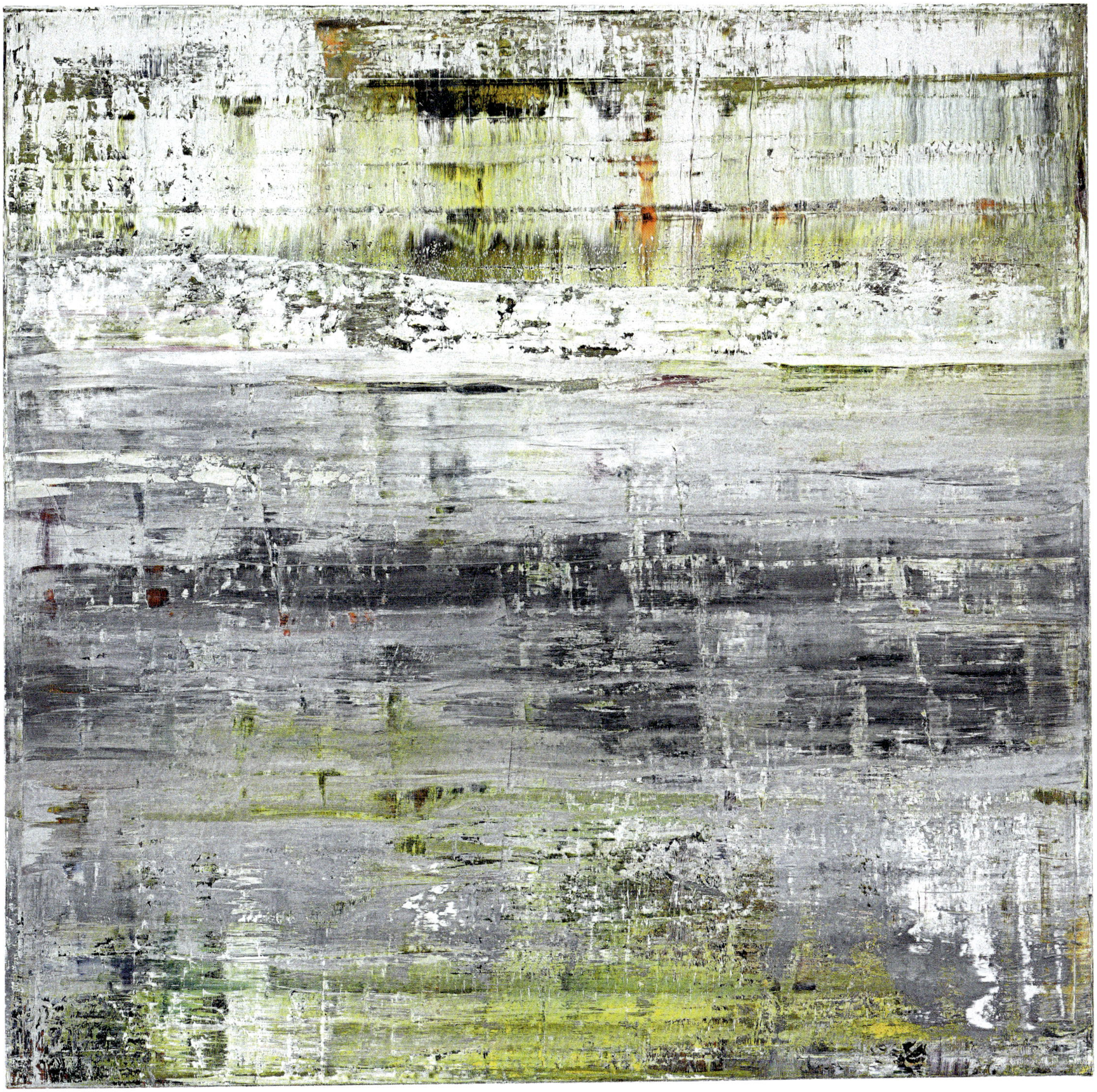

Cage (3), 2006   9 ft. 6 3/16 in. × 9 ft. 6 3/16 in. (290 × 290 cm)

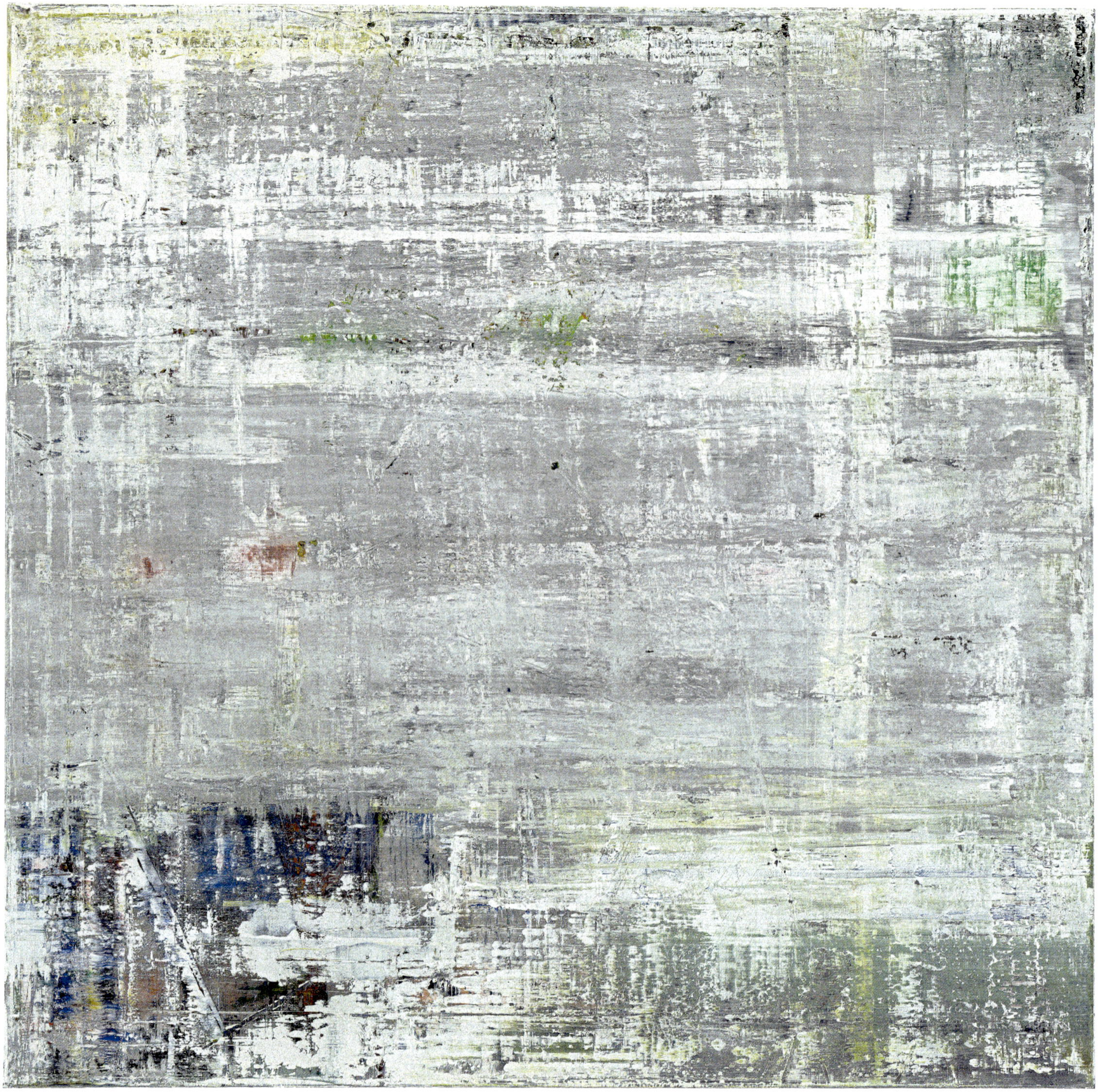

Cage (4), 2006 9 ft. 6 3⁄16 in. × 9 ft. 6 3⁄16 in. (290 × 290 cm)

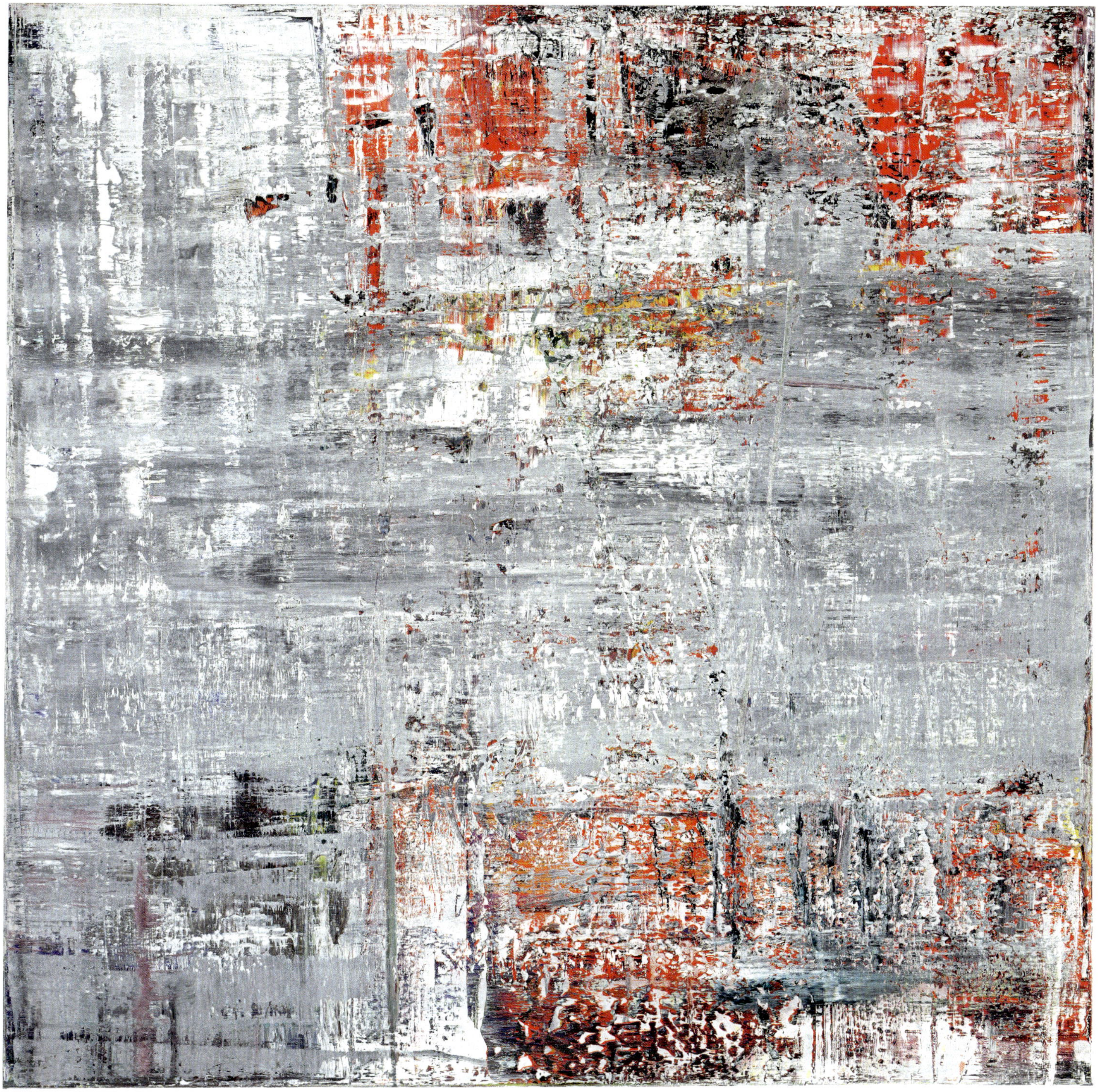

Cage (5), 2006 9 ft. 10 ⅛ in. × 9 ft. 10 ⅛ in. (300 × 300 cm)

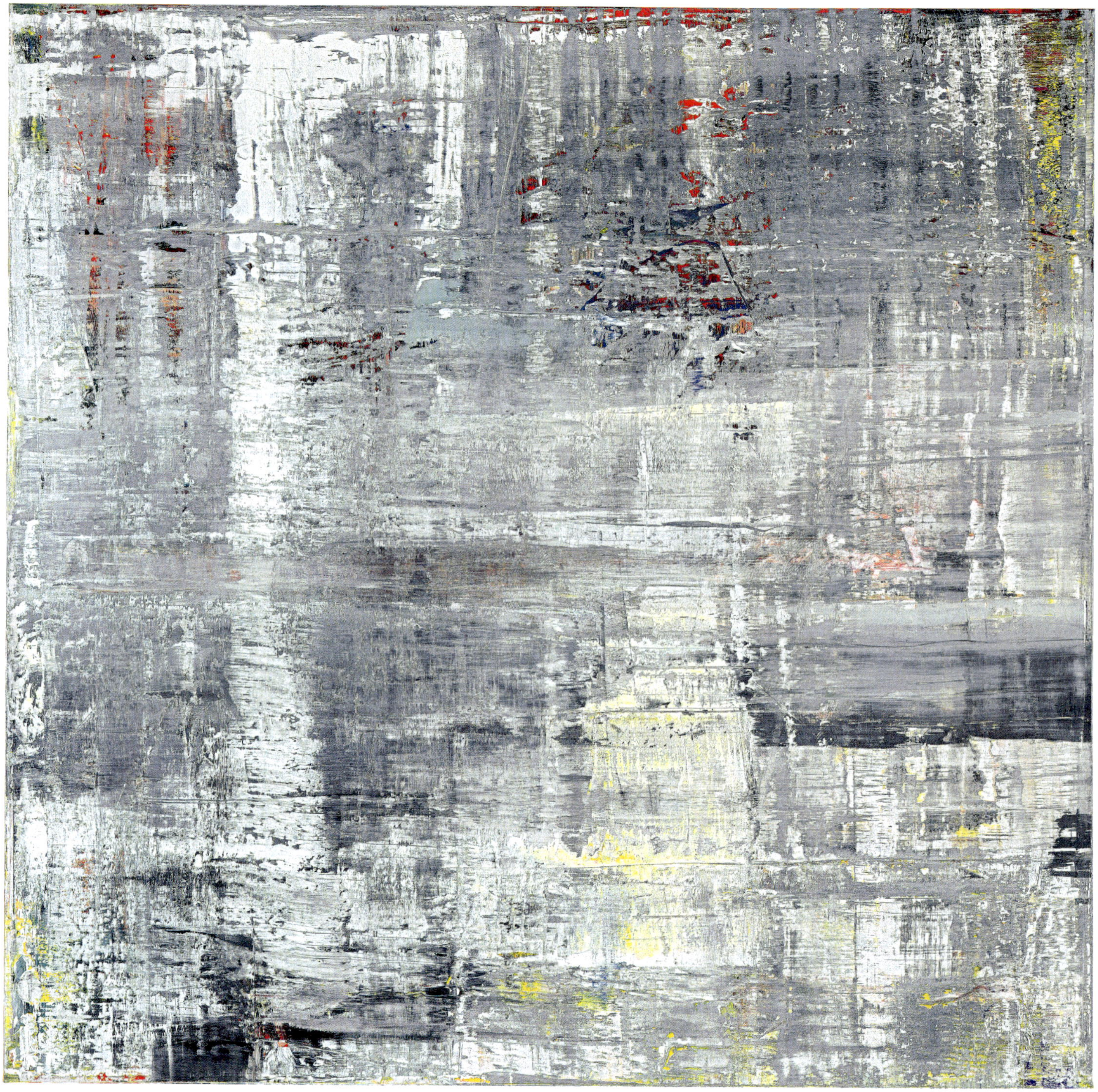

Cage (6), 2006 9 ft. 10 ⅛ in. × 9 ft. 10 ⅛ in. (300 × 300 cm)

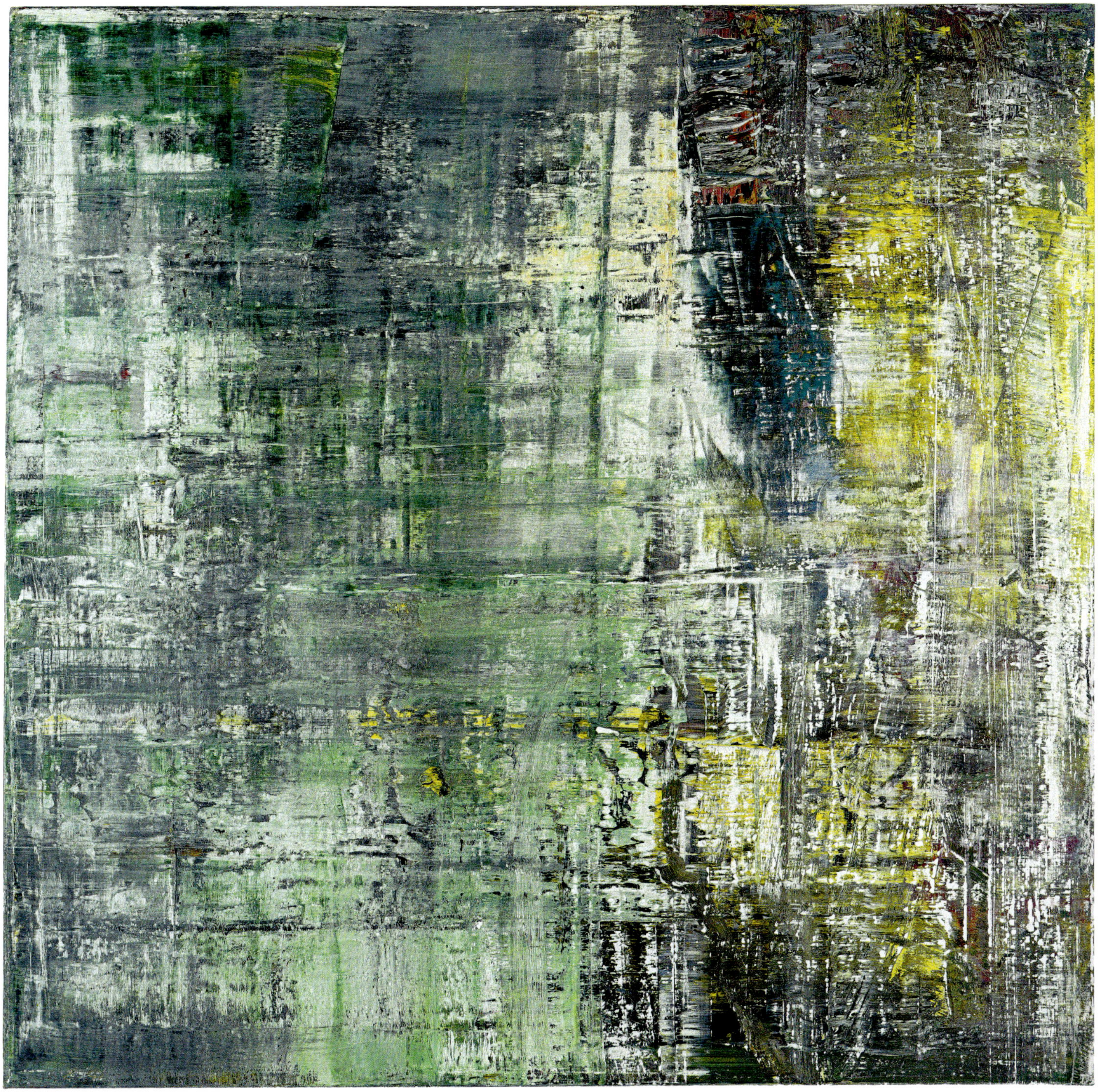

4,900 Colors, 2007 140 panels, each 19 ⅛ × 19 ⅛ in. (48.5 × 48.5 cm); 5 parts, total 11 ft. 1 11/16 in. × 76 ⅜ in. (339.5 × 194 cm)

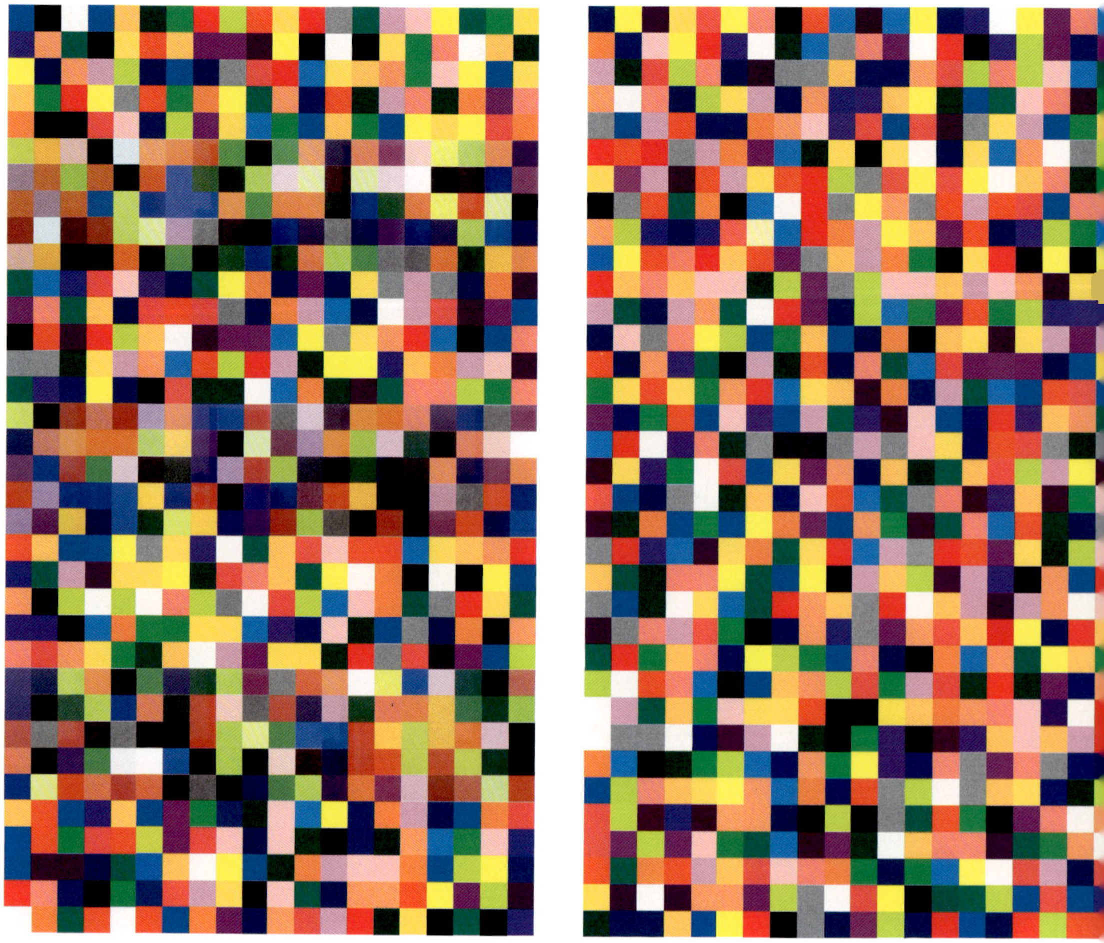

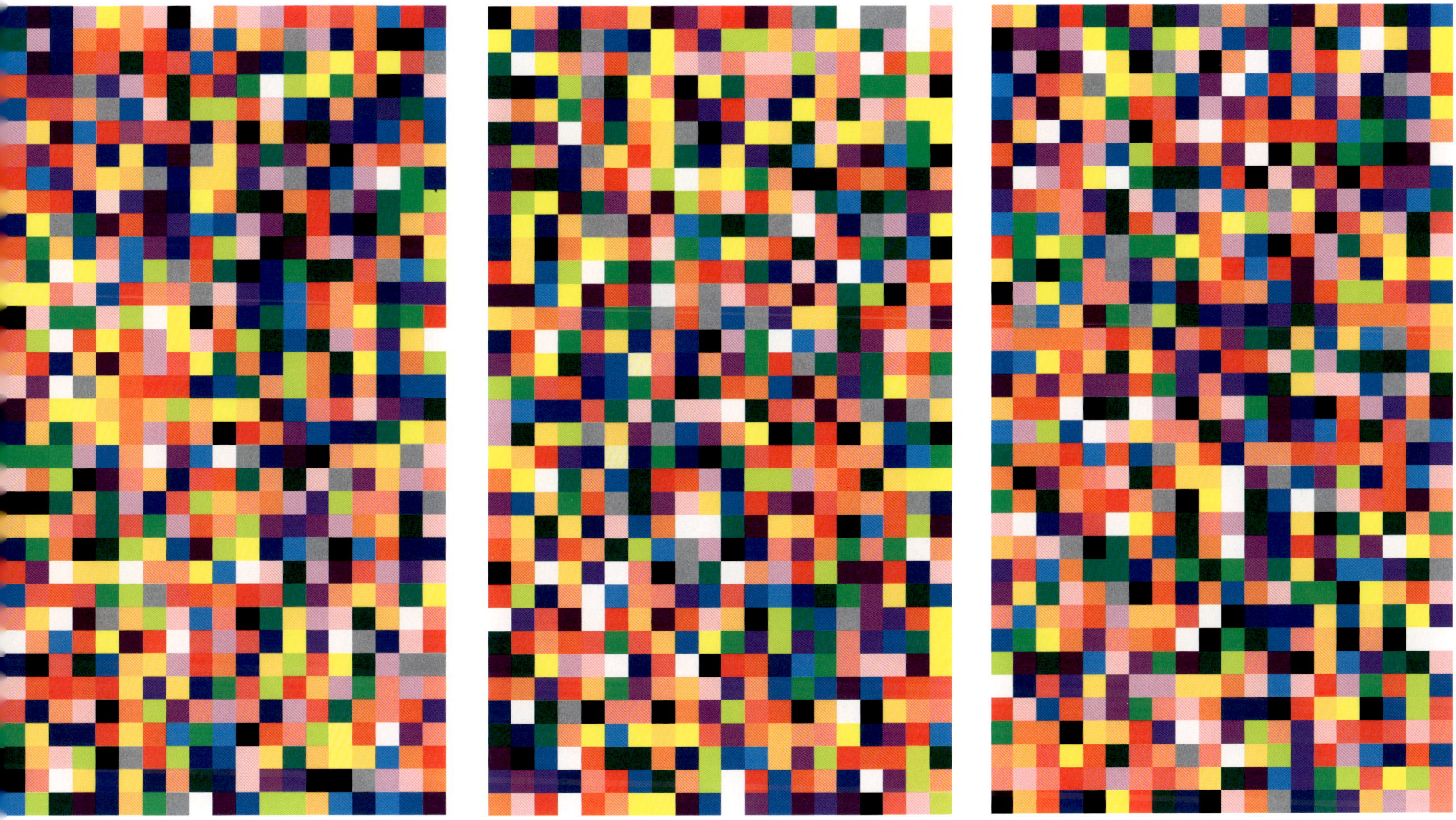

Ella, 2007   15 ¾ × 12 3/16 in. (40 × 31 cm)

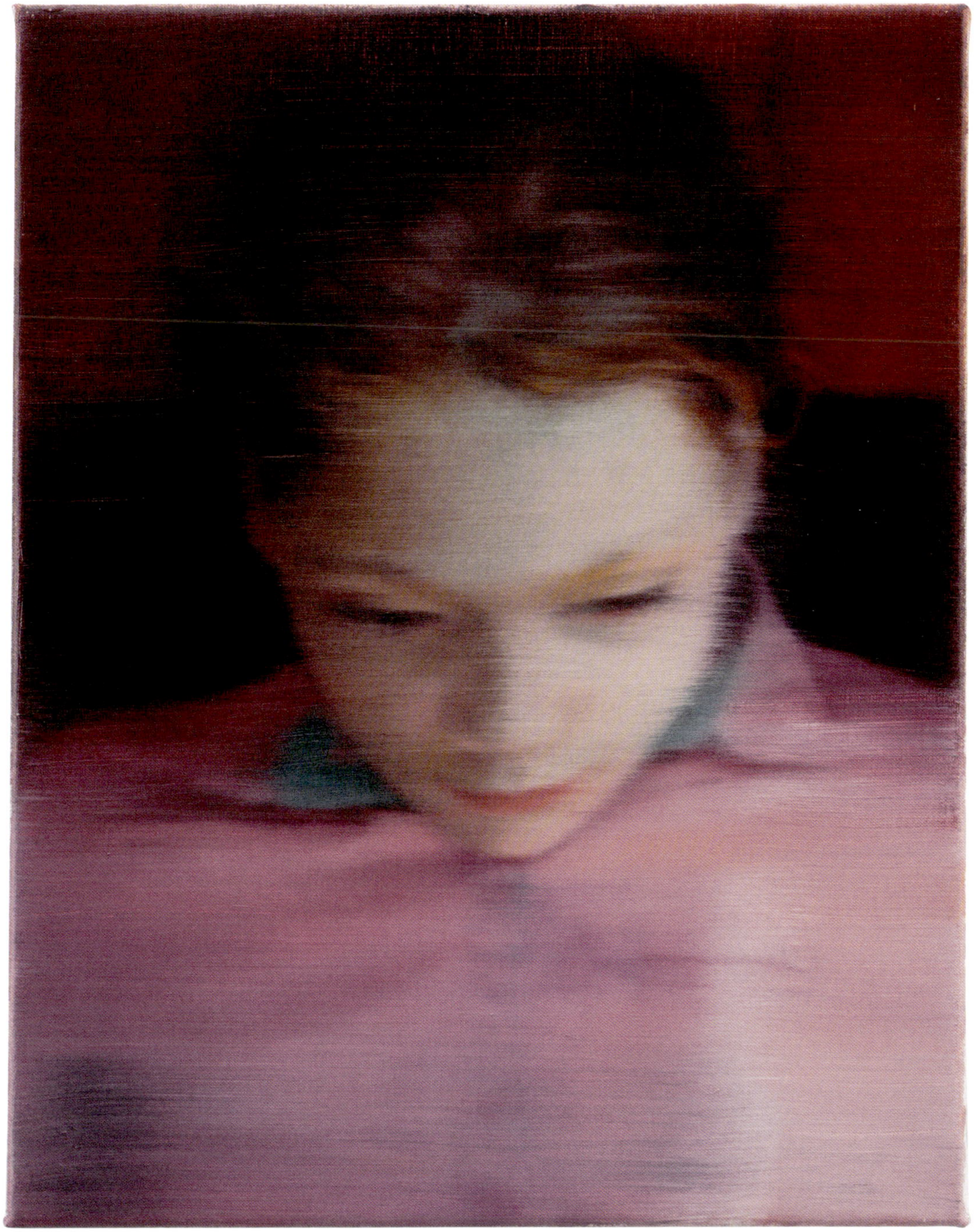

Abstract Painting, 2009 78 ¾ in. × 9 ft. 10 ⅛ in. (200 × 300 cm)

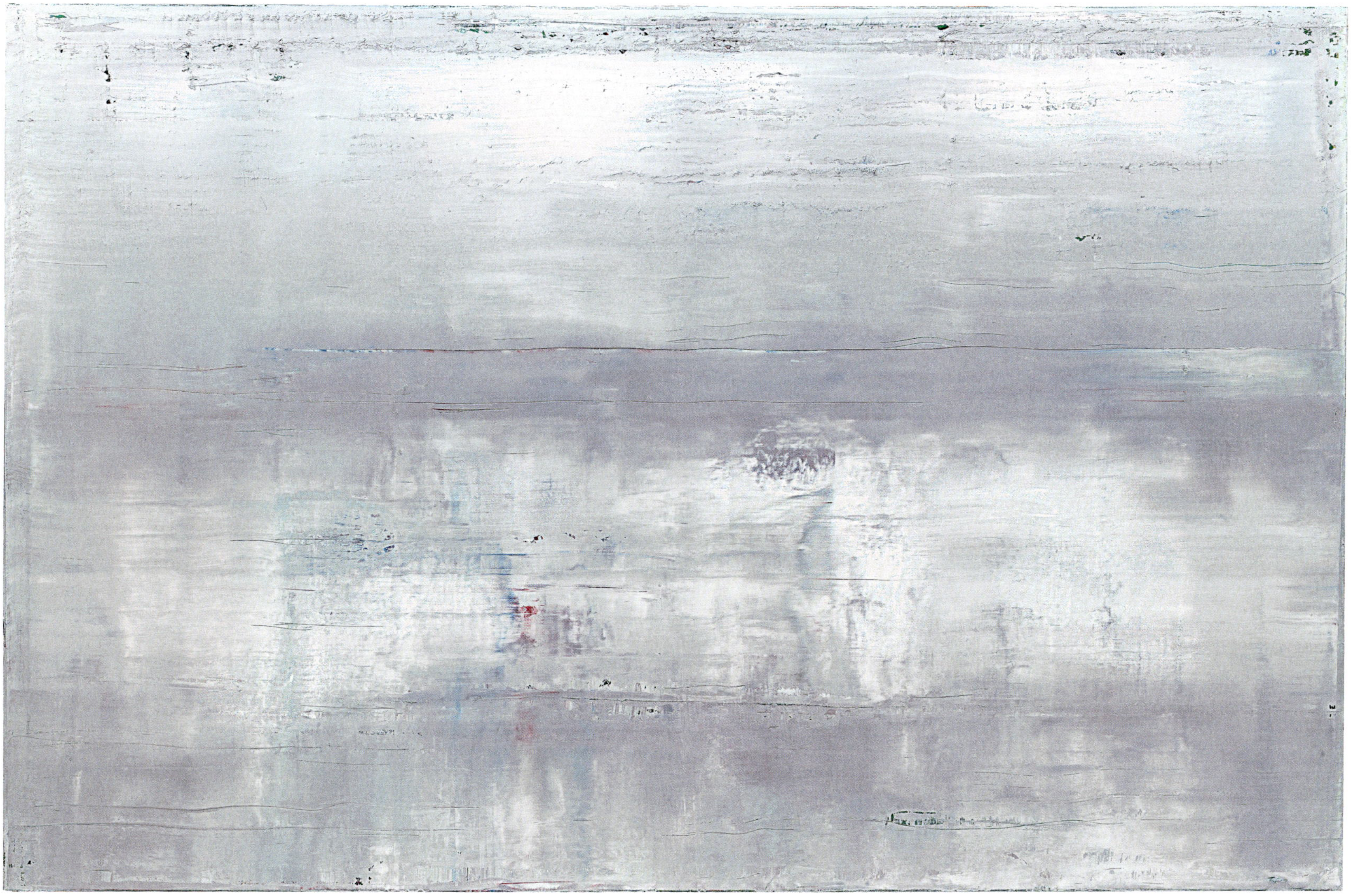

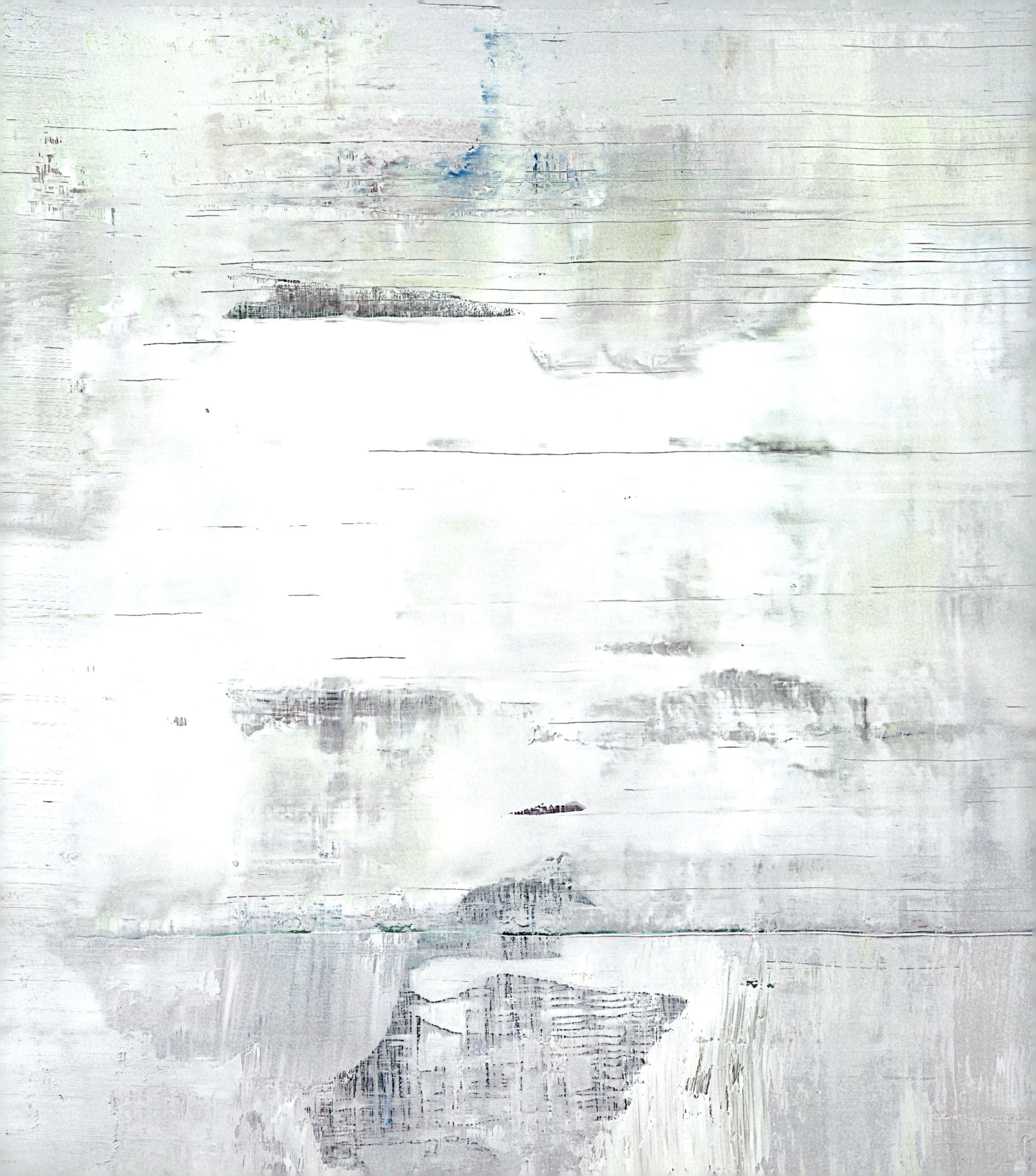

Abstract Painting, 2009 78 ¾ in. × 9 ft. 10 ⅛ in. (200 × 300 cm)

Elbe, 1957/2012 each 11 ⅝ × 8 ¼ in. (29.5 × 21 cm)

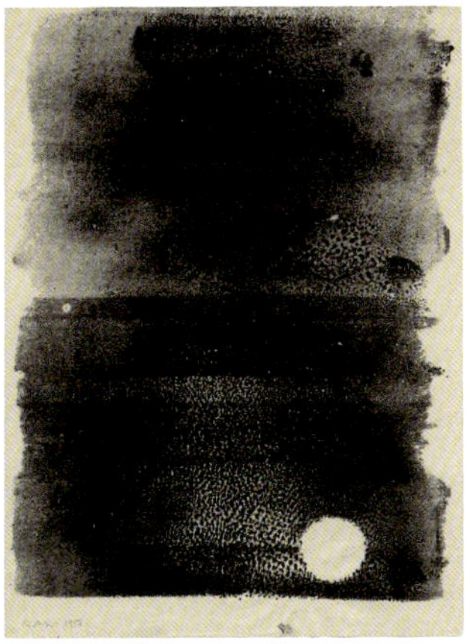
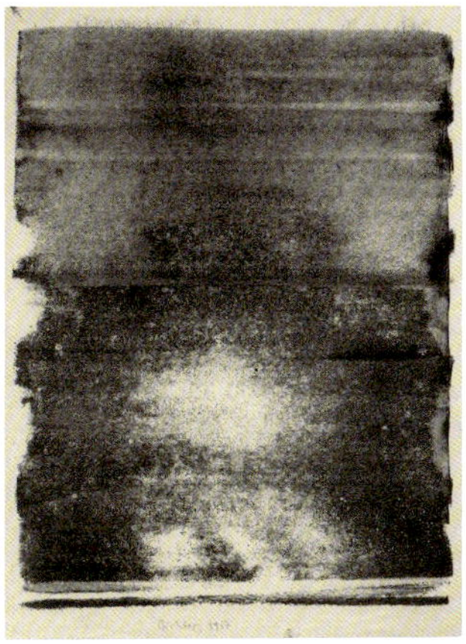

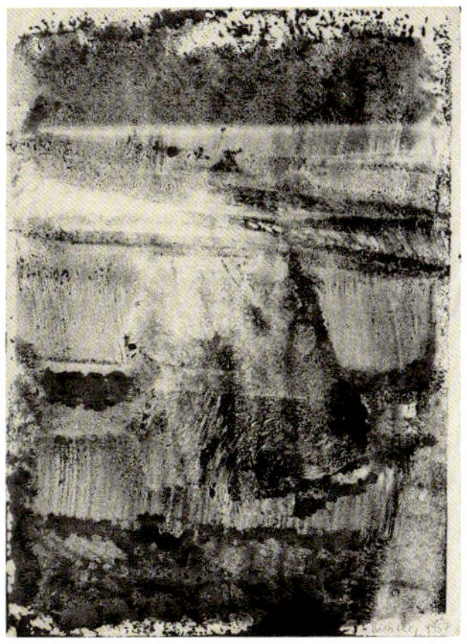
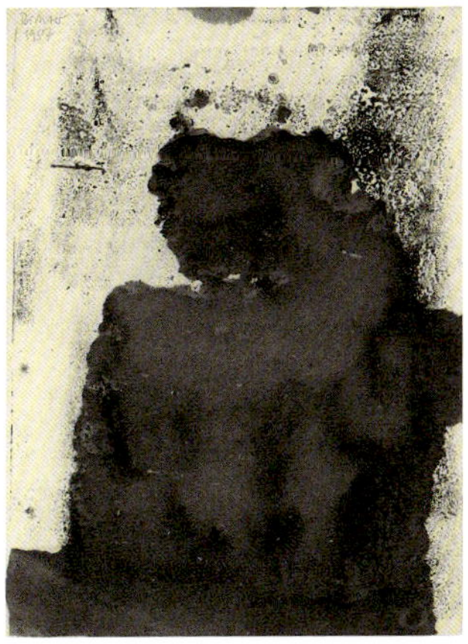
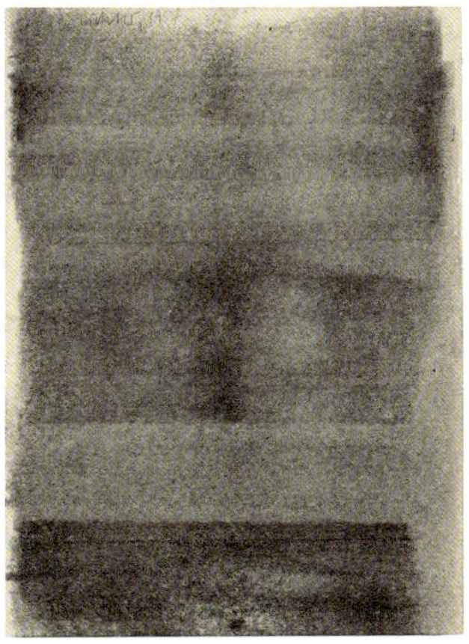
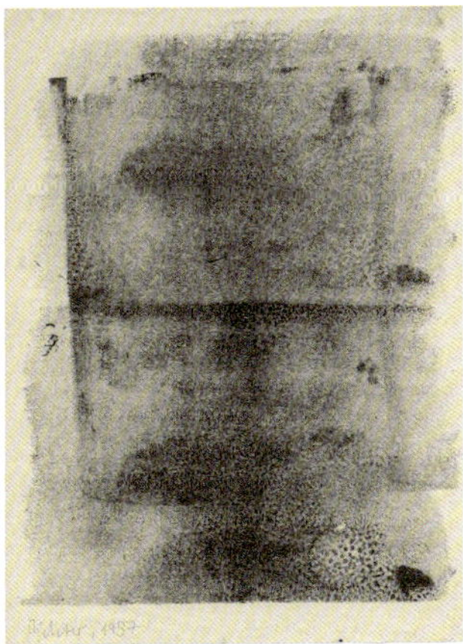
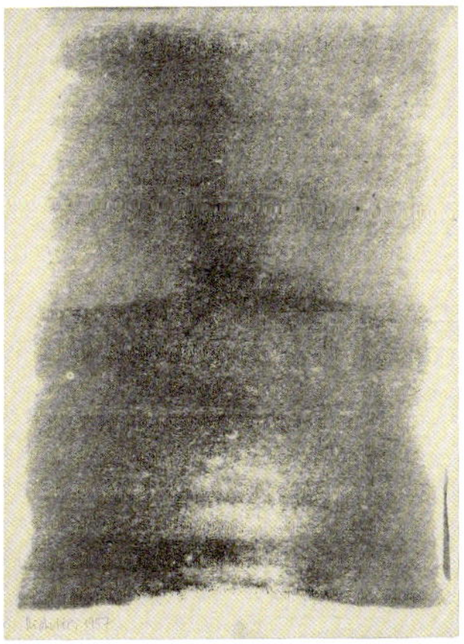
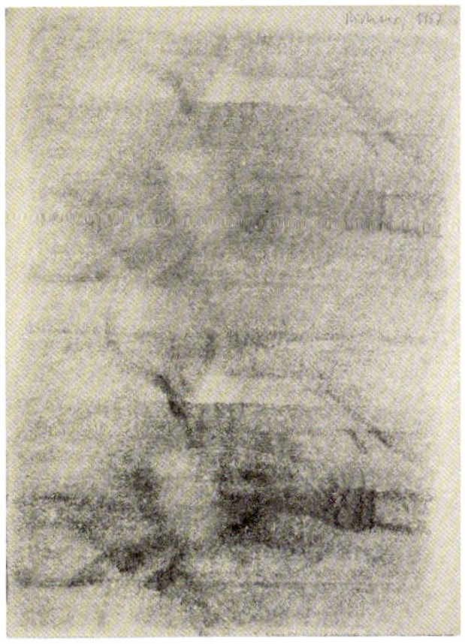
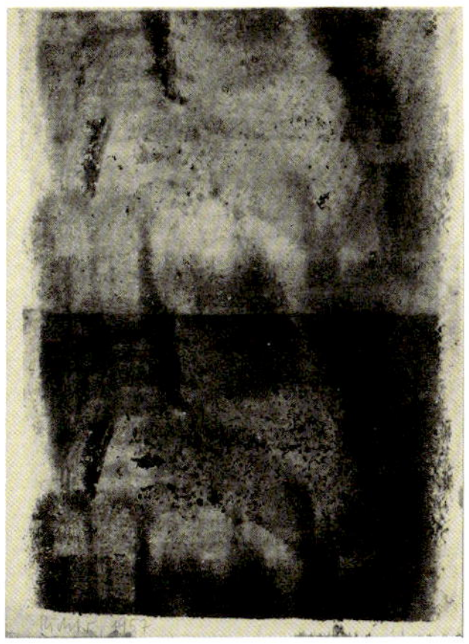
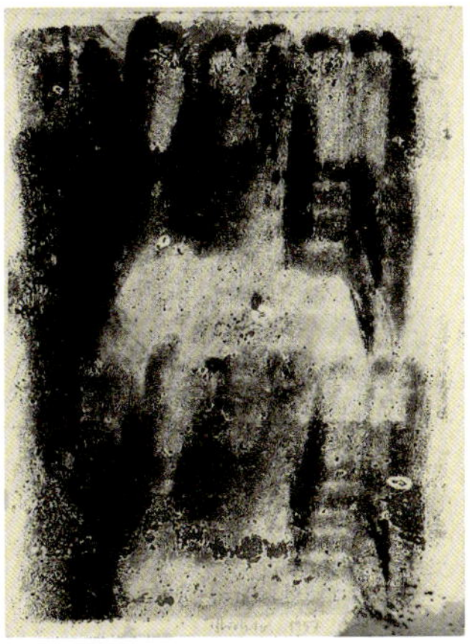
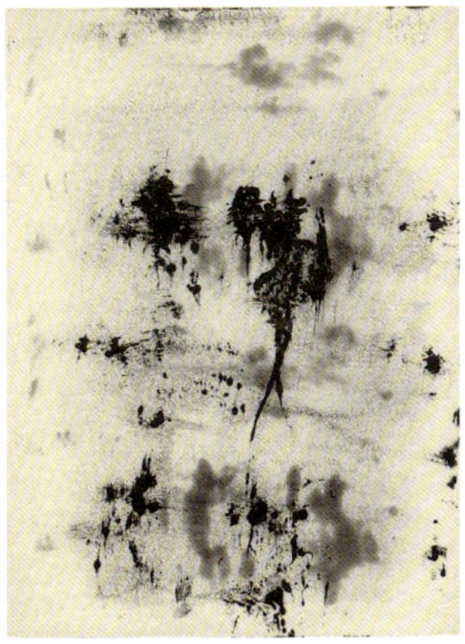
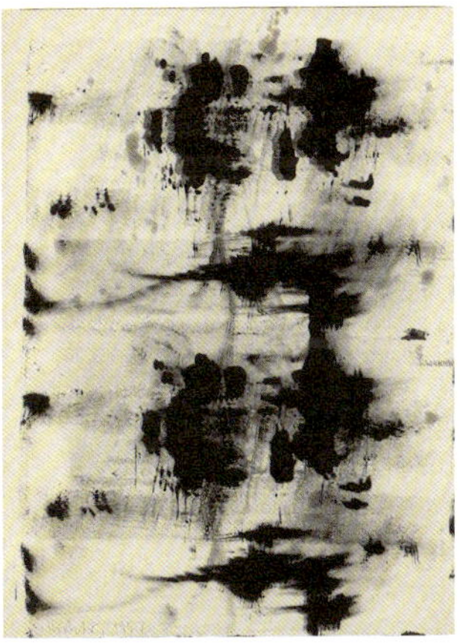
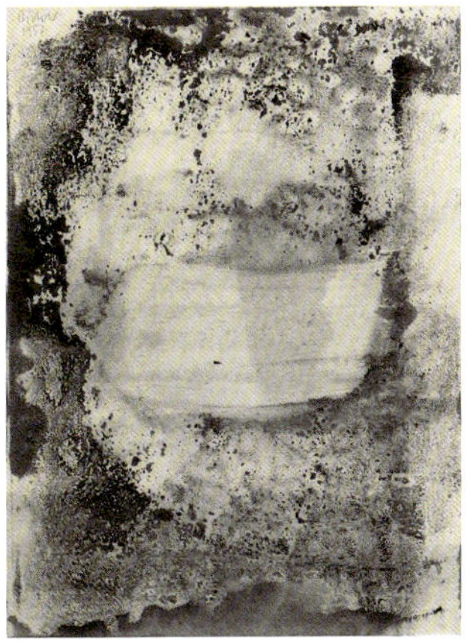
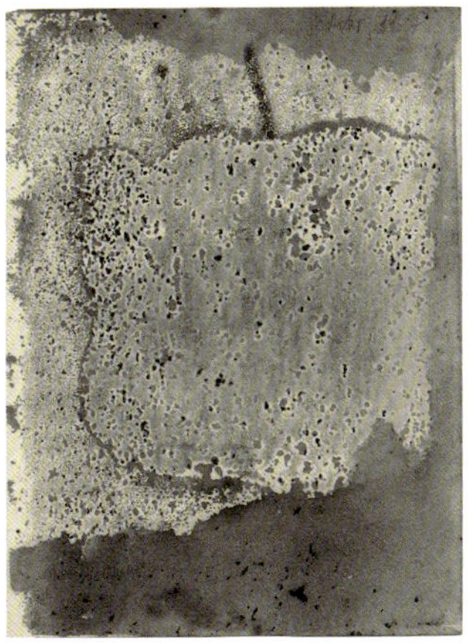
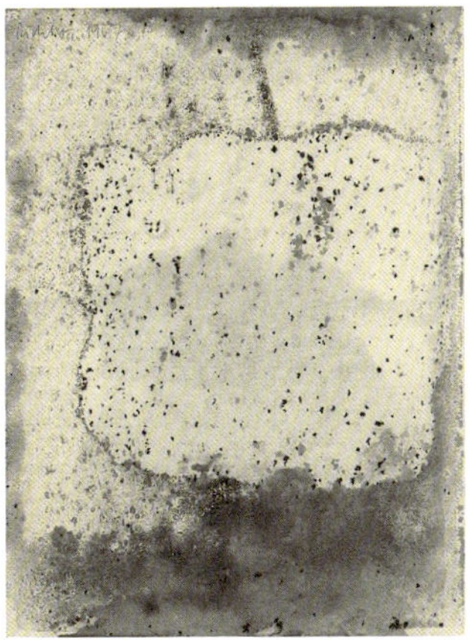
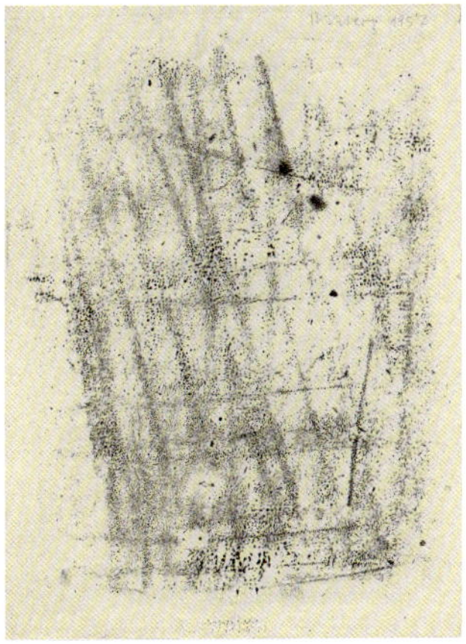
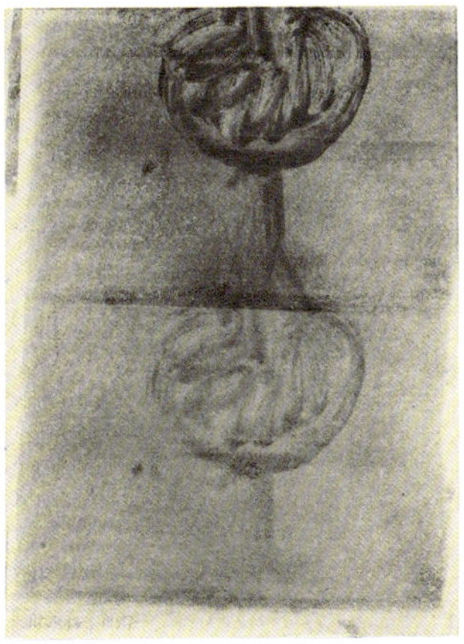

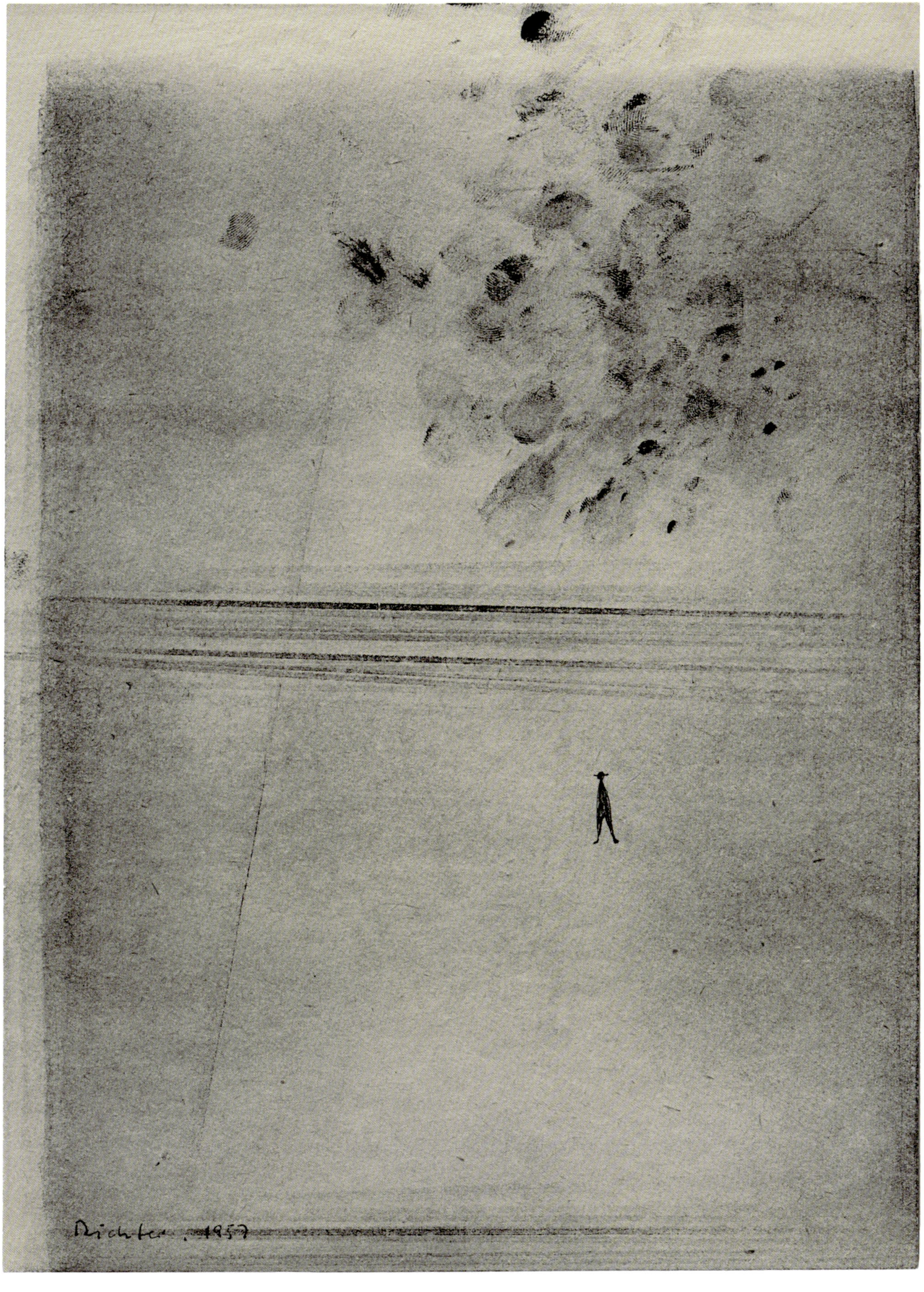

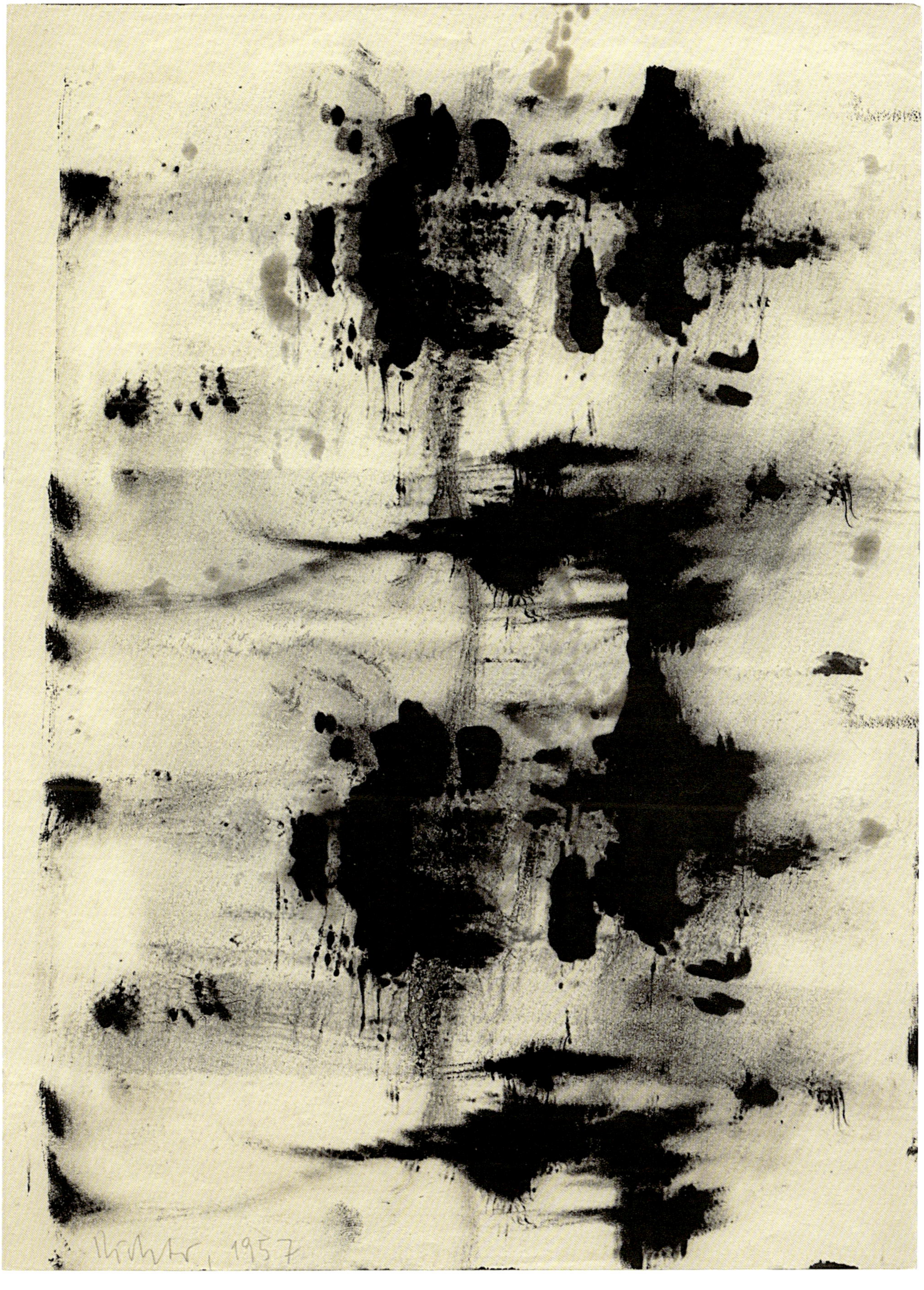
Richter, 1957

Flow, 2013 39 ⅜ × 78 ¾ in. (100 × 200 cm)

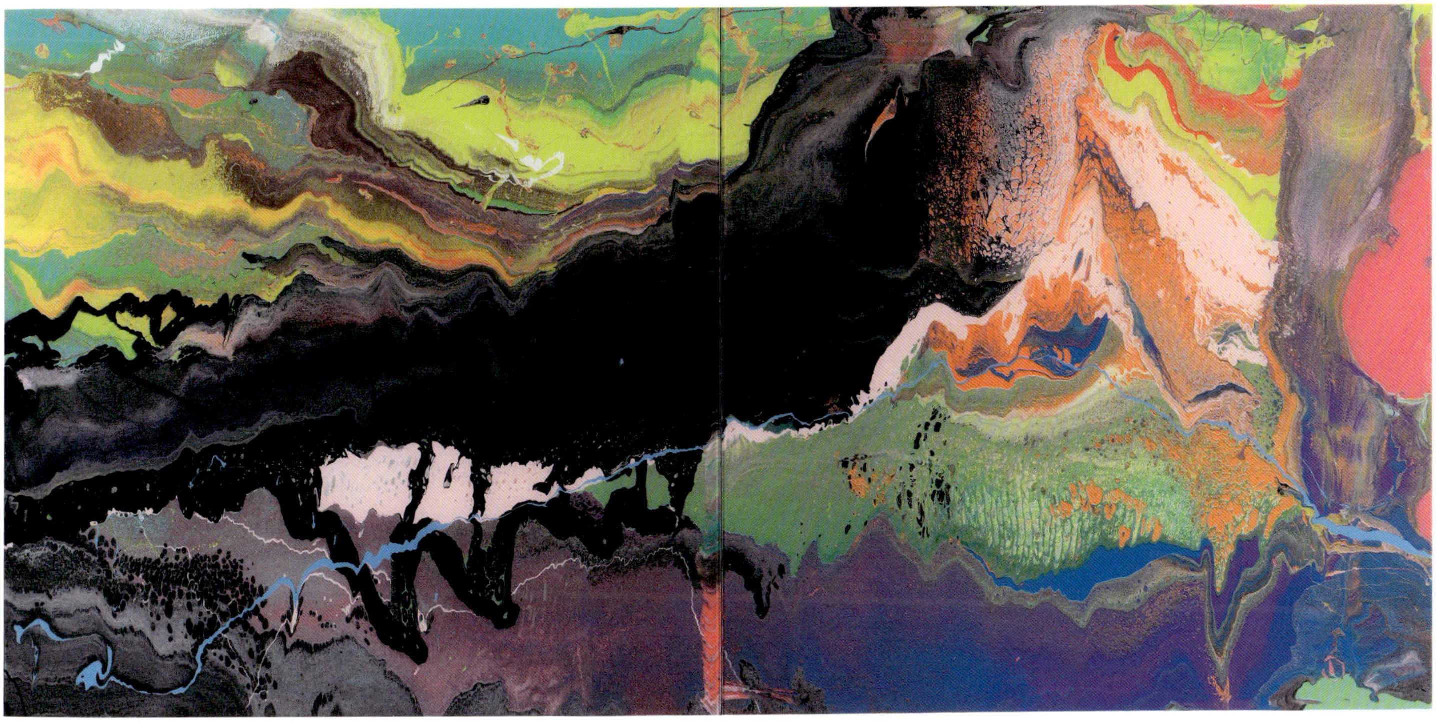

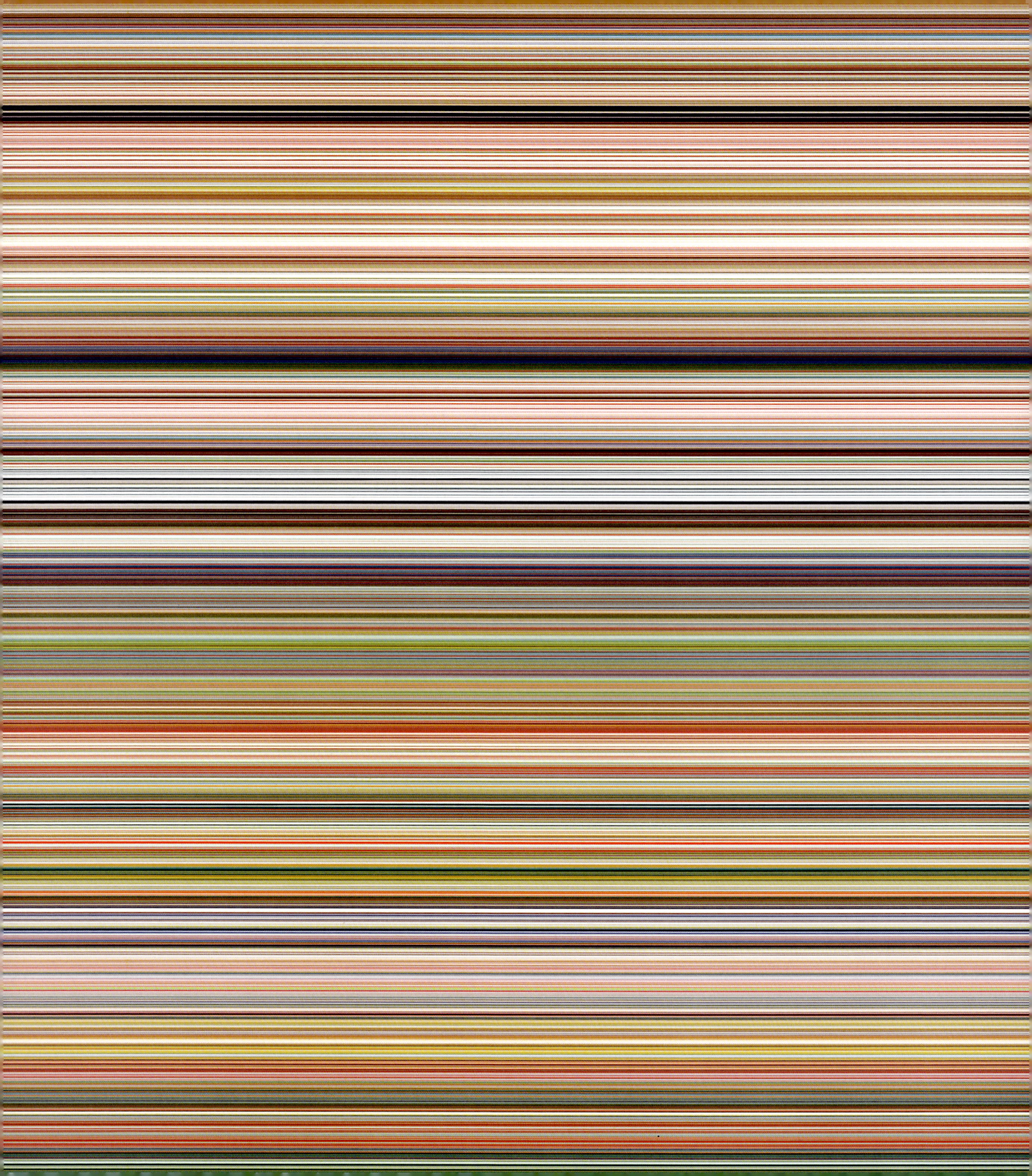

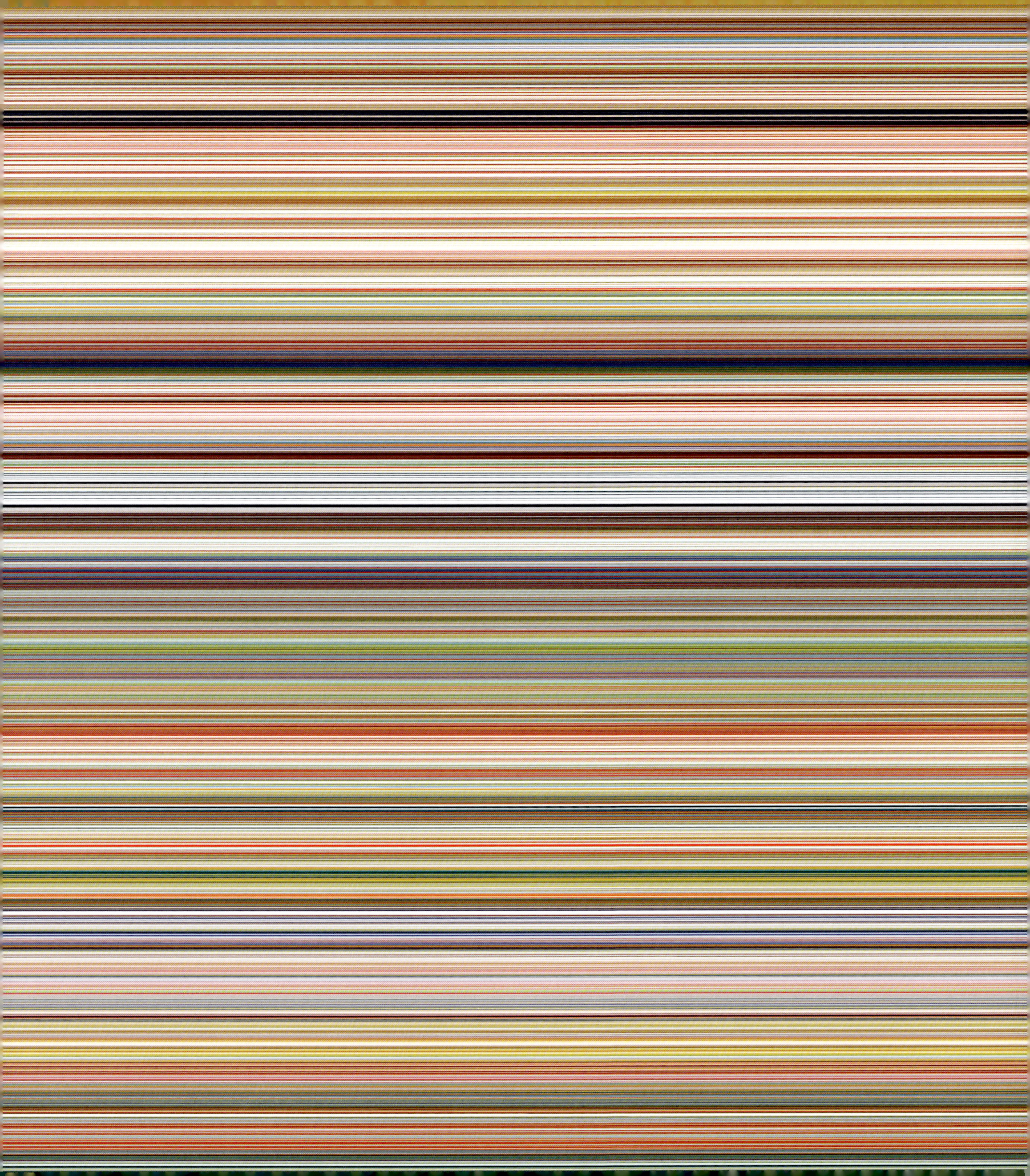

Strip, 2013   78 ¾ in. × 32 ft. 9 11⁄16 in. (200 × 1000 cm)

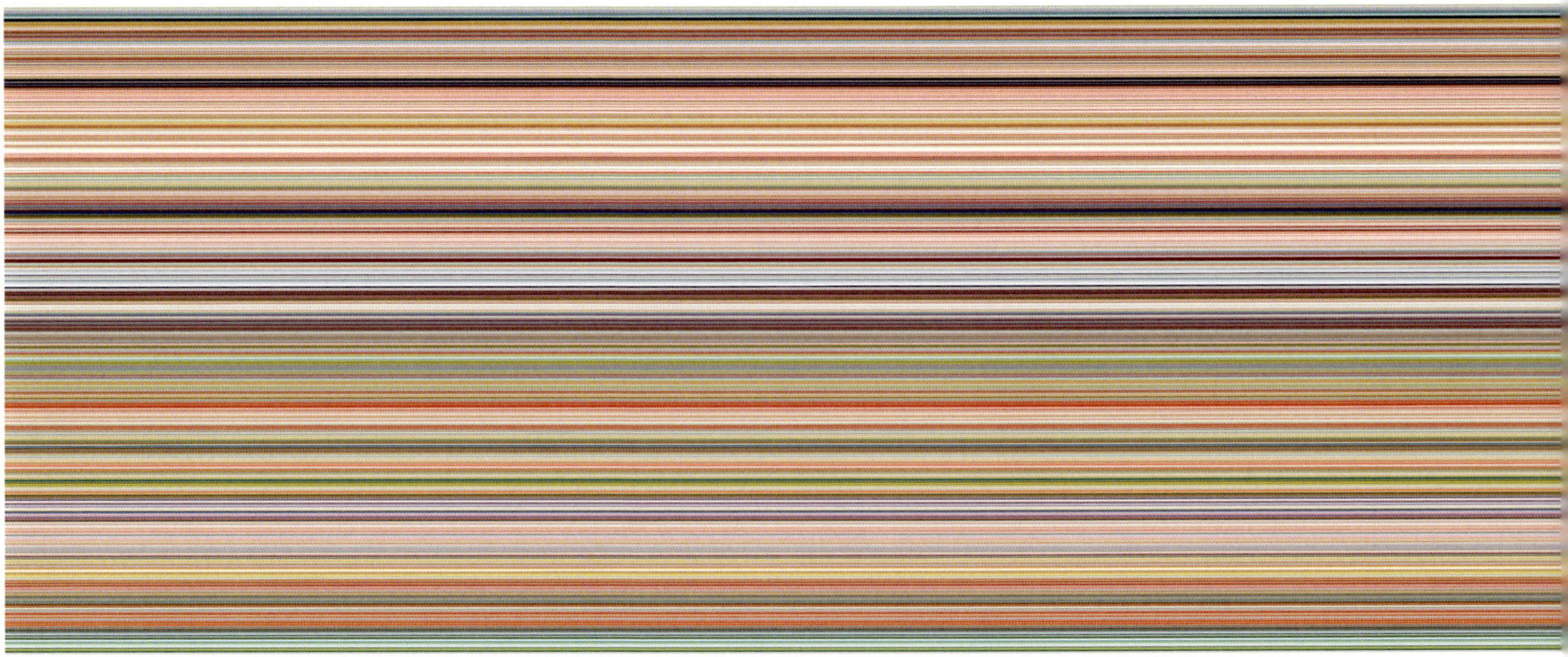

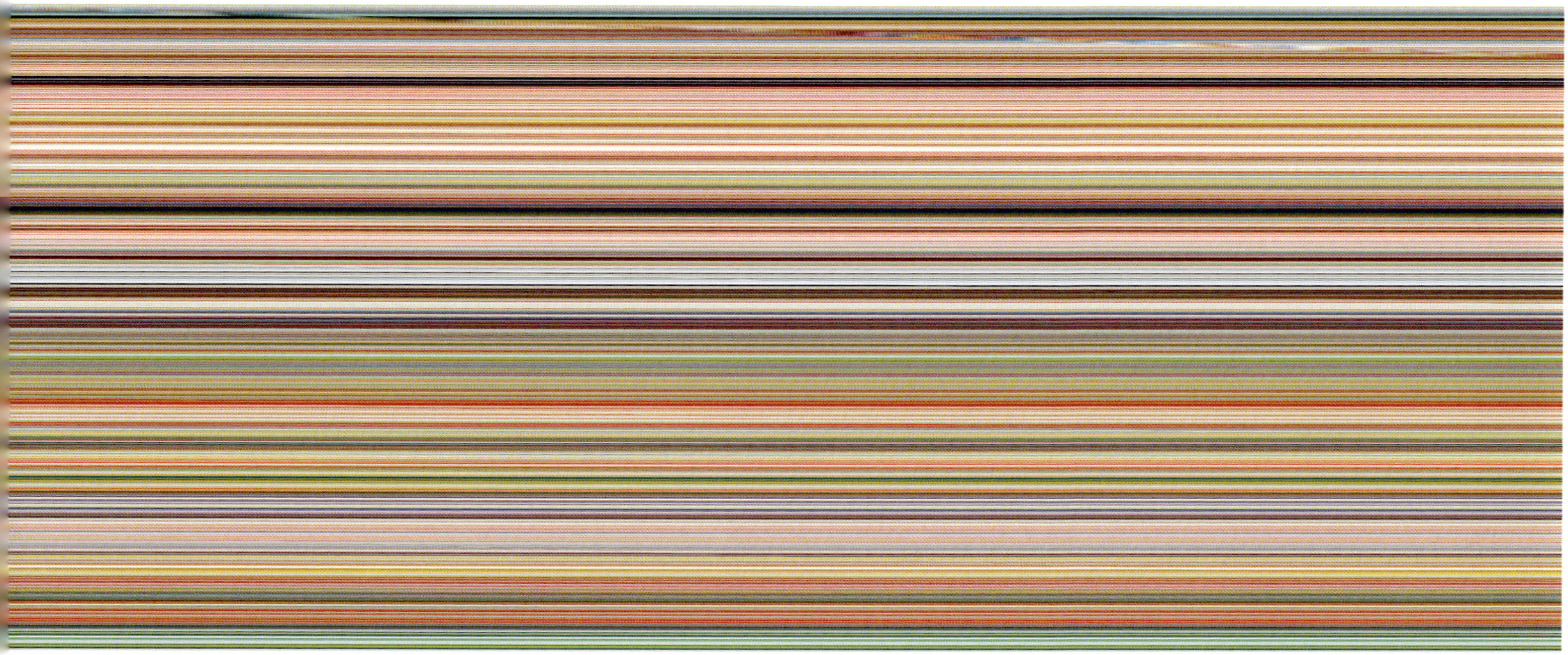

outside gatefold Birkenau, 2014 Diasec-mounted giclée prints, each 8 ft. 6 ⅜ in. × 78 ¾ in. (260 × 200 cm)

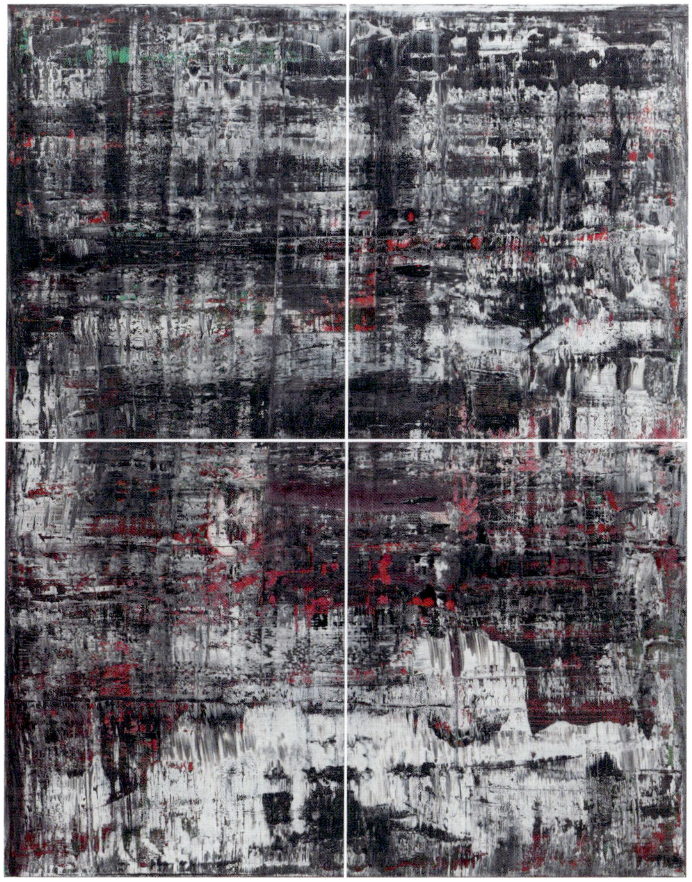

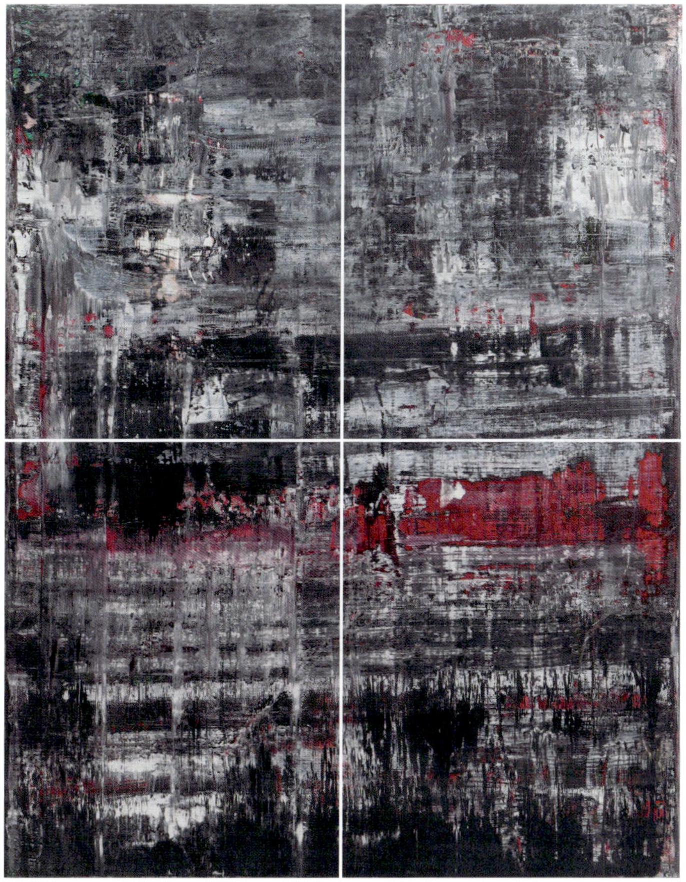

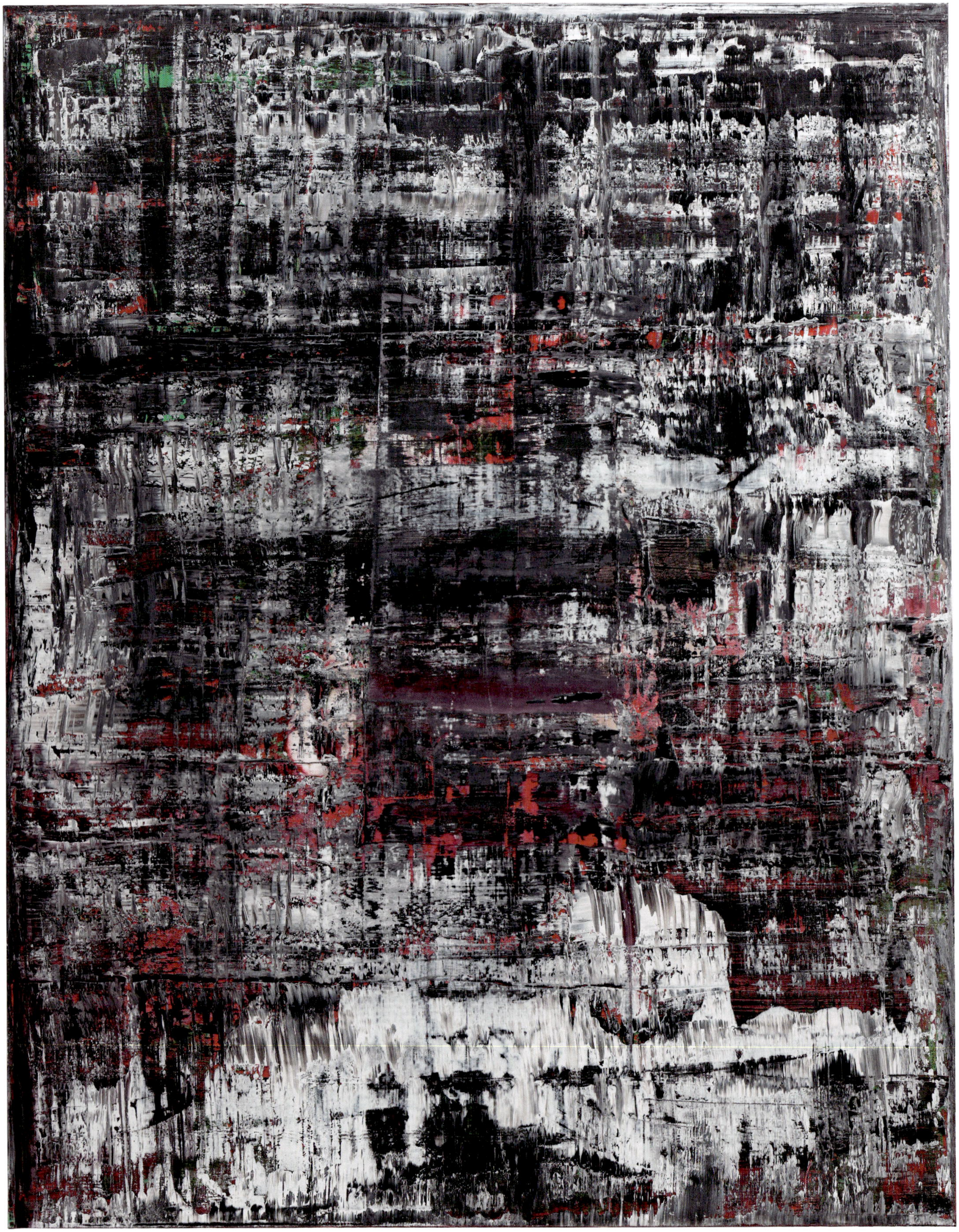

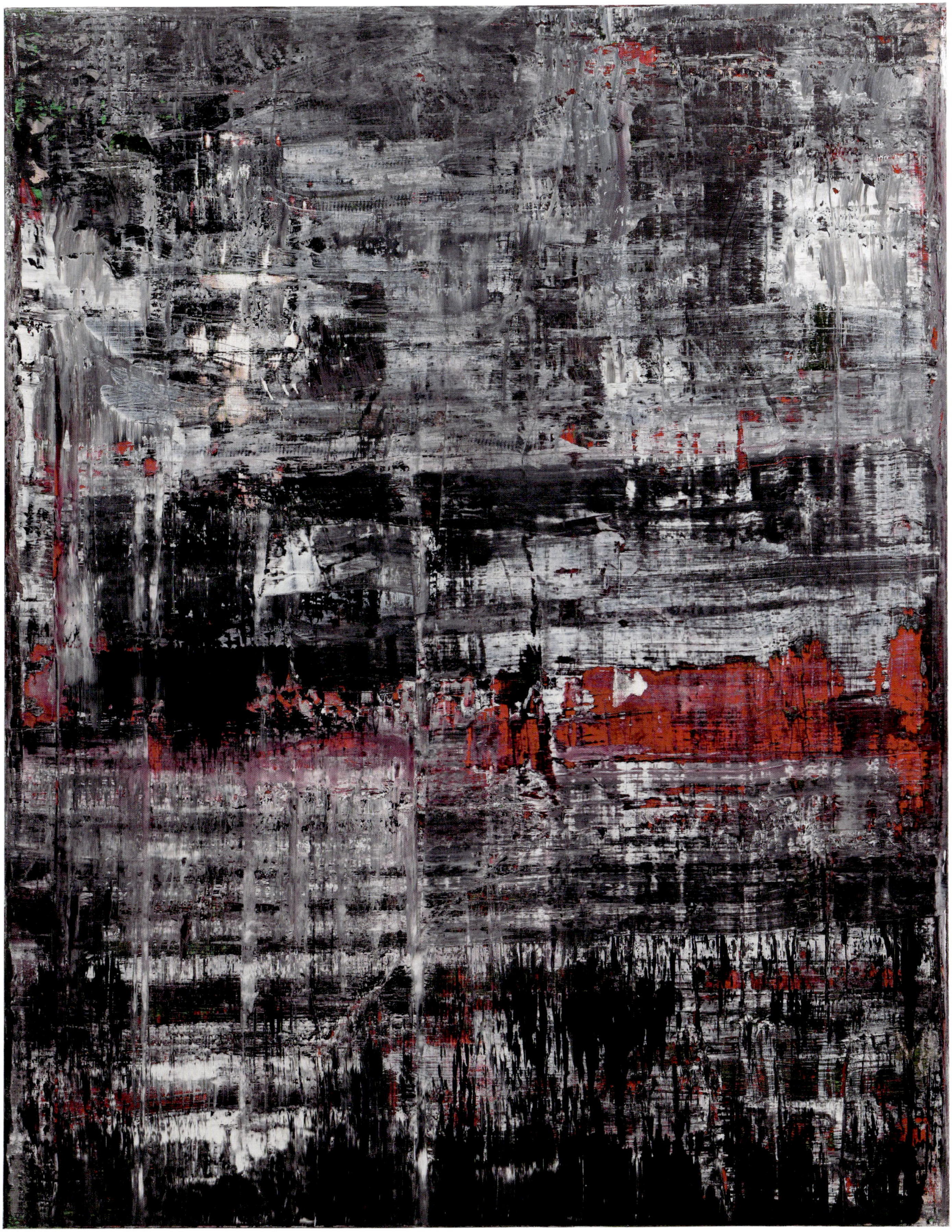

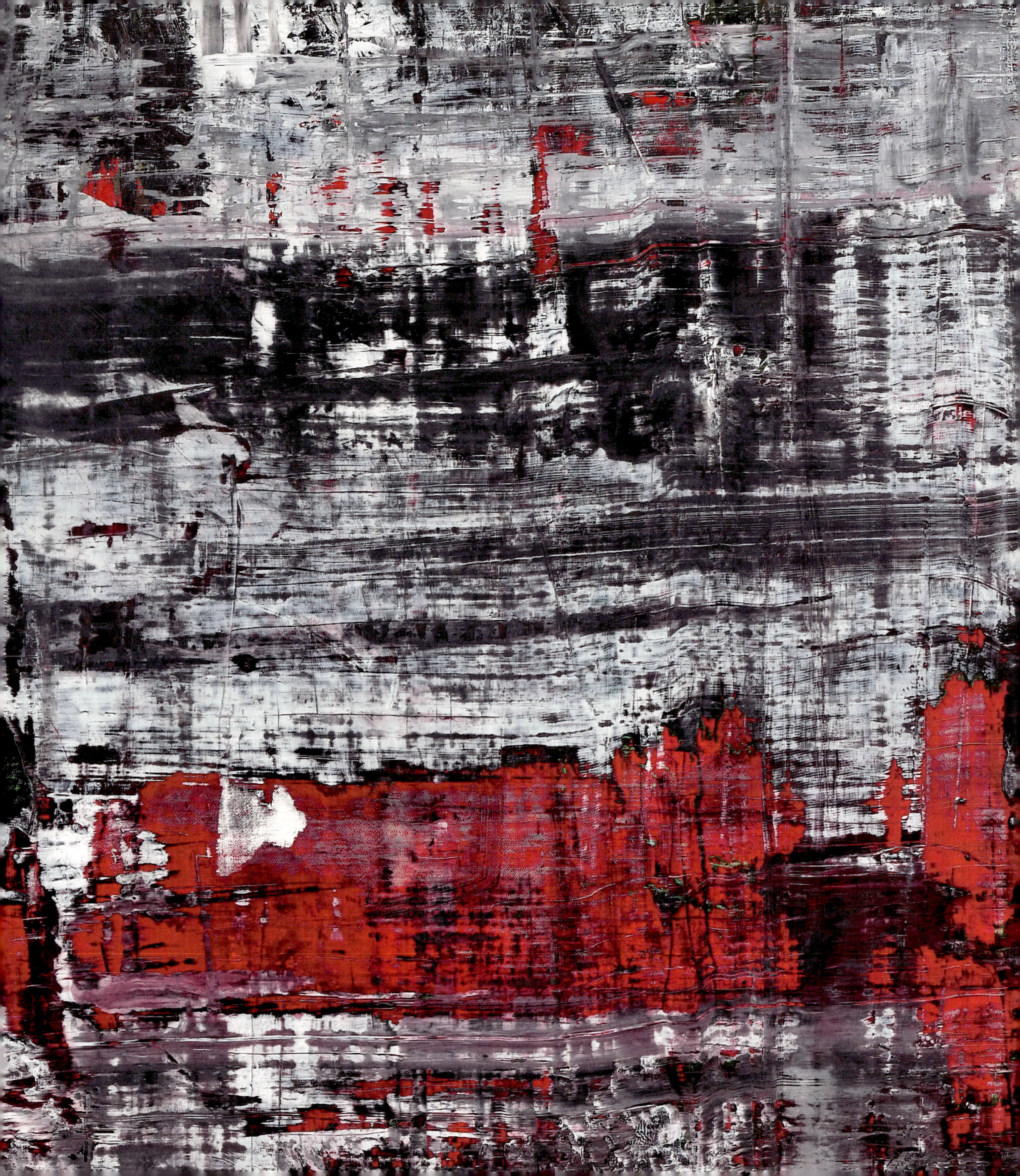

Sonderkommando photographs taken in KL Auschwitz II-Birkenau, Summer 1944; printed 2015 each 19 ⅛ × 15 ½ in. (48.5 × 39.3 cm)

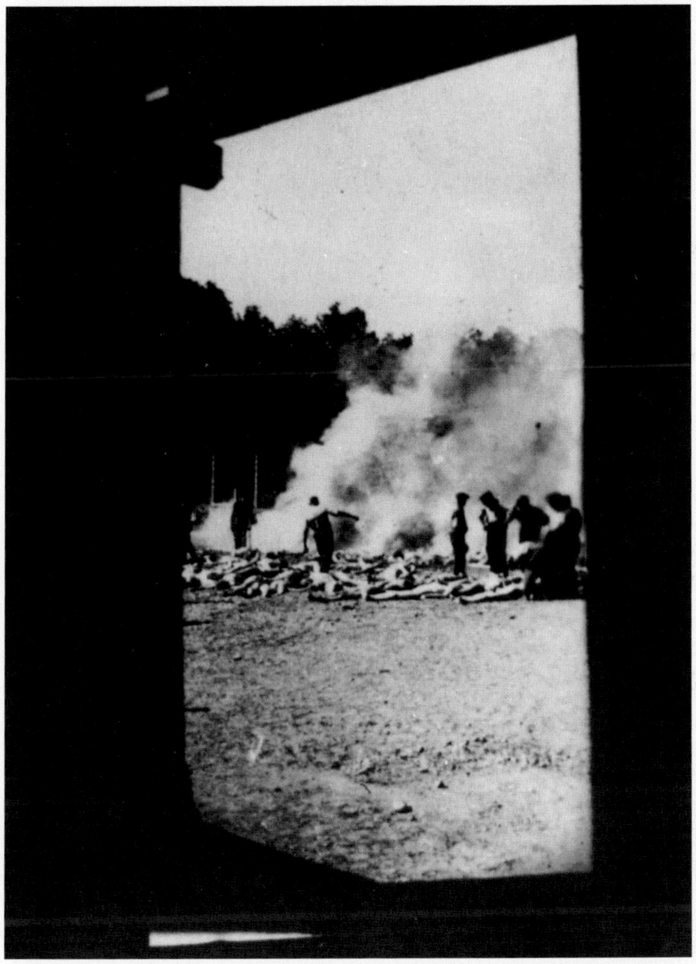

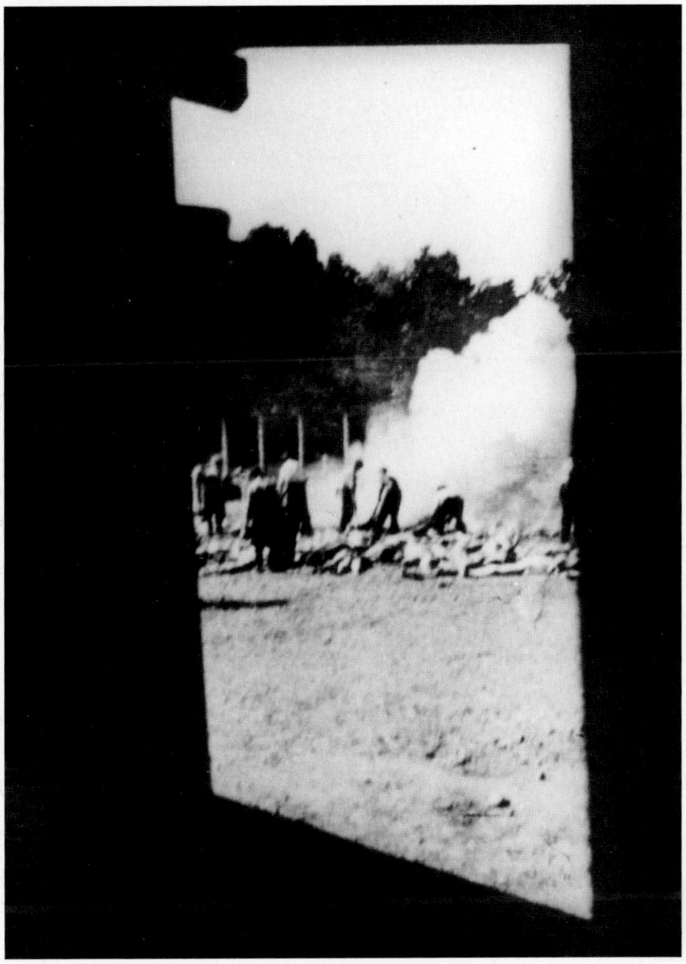

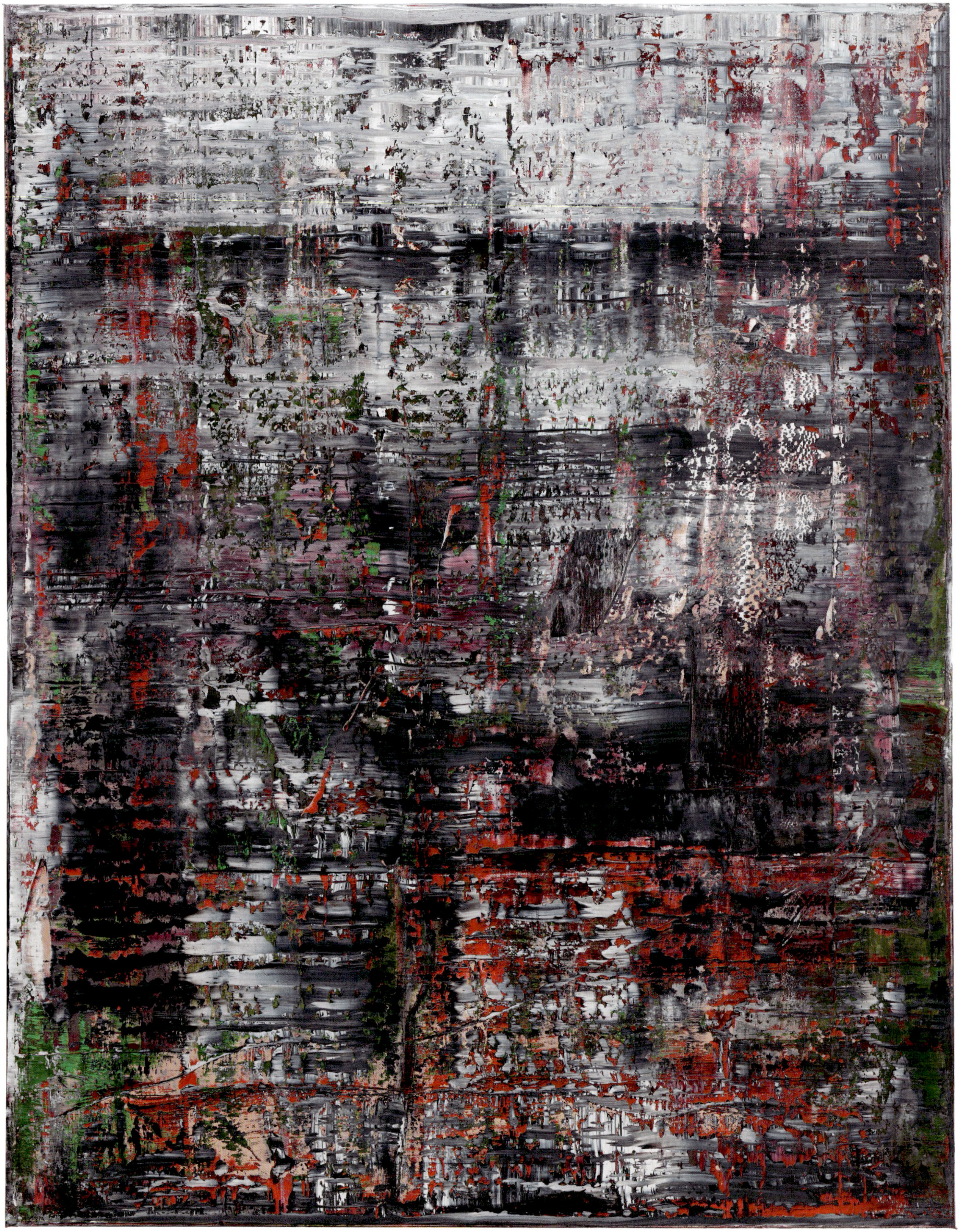

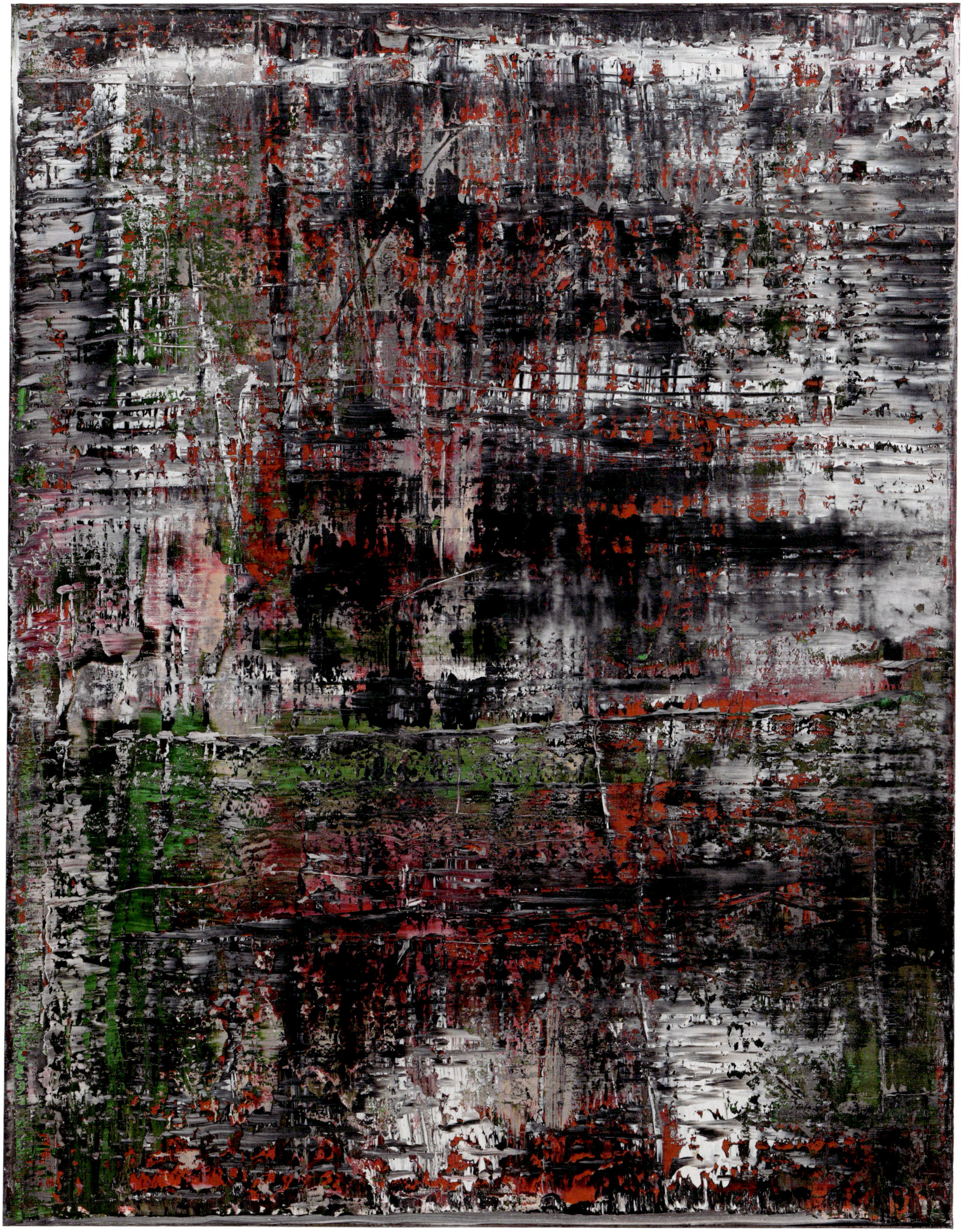

inside gatefold Birkenau, 2014 oil on canvas, each 8 ft. 6 ⅜ in. × 78 ¾ in. (260 × 200 cm)

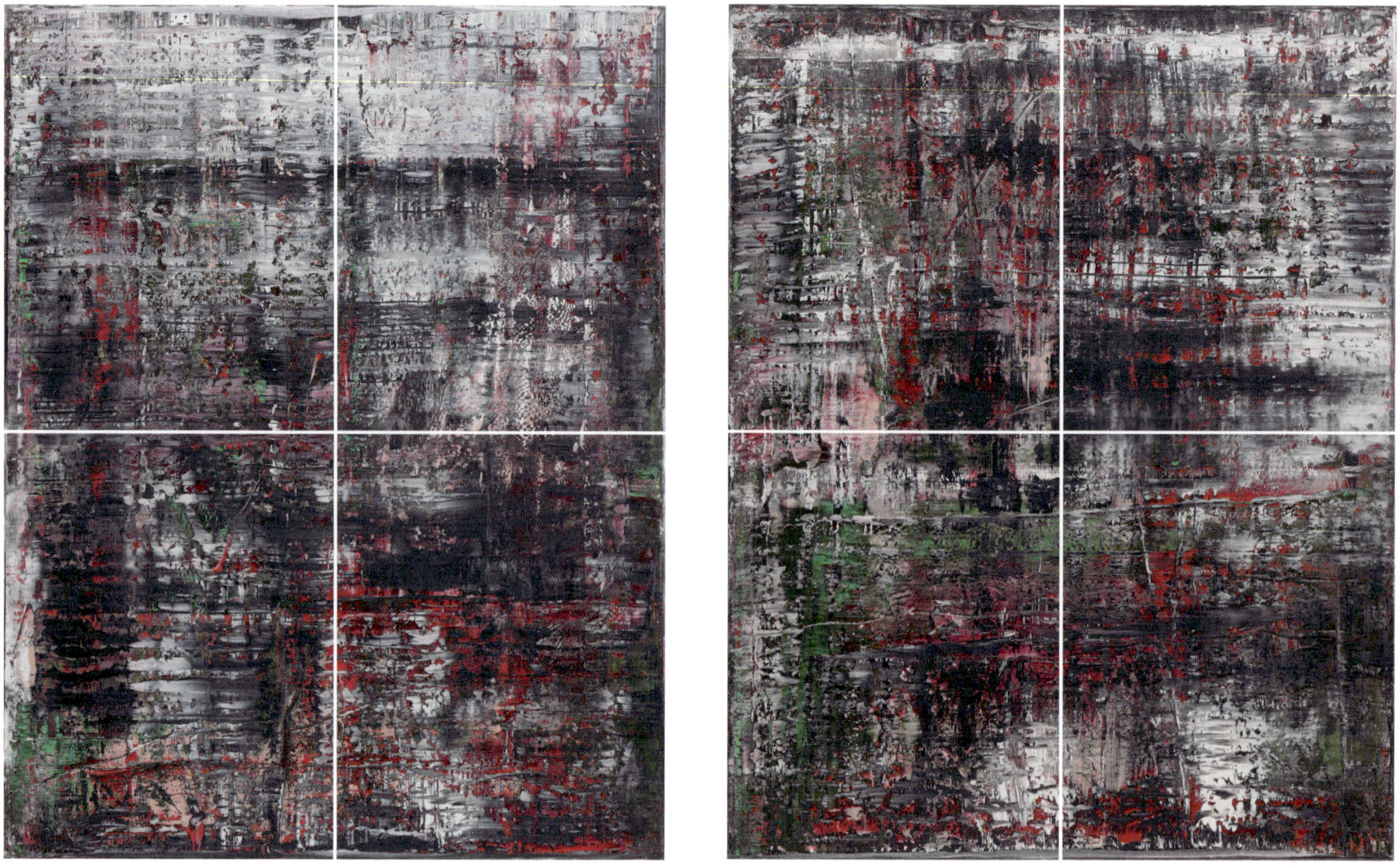

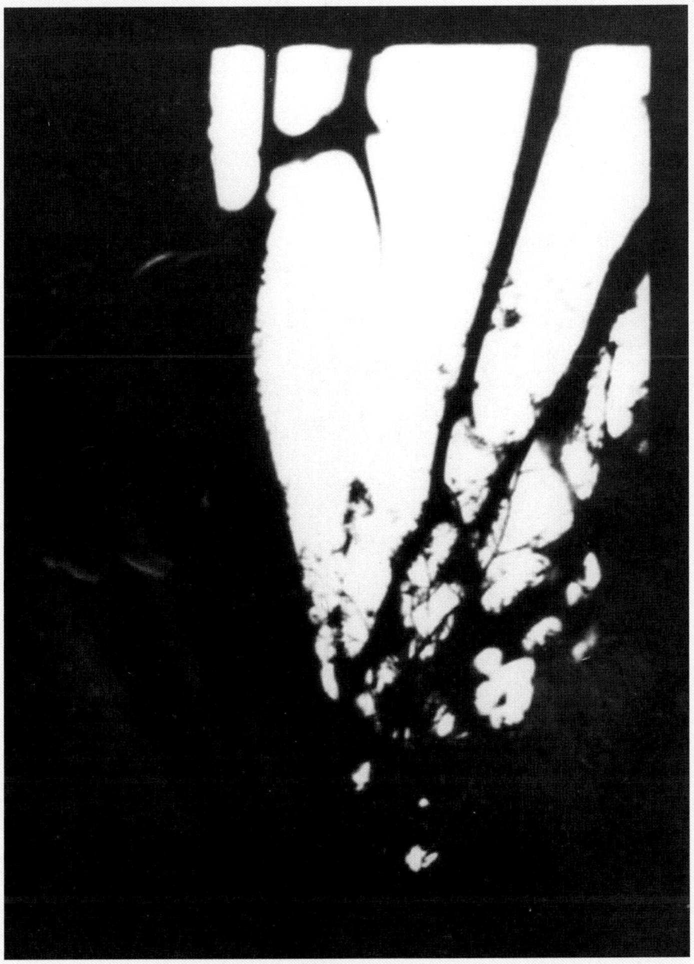

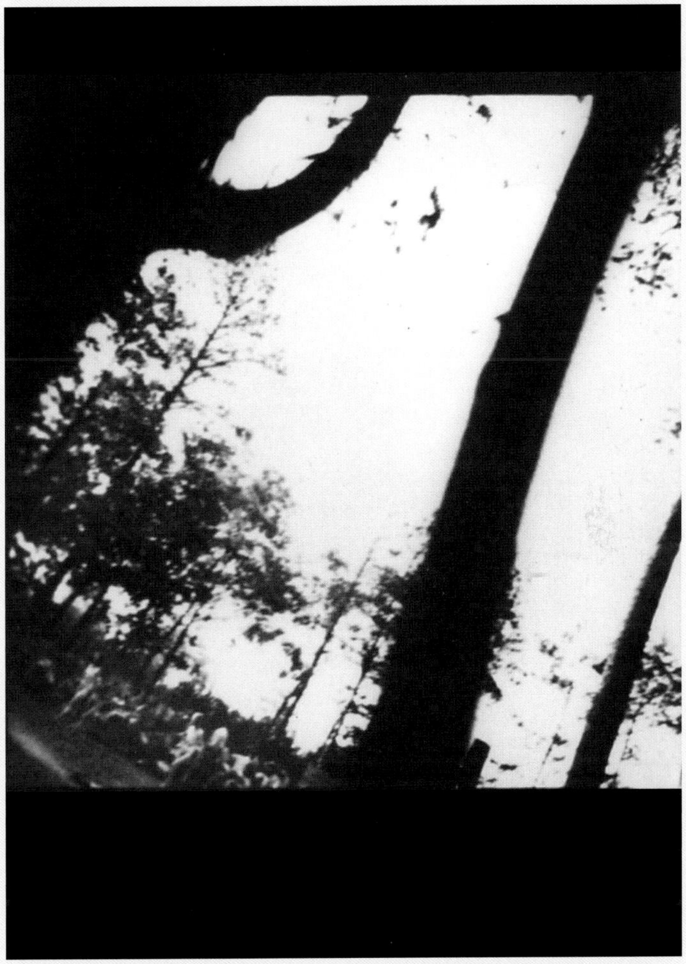

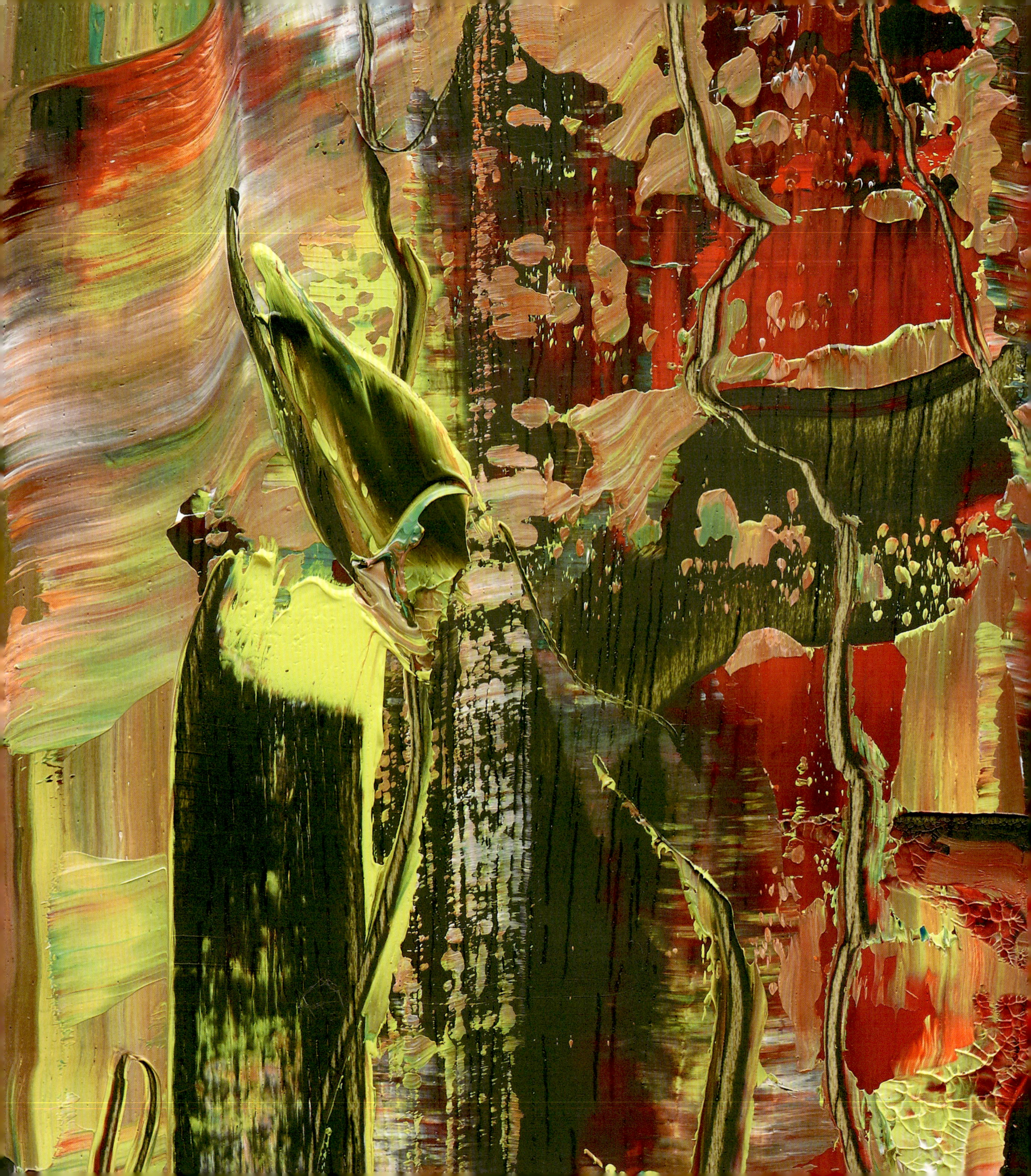

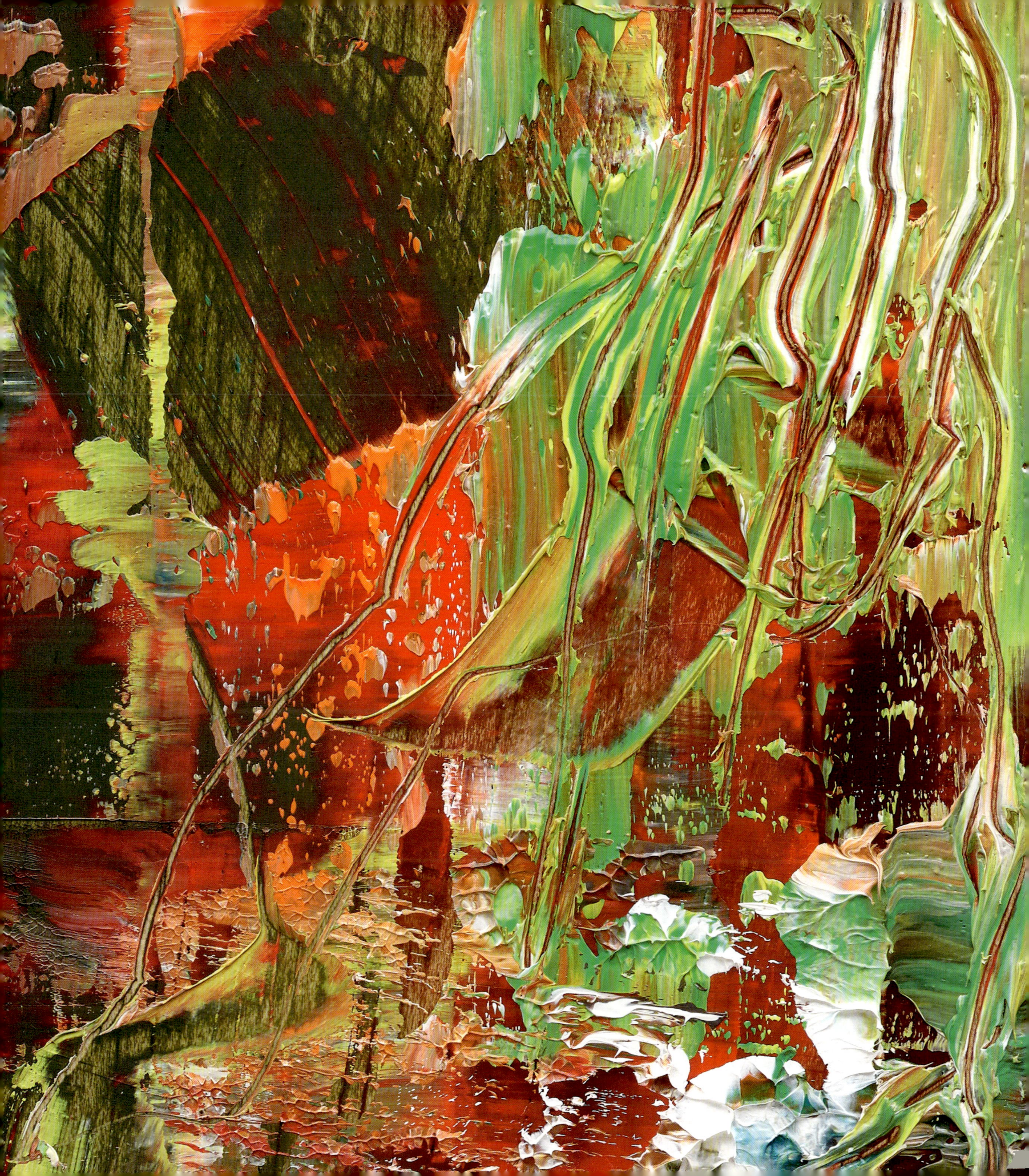

Abstract Paintings (1–7), 2016 each 15 ¾ × 11 13⁄16 in. (40 × 30 cm)

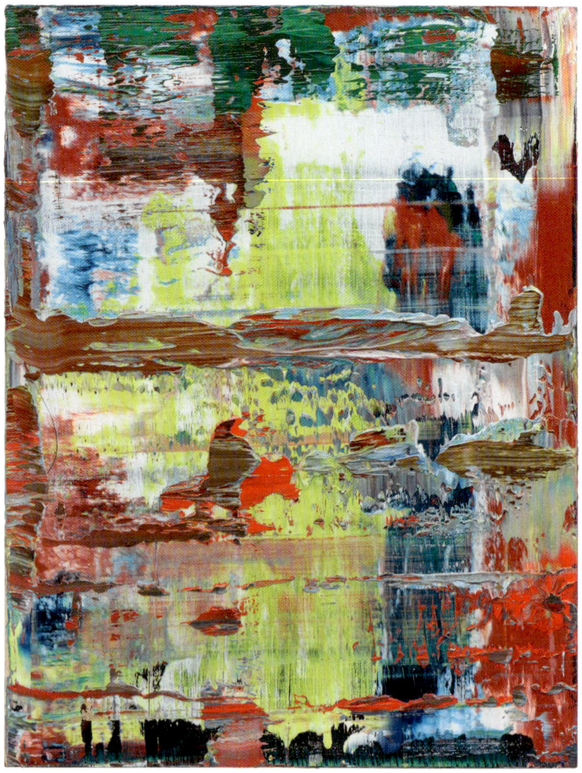

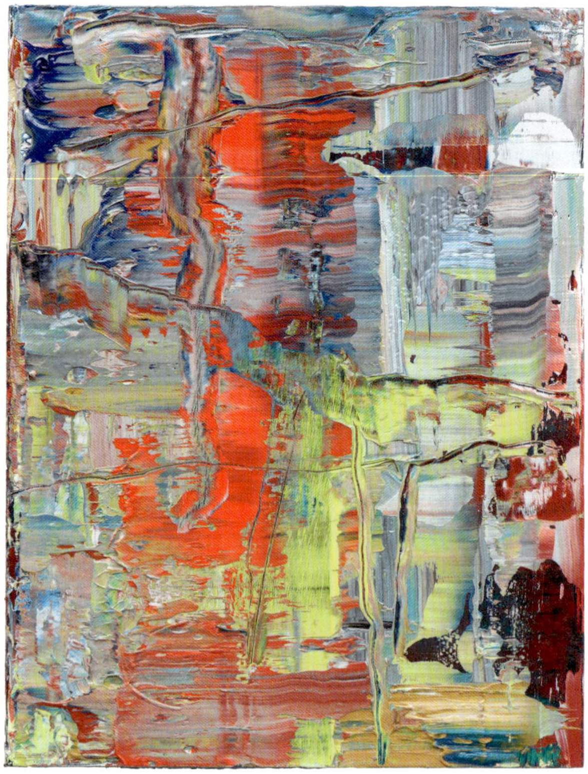

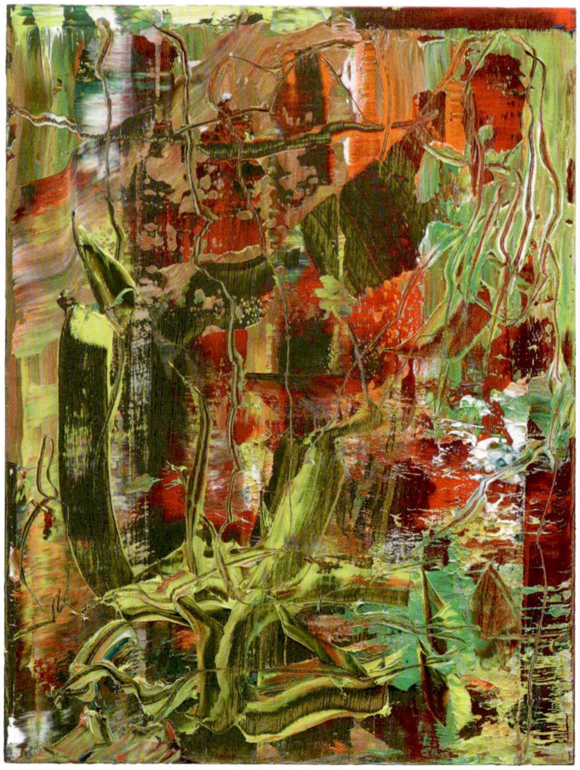

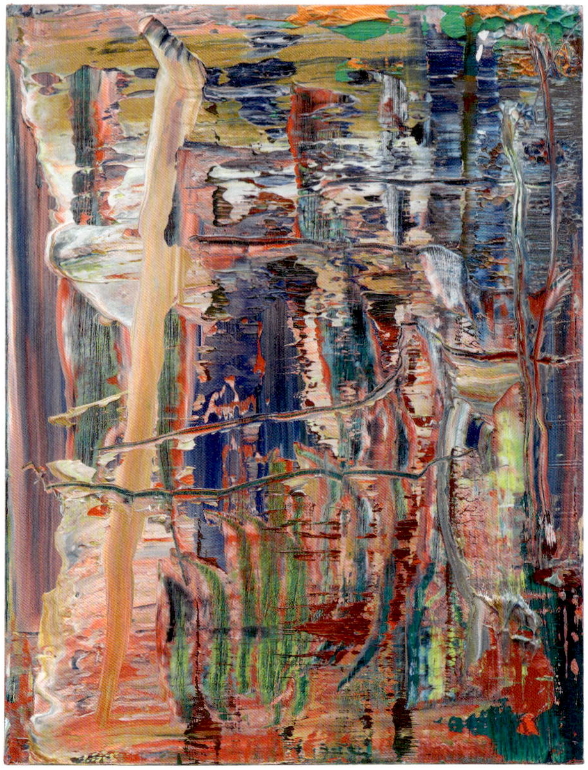

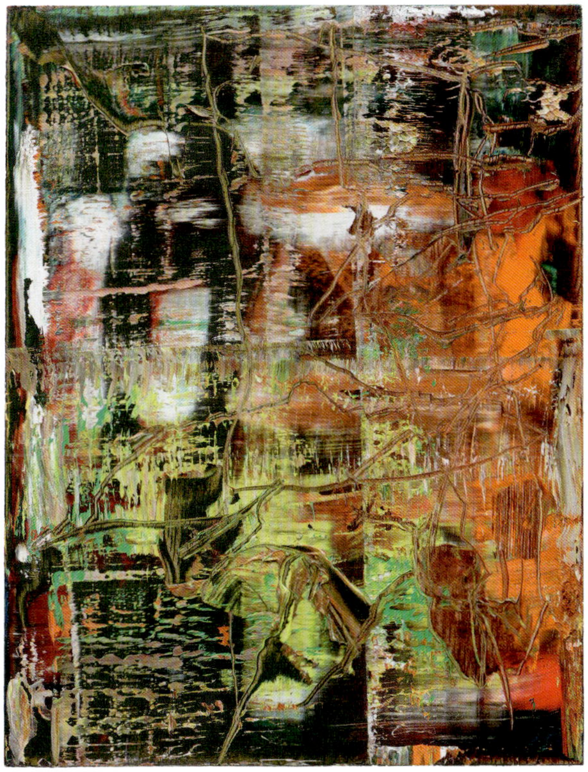

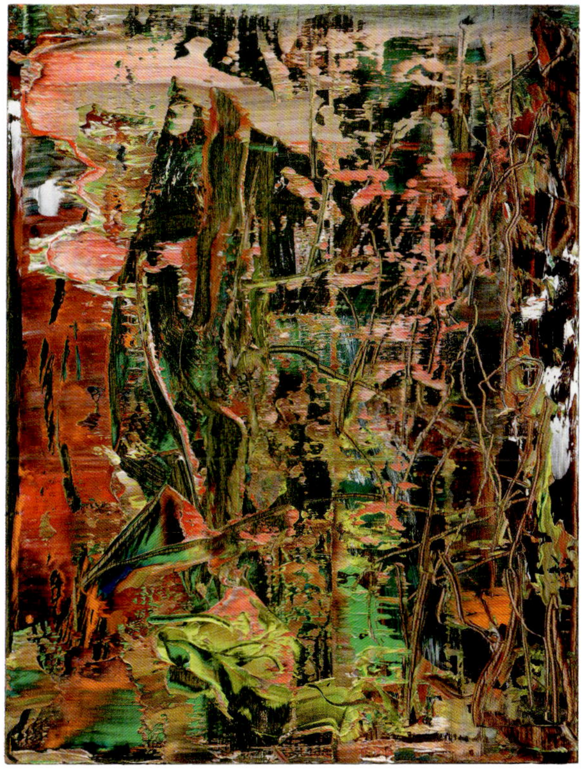

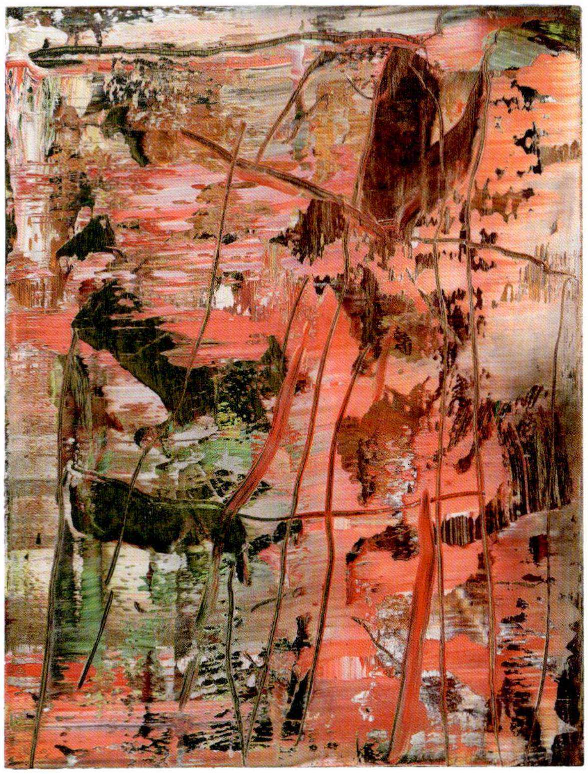

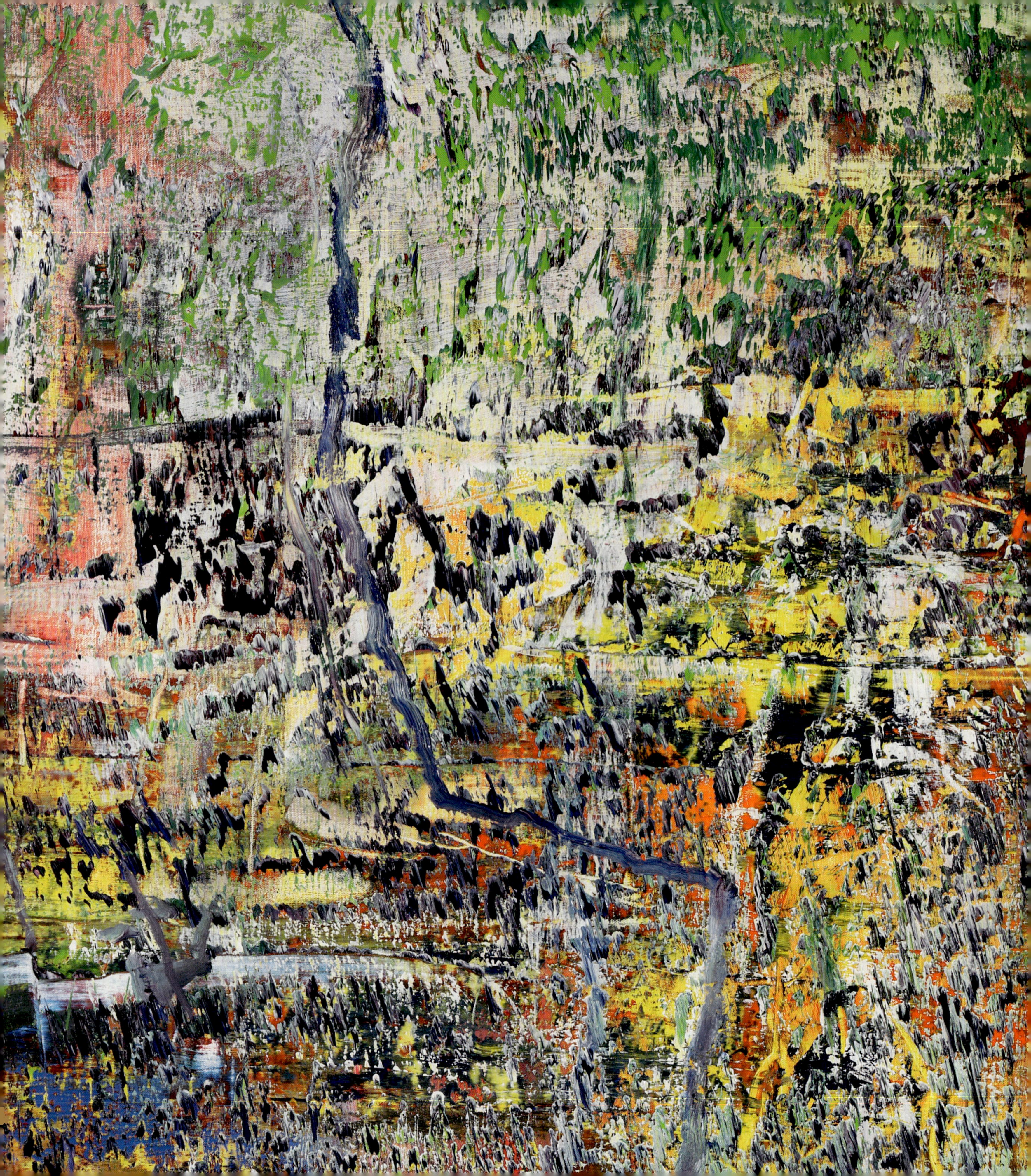

Abstract Painting, 2016 78 ¾ × 98 ⁷⁄₁₆ in. (200 × 250 cm)

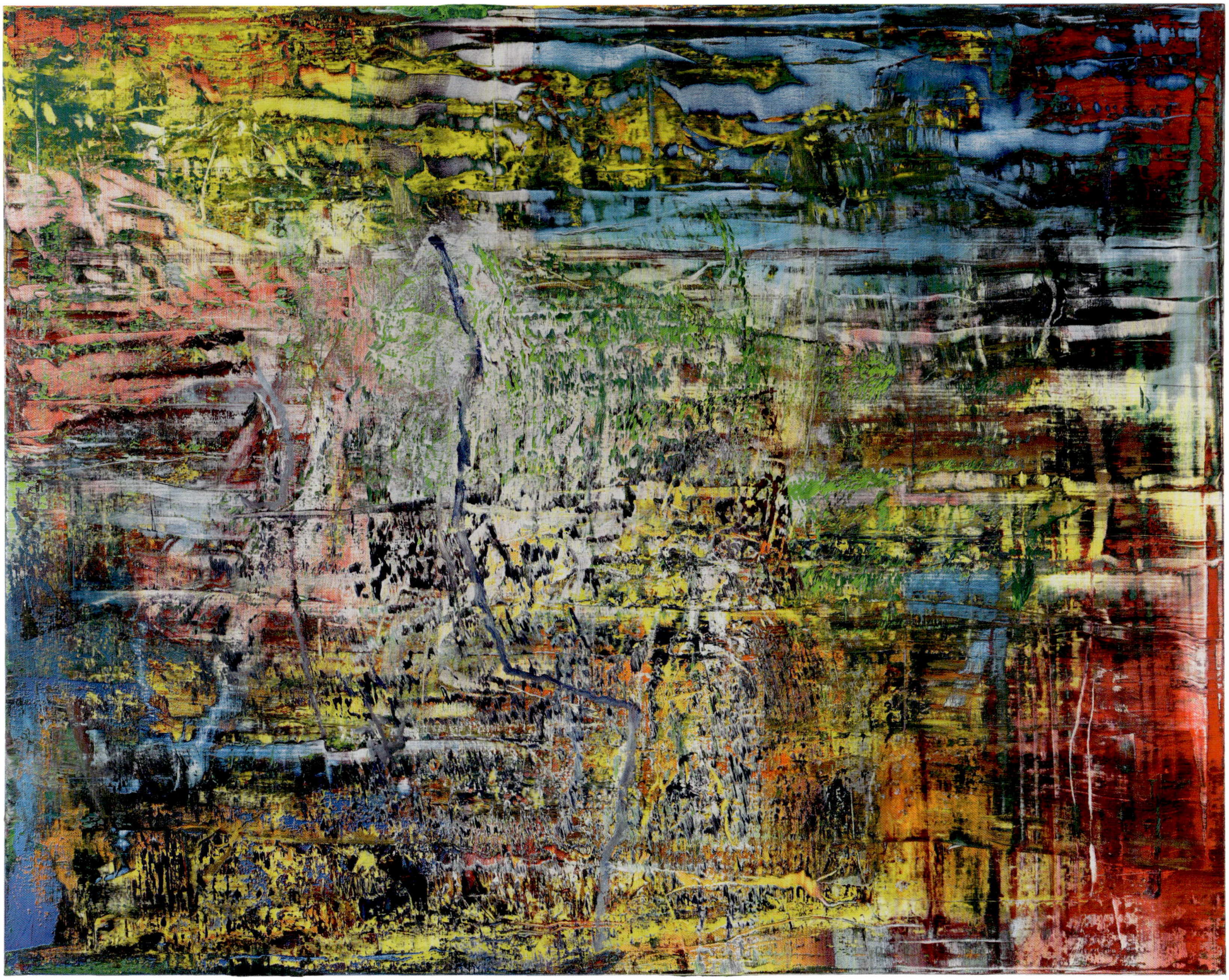

Abstract Painting, 2016   86 ⅝ × 56 11⁄16 in. (220 × 144 cm)

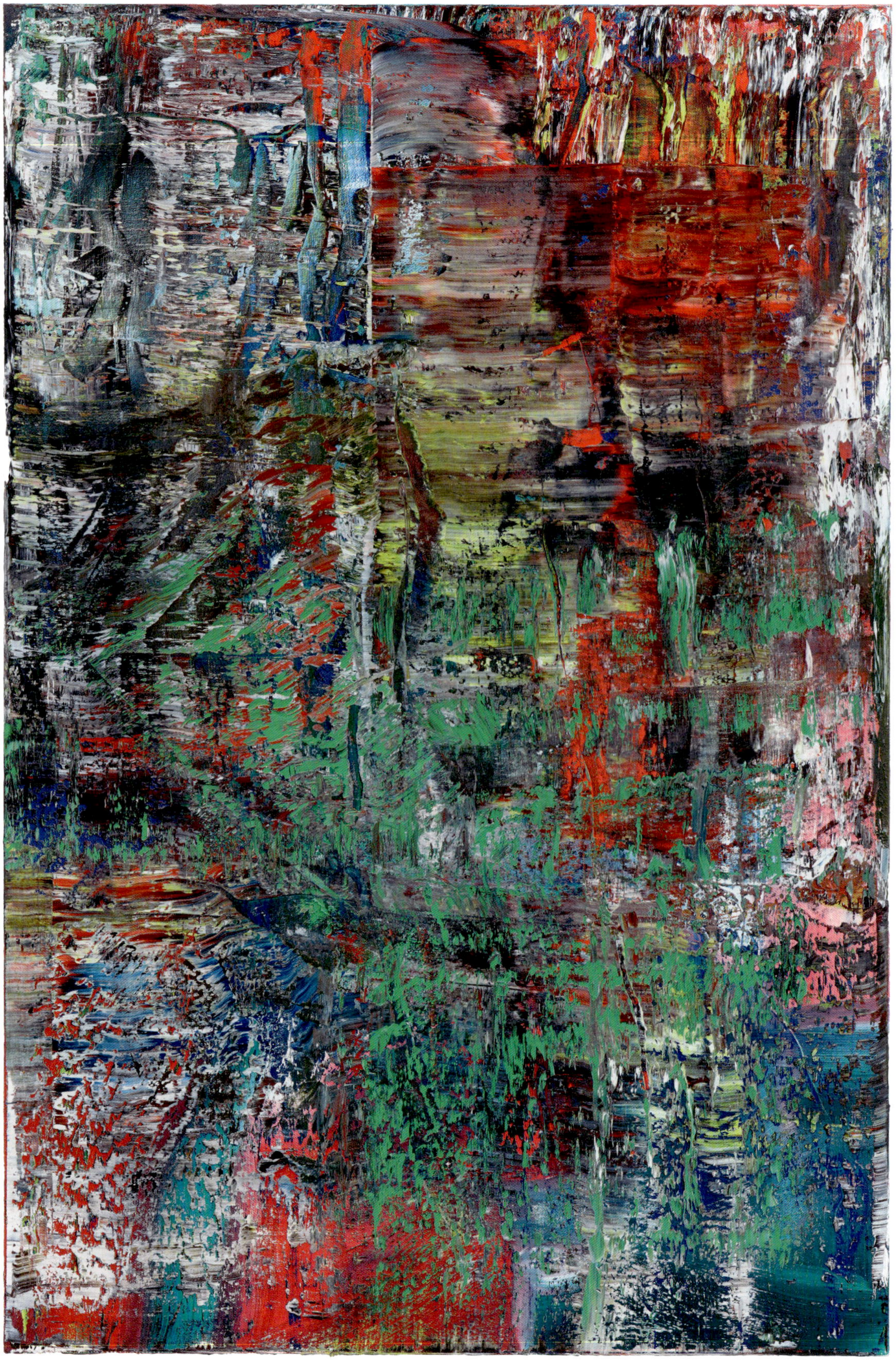

Abstract Painting, 2017 78 ¾ × 98 ⁷⁄₁₆ in. (200 × 250 cm)

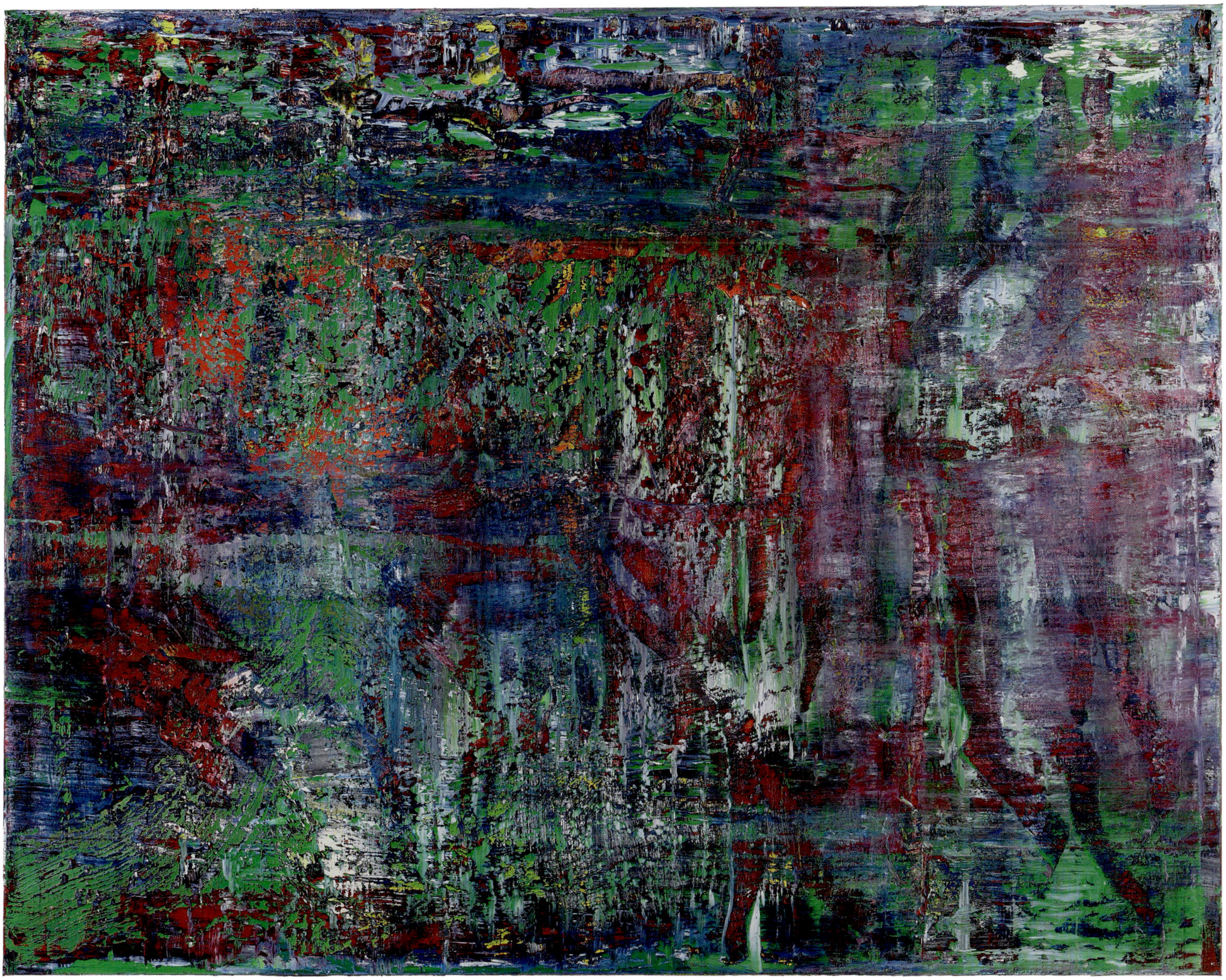

Abstract Painting, 2017 78 ¾ × 78 ¾ in. (200 × 200 cm)

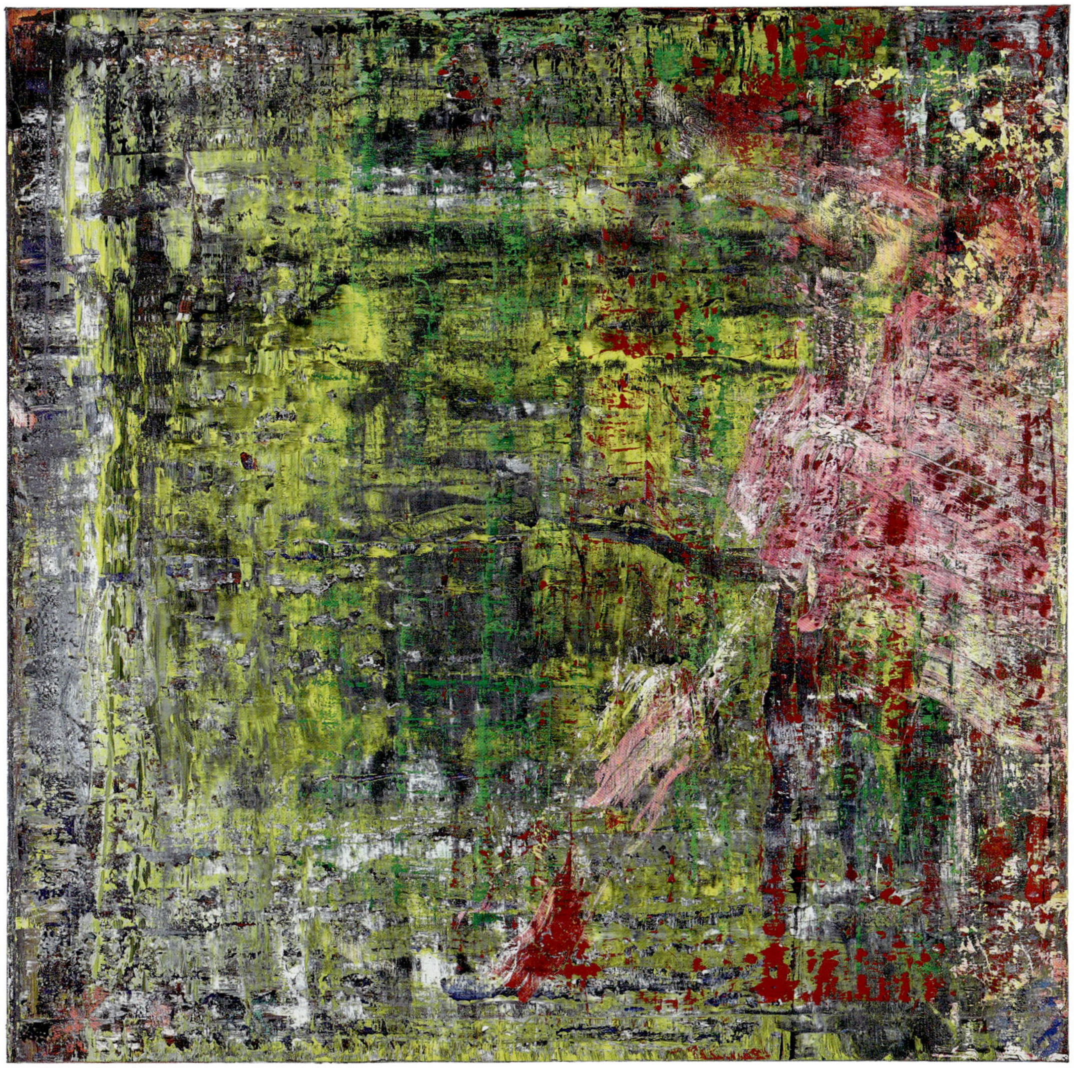

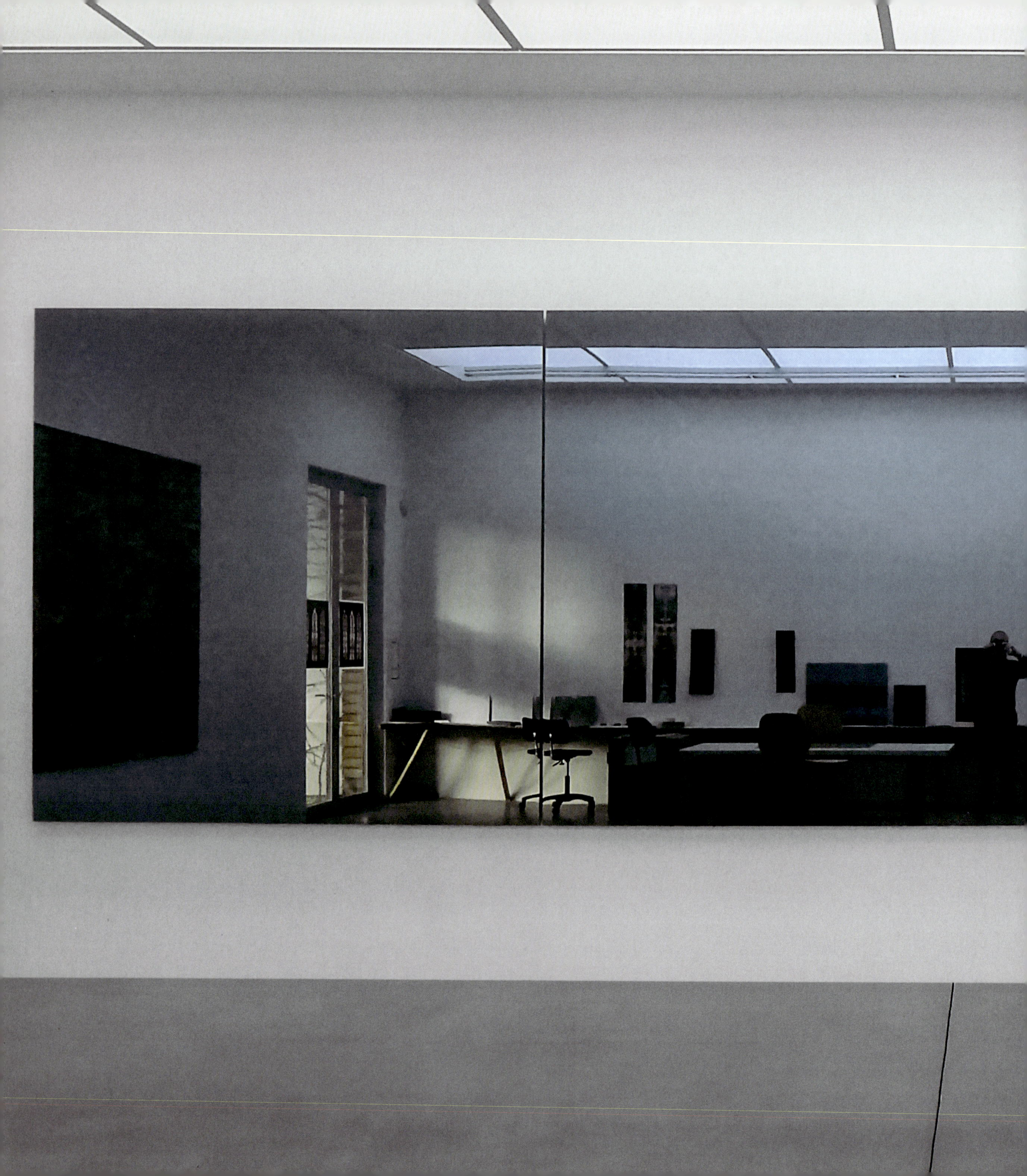

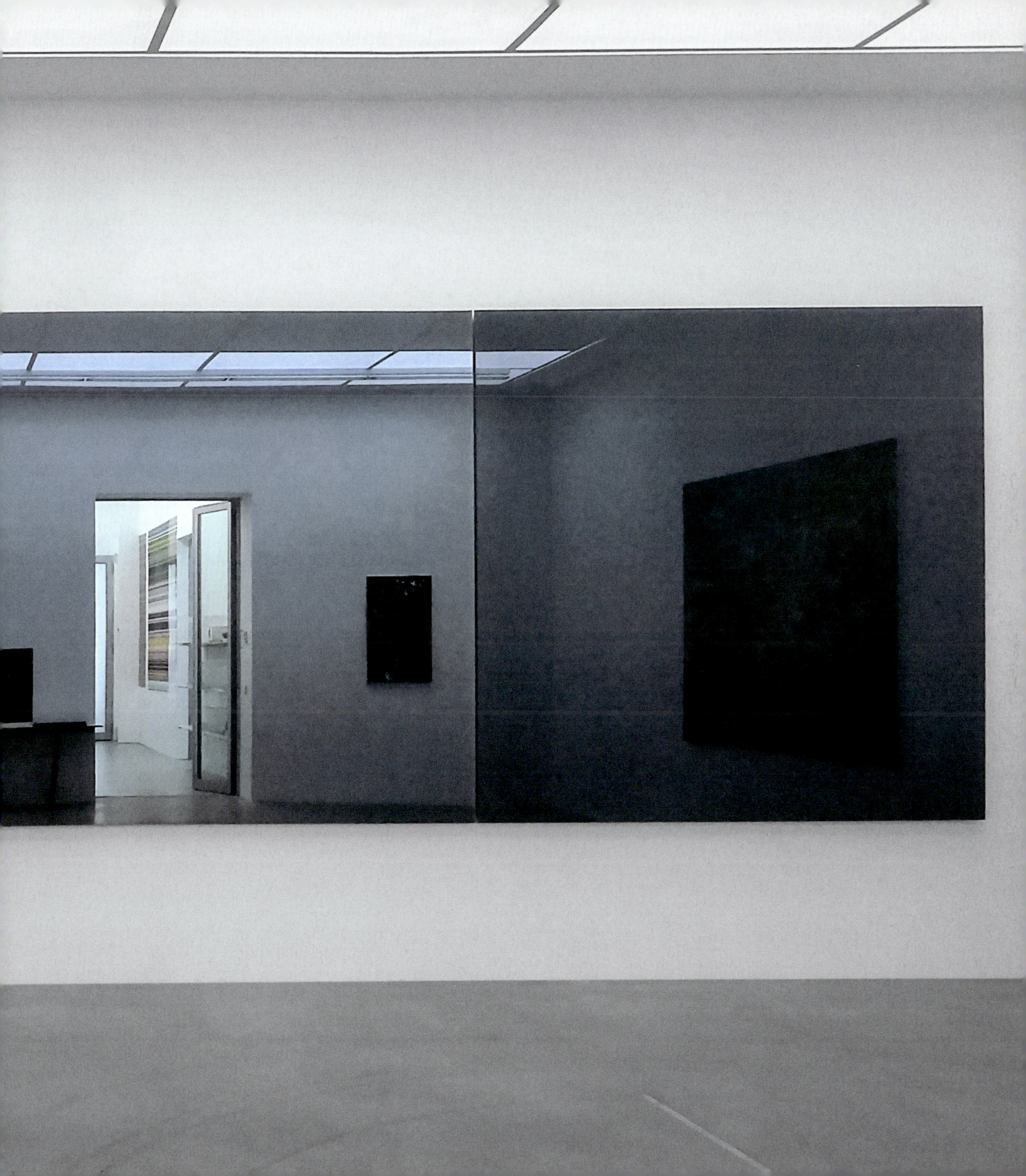

overleaf Gray Mirror (4 Parts), 2018 89 ¾ in. × 29 ft. 11 1⁄16 in. (228 × 912 cm)
right House of Cards (5 Panes), 2020 each pane 10 ft. 6 in. × 70 ⅞ in. × ⅜ in. (320 × 180 × 1 cm)

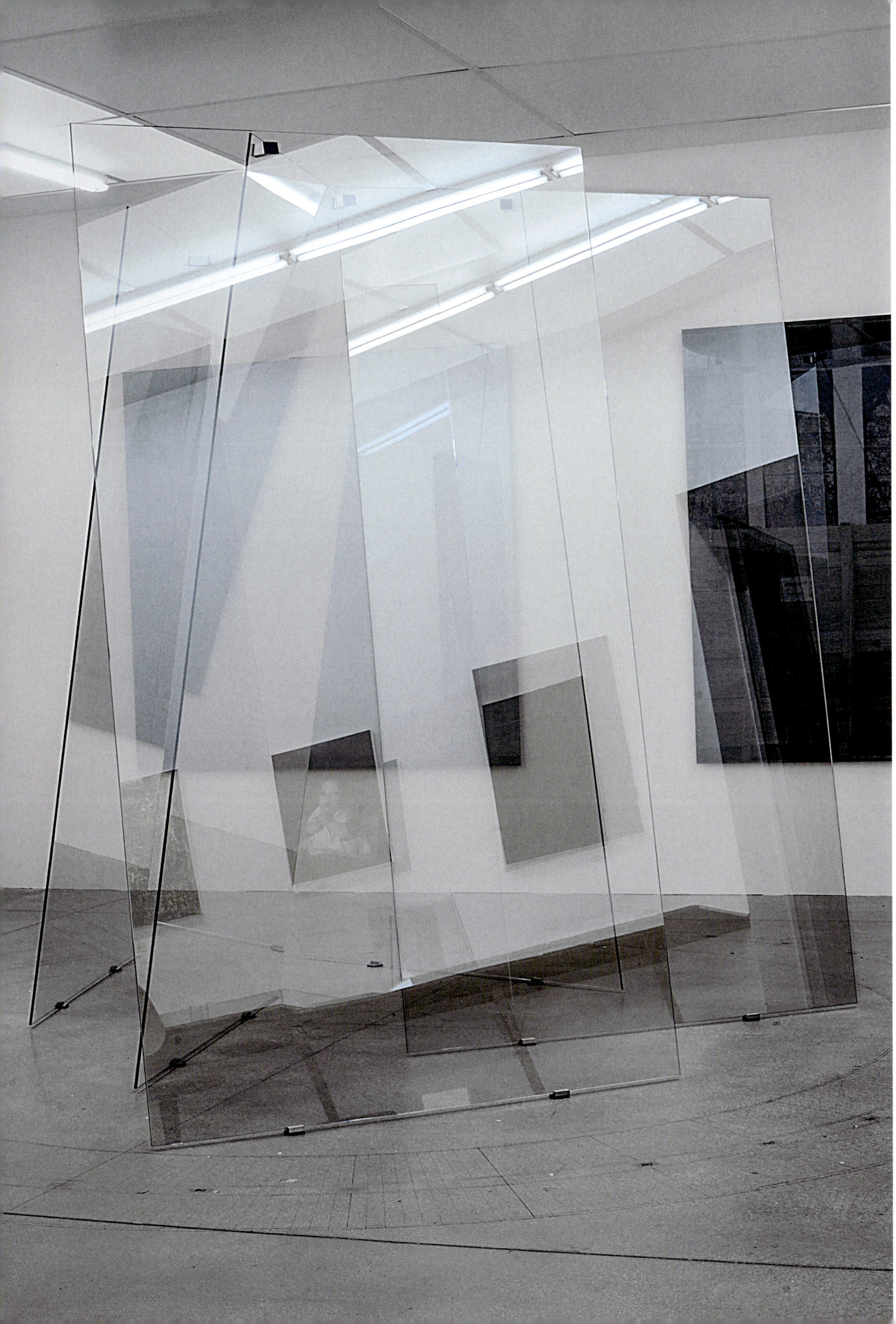

Works in the Exhibition

As of November 15, 2019

PAGE 104
Table (*Tisch*), 1962
Oil on canvas
35 7/16 × 44 1/2 in. (90 × 113 cm)
CR 1
Collection of Anne Simone Kleinman
and Thomas Wong

PAGE 105
Coffin Bearers (*Sargträger*), 1963
Oil on canvas
53 1/8 × 70 7/8 in. (135 × 180 cm)
CR 5
Bayerische Staatsgemäldesammlungen,
Pinakothek der Moderne, Munich. Acquired
in 1979 from PIN. Friends of the Pinakothek
der Moderne for the Collection of Modern Art

PAGE 106
Family at the Seaside (*Familie am Meer*), 1964
Oil on canvas
59 1/16 × 78 3/4 in. (150 × 200 cm)
CR 35
MKM Museum Küppersmühle für Moderne
Kunst, Duisburg / Germany, Ströher Collection

PAGES 107, 102–3 (DETAIL)
Administrative Building (*Verwaltungsgebäude*), 1964
Oil on linen
38 9/16 × 59 1/16 in. (98 × 150 cm)
CR 39
The Doris and Donald Fisher Collection at the
San Francisco Museum of Modern Art

PAGE 108
Aunt Marianne (*Tante Marianne*), 1965/2018
Digital print between Plexiglas and Alu Dibond
39 3/8 × 45 1/4 in. (100 × 115 cm)
Gerhard Richter Archiv, Staatliche
Kunstsammlungen Dresden

PAGE 109
Uncle Rudi (*Onkel Rudi*), 1965
Oil on canvas
34 1/4 × 19 3/4 in. (87 × 50 cm)
CR 85
Památník Lidice / Lidice Memorial

PAGES 111, 110 (DETAIL)
Group of People (*Personengruppe*), 1965
Oil on canvas
66 15/16 × 78 3/4 in. (170 × 200 cm)
CR 83
Private collection

PAGE 112
Kitchen Chair (*Küchenstuhl*), 1965
Oil on canvas
39 3/8 × 31 1/2 in. (100 × 80 cm)
CR 97
Kunsthalle Recklinghausen

PAGE 113
Mr. Heyde (*Herr Heyde*), 1965
Oil on canvas
21 5/8 × 25 9/16 in. (55 × 65 cm)
CR 100
Private collection

PAGES 114–15
Eight Student Nurses (*Acht Lernschwestern*), 1966
Oil on canvas
8 parts, each panel 37 3/8 × 27 1/2 in. (95 × 70 cm)
CR 130 (a, c, b, d, f, e, g, h)
Private collection, Zurich

PAGE 117
4 Panes of Glass (*4 Glasscheiben*), 1967
Glass and enameled steel
4 framed panes, each 77 3/16 × 41 3/4 in. (196 × 106 cm)
CR 160
Herbert Foundation, Ghent

PAGE 118
Townscape Paris (*Stadtbild Paris*), 1968
Oil on canvas
78 3/4 × 78 3/4 in. (200 × 200 cm)
CR 175
Froehlich Collection, Stuttgart

PAGE 119
Townscape Madrid (*Stadtbild Madrid*), 1968
Oil on linen
9 ft. 1 1/16 in. × 9 ft. 6 15/16 in. (277 × 292 cm)
CR 171
The Doris and Donald Fisher Collection at the
San Francisco Museum of Modern Art

PAGES 120–23
Alps (*Alpen*), 1968
Oil on canvas
78 3/4 in. × 21 ft. 3 7/8 in. (200 × 650 cm)
CR 189
Museum MMK für Moderne Kunst, Frankfurt
Former collection of Karl Ströher, Darmstadt

PAGE 124
Untitled (*Ohne Titel*), 1968
Oil on canvas
31 1/2 × 15 3/4 in. (80 × 40 cm)
CR 194-9
Hamburger Kunsthalle, on permanent
loan from the Collection of Elisabeth and
Gerhard Sohst

PAGE 125
Vintage (*Weinernte*), 1968
Oil on canvas
37 3/8 × 45 1/4 in. (95 × 115 cm)
CR 195
Private collection,
New Haven, Connecticut

PAGE 127
Star Picture (*Sternbild*), 1969
Oil on canvas
27 9/16 × 27 9/16 in. (70 × 70 cm)
CR 224-13
Collection of Stefan Asbrand-Eickhoff,
Hessen, Germany

PAGE 128
Star Picture (*Sternbild*), 1969
Oil on canvas
27 9/16 × 27 9/16 in. (70 × 70 cm)
CR 224-14
Collection of Stefan Asbrand-Eickhoff,
Hessen, Germany

PAGE 129
Star Picture (*Sternbild*), 1969
Oil on canvas
27 9/16 × 27 9/16 in. (70 × 70 cm)
CR 224-15
Collection of Stefan Asbrand-Eickhoff,
Hessen, Germany

PAGE 131
Study for Clouds (Contre-jour)
(*Wolkenstudie [Gegenlicht]*), 1970
Oil on canvas
31 1/2 × 39 3/8 in. (80 × 100 cm)
CR 276
Private collection

PAGE 132
Brigid Polk, 1971
Oil on linen
39 3/8 × 49 3/16 in. (100 × 125 cm)
CR 309
The Doris and Donald Fisher
Collection at the San Francisco
Museum of Modern Art

PAGE 133
Gray (Bark) (*Grau [Borke]*), 1973
Oil on canvas
35 7/16 × 25 9/16 in. (90 × 65 cm)
CR 348-7
Private collection

PAGE 134
Gilbert, 1975
Oil on canvas
25 9⁄16 × 23 5⁄8 in. (65 × 60 cm)
CR 381-1
ARTIST ROOMS: Tate and National Galleries of Scotland, Acquired jointly with the National Galleries of Scotland through The d'Offay Donation with assistance from the National Heritage Memorial Fund and the Art Fund 2008

PAGE 135
George, 1975
Oil on canvas
25 9⁄16 × 23 5⁄8 in. (65 × 60 cm)
CR 381-2
ARTIST ROOMS: Tate and National Galleries of Scotland, Acquired jointly with the National Galleries of Scotland through The d'Offay Donation with assistance from the National Heritage Memorial Fund and the Art Fund 2008

PAGE 136
Seascape (*Seestück*), 1975
Oil on canvas
78 3⁄4 in. × 9 ft. 10 1⁄8 in. (200 × 300 cm)
CR 375
Private collection, New York

PAGE 137
Seascape (*Seestück*), 1975
Oil on canvas
78 3⁄4 in. × 9 ft. 10 1⁄8 in. (200 × 300 cm)
CR 376
Collection of Lyn and Jerry Grinstein

PAGE 139
Vesuvius (*Vesuv*), 1976
Oil on wood
28 3⁄4 × 41 5⁄16 in. (73 × 105 cm)
CR 409
Collection of The Robert Lehrman Revocable Trust, Courtesy of Aimee and Robert Lehrman

PAGE 141
Betty, 1977
Oil on wood
11 13⁄16 × 15 3⁄4 in. (30 × 40 cm)
CR 425-4
Museum Ludwig, Cologne
Loan from private collection 2007

PAGE 143
Betty, 1977
Oil on canvas
19 11⁄16 × 15 3⁄4 in. (50 × 40 cm)
CR 425-5
Private collection

PAGES 144–45
Abstract Painting (*Abstraktes Bild*), 1978
Oil on canvas
78 3⁄4 in. × 10 ft. 11 7⁄8 in. (200 × 335 cm)
CR 434
Migros Museum für Gegenwartskunst, Zurich

PAGES 147, 146 (DETAIL)
Ice (*Eis*), 1981
Oil on canvas
27 9⁄16 × 39 3⁄8 in. (70 × 100 cm)
CR 476
Collection of Ruth McLoughlin, Monaco

PAGE 149
Iceberg in Mist (*Eisberg im Nebel*), 1982
Oil on canvas
27 9⁄16 × 39 3⁄8 in. (70 × 100 cm)
CR 496-1
Private collection, San Francisco

PAGE 151
Skull (*Schädel*), 1983
Oil on canvas
31 1⁄2 × 25 9⁄16 in. (80 × 65 cm)
CR 545-1
Private collection

PAGE 153
July (*Juli*), 1983
Oil on canvas
98 7⁄16 × 98 7⁄16 in. (250 × 250 cm)
CR 526
Private collection, Germany

PAGE 154
Mirror (*Spiegel*), 1986
Mirror
78 3⁄4 × 70 7⁄8 in. (200 × 180 cm)
CR 619
Gerhard Richter Archiv, Staatliche Kunstsammlungen Dresden (loan from a private collection)

PAGE 155
Cathedral Corner (*Domecke*), 1987
Oil on canvas
48 × 34 1⁄4 in. (122 × 87 cm)
CR 629-1
Collection of Samuel and Ronnie Heyman, Palm Beach, Florida

PAGES 157, 156 (DETAIL)
Squatters' House (*Besetztes Haus*), 1989
Oil on canvas
32 5⁄16 × 44 1⁄8 in. (82 × 112 cm)
CR 695-3
Private collection

PAGE 159
Passage (*Leipzig*), 1990
Oil on canvas
28 3⁄8 × 40 3⁄16 in. (72 × 102 cm)
CR 714
Würth Collection, Germany (Inv. 8554)

PAGES 161, 160 (DETAIL)
Abstract Painting (*Abstraktes Bild*), 1990
Oil on canvas
36 1⁄4 × 49 5⁄8 in. (92 × 126 cm)
CR 724-4
Private collection

PAGES 162–63
Six Photos. May 2–7, 1989
(*Sechs Fotos. 2.5.89–7.5.89*), 1991
Gelatin silver prints
Edition 12/50
Each 13 3⁄4 × 20 in. (35 × 50.8 cm)
National Gallery of Art, Washington, D.C., Patrons' Permanent Fund
Note: Illustrated images correspond to AP I/II

PAGE 165
Mirror, Blood Red (*Spiegel, blutrot*), 1991
Color-coated glass
35 1⁄16 × 36 1⁄4 in. (89 × 92 cm)
CR 736-4
Private collection

PAGE 167
I.G., 1993
Oil on canvas
32 1⁄4 × 36 1⁄4 in. (82 × 92 cm)
CR 790-3
"la Caixa" Collection of Contemporary Art

PAGE 168
I.G., 1993
Oil on canvas
28 3⁄8 × 40 3⁄16 in. (72 × 102 cm)
CR 790-4
Collection of Ruth McLoughlin, Monaco

PAGE 169
I.G., 1993
Oil on canvas
28 3⁄8 × 32 5⁄16 in. (72 × 82 cm)
CR 790-5
Friedrich Christian Flick Collection

PAGE 170
S. with Child (*S. mit Kind*), 1995
Oil on canvas
14 3⁄16 × 16 1⁄8 in. (36 × 41 cm)
CR 827-1
Hamburger Kunsthalle, on permanent loan from the Stiftung Hamburger Kunstsammlungen

PAGE 171
S. with Child (*S. mit Kind*), 1995
Oil on canvas
16 ⅛ × 14 3/16 in. (41 × 36 cm)
CR 827-2
Hamburger Kunsthalle

PAGE 172 TOP
S. with Child (*S. mit Kind*), 1995
Oil on canvas
20 ½ × 24 7/16 in. (52 × 62 cm)
CR 827-3
Hamburger Kunsthalle

PAGE 172 BOTTOM
S. with Child (*S. mit Kind*), 1995
Oil on canvas
20 ½ × 22 1/16 in. (52 × 56 cm)
CR 827-4
Hamburger Kunsthalle

PAGE 173
S. with Child (*S. mit Kind*), 1995
Oil on canvas
14 3/16 × 20 1/16 in. (36 × 51 cm)
CR 827-7
Hamburger Kunsthalle

PAGE 174
Self-Portrait (*Selbstportrait*), 1996
Oil on canvas
20 1/16 × 18 ⅛ in. (51 × 46 cm)
CR 836-2
Private collection

PAGE 175
Self-Portrait (*Selbstportrait*), 1996
Oil on linen
20 1/16 × 18 ⅛ in. (51 × 46 cm)
CR 836-1
The Museum of Modern Art, New York, Gift of Jo Carole and Ronald S. Lauder and Committee on Painting and Sculpture Funds, 1996

PAGE 177
Snow (*Schnee*), 1999
Oil on canvas
22 1/16 × 20 ⅛ in. (56 × 51 cm)
CR 861-2
Museum Frieder Burda, Baden-Baden

PAGES 179, 178 (DETAIL)
Farm (*Gehöft*), 1999
Oil on canvas
18 ⅛ × 20 1/16 in. (46 × 51 cm)
CR 861-1
Private collection

PAGE 180
Moritz, 2000
Oil on canvas
20 1/16 × 18 ⅛ in. (51 × 46 cm)
CR 863-1
De Pont Museum, Tilburg, The Netherlands

PAGE 181
Moritz, 2000
Oil on canvas
24 7/16 × 20 ½ in. (62 × 52 cm)
CR 863-2
De Pont Museum, Tilburg, The Netherlands

PAGE 183
11 Panes (*11 Scheiben*), 2004
Hard-coated tempered glass (Antelio silver) and wood
10 ft. 11 ⅞ in. × 82 11/16 in. × 22 13/16 in. (335 × 210 × 58 cm)
CR 886-3
High Museum of Art, Atlanta, Purchase with High Museum of Art Enhancement Fund (2005.217 a–o)

PAGES 185, 18 (DETAIL)
September, 2005
Oil on canvas
20 ½ × 28 ⅜ in. (52 × 72 cm)
CR 891-5
The Museum of Modern Art, New York, Gift of the artist and Joe Hage, 2008

PAGE 187
Juist, 2005
Oil on canvas
24 7/16 × 22 7/16 in. (62 × 57 cm)
CR 893-2
Private collection

PAGE 188 TOP LEFT
Forest (*Wald*) *(1)*, 2005
Oil on canvas
77 9/16 × 51 15/16 in. (197 × 132 cm)
CR 892-1
The Museum of Modern Art, New York, Gift of Warren and Mitzi Eisenberg, 2006

PAGES 188 TOP CENTER, 190
Forest (*Wald*) *(2)*, 2005
Oil on canvas
77 9/16 × 51 15/16 in. (197 × 132 cm)
CR 892-2
The Museum of Modern Art, New York, Gift of Warren and Mitzi Eisenberg and Leonard and Susan Feinstein, 2006

PAGE 188 TOP RIGHT
Forest (*Wald*) *(3)*, 2005
Oil on canvas
77 9/16 × 51 15/16 in. (197 × 132 cm)
CR 892-3
The Museum of Modern Art, New York, Promised gift of Leonard and Susan Feinstein, 2006

PAGES 188 BOTTOM LEFT, 192
Forest (*Wald*) *(7)*, 2005
Oil on canvas
77 9/16 × 51 15/16 in. (197 × 132 cm)
CR 892-7
The Museum of Modern Art, New York, Promised gift of Warren and Mitzi Eisenberg, 2006

PAGE 188 BOTTOM CENTER
Forest (*Wald*) *(8)*, 2005
Oil on canvas
77 9/16 × 51 15/16 in. (197 × 132 cm)
CR 892-8
The Museum of Modern Art, New York, Gift of Warren and Mitzi Eisenberg and Leonard and Susan Feinstein, 2006

PAGE 188 BOTTOM RIGHT
Forest (*Wald*) *(9)*, 2005
Oil on canvas
77 9/16 × 51 15/16 in. (197 × 132 cm)
CR 892-9
The Museum of Modern Art, New York, Gift of Warren and Mitzi Eisenberg, 2006

PAGE 189 TOP LEFT
Forest (*Wald*) *(4)*, 2005
Oil on canvas
77 9/16 × 51 15/16 in. (197 × 132 cm)
CR 892-4
The Museum of Modern Art, New York, Promised gift of Leonard and Susan Feinstein, 2006

PAGES 189 TOP CENTER, 191
Forest (*Wald*) *(5)*, 2005
Oil on canvas
77 9/16 × 51 15/16 in. (197 × 132 cm)
CR 892-5
The Museum of Modern Art, New York, Gift of Warren and Mitzi Eisenberg and Leonard and Susan Feinstein, 2006

PAGE 189 TOP RIGHT
Forest (*Wald*) *(6)*, 2005
Oil on canvas
77 9/16 × 51 15/16 in. (197 × 132 cm)
CR 892-6
The Museum of Modern Art, New York, Gift of Warren and Mitzi Eisenberg and Leonard and Susan Feinstein, 2006

PAGE 189 BOTTOM LEFT
Forest (Wald) (10), 2005
Oil on canvas
77 9/16 × 51 15/16 in. (197 × 132 cm)
CR 892-10
The Museum of Modern Art, New York, Gift of Warren and Mitzi Eisenberg and Leonard and Susan Feinstein, 2006

PAGE 189 BOTTOM CENTER
Forest (Wald) (11), 2005
Oil on canvas
77 9/16 × 51 15/16 in. (197 × 132 cm)
CR 892-11
The Museum of Modern Art, New York, Gift of Leonard and Susan Feinstein, 2006

PAGES 189 BOTTOM RIGHT, 193
Forest (Wald) (12), 2005
Oil on canvas
77 9/16 × 51 15/16 in. (197 × 132 cm)
CR 892-12
The Museum of Modern Art, New York, Gift of Warren and Mitzi Eisenberg and Leonard and Susan Feinstein, 2006

PAGE 196
Cage (1), 2006
Oil on canvas
9 ft. 6 3/16 in. × 9 ft. 6 3/16 in. (290 × 290 cm)
CR 897-1
Tate: Lent from a private collection 2007

PAGE 197
Cage (2), 2006
Oil on canvas
9 ft. 10 1/8 in. × 9 ft. 10 1/8 in. (300 × 300 cm)
CR 897-2
Tate: Lent from a private collection 2007

PAGE 198
Cage (3), 2006
Oil on canvas
9 ft. 6 3/16 in. × 9 ft. 6 3/16 in. (290 × 290 cm)
CR 897-3
Tate: Lent from a private collection 2007

PAGE 199
Cage (4), 2006
Oil on canvas
9 ft. 6 3/16 in. × 9 ft. 6 3/16 in. (290 × 290 cm)
CR 897-4
Tate: Lent from a private collection 2007

PAGES 200, 194–95 (DETAIL)
Cage (5), 2006
Oil on canvas
9 ft. 10 1/8 in. × 9 ft. 10 1/8 in. (300 × 300 cm)
CR 897-5
Tate: Lent from a private collection 2007

PAGE 201
Cage (6), 2006
Oil on canvas
9 ft. 10 1/8 in. × 9 ft. 10 1/8 in. (300 × 300 cm)
CR 897-6
Tate: Lent from a private collection 2007

PAGES 202–3
4,900 Colors (4,900 Farben), 2007
Lacquer on Alu Dibond [exhibition copy]
140 panels, each 19 1/8 × 19 1/8 in. (48.5 × 48.5 cm); 5 parts, total 11 ft. 1 11/16 in. × 38 ft. 2 1/4 in. (339.5 × 1,164 cm)
CR 901
Private collection

PAGE 205
Ella, 2007
Oil on canvas
15 3/4 × 12 3/16 in. (40 × 31 cm)
CR 903-1
Private collection

PAGE 207
Abstract Painting (Abstraktes Bild), 2009
Oil on canvas
78 3/4 in. × 9 ft. 10 1/8 in. (200 × 300 cm)
CR 911-1
Collection of James and Dana Tananbaum

PAGES 209, 208 (DETAIL)
Abstract Painting (Abstraktes Bild), 2009
Oil on canvas
78 3/4 in. × 9 ft. 10 1/8 in. (200 × 300 cm)
CR 911-2
Cranford Collection, London

PAGES 210–11, 213, 214, 215
Elbe, 1957/2012
Digital fine art prints on paper [exhibition copy]
31 prints, each 11 5/8 × 8 1/4 in. (29.5 × 21 cm)
Gerhard Richter Archiv, Staatliche Kunstsammlungen Dresden

PAGE 217
Flow, 2013
Lacquer on glass mounted on Alu Dibond
39 3/8 × 78 3/4 in. (100 × 200 cm)
CR 933-3
Private collection

PAGES 220–21, 218–19 (DETAIL)
Strip, 2013
Digital print on paper between Alu Dibond and Perspex (Diasec)
78 3/4 in. × 32 ft. 9 11/16 in. (200 × 1,000 cm)
CR 930-3
Private collection

PAGES 224, 229
Birkenau, 2014
Diasec-mounted giclée prints
4 prints, each 8 ft. 6 3/8 in. × 78 3/4 in. (260 × 200 cm)
Private collection

PAGE 225
Birkenau, 2014
Oil on canvas
8 ft. 6 3/8 in. × 78 3/4 in. (260 × 200 cm)
CR 937-1
Private collection

PAGES 226, 223 (DETAIL)
Birkenau, 2014
Oil on canvas
8 ft. 6 3/8 in. × 78 3/4 in. (260 × 200 cm)
CR 937-2
Private collection

PAGE 227
Birkenau, 2014
Oil on canvas
8 ft. 6 3/8 in. × 78 3/4 in. (260 × 200 cm)
CR 937-3
Private collection

PAGE 228
Birkenau, 2014
Oil on canvas
8 ft. 6 3/8 in. × 78 3/4 in. (260 × 200 cm)
CR 937-4
Private collection

PAGES 230–31
Sonderkommando photographs taken in KL Auschwitz II-Birkenau, Summer 1944 [Negative nos. 277, 278, 282, 283: Burning of corpses in the open air; Women driven to gas chambers; Tree branches]
Archive digital pigment prints, 2015
Each 19 1/8 × 15 1/2 in. (48.5 × 39.3 cm)
Private collection
Images from the Archive of the Auschwitz-Birkenau State Museum

PAGE 234 TOP LEFT
Abstract Painting (Abstraktes Bild), 2016
Oil on canvas
15 3/4 × 11 13/16 in. (40 × 30 cm)
CR 944-1
Private collection

PAGE 234 TOP RIGHT
Abstract Painting (Abstraktes Bild), 2016
Oil on canvas
15 3/4 × 11 13/16 in. (40 × 30 cm)
CR 944-2
Private collection

PAGES 234 BOTTOM LEFT, 232–33 (DETAIL)
Abstract Painting (*Abstraktes Bild*), 2016
Oil on canvas
15 ¾ × 11 13⁄16 in. (40 × 30 cm)
CR 944-5
Private collection

PAGE 234 BOTTOM RIGHT
Abstract Painting (*Abstraktes Bild*), 2016
Oil on canvas
15 ¾ × 11 13⁄16 in. (40 × 30 cm)
CR 944-6
Private collection

PAGE 235 TOP LEFT
Abstract Painting (*Abstraktes Bild*), 2016
Oil on canvas
15 ¾ × 11 13⁄16 in. (40 × 30 cm)
CR 944-3
Private collection

PAGE 235 TOP RIGHT
Abstract Painting (*Abstraktes Bild*), 2016
Oil on canvas
15 ¾ × 11 13⁄16 in. (40 × 30 cm)
CR 944-4
Private collection

PAGE 235 BOTTOM LEFT
Abstract Painting (*Abstraktes Bild*), 2016
Oil on canvas
15 ¾ × 11 13⁄16 in. (40 × 30 cm)
CR 944-7
Private collection

PAGES 237, 236 (DETAIL)
Abstract Painting (*Abstraktes Bild*), 2016
Oil on canvas
78 ¾ × 98 7⁄16 in. (200 × 250 cm)
CR 946-1
Private collection

PAGE 238
Abstract Painting (*Abstraktes Bild*), 2016
Oil on canvas
86 ⅝ × 56 11⁄16 in. (220 × 144 cm)
CR 945-5
Private collection

PAGE 239
Abstract Painting (*Abstraktes Bild*), 2017
Oil on canvas
78 ¾ × 98 7⁄16 in. (200 × 250 cm)
CR 952-4
Private collection

PAGE 241
Abstract Painting (*Abstraktes Bild*), 2017
Oil on canvas
78 ¾ × 78 ¾ in. (200 × 200 cm)
CR 952-2
Private collection

PAGES 242–43
Gray Mirror (4 Parts) (*Grauer Spiegel [4 Teile]*), 2018
Lacquer on back of glass
89 ¾ in. × 29 ft. 11 1⁄16 in. (228 × 912 cm)
CR 955
Private collection

PAGE 245
House of Cards (5 Panes)
(*Kartenhaus [5 Scheiben]*), 2020
Glass and steel construction
Each pane 10 ft. 6 in. × 70 ⅞ in. × ⅜ in.
(320 × 180 × 1 cm)
CR 956
Private collection

Notes

Introduction: The Excavation of Memory
Sheena Wagstaff

1. Gerhard Richter, interview with Rolf Schön, in Dieter Honisch, *Gerhard Richter: 36. Biennale di Venezia, Padiglione tedesco, 11.6.–1.10.72*, exh. cat. (Essen: Museum Folkwang, 1972), p. 23.

2. Gerhard Richter, "Comments on Some Works, 1991," in *Text: Writings, Interviews and Letters 1961–2007*, ed. Dietmar Elger and Hans Ulrich Obrist (London: Thames & Hudson, 2009), p. 259.

3. Tom McCarthy, "Blurring the Sublime: On Gerhard Richter," in *Typewriters, Bombs, Jellyfish: Essays* (New York: New York Review Books, 2017), p. 127.

4. N. R. Kleinfield, "U.S. Attacked; Hijacked Jets Destroy Twin Towers and Hit Pentagon in Day of Terror," *New York Times*, September 12, 2001.

5. Don DeLillo, "In the Ruins of the Future: Reflections on Terror and Loss in the Shadow of September," *Harper's*, December 2001, p. 39.

6. Doris McGonagill, *Crisis and Collection: German Visual Memory Archives of the Twentieth Century* (Würzburg: Königshausen & Neumann, 2015), p. 9. McGonagill's publication was important to my discussion of trauma addressed through visual art and literature.

7. Richter, "Interview with Hans Ulrich Obrist, 2006," in *Text*, p. 526.

8. Ibid., p. 527.

9. Buchloh originally made this comment in reference to the installation of *48 Portraits* at the 1972 Venice Biennale. "Divided Memory and Post-Traditional Identity: Gerhard Richter's Work of Mourning," *October* 75 (Winter 1996), p. 81.

10. "I Have Nothing to Say and I'm Saying It: Conversation between Gerhard Richter and Nicholas Serota, Spring 2011," in *Gerhard Richter: Panorama*, ed. Mark Godfrey and Nicholas Serota, exh. cat. (London: Tate Publishing, 2011; rev. ed. 2016), p. 26.

11. W. G. Sebald, "Air War and Literature," in *On the Natural History of Destruction*, trans. Anthea Bell (New York: Random House, 2003), p. 10.

12. Sebald, "Foreword," in ibid., p. ix.

13. Richter, "Notes, 1964–1965," in *Text*, pp. 33–34.

14. Georges Didi-Huberman, *Images in Spite of All: Four Photographs from Auschwitz*, trans. Shane B. Lillis (Chicago: University of Chicago Press, 2008).

15. Richter, "I Have Nothing to Say and I'm Saying It," p. 25.

16. Gerhard Richter, "Man kann Auschwitz nicht abmalen: Gespräch mit Julia Voss und Peter Geimer," *Frankfurter Allgemeine Zeitung*, February 25, 2016. Translation by Catherine Burns and Sabine Rewald.

17. Ibid.

18. McGonagill, *Crisis and Collection*, p. 101.

19. Theodor W. Adorno, "Marginalia on Mahler" (1936), in *Essays on Music*, ed. Richard Leppert, trans. Susan H. Gillespie (Berkeley: University of California Press, 2002), p. 612.

20. Kai-Uwe Hemken, quoted in McGonagill, *Crisis and Collection*, p. 161n119.

21. Richter, "I Have Nothing to Say and I'm Saying It," p. 15.

22. Ibid., p. 24.

Documents of Culture, Documents of Barbarism: Richter's *Birkenau* Paintings
Benjamin H. D. Buchloh

1. The Grundigs were Socialists who had been persecuted by the Nazi regime, forcing Lea, who was Jewish, into exile in Palestine, and Hans, a member of the Communist party, into the concentration camp of Sachsenhausen for several years. After their return to Dresden in 1949, both were appointed as faculty at the Dresden Academy. Richter did not study with either one, but rather with Heinz Lohmar, a German Jewish Surrealist painter who had immigrated to Paris and, as an anti-Fascist Communist, had also been appointed to the academy after returning to Dresden in 1949.

2. Dietmar Elger, Richter's biographer, states that the project originally comprised twelve drawings, four of which are still preserved in the Gerhard Richter Archive in Dresden. Four others, which seem to have disappeared, are recorded in one of Richter's photo albums in the Dresden archive. This project was most likely prompted not only by the initial publication of *The Diary of Anne Frank* in the German Democratic Republic in 1957 (a West German edition had already been published in 1950) but also by the 1956 premiere in Dresden of a play based on the diary by the American authors Frances Goodrich and Albert Hackett. See Kathrin Hoffmann-Curtius, *Judenmord: Art and the Holocaust in Post-war Germany* (London: Reaktion Books, 2018), pp. 182–84.

3. Lea Grundig published two portfolios in the immediate aftermath of the Holocaust, the first, *In the Valley of Slaughter*, in Tel Aviv in 1944, and the second, *Ghetto Uprising*, a series of drawings commemorating the uprising in the Warsaw Ghetto, in 1946. See Hoffmann-Curtius, *Judenmord*, pp. 68–90.

4. This exhibition was jointly organized by Konrad Lueg, Sigmar Polke, Manfred Kuttner, and Richter. It was touted as the beginning of "Capitalist Realism" and included six paintings by Richter.

5. Theodor W. Adorno, "Was bedeutet: Aufarbeitung der Vergangenheit" (1959), in *Gesammelte Schriften*, vol. 10.2, *Kulturkritik und Gesellschaft II* (Frankfurt: Suhrkamp, 1977), p. 5; published in English as "The Meaning of Working through the Past," in Adorno, *Critical Models: Interventions and Catchwords*, European Perspectives: A Series in Social Thought and Cultural Criticism, trans. Henry W. Pickford (New York: Columbia University Press, 1998), p. 101. Adorno initially presented this paper on November 6, 1959, during a conference on education hosted by the German Coordinating Council of the Societies for Christian-Jewish Cooperation in Wiesbaden, and it was broadcast as a radio lecture in 1960.

6. See Gerhard Richter, "Man kann Auschwitz nicht abmalen: Gespräch mit Julia Voss und Peter Geimer," *Frankfurter Allgemeine Zeitung*, February 25, 2016, p. 9.

7. Hannah Arendt, *Eichmann in Jerusalem: A Report on the Banality of Evil* (New York: Viking Press, 1963), p. 251.

8. Adorno returned from California to his native Frankfurt in 1949, and Arendt remained in the United States; both became among the most important intellectuals and philosophers of post-Holocaust history and post-totalitarian politics. Arendt returned to West Germany for the first time in 1949, on behalf of the Jewish Restitution Committee, and published her observations in the essay "The Aftermath of Nazi Rule: Report from Germany," *Commentary* 10 (1950), pp. 342–53. She provided a diagnosis that anticipates in almost all aspects Adorno's

1959 lecture. In this essay she speaks of the "German inability to mourn," a concept that the psychoanalyst Alexander Mitscherlich and his wife, Margarete, revisited in their book *Die Unfähigkeit zu Trauern* (Munich: Piper, 1967). They do not quote Arendt but rather deal with other psychoanalytical studies that have explored the difficulty of mourning. The first English translation of the book, *The Inability to Mourn*, was published by Grove Press, New York, in 1975.

9. Karl Jaspers, *Die Schuldfrage: Ein Beitrag zur deutschen Frage* (Zurich: Artemis, 1946), p. 11; published in English as *The Question of German Guilt*, trans. E. B. Ashton (New York: Doubleday/ Random House, 1948), p. 12.

10. Georges Bataille, "Réflexions sur la question juive," *Critique* 12 (May 1947), p. 471; reprinted as "Sartre," in Bataille, *Oeuvres complètes*, vol. 11 (Paris: Gallimard, 1988). My translation.

11. Enzo Traverso, *Understanding the Nazi Genocide: Marxism after Auschwitz*, trans. Peter Drucker (London: Pluto Press, 1999). Traverso's study was very important for the development of the questions sketched out in this essay.

12. Theodor W. Adorno, "Kulturkritik und Gesellschaft" (1949), in *Gesammelte Schriften*, vol. 10.1, *Kulturkritik und Gesellschaft I* (Frankfurt: Suhrkamp, 1970), pp. 30ff.

13. Walter Benjamin, "Theses on the Philosophy of History" (1940). My translation. Benjamin mailed a copy of the essay to Arendt, who shared it soon thereafter with Adorno. Against Benjamin's wish to not have the manuscript published, it was first circulated in a mimeographed booklet, "Walter Benjamin zum Gedächtnis," in 1947. The first English translation, by Harry Zohn, was published in Arendt's collection of Benjamin's essays, *Illuminations* (New York: Schocken Books, 1968).

14. Theodor W. Adorno, *Gesammelte Schriften*, vol. 6, *Negative Dialektik* (Frankfurt: Suhrkamp, 2003), p. 359. My translation.

15. Theodor W. Adorno, *Metaphysik: Begriff und Probleme* (1965), *Nachgelassene Schriften*, vol. 2 (Frankfurt: Suhrkamp, 1998), p. 172. Published in English as *Metaphysics: Concept and Problems*, ed. Rolf Tiedemann, trans. Edmund Jephcott (Stanford: Stanford University Press, 2001), p. 110.

16. Werner Heyde lived under a different name and continued his medical practice after the war. He was not exposed to the wider public as one of the key figures of the Nazi euthanasia program until preparations began for the Frankfurt Auschwitz trials. Heyde committed suicide in prison before facing the sentencing in his trial.

17. It is important to remember that the debasement of the portrait genre by the representation of criminal deviants had been executed by Andy Warhol in his infamous and censored series Thirteen Most Wanted Men at the 1964 World's Fair in New York. Richter's 1965 portraits of perpetrators also anticipate the negative counter-identification with the disavowed agents of German history that Anselm Kiefer would stage in 1969 by delivering Hitler salutes while traveling in various European countries.

18. One of many examples of the newly emerging West German intellectuals to actually address this history was the young art historian Martin Warnke, who was later central to the formation of social art history in Germany. He attended the Frankfurt trials and reported extensively on them in a German newspaper. See Martin Warnke, *Zeitgenossenschaft: Zum Auschwitz-Prozess 1964*, ed. Pablo Schneider and Barbara Wetzel (Berlin: Diaphanes, 2014). Another example is Klaus Theweleit, whose book *Male Fantasies* (Minneapolis: University of Minnesota Press, 1987) was one of the first major psychoanalytical studies of the formation of proto-Fascist German masculinity in the Weimar years.

19. At that moment, felt-tip markers were one of the most innovative bureaucratic marking devices (comparable in many ways to the ballpoint pens shockingly deployed in drawings by Andy Warhol and Sigmar Polke).

20. Founded in 1959, the radical group consisted of Lurie, Sam Goodman, and Stanley Fisher. Their extreme critiques of commercial consumer culture were often explicitly linked to images of Fascist history. Due to its shocking aggression, the work was largely sidelined and has almost never been shown in American institutions or galleries.

21. Ruth Klüger, quoted in Hoffmann-Curtius, *Judenmord*, pp. 310–11.

22. The Allies had circulated documentation in the immediate aftermath of the war. In his 1967 series of photographic references in the *Atlas*, Richter used pictures that had been taken by Private Harry Miller, a British soldier, on the occasion of the liberation of the Buchenwald concentration camp in 1945. Gerhard Schoenberner published the first German study of the different phases of the persecution and murder of the Jewish populations of Europe in his book *Der Gelbe Stern (The Yellow Star)* (Hamburg: Rütten & Loening, 1960), which Richter also knew.

23. In the 2012 film *Gerhard Richter Painting*, directed by Corinna Belz, Richter said that he saw the first images of the concentration camps while at the academy in Dresden in his mid-twenties: "Somebody had smuggled in an American publication, and we looked at it and it stayed with me ever since, the images and the reports on the atrocities." In an interview with Jan Thorn-Prikker, he stated, "In my mid-twenties I saw some concentration camp photographs that disturbed me very much. In my mid-thirties I collected and took photographs and tried to paint them. I had to give up. That was when I put the photographs together in that weird and seemingly cynical way in the *Atlas*." "Conversation with Jan Thorn-Prikker, 1989," in Gerhard Richter, *Text: Writings, Interviews and Letters 1961–2007*, ed. Dietmar Elger and Hans Ulrich Obrist (London: Thames & Hudson, 2009), p. 226. Richter and Konrad Lueg planned an exhibition for the Galerie Niepel in Düsseldorf that was to show concentration-camp photographs alongside images from pornographic magazines under the title *Sex and Mass Murder*. A psychoanalyst friend of Lueg's had introduced the artists to the material. As Richter stated in retrospect, in 2002: "I saw no possible moral or formal solution for how to exhibit the camp and the porno pictures as Konrad and I had planned.... We would have gotten a lot of attention, but it would have been unproductive and inadequate—at least inadequate." "Interview with Robert Storr, 2002," in Richter, *Text*, p. 289.

24. Completed in 2014, the *Birkenau* group was initially titled simply *Abstract Paintings* (CR 937 [1–4]) and was exhibited for the first time under the title *Birkenau* in March 2015 at the Albertinum in Dresden. The Birkenau camp at Auschwitz was built in 1940 and put into operation as a concentration camp the following year. It was one of the first death camps to adopt the system of execution in gas chambers, in the spring of 1942, and the last to end the industrialized murder, in November 1944, when it was liberated by the Soviet army.

25. See Georges Didi-Huberman, *Images in Spite of All: Four Photographs from Auschwitz*, trans. Shane B. Lillis (Chicago: University of Chicago Press, 2008). Richter's rediscovery of these images was triggered by Peter Geimer's review of Didi-Huberman's book in the *Frankfurter Allgemeine Zeitung*, February 11, 2008, on the occasion of the publication of Geimer's German

translation of the study. The artist had seen these images initially in Gerhard Schoenberner's book *Der Gelbe Stern* (see note 22, above). Didi-Huberman's essay was originally published in French in a catalogue for the 2001 exhibition *Mémoire des camps*, curated by Clément Chéroux. One of its main arguments at the time was directed at the prohibition of images of the Holocaust, as voiced programmatically by Claude Lanzmann's refusal to include any actual images and documents of the Holocaust in his important documentary, *Shoah*. Didi-Huberman responded to Lanzmann in his introductory sentence: "To know, we must imagine for ourselves." My initial essay on these works was published in a small volume, *Gerhard Richter's* Birkenau *Paintings* (Cologne: Walther König, 2016), parts of which have been revised and incorporated into this essay. Didi-Huberman subsequently published *Wo Es war: Vier Briefe an Gerhard Richter* [Four letters to Gerhard Richter] (Cologne: Walther König, 2018). I gratefully acknowledge Didi-Huberman's dialogic and critical responses to my essay, and I am indebted in many ways to his exceptional theoretical and historical elaborations, which have been crucial to my continuing reflections on Richter's extraordinary group of late paintings.

26. Guy Debord, *La société du spectacle* (Paris: Buchet/Chastel, 1967). The first English translation, by Fredy Perlman, was published by Black & Red Press, Detroit, in 1977; a later translation, by Donald Nicholson-Smith, was published in 1994 by Zone Books, New York.

27. It is well known that Piet Mondrian, for example, explicitly refrained from ever using green because he considered it irredeemably bonded with references to nature, and the color is similarly absent from the abstractions of Kazimir Malevich.

28. While one might assume that technical logistics necessitated the partitioning of the large-scale digital prints in order to have them match the actual size of the paintings, Richter emphasized that there were no such reasons for the division. This is also confirmed by the fact that Richter had initially produced two exact digital copies that were undivided. He had tried to install them in tandem with the paintings, but he ultimately rejected this solution.

29. The four *Birkenau* paintings are now in the collection of the Gerhard Richter Foundation, which cannot release any work for sale to a museum or private collection.

30. Kertész formulated his critical comments after seeing the American television series *Holocaust* and expressed them even more vociferously in response to Steven Spielberg's film *Schindler's List*, explicitly identifying both as kitsch; at that time he may also have been responding to the sudden fame accorded to Anselm Kiefer's paintings that pretended to address Holocaust history. See Imre Kertész, "Who Owns Auschwitz?," *Yale Journal of Criticism* 14, no. 1 (Spring 2001), p. 270.

31. Two major art-historical studies on representations of the Holocaust, while extremely helpful to this author's study of the scope and range of artists who have engaged with these historical demands, never even once ask the theoretical and ethical questions posed by Adorno and Claude Lanzmann. Nor do they question the actual aesthetic legitimacy and credibility of these artists' projects against the horizon of the major paradigms that defined artistic production in the twentieth century. See Ziva Amishai-Maisels, *Depiction and Interpretation: The Influence of the Holocaust on the Visual Arts* (Oxford: Pergamon Press, 1993), and Hoffmann-Curtius, *Judenmord*.

32. Theodor W. Adorno, "Commitment," in *The Essential Frankfurt School Reader*, ed. Andrew Arato and Eike Gebhardt (New York: Continuum Press, 1990), p. 312.

33. Mark Godfrey, *Abstraction and the Holocaust* (New Haven: Yale University Press, 2007). Given the book's comprehensive and complex historical and theoretical account, it is regrettable that Godfrey did not include a study of Eva Hesse's work.

34. Stella's first Black Painting was called *Reichstag*, followed by *Arbeit Macht Frei* (1958) and *Die Fahne Hoch!* (1959), painted a few months later. "Work Makes You Free" was the cynical, sadistic inscription over the gates at Auschwitz and Theresienstadt. *Die Fahne Hoch!* ("Raise the Flag!") was the first line of the "Horst Wessel Lied," the infamous Nazi marching song. Stella's sketches of the cruciform Black Paintings and their permutations, made in 1960, end with a notation reading "the final solution." For a more extensive discussion of these paintings, see Anna C. Chave, "Minimalism and the Rhetoric of Power," *Arts Magazine* 64, no. 5 (January 1990), pp. 44–63.

35. For an excellent discussion of Stella, see Godfrey, *Abstraction and the Holocaust*, pp. 96–105. See also my essay "Painting as Diagram: Five Notes on Frank Stella's Early Paintings, 1958–1959," *October* 143 (Winter 2013), pp. 126–44, which specifically discusses Stella's responses to what was perceived as the chauvinist flag cult of Jasper Johns in the mid-1950s.

36. We are limiting ourselves to symptomatic statements signaling the reemergence of anti-Semitic and proto-Fascist nationalist tendencies in the German context, assuming that American readers have ample access to similar symptoms that signal the seemingly inevitable transition from late monopoly capitalist structures to proto-Fascist policies.

37. Herbert Diess, the CEO of Volkswagen, made this remark in March 2019. *Ebit*, a near homonym of *arbeit* in German, refers to an accounting acronym that stands for "earnings before interest and taxes." It is a perfect example of the literally abysmal features of a proudly reconstituted national identity formed under the auspices of an apparently victorious economic superpower that seems to absolve itself from all historical guilt, precisely along the lines of the nation-state ideology that Adorno's 1959 essay had prophesied would become the carrier of renewed proto-Fascist thought.

38. Alexander Gauland, one of the central figures of the new right-wing populist-nationalist party in Germany, stated this at a conference in 2018.

39. Christiane Lange and Dirk Luckow, "Introduction," in Götz Adriani, *Baselitz, Richter, Polke, Kiefer: Die jungen Jahre der Alten Meister*, exh. cat. (Dresden: Sandstein, 2019), pp. 6–7. My translation.

40. Götz Adriani, ibid., pp. 13 and 28.

41. Theodor W. Adorno, *Aesthetische Theorie* (Frankfurt: Suhrkamp, 1995), p. 55. My translation.

Seeing One Medium through Another: Richter's Photo Paintings of the 1960s
Peter Geimer

1. Letter from Kuttner, Lueg, Polke, and Richter, quoted in Dietmar Elger, *Gerhard Richter: A Life in Painting*, trans. Elizabeth M. Solaro (Chicago: University of Chicago Press, 2009), p. 55.

2. Michel Foucault, "What Is an Author?," lecture given at the Collège de France, February 22, 1969; https://www.open.edu/openlearn/ocw/pluginfile.php/624849/mod_resource/content/1/a840_1_michel_foucault.pdf.

3. Benjamin H. D. Buchloh, "Gerhard Richter's *Tisch*: Memory Images and German Disavowal in 1962," in *Interiors and Interiority*, ed. Ewa Lajer-Burcharth and Beate Söntgen (Berlin: Walter De Gruyter, 2016), p. 401.

4. It was only in the 1970s that separate departments for photography were established in the Cologne, Bonn, Essen, and Munich museums, and even at Documenta in Kassel photography was not included until 1972.

5. Roland Barthes, *Camera Lucida: Reflections on Photography*, trans. Richard Howard (New York: Hill and Wang, 1981), p. 30.

6. This is wonderfully shown in the following note from Talbot's *The Pencil of Nature* (1844), which clearly rests on the fact that he measured the automatic nature of photography against the incomparably greater amount of time and labor involved in producing a drawing by hand: "Groups of figures take no longer time to obtain than single figures would require, since the Camera depicts them all at once, however numerous they may be." William Henry Fox Talbot, *The Pencil of Nature*, facsimile ed. (New York: Da Capo Press, 1969), unpaginated.

7. Walter Benjamin, "Kleine Geschichte der Photographie" (1931), published in English as "A Short History of Photography," trans. Stanley Mitchell, *Screen* 13, no. 1 (Spring 1972), p. 6.

8. In his semiotic theory, Charles Sanders Peirce distinguishes between different kinds of signs. He calls the photograph an example of the class of "indexical" signs, which are characterized by their direct relationship to the objects they represent—for instance, a weathervane, as an indicator of wind direction, is directly related to the wind that turns it. In this sense, Peirce sees photographs as photochemically fixed rays of light that have emanated from the depicted objects themselves. Accordingly, in photography there is an immediate physical connection between signifier and signified that does not exist in the same form in painting. This view was later expressed by theorists of photography such as André Bazin, Roland Barthes, Susan Sontag, and Rosalind Krauss. See Peter Geimer, "Image as Trace: Speculations about an Undead Paradigm," in "Indexicality: Trace and Sign," ed. Mary Ann Doane, special issue, *Differences: A Journal of Feminist Cultural Studies* 18, no. 1 (Spring 2007), pp. 7–28.

9. André Bazin, "Ontologie des photographischen Bildes" (1945), published in English as "The Ontology of the Photographic Image," trans. Hugh Gray, *Film Quarterly* 13, no. 4 (Summer 1960), p. 7.

10. Ibid.

11. Siegfried Kracauer, "Photography," in *Theory of Film: The Redemption of Physical Reality* (Princeton: Princeton University Press, 1997), p. 12.

12. Ibid., pp. 20, 19.

13. Ibid., p. 18.

14. For Steinert, see *Der Fotograf Otto Steinert*, ed. Ute Eskildsen, exh. cat. (Göttingen: Steidl, 1999); and Jörn Glasenapp, *Die deutsche Nachkriegsfotografie: Eine Mentalitätsgeschichte in Bildern* (Paderborn: Wilhelm Fink, 2008).

15. Otto Steinert, "Über die Gestaltungsmöglichkeiten der Fotografie" (1955), in *Theorie der Fotografie*, ed. Wolfgang Kemp, vol. 3, *1945–1980* (Munich: Schirmer/Mosel, 1983), p. 89.

16. Ibid., pp. 84, 89.

17. Ibid., p. 86.

18. See Ulrike Herrmann, "Otto Steinerts experimentelle Fotografie," in *Der Fotograf Otto Steinert*, pp. 125–26; and Glasenapp, *Die deutsche Nachkriegsfotografie*, p. 179.

19. For other examples of abstract photography, see Gottfried Jäger, ed., *The Art of Abstract Photography* (Stuttgart: Arnoldsche Verlagsanstalt, 2002).

20. Albert Renger-Patzsch, letter to the Boehringer firm (date unknown), quoted in Glasenapp, *Die deutsche Nachkriegsfotografie*, p. 180.

21. Albert Renger-Patzsch, "An Essay toward the Classification of Photography" (1956), *Untitled 12: Albert Renger-Patzsch 1897–1966: Photographs from the Collection of the Friends of Photography* (1977), pp. 18, 19, 23.

22. Karl Pawek, *Totale Photographie: Die Optik des neuen Realismus* (Olten, Switzerland: Walter, 1960), pp. 97, 206.

23. Glasenapp, *Die deutsche Nachkriegsfotografie*, pp. 216–17.

24. Roland Barthes, *Mythologies*, trans. Annette Lavers (New York: Hill and Wang, 1972), p. 101.

25. "A photograph is taken in order to inform. What matters to the photographer and to the viewer is the result, the legible information, the fact captured in an image. Alternatively, the photograph can be regarded as a picture, in which case the information conveyed changes radically. However, because it is very hard to turn a photograph into a picture simply by declaring it to be one, I have to make a painted copy." Gerhard Richter, "Notes, 1964–1965," in *The Daily Practice of Painting: Writings and Interviews 1962–1993*, ed. Hans Ulrich Obrist, trans. David Britt (Cambridge, Mass.: MIT Press; London: Anthony d'Offay Gallery, 1995), p. 31.

26. Uwe Schneede, "Gerhard Richter's Images of an Era," in *Gerhard Richter: Images of an Era*, ed. Uwe Schneede, exh. cat. (Munich: Hirmer, 2011), p. 14. See also Klaus Honnef, *Gerhard Richter* (Recklinghausen: Aurel Bongers, 1976), p. 20: "The picture symbolizes the dilemma of a painter who wishes to depict an everyday object by means of painting and has to accept the fact that one can accomplish this much more convincingly by photographic means."

27. Dietmar Elger, *Gerhard Richter: Maler* (Cologne: DuMont, 2018), p. 66.

28. For the particulars of the application of pigment and the various techniques of blurring, see Dietmar Elger, "The Painted Photo: Gerhard Richter in His Atelier," in *Gerhard Richter: Images of an Era*, pp. 60–69. See also Robert Storr, *Gerhard Richter: Forty Years of Painting*, exh. cat. (New York: Museum of Modern Art, 2002), p. 41.

29. Thierry de Duve, "Time Exposure and Snapshot: The Photograph as Paradox," *October* 5 (Summer 1978), p. 116.

30. Benjamin, "A Short History of Photography," p. 7.

31. See Gotthold Ephraim Lessing's canonical passage in his essay "Laocoon" (1766): "Since the artist can use but a single moment of ever-changing nature, and the painter must further confine his study of this one moment to a single point of view, while their works are made not simply to be looked at, but to be contemplated long and often, evidently the most fruitful moment... must be chosen." Gotthold Ephraim Lessing, *Laocoon: An Essay upon the Limits of Painting and Poetry*, trans. Ellen Frothingham (Boston: Roberts Brothers, 1874), p. 16.

32. For the theory of technical accident as the constitutive characteristic of a technique, see Paul Virilio, *L'accident originel* (Paris: Éditions Galilée, 2005).

33. Schneede, "Gerhard Richter's Images of an Era," p. 20.

34. "On Pop, East and West, and Some of the Picture Sources: Uwe M. Schneede in Conversation with Gerhard Richter," in Schneede, *Gerhard Richter: Images of an Era*, p. 108.

35. Karl Heinz Hering, "Zur Ausstellung Gerhard Richter," in *Gerhard Richter: Arbeiten 1962 bis 1971*, exh. cat. (Düsseldorf: Kunstverein für die Rheinlande und Westfalen, 1971), unpaginated. See also Hubertus Butin, "Hero Worship and the Rejection of Ideology: Gerhard Richter's 1966 Film *Volker Bradke*," in *Gerhard Richter: Images of an Era*, p. 89. Susanne Ehrenfried summarizes the core thesis of this pattern of interpretation as follows: "With the painted photo, clichés are exposed that serve as the basis for our naive or even critical engagement with photographs." Susanne Ehrenfried, *Ohne Eigenschaften: Das Portrait bei Gerhard Richter* (Vienna: Springer, 1997), p. 165.

36. Günther Anders, "Ikonomanie" (1956), in Kemp, *Theorie der Fotografie*, p. 110.

37. Ibid., p. 111.

38. Martin Heidegger, *Sojourns: The Journey to Greece* (1962), trans. John Panteleimon Manoussakis (Albany: State University of New York Press, 2005), p. 54.

39. Pierre Bourdieu, "The Social Definition of Photography" (1965), in *Photography: A Middle-brow Art*, trans. Shaun Whiteside (Stanford: Stanford University Press, 1990), p. 73.

40. Benjamin H. D. Buchloh, "Gerhard Richter's *Atlas*: The Anomic Archive," *October* 88 (Spring 1999), p. 143.

41. Ibid., p. 144.

42. Habbo Knoch, *Die Tat als Bild: Fotografien des Holocaust in der deutschen Erinnerungskultur* (Hamburg: Hamburger Edition, 2001), pp. 123, 128.

43. Cornelia Brink, "Secular Icons: Looking at Photographs from Nazi Concentration Camps," *History and Memory* 12, no. 1 (Spring/Summer 2000), p. 146.

44. Knoch, *Die Tat als Bild*, p. 163.

45. Hannah Arendt, "The Aftermath of Nazi Rule: Report from Germany" (1950), in *Essays in Understanding, 1930–1954: Formation, Exile, and Totalitarianism* (New York: Harcourt Brace, 1994), p. 245.

46. Gerhard Richter, "Man kann Auschwitz nicht abmalen: Gespräch mit Julia Voss und Peter Geimer," *Frankfurter Allgemeine Zeitung*, February 25, 2016, p. 9.

47. See *Mémoire des camps: Photographies des camps de concentration et d'extermination Nazis (1933–1999)*, ed. Clément Chéroux, exh. cat. (Paris: Marval, 2001), p. 162.

48. Benjamin H. D. Buchloh, *Gerhard Richter's* Birkenau *Paintings* (Cologne: Walther König, 2016), p. 6.

49. See, for example, Elger, *Gerhard Richter: Maler*, p. 125.

50. Richter, "Man kann Auschwitz nicht abmalen," p. 9.

51. "These faces imposed themselves as the traumatic emblem of the camps and their liberation with the same force as the piles of emaciated corpses; and they have been staring down the history of cinema ever since, offering themselves up as a generic form for modern cinema." Antoine de Baecque, *Camera Historica: The Century in Cinema*, trans. Ninon Vinsonneau and Jonathan Magidoff (New York: Columbia University Press, 2012), pp. 43–44.

52. Georges Didi-Huberman, "Returning an Image," in *Bild-gegen-Bild: Image Counter Image*, ed. Patrizia Dander and Julienne Lorz, exh. cat. (Munich: Haus der Kunst München; Cologne: Walther König, 2012), p. 79.

Chrono-Technics: Richter's Family Pictures
Briony Fer

1. For the most persuasive account of the complex contributing role of Richter's formation, "split as it was between East and West Germany, which serve, as well, as an analogue to postwar Germany's own conflicted relation to its past (which it must both disavow and work through)," see Benjamin H. D. Buchloh, "Divided Memory and Post-Traditional Identity: Gerhard Richter's Work of Mourning" (1996), in *Gerhard Richter*, ed. Benjamin H. D. Buchloh, October Files 8 (Cambridge, Mass.: MIT Press, 2009), p. 72.

2. I refer here specifically to the art of painting. This preoccupation with the family unit in painting is also at odds with the work of key feminist artists such as Mary Kelly, who would later analyze the mother-child axis in works such as *Post-Partum Document* (1973–79). In the history of photography, on the other hand, the family has been a constant resource. For an interesting discussion of Richter's family pictures, see also Rachel Haidu, "Arrogant Texts: Gerhard Richter's Family Pictures" (2007), in Buchloh, *Gerhard Richter*, pp. 153–68.

3. Copley painted the picture of his family when they were finally able to join him in England.

4. Christine Mehring has referred to the "grey zone between knowing and not knowing, between authenticity and cliché," in the family pictures in her insightful essay "East or West, Home Is Best: Friends, Family and Design in Richter's Early Years," in *Gerhard Richter: Panorama*, ed. Mark Godfrey and Nicholas Serota, exh. cat. (London: Tate Publishing, 2011), pp. 34–35.

5. Jean-Luc Nancy discusses what he calls "the spacing of time" in On Kawara's work, distinguishing its "chronomorphic poiesy" from the "chrono-metric" techniques of the clock or the calendar. See Jean-Luc Nancy, "The Technique of the Present," lecture given in January 1997 at the Nouveau Musée during *Whole and Parts: 1964–1995*, an exhibition of Kawara's works; "Technique du présent," *Les Cahiers: Philosophie de l'art* (1997).

6. It was revealed only in 2004 in the Danish newspaper *Politiken* that it was a photograph of the Danish royal princesses; see note in https://www.gerhard-richter.com/en/art/paintings/photo-paintings/families-11/three-siblings-5592.

7. Likewise, of the role models such as Vermeer that I discuss later in this essay, Richter has said, in conversation with Nicholas Serota, "And then when the paintings are finished, I might realize what they remind me of, for instance, *Reader* reminds me of Vermeer." See "I Have Nothing to Say and I'm Saying It," in *Gerhard Richter: Panorama*, p. 17.

8. Walter Benjamin, "The Image of Proust," in *Illuminations*, ed. Hannah Arendt, trans. Harry Zohn (London: Fontana, 1973), p. 213.

9. "This mania of Swann's for finding likenesses to people in pictures." Marcel Proust, *In Search of Lost Time*, vol. 2, *Within a Budding Grove*, trans. C. K. Scott Moncrieff and Terence Kilmartin (London: Chatto & Windus, 1992), p. 125.

10. Gerhard Richter, *The Daily Practice of Painting: Writings and Interviews 1962–1993*, ed. Hans Ulrich Obrist, trans. David Britt (Cambridge, Mass.: MIT Press; London: Anthony d'Offay Gallery, 1995), p. 37.

11. Freud first drew attention to the "king baby" and coined the term "His Majesty the baby" in his essay "On Narcissism" (1914), in Sigmund Freud, *On Metapsychology: The Theory of Psychoanalysis*, vol. 11, Penguin Freud Library (Harmondsworth, Middlesex: Penguin Books, 1984), p. 84.

12. Gerhard Richter, "Notes, 1964–1965," in Richter, *The Daily Practice of Painting*, p. 34.

13. For a critical analysis, see Benjamin Buchloh's seminal essay "Figures of Authority, Ciphers of Regression: Notes on the Return of Representation in European Painting," *October* 102 (Spring 1981), pp. 39–68.

14. *Gerhard Richter: 100 Pictures*, ed. Hans Ulrich Obrist, exh. cat. (Ostfildern-Ruit: Hatje Cantz, 1996).

15. Richter, "Notes, 1964–1965," p. 3.

16. Theodor W. Adorno, "Valéry Proust Museum," in *Prisms*, trans. Samuel and Shierry Weber (Cambridge, Mass.: MIT Press, 1983), p. 175.

17. Marcel Proust, *In Search of Lost Time*, vol. 6, *Time Regained*, trans. Andreas Mayor and Terence Kilmartin, revised by D. J. Enright (London: Vintage Books, 2000), p. 254.

18. See his comments on Vermeer's use of the camera obscura in relation to drawing in "Interview with Hans-Ulrich Obrist, 1993," in Richter, *The Daily Practice of Painting*, p. 260.

19. According to Peter Gidal, Richter had a postcard of *Woman Reading a Letter* tacked to the wall in an anteroom in his studio. He rightly stresses that Richter's 1994 painting *Reader* (*Lesende*) "could not exist in a less Vermeerian space"; see Peter Gidal, "The Polemics of Paint," in *Gerhard Richter: Painting in the Nineties*, exh. cat. (London: Anthony d'Offay Gallery, 1995), p. 26.

Terrains of Paint: Richter's Landscapes
Brinda Kumar

1. The exhibition toured to Berlin, Bern, and Vienna. Jürgen Harten, ed., *Gerhard Richter Bilder: Paintings 1962–1985*, exh. cat. (Cologne: DuMont, 1986).

2. Benjamin Katz et al., *Benjamin Katz: Gerhard Richter at Work*, exh. cat. (Dresden: Staatliche Kunstsammlungen; Munich: Hirmer, 2012), p. 115.

3. Harten, *Gerhard Richter Bilder*, p. 355.

4. Dietmar Elger, *Gerhard Richter: A Life in Painting*, trans. Elizabeth M. Solaro (Chicago: University of Chicago Press, 2009), p. 125.

5. The last such paintings were made in 1969 (CR 215, 216). Harten, *Gerhard Richter Bilder*, p. 25.

6. Mark Godfrey, "Damaged Landscapes," in *Gerhard Richter: Panorama*, ed. Mark Godfrey and Nicholas Serota, exh. cat. (London: Tate Publishing, 2011), p. 74.

7. Ibid., p. 78.

8. "Conversation with Mathias Schreiber, 1972," in Gerhard Richter, *Writings 1961–2007*, ed. Dietmar Elger and Hans Ulrich Obrist (New York: D.A.P./Distributed Art Publishers, 2009), p. 63.

9. For a fuller analysis of Richter's *48 Portraits* at the Venice Biennale, see Benjamin H. D. Buchloh, "Divided Memory and Post-Traditional Identity: Gerhard Richter's Work of Mourning" (1996), in *Gerhard Richter*, ed. Benjamin H. D. Buchloh, October Files 8 (Cambridge, Mass: MIT Press, 2009), pp. 83–94.

10. The juxtaposition of landscapes and politically charged images is paralleled in the organization of certain folios of the *Atlas*. "The transition to a large suite of colour landscape views . . . is accompanied, like strange intruders, by the two sheets 131 and 132 with photographs of Adolf Hitler and the shots of *Death in Safari Park* (sheet 133). Viewers are left on their own in their uncertainty as to which of the two motifs they should find more terrible. These images can in no way be incorporated into the parade of beautiful, even romantic landscapes." Gerhard Richter, *Atlas*, ed. Helmut Friedel (London: Thames & Hudson, 2006), pp. 9–10.

11. Oskar Bätschmann, "Landscapes at One Remove," in *Gerhard Richter: Landscapes*, ed. Dietmar Elger (Ostfildern-Ruit: Hatje Cantz, 2011), p. 61.

12. "Polke and Richter demonstrate the impotence of the artist in the year of the student revolt, using the incredible example of the transformation of a huge mountain simulated in photographs. . . . Well aware that the power of the picture is no greater than the faith that moves mountains, the artists conceal the misery of their never-ending powerlessness by imagining a temporary dematerialization, as if to say, at long last reality did us the favor of excelling itself. . . . For if the transformation of a mountain into a ball can be made to look like a fact by a skillful use of trick photos, the artist may hope, even if in vain, that one day he may really come to terms with reality." Harten, *Gerhard Richter Bilder*, pp. 28–29.

13. Elger, *Gerhard Richter: A Life in Painting*, p. 119.

14. "I liked them as outsiders, above all. . . . I liked the very nostalgic side. They were the first people who liked my landscapes. I think what impressed me the most was the way they took their own independence as a matter of course." "Interview with Hans Ulrich Obrist, 1993," in Richter, *Writings*, pp. 298–99.

15. Mark A. Cheetham, *Artwriting, Nation, and Cosmopolitanism in Britain: The "Englishness" of English Art Theory Since the Eighteenth Century*, British Art: Global Contexts (Farnham, Surrey: Ashgate, 2012), p. 120.

16. Harten, *Gerhard Richter Bilder*, p. 48.

17. Hans Ulrich Obrist, "Interview with Gerhard Richter," in *Gerhard Richter: Pictures/Series*, ed. Hans Ulrich Obrist, exh. cat. (Ostfildern-Ruit: Hatje Cantz, 2014), p. 93.

18. Gerhard Richter, "Notes, 1986," in *The Daily Practice of Painting: Writings and Interviews 1962–1993*, ed. Hans Ulrich Obrist, trans. David Britt (Cambridge, Mass.: MIT Press; London: Anthony d'Offay Gallery, 1995), p. 130.

19. "[Obrist:] In your *Atlas* there are sketches and designs for rooms that reveal an effort to find a place to fit the pictures, to create a kind of place-specific quality. [Richter:] That sort of thing only works in sketches, because the execution would be unendurable, overblown and bombastic. But it was good to design sanctuaries of that kind, for pictures with an incredible total effect. [Obrist:] Utopian spaces? [Richter:] And megalomaniac ones." "Interview with Hans Ulrich Obrist, 1993," p. 301.

20. Obrist, "Interview with Gerhard Richter," pp. 93–94.

21. "Interview with Irmeline Lebeer, 1973," as quoted in Benjamin H. D. Buchloh, "Readymade, Photography, and Painting in the Painting of Gerhard Richter" (1977), in *Neo-Avantgarde and Culture Industry: Essays on European and American Art from 1955 to 1975* (Cambridge, Mass: MIT Press, 2000), p. 384.

22. Godfrey, "Damaged Landscapes," p. 80.

23. "Just because landscape is beautiful, it's probably the most terrific thing there is. . . . I felt like painting something beautiful." "Interview with Rolf Gunther Dienst, 1970," in Richter, *The Daily Practice of Painting*, p. 64.

24. As quoted in Godfrey, "Damaged Landscapes," p. 79.

25. "For critics or observers of the scene still convinced that modern art is a sequence of ruptures, each one more radical than the last, Richter's landscapes may seem at best a kind of fence-sitting between the old and the new, and at worst an intellectually adroit and technically masterful form of backsliding. However, these paintings are no more a throwback to lapsed aesthetic conventions than they are an ironical recapitulation and then dismantling of them. The Janus-like position Richter occupies recognizes that those who work fully in the present always enter history in medias res. Looking both ways from such a position affords us a clearer perspective on the continuities and discontinuities of artistic practice than those available to anyone craning his or her neck to see the present from a vantage point in the hypothetical future or the reconstructed past." Robert Storr, *Gerhard Richter: Forty Years of Painting*, exh. cat. (New York: Museum of Modern Art, 2002), p. 68.

26. Godfrey, "Damaged Landscapes," p. 83.

27. Richter, "Notes, 1986," p. 158.

28. This was a period when Richter was experiencing difficulties in his first marriage, and he took the trip alone. Elger, *Gerhard Richter: A Life in Painting*, p. 202.

29. "Pierre Bourdieu has observed that landscapes photographed by tourists never really refer to landscape, but rather to the amateur photographer's experience associated with them. In an astonishing way, this corresponds to the groups of colored landscapes Richter has executed since 1968, using his own photographs as a working basis." Buchloh, "Readymade, Photography, and Painting," p. 384.

30. "These pictures are as beautiful as are their natural subjects and beautiful as painted artifacts, but they withhold any invitation to empathy. Whereas romantic paintings generally meet viewers halfway... Richter's paintings of this type are indifferent to the viewer's needs, acknowledging by that pointed indifference that the viewer and his or her needs exist. Thus they portray natural phenomena without symbolic amplification." Storr, *Gerhard Richter*, p. 53.

31. Harten, *Gerhard Richter Bilder*, p. 41.

32. "Conversation with Mathias Schreiber (1972)," in Richter, *Writings*, p. 63.

33. "For me, there's no difference between a landscape and an abstract painting. The term 'realism,' to my mind, has no meaning." "Interview with Irmeline Lebeer, 1973," in Richter, *The Daily Practice of Painting*, p. 72.

34. This process can also be seen in other series, including Tourist, Annunciation after Titian, S. with Child, and Moritz. It harks back to the first occlusion of the surface in Richter's seminal work *Table* (1962; p. 104).

35. "From a letter to Jean-Christophe Ammann, February 1973," in Richter, *Writings*, pp. 71–72.

36. "Somehow I tend to start off with very bright colours, and they get more and more veiled, or else brought forward again, or added on. But light is the right word, because these bright areas always have an illusionistic aspect to them." "Interview with Doris von Drathen (1992)," in Richter, *Writings*, p. 286.

37. "Interview with Sabine Schütz (1990)," in Richter, *Writings*, p. 253.

38. "I called this series of four paintings *Forest* [CR 731–34] after completion. There was no ironic meaning intended.... There seemed to me a romantic mood in these four paintings that reminded me of a forest. In the blue, there is the sensation of a diffuse light, which is why I came upon this title. I applied the paint across the canvas in two separate movements; across the middle one can see a caesura." "Comments on Some Works, 1991," in Richter, *Writings*, p. 270.

39. "One should also consider that many major series of abstracts in the 1990s were given titles like *River* and *Forest* because Richter was interested in what it means to see a painting, even one that is the result of chance accumulations and erasures, in relation to impressions familiar from our experience of the natural world." Godfrey, "Damaged Landscapes," p. 88.

40. Many of these were later compiled in the artist's book also titled *Wald* (Forest).

41. Obrist, "Interview with Gerhard Richter," p. 98.

42. Benjamin H. D. Buchloh, *Gerhard Richter's* Birkenau *Paintings* (Cologne: Walther König, 2016), p. 26.

43. For an analysis of these images, see Georges Didi-Huberman, *Images in Spite of All: Four Photographs from Auschwitz*, trans. Shane B. Lillis (Chicago: University of Chicago Press, 2008).

44. Mark Godfrey, "A Curtain of Trees," lecture given at Tate Modern, London, October 21, 2011, https://www.youtube.com/watch?v=njrU715rW9Y (accessed May 29, 2019).

Randomizing Painting: Notes on Richter's Abstractions
André Rottmann

1. Gerhard Richter, "Notes, 1964–1965," in *The Daily Practice of Painting: Writings and Interviews 1962–1993*, ed. Hans Ulrich Obrist, trans. David Britt (Cambridge, Mass.: MIT Press; London: Anthony d'Offay Gallery, 1995), p. 37.

2. Peter Osborne, "Abstract Images: Sign, Image, and Aesthetic in Gerhard Richter's Painting," in *Gerhard Richter*, ed. Benjamin H. D. Buchloh, October Files 8 (Cambridge, Mass.: MIT Press, 2009), p. 96.

3. Hal Foster, *The First Pop Age: Painting and Subjectivity in the Art of Hamilton, Lichtenstein, Warhol, Richter, and Ruscha* (Princeton: Princeton University Press, 2012), p. 174.

4. Friedrich Kittler, "Gramophone, Film, Typewriter," trans. Dorothea von Mücke with Philippe L. Similon, *October* 41 (Summer 1987), p. 102.

5. Ibid.

6. In his own words, *Gestell* for Heidegger "means the gathering together of that setting-upon which sets upon man, i.e., challenges him forth, to reveal the real, in the mode of ordering, as standing-reserve" and signals "that way of revealing which holds sway in the essence of modern technology and which is itself nothing technological." Martin Heidegger, "The Question Concerning Technology" (1954), in *The Question Concerning Technology and Other Essays*, trans. William Lovitt (New York: Harper & Row, 1977), p. 20.

7. For a discussion of such a "colorless" aesthetic beyond any symbolism, see Roland Barthes, *Writing Degree Zero*, trans. Annette Lavers and Colin Smith (London: Jonathan Cape, 1967).

8. See Michel Serres, *The Parasite*, trans. Lawrence R. Schehr (1980; new ed., Minneapolis: University of Minnesota Press, 2007), esp. pp. 38–39.

9. "Such painting is 'postconceptual' to the extent that it is constituted as art by its critical, reflective relationship to the historical constitution and destruction of the *concept* of painting, rather than merely by its continuation of the practice of painting at the level of craft, medium, and technique." Osborne, "Abstract Images," p. 96. In his recent writings, Osborne has further developed the "single and simple, speculative

proposition: *contemporary art is postconceptual art.*" Peter Osborne, *Anywhere or Not at All: Philosophy of Contemporary Art* (London: Verso, 2013), p. 3. On the mutual definitions of the two terms, see ibid., pp. 51–53.

10. It would seem that Richter's tentative foray into the realm of abstraction was partially prompted by Palermo's Cloth Pictures (1966–72). On this body of work, see Christine Mehring, *Blinky Palermo: Abstraction of an Era* (New Haven: Yale University Press, 2008), pp. 45–85. About starting to paint nonfigurative pictures, Richter has said, "It did have something to do with Palermo and his interests, and later with Minimal Art as well; but when I painted my first Color Charts in 1966, that had more to do with pop art. They were copies of paint sample cards, and what was effective about them was that they were directed against the efforts of the neoconstructivists, Albers and the rest." Quoted in Benjamin H. D. Buchloh, "An Interview with Gerhard Richter" (1986), in Buchloh, *Gerhard Richter*, p. 10. In another oft-quoted interview, with Irmeline Lebeer, the artist said: "The first colour charts were unsystematic. They were based directly on commercial colour samples. They were still related to Pop Art." Gerhard Richter, "Interview with Irmeline Lebeer" (1973), in *Text: Writings, Interviews and Letters 1961–2007*, ed. Dietmar Elger and Hans Ulrich Obrist (London: Thames & Hudson, 2009), p. 82.

11. On these conjectures, see Benjamin H. D. Buchloh, "The Chance Ornament: Aphorisms on Gerhard Richter's Abstractions," *Artforum* 50, no. 6 (February 2012), p. 170. Thierry de Duve has summarized Duchamp's 1961 argument as follows: "Just as the prerequisite of the painter's work is a manufactured product, so 'all paintings in the world' now partake of an industrial culture. An artist who has stopped painting but now chooses a readymade thus belongs to the same tradition as the painter, because the fact that colors are produced industrially both annihilates this tradition and sets up its new conditions." Thierry de Duve, *Kant after Duchamp* (Cambridge, Mass.: MIT Press, 1996), p. 163.

12. See Carol Armstrong, "Seurat's Media, or a Matrix of Materialities," *Grey Room* 58 (Winter 2015), pp. 6–25.

13. See Sven Lütticken, *Idols of the Market: Modern Iconoclasm and the Fundamentalist Spectacle* (Berlin: Sternberg Press, 2009), p. 139. In her analysis of Richter's *Singer* (*Sänger*) of 1965–66, which shortly preceded the first Color Charts (and the backside of which arguably prompted them), art historian Jaleh Mansoor has likewise stressed that the artist's nonobjective work acknowledges "the degree to which history, if it is accessible at all, is mediated, which is to say, redrawn through a sociopolitical field itself determined by abstraction." However, Mansoor focuses her argument on the intersections between visual abstraction and a capitalist economy and "mode of production predicated on the occlusion of resources and labouring bodies, on the exchange of materials and labour power, reintegrated as products and ultimately realised as value by the money form (the ultimate abstraction)." Jaleh Mansoor, "Minima Moralia: Notes on Richter's Readymade Red in *Singer* of 1965/66," in Dietmar Elger, Hubertus Butin, and Jaleh Mansoor, *Gerhard Richter: Colour Charts* (London: Dominique Lévy, 2016), p. 31.

14. Ibid., p. 140.

15. Rosalind E. Krauss, "Grids" (1979), in *The Originality of the Avant-Garde and Other Modernist Myths* (Cambridge, Mass.: MIT Press, 1985), pp. 8–22.

16. Ibid., pp. 18–19.

17. Ibid., p. 18.

18. On the relation between diagrammatic and geometric painterly abstraction, as first analyzed by Benjamin H. D. Buchloh, see below.

19. Krauss, "Grids," p. 21.

20. Rosalind E. Krauss, "The Originality of the Avant-Garde," in *The Originality of the Avant-Garde*, p. 161.

21. Ibid.

22. See ibid.

23. See Bernhard Siegert, "(Not) in Place: The Grid, or, Cultural Techniques of Ruling Spaces," in *Cultural Techniques: Grids, Filters, Doors, and Other Articulations of the Real*, trans. Geoffrey Winthrop-Young (New York: Fordham University Press, 2015), p. 97.

24. Bernhard Siegert, "Cultural Techniques: Or the End of the Intellectual Postwar Era in German Media Theory," *Theory, Culture & Society* 30, no. 6 (2013), p. 58. The most basic cultural techniques within the history of media are writing (prior to the alphabet or scripture), image making (preceding the notions of painting or even pictures), counting (before the introduction of numbers), and making music (independent of notations and scores).

25. Ibid., p. 61. As Siegert has written: "Every culture begins with the introduction of distinctions: inside/outside, pure/impure, sacred/profane, female/male, human/animal, speech/absence of speech, signal/noise, and so on." Ibid.

26. Siegert, "(Not) in Place," p. 97.

27. Ibid., p. 98.

28. Ibid., p. 97.

29. Benjamin H. D. Buchloh, "The Diagram and the Colour Chip: Gerhard Richter's *4900 Colours*," in Benjamin H. D. Buchloh, Peter Gidal, and Birgit Pelzer, *Gerhard Richter: 4900 Colours*, exh. cat. (London: Serpentine Gallery; Ostfildern-Ruit: Hatje Cantz, 2008), pp. 63–64.

30. Ibid., p. 64.

31. Buchloh has stressed, "Least of all would the diagram pretend to serve as a universal language that could transcend all boundaries of the nation state, or of class and gender." Ibid.

32. Ibid. On this crucial difference between Mondrian's and Richter's grids, see ibid., p. 65.

33. Krauss, "Grids," p. 12.

34. Siegert, "(Not) in Place," p. 103. Siegert here refers to Martin Heidegger's reading of the very term *repraesentare* in the essay "The Age of the World Picture" (1938), in *The Question Concerning Technology*, pp. 115–54, esp. pp. 131–33.

35. Robert Storr, *Gerhard Richter: Forty Years of Painting*, exh. cat. (New York: Museum of Modern Art, 2002), p. 51.

36. Birgit Pelzer, "The Asymptote of Chance," in *Gerhard Richter: 4900 Colours*, p. 121.

37. See ibid.

38. "Platz der Luftbrücke: Stefan Banz im Gespräch mit Friedrich Kittler, Berlin-Tempelhof, Manfred von Richthofen-Strasse, 28. Juni 1996," in Friedrich Kittler, *Platz der Luftbrücke: Ein Gespräch mit Stefan Banz* (Nuremberg: Verlag für moderne Kunst, 2011), pp. 50–51. My translation.

39. Friedrich A. Kittler, "There Is No Software" (1993), in *The Truth of the Technological World: Essays on the Genealogy of Presence*, trans. Erik Butler (Stanford: Stanford University Press, 2013), p. 219.

40. For a more detailed analysis of the conception of *4,900 Colors*, see Pelzer, "The Asymptote of Chance," pp. 122–25.

41. Branden W. Joseph, *Experimentations: John Cage in Music, Art, and Architecture* (New York: Bloomsbury Academic, 2016), p. 143.

42. "The phonograph does not hear as do ears that have been trained immediately to filter voices, words, and sounds out of noise; it registers acoustic events as such." Friedrich A. Kittler, *Gramophone, Film, Typewriter*, trans. Geoffrey Winthrop-Young and Michael Wutz (Stanford: Stanford University Press, 1999), p. 23. Following Lacan's tripartite structure of the symbolic, the imaginary, and the real, the latter in Kittler's media theory connotes "the waste or residue that neither the mirror of the imaginary nor the grid of the symbolic can catch: the physiological accidents and stochastic disorder of bodies." Ibid., pp. 15–16.

43. See Joseph, *Experimentations*, pp. 147–48. In this passage Joseph draws on Gilles Deleuze's study *Bergsonism* (trans. Hugh Tomlison and Barbara Habberjam [New York: Zone Books, 1988]).

44. Buchloh, "The Diagram and the Colour Chip," p. 67.

45. Along these lines, art historian Briony Fer writes: "The number of permutations and variations Richter devises… suggests that the color chart offers him a remarkably elastic template to work with, suggests even that the more rigid the control of the grid, the more variable what goes on within it. A precarious balance is struck between control and chance." Briony Fer, "Color Manual," in *Color Chart: Reinventing Color, 1950 to Today*, ed. Ann Temkin, exh. cat. (New York: Museum of Modern Art, 2008), p. 32.

46. See Pelzer, "The Asymptote of Chance," p. 125.

47. Gilles Deleuze, "Postscript on the Societies of Control," *October* 59 (Winter 1992), pp. 5–6.

48. See ibid., p. 4

49. Ibid., p. 5.

50. Ibid., p. 4.

51. Branden W. Joseph, "Societies of Control," *Texte zur Kunst* 17, no. 66 (June 2007), p. 94.

52. Richter's process is meticulously detailed and documented in a monograph by Robert Storr: *Gerhard Richter: The Cage Paintings* (London: Tate Publishing, 2009), pp. 92–166.

53. See also ibid., p. 70.

54. Buchloh, "The Chance Ornament," p. 173.

55. Benjamin H. D. Buchloh, "Richter's Abstractions: Silences, Voids, and Evacuations," in *Gerhard Richter: Paintings from 2003–2005*, exh. cat. (New York: Marian Goodman Gallery; Cologne: Walther König, 2005), p. 17.

56. The discrete steps of this process are illustrated as plates in Richter's artist book *Patterns: Divided, Mirrored, Repeated* (London: Heni Publishing; Cologne: Walther König, 2012).

57. Kittler, *Gramophone, Film, Typewriter*, p. xl.

58. Benjamin H. D. Buchloh, "The Chance Ornament: Painting Progress, Painting Loss," in *Gerhard Richter: Strip Paintings*, exh. cat. (New York: Marian Goodman Gallery, 2012), p. 16.

59. Friedrich A. Kittler, *Text als kalkulierter Zufall* (Hamburg: Material-Verlag, 1996), p. 5. My translation.

60. Ibid., p. 7.

In a Glass, Darkly
Hal Foster

1. Gerhard Richter, "Note, 1971," in *Text: Writings, Interviews and Letters 1961–2007*, ed. Dietmar Elger and Hans Ulrich Obrist (London: Thames & Hudson, 2009), p. 57. I am greatly indebted, as are all who write on Richter, to Benjamin Buchloh, to whom this essay is dedicated.

2. Richter, "Interview with Peter Sager, 1972," in *Text*, p. 67.

3. See Donald Judd, "Specific Objects," *Arts Yearbook 8* (1965), repr. in *Donald Judd, Complete Writings 1959–1975* (Halifax: Press of the Nova Scotia College of Art and Design, 1975), pp. 181–89.

4. Richter, "From a Letter to Benjamin H. D. Buchloh, 1977," in *Text*, p. 93.

5. Richter, "Notes, 1981," in *Text*, p. 120. Richter adds immediately, "Berges furnishing store," a reference to the store where, in 1963, Richter and Konrad Lueg staged a performance in the context of the show *Living with Pop—A Demonstration for Capitalist Realism*. Not incidentally, for Richter the glass pieces allude to Duchamp only negatively, if at all. He says that he is opposed in particular to the "pseudo-complexity" and "manufactured mystery" of *The Large Glass* (1915–23) ("Interview with Jonas Storsve, 1991," in *Text*, p. 272).

6. Richter, "Notes, 1981," p. 120.

7. Richter, "Interview with Hans Ulrich Obrist, 1993," in *Text*, p. 305.

8. Ibid.

9. Richter, "Interview with Jonas Storsve," p. 272.

10. The monochrome, it can be argued, did not void these paradigms so much as it sublated them—negated them in a way that also preserved them. See my contribution to "Abstraction, 1910–1925: Eight Statements," *October* 143 (Winter 2013), pp. 33–34.

11. See Benjamin H. D. Buchloh, "Gerhard Richter's Glass: Painting's Double," in *Gerhard Richter*, exh. cat. (London: Marian Goodman Gallery, 2014).

12. Benjamin H. D. Buchloh, "Gerhard Richter's *Eight Gray*: Between *Vorschein* and *Glanz*," in *Gerhard Richter: Eight Gray*, exh. cat. (New York: Guggenheim Museum Publications, 2002), p. 15.

13. Buchloh, "Gerhard Richter's Glass," pp. 87, 92.

14. See Michel Foucault, *The Order of Things: An Archaeology of the Human Sciences* (New York: Vintage, 1973), pp. 3–16; and Louis Marin, "Toward a Theory of Reading in the Visual Arts: Poussin's *The Arcadian Shepherds*," in *The Reader in the Text: Essays on Audience and Interpretation*, ed. Susan R. Suleiman and Inge Crosman (Princeton: Princeton University Press, 1980), p. 310.

15. See Craig Owens, "Representation, Appropriation, and Power," *Art in America* 70 (May 1982), pp. 9–21.

16. Pliny the Elder regarded it as long established that the tracing of the outline of a human shadow initiated the art of painting and that this image was monochromatic. See David Summers, *Vision, Reflection, and Desire in Western Painting* (Chapel Hill: University of North Carolina Press, 2007).

17. Richter, "Interview with Hans Ulrich Obrist," p. 305. Until recently, these models lingered on in photo discourse, as in the 1978 exhibition *Mirrors and Windows*, curated by John Szarkowski at the Museum of Modern Art in New York.

18. Even the aleatory takes on a somewhat sinister cast, very different from the delight in "the airports for the lights, shadows, and particles" that John Cage experienced before the White Paintings (1951) of Robert Rauschenberg.

19. Jacques Lacan, *The Four Fundamental Concepts of Psychoanalysis*, trans. Alan Sheridan (New York: W. W. Norton, 1978), p. 101.

20. Roger Caillois, "Mimicry and Legendary Psychasthenia" (1935), *October* 31 (Winter 1984), p. 30.

21. Richter expressed this ambivalence, or doubt mixed with disappointment, in a statement from January 26, 1983: "Minimal art: I saw this as an attempt to develop a new alphabet for the art of the future. And although it doesn't look as if it is being used in that way, my hopes still go in that direction. But then perhaps that is a completely wrong way of looking at it" ("Notes, 1993," in *Text*, p. 129).

22. This is how I put it in *The Art-Architecture Complex* (London: Verso, 2011): "For years I took Donald Judd at his word: that Minimalist objects are opposed to any pictorial illusionism or virtual space whatsoever. . . . In my literalism, which was deepened by the literalism of Postminimalist practices such as process, body, and site-specific art, I did not attend to how illusionism might be preserved in Minimalism, even expanded by it (think of the reflective surfaces and refractive depths in some Judd boxes, or the brilliant color and immersive light in all Flavin lights); or, further, how illusionism might be released in the optical effects of the 'light and space' art that developed with Minimalism and after (think of the reflective glass cubes of Larry Bell, the haloed light disks of Robert Irwin, the colored light ambiances of James Turrell, and so on). In short, if Minimalism contested the illusionistic remainder in late-modernist painting, how thoroughly did it do so, and for how long? Was its break with pictorial virtuality only partial and temporary, a historical ruse on the way to the recent triumph of the virtual (in the digital pictorialism of recent photography, say, or the projected images of recent video installations)—a triumph that is hardly restricted to art (as we have seen, it is pervasive in architecture, too)? This possibility leads me to ask whether, even as Minimalism remains a crux in twentieth-century practice, its aftermath might not also be, at least in part, a *catastrophe*" (pp. 182–84).

23. See Michael Fried, "Art and Objecthood," *Artforum* 5 (Summer 1967), pp. 12–23. Perhaps this is the place to note a possible connection to Richard Serra, whom Richter admires. Richter gave *7 Panes of Glass* (2013) the subtitle *House of Cards*, an allusion to the key work in lead by Serra, *One-Ton Prop (House of Cards)* (1969). Yet, apart from the precarious propping of the elements, I see little in common between the works. Serra is concerned with the structural limits of lead, Richter with the imagistic effects of glass.

24. Richter, "MoMA Interview with Robert Storr, 2002," in *Text*, p. 421.

25. Roland Barthes, *The Neutral*, trans. Rosalind Krauss and Denis Hollier (New York: Columbia University Press, 2007), pp. 6–7. The *Oxford English Dictionary* defines "baffle" as a plate that regulates passage in and out, and "to baffle" as "to reduce to perplexity."

26. Richter, "Interview with Jonas Storsve," p. 272. In Barthesian terms, "the third meaning"—defined, saliently here, as an "obtuse meaning" ("*obtusus* means *that which is blunted, rounded in form*")—allows for both "a certain emotion" and a certain "drifting" of sense. See Roland Barthes, "The Third Meaning" (1970), in *Image-Music-Text*, trans. Stephen Heath (New York: Hill and Wang, 1977).

27. See note 21.

28. I am inspired here by a series of stringent questions posed by Buchloh: "What have been the actual gains of painting whenever it has affirmed technoscientific impact? What have been its actual results in everyday life when it has claimed an intricate relationship between the surfaces of pigment and the surfaces of machines, or the surfaces of pigment and the surfaces of architecture, or the morphologies of geometric abstraction and the morphologies of scientific knowledge? What has been the actual progress demarcated by these technological assimilations? And whose actual perceptual interests or cognitive benefits has the technoscientific mimicry ultimately served?" Benjamin H. D. Buchloh, "Painting Progress, Painting Loss," in *Gerhard Richter: Painting 2010–2011*, exh. cat. (New York: Marian Goodman Gallery, 2011), p. 26.

29. Colin Rowe and Robert Slutzky, "Transparency: Literal and Phenomenal," *Perspecta* 8 (1963), p. 46.

30. Anthony Vidler, *The Architectural Uncanny* (Cambridge, Mass.: MIT Press, 1992), p. 221.

31. If transparency (let alone materialism) meant anything at all in modernism, it meant *de*fetishization, a motive announced as such from the Russian Constructivists through to Carl Andre and Richard Serra. For more on fetishization vis-à-vis the glass pieces, see Buchloh, "Gerhard Richter's *Eight Gray*."

32. Buchloh, "Gerhard Richter's Glass," p. 89.

Selected Bibliography

Adriani, Götz. *Baselitz, Richter, Polke, Kiefer: Die jungen Jahre der Alten Meister*. Exh. cat. Dresden: Sandstein, 2019.

———. *Gerhard Richter: Paintings from Private Collections*. Exh. cat. Ostfildern-Ruit: Hatje Cantz, 2008.

Bischoff, Ulrich, Elisabeth Hipp, and Jeanne Anne Nugent. *From Caspar David Friedrich to Gerhard Richter: German Paintings from Dresden*. Exh. cat. Los Angeles: J. Paul Getty Museum, 2006.

Buchloh, Benjamin H. D. "The Chance Ornament: Aphorisms on Gerhard Richter's Abstractions." *Artforum* 50, no. 6 (February 2012), pp. 168–79.

———. "Divided Memory and Post-Traditional Identity: Gerhard Richter's Work of Mourning." *October* 75 (Winter 1996), pp. 60–82.

———. *Gerhard Richter*. Exh. cat. London: Marian Goodman Gallery, 2014.

———, ed. *Gerhard Richter*. October Files 8. Cambridge, Mass.: MIT Press, 2009.

———. *Gerhard Richter: Eight Gray*. Exh. cat. New York: Guggenheim Museum Publications, 2002.

———. *Gerhard Richter: Paintings from 2003–2005*. Exh. cat. New York: Marian Goodman Gallery; Cologne: Walther König, 2005.

———. *Gerhard Richter: Painting 2010–2011*. Exh. cat. New York: Marian Goodman Gallery, 2011.

———. *Gerhard Richter: Strip Paintings*. Exh. cat. New York: Marian Goodman Gallery, 2012.

———. "Gerhard Richter's *Atlas*: The Anomic Archive." *October* 88 (Spring 1999), pp. 117–45.

———. *Gerhard Richter's* Birkenau *Paintings*. Cologne: Walther König, 2016.

———. "Gerhard Richter's *Tisch*: Memory Images and German Disavowal in 1962." In *Interiors and Interiority*. Edited by Ewa Lajer-Burcharth and Beate Söntgen, pp. 389–412. Berlin: Walter De Gruyter, 2016.

———. "Readymade, Photography, and Painting in the Painting of Gerhard Richter" (1977). In *Neo-Avantgarde and Culture Industry: Essays on European and American Art from 1955 to 1975*, pp. 365–403. Cambridge, Mass: MIT Press, 2000.

Buchloh, Benjamin H. D., Peter Gidal, and Birgit Pelzer. *Gerhard Richter: 4900 Colours*. Exh. cat. London: Serpentine Gallery; Ostfildern-Ruit: Hatje Cantz, 2008.

Curley, John J. *A Conspiracy of Images: Andy Warhol, Gerhard Richter, and the Art of the Cold War*. New Haven: Yale University Press, 2013.

Didi-Huberman, Georges. *Images in Spite of All: Four Photographs from Auschwitz*. Translated by Shane B. Lillis. Chicago: University of Chicago Press, 2008.

———. "Sortir du plan: Deux lettres à Gerhard Richter." *Les Cahiers du Musée national d'art moderne* 135 (Spring 2016), pp. 74–105.

———. *Wo Es war: Vier Briefe an Gerhard Richter*. Cologne: Walther König, 2018.

Ehrenfried, Susanne. *Ohne Eigenschaften: Das Portrait bei Gerhard Richter*. Vienna: Springer, 1997.

Elger, Dietmar. *Gerhard Richter: A Life in Painting*. Translated by Elizabeth M. Solaro. Chicago: University of Chicago Press, 2009.

———, ed. *Gerhard Richter: Catalogue Raisonné*. Vols. 1–4. Ostfildern-Ruit: Hatje Cantz, 2011–17.

———, ed. *Gerhard Richter: Landscapes*. Ostfildern-Ruit: Hatje Cantz, 2011.

———. *Gerhard Richter: Maler*. Cologne: DuMont, 2018.

Elger, Dietmar, Hubertus Butin, and Jaleh Mansoor. *Gerhard Richter: Colour Charts*. London: Dominique Lévy, 2016.

Foster, Hal. *The First Pop Age: Painting and Subjectivity in the Art of Hamilton, Lichtenstein, Warhol, Richter, and Ruscha*. Princeton: Princeton University Press, 2012.

Friedel, Helmut, and Robert Storr. *Gerhard Richter: Red-Yellow-Blue*. Munich: Prestel, 2007.

Gidal, Peter. *Gerhard Richter: Painting in the Nineties*. Exh. cat. London: Anthony d'Offay Gallery, 1995.

Godfrey, Mark, and Nicholas Serota, eds. *Gerhard Richter: Panorama*. Exh. cat. London: Tate Publishing, 2011.

Harten, Jürgen, ed. *Gerhard Richter Bilder: Paintings 1962–1985*. Exh. cat. Cologne: DuMont, 1986.

Hering, Karl-Heinz, ed. *Gerhard Richter: Arbeiten 1962 bis 1971.* Exh. cat. Düsseldorf: Kunstverein für die Rheinlande und Westfalen, 1971.

Hoffmann-Curtius, Kathrin. *Judenmord: Art and the Holocaust in Post-war Germany.* London: Reaktion Books, 2018.

Honisch, Dieter. *Gerhard Richter: 36. Biennale di Venezia, Padiglione tedesco, 11.6.–1.10.1972.* Exh. cat. Essen: Museum Folkwang, 1972.

Honnef, Klaus. *Gerhard Richter.* Recklinghausen: Aurel Bongers, 1976.

Katz, Benjamin, Dietmar Elger, Wilfried Wiegand, Stephan von Wiese, and Paul Moorhouse. *Benjamin Katz: Gerhard Richter at Work.* Dresden: Staatliche Kunstsammlungen; Munich: Hirmer, 2012.

McCarthy, Tom. "Blurring the Sublime: On Gerhard Richter." In *Typewriters, Bombs, Jellyfish: Essays*, pp. 125–36. New York: New York Review Books, 2017.

McGonagill, Doris. *Crisis and Collection: German Visual Memory Archives of the Twentieth Century.* Würzburg: Königshausen & Neumann, 2015.

Mehring, Christine, Jeanne Anne Nugent, and Jon L. Seydl, eds. *Gerhard Richter: Early Work, 1951–1972.* Los Angeles: J. Paul Getty Museum, 2011.

Nasgaard, Roald. *Gerhard Richter: Paintings.* Exh. cat. New York: Thames & Hudson, 1988.

Obrist, Hans Ulrich, ed. *Gerhard Richter: 100 Pictures.* Exh. cat. Ostfildern-Ruit: Hatje Cantz, 1996.

———, ed. *Gerhard Richter: Pictures/Series.* Exh. cat. Ostfildern-Ruit: Hatje Cantz, 2014.

Richter, Gerhard. *Atlas.* Edited by Helmut Friedel. London: Thames & Hudson, 2006.

———. *Atlas: The Reader.* London: Whitechapel Gallery, 2012.

———. *The Daily Practice of Painting: Writings and Interviews 1962–1993.* Edited by Hans Ulrich Obrist. Translated by David Britt. Cambridge, Mass.: MIT Press; London: Anthony d'Offay Gallery, 1995.

———. "Man kann Auschwitz nicht abmalen: Gespräch mit Julia Voss und Peter Geimer," *Frankfurter Allgemeine Zeitung*, February 25, 2016.

———. *Patterns: Divided, Mirrored, Repeated.* London: Heni Publishing; Cologne: Walther König, 2012.

———. *Text: Writings, Interviews and Letters 1961–2007.* Edited by Dietmar Elger and Hans Ulrich Obrist. London: Thames & Hudson, 2009.

———. *Writings 1961–2007.* Edited by Dietmar Elger and Hans Ulrich Obrist. New York: D.A.P./Distributed Art Publishers, 2009.

Richter, Gerhard, and Dieter Schwarz. *Elbe: 31 Monotypien 1957.* Cologne: Walther König, 2009.

Schneede, Uwe, ed. *Gerhard Richter: Images of an Era.* Exh. cat. Munich: Hirmer, 2011.

Silverman, Kaja. "Photography by Other Means." In *Flesh of My Flesh*, pp. 168–221. Stanford: Stanford University Press, 2009.

Storr, Robert. *Gerhard Richter: The Cage Paintings.* London: Tate Publishing, 2009.

———. *Gerhard Richter: Doubt and Belief in Painting.* New York: Museum of Modern Art, 2003.

———. *Gerhard Richter: Forty Years of Painting.* Exh. cat. New York: Museum of Modern Art, 2002.

Temkin, Ann, ed. *Color Chart: Reinventing Color, 1950 to Today.* Exh. cat. New York: Museum of Modern Art, 2008.

Index

Page references in *italics* refer to illustrations.

Photograph Credits

Archive of the Auschwitz-Birkenau State Museum: pp. 230, 231; Art Institute of Chicago / Art Resource, NY: fig. 27; © 2020 Artists Rights Society (ARS), New York / VG Bild-Kunst, Bonn: fig. 10; Photo by Iwan Baan: fig. 81; © Association Marcel Duchamp / ADAGP, Paris / Artists Rights Society (ARS), New York 2020. Yale University Art Gallery: fig. 68; Collection of the Gemeente-museum Den Haag: fig. 69; © Dan Graham. Image © The Metropolitan Museum of Art: fig. 79; Photo © President and Fellows of Harvard College: fig. 29; Photo by Christoph Irrgang, Hamburg: figs. 25, 26; © 2020 Judd Foundation / Artists Rights Society (ARS), New York. Digital Image © The Museum of Modern Art/Licensed by SCALA / Art Resource, NY: fig. 78; © 2020 Ellsworth Kelly. Digital Image © The Museum of Modern Art/ Licensed by SCALA / Art Resource, NY: fig. 70; © Kunsthistorisches Museum-Museumsverband: fig. 46; Foto Marburg / Art Resource, NY: fig. 80; Image © The Metropolitan Museum of Art: fig. 50; © 2020 The Estate of Robert Morris / Artists Rights Society (ARS), New York. © Tate, London / Art Resource, NY: fig. 75; © Museo Nacional del Prado / Art Resource, NY: fig. 76; Museum MMK, © Gerhard Richter, photo: Axel Schneider: pp. 120–23; © National Gallery, London / Art Resource, NY: figs. 44, 77; © 2020 The Kenneth Noland Foundation / Licensed by VAGA at Artists Rights Society (ARS), NY. Digital image © Whitney Museum of American Art / Licensed by Scala / Art Resource, NY: fig. 73; © 2020 Estate of Pablo Picasso / Artists Rights Society (ARS), New York. The Art Institute of Chicago / Art Resource, NY: fig. 37; © 2020 Albert Renger-Patzsch Archiv / Ann and Jürgen Wilde, Zülpich / Artists Rights Society (ARS), New York. Grisebach GmbH: fig. 31; © Gerhard Richter 2020 (03032020): figs. 1, 2, 3, 4, 7, 8, 9, 11, 12, 13, 14, 15, 16, 17, 20, 22, 23, 24, 32, 33, 34, 35, 36, 38, 40, 41, 42, 43, 47, 48, 49, 51, 52, 53, 54, 55, 56, 57, 58, 59, 61, 62, 63, 64, 65, 66, 67, 71, 72, pp. 105, 106, 107, 108, 109, 111, 112, 113, 114, 115, 117, 118, 119, 124, 125, 127, 128, 129, 131, 132, 133, 134, 135, 136, 137, 139, 141, 143, 144–45, 147, 149, 151, 153, 154, 155, 157, 159, 161, 162, 163, 165, 167, 168, 169, 170, 171, 172, 173, 174, 175, 177, 179, 181, 185, 187, 188, 189, 190, 191, 192, 193, 196, 197, 198, 199, 200, 201, 202–3, 205, 207, 209, 210, 211, 213, 214, 215, 217, 220–21, 224, 225, 226, 227, 228, 229, 234, 235, 237, 238, 239, 241, 242–43; © Gerhard Richter 2020 (03032020), © Hubert Becker 2020: p. 245; © Gerhard Richter 2020 (03032020), photo by Jennifer Bornstein: p. 104; © Gerhard Richter 2020 (03032020). Gerhard Richter, Eis, Köln, Verlag der Buchhandlung Walther König, 2011. Image © The Metropolitan Museum of Art, photo by Heather Johnson: fig. 60; © Gerhard Richter 2020 (03032020), photo by Joe Hage: fig. 6; © Gerhard Richter 2020 (03032020), courtesy of Frank Kranstedt, zero one film: fig. 5; © Gerhard Richter 2020 (03032020). Neue Bilder, Galerie Heiner Friedrich, München 1967: fig. 74; © Gerhard Richter 2020 (03032020), Printmanagement Plitt GmbH, Oberhausen: figs. 18, 19; © Gerhard Richter 2020 (03032020), photo by James Schoomaker: p. 183; Rijksmuseum Amsterdam: fig. 45; © Ed Ruscha. Image © The Metropolitan Museum of Art, photo by Hyla Skopitz: fig. 39; Estate Otto Steinert, Museum Folkwang, Essen: fig. 28; Estate Otto Steinert, Museum Folkwang, Essen - ARTOTHEK: fig. 30; © 2020 Frank Stella / Artists Rights Society (ARS), New York: fig. 21

This catalogue is published in conjunction with *Gerhard Richter: Painting After All*, on view at The Metropolitan Museum of Art, New York, from March 4 through July 5, 2020, and at the Museum of Contemporary Art, Los Angeles, from August 14, 2020, through January 19, 2021.

The exhibition is made possible by the Barrie A. and Deedee Wigmore Foundation.

Corporate sponsorship is provided by Morgan Stanley.

Morgan Stanley

Major support is provided by David S. Winter and the Modern and Contemporary Art Visiting Committee.

Additional funding is provided by Angela A. Chao and Jim Breyer, Jane C. Carroll, the Horace W. Goldsmith Foundation, Kenneth and Rosalind Landis, and Stuart and Gina Peterson.

The catalogue is made possible by the Mary C. and James W. Fosburgh Publications Fund.

Additional support for the catalogue is provided by Christie's, and by Sharon Wee and Tracy Fu.

PUBLISHED BY THE METROPOLITAN MUSEUM OF ART, NEW YORK

Mark Polizzotti, Publisher and Editor in Chief
Gwen Roginsky, Associate Publisher and General Manager
Peter Antony, Chief Production Manager
Michael Sittenfeld, Senior Managing Editor

Edited by Elisa Urbanelli
Designed by Daphne Geismar
Production by Paul Booth
Bibliographic editing by Kate Norment
Image acquisitions and permissions by Josephine Rodriguez-Massop
Translations from German by Russell Stockman

Photography credits appear on page 269.

Gerhard Richter's *Atlas* is in the collection of the Städtische Galerie im Lenbachhaus und Kunstbau München, Munich.

Typeset in Greta Text Pro
Printed on 150 gsm Perigord
Color separations, printing, and binding by Trifolio S.r.l., Verona, Italy

Front cover: *Table*, 1962 (p. 104); back cover: *Abstract Painting*, 2016 (p. 234 top right)

First printing

The Metropolitan Museum of Art
1000 Fifth Avenue
New York, New York 10028
metmuseum.org

Distributed by
Yale University Press, New Haven and London
yalebooks.com/art
yalebooks.co.uk

Cataloguing-in-Publication Data is available from the Library of Congress.
ISBN 978-1-58839-685-3